MICRO- ECONOMICS

THIRD EDITION

B. CURTIS EATON
Simon Fraser University

DIANE F. EATON

PRENTICE HALL INC.
Englewood Cliffs, New Jersey 07632

Canadian Cataloguing in Publication Data

Eaton, B. Curtis, 1943-
  Microeconomics

3rd ed.
ISBN 0-13-147331-X

1. Microeconomics.   I. Eaton, Diane F.
II. Title.

HB172.E38   1995   338.5   C94-93167-X

Library of Congress Cataloging-in-Publication Data
Eaton, Buford Curtis, 1943-
    Microeconomics / B. Curtis Eaton, Diane F. Eaton. — 3rd ed.
        p.   cm.
    Includes index.
    ISBN 0-13-147331-X
    1. Microeconomics.   I. Eaton, Diane F.   II. Title
    HB172.E23   1995   94-22281
    338.5—dc20   CIP

© 1995 Prentice-Hall, Inc.,
Englewood Cliffs, New Jersey 07632

Previous editions were published as *Microeconomics*
Copyright © 1991, 1988 W. H. Freeman and Company

Prentice-Hall Canada Inc., Scarborough
Prentice-Hall International (UK) Limited, London
Prentice-Hall of Australia, Pty. Limited, Sydney
Prentice-Hall Hispanoamericana, S.A., Mexico City
Prentice-Hall of India Private Limited, New Delhi
Prentice-Hall of Japan, Inc., Tokyo
Simon & Schuster Asia Private Limited, Singapore
Editora Prentice-Hall do Brasil, Ltda., Rio de Janeiro

ISBN 0-13-147331-X

Acquisitions Editor: Jacqueline Wood   Cover Design: Monica Kompter
Developmental Editor: Maurice Esses   Cover Image: J.A. Kraulis/Masterfile
Copy Editor: Ruth Chernia   Page Layout: Steve Lewis
Production Editor: Norman Bernard

1 2 3 4 5   RRD   99 98 97 96 95

Printed and bound in the United States of America.

Every reasonable effort has been made to obtain permissions for all articles and data used in this edition.
If errors or omissions have occurred, they will be corrected in future editions provided written notification has been received by the publisher.

Brief Table of Contents

Preface   xviii

PART I   An Introduction to Microeconomics   1

Chapter 1   Microeconomics: A Working Methodology   2

PART II   Individual Choice   39

Chapter 2   A Theory of Preferences   40

Chapter 3   Getting and Spending: The Problem of
             Economic Choice Making   69

Chapter 4   Vicarious Problem Solving: Applications of the
             Theory of Choice   110

Chapter *5   Choice Making under Imperfect
             Information   140

PART III The Firm   177

Chapter *6   The Theory of the Firm   178

Chapter 7   Production and Cost: One Variable Input   205

Chapter 8   Production and Cost: Many Variable
             Inputs   238

PART IV Goods Markets   271

Chapter 9   The Theory of Perfect Competition   272

Chapter 10   Monopoly   315

Chapter 11   **Game Theory and Oligopoly**   359

Chapter *12   **Product Differentiation**   398

PART V   Resource Markets and General Equilibrium   427

Chapter 13   **Input Markets and the Allocation of Resources   428**

Chapter 14   **The Distribution of Income   462**

Chapter 15   **Intertemporal Resource Allocation   485**

Chapter 16   **Efficiency and the Allocation of Resources: A General Equilibrium Approach   516**

Chapter 17   **Externalities and Public Goods   545**

Answers to Problems   570

Index   595

Table of Contents

Preface   xviii

PART 1   An Introduction to Microeconomics   1

Chapter 1   Microeconomics: A Working Methodology   2

1.1   Choice of Production Technique   3
1.2   The Water Shortage Problem   3
    Common Property Problems   8

1.3   Agricultural Price Support Programs   9
    Competitive Equilibrium Price and Quantity   10
    Price Supports   11

1.4   Describing an Economy   14
    A Resource Endowment   15
    A Technology   15
    Preferences of Individuals   15
    Self-Interest and Economic Choice Making   16
    Institutions   17

1.5   The Equilibrium Method   18
1.6   Positive and Normative Economics   19
    The Pareto Criterion   20
    Cost-Benefit Analysis   21

1.7   The Market Economy   22
    The Circular Flow of Economic Activity   23
    The Plan of the Book   24

    Summary   24
    Exercises   25
    Appendix: Model Building   27
    References   37

PART II   Individual Choice   39

Chapter 2   A Theory of Preferences   40

2.1   Completeness and Consistency of Preferences   40
    The Two-Good Case   41

A Preference Ordering   41
Completeness Assumption   42
Two-Term Consistency Assumption   42
Transitivity (or Three-Term Consistency) Assumption   42

2.2   Tradeoffs and Indifference Curves   44
Nonsatiation   46
The Slope of Indifference Curves   47
Non-Intersecting Indifference Curves   48

2.3   Tradeoffs and the Marginal Rate of Substitution   50
Diminishing Marginal Rate of Substitution   52
Kinked Indifference Curves   52
Shapes of Indifference Curves   53

2.4   Applications   56
Overtime Pay   56
Pollution   57
Snap Courses   59

2.5   Utility Functions   61
Constructing a Utility Function   61
Many Utility Functions   63
The Meaning of Utility Numbers   64

2.6   The Many-Goods Case   65

Summary   66
Exercises   67
References   68

Chapter 3   Getting and Spending: The Problem of Economic Choice Making   69

3.1   Economic Choices   69
3.2   The Budget Constraint   71
Attainable Consumption Bundles   71
Opportunity Cost   72

3.3   The Consumer's Choice Problem   73
The Choice Problem   73
The Solution: Demand Functions   74

3.4   Graphic Analysis of Utility Maximization   76
Interior Solutions   76
Corner Solutions   78

3.5   Elasticity   81
Elasticity of the Number of Smokers with Respect to Price   84

3.6   Comparative Statics Analysis of Demand   85
3.7   Consumption Response to a Change in Income   86
        Normal Goods and Inferior Goods   86
        Engel Curves   87
        Some Income Elasticities of Demand   88

3.8   Consumption Response to a Change in Price   89
        The Price-Consumption Path   91
        The Demand Curve   91
        Some Price Elasticities of Demand   91

3.9   Income and Substitution Effects   92
        Income and Substitution Effects for a Price Increase   93
        Income and Substitution Effects for a Price Decrease   94
        The Negative Substitution Effect   96
        The Ambiguous Income Effect   96
        The Slope of the Demand Curve   97

*3.10   The Compensated Demand Curve   97
        The Substitution Effect Revisited   97
        The Compensated Demand Function   99

3.11   Complements and Substitutes   101
        Some Cross-Price Elasticities of Demand   102

3.12   Composite Commodities   103
*3.13   Two General Properties of Demand Functions   104
        No Money Illusion   104
        Engel's Aggregation Law   106

        Summary   106
        Exercises   107
        References   109

Chapter 4   Vicarious Problem Solving: Applications of the Theory of Choice   110

4.1   Lump-Sum Versus Excise Taxes   110
        Excise Tax Versus Lump-Sum Tax   110
        An Application to the Theory of Clubs   113
        Government Subsidies   113

4.2   Measuring Benefits and Costs   114
        Equivalent Variation for a New Good   114
        Compensating Variation for a New Good   114
        Equivalent Variation for a Price Change   117
        Compensating Variation for a Price Change   117

      Comparing Equivalent Variation and Compensating Variation   117
      Consumer's Surplus   118

*4.3   The Demand for Consumer Capital   121
*4.4   Two-Part Tariffs   124
4.5   The Demand for Leisure and the Supply of Labor   127
      Work, Leisure, and Income   127
      Time and Money Prices   128

*4. 6   The Tragedy of the Commons   129
      Racquetball and the Tragedy of the Commons   130
      First Come, First Served Allocation   130
      Institutional Mechanisms for Allocation   131

*4.7   Index Numbers   133
      Quantity Indexes   133
      Price Indexes   135

      Summary   137
      Exercises   137
      References   139

Chapter *5   Choice Making under Imperfect Information   140

5.1   Expected-Utility Theory   140
      Calculating Expected Monetary Value   141
      The Expected-Utility Hypothesis   142
      The Expected-Utility Function   143

5.2   Generalizing the Expected-Utility Approach   146
      Subjective Probabilities   147
      State-Dependent Preferences   148

5.3   Attitudes Towards Risk   148
5.4   Shedding Risk   152
      Informal Risk Pooling   152
      The Market for Insurance   154
      Risk Spreading   157
      The Case for Risk Aversion   158

5.5   The Economics of Asymmetric Information   158
      Hidden Characteristics   159
      Adverse Selection: The "Lemons Principle"   161
      Signaling   162
      Moral Hazard Problems: Hidden Actions   165

      Summary   167
      Exercises   167

Appendix: The Expected-Utility Theorem   171
    The Substitution Assumption   172
    The Ordering Assumption   173
    Expected Utility Theorem   174

References   175

PART III The Firm   177

Chapter *6   The Theory of the Firm   178

6.1   Organizational Issues   178
    Three Structures of the Firm   179
    Cooperation from Noncooperative Behavior   180
    A Key to the Puzzle: Institutions   181
    The Existence of Multiperson Firms   182

6.2   Organizational Issues   183
    The One-Person Firm   183
    A Two-Person Alternative   185
    The Partnership Equilibrium   187
    Pareto Optimality and Choice of Institutions   189

6.3   Team Production   189
    Productivity of Teams   190
    Partnership with Team Production   190
    The Owner-Managed Team   192
    Contracting and Monitoring Costs   193

6.4   The Pareto-Preferred Organizational Forms   195
6.5   Specialization and the Division of Labor   197
    Transactions Costs   199
    Generic Inputs   199
    Specific Inputs   200

Summary   201
Exercises   202
References   204

Chapter 7   Production and Cost: One Variable Input   205

7.1   The Production Function   205
    Defining the Production Function   206
    A Fixed-Proportions Production Function   206
    Variable-Proportions Production Functions   207

7.2   The Short- and Long-Run Cost-Minimization Problems   209
       The Long-Run Cost-Minimization Problem   209
       Input Prices   210
       Short-Run Cost-Minimization Problems   210

7.3   Production: One Variable Input   210
       Total Product   211
       Marginal Product   212
       Diminishing Marginal Productivity   213
       Average Product   216

7.4   Costs of Production: One Variable Input   219
       The Variable Cost Function Illustrated   220
       Deriving the Variable Cost Function   221
       Average Variable Cost and Short-Run Marginal Cost   221
       Average Product and Average Cost   225
       Marginal Product and Marginal Cost   225
       Fixed Cost   226
       Short-Run Total Cost and Short-Run Average Cost   226

*7.5   Applications: Traffic Congestion and Multiplant Firms   228
       The Allocation of Output among Different Plants   233

       Summary   234
       Exercises   235
       References   237

Chapter 8   Production and Cost: Many Variable Inputs   238

8.1   Isoquants and Input Substitution   238
       The Shape of Isoquants   239

8.2   Marginal Rate of Technical Substitution   240
       Perfect Substitutes and Perfect Complements   243
       Diminishing Marginal Rate of Technical Substitution   243
       MRTS as a Ratio of Marginal Products   244

8.3   Returns to Scale   245
8.4   The Cost-Minimization Problem: A Perspective   248
8.5   Solving Cost-Minimization Problems   249
       The First Principle of Cost Minimization   251
       The Second Principle of Cost Minimization   251

8.6   Comparative Statics for Input Prices   254
8.7   Comparative Statics for the Level of Output   256
       Normal and Inferior Inputs   257
       Long-Run Costs and Output   258

8.8   Comparing Long-Run and Short-Run Costs   261
8.9   A Theory of Market Structure   265

        Summary   267
        Exercises   268

Part IV Goods Markets   271

Chapter 9   The Theory of Perfect Competition   272

9.1   Competitive Model of Exchange   272
        Market Demand   273
        Market Supply   274
        The Walrasian Auctioneer   275
        Competitive Equilibrium   275
        Pareto Optimality, or Efficiency   277
        The Role of Initial Allocation   277
        The Function of Price   278

9.2   Potential Difficulties with the Competitive Model   279
        Price Taking or Price Manipulating   279
        Large Numbers and Price-Taking Behavior   281
        Price Making: The Walrasian Auctioneer   281
        Perfect Information   282
        Robustness of the Competitive Model   282

9.3   The Assumptions of Perfect Competition   283
9.4   The Firm's Short-Run Supply Decision   284
9.5   Short-Run Competitive Equilibrium   290
        Aggregating Demand   290
        Aggregating Short-Run Supply   291
        Short-Run Competitive Equilibrium   292

9.6   Efficiency of the Short-Run Competitive Equilibrium   294
9.7   Long-Run Competitive Equilibrium   296
        No-Exit, No-Entry, and Long-Run Equilibrium   296
        Price Equal to Minimum Average Cost   297
        The Individual Firm in Long-Run Equilibrium   298
        Long-Run Supply Function   298
        The Constant-Cost Case   299
        A Dynamic Story   299
        The Increasing-Cost Case   301
        The Decreasing-Cost Case   304

9.8   Comparative Statics   304

*9.9   Rent Control   305
            The Rent Control Model   305
            Apparent Effects of Rent Control   307
            Short-Run Effects   307
            Long-Run Effects   309

        Summary   310
        Exercises   311
        References   314

Chapter 10   **Monopoly**   315

10.1   Monopoly Defined   315
10.2   The Monopolist's Revenue Functions   316
            Marginal Revenue   317
            Marginal Revenue and the Price Elasticity of Demand   319
            Linear Demand Curve   319

10.3   Maximizing Profit   321
10.4   The Inefficiency of Monopoly   324
10.5   Sources of Monopoly   327
            Government Franchise Monopoly   327
            Patent Monopoly   327
            Resource-Based Monopoly   327
            Technological (or Natural) Monopoly   327
            Monopoly by Good Management   330

*10.6   Regulatory Responses to Monopoly   330
            Divestiture in a Resource-Based Monopoly   331
            Responses to Patent Monopoly   331
            Responses to Natural Monopoly   331
            Average Cost Pricing   331
            Rate-Of-Return Regulation   332
            Efficient Regulatory Mechanisms   334
            Franchise Monopoly   338

10.7   Price Discrimination   338
            Market Segmentation   338
            Perfect Price Discrimination   339
            Ordinary Price Discrimination   339
            Market Segmentation Revisited   344
            Multipart or Block Pricing   345

*10.10   Patent Policy   348
            The Appropriability Problem   349

A Model of Inventions   349
Product Development in the Absence of Patents   351
The Effects of Patents   352
Optimal Patent Policy   352

Summary   355
Exercises   356
References   358

Chapter 11   Game Theory and Oligopoly   359

11.1   Game Theory   360
11.2   Monopoly Equilibrium   361
11.3   Duopoly as a Prisoners' Dilemma   362
    The Oligopoly Problem   363
    The Prisoners' Dilemma   364

11.4   The Cournot Duopoly Model   364
    Mock Dynamics in the Cournot Model   367
    Generalizing Results   368
    Isoprofit Curves   368

11.5   The Cournot Model with Many Firms   371
11.6   The Bertrand Model   372
    Dynamics in the Bertrand Model   374

11.7   The Collusive Model of Oligopoly   375
11.8   Experimental Evidence   377
11.9   Repeated Play, Supergames, and Richer Strategies   377
11.10   The Limit Output Model   379
    Barriers to Entry   380
    The Inducement to Entry   381
    Strategic Choice of Industry Output   383
    Critique of the Model   384

11.11   Refinements of Limit Output   384
11.12   Positioning and Reacting   388

Summary   389
Exercises   390
Appendix: Collusion in Supergames   392
    Trigger Strategies   392
    The Credibility Problem   395
    Subgame Perfection   396
    Critique of the Collusive Model   396

References   397

Chapter *12   Product Differentiation   398

12.1   Chamberlin's Symmetrically Differentiated Products   399
Symmetric Preferences   400
Symmetric Demand Functions   401

12.2   Chamberlin's Small-Numbers Case   404
The Nash Price Equilibrium   405
The Collusive Price   405
The Oligopoly Problem Again   407
Entry   408

12.3   Chamberlin's Large-Numbers Case   409
Short-Run Equilibrium   409
Long-Run Equilibrium   409
Efficiency and the Chamberlin Model   409

12.4   Address Models of Monopolistic Competition   412
A Model of Spatial Competition   412
Short-Run Price Equilibrium   413
Long-Run Equilibrium   417
Profit in Long-Run Equilibrium   418
Product Proliferation   420
Generalizing the Model   420
Efficiency   421
Product Diversity: Equilibrium Versus Cost-Benefit Efficiency   422

Summary   422
Exercises   424
References   424

PART V   Resource Markets and General Equilibrium   427

Chapter 13   Input Markets and the Allocation of Resources   428

13.1   The Role of Input Markets   428
13.2   Perfectly Competitive Input Markets   429
13.3   The Supply of Non-Labor Inputs   431
13.4   The Supply of Labor   431
Responses to Changes in Non-Work Income   433
Responses to a Change in the Wage Rate   434
Labor Supply Curves   435

13.5   The Firm's Demand for One Variable Input   437
         Input Demand in a One-Good Economy   437
         Value of the Marginal Product   441

13.6   Input Demand with Many Variable Inputs   442
         Downward-Sloping, Long-Run Input Demand Curve   442
         A Comparison of Long-Run and Short-Run Input Demand   444

13.7   Competitive Equilibrium in an Input Market   445
13.8   Monopsony in Input Markets   447
         The Monopsonist's Factor Cost Functions   447
         The Short-Run Monopsony Equilibrium   450
         The Inefficiency of Monopsony   452

13.9   Sources of Monopsony Power   453
         Immobility   454
         Monopoly and Specialized Inputs   455

13.10   Monopsonistic Price Discrimination   455

         Summary   458
         Exercises   459
         References   461

Chapter 14   The Distribution of Income   462

14.1   Distributive Justice   462
         The Productivity Principle   463
         Product Exhaustion   463
         Thought Experiments for the Productivity Principle   464
         Input Prices and Scarcity   465
         The Redistributionist Principle   465

14.2   Minimum-Wage Legislation   468
         Competitive Labor Markets   468
         Monopsonistic Labor Markets   470
         Union Wage Rates: Some Analogous Issues   472

14.3   Wage Floors in a Two-Sector Model   473
         The Underemployment Equilibrium   474
         The Unemployment Equilibrium   474

14.4   Income Maintenance   476
         The Efficient Transfer Mechanism   477
         Topping Up and Welfare   478
         The Negative Income Tax   480

         Summary   482
         Exercises   482
         References   484

Chapter 15   Intertemporal Resource Allocation   485

15.1   Intertemporal Value Comparisons   486
     A Perfect Market for Loanable Funds   487
     The Separation Theorem   487
     Present Value   488

15.2   The Life-Cycle Model   489
     The Budget Line   489
     The Intertemporal Allocation of Lifetime Income   492
     Comparative Statics   494
     Supply and Demand for Loanable Funds   498

15.3   Human Capital   499
15.4   Intertemporal Allocation of Nonrenewable Resources   504
     Individual Supply Behavior   505
     Hotelling's Law   506
     Determining the Competitive Equilibrium   506

15.5   The Firm's Demand for Capital Inputs   508
15.6   The Market for Loanable Funds   511

     Summary   512
     Exercises   513
     References   515

Chapter 16   Efficiency and the Allocation of Resources: A General Equilibrium Approach   516

16.1   Efficiency in an Exchange Economy   517
     The Edgeworth Box Diagram   517
     Preference Assumptions   519
     Efficiency in Consumption   520
     The Contract Curve   521

16.2   Competitive Equilibrium in an Exchange Economy   522
     Budget Lines in an Exchange Economy   522
     Finding the Competitive Equilibrium   524
     The First Theorem of Welfare Economics   526
     The Second Theorem of Welfare Economics   526

16.3   Efficiency in General Equilibrium with Production   527
     Production Assumptions   527
     Efficiency in Consumption   528
     Production Possibilities Set   528
     Efficiency in Production   529
     The Marginal Rate of Transformation   530
     Efficiency in Product Mix   533

16.4   Efficiency and General Competitive Equilibrium   535
16.5   Sources of Inefficiency   537
       The Inefficiency of Monopoly   537
       Taxation and Efficiency   539

       Summary   539
       Exercises   540
       Appendix: Efficiency   541
       References   544

Chapter 17   Externalities and Public Goods   545

17.1   The Smoker's Externality   546
17.2   A Taxonomy of Externalities   550
       Consumption–Consumption Externalities   550
       Production–Production Externalities   551
       Consumption–Production Externalities   551
       Production–Consumption Externalities   551

17.3   Responses to Externalities: An Overview   551
       Private Negotiations   552
       Internalization   552
       Governmental Responses   552
       Assigning Property Rights   552
       Public Regulation   553
       Nonintervention   553

17.4   Privately Negotiated Solutions   553
17.5   Internalizing the Externality   558
17.6   Regulatory Solutions   559
       Cost-Benefit Analysis   560
       Hitting the Regulatory Target   562

17.7   Public Goods   563
       Nonrivalrous Goods   564
       Nonexcludable Goods   564
       Pure Public Goods   564
       Public Provision of Nonrivalrous Goods   565
       Cost-Benefit Analysis and Revealed Preference   566

       Summary   567
       Exercises   568
       References   569

Answers to Problems   570
Index   595

Preface

To the Student

We are all curious about the world around us, and we want understand it. Economics provides a systematic way of understanding the economic activity that we see every day. These are just a sampling of the many questions you will come to think about more clearly by applying the tools of microeconomic theory: Why did the Portuguese cod fleet use fishing techniques in the 1970s that were strikingly different from the techniques used by the American and Canadian cod fleets? Are the seasonal water shortages that afflict so many communities inevitable, or do they sometimes result from poor resource management? Once a government decides to support the price of an agricultural product, what is the best way to do it?

Throughout the book we present the working methodology of the microeconomic theorist, not by talking about it, but by showing you how to create economic models to answer specific economic questions like the three examples just mentioned. In fact, we open Chapter 1 by showing you how economists typically tackle these three problems. And we end the chapter with an appendix that takes you step by step through the process of building an economic model.

Chapter 1 — with its hands-on, problem-solving approach to microeconomic theory — sets the tone for the following chapters. We typically begin with an intriguing question from ordinary life and then work outward from specific problem to more general theory. This approach lets you see immediately how useful microeconomic theory can be in making sense of real-life economic events.

This hands-on approach to microeconomic theory is reinforced throughout by the use of in-chapter problems. These problems are meant to encourage *active* reading in two ways: by encouraging you to check your understanding of material that you have just read and, sometimes, by challenging you to extend what you have learned one step farther or apply what you have learned to a related problem. (We provide answers to all the in-chapter problems at the back of the book.) Our philosophy is that the only real way to learn microeconomics is to *do* it — every step of the way.

Of course, microeconomics is a field that is changing rapidly — and that is its real challenge. We not only cover the standard topics in microeconomics; we also provide you with an overview of current research in many important areas. By putting you in touch with modern trends in economics — with the "frontiers" of microeconomic research — we bring you right up to date and also let you see just how much exciting work in microeconomics remains to be done.

To the Instructor

Thinking like an economist

The major focus of our book is to try to teach students how to think like economists. We almost always start with an interesting question and ask, "How would an economist try to answer this particular question?" Then we construct the solution — an economic model — from the ground up. We have been careful to choose applications that are interesting and not too difficult — applications that are well within students' grasp — and then to present them in clear, consistent, step-by-step discussions. We then show how the model can be generalized to apply to other, similar problems. In this way, students are actively engaged in developing the standard tools of microeconomic analysis. More importantly, they see how economists create those tools and get a chance to do economics for themselves. The benefit of this approach is that students learn that abstract economic thinking (that is, economic model building) is essentially about very real and familiar problems.

This problem-solving approach is reinforced by many in-chapter problems and end-of-chapter exercises. The point of the in-chapter problems — a feature that we introduced to the intermediate microeconomics market in the first edition of *Microeconomics* — is to draw students into the material and to keep them actively engaged in their reading. Full problem answers in the textbook guarantee that students will not be frustrated if they fail to hit on solutions quickly. A very complete set of end-of-chapter exercises for each chapter reinforces students' learning. These exercises contain a large number of easy-to-do problems and a small number of more challenging problems.

A balance of theory and application

Because our whole approach is applied — we almost always work from the specific application to more general theory — our book is full of lively and interesting examples. But our objective throughout is to use these applications as a means of developing economic theory in as precise and rigorous a way as possible. Our major aim is to give students a thorough grounding in microeconomic theory. Several of our reviewers have commented that this book provides an optimal balance between interesting applications and carefully developed theory.

Up-to-date economics

We also provide a balance between traditional economic theory and modern developments in microeconomics. Our treatment of the standard topics of microeconomics is careful and comprehensive. Students using our book will acquire a thorough understanding of the traditional tools of the microeconomic theorist. However, we have also been trendsetters in introducing current research topics at the intermediate level. We provide students with in-depth treatments of many modern topics in microeconomics, including the theory of uncertainty and imperfect information (Chapter 5); the theory of the firm (Chapter 6); game theory, with applications to oligopoly and market structure (Chapter 11); and the address (or characteristics) approach to product differentiation (Chapter 12).

Accessible presentation and readable style

This book is analytically rigorous but still widely accessible to undergraduate students. The analysis is presented in an engaging and highly readable style. (One of the authors, Diane Eaton, is a professional textbook writer.) Each topic flows naturally from what came before it and leads smoothly into what follows. The seamless, well-paced "narrative" style of presentation allows students to progress from one topic to the next with ease.

We do not use calculus in the text itself, where we rely on carefully explained graphic techniques. However, we do provide complete calculus footnotes for students with a solid background in mathematics. We have also introduced new graphic aids to help students identify and review major concepts. Key terms in every chapter are in boldface in the text and set out in the margin, and important assumptions and results are also graphically highlighted for easy identification. More technically-demanding material has been placed in appendices, and challenging end-of-chapter exercises are marked with an asterisk.

Changes to the third edition

Broadly speaking, the organization and content remain unchanged in the third edition of *Microeconomics*. Several chapters that have been perennial favorites with instructors — including Chapter 4 (Vicarious Problem Solving), Chapter 6 (The Theory of the Firm), Chapter 12 (Product Differentiation), and Chapter 16 (General Equilibrium and Welfare) — are updated but essentially unchanged. However, the remaining chapters have all been thoroughly revised from beginning to end. We have substantially reworked specific material at many points and introduced completely new material at many other points in these chapters. In addition, we have added a brand-new chapter on intertemporal resource allocation (Chapter 15).

We have designed this book so that a number of differentiated courses can be taught from it. The chapters that form the core of a standard one-semester microeconomics course are Chapters 1–4 and Chapters 7–10. A number of specialized courses — for example, courses that emphasize comparative institutional analysis, labor economics, industrial organization, or consumer theory — can easily be built on this core by assigning the relevant additional chapters. (Note that chapters and sections marked with an asterisk can be skipped without loss of continuity.)

Additional resources

Our textbook is supplemented by a range of additional resources for instructors. The *Instructor's Manual* provides answers to the end-of-chapter exercises as well as suggestions for lectures, a series of easy-to-administer classroom experiments, and transparency masters for all figures in the text. A complete *Test Item File* of multiple-choice questions is also available on computer disk and in booklet form.

In the accompanying study guide, *Problem Solving in Microeconomics*, Nancy Gallini of the University of Toronto, has done a superb job of providing further study material for students. In addition to chapter summaries, case studies, lists of key words, multiple-choice questions, and true-false questions, this study guide offers many useful and fascinating real-world problems.

Finally, we would like to acknowledge all those at Prentice Hall Canada who worked on the third edition, especially our copy editor Ruth Chernia, Jackie Wood, Maurice Esses, Norman Bernard, Monica Kompter, and Steve Lewis.

REVIEWERS

We would like to acknowledge the useful suggestions and encouragement given to us by the reviewers of this text. Reviewers of the third edition include:

William Baldwin, Dartmouth College
Price Fishback, University of Arizona
Mason Gerety, University of Maryland
Michael Leeds, Temple University

Robin Neill, Carleton University
Ingrid Peters-Fransen, Wilfrid Laurier University
Leonid Polishchuck, The University of British Columbia
William A. Sims, Concordia University
Paul M. Taube, University of Texas-Pan American
Gary N. Tompkins, University of Regina
Linda Welling, University of Victoria
Gilbert N. Wolpe, Middlesex Community College
Ian Wooton, The University of Western Ontario

Reviewers of the second edition include:

Robert A. Becker, Indiana University
Arlo Biere, Kansas State University
George D. Brower, Allegheny College
Mukesh Eswaren, The University of British Columbia
Larry Herman, Kenyon College
Anthony Y. C. Koo, Michigan State University
James P. Lesage, University of Toledo
Lynne Pepall, Tufts University
Malcolm Rutherford, University of Victoria
Nicolas Schmitt, Simon Fraser University
Alan Slivinski, University of Western Ontario
Roger Ware, University of Toronto
Douglas S. West, University of Alberta

Reviewers of the first edition include:

Thomas Barthold, Dartmouth College
George Borjas, University of California, Santa Barbara
Oscar T. Brookins, Northeastern University
Norman Clifford, University of Kansas
William T. Dickens, University of California, Berkeley
Joseph C. Gallo, University of Cincinnati
Charles Geiss, University of Missouri
Edward Greenberg, Washington University
Richard Hofler, University of Tennessee
Joseph Hughes, Rutgers University
Michael Jones, Yale University
Edward C. Kienzle, Boston College
Anthony Y. C. Koo, Michigan State University
Martin McGuire, University of Maryland
Paul L. Menchik, Michigan State University
Michael Morgan, College of Charleston

Paul Glen Munyon, Grinnell College
Jack Ochs, University of Pittsburgh
William B. O'Neil, Colby College
Paul Roman, St. Louis University
William Schaffer, Georgia Institute of Technology
John Schroeter, Iowa State University
Alan Slivinski, University of Western Ontario
Paul M. Sommers, Middlebury College

B. Curtis Eaton
Diane F. Eaton
1995

PART I

An Introduction to Microeconomics

Chapter 1 is your introduction to the working methodology of the micro-economist theorist. We begin with a sampler of interesting microeconomic questions and show you how economists go about building specific economic models to answer these questions. We then use these examples to present a more systematic discussion of the subject matter and method of economics. We describe an economy, explore the equilibrium method that economists use to analyze economic problems, define positive and normative economics, and consider Pareto optimality and cost-benefit analysis. This introduction concludes with a brief discussion of a market economy and an outline of the remainder of the book.

Microeconomics: A Working Methodology

Why do you sometimes find two or three gas stations at the same intersection? Why does the value of a new car plummet the instant you drive it off the lot? Why do people have to spend so much time searching for an apartment in rent-controlled areas? Why do amusement parks often charge a whopping admission price to the park and almost nothing for the rides? Why does McDonald's break down the job of making hamburgers into so many little tasks and hire different workers to do each one? Why does IBM produce a whole spectrum of products? Why are some markets (like the market for local telephone services) monopolized and others (like the markets for carpet cleaning services) highly competitive? What is the best way to ease the annoying traffic congestion that plagues so many cities around the world?

As you work your way through this book, you will discover answers to these and many other questions. But microeconomics is not just a listing of specific economic questions and their answers. The real economic environment poses so many complex questions that we cannot expect to find ready-made answers to them all. The only way to do microeconomics successfully is to find a method for setting out and then solving microeconomic problems. Throughout the book, you will be introduced to the tools of economic analysis and shown how to use those tools to answer many economic questions.

Chapter 1 is an introduction to the working methodology of microeconomics.[1] We begin the chapter with several short, nonrigorous explorations of different microeconomic problems. Why did the Portuguese cod-fishing fleet use techniques in the 1970s that were strikingly different from the techniques used by the American and Canadian cod fleets? Are the seasonal water shortages that afflict so many communities inevitable, or do they sometimes result from poor resource management? Once a government decides to support the price of an agricultural product, what is the best way to do it?

Our aim is to show you how economists typically approach such questions. In the concluding sections of the chapter, we use these problems as examples as we provide a more systematic discussion of the subject matter and method of economics. We show how to describe an economy, we look at the equilibrium method economists use to explore economic problems, and we consider two kinds of questions addressed by economists — positive and normative questions. We conclude with a brief discussion of a market economy and an outline of the book.

---

1 See Larry Boland's entry on "methodology" in *The New Palgrave: A Dictionary of Economics* for an accessible discussion of modern views on methodology.

1.1
Choice of Production Technique

International travelers often comment on the many ways that firms from different parts of the world do the same job. Fishing for cod off the coast of Newfoundland is our favorite example. When we visited St. John's, Newfoundland, in the spring of 1970 the Portuguese cod-fishing fleet was in the harbor. The fleet consisted of some sailing ships, each equipped with numerous small rowing dinghies, some fishers (one for each dinghy), fishing lines (two for each fisher), and a cook-captain. Each fisher set out in a dinghy every day with two fishing lines to jig for cod by hand while the cook-captain tended the ship and cooked dinner. Interestingly, the American and Canadian fleets that were operating in the same waters fished in quite a different way. They caught cod using electronic fish-locating gear, expensive nets that were set and pulled with powerful winches, motorized boats, and relatively few fishers. Another striking example comes from the shrimp-packing industries situated on either side of the Mexico - United States border along the Gulf of Mexico. Shrimp-packers in Texas use many special-purpose labor-saving machines and relatively few workers, while shrimp-packers in Mexico use many workers and very few machines to do the same job. In India, you may see large water-diversion systems and canals dug by hand and the dirt carried away in baskets by dozens of laborers, while in North America and Europe the same job is done using huge earth-moving machines and relatively few workers.

To an economist, these observations pose a question: How can these marked differences in the choice of a production technique be explained? The economist's explanation is this: Among all the techniques that can be used to accomplish a particular task, the firm chooses the technique that is least costly. As a result, in countries where machines are relatively more expensive than labor, firms use fewer machines and more workers. And in countries where labor is relatively more expensive than machines, the reverse is true. In 1970 in Portugal, labor was cheap relative to machines, but in Canada and the United States, machines were cheap relative to labor. So the Portuguese fleet used labor-intensive fishing techniques while the Canadian and American fleets used machine-intensive techniques. Similarly, in India labor is relatively cheaper than machines, so labor-intensive techniques are used to construct water works, while in North America and Europe, machinery is relatively cheaper, so machine-intensive techniques are used.

> ### PROBLEM 1.1
>
> You may have noticed that the materials used to package consumer products sometimes change. For example, steel cans are sometimes substituted for aluminum cans and plastic bottles for glass bottles. How would you begin to explain these changes in packaging materials?

1.2
The Water Shortage Problem

International travelers are also likely to encounter the seasonal water shortages experienced by communities around the world. For example, in many parts of North America late summer is often a time of drought. Cities in drier regions like Arizona and California often have severe water shortages in August, but even cities in regions where water is relatively abundant, like Oregon and British Columbia, can suffer from late-summer water problems. To an economist, these events pose a question: Can anything be done to ease the severity of such recurring water shortages?

Let us take an economist's approach to this question. The first step is to simplify what is in reality a multitude of complex problems to a single, simple problem. We will explore the water-shortage problem in the context of a very simple, public water system on an imaginary vacation island in the Pacific Ocean. (This imaginary water problem, however, is based on a real water problem on an island northwest of Seattle, Washington.) Even though our story — or our model — is a simple one, it captures important features of many real water-shortage problems, and it allows you to see how economists typically approach this kind of problem.

Let us imagine that a parcel of land on this hypothetical vacation island was subdivided in the mid-1970s and named the Village Point Estates. At the same time, the Village Point Water District was also developed to provide water for the new subdivision. Today, the Village Point Water District still owns and operates a number of wells and a network of pipes connecting 100 homes to the wells. The water district pumps water from the wells and distributes it to the homes.

In effect, the Village Point Water District is jointly owned by the homeowners in Village Point Estates. Not only do these homeowners elect the board of directors that manages the water district's affairs, they also jointly pay for all of the water district's costs, composed of a salary for one part time employee, the cost of the electricity for pumping the water, the cost of maintaining the system, and a large payment to the original developers who lent money to the Village Point Water District to cover the costs of drilling the wells and constructing the delivery system. These costs total $50,000 per year.

To generate the $50,000 required to cover its costs, the Village Point Water District levies a fixed annual fee of $500 per householder. Notice that the water district does *not charge* each of the 100 householders on the basis of amount of water used. Instead, *every householder pays $500 a year, regardless of how much or how little water it uses.* Because every householder pays the *same fixed fee* for water regardless of quantity used, we will call this arrangement a *non-metered scheme.*

Imagine that all the houses supplied by the Village Point Water District are vacation cottages occupied only during July and August. As a result, water is demanded only in these months. The water supply comes from winter rain that accumulates in the aquifers from which the water district pumps its water. For the first few years, there were only a few houses in Village Point Estates, and the water system worked quite well. However, as the number of homes served by the water district grew, a serious problem developed. In August, the water in the wells was often very low and water was available only intermittently. This is the problem we want to explore.

To grasp the essence of the problem, we will ignore the very real differences in yearly rainfall and in water usage among householders and think in terms of a *representative householder* in a representative year. That is, we will suppose that as far as water consumption is concerned, *all the Village Point householders are identical* and that this representative Village Point householder uses 20,000 gallons of water over the crucial two-month summer period. He or she uses 15,000 gallons in July, and — if the water were available — he or she would use 15,000 gallons in August as well. But in August, water is not always available. Some days there is water in the wells and the water district can supply water to Village Point. Other days the wells are completely dry and the water district's pipes are empty. All told, in August the representative Village Point householder is able to use just 5,000 gallons of water. To summarize: the householder currently has what we can call the *unbalanced water use profile* consisting of 15,000 gallons of water in July and only 5,000 gallons in August.

The water district has looked into the possibility of increasing the water supply to ease the August shortage, but the necessary improvements — including an expensive desalinization plant — are just too costly. So it seems that the Village Point householder will have to make do with just 20,000 gallons of water over the two-month period.

Interestingly, this householder would actually prefer to spread his or her water use evenly across the two month period, using 10,000 gallons of water in July and 10,000 gallons in August, rather than 15,000 gallons in July and only 5,000 gallons in August. That is, the householder prefers what we can call the *balanced water use profile*, consisting of 10,000 gallons per month, to the current unbalanced water use profile. However, under the current scheme, there is no way that the householder can achieve the preferred balanced water use profile by his or her own efforts — *even though the total amount of water in the two profiles is identical*.

To see why, imagine what would happen if just one householder in Village Point Estates reduced personal water use from 15,000 gallons to 10,000 gallons in July, thereby leaving 5,000 additional gallons of water available for use in August. In August, this water-conserving householder would not get to use the full 5,000 gallons he or she saved in July. Instead, every one of the 100 householders served by the Village Point Water District would draw on the extra water supply, increasing their August water use by 50 gallons each (5,000 gallons divided by 100 householders). In other words, by reducing personal water use by 5,000 gallons in July, the single water-conserving householder increases personal water use in August by *only* 50 gallons.

In Figure 1.1 we have shown all the water use profiles that this householder can attain personally under the non-metered scheme. Gallons of water used in July are measured on the horizontal axis and gallons of water in August on the vertical axis. The householder is initially at point U, where he or she has the unbalanced water use

FIGURE 1.1   Attainable water use profiles

Under the non-metered scheme, the householder can attain any water use profile on line DCU, and he or she chooses the unbalanced water use profile. Hence, the equilibrium for the representative householder under the non-metered scheme is the unbalanced water use profile at U. The balanced water use profile at B (which uses the same amount of water and is preferred to the unbalanced profile) is unattainable under the non-metered scheme.

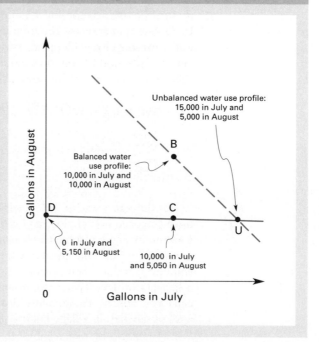

profile composed of 15,000 gallons in July and 5,000 gallons in August. As we saw above, starting from the unbalanced water use profile, this householder can attain point C by conserving 5,000 gallons in July. At point C, the householder uses 10,000 gallons in July and 5,050 gallons in August. Starting again from the unbalanced water use profile, this householder can attain point D by reducing personal water use in July to nothing. At point D, he or she uses no water in July and 5,150 gallons in August. In other words, if this householder reduces personal water use in July by 15,000 gallons, the result is an increase in personal water use in August of just 150 gallons because the 15,000 additional gallons now available in August are evenly split among all 100 Village Point householders who draw water from the system. Notice that the slope of the line DCU is -1/100. This slope reflects the fact that when this householder decreases July water use by one gallon, he or she gets to use only a hundredth of that gallon in August.

What is the best, or most preferred, profile on the line DCU from the individual householder's point of view? We know two facts relevant to this question. 1. All householders actually choose the unbalanced consumption profile at point U in each year. 2. The line DCU describes the water use profiles that the householder can attain by his or her own actions. It seems natural to assume that, from the water use profiles on line DCU, the householder actually chooses the profile that is most preferred. Given this assumption, we conclude that the unbalanced water consumption profile U is the most preferred profile on line DCU.

Because all 100 householders in Village Point Estates see the problem in exactly the same way, they find themselves in an *equilibrium* in which every householder has the unbalanced water use profile containing 15,000 gallons of water in July and only 5,000 gallons in August. This situation is an equilibrium because there is nothing any individual householder can do to attain a more preferred water use profile. In other words, among the the water use profiles that the householder can attain by his or her own actions, the unbalanced profile is most preferred.

Yet this equilibrium is unattractive because every householder would actually prefer to reallocate 5,000 gallons of water from July to August. That is, every householder prefers the balanced profile at point B in Figure 1.1 to the unbalanced profile at point U. Notice that because the total amount of water in the balanced and unbalanced water use profiles is identical, every single householder could be made *better off* if only a way could be found to induce *every* Village Point householder to save 5,000 gallons of water in July for use in August.

> ### PROBLEM 1.2
>
> Under the non-metered scheme, what happens to an individual householder's private incentive to conserve water in July for use in August as the number of householders decreases?

Is there any way to make everyone in the Village Point Water District better off by giving each householder an incentive to use 10,000 gallons each month? What this community needs is some mechanism to motivate each householder to reduce personal water use in July. One possibility is to mount a campaign in which everyone is urged to voluntarily reduce their private water use for the common good. This sort of campaign is likely to work well where the community is small and where people in the community can easily observe the amounts of water used by their neighbors. But these conditions are not satisfied in Village Point Estates, so something else is required.

An economist might suggest trying what we will call a *metered scheme*. Suppose that the water district decided to install meters to monitor every householder's water use and began to charge a *price per gallon* for water used during July and August. As you know from introductory economics, consumption of a good rises or falls depending on the price of that good. We could reasonably expect that a very high price per gallon for water would dramatically reduce water use while a more moderate price would lead to a less dramatic reduction. We can imagine that the water district might experiment with different prices to find the price that would result in each Village Point householder using just 10,000 gallons per month. Let us suppose the magic price is $.02 per gallon. The representative householder's water bill would then be $200 per month for a total bill of $400 over the two-month period.

This price-per-gallon charge does succeed in achieving the desired reallocation of water use. But does it in fact make each householder better off? The answer depends on how much it costs to monitor the amount of water used by each householder. Suppose for the moment that monitoring water use is costless. The water district could then use the $400 collected from each householder to reduce the fixed yearly fee of $500 per householder to a fixed yearly fee of just $100. Each householder still pays the water district a total of $500 per year, but because the price-per-gallon charge brings about the desired reallocation of water use, each householder is better off.

Let us describe these two institutions more carefully. The metered scheme is composed of a fixed yearly fee of $100 per householder plus a $.02 price-per-gallon charge for water used in July and August. The non-metered scheme is composed of a fixed yearly fee of $500 per householder and a price-per-gallon charge equal to zero.

Now let us see why the metered scheme is preferred. Both schemes yield an equilibrium in which the Village Point householder uses 20,000 gallons of water over the two-month period and pays a total of $500 per year for water. The crucial difference is that under the metered scheme, the householder achieves the balanced water use profile. Under the non-metered scheme, he or she is left with the unbalanced water use profile. Since this householder prefers the balanced to the unbalanced profile, the metered scheme is preferred.

Finally, let us summarize how the metered scheme works. As we saw, under the non-metered scheme, the Village Point householder has no real incentive to limit water use in July: if this householder reduces personal water use by one gallon in July, he or she gets only an additional 1/100 of a gallon in August. Clearly, it is not in this householder's personal self-interest to conserve water in July for use in August. Consequently, the non-metered scheme produces an equilibrium in which too much water is used in July, and too little in August. By imposing a *price* on water use, however, the metered scheme does provide this householder with a *personal incentive to conserve water*. The higher the price, the larger the incentive. When the water district chooses the $.02 per gallon price, the Village Point householders use 10,000 gallons per month, and the metered scheme generates the balanced water use profile preferred by the householder. Since we have assumed that it costs nothing to monitor householders' water use, all the revenue generated by the per-gallon price for water can be used to reduce the householders' fixed yearly fee. We see, then, that in this very simple model, *price serves only to allocate water use* across the two summer months. A clever choice of price produces the optimal allocation.

Of course, it is not really costless to monitor water use. Meters have to be bought and installed, someone has to be paid to read the meters, and water bills have to be prepared and mailed. Once these *monitoring costs* enter the picture, how can we determine if the metered scheme is better or worse than the non-metered scheme? Let C be the sum of all these monitoring costs, expressed as a yearly cost per householder. In other words, C is the *cost* to each householder of the metered scheme. What is the *benefit* to the householder of having the balanced water use profile? Let R represent the highest price that the householder is willing to pay for the balanced water use profile — given that the alternative is the unbalanced water use profile. This sum, R, is a measure of the benefit to the Village Point householder of the metered scheme. If R is larger than C, then the metered scheme is preferred to the non-metered scheme. But if R is smaller than C, then the opposite is true.

Common Property Problems

common
property
problem

This water shortage problem is one example of a what's called a **common property problem.**[2] The non-metered scheme produced an unattractive equilibrium because the water in the district's wells is property that is *held in common* by the 100 householders of Village Point Estates. As a result, the individual householder is able to use in August only 1/100 of any water personally saved in July. In other words, because the water is common property, the individual householder has insufficient incentive to conserve water in July. A similar common property problem bedeviled the oil industry in North America in the early part of this century. To understand this problem we need to know something about the geology of oil and something about the legal institution that allows someone to establish a property right to oil.

Two things are important here about the geology of oil. First, oil occurs in very large subterranean reservoirs. Second, the total amount of oil that is recovered from a reservoir depends on the rate at which oil is extracted from it. If the oil is extracted too rapidly, there is an inverse relationship between the rate of extraction and the total amount of oil recovered from a reservoir: the faster oil is pumped out of a reservoir, the smaller is the total amount of oil that can be recovered. In extreme cases of very rapid extraction, the amount of oil actually extracted is only one-fifth of the maximum amount that could have been extracted.

rule of capture

The legal institution that governs property rights in oil extraction is the **rule of capture**. Surface landowners hold the right to drill for oil on their land (as well as other mineral rights). But to establish a property right to any oil beneath the surface, the owner must actually capture the oil; that is, the owner must drill one or more wells and pump the oil out of the ground. Notice that under the rule of capture, oil in any reservoir is the common property of everyone who owns drilling rights to land located above the reservoir. And because oil reservoirs typically are very large, there are many such landowners.

In the associated equilibrium, many landowners drill wells to tap the reservoir, and each well is pumped at or near maximum capacity. This equilibrium is unattractive for two reasons. Too many wells are drilled, and oil is pumped out so rapidly that the total quantity of oil actually extracted is only a fraction of the quantity that could have been extracted from the reservoir. Indeed, all those who pump oil from the reservoir would be better off if a way could be found to reduce the number of wells and/or the rate of extraction.

Notice that if only *one* person or organization managed the drilling rights to a whole oil field, oil in the reservoir would cease to be common property, and the incentive to drill too many wells and to extract oil too quickly would disappear. This institutional

---

2 Two entries in *The New Palgrave* are quite useful as introductions to the important economic role of private property rights and the implications of imperfect property rights: "property rights" by Armen Alchian and "common property rights" by Steven Cheung. See also Coase (1960).

unitization

solution to the common property problem is called **unitization** since it results in the entire reservoir being managed as a unit. Beginning in the mid-1940s, all the major oil-producing states except Texas adopted laws that encourage unitization. These laws compel unitization if a majority of producers agree to a sharing formula.

Common property problems occur in many different forms in open ocean fisheries. Here, too, the source of the problem is the law of capture. To establish a property right to fish in the ocean, a fisher must actually harvest the fish. As a result, too many resources (boats, labor, fishing gear) are used to harvest the fish that are caught. And too many fish are caught because individual fishers have only a limited incentive to leave fish in the ocean so they can reproduce. This, of course, can lead to the extinction of the fishery. Put yourself in the place of a whaler who has the chance to harvest the last pair of whales of some species. If your motivation was narrowly economic, almost certainly you would choose to harvest the whales, and the species would become extinct. If you did decide to harvest the whales, you would then sell them at their current market value. On the other hand, if you decided to leave them alive, someone else might harvest them. In this case, you would get nothing and the species would still become extinct. And even if the whales managed to survive and reproduce, chances are small that you would have the opportunity to harvest and sell their offspring. If you placed no direct value on the survival of the species, this line of reasoning would lead you to harvest the whales yourself.

In the following problem you can explore a simple game that captures the essence of common property problems.

PROBLEM 1.3

This game involves a host and four players in separate rooms. The host gives each player $90 and an envelope. Each player must choose either to keep the $90 or to put it into the envelope. Then the players assemble in a common room where the host collects the four envelopes, takes the money out, and puts it all into a common pool. For every $90 from an envelope, the host adds an additional $120 to the common pool. The common pool is then divided equally among the four players. Before the players make their choice about keeping the $90 or putting it into the envelope, the host describes the entire sequence of events to each player.

1. Would a player motivated only by private gain choose to keep the $90 or put it into the envelope?
2. Suppose that all the players are forced to make the same choice and that the choice is determined by a vote. How will a player motivated only by private gain choose to vote?

1.3

Agricultural Price Support Programs

For the last 50 years, farmers' groups have successfully lobbied governments in Europe, North America, Australia, and elsewhere to support prices for a whole range of agricultural products — including wheat, corn, butter, wine, and wool — at artificially high levels. As you will see in later chapters, there are good economic reasons to oppose price supports. However, given that a political decision has been made to institute an agricultural price support program, what is the best way to do it? Let us create a simple model to explore and compare two possible price support programs.

Imagine, then, that a government agency known as the Agricultural Price Support Authority is about to institute one of two programs to support the price of a particular agricultural good. Under what we will call the *buy-and-store program*, the Agricultural Price Support Authority would offer to buy the good at a designated support price, and then it would store whatever quantity it ultimately bought. By contrast, under what we will call the *price subsidy program*, the Agricultural Price Support Authority would not actually offer to buy the agricultural good; instead, it would pay agricultural producers a subsidy per unit produced equal to the difference between the designated support price and the price the good actually sold for in the marketplace. Is there any reason to prefer one of these programs to the other?

Before we tackle this question, we need to set out the relevant theory of price in markets for agricultural goods. (You will have the opportunity to explore this theory in detail in Chapter 9.) In many agricultural markets, neither buyers nor sellers have any real control over the price of the good because the amount that any single buyer (seller) offers to buy (sell) is small relative to the total quantity transacted. In other words, in large agricultural markets characterized by many buyers and sellers, prices are taken as given. Economists refer to such markets as **perfectly competitive markets**.

perfectly competitive markets

Since neither buyers nor sellers in perfectly competitive markets can choose the price at which they either buy or sell the good in question, the only decisions they can make are decisions about what *quantity* to buy or sell. In the following treatment of demand and supply, we will use the market for butter as our example; however, this discussion is applicable to any perfectly competitive market.

On the demand side of the market for butter, a consumer's behavior can be described by the quantity of butter purchased at any given price. This relationship between quantity demanded and price is called the individual's demand curve. For example, one particular consumer might buy three pounds of butter per week at $.50 per pound, two pounds per week at $1.50 per pound, and just one pound per week at $3 per pound. These are three points on that person's individual demand curve for butter.

market demand curve

We can add up the demand curves for every single consumer in an economy to get a **market demand curve**, labeled *DD* in Figure 1.2a. It tells us how much butter all individual demanders will buy at any given price in any given week. If, for example, the price of butter is $2 per pound, then 180 million pounds will be demanded. If the price is higher, for example $3, then only 120 million pounds will be demanded. Demand curves are usually thought to be downward-sloping: the higher the price, the smaller the quantity demanded.

market supply curve

On the supply side of the market, an individual producer's behavior can be described by the quantity of butter the producer will supply at any given price. Once again, we can add up the supply curves for every single producer in an economy to get a **market supply curve**, labeled *SS* in Figure 1.2b. It tells how much butter all producers will supply at any given price. If, for example, the price of butter is $3 per pound, then 210 million pounds will be supplied. If the price is lower, for example $2 per pound, then only 90 million pounds will be supplied. Supply curves are usually thought to be upward-sloping: the higher the price, the larger the quantity supplied.

Competitive Equilibrium Price and Quantity

competitive equilibrium price

competitive equilibrium quantity

The **competitive equilibrium price** is the price where quantity demanded is equal to quantity supplied. We can identify the competitive equilibrium price and the **competitive equilibrium quantity** by combining the demand and supply sides of the butter market into a single figure. As you can see from Figure 1.3, the equilibrium price is $2.50, and the equilibrium quantity is 150 million pounds.

FIGURE 1.2   Demand and supply

The market demand curve *DD* specifies the quantity of butter demanded at any given price, and the market supply curve *SS* specifies the quantity of butter supplied at any given price.

For example, when butter is $3 per pound, 120 million pounds are demanded and 210 million pounds are supplied.

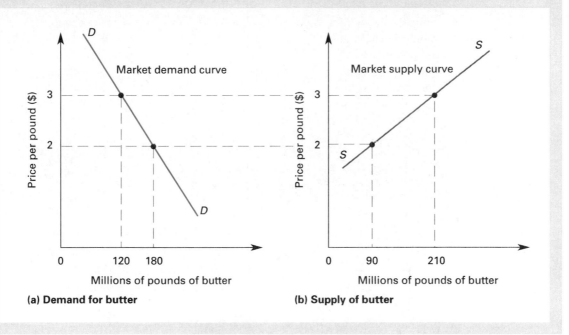

(a) Demand for butter

(b) Supply of butter

At prices higher than the $2.50 equilibrium price, butter is in excess supply: not all the butter supplied can be sold. As a result, the price will tend to drop towards the equilibrium price of $2.50 per pound. For example, when the price is $3 per pound, producers supply 210 million pounds of butter, but consumers demand only 120 million pounds, so there is an excess supply of 90 million pounds of butter. Conversely, at prices lower than the $2.50 equilibrium price, butter is in excess demand: more butter is demanded than is available. (How large is the excess demand when the price of butter is $2 per pound?) As a result, the price will tend to rise towards the $2.50 equilibrium price.

Notice how *price* serves to coordinate economic decision making in this model: *Producers and consumers base their supply and demand decisions on price.* If their decisions are not mutually consistent — that is, if there is either excess demand or excess supply — the resulting pressure in the marketplace will tend to push price either up or down. Only at the equilibrium price are the decisions of producers and consumers mutually consistent, and, therefore, only at this price is there no pressure for price to change.

Price Supports

Now that we have some understanding of how price is determined in a competitive market, we can begin to understand the implications of price support programs. In the absence of any government intervention, we would expect to see an equilibrium price of $2.50 per pound in the marketplace for butter. Let us suppose then that the

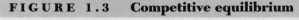

FIGURE 1.3   Competitive equilibrium

In a competitive equilibrium, price is such that quantity demanded equals quantity supplied. The competitive equilibrium price is $2.50 per pound, and 150 million pounds of butter are supplied and demanded at this price.

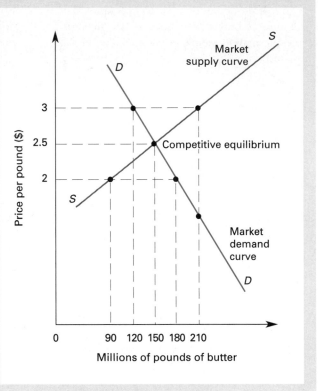

Agricultural Price Support Authority wants to institute a support price that is higher than the equilibrium price — for example, a support price of $3 per pound.

What happens if the Agricultural Price Support Authority opts for the buy-and-store program, where it offers to buy butter at the $3 support price and then stores all the butter it buys, thereby removing it from the market? Given the support authority's offer to buy butter at $3 per pound, butter producers will accept nothing less in the marketplace. As a result, consumers of butter will also have to pay a market price of $3 per pound. As you can see from Figure 1.4, when the price of butter is $3, then 210 million pounds of butter will be supplied each week. Notice, however, that only 120 million pounds will be sold in the marketplace at the $3 price. The support authority will therefore have to buy and store an amount equal to the difference between the quantity supplied and the quantity demanded, or 90 million pounds of butter. This means, of course, that if the support authority opts for the buy-and-store program, it will have to spend at least $270 million per week to achieve the $3 support price. In addition, it will have to pay the costs of storing the butter.

What happens if the support authority decides instead to implement the price subsidy program, where it pays producers a subsidy per unit produced equal to the difference between the $3 support price and the market price? Under the price subsidy program, butter producers first sell their butter in the marketplace for whatever price they can get, and then the support authority pays them a subsidy per pound of butter sold equal to the difference between the $3 support price and the market price. As you can see from Figure 1.4, because producers once again get a total of $3 per pound for their butter, they will once

FIGURE 1.4   Price support programs

Because under both programs the producer gets $3.00 per pound of butter, 210 million pounds are supplied. Under the buy-and-store program, 120 million pounds are sold to consumers at $3.00 per pound and the Price Support Authority buys and stores the remaining 90 million pounds. Under the price subsidy program, all 210 million pounds are sold to consumers at $1.50 per pound, and the Price Support Authority pays producers a subsidy equal to $1.50 per pound.

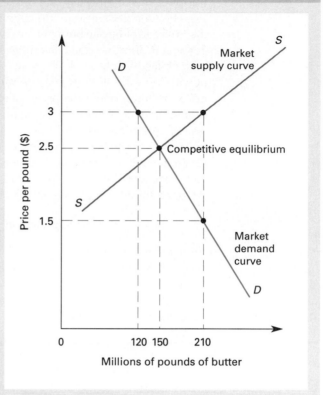

again supply 210 million pounds of butter. However, under the price subsidy program, all 210 million pounds of butter will be sold in the marketplace at a price of $1.50 per pound. The support authority will therefore have to pay butter producers a subsidy of $1.50 per pound, equal to the difference between the $3 support price and the $1.50 market price. This means that if the support authority opts for the price subsidy program, it will have to spend $315 million per week to achieve the $3 support price.

What can we say about which of these programs is preferred? First, look at the question from the point of view of the sellers in this market. Butter producers are indifferent between the buy-and-store and the price subsidy programs since both programs result in the same $3 support price. What about the buyers in this market? Consumers prefer the price subsidy program, where they pay just $1.50 per pound for butter, to the buy-and-store program, where they pay $3 per pound. Of course, as taxpayers, producers and consumers collectively will have to pay the costs incurred by the Agricultural Price Support Authority. Those costs are $315 million under the price subsidy program, and $270 million plus storage costs under the buy-and-store program.

We can easily establish the following results: If storage costs are larger than $45 million ($315 million minus $270 million), then the price subsidy program is preferred. Producers as producers are indifferent between the two programs; consumers as consumers prefer the price subsidy program; and, collectively as taxpayers, both producers and consumers prefer the cheaper, price subsidy program. However, if costs of storage are less than $45 million, the situation is more complex because the price subsidy program is then more expensive than the buy-and-store program. To compare programs in this case, we need to know just how much consumers as a group value the lower market price for butter that emerges under the price subsidy program.

How could we measure the aggregate benefit that consumers as a group place on the privilege of buying butter at a market price of $1.50 compared with buying it at $3 per pound? First, we could determine the largest amount each consumer would pay for this privilege for one week. Then, we simply add up all these amounts to get a measure of what we will call the *aggregate consumers' benefit* per week of the lower market price for butter under the price subsidy program. Let $ACB denote aggregate consumers' benefit. We want to compare $ACB with what we will call the *aggregate taxpayers' cost* of the price subsidy program relative to the buy-and-store program. Let $ATC denote aggregate taxpayers' costs. We know from above that the price subsidy program costs taxpayers $315 million per week and that the buy-and-store program costs taxpayers $270 million plus storage costs. Therefore, aggregate taxpayers' costs of the price subsidy program relative to the buy-and-store program are:

$$\$ATC = \$315 \text{ million} - (\$270 \text{ million} + \text{storage costs})$$

From this calculation we know that the price subsidy program is preferred if $ACB exceeds $ATC, and that the buy-and-store program is preferred if $ATC exceeds $ACB.

One important determinant of the Agricultural Price Support Authority's costs is the responsiveness of quantity demanded to a change in price. You can explore just how this affects costs in the following problem.

> **PROBLEM 1.4**
>
> We will continue to suppose that the market demand curve is linear and that it passes through the competitive equilibrium point in Figure 1.4. We want to explore the implications of a change in the slope of the market demand curve. Specifically, how do the Agricultural Price Support Authority's costs under the two programs change as the demand curve gets steeper?

1.4
Describing an Economy

Now that we have some concrete examples of economic analysis in place, we can begin a more structured discussion of economics and the economy. The purpose of economic activity is to transform resources into goods and services. Goods and services — or

goods

resources

economics

goods, for short — are what individuals value: T-shirts, haircuts, artichokes, 18 holes of golf, and so on. **Resources** are what are used to produce such goods. Land in the Salinas Valley of California, for example, is a resource because it can be used to produce artichokes (or cotton or a shopping mall or a golf course). Using the concepts of goods and resources, we can provide an informal but revealing definition of **economics**: *It is the study of the allocation of scarce resources to the production of alternative goods.*

Two words in this definition deserve special attention: *scarce* and *alternative*. It is almost impossible to think of a resource that is not scarce, that is, in limited supply. Because resources are normally in limited or finite supply, how they are allocated to alternative uses is a fundamental economic question. It is also hard to imagine a resource with only one possible use. Think, for example, of the many ways in which water and oil are used in different production processes. Because resources are almost invariably used in a range of productive processes, a central aim of economics is studying how those scarce resources are allocated to different uses. For example, you have already learned something about the allocation of several scarce resources, including water, oil, and fish.

This informal definition of economics is useful but limited. To develop a deeper understanding of what economics is all about, we first need to know just what an economy is. We can describe an **economy** by breaking it down into four basic building blocks: a *resource endowment,* a *technology, preferences of individuals*, and *institutions.*

economy

A Resource Endowment

resource
endowment

A resource endowment consists of all the resources available to an economy. For example, the North American economy's resource endowment could be described by cataloguing the quantities of all available resources: X million gallons of water in the Ogallala aquifer, the labor of Y million people, Z million barrels of oil in the Beaufort Sea oil fields, Q million tons of shrimp in the Gulf of Mexico, U million acres of Class A farm land in Iowa, V million tons of coal in the Appalachian mountains, and so on until the catalogue was complete. In essence, then, a resource endowment is simply a listing of everything in an economy that can be used to produce goods. Notice that — as we have said — these resources are in limited or scarce supply: there is only a certain amount available for use in an economy.

A Technology

technology

An economy's **technology** specifies how those resources can be used to produce goods. We already touched on technology in Section 1.1 when we described alternative choices of technology in the cod-fishing and shrimp-packing industries and in water-system construction. Figuratively speaking, a technology is the economy's cookbook because it tells us all the different combinations of resources that can be used to produce a good. For example, suppose that we were thinking about producing 10 tons of frozen shrimp for New Year's Eve in Boston. The economy's technology would tell us all the different combinations of resources that could do the job: all the labor-intensive techniques and all the capital-intensive techniques for catching shrimp, the various techniques for freezing shrimp, and the various techniques for transporting frozen shrimp to Boston. Notice that our technological cookbook differs from an ordinary cookbook in that it provides not just one but potentially a very large number of resource combinations that will all achieve a given result.

Preferences of Individuals

preferences of
individuals

preference
ordering

Very loosely, which goods are actually produced in an economy depends upon what people would like to buy — that is, it depends upon the **preferences of individuals**. In principle, describing any person's preferences requires us to construct that individual's **preference ordering**. In Chapter 2 we will provide a full treatment of the concept of a preference ordering. Here we will simply give you an example of a very limited and specific preference ordering from the water shortage problem of Section 1.2.

From the Village Point householder's point of view, what matters is the amount of water used in each of the two summer months and, of course, the amount of money paid to the water district (since money paid to the water district is not available to buy other goods). A consumption profile can then be described as follows: (gallons used in July, gallons used in August, dollars spent on water). In this notation, the unbalanced profile produced by the non-metered scheme is (15,000 gal., 5,000 gal., $500), and the balanced profile produced by the metered scheme is (10,000 gal., 10,000 gal., $500). A preference ordering in this very limited context is a complete listing of all conceivable water use profiles for the Village Point householder in descending order of desirability. For example, we know that in this householder's preference ordering, the balanced water use profile (10,000 gal., 10,000 gal., $500) is higher than the unbalanced water use profile (15,000 gal., 5,000 gal., $500).

But many other water use profiles are also conceivable and will therefore appear in this preference ordering. For example, that preference ordering would tell how this householder ranks the following water use profiles: (11,000 gal., 14,000 gal., $300), (7,000 gal., 17,000 gal., $495), and (5,000 gal., 3,000 gal., $1500). A preference ordering for the Village Point householder is a complete ranking of these and every other conceivable profile in descending order of desirability. To check your understanding of this concept, try writing down your own preference ordering in another very limited context in the following problem.

PROBLEM 1.5

Write down your own preference ordering for the following bundles of bills.
a. three $100 bills, ten $20 bills, seventeen $5 bills
b. two $100 bills, thirteen $20 bills, four $5 bills
c. four $100 bills, one $20 bill, fourteen $5 bills
d. one $100 bill, thirty $20 bills, one $5 bills

Self-Interest and Economic Choice Making

The preferences of individuals are the keystone of the economist's vision of the economy because preferences provide the motivation for all economic activity. Put briefly, the economist's theory of behavior is this: *in any choice situation, the individual makes the choices that allow him or her to attain the highest possible ranking in his or her preference ordering.* This theory of economic choice making — often called the **theory of self-interest** — is at the core of virtually all economic analysis.

theory of self-interest

We have already used the theory of self-interested choice making at a number of points. We used it in the water shortage problem when we argued that under the nonmetered scheme, the unbalanced profile (15,000 gal., 5,000 gal., $500) was an equilibrium. First we identified all the water use profiles the householder could achieve by his or her own actions. These were the profiles on the line DCU in Figure 1.1. Then we argued that Village Point householder stayed with the unbalanced profile because he or she could not personally attain a more preferred profile. Obviously, this argument was based on the notion of self-interested choice making by the Village Point householder.

Less obviously, we also implicitly used the theory of self-interested choice making in Section 1.1 to explain the way in which firms chose a production technique. Let us return to that example to see how the self-interest of individuals lies behind a firm's decisions. Recall that the economist's explanation is that a firm chooses the production technique that costs the least. Why? Because the least costly production technique maximizes the firm's profits. But a firm is just the agent for its owners, and a firm's profit is just income for its owners. Therefore, when a firm maximizes its profit, it is maximizing the income of its owners. And as the income of an individual owner increases, the set of consumption choices available to that individual expands. Or, in the language of self-interest, as personal income increases, the individual can attain a higher ranking in his or her preference ordering. Thus, the self-interested choice making of individuals is also at the core of the profit-maximizing activities of firms.

Institutions

institutions

Notice that all three of the building blocks we have so far considered — an economy's resource endowment, its technology, and the preferences of individuals — are not easily changed over short periods of time. Indeed, in most economic theory, these building blocks are assumed to be unchangeable.[3] By contrast, **institutions** — the fourth building block — can be changed in important ways. You have already encountered a number of institutions. For example, in the water shortage problem, you looked at two different institutions for regulating water allocation — a metered scheme and a non-metered scheme. In the common property oil extraction problem, you encountered two legal institutions for regulating oil extraction — the rule of capture and unitization. And in the agricultural price support problem, you compared two institutions designed to support the price of butter — the buy-and-store program and the price subsidy program.

In almost any newspaper you can find articles about changes to major economic institutions. Since the early 1990s, for example, there have been thousands of articles about the Maastricht Treaty between member nations of the European Community (EC) and there have been thousands more about the North American Free Trade Agreement (NAFTA) between Canada, Mexico, and the United States. Recently, almost every American newspaper has carried stories on institutional reforms in the delivery of health care services in the United States. These are just a few examples of the multitude of institutions that affect economic life around the globe.

Because institutions are changeable, they play an especially interesting role in economics. If we think of economic activity as a game in which the objective of each participant is to reach the highest possible ranking in his or her own preference ordering, then economic institutions are the *rules* by which the game in a particular economy must be played. For example, what we called the rule of capture established the rules for exploiting two different resources — oil and fish. Under the rule of capture, an owner can only establish a property right to oil in the ground by pumping it out of the ground — that is, by "capturing" it. And a fisher can only establish a property right to fish in the sea by hauling them out of the sea. If an oil producer chooses not to pump oil today, under the rule of capture the producer has no legal right to that oil tomorrow. If a whaler chooses not to catch a particular whale today, under the rule of capture the whaler has no legal right to that whale (or its offspring) tomorrow. Thus, these institutions define the rules of the economic game and affect the behavior of individuals in important ways. If an institution is changed, we would expect to see individual participants change their actions in response to that institutional change. For example, the water consumption of Village Point householders was different under the metered and the non-metered schemes. Institutions are thus a powerful force for organizing and directing economic activity.

Many institutions are formally codified in law. For example, property law formally specifies how ownership of property may be acquired and transferred. Other important legal institutions that regulate economic behavior include tax laws, antitrust laws, labor laws, minimum-wage laws, rent-control laws, and agricultural price-support laws.

---

3 In an intertemporal framework, technology changes from period to period. Furthermore, it is possible to promote technological change by appropriate policy measures. Nuclear power is just one example of a policy-promoted technology.

PROBLEM 1.6

Governments often require retailers to collect a 10-cent deposit on pop bottles from their customers. What is the purpose of this institution and how does it work?

Less obvious but nevertheless important are the many private and often informal institutions that regulate everyday economic activity. For example, private rental deposit arrangements of various kinds are very much like the public institution you considered in Problem 1.6. If you want to rent certain kinds of merchandise like VCRs, ski equipment, furniture, or power tools, you will probably be asked to leave a sizable deposit to guarantee the return of the merchandise. If you rent an apartment, you will probably be asked to pay a damage deposit — a similar institution. And if you fly into certain airports, you will have to deposit four quarters in a coin box before you can take a baggage cart from a specially designed lock-up device. The clever twist is that you can get your money back if you return your cart (or any other cart) to the lock-up devise. What is the special function of this refund-for-cart-return institution? These informal institutions, like more public and formal institutions, also organize and direct the actions of individuals.

1.5

The Equilibrium Method

Now that we have described an economy, let us see how economists study real economies. Economists study real economies by selecting certain segments of an economy and then constructing *economic models* of those segments. For example, there are many different kinds of water systems in any modern economy. None of these real systems is identical to the hypothetical Village Point Water District described in the water shortage problem of Section 1.2. Real water systems are vastly more complex. Yet our simple economic model of the Village Point Water District captures important features of many real water systems.

The four features captured by the model of the hypothetical water district in Section 1.2 correspond to the four building blocks of an economy. First, there is a *scarce resource*: the water district has only 2,000,000 gallons of water for the three-month summer period. Second, there is a specific *technology* for water distribution in which the water district's costs depend only on the total amount of water pumped through the system. Third, there are the *preferences of individuals:* each householder prefers the balanced to the unbalanced water use profile. And fourth, there are two possible *institutions* — a metered scheme and a non-metered scheme — that establish the rules of the economic "game" in which each of 100 Village Point householders chooses how much water to use in each month.

social state

As we said, the driving forces in any economic model are the choices made by individuals. Collectively, these choices give rise to what we will call a **social state**. In the water shortage model of Section 1.2, for example, a social state is described by the amount of water each of the 100 householders uses in each month and the amount each householder pays for water. The social state that arose from the choices of the Village Point householders under the metered scheme was the one in which each of 100 householders used 10,000 gallons in each month, and paid $500 dollars for their water. In contrast, the social state that arose from the choices of the Village Point householders under the non-metered scheme was the one in which each of 100 householders used 15,000 gallons in July and 5,000 gallons in August, and paid $500 dollars for their water.

method of equilibrium

equilibrium

The economist's aim is to explain or predict the social state that will arise from the choices of the individual economic participants. The method used to make these predictions is the **method of equilibrium**. At the heart of this method is the concept of an **equilibrium**. It can be defined this way: *an equilibrium consists of a set of choices for the individuals and a corresponding social state such that no individual can make himself or herself better off by making some other choice.*

This concept of equilibrium is, of course, built squarely on the economist's theory of self-interested choice making: an economy, or a model of it, is in equilibrium only when no individual participant can reach a higher ranking in his or her preference ordering by making a different choice.

comparative statics analysis

An important part of the method of equilibrium is a technique known as **comparative statics analysis**. Notice that in these simple models, we have sometimes substituted one institution for another and compared the resulting equilibria. For example, in the water shortage model, we compared the equilibrium arising from the non-metered scheme with the equilibrium under the metered scheme. And in the agricultural price support problem, we compared the equilibrium arising from the buy-and-store program with the equilibrium arising from the price subsidy program. These are just two examples of comparative statics analysis. *Comparative statics analysis is the method of analyzing the impact of a change in a model by comparing the equilibrium that results from the change with the original equilibrium.* As Timothy Kehoe points out, comparative statics analysis is as old as economics itself. It was used by the British economist David Hume in 1752 to analyze the effects of an increase in the stock of gold on the price level in an economy.[4]

1.6

Positive and Normative Economics

positive economics

Comparative statics analysis is in the domain of what is called **positive economics**. Positive economics is concerned with the social states that actually arise in different economic settings. For example, in the water shortage problem, we were posing a positive question in asking how patterns of water consumption might change when a metered scheme was substituted for a non-metered scheme. Similarly, in the agricultural price support problem, we were posing a positive question in asking how the price consumers pay for butter changes when a price subsidy program is substituted for a buy-and-store program.

Comparative statics analysis is one of the most important techniques used in policy making. It is often used to make predictions in answer to questions that policy makers grapple with day in and day out. For example, recently our municipality decided that for environmental reasons, household garbage had to be cut by 50 percent per capita by the year 2000. The municipal council is now trying to decide whether to pass a by-law that will reduce the maximum amount of garbage collected from a single-family residence from 13 to 3 cans per week. However, under the proposed by-law, residents would be permitted to put out more than 3 cans for collection, if they bought special tags costing $1.50 each and attached a tag to each additional can. The municipal council hopes that by substituting this new by-law for the old one, they will encourage residents to reduce household waste. Are the council members right? Comparative statics analysis can be used to help policy makers like these council members make more informed policy decisions.

Positive economics involves questions about the *facts* of economics activity. Therefore, answers to positive questions are always supported (or refuted) by factual observations.

---

4 See Kehoe's entry on "comparative statics" in *The New Palgrave*.

Making careful empirical observations of the facts of the real world — however difficult collecting and interpreting those facts may sometimes be — is a way of testing the predictions of economic models. Does the cod fishing fleet actually switch from labor-intensive techniques to machine-intensive techniques when the price of labor rises relative to the price of machines? Is the amount of oil pumped from a reservoir under unitization actually larger than under the ordinary rule of capture? Supporting evidence for the positive predictions of economic models is provided by careful empirical research.

normative
economicsOn the other hand, **normative economics** involves value judgments and therefore cannot be answered by reference to factual observations alone. Answers to normative questions also depend on our commitment to certain values or *norms* that are outside the scope of positive economics. Should government try to aid butter producers? Should it attempt to protect and preserve particular species of fish or specific types of forests or designated watersheds? Answers to questions like these are necessarily based, at least in part, on normative judgments that we, as members of society, make about what is desirable or undesirable, good or bad, right or wrong.

Policy making often involves a subtle interplay between normative and positive economics. Normative considerations tell us what are and are not desirable social states, while positive theoretical and empirical analysis tells us what are (and are not) sensible ways of trying to achieve a particular desirable social state. Setting social and economic goals is clearly in the realm of normative economics. For example, our municipal government's decision that household garbage should be cut by 50 percent per capita by the year 2000 is a value judgment concerning what is right for our community. However, once certain social and economic goals are accepted, implementing those goals — and, indeed, discovering whether those goals can actually be achieved — is in the realm of positive economics. For example, will the proposed scheme in which households must pay $1.50 per can if they want to dispose of more than three cans per week achieve the normative goal of a 50 percent reduction in household garbage? Or will it be necessary to charge $3 per can? Are other measures — for example, creating a curbside recycling program or distributing compost boxes to local households — called for?

The Pareto Criterion

Given the importance of normative evaluations in policy making, it would clearly be useful to have some kind of normative yardstick for comparing different social states. One such normative yardstick — the one that is most widely used by economists — is the Pareto criterion**Pareto criterion**. It takes its name from Vilfredo Pareto, the turn-of-the-century Italian economist who first developed it. The Pareto criterion can be defined this way: *In comparing any two social states—say, state I and state J — state I is Pareto-preferred to state J if no one in state I is worse off than in state J, and if at least one person is better off in state I than in state J.*

Now let us apply the Pareto criterion to the familiar water shortage problem. Recall that we looked at just two social states. We will call the state in which all 100 householders have the balanced water use profile (10,000 gal., 10,000 gal., $500) state *I*. And we will call the state in which all 100 householders have with the unbalanced water use profile (15,000 gal., 5,000 gal., $500) state *J*. As you know, everyone in Village Point is better off in state *I* than in state *J* because everyone prefers the balanced water use profile to the unbalanced water use profile. Using the Pareto criterion, we can say, then, that state *I* is Pareto-preferred to state *J*. Although the Pareto criterion *is* a value judgment, it is not a very difficult one to accept. Moreover, it plays a central role in economic analysis, and we will be using it throughout the book.

Pareto optimality

efficiency

Another concept that also plays a central role in economic analysis — and one that we will also be using throughout the book — follows directly from the Pareto criterion. It is called **Pareto optimality**, and it can be defined this way: *A social state is Pareto-optimal if no other attainable social state is Pareto-preferred to it.* To an economist, Pareto optimality is synonymous with economic **efficiency**, and we will therefore be using the terms *Pareto-optimal*, and *efficient* interchangeably. Do notice, however, that the concept of Pareto optimality (or efficiency) does *not* identify the best possible social state. Consider the following problem.

PROBLEM 1.7

Two gluttons must split a pecan pie. A social state in this context is simply a particular division of the pie: X% to one glutton and $(100 − X)$% to the other. What values of X are Pareto-optimal or efficient?

The Pareto criterion is problematical for policy makers because it says that one state is preferred to another *only* if no one is worse off in one state than in the other. It is the business of policy makers to make judgments about the relative desirability of different policies. Yet few policies, if any, are free of adverse consequences for at least *some* individuals. In other words, any change in policy is almost bound to make at least one person worse off, even though it might make many other people better off. Guided only by the Pareto criterion, then, policy makers might always decide against a policy change and stick with the status quo.

Cost-Benefit Analysis

cost-benefit criterion

There is another, less widely accepted criterion — called the **cost-benefit criterion** — that can be used to compare social states. It differs from the Pareto criterion in that it *does* incorporate trade-offs between making some individuals worse off and making other individuals better off. The cost-benefit criterion is attractive to many policy makers because it will rank social states where the Pareto criterion will not.

To see how cost-benefit analysis is done, let us consider a move from any social state to any other; say, from state I to state J. We begin by calculating the social benefits from this move. First we will identify the "winners" — that is all those who benefit as a result of the move from state I to state J. Then we compute a dollar measure of each winner's personal benefit. Finally, we add up all the measures of individual benefit to arrive at the **gross social benefit**. Now let us calculate the social costs from this move. First we identify the "losers" — all those who are made worse off as a result of the move from state I to state J. Then we compute a dollar measure of each loser's personal cost. Finally, we add up all the measures of individual cost to arrive at the **gross social cost**. (You will learn more about how to make these calculations in Chapter 4.)

gross social benefit

gross social cost

net social benefit

If we then subtract the gross social cost from the gross social benefit, we have the **net social benefit**. We can use net social benefit to define the cost-benefit criterion: *In the move from social state I to social state J, if net social benefit is positive, then the cost-benefit criterion ranks state J as preferred to state I. On the other hand, if net social benefit is negative, then the cost-benefit criterion ranks state I as preferred to state J.*

We used the cost-benefit criterion in Section 1.3 to compare the buy-and-store program for supporting the price of butter with the price support scheme. We organized our data by looking at how individuals in three groups — producers, consumers, and taxpayers — were affected by a move from the social state with the buy-and-sell program to the social state with the price subsidy program. Producers as producers were indifferent between the institutions because the support price was $3 per pound under both institutions. Consumers as consumers clearly preferred the price subsidy program because butter was $1.50 per pound under this program and $3 per pound under the buy and store program. Collectively, producers and consumers as taxpayers preferred the buy-and-store program if the storage costs were less than $45 million per week, and they preferred the price subsidy program if the storage costs were more than $45 million per week. To compare programs, we first computed the aggregate consumers' benefit $ACB and the aggregate taxpayers' cost $ATC in a move from the buy-and-store to the price subsidy program. We then used the cost-benefit criterion to rank the two programs. The price subsidy (buy-and-store) program was preferred if $ACB was larger (smaller) than $ATC.

The normative assumption of cost-benefit analysis is that a dollar of cost to one person can always be offset by a dollar of benefit to any other person. Which individuals enjoy greater benefits or suffer greater costs is *not* an issue in cost-benefit analysis. This assumption, like the Pareto criterion, is clearly a value judgment. Many economists do not accept it and therefore will not use the cost-benefit criterion.

> **PROBLEM 1.8**
>
> To see that the cost-benefit criterion does in fact trade off gains for some individuals against losses for others, imagine a situation in which aggregate taxpayers' costs are larger for the price subsidy scheme than for the buy-and-store scheme, and yet, according to the cost-benefit criterion, the price subsidy scheme is preferred. Which individuals will be made worse off, and which individuals will be made better off by the move from the buy-and-store program to the price subsidy program? (Hint: not everyone buys butter and not everyone pays taxes.)

The Market Economy

pure-market economy

A quick glance at economies around the world is enough to remind us how much real economies vary from place to place. In making comparisons between different economic institutions, it is often convenient to use a specific set of institutions as a reference point. We will use a hypothetical **pure-market economy** — or what is often called a free-enterprise economy — as our baseline model of an economy. The only institutions regulating economic activity in this pure-market economy are the institutions of private property. These pure-market institutions create property rights and promote unrestricted voluntary exchange as the primary mode of economic interaction. The only role government plays in this hypothetical model is to enact and enforce private property laws.

The hypothetical pure-market economy allows us to pose many interesting questions about alternative institutions that we see in real economies. These are a few of the questions you will encounter in later chapters: Relative to the pure-market economy, what are the implications of a minimum-wage law? Of a rent-control law? Of a price subsidy for agricultural goods? Of a negative income tax? In addition, the institutions of a pure-market economy are interesting because a good portion of economic activity in countries like Australia, Great Britain, France, Germany, Canada, and the United States *is* coordinated through markets. Understanding a pure-market economy is therefore useful in interpreting much of the economic activity we see around us.

The Circular Flow of Economic Activity

The circular-flow diagram in Figure 1.5 is a useful way of visualizing a market economy. In this diagram, two sets of participants play crucial economic roles: *individuals* and *firms*. From an economist's perspective, every individual on the left in Figure 1.5 can be described by his or her preferences and by the resources he or she owns. In a pure-market economy, all resources — including resources nominally owned by firms — are ultimately owned by individuals because firms are owned by individual people. Every firm on the right in Figure 1.5 can be described by its technology (the terms on which it can transform resources into goods) and by its organizational structure (the set of internal institutions used to organize the firm).

FIGURE 1.5   The circular-flow diagram of an economy

Individuals, who can be described by their preferences and the resources they own, supply resources to firms and demand goods from firms. Firms, which can be described by their technology and their organizational structure, demand resources from individuals and supply goods to them. Firms and individuals interact in resource markets and in goods markets, in both of which prices and quantities are determined.

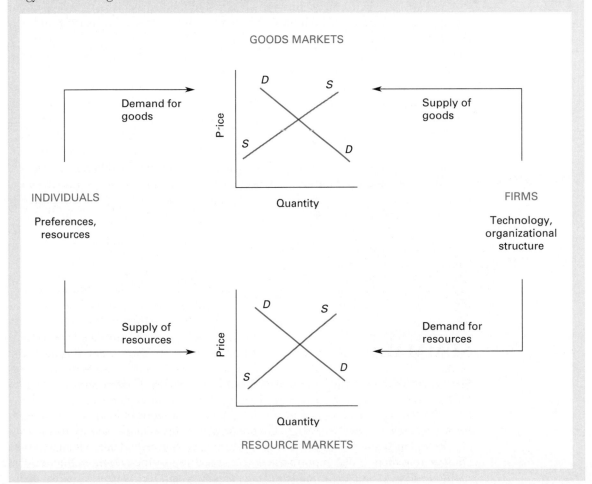

These individuals and firms interact in two sets of markets: *resource markets* and *goods markets*. In the resource markets at the bottom of Figure 1.5, individuals are the suppliers of labor and other resources, and firms are the demanders. In the goods markets at the top of Figure 1.5, firms are the suppliers of goods and services, and individuals are the demanders. In equilibrium, there is a price and a quantity in every resource market and in every goods market.

The Plan of the Book

Figure 1.5 provides a handy reference point for previewing the rest of the book. In Part II, Individual Choice, we concentrate on the individuals on the left side of our circular-flow diagram. In Chapter 2, we set out the standard economic theory of individual preferences. In Chapter 3, we analyze the individual's choice-making behavior. In the process, we derive demand curves for goods and supply curves for resources, thereby filling in the demand side of the markets for goods at the top and the supply side of the markets for resources at the bottom of Figure 1.5. In Chapter 4, we use tools from earlier chapters to explore a range of applications drawn from everyday life. In Chapter 5, we extend the theory of preferences to include economic decisions with risky outcomes. We then use this theory to explain some otherwise puzzling real-life phenomena.

In Part III, The Firm, we turn our attention to the firms on the right side of our circular flow diagram. In Chapter 6, we try to understand why firms exist and why they take the particular organizational forms they do. In Chapters 7 and 8, we introduce the idea of a production function and then use it to derive a number of cost relationships for a firm in the short run and the long run.

In Part IV, Goods Markets, we consider the forces that determine both the prices of the goods available in the goods markets at the top of our circular flow diagram and the quantities in which they are produced. In Chapter 9, we look at perfectly competitive markets; in Chapter 10, at monopolistic markets; in Chapter 11, at an undifferentiated oligopoly, a market in which a small number of firms sell an identical good; and in Chapter 12, at a differentiated oligopoly, a market in which a small number of firms sell differentiated goods.

In Part V, Resource Markets and General Equilibrium, we turn to the resource markets at the bottom of our circular flow diagram. Chapter 13 explores both perfectly competitive and monopsonistic resource markets. Chapter 14 takes up the distribution of income and examines the conflict between economic efficiency and equity in the distribution of income. Chapter 15 focuses on the intertemporal allocation of resources. Chapter 16 draws together many of the concepts from earlier chapters to build a model of general equilibrium — equilibrium in all markets at once. Finally, Chapter 17 explores externalities and, more briefly, public goods.

SUMMARY

We began the chapter with several simple economic models. These served as examples in the more systematic discussion of the subject matter of economics that followed. Any economy can be described by breaking it down into four building blocks: the *resource endowment*, the *technology*, the *preferences of individuals*, and its *institutions*.

Economists study real economies by selecting certain segments of them and then constructing models that capture the essential features of the chosen segments. The method used to study these models is the *method of equilibrium*. An *equilibrium* is a social state in which the choices of individuals are such that no individual can make himself or herself better off by making a different choice. An important part of the method of equilibrium is a procedure called *comparative statics analysis* — the method of analyzing the impact of a change in a model by comparing the equilibrium that results from the change with the original equilibrium.

Three of an economy's building blocks — the resource endowment, the technology, and individual preferences — are assumed to be unchanging, or fixed, in most economic analyses. Only the fourth building block — *institutions* — is changeable, which makes institutions particularly interesting. Many interesting comparative statics questions concern changes in institutions: What happens when we substitute one institution for another? To answer such questions consistently, however, we need a point of comparison. That is, we need a baseline set of institutions as a reference point. In this book, the baseline is the set of institutions defining a *pure-market (or free-enterprise) economy*.

The *preferences of individuals* play a crucial role in economic theory. First, preferences play a key role in positive economics, since the economist's *theory of self-interested choice making* is that every individual will chose to undertake the course of economic action that makes him or her as well off as possible. *Positive economics* provides predictions about what that course of action will be. Those predictions are supported or refuted by careful empirical observations of the relevant facts of economic life.

Preferences also play a key role in *normative economics,* because preferences give meaning to the expressions *better than* and *worse than* in characterizing the well-being of individual members of society. Economists use two different normative criteria to compare social states. The most widely accepted is the *Pareto criterion.* In comparing any two social states, say I and J, the Pareto criterion says that state I is Pareto-preferred to state J if no one is worse off and if at least one person is better off in state I than in state J. A social state is *Pareto-optimal* if no other attainable social state is Pareto-preferred to it. To an economist, *Pareto optimality* and *efficiency* are synonymous. Some economists also use the more controversial *cost-benefit criterion* to compare social states. In comparing any two social states, say I and J, the cost-benefit criterion says that if a move from state I to state J results in a positive (negative) net social benefit, then state J (state I) is preferred.

EXERCISES

1. "In economics any equilibrium is always optimal; in fact, the terms equilibrium and optimum are synonymous." Discuss.

2. Consider the following supply and demand functions:

$$x_D = 20 - p \qquad \text{(demand)}$$

$$x_S = p - 6 \qquad \text{(supply)}$$

   a. Find the competitive equilibrium price and quantity.

   b. Now suppose that consumers' incomes increase, shifting the demand curve up and to the right as follows:

$$x_D = 28 - p \qquad \text{(demand)}$$

Find the new equilibrium price and quantity. Show both equilibria on a carefully constructed diagram.

3. One of the social problems associated with the use of illegal drugs is street crime. Drug addicts sometimes become muggers and thieves as they seek to raise money to support their addiction. If the police manage to restrict the supply of illegal drugs, what will be the effect on the price of illegal drugs? On the level of street crime?

4. Until very recently, the money prices of most consumer goods in Russia were fixed, and goods were allocated to consumers on a first come, first served basis. If money prices are not allowed to perform the role of allocating consumer goods to consumers, on what basis will such goods be allocated?

5. Suppose that the U.S. government convinced Japanese automakers to voluntarily restrict the number of Japanese cars they sold in the U.S. market. What effect would these voluntary export restraints have on the price of Japanese cars in the United States? On the price and quantity of American cars sold in the United States?

6. At a recent meeting of the Board of Directors of the West Van Municipal Library, a director moved that the library eliminate fines for late books. In support of her motion, the director argued that the fines served no real purpose because very few people returned their books late. If you were a user of this library, would you support or oppose this motion? As a user of this library, do you think you would be better off or worse off if fines were eliminated? Justify your answers.

7. The disposal of household refuse is now a major problem all across the United States. In many cities, refuse disposal is provided by the city free of charge. (The cost of disposal is financed by tax revenue in these cities.) However, some cities use a refuse disposal fee, charging the household, for example, $2 per bag of trash. Under which system will the quantity of trash hauled to the official trash dump be larger? Under which system will the quantity of trash illegally dumped by the roadside be larger?

8. By volume, paper is the single largest source of household refuse in the United States, accounting for 40% of the total volume of trash by some estimates. Newspapers alone account for 15% of the total volume.

   a. For purposes of argument, suppose that the total cost of disposal is 1/10 of a cent per page of newspaper. What would be the effect of a law requiring newspapers to pay a refuse disposal tax equal to 1/10 of a cent per page printed on the price and quantity of newspapers? On the size of newspapers? On the format of newspapers? On the size of magazines? On the demand for radio and television ads?

   b. More generally, what would be the effects of such a disposal tax levied on the sale of all paper products?

   c. What sorts of institutions would encourage recycling of paper?

*9. This game involves a host and N players in separate rooms. The host gives each player X and an envelope. Each player must choose either to keep the X or to put it into the envelope. Then the players assemble in a common room where the host collects the envelopes, takes the money out, and puts it all into a common pool. For every X from an envelope, the host adds an additional Y to the common pool. The common pool is then divided equally among the N players. Before the players make their choice about keeping the X or putting it into the envelope, the host describes the entire sequence of events to each player.

   a. Under what circumstances would a player motivated only by private gain choose to keep the X, and under what circumstances would such a player choose to put X into the envelope?

   b. Does an increase in N make it more or less likely that a player motivated only by private gain will keep the X? How does an increases in X affect this choice? How does an increase in Y affect this choice?

   c. Now suppose that the players are all forced to make the same choice, and that the choice is determined by a vote. How will a player motivated only by private gain choose to vote?

1A

Appendix: Model Building

We have explored several different economic models in this chapter, but we paid very little attention to how these models were constructed. In this appendix, we will show you how an economist builds a model by looking in some detail at one very useful model: the *Hotelling model of minimum differentiation*.

Choosing a Question

We will begin the process of model building with a casual observation from our own experience. We noticed that Bay-Bloor Radio has about 24 different portable radios in stock, and asked ourselves *why* a retailer would offer so many different radios for sale.

economic model Any attempt to answer that question is an **economic model**, or theory, although not necessarily a carefully formulated, accurate, or even conscious one. Suppose we answered the question this way: Not everybody wants the same kind of radio, so it pays a retailer to carry a selection of models. But this "answer" is not really a statement of

assumptions fact. Rather, it is a tentative theory based on a series of implicit **assumptions** from which we have derived a conclusion or prediction. For example, we have implicitly assumed that different people have different preferences, that portable radios are significantly different, and that retailers are motivated by profit.

deduction From implicit assumptions like these, we have made a very loose **deduction**: the retailer will offer a wide range of models because it can then sell more radios and thus

prediction make more profit. Our deduction is also a **prediction** about what we would discover if we attempted to verify our casual observation by making systematic empirical observations of many audio retailers. That is, we have predicted that audio retailers in general will offer a range of models for sale. But is this tentative theory well-founded?

The basic method of thinking through an economic model is by using deductive reasoning, in which conclusions are drawn from carefully selected and clearly defined assumptions. First, we explicitly choose and state the assumptions that we think are relevant. Then we draw deductions from those assumptions. These deductions (like deductions in geometry) must satisfy the rules of logic by following from the assumptions. They are also the predictions of our model; they are the statements about what we would actually expect to find in the world. We can test the accuracy of our model's predictions by conducting careful empirical investigations that will tend either to support or to refute them.

Now let us begin to build an economic model from the ground up. We will start by asking some other intriguing questions based on casual observation. Why do two, three, or even four gas stations sometimes locate at the same intersection? Why do large grocery stores seem so similar in terms of the range and quality of goods they offer us? Why do supposedly different brands of premium beer or tennis rackets or economics textbooks seem almost indistinguishable?

These were the kinds of questions that Harold Hotelling attempted to answer in a now classic paper, "Stability in Competition" (1929). Just as we began with a casual observation about the range of models offered by an audio retailer, so Hotelling began with the observation that firms tend to cluster together in their locations or in the range or quality of their goods. Gas stations "cluster" at certain intersections, and premium beer makers "cluster" along certain characteristics of the beer they produce. In short, Hotelling began with the observation that firms seem to produce *minimally differentiated products* — products that are only slightly different from one another.

Our challenge is to create a model or theory that helps us to understand the phenomenon of clustering, or **minimum differentiation**. However, you need to remember that any particular model is not the final or "right" one in any absolute sense. Your role is to think through this model for yourself rather than to simply accept it.

minimum
differentiation

Choosing Assumptions

Because the multitude of economic "facts" relevant to any economic question is overwhelming, we need to reduce the question to a manageable size. That is, we need to choose a few simple assumptions that seem to approximate the key elements of the complex reality we are attempting to understand. Building models is something like drawing maps. Although real cities look nothing like maps of cities, maps are useful precisely because they ignore unnecessary information like the color of the second house from the corner on Main and First Streets. Maps give us only what we need to know to get from one point to another. Similarly, economic models abstract what we hope is the relevant information from a welter of economic details.

Let us begin this process of abstraction by thinking about the different ways in which products can cluster, or be minimally differentiated, and then selecting the simplest kind of product differentiation. Firms can cluster in *geographic space* by locating their stores together, or they can cluster in *characteristics space* by producing products that have similar mixes of characteristics. Gas stations located at the same intersection are clustered in geographic space. Different brands of tennis rackets that are similar in weight, balance, size, and strength are clustered in characteristics space. Because choosing a location in geographic space is easier to understand than choosing a point, or location, in characteristics space, let us ask where in a particular geographic market firms will choose to establish their businesses.

Having chosen to concentrate on clustering in a geographic space, these questions naturally arise: How many firms are there? What are the potential geographic locations of their stores? What kinds of firms are we concerned with? What goods do they sell, and at what prices? What are the firms' costs? What characterizes the customers who buy the firms' goods? What motivates these buyers and sellers?

Our next step is to reduce the vast number of firms and of goods sold to the simplest possible case. At a minimum, we need two competing firms. We can also reduce the vast array of products these two firms might sell to identical goods. We will assume that both firms offer exactly the same good, which we will call groceries, for sale. We will also assume that no price competition exists between the two firms and that both sell groceries at the same *fixed price*, denoted by *P*. We will assume, too, that the cost of each unit of groceries, denoted by *C*, is exactly the same for both firms, and that the price *P* is greater than the cost *C*. We can combine these restrictions in our first assumption.

ASSUMPTION 1

There are two firms selling an identical good, groceries, at a fixed price *P* per unit. The firm's cost of groceries is *C* per unit, and *P* is greater than *C*.

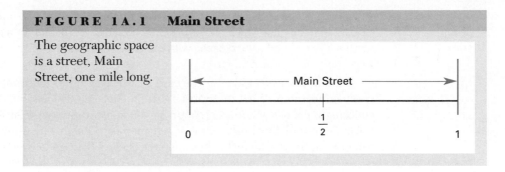

FIGURE 1A.1   Main Street

The geographic space is a street, Main Street, one mile long.

Where firms choose to locate obviously has a great deal to do with where their potential customers are located. Our model must therefore include a geographic space that locates potential buyers in a particular pattern. Because we need to reduce the actual geographic space to something manageable, let us imagine that all the customers live along a single street called Main Street. We can then represent the geographic space where these customers live by a straight line that, for simplicity, we will assume is one mile long. This brings us to the second simplifying abstraction in our model.

ASSUMPTION 2
The geographic space is a street, Main Street, that is one mile long.

In Figure 1A.1, we have represented Main Street by a line segment extending from 0 to 1. We can then think of numbers between 0 and 1 as *addresses* on Main Street. For example, 1/2 is the address at the midpoint or middle of Main Street.

Now what assumptions should we make about the number and distribution of these buyers? We know, of course, that population density differs from place to place and even from block to block. For instance, a thousand people may be living in a high-rise development on one block but only a hundred people may be living in large, single-family houses on the next block. Nevertheless, to assume that the customers are spaced evenly, or *uniformly*, along Main Street is a useful simplification. Imagine, then, that a specific number of customers, N, are uniformly distributed along Main Street.

ASSUMPTION 3
There are N customers uniformly distributed along Main Street.

PROBLEM 1A.1
Suppose that N is equal to 128. How many customers live between addresses 1/2 and 3/4? Between addresses 1/4 and 1? Between addresses 0 and 1/8?

Although in reality customers buy groceries at different times and places and in different amounts, we can simplify this analysis by making a fourth assumption: each customer buys one unit of groceries at the fixed price P from one of the two firms described in assumption 1.

ASSUMPTION 4
In each period, each customer buys one unit of groceries at the fixed price P.

We will also assume that getting to the store and back is expensive for the customer and that the farther it is to the store, the more expensive it is to make the trip back and forth.

ASSUMPTION 5
Travel to either store is costly for the customer, and the customer's cost of travel increases with the distance traveled.

Finally, we need to identify the basis on which firms and customers make their respective decisions. What motivates a firm in choosing its location, and customers in choosing the store where they shop? As you know, the economist's answer to questions about individual motivation is *self-interest*. Our final assumption is that consumers and firms alike make the economic choices that are in their own self-interest.

ASSUMPTION 6
Both firms and customers are motivated by self-interest.

The precise meaning of the term self-interest varies from model to model. In this model, it is in the *firms' self-interest to make the largest possible profit*. Since both firms offer groceries at the same price, it is in *customers' self-interest to minimize travel costs*.

Finding the Equilibrium

Now that our assumptions are in place, what predictions can we derive from them? Notice that *location* is the only variable firms can choose because our other assumptions have equalized prices, products offered, and other relevant variables. According to assumption 6, our two firms — let us call them All-Valu and Bestway — *will attempt to maximize their profits through the locations of their stores*.

Let us concentrate on All-Valu's choice of location. Notice that All-Valu's profit in any period is just profit per unit multiplied by number of units sold in the period; that is,

All-Valu's profit = (profit per unit)(units sold)

Profit per unit is just $P - C$ since All-Valu pays C for a unit of groceries and sells it for P. Because each customer buys exactly one unit, the number of units sold is equal to the number of customers whom the store attracts; therefore,

All-Valu's profit = $(P - C)$(number of All-Valu's customers)

To discover the number of customers who choose to shop at All-Valu, we need to look at the locations of the two stores. In Figure 1A.2, the line from address 0 on the left to address 1 on the right represents Main Street. We will refer to addresses 0 and 1 as the *market boundaries* of Main Street. Let us arbitrarily locate Bestway at point b, somewhere to the right of the halfway point on Main Street ($b > 1/2$). Now let us arbitrarily locate All-Valu's store at point a, somewhere to the left of Bestway's store ($a < b$). Given the locations represented in Figure 1A.2, how many customers will shop at All-Valu?

To answer this question, we need to derive a prediction about how individual customers will choose the stores where they shop. According to assumption 6, the customers — like the firms — are motivated by their own self-interest. Because the firms' prices are identical and because travel to the store is costly, self-interest will lead customers to buy their groceries at the closer store. We can now state the first prediction of our model:

Customers will patronize the closer store.

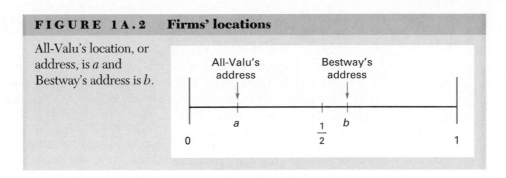

FIGURE 1A.2   Firms' locations

All-Valu's location, or address, is a and Bestway's address is b.

method of
equilibrium

Notice how we used the **method of equilibrium** to derive this prediction. By definition, a model is in equilibrium when no individual economic participant can reach a higher ranking in his or her preference ordering by making a different choice. To get this prediction, we fixed the locations, or addresses, of the two firms at points a and b in Figure 1A.2, thereby creating a new model in which the only choices to be determined are the customers' choices of where to shop. This new model is, in a sense, a sub-model of the complete model. The point is that we used the method of equilibrium in this sub-model to derive the prediction that customers will shop at the closer store.

Knowing that customers will choose the closer store, we can calculate the number of customers who will shop at All-Valu. Let us begin by identifying the address of the customer who is indifferent between the two stores. Notice that in Figure 1A.3, the address $(a + b)/2$ is *midway* between points a and b, or equidistant from All-Valu and Bestway. The customer at address $(a + b)/2$ is therefore *indifferent* between shopping at All-Valu or at Bestway. However, customers to the left of this point prefer All-Valu because it is closer. Customers to the right of this point prefer Bestway for the same reason. We will call the address $(a + b)/2$ the *point of market segmentation* since it divides the total market into All-Valu's and Bestway's market segments. All-Valu's market segment extends from 0 to $(a + b)/2$, and Bestway's market segment extends from $(a + b)/2$ to 1. Because the N customers are uniformly distributed from 0 to 1, the number of All-Valu's customers is equal to the length of its market segment, $(a + b)/2$, multiplied by the total number of customers in the market, N; that is,

$$\text{number of All-Valu's customers} = N(a + b)/2$$

Combining this expression with the previous expression for All-Valu's profit, we have

$$\text{All-Valu's profit} = (P - C)[N(a + b)/2] \qquad \text{when } a < b$$

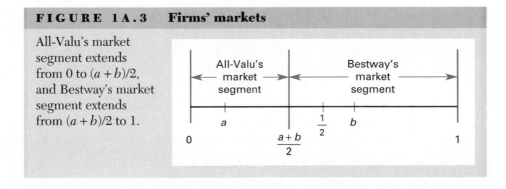

FIGURE 1A.3   Firms' markets

All-Valu's market segment extends from 0 to $(a + b)/2$, and Bestway's market segment extends from $(a + b)/2$ to 1.

PROBLEM 1A.2

Suppose that N is 128, b is 3/4, and $P - C$ is 1. When a is 0, what is the point of market segmentation? How many customers shop at All-Valu? What is All-Valu's profit? When a is 1/4? When a is 1/2? Does the number of All-Valu's customers increase or decrease as a increases?

Given that the only decision All-Valu can make that affects its profit is where to locate, which value of a maximizes All-Valu's profit? As you saw in Problem 1A.2, as a increases, the point of market segmentation, $(a + b)/2$, moves to the right, and All-Valu's market segment increases. Because All-Valu's profit is *directly proportional* to its market segment, its profit increases as a increases.[5] Thus, our model predicts that: when $a < b$, All-Valu will locate as close to b as possible; that is, a will be just less than b.

Of course, All-Valu is also free to locate anywhere to *the right* of Bestway; that is, to choose $a > b$. If it does so, All-Valu's market segment extends from $(a + b)/2$ to 1, and its profit is therefore

$$\text{All-Valu's profit} = (P - C)\, N\, [1 - (a + b)/2] \qquad \text{when } a > b$$

When All-Valu locates to the right of Bestway $(a > b)$, it is clear that as it relocates farther and farther to the right, it loses customers to Bestway, and its profit drops. Thus, when $a > b$, All-Valu's profit is largest when a is just to the right of b.

In Figure 1A.4, we have used the two algebraic expressions for All-Valu's profit to graph its profit as a varies from 0 to 1. Possible locations for All-Valu along Main Street are on the horizontal axis, and its profit is on the vertical axis. So that you can verify the details, in constructing Figure 1A.4, we have supposed that N, b, and $P - C$ are the values specified in Problem 1A.2. We have also assumed that when a is equal to b, the stores split the market evenly. From Figure 1A.4, we see that, because we have assumed that b exceeds 1/2, All-Valu will locate just to the left of Bestway. However, if b is less than 1/2, All-Valu will instead decide to locate just to the right of b. The general inference that we have made is that All-Valu will locate adjacent to its competitor on one side or the other. Whether it chooses to be on the right or on the left will depend on whether b is smaller or larger than 1/2. All-Valu will choose whichever side gives it the larger segment of the market. Of course, Bestway will choose its location in exactly the same way. As a result, we have our second prediction:

When a store is relocating, it will always choose to establish itself adjacent to its competitor on the side farther from a market boundary (points 0 and 1).

In deriving this prediction, once again we used the method of equilibrium. The second prediction tells us what will happen when one firm's address is fixed. Notice that when we fix one firm's address, we are creating a sub-model in which the choices to be determined are the other firm's choice of an address and each customer's choice of which store to patronize. In the equilibrium of this sub-model, the firm that is picking

---

5 In this exercise, All-Valu is choosing its location a to maximize its profit. The partial derivative of this profit function with respect to a is $[(P - C)N]/2$, which is positive. All-Valu's profit is thus an increasing function of a. All-Valu will therefore locate as near to b as possible.

FIGURE 1A.4   Profit as a function of location

The two colored line segments give All-Valu's profit for all addresses *a* from 0 to 1, given that Bestway is located at 3/4. Because All-Valu's profit is largest when *a* is just less than 3/4, it will locate there.

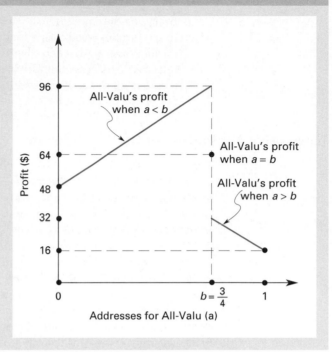

All-Valu's profit when $a < b$

All-Valu's profit when $a = b$

All-Valu's profit when $a > b$

Profit ($)

$b = \frac{3}{4}$

Addresses for All-Valu (a)

an address chooses to establish itself adjacent to its competitor on the side farther from a market boundary, and (consistent with our first prediction) customers choose to patronize the closer store.

This second prediction begins to make sense of our earlier observations about how gas stations tend to cluster at the same intersection. Using this prediction we can deduce the equilibrium of locations in the complete model. We can find the equilibrium by discovering what would happen if both stores were to locate to one side of the midpoint (1/2) of Main Street.

In Figure 1A.5, Bestway is initially located at b_1. Because it is closer than its competitor to the midpoint and therefore commands the larger share of the market, it will stay put. However, because All-Valu is initially located at a_1, it will "leapfrog" its competitor and relocate adjacent to its competitor on the side closer to the midpoint at a_2. As a result of All-Valu's move, Bestway's share of the market will drop. It will then leapfrog All-Valu to recapture its market advantage. This process will continue until both grocery stores are finally located together at the center of Main Street. Of course, this leapfrogging is not something we would actually expect to see, but rather something these two firms would play out in their minds before choosing their equilibrium locations at the center of the market. We have reached our third prediction:

Both stores will locate together at the center of the market.

This third prediction concerns not a sub-model but the *complete model* in which the choices to be determined are Bestway's and All-Valu's choice of an address and also each customer's choice of where to buy groceries. In the equilibrium of the complete model, the stores are located together at the center of the market and customers patronize either firm since both firms are the same distance away from any one customer.

PROBLEM 1A.3

In finding the equilibrium of Hotelling's duopoly model, we assumed that the two grocers could change their locations at no cost. Consider the opposite extreme: assume that once they have chosen a location, the grocers cannot relocate their stores. Let All-Valu choose its location first and assume that it understands that once its location is chosen, Bestway will choose the location that maximizes its own profit. Which locations will the firms choose?

Normative Evaluation of the Equilibrium

The next question is a normative question. Is the minimally differentiated equilibrium of the Hotelling model *socially desirable*? Using the Pareto criterion, we cannot say very much in answer to that question. If we start with any configuration of locations for the two firms, and then move one or both firms, someone is inevitably made worse off. In the new configuration of locations, some customer has to travel farther to get groceries, or some firm's profit declines. This means that *any* social state is Pareto-optimal.

By contrast, the cost-benefit criterion can be used to identify the single *best* configuration of locations in the model. Notice first that the aggregate profit of the two firms is independent of their locations. Aggregate profit per period is just $N(P - C)$ since each of N customers buys one unit per period. Of course, the distribution of this profit is determined by the firms' locations, but the aggregate amount is independent of locations. In the language of cost-benefit analysis, a dollar of cost to one firm is always offset by a dollar of benefit to the other firm. So, in comparing any two configurations of locations, the cost-benefit criterion tells us that the preferred configuration is the one in which customers' aggregate travel costs are lower: *the cost-benefit optimal configuration of locations is a configuration in which customers' aggregate travel costs are minimized*. Which configuration is cost-benefit optimal will depend on the details of travel costs. Except in very odd cases, however, there will be a *unique* cost-benefit optimal configuration; that is, there will be a single configuration of locations that minimizes aggregate travel costs.

For example, let us suppose that the relationship between distance traveled and costs incurred is proportional to distance and is the same for all customers. Then the

FIGURE 1A.5   The equilibrium of locations

The firms are initially located at a_1 and b_1. All-Valu relocates at a_2, inducing Bestway to relocate at b_2. This process of relocation by leapfrogging stops only when the firms are both located at the midpoint of the market; that is, $a = b = 1/2$ is the equilibrium pair of locations.

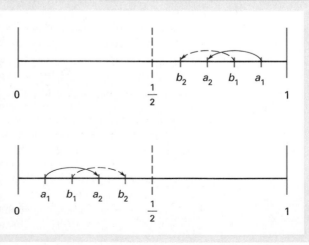

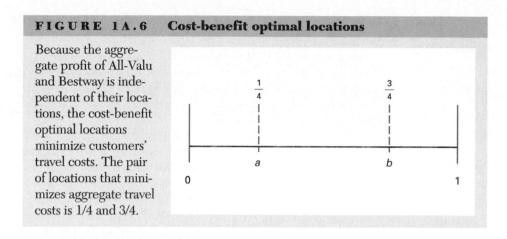

FIGURE 1A.6   Cost-benefit optimal locations

Because the aggregate profit of All-Valu and Bestway is independent of their locations, the cost-benefit optimal locations minimize customers' travel costs. The pair of locations that minimizes aggregate travel costs is 1/4 and 3/4.

configuration of locations that minimizes travel costs is the configuration in Figure 1A.6, where one firm is located at address 1/4 and the other firm at address 3/4. In this configuration, no customer is farther than 1/4 mile from the closer store. By comparison, in the equilibrium of our location model, where both firms are located at address 1/2, half the population (the customers between 0 and 1/4 and between 3/4 and 1) must travel more than 1/4 mile to the closer store.

Further Applications of the Model

Although this model concerns how two firms locate in geographic space, many of the economists who first thought about minimum differentiation, including Hotelling and Kenneth Boulding, believed that the prediction about clustering at a central location could be used to a understand many other intriguing economic questions.[6] For instance, Boulding (1966) described some of the other observations that he thought the principle of minimum differentiation explained:

> It explains why all the dime stores are usually clustered together, often next door to each other; why certain towns attract large numbers of firms of one kind; why an industry, such as the garment industry, will concentrate in one quarter of a city. It is a principle which can be carried over into other "differences" than spatial differences. The general rule for any new manufacturer coming into an industry is: "Make your product as like the existing products as you can without destroying the differences." It explains why all automobiles are so much alike. ... It even explains why Methodists, Baptists, and even Quakers are so much alike, and tend to get even more alike, for if one church is to attract the adherents of another, it must become more like the other but not so much alike that no one can tell the difference. (601)

As Boulding suggested, this model seems helpful in explaining other observations. It not only seems to tell us something about why firms tend to locate together. It also appears to explain why rival firms tend to imitate one another in the range or qualities

---

6 Hotelling's original location model stimulated a good deal of subsequent research. These are but a few of many papers inspired by Hotelling's model: Lerner and Singer (1937); Smithies (1941); Eaton and Lipsey (1975); and d'Aspremont, Gabsewicz, and Thisse (1979). The model has also been applied to politics: see Downs (1957).

of the products they sell. For example, it might explain why Microsoft Corporation imitated the user-friendly interface pioneered by Apple Computer in its Windows operating system for IBM computers and clones. Thus, this model can be *generalized* from the clustering of firms in geographic space to apply to the clustering of products in other domains. However, in each new application of the model, it is important to reinterpret the model's assumptions to see that the model does in fact capture the essential features of the new problem.

To see what is involved, let us apply the model in another context: the morning scheduling decisions made by competing airlines on the route from Chicago to Atlanta. Let us assume that most people prefer to arrive within an hour of 8 A.M., a time that is neither too early for most travelers to arrive nor too late to leave them a good part of the day to spend in Atlanta. The assumption is, then, that most morning passengers prefer to fly in the early morning, but they will accept arrival times before or after their most preferred time.

If one airline picks 8 A.M. as its arrival time, when will its rival schedule its morning arrival? As we discovered in the leapfrogging exercise, the best strategy is to get between one's rival and the mass of customers by locating just next to the rival on the side with the larger market segment. If more customers prefer to arrive after rather than before 8 A.M., we can predict that the rival airline will schedule an arrival just slightly after 8 A.M. Notice that we have implicitly modified the assumption about distance: we have substituted *time* — the stretch of time within which morning arrivals are acceptable to air travelers — for *distance*. How have we also implicitly redefined our assumption about what constitutes the self-interest of airline passengers?

By scheduling a flight that arrives just after 8. A.M, the rival airline picks up all the midmorning traffic — passengers who have no flights available to them later in the morning — yet it does not lose customers who prefer times closer to 8 A.M. We then predict that the two rivals will locate at the center of the market for morning air travel. We can test the prediction in a rough way by looking at how airlines actually schedule flights. For example, one day at Atlanta's Hartsfield Airport, 45 commercial flights were scheduled to land between 8 A.M. and 8:10 A.M.

SUMMARY

The objective of this appendix has been to set out the working methodology of the economic theorist. Because economic theory attempts to explain economic reality, what often sparks the theorist's interest is an intriguing observation from ordinary life coupled with the question, "Why?" For example, "Why do two, three, or even four gas stations sometimes locate at the same intersection?"

The theorist then builds a model (or theory) to explain the observation. This model building is the process of judiciously selecting a set of assumptions that capture the essential features of that economic reality and then deriving conclusions, or predictions, from those assumptions. The method used to derive those predictions is the method of equilibrium. An equilibrium consists of a set of choices for individuals and a corresponding social state such that no individual can make himself or herself better off by making some other choice. Thus, the force that drives this deductive process is the *self-interest* of individual economic agents. Indeed, the systematic application of this method of analysis distinguishes economics from other social sciences.

Having identified an equilibrium, the theorist then engages in normative evaluation of some kind in an attempt to determine the social desirability of the equilibrium. The tools used for this purpose are the Pareto criterion and and the cost-benefit criterion. Often, a theorist will also try adapting the model to explore other, similar problems. Of course, as we saw in the body of this chapter, the real test of any model is its ability to explain and predict economic reality.

REFERENCES

Alchian, A. 1987. "Property Rights," in *The New Palgrave: A Dictionary of Economics*, J. Eatwell, M. Milgate, and P. Newman (eds.), London: The Macmillan Press.

Boland, L. 1987. "Methodology," in *The New Palgrave: A Dictionary of Economics*, J. Eatwell, M. Milgate, and P. Newman (eds.), London: The Macmillan Press.

Boulding, K. 1966. *Economic Analysis*, New York: Harper & Row.

Cheung, S. 1987. "Common Property Rights," in *The New Palgrave: A Dictionary of Economics*, J. Eatwell, M. Milgate, and P. Newman (eds.), London: The Macmillan Press.

Coase, R. H. 1960. "The Problem of Social Cost," *Journal of Law and Economics*, 3:1–44.

d'Aspremont, C., J. Gabsewicz, and J. Thisse. 1979. "On Hotelling's 'Stability in Competition'," *Econometrica*, 47:1145–50.

Downs, A. 1957. "An Economic Theory of Political Action in a Democracy," *Journal of Political Economy*, 65:135–50.

Eaton, B. C., and R. G. Lipsey. 1975. "The Principle of Minimum Differentiation Reconsidered: Some New Developments in the Theory of Spatial Competition," *Review of Economic Studies*, 42:27–49.

Eatwell, J., M. Milgate, and P. Newman (eds.). 1987. *The New Palgrave: A Dictionary of Economics*, London: The Macmillan Press.

Hotelling, H. 1929. "Stability in Competition," *The Economic Journal*, 39:41–57.

Kehoe, T. 1987. "Comparative Statics," in *The New Palgrave: A Dictionary of Economics*, J. Eatwell, M. Milgate, and P. Newman (eds.), London: The Macmillan Press.

Lerner, A., and H. Singer. 1937. "Some Notes on Duopoly and Spatial Competition," *Journal of Political Economy*, 45:145–86.

Smithies, A. 1941. "Optimum Location in Spatial Competition," *Journal of Political Economy*, 49:423–39.

Individual Choice

In Part II, we concentrate on the behavior of individuals as economic agents as we see how consumers decide which goods to buy in the goods market at the top of the circular-flow diagram in Chapter 1 (Figure 1.5) and which labor services and other personal resources to sell in the resources markets at the bottom of the diagram.

In Chapter 2, we set out the most widely used economic theory of individual preferences, we examine an individual's willingness to make tradeoffs among goods, and we show how to construct utility functions from data about individual preferences. We also see how the theory of preferences can be used to explore several intriguing observations from ordinary life.

In Chapter 3, we see how a consumer allocates a limited income across consumption goods to maximize his or her own utility. The solution to this problem is a set of demand functions specifying how much of each good a consumer buys, given the consumer's income and any set of prices for consumption goods.

In Chapter 4, we apply the techniques of Chapter 3 to a grab-bag of situational problems. We ask, for example, why the allocation of court time at the University of Colorado Recreation Center is wasteful and how it could be improved. Our intention is to let you see just how widely applicable the theory of choice actually is.

Because the theory of preferences in Chapter 2 does not apply to situations that are "risky," in Chapter 5 we extend the theory to include risk. We create an economic model known as the theory of expected utility and then use it to explain a whole range of otherwise puzzling observations. For example, the theory explains why people buy insurance.

CHAPTER 2

A Theory of Preferences

All social sciences — including political science, sociology, psychology, and economics — are concerned with human behavior. Yet each discipline in the social sciences views human nature from a different vantage point and therefore illuminates different facets of behavior. What distinguishes the economist's approach to the study of human behavior is the universality of the hypothesis of the pursuit of *self-interest*. Economists see self-interest at work everywhere in economic life.

In Chapter 1, we introduced you to the concept of self-interest, and we saw that — for economists — self-interest motivates all economic activity, including the profit-maximizing activities of firms. We also saw that — for economists — self-interest means that individuals make the choices that allow them to attain the highest possible ranking in their own preference orderings. In this chapter, we will set out the foundations of this approach in some detail as we explore the theory of preferences.

This theory is based on two fairly simple ideas. The first is that individuals have consistent preferences. The second is that they are willing to make tradeoffs. We begin the chapter by considering precisely what it means to say that individual preferences are consistent, and then we explore an individual's willingness to make tradeoffs — that is, at his or her willingness to give up one thing in order to get another. Here we are in fact constructing a theory of preferences.

We then describe a useful measure of an individual's willingness to make tradeoffs called the marginal rate of substitution, we introduce an additional and widely used assumption known as a diminishing marginal rate of substitution, and we explore alternatives to it. Next, we look at several applications of the theory of preferences. Then we introduce utility functions and show how to construct a utility function from preference data. Finally, we discuss how to extend the theory of preferences from the two-good case used throughout the chapter to the many-good case.

2.1
Completeness and Consistency of Preferences

preferences

Clearly, what people like and what economic choices they make are directly linked: people's **preferences**, or personal tastes, dictate their economic decisions. But preferences may cover more territory than you at first imagine. Individuals clearly have preferences about goods such as CDs, running shoes, and paperback books and about services such as house cleaning, car washing, and banking. These are the kinds of economic goods that ordinarily come to mind when we think about individuals making economic choices.

However, people also have preferences about a whole range of other, less tangible economic goods. These include preferences about how to spend time (working, studying, watching TV, shopping), possible occupations (construction work, dentistry, massage therapy, accounting), social relations (living in the hometown or traveling the world), different environmental settings (large cosmopolitan cities or remote wilderness areas), and charitable activities (donating to a food bank or volunteering for a charity fund drive). Notice that "self-interested" does *not* mean "selfish." For example, charitable actions of all kinds are perfectly in keeping with this theory of preferences. Although we will develop the theory of preferences in the context of ordinary consumption goods and services like T-shirts and haircuts, later in the chapter we will apply it to other kinds of preferences, including workers' preferences about allotting time between work and leisure.

The Two-Good Case

To keep the analysis of individual preferences simple, we will assume that there are just two goods. (In Section 2.6, we show how to extend the theory from this two-good case to the many-good case.) In this case, the person is faced with choices among different combinations (or bundles) containing varying amounts of these two goods. We will use the terms *good 1* and *good 2* to represent the goods themselves. For example, good 1 might be T-shirts and good 2 haircuts. We will use the symbols x_1 and x_2 to denote corresponding quantities of good 1 and good 2. For example, $x_1 = 2$ means two

consumption bundle

T-shirts and $x_2 = 5$ means five haircuts. A **consumption bundle** is simply *a combination of a specific quantity of each good*. We will denote a consumption bundle by (x_1, x_2). For example, the consumption bundle (2,5) contains 2 units of good 1 (T-shirts) and 5 units of good 2 (haircuts). The consumption bundle (62,17) contains 62 units of good 1 and 17 units of good 2 , and so on.

A Preference Ordering

preference statements

Notice that implicit in choosing one consumption bundle or another is a person's ability to make one of two **preference statements** — the ability to say either "I like this bundle better than that one: I prefer it," or to say "I like both equally well: I'm indifferent between them." We can make use of a person's statements of preference and indifference to compare the relative attractiveness of two particular consumption bundles.

preference ordering

By making a whole series of such comparisons, we may be able to construct a **preference ordering** for that person — a ranking from top to bottom, from most-preferred to least-preferred — of all consumption bundles. More precisely, we can use these preference statements to construct a complete preference ordering *if two conditions are satisfied: 1. a person is always able to make such preference statements, and 2. his or her preference statements are consistent.*

Our first challenge, then, is to find a set of assumptions that imply these two conditions. To begin, let us imagine that a particular person named Eleanor has made the following three preference statements about four consumption bundles containing good 1 (T-shirts) and good 2 (haircuts): a. she prefers bundle (20,17) to bundle (4,12); b. she is indifferent between bundle (4,12) and bundle (10,5); and c. she prefers bundle (10,5) to bundle (2,3). Now let us try to rank, or order, Eleanor's preferences over these four consumption bundles. This seems to be the obvious ordering:

> First: bundle (20,17)
> Second: bundles (4,12) and (10,5)
> Third: bundle (2,3)

But this is just a tentative beginning in our attempt to create a preference ordering for Eleanor. First, do we know that her preference ordering is *complete*? Eleanor

completeness

was able to make preference statements about these four bundles, but do we know that she can do so for every pair of consumption bundles? If she cannot make such preference statements about *all possible pairs of consumption bundles*, then we cannot construct a complete preference ordering for her. We therefore need the following assumption about the **completeness** of an individual's preferences:

COMPLETENESS ASSUMPTION
Given any two consumption bundles, one of the following statements is true:

Bundle 1 is preferred to bundle 2
Bundle 2 is preferred to bundle 1
Bundle 1 is indifferent to bundle 2

This seems to be a perfectly straightforward assumption, but you should be aware that it is also a strong one. For example, the completeness assumption implies that a person is familiar with every good in the consumption bundles. Yet someone who has never eaten say, a papaya, cannot be expected to satisfy this assumption if papayas are included in those bundles. The completeness assumption therefore rules out interesting economic issues about how individuals explore, or find out about, their own preferences.

Second, do we know that Eleanor's preferences over these four bundles and all other bundles are *consistent*? For example, we placed bundle (20,17) first in her preference ordering and bundle (2,3) third. But can we be sure that if we asked Eleanor to compare these two bundles, she would say that she prefers bundle (20,17) to bundle (2,3)? What if she tells us instead that she prefers bundle (2,3) to bundle (20,17)? Or that she is indifferent between them? Then Eleanor's preferences are not consistent, and we cannot construct a complete preference ordering for her. We therefore need to make two assumptions about the *consistency* of an individual's preferences.

two-term
consistency

The first consistency assumption is known as **two-term consistency**. Common sense suggests that the three preference statements in the completeness assumption are mutually exclusive. That is, for any two consumption bundles, only *one* of the three statements is true:

TWO-TERM CONSISTENCY ASSUMPTION
Given any two consumption bundles, only one of the following statements is true:

Bundle 1 is preferred to bundle 2
Bundle 2 is preferred to bundle 1
Bundle 1 is indifferent to bundle 2

transitivity

The second consistency assumption is known as three-term consistency or **transitivity**. It guarantees, for example, that if Eleanor says that she prefers (20,17) to (4,12) and that she prefers (4,12) to (2,3), she will also say that she prefers (20,17) to (2,3). As you can see, transitivity is slightly more complicated than two-term consistency, but it makes equally good sense.

TRANSITIVITY (OR THREE-TERM CONSISTENCY) ASSUMPTION
Given any three consumption bundles:

1. If bundle 1 is preferred to bundle 2 and bundle 2 is preferred to bundle 3,
then bundle 1 is preferred to bundle 3

2. If bundle 1 is preferred to bundle 2 and bundle 2 is indifferent to bundle 3,
then bundle 1 is preferred to bundle 3

3. If bundle 1 is indifferent to bundle 2 and bundle 2 is preferred to bundle 3,
then bundle 1 is preferred to bundle 3

4. If bundle 1 is indifferent to bundle 2 and bundle 2 is indifferent to bundle 3, then bundle 1 is indifferent to bundle 3

To check your understanding of the transitivity assumption, try the following problem.

PROBLEM 2.1

Does the following set of preference statements violate the transitivity assumption? Bundle (11,17) is indifferent to bundle (14,21); bundle (10,19) is preferred to bundle (14,21); bundle (14,21) is preferred to bundle (15,8); bundle (15,8) is preferred to bundle (11,17).

The transitivity assumption seems straightforward enough, but does it actually describe human behavior? To try to answer that question, a number of economists have devised laboratory experiments to test the transitivity of preferences. In surveying experiments about the transitivity of preferences among adults, Bradbury and Moscato (1982) conclude that the preferences of the great majority of adults are consistent. Interestingly, experiments about children's preferences for different colors reveals that the preferences of younger people tend to be inconsistent, or intransitive.

Although the three-term or transitivity assumption *is* necessary to construct a complete preference ordering, a four-term consistency assumption is not. It is implied by the transitivity assumption. That is, four-term consistency can be derived from three-term consistency. And just as four term consistency can be derived from three-term consistency, five-term consistency can be derived from four-term consistency, six-term consistency from five-term consistency, and so on. In combination with the two-term-consistency assumption, this chain of consistency results means that an individual is incapable of making any inconsistent set of preference statements. In other words, they guarantee that an individual's preferences are consistent.

To see why, consider the following statement — one of the eight preference statements needed to describe four-term consistency: If bundle 1 is preferred to bundle 2, bundle 2 is preferred to bundle 3, and bundle 3 is preferred to bundle 4, then bundle 1 is preferred to bundle 4. Now, suppose that Eleanor's preferences satisfy the transitivity assumption and that she makes the following three preference statements: she says that a. she prefers bundle (20,17) to bundle (4,12); b. she prefers bundle (4,12) to bundle (2,3); c. she prefers bundle (2,3) to bundle (1,2). To show that Eleanor's preferences also satisfy four-term consistency, we must show that she prefers bundle (20,17) to bundle (1,2). Using statements a. and b. in conjunction with part 1 of the transitivity assumption, we can infer that Eleanor would also make the statement that d. she prefers bundle (20,17) to bundle (2,3). Now, using statements d. and c., again in conjunction with part 1 of the transitivity assumption, we can infer that — just as four-term consistency requires — Eleanor would also say that she prefers bundle (20,17) to bundle (1,2). In the following problem you can adapt this argument to see more generally that three-term consistency does imply four-term consistency.

PROBLEM 2.2

The following is another of the eight statements needed to describe four-term consistency: If bundle 1 is indifferent to bundle 2, bundle 2 is preferred to bundle 3, and bundle 3 is preferred to bundle 4, then bundle 1 is preferred to bundle 4. Show that this statement is true if the transitivity assumption is satisfied. Then write down the other six statements that describe four-term consistency.

These three assumptions — completeness, two-term consistency, and transitivity — are basic or *core assumptions* about preferences. Taken together they tell us precisely what it means to say that an individual has consistent preferences. The first assumption guarantees that a person can always make preferences statements. The second and third assumptions guarantee that a person will not make inconsistent preference statements. In summary:

> Taken together, the completeness, two-term consistency, and transitivity assumptions guarantee that an individual can consistently rank any set of consumption bundles.

To remind you that these assumptions are *always* in the background when we use the concept of self-interest, we have set each assumption out formally in the text.

2.2

Tradeoffs and Indifference Curves

The idea that individuals have consistent preferences is one key concept in the economist's theory of human behavior. The idea that individuals are willing to make tradeoffs is another. Now it is time to look at precisely what economists mean by the term *tradeoffs* and to see how tradeoffs and *indifference curves* are inextricably linked.

Let us return to the tentative preference ordering we constructed for Eleanor. By definition, the bundles among which she is indifferent will occupy the same position in her preference ordering. For example, because she is indifferent between bundle (4,12) and bundle (10,5), we know that these two bundles occupy the same position in her preference ordering. The list of all bundles occupying the same position in a preference ordering is called an **indifference curve**. An indifference curve for Eleanor, labeled *I*, is presented in Figure 2.1. We know that any two consumption bundles on this indifference must satisfy the indifference statement. For example, we know that Eleanor is also indifferent between bundle (10,5) and bundle (5,10) and that she is indifferent between bundle (4,12) and bundle (5,10).

indifference
curve

Now let us look at the relationship between indifference curves and the willingness to make tradeoffs. Suppose that Eleanor is initially at bundle (4,12) in Figure 2.1 where she has a consumption bundle containing 4 T-shirts and 12 haircuts. We know that she is willing to give up 2 haircuts in order to get 1 more T-shirt because the consumption bundle (5,10) is on the same indifference curve. Beginning at bundle (4, 12), we also know that she is willing to give up 7 haircuts to get 6 T-shirts because the bundle (10,5) is also on the same indifference curve. As you can see, tradeoffs concern movements along indifference curves. Given an initial bundle, as we move along the associated indifference curve, we encounter all of the tradeoffs that a particular person is willing to make from the initial bundle.

Continuity of Preferences

There were a number of bundles that Eleanor found equally acceptable. The indifference curve in Figure 2.1 reflects the fact that she was willing to trade off one good against the other. Is it conceivable that there are consumption bundles for which a particular person finds *no* acceptable substitutes? If so, what will the resulting indifference curve look like? Try the following problem to find out.

FIGURE 2.1   An indifference curve for Eleanor

Curve *I* is an indifference curve because Eleanor is indifferent between any two consumption bundles on it. For example, she is indifferent between bundle (10,5) and bundle (4,12).

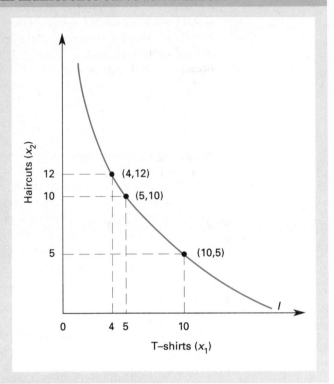

PROBLEM 2.3

Clem is obsessed with good 1. Given any two bundles with unequal quantities of good 1, Clem prefers the bundle with the larger quantity of good 1. Given any two bundles with equal quantities of good 1, Clem prefers the bundle with the larger quantity of good 2. Consider bundle (2,3), and show that there is no other bundle, say bundle *B*, for which Clem will say that he is indifferent between bundle (2,3) and bundle *B*. Now, consider an arbitrary consumption bundle and show that it, too, is a single-point indifference curve.

As you discovered, Clem's indifference curves are simply points. This reflects the fact that Clem is completely *unwilling* to make tradeoffs of one good for another: there is no amount of good 2 large enough to persuade him to give up even a very small amount of good 1. However, few people's preferences are like Clem's. Most individuals are willing to make tradeoffs among goods. To insure that individuals are willing to make tradeoffs, we need an additional assumption known as the **continuity of preferences**:

continuity of preferences

CONTINUITY OF PREFERENCES ASSUMPTION
Through any consumption bundle in which the quantity of at least one good is positive, there is a continuous indifference curve.

This assumption — the fourth and last of the core assumptions of the theory of preferences — is a fundamental assumption: The continuity of preferences assumption guarantees that individuals are always willing to make tradeoffs. We have therefore set the assumption out formally in the text as a reminder that it, too, is always in the background when we use the theory of preferences.[1]

To see what the continuity assumption means in graphic terms, place your pencil on any consumption bundle in Figure 2.1. The continuity assumption means that you can draw the indifference curve through that bundle without lifting your pencil from the paper — that is, the indifference curve is continuous. In the following problem, you can try your hand at constructing indifference curves for a particularly simple preference ordering.

PROBLEM 2.4

Amy likes eating fish, but she only eats two kinds: trout (good 1) and salmon (good 2). Her preferences are such that, given a choice between two bundles containing trout and salmon, she always prefers the bundle that weighs more. Let x_1 and x_2 denote pounds of trout and salmon respectively.
a. What is Amy's preference ordering over the following six bundles: (10,15), (20,30), (25,0), (15,15), (20,15), (40,10)?
b. On one diagram draw the indifference curves defined by each of the following bundles: (10,15), (20,30), (20,15), (40,0).

Nonsatiation

nonsatiation
assumption

When consumption bundles contain only goods, it is convenient to assume that "more is better" — that a consumer always prefers a consumption bundle with more of both goods to a bundle with less. Or, to put it more precisely, *given two consumption bundles, if bundle 1 contains more of one good than bundle 2, and if it does not contain less of the other good, then bundle 1 is preferred to bundle 2.* This assumption is known as the **nonsatiation assumption**. Nonsatiation means, for example, that Eleanor would rather have bundle (17,51) — that is, 17 T-shirts and 51 haircuts — than bundle (4,5) — that is, 4 T-shirts and 5 haircuts. To check your understanding of the nonsatiation assumption, try the following problem.

PROBLEM 2.5

Which of the following preference statements violate the nonsatiation assumption? Bundle (12,35) is preferred to bundle (10,30); bundle (17,98) is preferred to bundle (17,97); bundle (10,9) is preferred to bundle (10,10); bundle (42,67) is preferred to bundle (42,60); bundle (6,9) is preferred to bundle (7,8); bundle (99,43) is preferred to bundle (101,45).

Nonsatiation is *not*, however, a core assumption like the four preceding assumptions. It is easy to imagine that at some point "enough is enough." For example, Eleanor might decide that 912 T-shirts was enough, and she therefore might say that a consumption bundle containing 913 T-shirts and 6 haircuts was not really preferable to a bundle containing 912 T-shirts and 6 haircuts. If this happens, then Eleanor's preferences do not satisfy the nonsatiation assumption.

---

1 Students interested in a mathematical treatment of this theory should consult Arrow (1959) or Chapter 3 of Debreu (1959). The basic elements of this theory are attributable to Slutsky (1915) and to Hicks and Allen (1934). See also the following entries in *The New Palgrave*: "preferences" (G.H. von Wright); "utility theory and decision theory" (R.D. Collison Black).

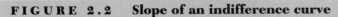

FIGURE 2.2   Slope of an indifference curve

Nonsatiation implies that any bundle in the green area is preferred to bundle (2,2) and that bundle (2,2) is preferred to any bundle in the gray area. Accordingly, the indifference curve through (2,2) cannot pass through either the green or the gray area, and its slope is therefore negative.

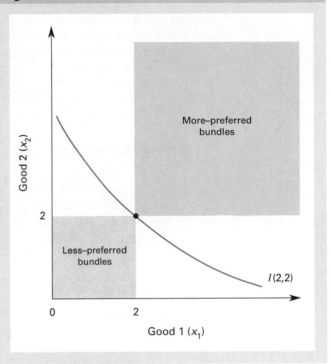

In other cases, the nonsatiation assumption is not applicable. For example, in cases where consumption bundles contain what are sometimes called economic "bads" like air pollution, less — not more — is better. We will consider some economic bads in the applications of Section 2.4.

The Slope of Indifference Curves

In Figure 2.2, we have drawn an indifference curve and, for convenience, we have labeled it $I(2,2)$ since it passes through consumption bundle (2,2). Notice that its slope is negative. When the nonsatiation assumption is satisfied, the slope of *any* indifference curve is negative. To see why, notice that any bundle in the green area of Figure 2.2 is preferred to bundle (2,2) because bundles in that area contain at least 2 units of both goods and more than 2 units of either good 1 or good 2. Similarly, bundle (2,2) is preferred to any bundle in the gray area, because those bundles contain less of at least one good and no more of the other good than consumption bundle (2,2). If we now draw an indifference curve through bundle (2,2), it cannot enter the green (more preferred) area or the gray (less preferred) area. The indifference curve $I(2,2)$ in Figure 2.2 must therefore slope downward and to the right:

The nonsatiation assumption implies that indifference curves have a negative slope.

The Indifference Map

There is another important observation to make about indifference curves. Because the preference ordering is a complete ordering, we know that there is an indifference curve through *every* bundle. Thus, the (x_1, x_2) plane, or quarter plane, is filled with indifference curves like those in Figure 2.3. Because of the nonsatiation assumption, bundles with more of both goods are preferred to those with less. As we move upward and to the right from indifference curve $I(2,2)$ to $I(3,3)$ to $I(4,4)$ to $I(5,5)$ in Figure 2.3, we encounter indifference curves containing more-preferred consumption bundles. For example, any bundle on $I(3,3)$ is preferred to any bundle on $I(2,2)$. In summary:

The nonsatiation assumption implies that bundles on indifference curves farther from the origin are preferred to bundles on curves closer to the origin.

PROBLEM 2.6

Amy from Problem 2.4 is indifferent between two consumption bundles if the combined weight of trout (good 1) and salmon (good 2) in the two bundles is identical. Show that there is an indifference curve through every consumption bundle (x_1, x_2). Hint: pick an arbitrary bundle and construct her indifference curve.

Non-Intersecting Indifference Curves

Notice that the indifference curves in Figure 2.3 do not intersect each other. Because this is an important general property of indifference maps, it deserves closer attention. Specifically, we want to show that the transitivity assumption implies that

FIGURE 2.3   An indifference map

The space of consumption bundles is filled with indifference curves. Four indifference curves are shown here. Any bundle on $I(5,5)$ is preferred to any bundle on $I(4,4)$, any bundle on $I(4,4)$ is preferred to any bundle on $I(3,3)$, and any bundle on $I(3,3)$ is preferred to any bundle on $I(2,2)$.

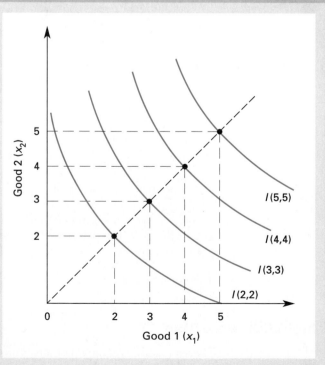

indifference curves cannot intersect. To do so, let us begin by assuming — strictly for purposes of argument — that two indifference curves *do* cross. We will then show that this leads to a violation of the transitivity assumption.

Let us assume, then, that two indifference curves do intersect as shown in Figure 2.4. Now pick a bundle other than bundle 3 from each indifference curve — say, bundle 1 from indifference curve I_1 and bundle 2 from indifference curve I_2. Since bundles 1 and 2 are on different indifference curves, one bundle must be preferred to the other. Suppose bundle 1 is the preferred bundle; then we have preference statement a: bundle 1 is preferred to bundle 2. In addition, since bundles 2 and 3 are on indifference curve I_2, we have preference statement b: bundle 2 is indifferent to bundle 3. Similarly, since bundles 1 and 3 are on indifference curve I_1, we have preference statement c: bundle 1 is indifferent to bundle 3. Notice that these three preference statements violate part 2 of the transitivity assumption that demands that if statements a. and b. are true, then bundle 1 must be preferred to bundle 3. Therefore, it cannot be the case that indifference curves intersect and that preferences also satisfy the transitivity assumption. In other words, intersecting indifference curves and transitive preferences are contradictory notions:

The transitivity assumption implies that indifference curves cannot intersect.

FIGURE 2.4   Impossible indifference curves

Since bundles 1 and 2 are on different indifference curves, bundle 1 must be preferred to bundle 2 or vice versa. Since bundle 1 is on the same indifference curve as bundle 3, bundle 1 must be indifferent to bundle 3. Similarly, bundle 2 must be indifferent to bundle 3. Therefore bundle 1 must be indifferent to bundle 2. Of course, this contradicts our first statement. Therefore we conclude that indifference curves cannot intersect.

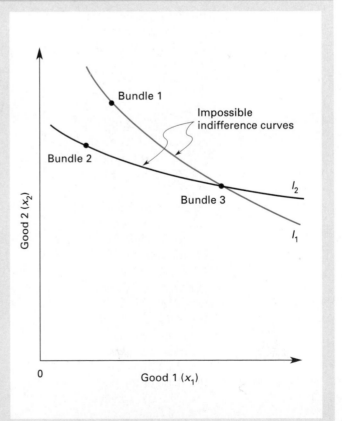

2.3

Tradeoffs and the Marginal Rate of Substitution

Basic to the theory of consumer choice in Chapter 3 is the *rate* at which someone is willing to trade off, or substitute, one good for another — the rate at which the quantity of one good must be increased as the quantity of another is decreased in order to keep a consumer on the same indifference curve. As you have discovered, Amy is always willing to trade off or *substitute* a pound of salmon for a pound of trout. Our goal in this section is to develop a measure to quantify the amount of one good a person will give up to obtain more of another good. That measure is known as the *marginal rate of substitution*.

To begin, let us suppose that the person whose preferences are represented in Figure 2.5 is initially at bundle A. Now suppose that we make a reduction the quantity of good 1 in bundle A, denoted by Δx_1. What increase in the quantity of good 2, denoted by Δx_2, will compensate for that reduction in quantity of good 1? For example, what happens if good 1 is reduced by 9 units — $\Delta x_1 = 9$? As you can see from Figure 2.5, to get this person back to indifference curve I, good 2 must be increased by 15 units — $\Delta x_2 = 15$. The ratio $\Delta x_2/\Delta x_1$ is called a *rate of substitution* because it tells us the rate at which quantity of good 2 must be increased per unit reduction in quantity of good 1. In this case, the rate of substitution is 15/9, or approximately 1.67, which is equal to the absolute value of the slope of the dashed line AB in Figure 2.5.

FIGURE 2.5   Marginal rate of substitution

Beginning at bundle A, if the quantity of good 1 is reduced by 9 — $\Delta x_1 = 9$ — then quantity of good 2 must be increased by 15 — $\Delta x_2 = 15$ — to get back to indifference curve I. The rate of substitution of good 2 for good 1 is $\Delta x_2/\Delta x_1$, which is equal to the absolute value of the slope of the dashed line from bundle A to bundle B. To find the marginal rate of substitution, *MRS*, let Δx_1 approach zero. As it does, the rate of substitution approaches the absolute value of the slope of the tangent line *TT*, which is *MRS* at bundle A.

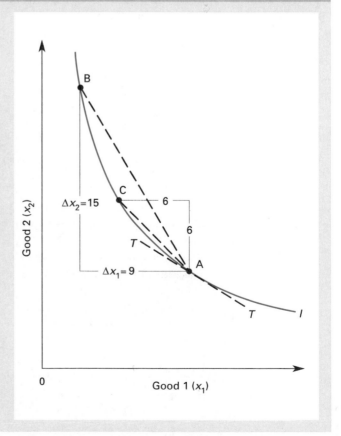

marginal change

The rate of substitution that we just calculated is termed a *nonmarginal rate of substitution* because the initial 9-unit reduction in quantity of good 1 is clearly a *measurable* change. By contrast, a **marginal change** is immeasurably small, or *infinitesimal*. We will look more carefully at the marginal rate of substitution in a moment. But first, let us see why the nonmarginal rate of substitution is problematical.

The difficulty with the nonmarginal rate of substitution is that its *value* changes as the initial reduction in quantity of good 1 changes. For example, starting at bundle A in Figure 2.5, we initially reduced the quantity of good 1 by 9 units to get a nonmarginal rate of substitution of 15/9, or approximately 1.67. However, if instead we had reduced the quantity of good 1 by only 6 units, then we would have had to increase good 2 by 6 units to get this person back to indifference curve *I*. In this case, the nonmarginal rate of substitution is 6/6, or 1, which is equal to the absolute value of the slope of dashed line AC in Figure 2.5. There is an ambiguity here: Is the rate of substitution of good 2 for good 1 equal to 1.67, or is it equal to 1?

marginal rate of substitution

To resolve this ambiguity, economists use the **marginal rate of substitution**, *MRS*. *MRS* is the rate of substitution associated with a marginal reduction in quantity of good 1. To find *MRS*, just imagine what happens to the nonmarginal rate of substitution as Δx_1 gets smaller and smaller, eventually approaching zero. For $\Delta x_1 = 9$, the nonmarginal rate of substitution is determined by the slope of the dashed line segment AB. For $\Delta x_1 = 6$, it is determined by the slope of the dashed line segment AC. Notice that as Δx_1 approaches zero, the dashed line segment approaches the line labeled *TT* that is tangent to indifference curve *I* at bundle A. Therefore, the marginal rate of substitution is the absolute value of the slope of *TT*. That is, the marginal rate of substitution *MRS* of good 2 for good 1 at bundle A is the absolute value of the slope of the indifference curve at bundle A. More generally: *The marginal rate of substitution of good 2 for good 1 at any point (x_1,x_2), denoted by $MRS(x_1,x_2)$, is the absolute value of the slope of the indifference curve at that point.*[2]

2 In Section 2.5, we show how to represent preferences by a utility function, $U(x_1,x_2)$. Using the implicit function theorem we can express *MRS* in terms of the partial derivatives of the utility function. An indifference curve can be written as

$$u' = U(x_1, x_2)$$

where u' is fixed and x_1 and x_2 are free to vary. Since the indifference curve defines x_2 as an implicit function of x_1, we can use the implicit function theorem to express this indifference curve as

$$x_2 = g(x_1)$$

MRS is, of course, just $-g'(x_1)$, where $g'(x_1)$ is the derivative of $g(x_1)$. Combining these equations, we have the following identity

$$u' = U[x_1, g(x_1)]$$

Differentiating the identity with respect to x_1 gives us

$$U_1[x_1, g(x_1)] + g'(x_1)U_2[x_1, g(x_1)] = 0$$

where $U_1(\cdot)$ and $U_2(\cdot)$ denote the partial derivatives of $U(\cdot)$ with respect to x_1 and x_2. (The partial derivative $U_i(\cdot)$ is sometimes called the *marginal utility* of good i.) Rearranging this equation, we get

$$-g'(x_1) = \frac{U_1(x_1, x_2)}{U_2(x_1, x_2)}$$

But the left side of this equation is just *MRS*; hence

$$MRS(x_1, x_2) = \frac{U_1(x_1, x_2)}{U_2(x_1, x_2)}$$

Thus, for example, for the utility function $U(x_1, x_2) = x_1 x_2$, $MRS(x_1, x_2) = x_2/x_1$.

Notice that if we had picked some bundle other than bundle A in Figure 2.5, we would have found a *different* value for *MRS* because the slope of indifference curve *I* varies from point to point. For instance, because the indifference curve is steeper at bundle C than at bundle A, *MRS* is larger at bundle C than at bundle A. And *MRS* is larger still at bundle B. In other words, $MRS(x_1, x_2)$ ordinarily takes on different values at different bundles, and is therefore a *function*, and not simply a number.

In the following problem, you can explore one case in which *MRS* is the same at all bundles. Be sure to notice the unusual shape of the indifference curves.

PROBLEM 2.7

1. Amy is indifferent between any two bundles in which the combined weight of trout and salmon is 10 pounds. The indifference curve for such bundles is $10 = x_1 + x_2$, where x_1 is pounds of trout and x_2 is pounds of salmon. What is Amy's *MRS* for any bundle on this indifference curve?
2. Amy's cousin Arno likes eating fish, too, but his preferences are different from Amy's. He is only interested in the nutritional value of the fish he eats, and he believes that a pound of salmon is twice as nutritious as a pound of trout. Find an indifference curve for Arno, and then show that Arno's *MRS* of salmon for trout is 1/2.

Diminishing Marginal Rate of Substitution

Notice that in Figure 2.5, *MRS* declines or *diminishes* in a move down the indifference curve. This means that the person whose preferences are represented in Figure 2.5 is less willing to substitute good 2 for good 1 at point B than at point A. This seems reasonable since — relative to good 1 — good 2 is more abundant at point B than it is at point A. Economists often make the assumption of a diminishing marginal rate of substitution because in many circumstances it seems to capture the reality of people's preferences.

Just imagine your own willingness to substitute food (good 2) for clothing (good 1). If you now have a consumption bundle in which food is plentiful relative to clothes, you might be reluctant to give up still more clothes to get additional food. On the other hand, if you have a bundle in which food is scarce relative to clothes, you might be quite willing to give up clothes to get additional food. If these speculations about your willingness to substitute food for clothes are right, then — in terms of food and clothing — your preferences satisfy the **assumption of a diminishing marginal rate of substitution**: in moving down an indifference curve, the marginal rate of substitution diminishes. As you will see in the applications of Section 2.4, a diminishing marginal rate of substitution can be used to explain some familiar observations from ordinary experience.

diminishing
marginal rate of
substitution
assumption

Kinked Indifference Curves

Even though *MRS* is a very useful concept, it is not always well defined. Notice that the indifference curve in Figure 2.6 has a *kink* at bundle K. At any bundle to the right or to the left of the kink, it is possible to construct a unique line tangent to the indifference curve. Consequently, *MRS* is well defined for any such bundle. Notice, however, that we can draw any number of straight lines that pass through point K but do not intersect, or cross, the indifference curve. The dashed lines labeled *TT* and *T′T′* are two such lines. Is it the slope of *TT* or the slope of *T′T′* that determines *MRS*? The answer is neither one. Rather, because the indifference curve is kinked at bundle K, *MRS* is simply not defined for bundle K.

FIGURE 2.6   Kinked indifference curve

Indifference curve I has a kink at bundle K. Through bundle K, any number of lines can be drawn that do not intersect the indifference curve. Hence, there is no tangent line to the indifference curve at bundle K, and MRS is not defined.

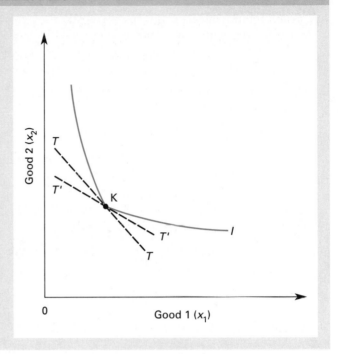

This leads us to an important understanding. If indifference curves are smooth — that is, if they have no kinks — then MRS is always well defined. But for any bundle at which the indifference curve is kinked, MRS is not defined.[3] In the following problem, you can consider another case in which MRS is not everywhere well defined.

PROBLEM 2.8

Suppose the two goods are right shoes and left shoes. Then, if we begin at any point where the number of right shoes is equal to the number of left shoes, it seems sensible to suppose that we stay on the same indifference curve if 1. we hold the number of left shoes constant and increase the number of right shoes, or if 2. we hold the number of right shoes constant and increase the number of left shoes. Draw an indifference curve, and identify the kink in it. What is MRS to the right of the kink? Above the kink? At the kink?

Shapes of Indifference Curves

Finally, we want to introduce some useful terminology to describe the *shape* of indifference curves. We can distinguish three kinds of indifference curves: *strictly convex* indifference curves, shown in Figure 2.7a; *weakly convex* indifference curves, shown in Figure 2.7b; and *nonconvex* indifference curves, shown in Figures 2.7c and 2.7d.

---

3 Mathematically, smoothness of indifference curves is related to differentiability of the utility function (discussed in Section 2.5). From footnote 2, we know that $MRS(x_1, x_2) = U_1(x_1, x_2)/U_2(x_1, x_2)$. If these partial derivatives are continuous functions, then so is their ratio, $MRS(x_1, x_2)$; hence, if $U(x_1, x_2)$ is differentiable and if its partial derivatives are continuous, then its indifference curves are smooth.

FIGURE 2.7   **Shapes of indifference curves**

The indifference curve in (a) is strictly convex, the indifference curves in (c) and (d) are non-convex, and the indifference curve in (b) is weakly convex.

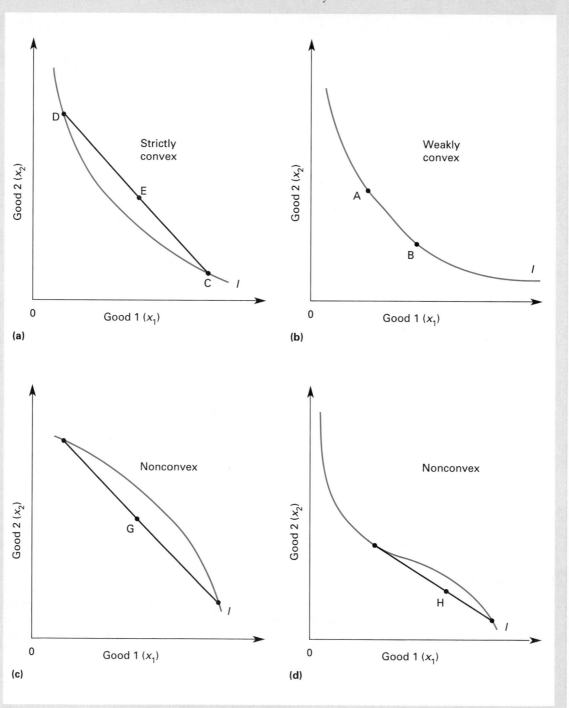

(a)

(b)

(c)

(d)

Let us begin with Figure 2.7a, and use a particular criterion to show that the indifference curve is strictly convex. First we choose two bundles — bundles C and D — and then construct the line segment connecting them. Notice that (with the exception of the original bundles C and D) every bundle on this line segment lies above the indifference curve. From the nonsatiation assumption, we know that any bundle on the line segment — for example, bundle E — is preferred to bundles C and D and also to any other bundle on indifference curve *I*. Notice that this property holds regardless of which two bundles we choose on the indifference curve. This is what we mean when we say that an indifference curve is **strictly convex**.[4]

strictly convex

Now let us turn to Figures 2.7c.and 2.7d. Here we have a simpler criterion to show that   indifference curve is nonconvex. We simply choose one pair of bundles on the indiffe   nce curve, draw the line segment connecting them, and then identify one bundle on   he line segment that is less preferred than a bundle on the indifference curve. For example, because any bundle on the indifference curve in Figure 2.7c is preferred to bundle G, we know that this indifference curve is *nonconvex*. Similarly, because any bundle on the indifference curve in Figure 2.7d is preferred to bundle H, we also know that this indifference curve is **nonconvex**.

nonconvex

The indifference curve in Figure 2.7b is slightly more complex. Because this indifference curve has a linear segment AB, it fails to satisfy the convexity criterion. To see why, suppose we begin by picking bundles A and B at the ends of the linear segment of the indifference curve. Because the line segment connecting these two bundles is *coincident* with segment *AB* of the indifference curve, we know that bundles on this line segment are neither more preferred nor less preferred than the bundles on the indifference curve. And yet, it also fails to satisfy the nonconvexity criterion. Because this indifference curves fails to satisfy the criterion for convexity and for nonconvexity, it is called **weakly convex**.

weakly convex

We can use the concept of *MRS* to explain these distinctions in a different way. What happens to *MRS* as we move from left to right along the strictly convex indifference curve in Figure 2.7a? Since the indifference curve gets continually flatter as we move from left to right, *MRS* is decreasing or diminishing. Accordingly, *strict convexity is associated with a diminishing MRS*. In contrast, as we move from left to right along either of the nonconvex indifference curves in Figures 2.7c and 2.7d, *MRS* does not continually diminish. In fact, in Figure 2.7c, *MRS* continually increases, while in Figure 2.7d, it initially diminishes and subsequently increases. Accordingly, *nonconvexity is associated with an increasing MRS for at least some portion of the indifference curve*. Finally, as we move from left to right along the weakly convex indifference curve in Figure 2.7b, *MRS* either diminishes or remains constant, but does not increase. Therefore, *weak convexity is associated with a non-increasing MRS*. As we have said, in many circumstances a diminishing *MRS* is a reasonable assumption. Thus, most of the indifference curves in the remainder of the book are strictly convex.

---

4 Strict convexity of an indifference curve can be defined in more mathematical terms. Pick any two bundles on the indifference curve, say B′ and B″. Form a new bundle B‴ as follows:

$$B''' = tB' + (1 - t)B''$$

where *t* is any number larger than 0 and less than 1. The bundle B‴ is said to be a convex combination of B′ and B″. Suppose, for example, that B′ = (2, 4), B″ = (4, 0), and $t = \frac{1}{2}$; the the convex combination B‴ is (3, 2). If for all B′ and B″ on the indifference curve and for all permissible values of t the convex combination B‴ is preferred to the original bundles B′ and B″, the indifference curve is strictly convex.

PROBLEM 2.9

Construct the following indifference curves and indicate whether they are strictly convex, weakly convex, or nonconvex.

$$2 = x_1 + x_2$$
$$36 = x_1 x_2$$
$$1 = (x_1)^2 + (x_2)^2$$

Applications

To show you just how powerful and wide-ranging the theory of preferences is, let us use it to analyze three problems from everyday life. First, we can use it to explain why we so often see higher wage rates — "time-and-a-half" or "double time" — for overtime work. Then we can use it to create a measure of the harm done by air pollution. Finally, we can use it to explain why students typically spend almost no time studying for "snap courses" in which they can get high grades with little effort.

Overtime Pay

Collective agreements between firms and their employees typically have provisions specifying a base work day, a base wage rate, and an overtime wage rate — often 1.5 times the base wage rate. For example, a collective agreement might have a provision establishing an 8-hour base work day, a $10/hour base wage rate, and a $15/hour overtime wage rate. These provisions for overtime pay raise a question: Why do workers demand higher wage rates for overtime? Or, to put it another way, why don't workers negotiate a single wage rate applying to all hours of work?

First we need to represent the particular preferences relevant to this problem. The goods in this case are clearly not ordinary consumption goods like T-shirts and haircuts. How can we characterize the two rather different "goods" in these particular consumption bundles? Because people work to make money to spent on consumption goods, one good in this case is *income* or expenditure on all goods. What is the second good in these consumption bundles? It could be hours of work. (You are asked to take this approach in Problem 3.f at the end of the chapter.) Traditionally, however, economists have approached the problem in a slightly different, but equivalent, way. They think of the 24 hours in a day as being divided into work time and leisure time. Because people trade off income (or work time) against leisure time, they use hours of *leisure* as the second "good" in these bundles. These particular consumption bundles are then of the following sort: (L,I) where L is hours of leisure and I is dollars of income. Bundle $(16,80)$, for example, is the bundle containing 16 hours of leisure (and therefore 8 hours of work) and $80 of income per day (8 hours at a wage rate of $10 per hour).

Now let us build a model of employee preferences over income and leisure. As always, we will use the four core assumptions of the theory of preferences — completeness, two-term consistency, transitivity, and continuity. We will also use the nonsatiation assumption because most people seem to prefer more income to less and more leisure to less. Notice that we already created a very basic model of employee preferences over income and leisure: the model implies that employee indifference curves are continuous and downward sloping.

In addition, we will make the assumption of a diminishing marginal rate of substitution. This assumption implies that the less leisure time an employee has, the less willing he or she is to give up additional leisure time to get additional income. These employee preferences are represented by the downward sloping indifference curve in (*L,I*) space in Figure 2.8. Notice that *MRS* at bundle B (equal to the absolute value of the slope of tangent line *TT*) exceeds *MRS* at bundle A (equal to the absolute value of the slope of tangent line *T'T'*). In other words, the rate at which an employee's income must be increased to compensate for a marginal decrease in leisure is larger at bundle B (where the employee has only 16 hours of leisure a day) than it is at bundle A (where the employee has 20 hours of leisure a day).

More generally, diminishing *MRS* implies that an employee becomes less and less willing to trade off leisure for income as work time increases and leisure time decreases. This provides a tentative answer to the question about higher pay for overtime:

Employees demand more money for overtime work because the more hours they are working, the less willing they are to trade off leisure time for income.

Pollution

Air pollution is an ugly fact of life in most urban settings. Because air pollution is something that most of us would prefer to avoid, it is a "bad," not a good. Let us develop a model of preferences that incorporates the economic bad of air pollution and then

FIGURE 2.8 **Employee preferences for leisure and income**

The *MRS* at bundle B (equal to the absolute value of the slope of tangent line *TT*) exceeds *MRS* at bundle A (equal to the absolute value of the slope of tangent line *T'T'*). More generally, *MRS* diminishes in moving down the indifference curve. That is, the fewer hours of leisure this person has, the less willing he or she is to trade off income for leisure.

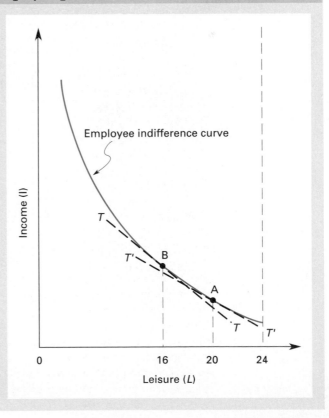

use that model to create *an economic measure of the cost of air pollution* to a particular person. Once again, notice that these consumption bundles clearly do not contain ordinary consumption goods. Instead, these bundles will necessarily contain a *measure of pollution* and expenditure on all other goods, or *income*, and they are therefore of the following kind: (P,I) where P is a measure of pollution and I is dollars of income. Once again, we will use the four core assumptions of the theory of preferences. We can then use our understanding of an individual's willingness to trade off income against pollution to create an economic measure of the cost of air pollution to that person. For example, many city dwellers choose to put up with the polluted air of large urban areas because they can make more money working in cities than in less-polluted rural communities. That is, they are trading off higher levels of pollution for higher incomes. As we said earlier, the nonsatiation assumption is not applicable in cases where consumption bundles contain economic "bads," and therefore where less — not more — is preferable. Therefore, we will not be using it here.

Recall that nonsatiation implied that indifference curves have a negative slope. In the absence of the nonsatiation assumption, what will the be the slope of indifference curves in this case? Notice that the indifference curves shown in Figure 2.9 — which contain a "bad" (pollution) and a "good" (income) — are upward sloping in the (P,I) space. Let us see why. Beginning at bundle A on indifference curve 1, suppose that the level of air pollution rises by ΔP. Because pollution is a bad, this rise in air pollution (holding income constant) will put the person whose preferences are represented in Figure 2.9

FIGURE 2.9 **The cost of pollution**

Because these indifference curves incorporate a "bad" (pollution) and a "good" (income), they are upward sloping in (P,I) space. If this person is initially at point A, the smallest increase in income that he or she is willing to accept for a ΔP increase in air pollution is ΔI. Therefore ΔI is a measure of what a ΔP increase in air pollution costs this person.

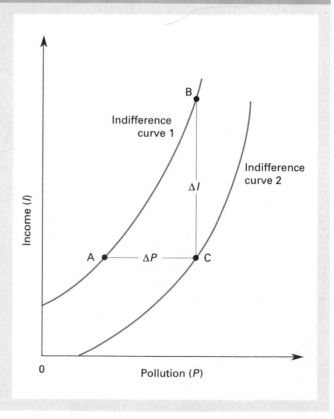

at bundle C, on the less preferred indifference curve 2. What change in income is needed to get this person back onto indifference curve 1? The answer is an increase in income of ΔI, which puts the individual back onto indifference curve 1 at bundle B. Notice that bundle B is necessarily *above* and *to the right* of bundle A. Therefore, the indifference curve connecting bundles A and B is necessarily upward sloping. More generally:

**When consumption bundles contain a bad and a good
the indifference curves are upward sloping.**

Now we can use this model of preferences over pollution and income to create a measure of the personal cost of pollution. We can do so by exploring the tradeoffs that an individual is willing to make between pollution and income. Let us imagine that the person in Figure 2.9 is initially at bundle A and asks, "What does an increase in air pollution of $\varnothing P$ cost this person?" Or, to put it another way, "What increase in income will compensate this person for an increase in air pollution of $\varnothing P$?" From Figure 2.9 we can see that $\varnothing I$ *is the smallest increase in income such that he or she would voluntarily accept for the increase in pollution of $\varnothing P$.* Therefore, $\varnothing I$ is one useful measure of what $\varnothing P$ costs this person.

Notice that the slope of the indifference curve gives us the rate at which income must be increased to compensate for a marginal increase in pollution. Therefore, we can interpret the slope of an indifference curve at any point in Figure 2.9 as the *MRS* of income for pollution. *MRS* can then be interpreted as the *marginal cost of pollution* to this person. Notice that in constructing Figure 2.9, we have assumed that the *MRS* increases as we move from left to right along an indifference curve. That is, we have assumed that the higher the initial level of pollution, the higher the marginal cost of air pollution.

Snap Courses

Why do students spend little or no time studying for a *snap course*? This question is prompted by our own university experience. During the early years of the war in Vietnam, a male student who had to leave an American college because of low grades faced the possibility of being drafted for military service. To try to protect students from the draft, a small number of instructors in some American universities promised to give *all* the students in their courses A grades. These were the ultimate snap courses. You can guess how many students responded: they spent little or no time studying for these courses.

To model student preferences in this situation, it is useful to think of bundles composed of *time per day* spent studying for a snap course, denoted by T, and the *course grade*, denoted by G. Let us suppose that grades are assigned in the interval from 0 to 100%. Then (T,G) denotes a consumption bundle. The question is this: If a certain student responds to a guaranteed grade of 100% by spending no time studying for the snap course, what can we infer about that student's preferences?

As always, we will use the completeness, two-term consistency, transitivity, and continuity assumptions in developing a model of student preferences over study time and course grade. The heart of our model of student preferences, however, is this: G is a "good" (the student prefers a higher grade to a lower grade), and T is a "bad" (time spent on one course is time lost on other courses). Since we have a good and a bad in these consumption bundles, the indifference curves in Figure 2.10 have a positive slope. (Since there seems to be no compelling reason to make further assumptions about the shape of these indifference curves, we have constructed them as wavering but upward sloping lines.)

FIGURE 2.10   Student preferences

These curves are upward sloping because they incorporate a "good" (the course grade, *G*) and a "bad" (study time for the course, *T*). Holding *T* constant, as *G* increases, more preferred bundles are encountered. Holding *G* constant, as *T* increases, less preferred bundles are encountered. The most preferred bundle is bundle A, which corresponds to no time spent studying and a grade of 100%.

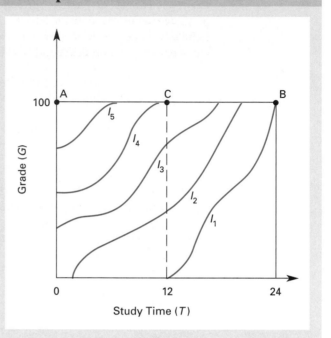

Notice that if we hold *T* constant in Figure 2.10 while increasing *G*, we move upward in (*T,G*) space, encountering more preferred indifference curves. And if we hold *G* constant while increasing *T*, we move rightward in (*T,G*) space, encountering less preferred indifference curves. Given our assumptions, the most preferred bundle in Figure 2.10 is (0,100). This bundle corresponds to no time spent studying and a grade of 100%.

From an economist's perspective, the primary function of a grading scheme is to motivate students by tying their final grades to time spent studying for the course. That is, an effective grading scheme is an *incentive mechanism* that induces students to spend time studying for a course by rewarding them with higher grades if they study harder. However, in the ultimate snap course, students get a grade of 100%, regardless of performance on exams and assignments. As a result, they have no incentive to spend time studying. Given this grading scheme, the student in Figure 2.10 can choose any point on line segment ACB. For example, this student can choose bundle B, where he or she spends 24 hours studying for the course and gets a grade of 100%; or bundle C, where he or she spends 12 hours studying and gets 100%; or bundle A, where he or she spends no time studying and gets 100%. Given our model of student preferences, the most-preferred bundle on line segment ACB is bundle (0,100). Our model leads us to the following conclusion:

The student will choose to spend no time studying for the ultimate snap course.

Notice that this model does not necessarily imply that the student finds the course material inherently uninteresting. In fact, most of us who signed up for these ultimate snap courses in the Vietnam era spent little or no time studying for them — not because we found the courses themselves boring — but because we found it *more attractive* to spend our limited time studying for other courses in which instructors used conventional grading schemes. Complete lack of interest in the snap course is *sufficient* to generate the upward sloping indifference curves in Figure 2.10, but it is *not necessary* since time spent studying for a snap course cannot be spent studying for other courses. In other words, there is an opportunity cost of studying for a snap course. If the opportunity cost is large enough, indifference curves for the snap course will be upward sloping as we have constructed them — no matter how interesting these courses might be.

2.5

Utility Functions

utility function

utility number

Economists have developed a mathematical tool for representing an individual's preference ordering. That tool is called a **utility function**. Although the term utility function may be a bit intimidating, the basic concept is simple. A utility function assigns a number — called a **utility number** — to every consumption bundle in a person's preference ordering in accordance with two rules. *First, if someone is indifferent between two bundles, the utility function assigns the same utility number to both bundles. Second, if he or she prefers one bundle to another, the utility function assigns a larger utility number to the preferred bundle.* We will use the notation $U(x_1, x_2)$ to represent a utility function.

To see for yourself just what utility functions and utility numbers are and do, pay careful attention to the following important problem.

> **PROBLEM 2.10**
>
> Let us return to Amy. Recall that she eats only trout (good 1) and salmon (good 2), and that her preferences are such that — given a choice between two bundles — she always prefers the bundle that weighs more. Let x_1 and x_2 denote pounds of trout and salmon respectively. We want to show that the following function is a utility function for Amy:
>
> $$U(x_1, x_2) = x_1 + x_2$$
>
> a. What utility numbers does this function assign to the following six bundles: (10,15), (20,30), (25,0), (15,15), (20,15), (40,10)? Do these utility numbers accurately reflect her preference ordering over these bundles?
> b. More generally, show that this function is a utility function for Amy. To do so, show that the answer to each of the following questions is "yes." Question 1: Does this function assign the same utility number to two bundles whenever Amy is indifferent between them? Question 2: Does this function assign a larger utility number to the preferred bundle when Amy prefers one bundle to another? Question 3: Does this function assign a utility number to all consumption bundles that contain trout and salmon?

Constructing a Utility Function

Now we want to generalize what you learned in this problem by establishing a rule for assigning utility numbers to consumption bundles that will allow us, in principle at least, to construct a utility function for any set of individual preferences that satisfy these five assumptions: completeness, two-term consistency, transitivity, continuity, and nonsatiation. Notice that now we are *not* dealing with specific preferences like Amy's preferences for trout and salmon, but rather with *any preferences* that satisfy these five assumptions. Therefore, our objective is not to find a particular utility function such as the utility function $U(x_1, x_2) = x_1 + x_2$, but to show that *some utility function exists for any preferences that satisfy these five assumptions*.

In Figure 2.11, we have constructed a ray through the origin (the line $x_2 = x_1/2$). We will be using this ray in setting out the following rule for assigning utility numbers. For any bundle on the ray $x_2 = x_1/2$, first identify the associated indifference curve. Then, note the quantity of good 1 in the original bundle on the ray, and use this quantity as the utility number for every bundle on the indifference curve. For example, consider bundle (2,1) on the ray in Figure 2.11. The associated indifference curve is $I(2,1)$, and the number 2 is therefore the utility number for every bundle on $I(2,1)$. Now consider a different bundle on the ray, bundle (4,2). The associated indifference curve is $I(4,2)$, and the number 4 is therefore the utility number for every bundle on $I(4,2)$. Because we are using the non-satiation assumption, the indifference curves in Figure 2.11 are negatively sloped.

By considering the same questions you looked at in Problem 2.10, we can show that this rule does allow us to construct a utility function for any set of preferences that satisfy the five assumptions. We need to show that the answer to the following three questions is "yes." Question 1: Does this rule assign the same utility number to two bundles whenever the individual is indifferent between them? Question 2: Does this rule assign a larger utility number to the preferred bundle whenever the individual prefers one bundle to another? Question 3: Does this rule assign a utility number to all consumption bundles?

The answer to the first question is clearly yes. Because indifference curves are negatively sloped and because the ray is positively sloped, any indifference curve will intersect the ray once and only once. Therefore, we know that this rule does assign the same utility number to all bundles on the same indifference curve.

FIGURE 2.11   Constructing a utility function

To construct a utility function, for every bundle on the ray $x_2 = x_1/2$, identify the associated indifference curve, and assign the quantity of good 1 in the bundle as a utility number to all bundles on the indifference curve. This rule assigns utility number 2 to all bundles on $I(2,1)$, utility number 4 to all bundles on $I(4,2)$, and utility number 6 to all bundles on $I(4,5)$.

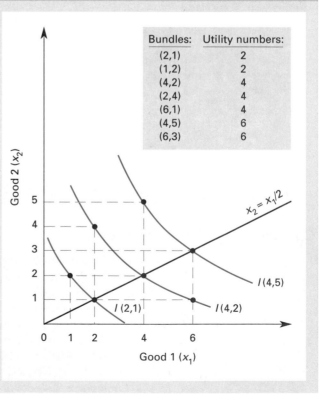

Bundles:	Utility numbers:
(2,1)	2
(1,2)	2
(4,2)	4
(2,4)	4
(6,1)	4
(4,5)	6
(6,3)	6

Let us turn to the second question and consider two bundles in Figure 2.11 that are *not* on the same indifference curve, say bundles (6,1) and (1,2). Which is the preferred bundle? The answer is bundle (6,1) because it is on the indifference curve farther from the origin. Does this rule assign a larger number to bundle (6,1) than to bundle (1,2)? Yes; the utility number for bundle (6,1) is 4 and the utility number for bundle (1,2) is 2. That is, for this particular pair of bundles, the rule does assign a higher utility number to the more preferred bundle. Now consider an arbitrary pair of bundles on distinct indifference curves. The nonsatiation assumption implies that the preferred bundle is on the indifference curve that is farther from the origin. The point of intersection of the more distant indifference curve and the ray through the origin is farther from the origin than is the point of intersection of the nearer indifference curve and the ray. Therefore, given our rule for assigning utility numbers, the bundle on the more distant indifference curve will be assigned a larger utility number than the bundle on the nearer indifference curve.

Now let us turn to the third question and consider some consumption bundle in Figure 2.11 that is not on the ray $x_2 = x_1/2$ — for example, bundle (4,5). The continuity assumption implies that there is a continuous indifference curve, labeled $I(4,5)$, that passes through this bundle. Furthermore, the indifference curve $I(4,5)$ must intersect the ray through the origin because it is negatively sloped and the ray is positively sloped. Because $I(4,5)$ intersects the ray at (6,3) in Figure 2.11, the rule assigns utility number 6 to consumption bundle (4,5). In other words, our rule for assigning utility numbers does in fact assign a utility number to every consumption bundle:

If preferences satisfy the five stated assumptions about preferences, there is a utility function that represents those preferences.

Even though we used the nonsatiation assumption to argue this result, it is in no way necessary. As you know, the core assumptions are the first four assumptions — completeness, two-term consistency, transitivity, and continuity. If these assumptions are satisfied, then a person's preferences can be represented by a utility function.

Many Utility Functions

Now we want to argue that, given preferences satisfying these assumptions, *any number of utility functions* can be constructed that represent these preferences. But first, try the following problem.

PROBLEM 2.11

This problem is also about Amy's preferences. In the preceding problem, you showed that the following function is a utility function for Amy:

$$U(x_1,x_2) = x_1 + x_2$$

Using the approach from that problem, show that the following are also utility functions for Amy:

1. $U(x_1,x_2) = 16(x_1 + x_2)$
2. $U(x_1,x_2) = (x_1 + x_2)^2$
3. $U(x_1,x_2) = \log(x_1 + x_2 + 1)$
4. $U(x_1,x_2) = 5073 + x_1 + x_2$

In Problem 2.11 you discovered that many different functions will represent the same preference ordering. This is an important point because it helps us to see what utility numbers do and do not mean. It is therefore worth examining more carefully. Consider some utility function $U(x_1,x_2)$ that represents Harry's preferences for goods 1 and 2, and two consumption bundles, (17,9) and (15,10). Harry prefers bundle (17,9) to bundle (15,10). Since $U(x_1,x_2)$ is a utility function for Harry, it is therefore true that the utility number $U(17,9)$ exceeds the utility number $U(15,10)$. Keep in mind that $U(17,9)$ and $U(15,10)$ are just the utility numbers that emerge when the utility function is evaluated first at (17,9) and then at (15,10). Now let us form a new function by multiplying the utility number associated with any bundle by some constant c. The new function, which we will call $V(x_1,x_2)$, is simply

$$V(x_1,x_2) = cU(x,x_2)$$

Is $V(x_1,x_2)$ also a utility function for Harry? It is, if it always assigns a larger utility number to the preferred bundle. In particular, does $V(17,9)$ exceed $V(15,10)$? Or, equivalently, does $cU(17,9)$ exceed $cU(15,10)$? If c is positive, it does. Therefore, when c is positive, $V(x_1,x_2)$ is also a utility function for Harry.

The point is this: if we have one utility function, we can generate others that represent the same preference ordering by multiplying the original utility function by a positive constant, just as we multiplied Amy's original utility function by the positive constant 16 to get another utility function for her. Clearly, this is not the only way to construct a new utility function. For example, adding a constant to a utility function will generate another function that represents the same preference ordering as the original utility function.[5]

The Meaning of Utility Numbers

ordinal utility

These observations should make it clear that the economist's theory of utility is a theory of **ordinal utility**, not cardinal utility. Utility numbers reveal only the relative ordering of consumption bundles (first, second, or third) and nothing about the distance between bundles in terms of desirability (twice as desirable or one-third as desirable). In comparing two bundles, utility numbers tell us one of three things: the first bundle is preferred to the second, the second bundle is preferred to the first, or the individual is indifferent between the two bundles — and *nothing more*. In particular, we *cannot* use utility numbers to make comparisons among individuals. The notion of preference — not utility— is the primitive, or irreducible, concept at the heart of our analysis.

---

5 In general, we can form a new function $V(x_1,x_2)$ from $U(x_1,x_2)$ by feeding utility numbers into another function, which we will call f. Symbolically, the new function is

$$V(x_1,x_2) = f[U(x_1,x_2)]$$

If f has the property that the larger the number you feed into it, the larger the number that comes out, then $V(x)$ is also a utility function. (Any function f that has this property is said to be a *monotonically increasing function*.) Suppose that f is monotonically increasing. Then 1. when $U(B_1) > U(B_2)$, $V(B_1) > V(B_2)$, and 2. when $U(B_1) = U(B_2)$, $V(B_1) = V(B_2)$. In other words, the functions $V(x_1,x_2)$ and $U(x_1,x_2)$ represent the same preference ordering. Thus, given a utility function, we can create others by operating on it with any monotonically increasing function.

2.6
The Many-Goods Case

In this last section of the chapter, we will briefly indicate how the theory can be extended to the case in which there are an arbitrary number of goods — the n-good case. In this n-good case, a consumption bundle is an ordered list of quantities of n goods, written as $(x_1, x_2, \ldots, x_n)$. Here, x_1 is the quantity of good 1, x_2 is the quantity of good 2, and x_n is the quantity of good n. To see how the core theory extends to this n-good case, let us consider the following question: What assumptions guarantee that an individual has consistent preferences and that those preferences can be represented by a utility function?

The first question is easily answered. The three assumptions that guarantee a complete preference ordering in the two-good case do the same job in the n-good case. If a person can compare any pair of bundles, and if those comparisons exhibit two-term consistency and three-term consistency (transitivity), then that person's preferences are consistent. The existence of many goods therefore presents no problem in this part of the theory.

To assure that preferences can be represented by a utility function, a continuity assumption is required. In this case, however, the assumption is more technical. Given any consumption bundle — say, bundle B — we can define the set of bundles that are either preferred to bundle B or indifferent to it. This set is called the *no-worse-than set* because the bundles in it are no worse than B. Similarly, we can define the *no-better-than set*, which contains all the bundles to which B is preferred or to which *B* is indifferent. The continuity assumption in the n-good case is that the no-worse-than and the no-better-than sets are closed sets — that is, they are sets that contain their boundaries. If these four assumptions are satisfied, then a preference ordering can be represented by a utility function, which we can write as $U(x_1, x_2, \ldots, x_n)$. The core of the theory of self-interest in the n-good case is therefore essentially the same as in the two-good case. The only new feature is the more technical continuity assumption.

Finally, we should briefly indicate how the concept of *MRS* is defined in the n-good case. Suppose that from the list of n goods, we pick two goods — say, good i and good j — and then hold constant, or fix, all other quantities in the utility function. For example, we might fix all these quantities at zero, or we might fix some quantities at zero and others at two or, indeed, at any values. What matters is that all quantities other than x_i and x_j are fixed. As a result, we have a function with just the two variables, x_i and x_j — that is, a utility function very much like those we explored earlier in this chapter. The only difference is that this utility function with just two variables has been created from a utility function with n variables by fixing the values of all but two of the n variables. Like the two-variable utility functions explored earlier, the indifference curves associated with this utility function can be plotted in a two-dimensional diagram with x_i on the horizontal axis and x_j on the vertical axis. We can then use this type of diagram to define $MRS(x_i, x_j)$ as follows: *the absolute value of the slope of an indifference curve at some bundle is the MRS of good j for good i at that bundle.*

The following problem will help you check your understanding of a very simple utility function in the three-good case — a utility function in which marginal rates of substitution are constant.

PROBLEM 2.12

The following function is Brett's utility function for good 1 ($100 bills), good 2 ($20 bills), and good 3 ($10 bills). (It may also express your preference ordering over these goods.)

$$U(x_1, x_2, x_3) = 100x_1 + 20x_2 + 10x_3$$

Fix x_1 at 10, and plot an indifference curve of the resulting function with x_2 on the horizontal axis and x_3 on the vertical axis. What is *MRS* of good 3 for good 2? Now fix x_2 at 10, and plot an indifference curve with x_1 on the horizontal axis and x_3 on the vertical axis. What is *MRS* of good 3 for good 1? Finally, what is *MRS* of good 2 for good 1?

SUMMARY

The economist's approach to human behavior is founded on two simple ideas. First, individuals have consistent preferences. Second, they are willing to make tradeoffs. As we saw in Section 2.1, an individual's preferences are consistent if they satisfy three assumptions: *completeness assumption* — the individual can compare any two consumption bundles; *two-term consistency assumption* — the individual's preferences are consistent over any pair of consumption bundles; and *transitivity assumption* — the individual's preferences are consistent over any three bundles. As we saw in Section 2.2, an individual is willing to make tradeoffs if the *continuity assumption* is satisfied. These four assumptions form the core of our *theory of preferences*.

We also explored the important concept of the *marginal rate of substitution MRS*. *MRS* is a measure of the willingness of a person to trade off an increase in the quantity of one good for a decreases in the quantity of another. The *MRS* of good 2 for good 1 is the rate at which the consumption of good 2 must be increased as the consumption of good 1 is decreased in order to keep an individual on the same indifference curve. At any point, *MRS* is equal to the absolute value of the slope of the indifference curve through that point. We then introduced an important empirical assumption concerning the shape of indifference curves — the *assumption of a diminishing MRS*.

We used this theory of preferences to tackle some interesting questions. Why do employees often demand premium rates of pay for overtime work? Because their indifference curves for bundles of leisure and income satisfy the hypothesis of diminishing *MRS*. How can we measure the cost of air pollution to a particular person? By looking at that person's willingness to substitute income for pollution — or that person's *MRS* of income for pollution. Why do students devote so little time to snap courses? Because time spent studying for such courses is an economic bad.

We ended by showing how to construct a *utility function* to represent any individual preference ordering. You discovered that *utility numbers* are ordinal, not cardinal, and that, given individual preferences that satisfy these assumptions, any number of utility functions can be constructed to represent those preferences. Finally, we showed how the two-good case could be extended to the *many-goods case*.

EXERCISES

1. Could the following two equations represent two different indifference curves for the same individual?

$$x_1 + x_2 = 100$$
$$x_1 x_2 = 100$$

2. Given a choice between two bundles containing good 1 and good 2, Dizzy says that (i) he prefers the bundle with the larger quantity of good 1 and (ii) if the quantity of good 1 is the same in the two bundles, he is indifferent between them.

   a. Draw one of Dizzy's indifference curves.
   b. Construct three utility functions that represent Dizzy's preferences.
   c. Can you find two goods such that your preferences are like Dizzy's?

3. Construct a representative indifference curve for each of the following situations. In so doing, you are creating a model of preferences for each situation much as we did in the applications section of this chapter. Keep in mind that a good theory is one that you can defend.

   a. The two goods are $5 bills and $20 bills. (What is the marginal rate of substitution of $20 bills for $5 bills?)
   b. The two goods are right shoes and left shoes, and the consumer has two feet; the consumer has only one foot.
   c. The two goods are money and cocaine, and the more cocaine the individual consumes, the more money he or she is willing to give up to get even more cocaine.
   d. The two goods are money and lobster tails, and eating more than a certain number of lobster tails makes the consumer sick. (Assuming that the consumer can dispose of unwanted lobster tails at no cost, how do the indifference curves change?)
   e. The two goods are Coke and Pepsi, and the consumer perceives no difference between the two soft drinks.
   f. There is one bad — hours spent working — and one good — income.

4. Consider the following utility functions:

   (i) $U(x_1, x_2) = x_1 x_2$
   (ii) $U(x_1, x_2) = 10 x_1 x_2$
   (iii) $U(x_1, x_2) = (x_1 x_2)^2$

   a. Construct an indifference curve for each of these functions. For (i), use utility number 20; for (ii), use utility number 200; for (iii), use utility number 400.
   b. Do these utility functions represent different preference orderings?

5. Althea's preferences are captured in the following utility function:

   $$U(x_1, x_2) = \min(2x_1, 7x_2)$$

   a. Draw an indifference curve for Althea.
   b. Which of the assumptions in Chapter 2 do not apply to Althea?

6. Consider the following utility function:

   $$U(x_1, x_2) = x_2 + x_1^{1/2}$$

   a. Very carefully draw the indifference curves associated with utility numbers 64, 49, and 36. For all three indifference curves, find the quantity of x_2 when x_1 is 0, 1, 4, 9, 16, 25, and 36.
   b. How does MRS change as you move from one indifference curve to another along the *vertical line $x_1 = 4$*? Or $x_1 = 16$? Or any vertical line?

7. In their theory of economic development, Eswaran and Kotwal (1994) use what they call *hierarchical preferences*. They look at bundles (F, T) composed of pounds of food F and yards of textiles T. The following utility function illustrates hierarchical preferences:

   $$U(F, T) = \begin{cases} F & \text{if } F \le 100 \\ T & \text{if } F > 100 \end{cases}$$

   a. Illustrate the indifference map for this utility function.
   b. Write a verbal description of the preferences captured by this utility function.
   c. Why do Eswaran and Kotwal use the adjective *hierarchical* to describe these preferences?
   d. Can you write a utility function that exhibits hierarchical preferences for bundles that contain three goods: pounds of food F, yards of textiles T, and quantity of luxury goods L?

8. Suppose that someone's preferences satisfy all the assumptions made in this chapter. Suppose, too, that for any value of x_1, MRS is the same regardless of the value of x_2. Draw two indifference curves. Do the indifference curves you constructed in Exercise 6 meet these conditions?

*9. Jack's preferences over goods 1 and 2 can be described as follows: bundle (x_1', x_2') is preferred to bundle (x_1'', x_2'') if the maximum of x_1' and x_2' is larger than the maximum of x_1'' and x_2''; if the maximums are equal, he is indifferent between the bundles.

    a. Show that Jack is indifferent between (10,8) and (2,10). Draw the entire indifference curve through these two bundles.

    b. Find a utility function to represent these preferences.

    c. Are Jack's indifference curves convex? Do these preferences satisfy the nonsatiation assumption? Are Jack's indifference curves kinked?

10. Jo says that (i) she has convex indifference curves for bundles that contain more than three units of good 1; (ii) she prefers any bundle with more than three units of good 1 to any bundle with three or less units of good 1; and (iii) for bundles with three or less units of good 1, the function $U(x_1, x_2) = x_1$ represents her preferences. Illustrate Jo's indifference map.

REFERENCES

Arrow, K. J. 1959. "Rational Choice Functions and Orderings," *Economica* 26:121–27.

Bradbury, H., and M. Moscato. 1982. "Development of Transitivity of Preferences: Novelty and Linear Regularity," *The Journal of Genetic Psychology* 140: 265–81.

Collison Black, R.D. 1987. "Utility Theory and Decision Theory," in *The New Palgrave: A Dictionary of Economics*, J. Eatwell, M. Milgate, and P. Newman (eds.), London: The Macmillan Press.

Debreu, G. 1959. *Theory of the Value*, New York: Wiley.

Eswaran, M., and A. Kotwal. 1994. *Why Poverty Persists in India*, New Delhi: Oxford University Press.

Hicks, J. R., and R. G. D. Allen. 1934. "A Reconsideration of the Theory of Value," *Economica* 1:52–75, 196–219.

Slutsky, E. 1915. "Sulla teoria del bilancio del consumatore," *Giornale degli economisti e rivista di statistica* 51:1–26. English translation: "On the Theory of the Budget of the Consumer," in *Readings in Price Theory*, G. J. Stigler and K. E. Boulding (eds.), Homewood, Ill: Richard D. Irwin, 27–56.

von Wright, G. H. 1987. "Preferences," in *The New Palgrave: A Dictionary of Economics*, J. Eatwell, M. Milgate, and P. Newman (eds.), London: The Macmillan Press.

CHAPTER 3

Getting and Spending: The Problem of Economic Choice Making

In the nineteenth century, the English poet William Wordsworth lamented what he saw as a society obsessed with "getting and spending." However lamentable such concern with getting and spending may still seem today, economic choice making inevitably threads its way through our lives. Some choices are relatively unimportant: Should I spend the evening watching television? Should I buy new running shoes? Some are more significant: Should I spend the next eight years of my life studying to be a doctor? As we will see in this chapter, all economic decisions, large or small, have certain elementary but important factors in common. In this chapter, we develop a set of graphic tools that can be used to analyze a whole range of consumer-choice problems.

3.1

Economic Choices

In the theory of economic choice making, the word *constrained* is crucial. Constraints are basic to all economic choices. These constraints include limits on income, time, and human resources. Implicit in the word *choice* is the notion that we must make economic choices among competing alternatives. That is, our choices are limited, or constrained: we cannot "have it all." *Income* is one constraint. For example, if I choose to buy a new pair of running shoes, I have implicitly decided to give up other consumption possibilities — perhaps buying a new tennis racket or having dinner at a favorite restaurant. I cannot afford all three choices because my income — my command over goods — will not stretch that far.

Time is another constraint. By deciding to spend the evening watching television, I am implicitly giving up other activities that compete for my time — say, playing squash or reading. In fact, the most fundamental economic choice we all face is what to do with the one life span we have. By deciding to become a doctor, for example, I give up the chance to become a carpenter, a writer, an accountant, or a computer scientist.

Our endowment of *human resources* also limits, or constrains, our choices. For example, someone who tips the scales at 95 pounds cannot choose to become a heavy-weight boxer. Of course, we can choose to augment the human resources we do have — for example, by choosing further schooling — but in making this choice, we must forego other opportunities such as getting work experience or traveling. Because our limited endowments of income, time, and human resources necessarily restrict the possibilities open to us, we must make choices among competing alternatives.

Moreover, when we make choices about getting and spending our limited resources, we have to rely on imperfect information to guide us. In an ideal world, we would know exactly what our alternatives were when we made choices. In reality, however, we almost always make choices without anything like complete information about our alternatives. In other words, most choice problems are choice problems under *imperfect information*: We do not know the complete list of available alternatives. For example, we might not be familiar with all the novels currently for sale or all the jobs openings presently available. Furthermore, we lack complete information about the prices of these alternatives.

Being informed about today's alternatives clearly is problematical. Being informed about tomorrow's alternatives is even more difficult. For example, jobs as bank tellers, secretaries, and automobile assembly line workers — at least, as we know them today — will almost certainly not exist in 20 years. However, we cannot know precisely how and when these occupations will change. Furthermore, we cannot know for certain what wages will be paid for specific job skills in the future. It is hard to know, for example, what computer scientists will be paid ten or even five years from now. Yet this information — or reasonable "guesstimates" about it — is essential to those who are now choosing careers as computer scientists (or bank tellers or secretaries). Such choices are inherently intertemporal (we spend time today to acquire skills that we hope to market in the future), and we make them using imperfect information (we cannot know the future). In fact, all economic decisions are intertemporal. By spending income today, I am giving up the chance to spend it tomorrow. By acquiring the skills of a computer scientist today, I am passing up the opportunity to study physiotherapy and therefore the chance to become a physiotherapist in the future. These simple observations illustrate what a complex affair economic choice making is. In a sense, making a choice today affects all the economic choices we must make in a lifetime — and we make each choice in an environment about which we have imperfect information.

To even begin to understand consumer choice making, we need to reduce the bewildering complexity of choice problems to a few basic elements. In this chapter, we will explore a relatively simple choice problem in which a particular consumer — knowing his or her budget and the price of all goods — chooses a consumption bundle in some period (this week, for instance). Clearly, this simple choice problem is unlike the real problems consumers actually face because it is an atemporal problem rather than an intertemporal problem, and because it involves perfect information rather than imperfect information.[1]

This choice problem is *atemporal* because we are assuming that this consumer has already decided to spend a particular sum of money — what we have called the consumer's budget — on consumption goods *in a given period*. Thus, we are supposing that this person has somehow resolved the potentially complex interactions between today's consumption decisions and tomorrow's. This problem also involves *perfect information* because we are assuming that this consumer knows all relevant prices. Thus, we are also supposing that this person has somehow solved the problem of how to generate information on prices. In later chapters, we will see how to analyze both intertemporal

---

1 Following the lead of Nobel prize winner Herbert Simon, behavioral economists have done a great deal of interesting work on the ways in which limitations on knowledge and computational capacity affect the actual decison-making process. The term *bounded rationality* is used to designate this approach to the study of choice making. For an introduction to behavioral economics see the entries in the *New Palgrave* by Herbert Simon entitled "bounded rationality" and "behavioral economics."

choice making and choice making under imperfect information. In this chapter, however, we will limit our analysis to a very simple choice problem characterized by atemporality and perfect information.

We will also assume throughout the chapter that this consumer's preferences satisfy five of the assumptions discussed in Chapter 2 — completeness, two-term consistency, transitivity, continuity, and nonsatiation. We therefore know that this consumer's preferences are consistent and that he or she is willing to make tradeoffs. In addition, these assumptions allow us to represent this consumer's preferences by a utility function. Finally, we will assume that there are just *two goods* in the consumption bundles. In Section 3.12, you will see why this two-good case is not as restrictive as it might appear to be at first.

3.2
The Budget Constraint

We will begin our exploration of the consumer's choice problem by examining the consumer's budget constraint and identifying the consumer's attainable consumption bundles — that is, the bundles that this consumer can actually afford to buy. For example, we can all imagine owning a Ferrari, but few of us can actually afford to do so. Our choices are limited, or constrained, by our budgets and by the prices of the goods we want to buy. An *attainable consumption bundle* is one that is affordable, given the consumer's budget constraint.

Attainable Consumption Bundles

Some notation will allow us to define attainable bundles more precisely. We will call the two goods in the consumption bundles good 1 and good 2, and we will denote their respective prices by p_1 and p_2. In addition, we will denote the consumer's budget (or income) by M. The total cost of bundle (x_1, x_2) is just the sum of prices multiplied by quantities, $p_1 x_1 + p_2 x_2$, and attainable bundles are just bundles whose total cost does not exceed M. Thus, an

attainable consumption bundle

attainable consumption bundle is any bundle that satisfies the following inequality:

$$p_1 x_1 + p_2 x_2 \leq M$$

budget constraint

The inequality itself is called the **budget constraint**.

In Figure 3.1, the set of attainable bundles is indicated by the shaded area. The attainable bundles on the line

$$p_1 x_1 + p_2 x_2 = M$$

budget line

use up all of the consumer's budget, whereas attainable bundles below the line do not. The line itself is commonly called the **budget line**. Because it important to understand what a budget line is, give the following problem careful attention.

> **PROBLEM 3.1**
>
> Why does the budget line intersect the x_1 axis at M/p_1 and the x_2 axis at M/p_2? What is the slope of the budget line? On the budget line, how many units of good 2 must the consumer give up to get an additional unit of good 1? What happens to the budget line as p_1 approaches zero? As p_2 approaches zero?

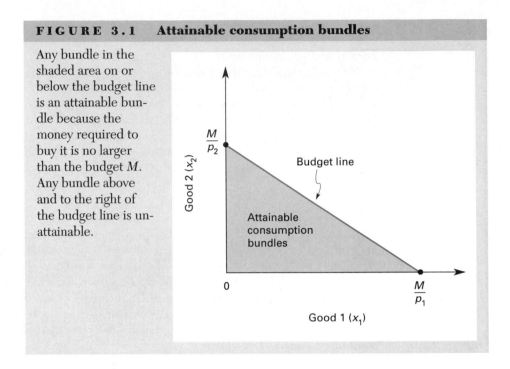

FIGURE 3.1 **Attainable consumption bundles**

Any bundle in the shaded area on or below the budget line is an attainable bundle because the money required to buy it is no larger than the budget M. Any bundle above and to the right of the budget line is unattainable.

Opportunity Cost

opportunity cost

For many purposes, it is useful to think of the prices of goods in terms of real alternatives or opportunities forgone, rather than in monetary terms. In Problem 3.1, you discovered that, on the budget line, the consumer must give up p_1/p_2 units of good 2 to get an additional unit of good 1. That is, the **opportunity cost** of good 1 is p_1/p_2 units of good 2. Conversely, the opportunity cost of good 2 is p_2/p_1 units of good 1.

Imagine that you live in Chicago and that good 1 is tickets to Chicago Blackhawks hockey games and good 2 is tickets to Chicago Bulls basketball games. If the ticket price of a Blackhawks hockey game (p_1) is $40 and the ticket price of a Bulls basketball game (p_2) is $20, then the *opportunity cost* of buying a ticket to one Blackhawks game — equal to p_1/p_2 — is not buying tickets to two Bulls games. If instead the ticket prices were identical, the opportunity cost of one ticket to a Blackhawks game would be one ticket to a Bulls game. In Problem 3.1, you also learned that the slope of the budget line is $-p_1/p_2$. We see then that the absolute value of the slope of the budget line has an important economic interpretation: it is the opportunity cost of good 1 in terms of good 2.

It is useful to interpret opportunity cost in a slightly different way. The opportunity cost of good 1 in terms of good 2 is the rate at which the individual can substitute good 2 for good 1. Suppose again that the ticket price of a Blackhawks game (good 1) is $40 and the ticket price of a Bulls game (good 2) is $20. Suppose, too, that a Chicago sports fan wants to substitute more tickets to Bulls games for fewer tickets to Blackhawks games. Giving up one ticket to a Blackhawks game frees up $40, which can be used to buy two ($40/$20) additional tickets to Bulls games. To summarize:

The price ratio p_1/p_2 has the following interpretations: it is the opportunity cost of good 1 in terms of good 2; it is the absolute value of the slope of the budget line; it is the rate at which good 2 can be substituted for good 1.

As you saw in Chapter 2, the marginal rate of substitution *MRS* measures the *willingness* of the individual to substitute good 2 for good 1. As you will soon see, the interplay between opportunity cost — the rate at which an individual is able to substitute good 2 for good 1 — and marginal rate of substitution — the rate at which the individual is willing to substitute good 2 for good 1 — determines the consumption bundle that the consumer actually chooses. But first it is helpful to set out a precise statement of the consumer's choice problem.

3.3

The Consumer's Choice Problem

Consumer theory is built on the assumption that individual consumers make the most of their opportunities in light of their preferences. Because higher indifference curves are preferred to lower indifference curves, a consumer's problem is to reach the highest indifference curve permitted by his or her budget constraint — that is, the highest attainable indifference curve. We can use the consumer's utility function $U(x_1, x_2)$ to reformulate the consumer's problem. Rather than seeing a consumer as trying to reach the highest attainable indifference curve, we can think of him or her as maximizing utility, given the budget constraint. More precisely, we can think of the consumer as choosing the quantities of the two goods that maximize utility, subject to the budget constraint. We will call the consumption bundle that the consumer chooses the **utility-maximizing bundle**, denoted by $(x_1{}^*, x_2{}^*)$.

utility-
maximizing
bundle

We can infer one important characteristic of the utility-maximizing consumption bundle: it must lie *on* the budget line. To see why, consider the bundle at point A in Figure 3.2, which lies inside the budget line. This cannot be the utility-maximizing bundle $(x_1{}^*, x_2{}^*)$ because the nonsatiation assumption implies that any of the bundles on segment CD of the budget line — every one of which contains more of both goods — is preferred to the bundle at point A. In other words, the nonsatiation assumption implies that a consumer will always pick a consumption bundle on the budget line:

The nonsatiation assumption implies that the utility-maximizing consumption
bundle $(x_1{}^*, x_2{}^*)$ lies on the budget line.

The Choice Problem

We can use this result to write the consumer's choice problem as follows:

$$\text{maximize } U(x_1, x_2) \text{ by choice of } x_1 \text{ and } x_2$$
$$\text{subject to the constraint } p_1 x_1 + p_2 x_2 = M$$

This expression is a compact way of writing out the consumer's choice problem. It tells what the consumer's objective is — maximizing utility. It tells what the consumer is choosing — a consumption bundle. And it tells what constraint the consumer faces — the budget line.

Just what is the solution to a consumer's choice problem? It is very much like the solution to that recurring problem: What should I wear today? In New York, for example, late fall weather is notoriously unpredictable. One day may be warm and sunny, the next cold and dry, the next very rainy, and the next snowy. Before choosing what clothing to venture out in, the sensible New Yorker looks out the window to see what the weather is like.

FIGURE 3.2 **Nonsatiation and the utility-maximizing consumption bundle**

Nonsatiation implies that the utility-maximizing consumption bundle will be on the budget line. For example, bundle A could not be the utility-maximizing bundle because any bundle on segment CD of the budget line is preferred to it.

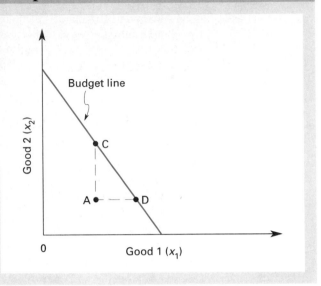

We could describe the solution to the New Yorker's choice problem by a series of rules of thumb. If it's warm and sunny, wear a light windbreaker. If it's raining, wear rain gear. If it's cold and dry, wear a down jacket. The items of clothing that we choose to wear are **endogenous variables** because we do the choosing. But the particular items we choose on any day are determined by the **exogenous variables** that we collectively call weather, over which we have no control. That is, according to the New Yorker's rules for choosing what to wear, the endogenous variables (items of clothing) are determined by the exogenous variables (weather).

endogenous variables

exogenous variables

The Solution: Demand Functions

The solution to the consumer choice problem in this chapter has the same form. Here, too, the endogenous variables are determined by the exogenous variables. Of course, in the consumer's utility-maximizing problem, the endogenous variables are the quantities of the two goods to be chosen: x_1 and x_2. The exogenous variables are the two prices p_1 and p_2 and the budget M; these are the givens, the constraints within which an individual consumer must operate. In the solution to this choice problem, then, the utility-maximizing values of x_1 and x_2 (the endogenous variables) are determined by p_1, p_2, and M (the exogenous variables).

Before taking up this general choice problem, it may be helpful to actually solve a specific choice problem — that is, to find $(x_1{}^*, x_2{}^*)$ for a specific utility function. We will use the following utility function, which captures the preferences of Amy from the problems in Chapter 2:

$$U(x_1, x_2) = x_1 + x_2$$

Here, x_1 is pounds of trout and x_2 is pounds of salmon. Given a choice between any two bundles, Amy prefers the bundle that weighs more, and she is indifferent between the bundles if they weigh the same. Therefore, this function — which gives us the total weight of any consumption bundle — is a utility function for Amy.

For Amy trout and salmon are *perfect substitutes* because an additional pound of either fish is equally attractive. In effect, Amy sees no real difference between the two kinds of fish. Therefore, she maximizes her utility by spending her whole budget on the cheaper fish; that is,

$$x_1{}^* = M/p_1 \text{ and } x_2{}^* = 0 \text{ if } p_1 < p_2$$

$$x_1{}^* = 0 \text{ and } x_2{}^* = M/p_2 \text{ if } p_1 > p_2$$

If the prices are identical, *any* bundle on the budget line is utility-maximizing since the budget line is then coincident with an indifference curve.

Notice how similar the solution of Amy's problem is to the solution to the New Yorker's what-to-wear problem. Both solutions have essentially the same form: the variables that are to be chosen (the endogenous variables) are determined by the variables that are given (the exogenous variables). If it is raining, wear rain gear (and leave the down parka in the closet). If $p_1 < p_2$, spend M/p_1 on good 1 and nothing on good 2.

In fact, the solution to *any* consumer choice problem has this form. We will therefore write the solution to the general two-good choice problem in the following symbolic way:

$$x_1{}^* = D_1(p_1, p_2, M)$$

$$x_2{}^* = D_2(p_1, p_2, M)$$

demand functions

The functions D_1 and D_2 are **demand functions**.[2] The first of them says that the utility-maximizing quantity of good 1 (denoted by $x_1{}^*$) is some function D_1 of the exogenous variables p_1, p_2, and M. This equation is simply a symbolic way of saying that the choice of $x_1{}^*$ is determined by (or depends on) the prices of all items in the consumption bundle and the budget to be devoted to the whole bundle.

---

2 One method for solving the consumer's choice problem when the utility function is differentiable and the solution is interior is the *method of Lagrange multipliers*, developed in most basic calculus texts. The mechanics of the method are simple. First, combine the utility function and the budget line by introducing a Lagrange multiplier λ to form what is called the Lagrangian function, as follows:

$$L(x_1, x_2, \lambda) = U(x_1, x_2) - \lambda(M - p_1 x_1 - p_2 x_2)$$

Now, differentiate with respect to x_1, x_2, and λ and set these derivatives equal to zero to obtain

$$U_1(x_1{}^*, x_2{}^*) - \lambda^* p_1 = 0$$
$$U_2(x_1{}^*, x_2{}^*) - \lambda^* p_2 = 0$$
$$M - p_1 x_1{}^* - p_2 x_2{}^* = 0$$

(The symbol U_i denotes the partial derivative of U with respect to x_i.) We then have a system of three simultaneous equations in three unknown endogenous variables, $x_1{}^*$, $x_2{}^*$, and λ^*. Solving for these unknown endogenous variables in terms of the three exogenous variables, p_1, p_2, and M, yields two demand functions and a function that determines a value for λ^*. For example, if

$$U(x_1, x_2) = x_1 x_2$$

then

$$x_1{}^* = \frac{M}{2p_1}$$

$$x_2{}^* = \frac{M}{2p_2}$$

$$\lambda^* = \frac{M}{2p_1 p_2}$$

system of
demand
functions

A single demand function describes the functional relationship between the quantity of a good demanded and all the factors that influence demand: the price of that good, the prices of other goods, and the size of the individual consumer's budget. A **system of demand functions**, D_1 and D_2, tells us how much of both goods will be chosen, given the exogenous variables. In the following problem, you are asked to solve another relatively simple utility-maximization problem, thereby generating the demand functions for another specific utility function.

PROBLEM 3.2

Consider the following utility function:

$$U(x_1, x_2) = \min(x_1, x_2)$$

Show that the demand functions are

$$x_1{}^* = M/(p_1 + p_2)$$

$$x_2{}^* = M/(p_1 + p_2)$$

Hint: First draw an indifference curve and observe that it has a right-angled kink where it intersects the line $x_2 = x_1$. Then show that the utility-maximizing bundle lies on the line $x_2 = x_1$. Finally, use this information in combination with the budget line to derive the demand functions.

Graphic Analysis of Utility Maximization

interior solution

corner solution

essential good

inessential good

In this section, we will use powerful graphic techniques to describe the solution to the utility-maximizing problem when indifference curves are *smooth* and *strictly convex*. We will distinguish two types of solution to the problem — interior and corner solutions — and two kinds of goods — essential and inessential goods. An **interior solution** to the utility-maximizing problem is one in which the quantities of both goods are positive. A **corner solution** is one in which the quantity of one good is positive and the quantity of the other good is zero. An **essential good** is a good that is indispensable, such as water or air. Regardless of how high the price of an essential good may be, the consumer will still decide to buy some of it. In contrast, an **inessential good** is one like fresh raspberries in January or cut flowers for the kitchen table: if the price of an inessential good is high enough, the consumer will decide not to buy any of it.

Interior Solutions

As you already know, the nonsatiation assumption implies that the solution to the utility-maximizing problem will lie on the budget line. This is one of the two statements that describe, or characterize, an interior solution:

$$p_1 x_1{}^* + p_2 x_2{}^* = M$$

For example, the utility-maximizing bundle in Figure 3.3 lies on the budget line at bundle A.

The second statement tells us just which bundle on the budget line maximizes utility. Notice that at the utility-maximizing bundle in Figure 3.3, the indifference curve I_2 is *tangent* to the budget line. As long as indifference curves are smooth and the solution is an interior rather than a corner solution, this tangency result always holds: an indifference curve is tangent to the budget line at the utility-maximizing bundle. Why? The indifference curve through any bundle on the budget line will 1. intersect the budget line from above, 2. intersect it from below, or 3. be tangent to it. The first case is shown at bundle D in Figure 3.3. Because bundles along the budget line to the right of D (and to the left of F) are preferred to it, D cannot be the utility-maximizing bundle. The second case is shown at bundle F in Figure 3.3. Because bundles along the budget line to the left of F (and to the right of D) are preferred to it, F cannot be the utility-maximizing bundle. This means that the third case, where the indifference curve is tangent to the budget line, must be the utility-maximizing bundle.

This tangency result is the second statement that characterizes an interior solution. As you learned in Problem 3.1, the absolute value of the slope of the budget line is p_1/p_2 and, as you learned in Chapter 2, the absolute value of the slope of an indifference curve at any bundle (x_1, x_2) is $MRS(x_1, x_2)$. Because the budget line and the indifference curve are tangent at bundle A, their slopes must be identical at this point. In other words,

$$MRS(x_1^*, x_2^*) = p_1/p_2$$

This is the second statement that characterizes an interior solution.[3]

But what does this tangency condition really mean? Suppose that the consumer is thinking about choosing some bundle on the budget line where MRS is less than p_1/p_2 — say, bundle *F* in Figure 3.3. As we argued in Chapter 2, MRS is the rate at which the consumer is *willing* to substitute good 2 for good 1. On the other hand, as we saw in our discussion of opportunity cost, p_1/p_2 is the rate at which the consumer *can* substitute good 2 for good 1. At bundle *F*, MRS is less than p_1/p_2 — that is, the rate at which the consumer is willing to substitute good 2 for good 1 is less than the rate at which good 2 can be substituted for good 1. Therefore, the consumer will be better off as he or she substitutes good 2 for good 1. Accordingly, the consumer will move to the left from F

---

3 Let us derive this characterization of the utility-maximizing solution by using the method of Lagrange multipliers introduced in footnote 2. The Lagrangian function is

$$L(x_1, x_2, \lambda) = U(x_1, x_2) - \lambda(M - p_1 x_1 - p_2 x_2)$$

Differentiating with respect to x_1, x_2, and λ and setting the results equal to zero, we obtain

$$U_1(x_1^*, x_2^*) - \lambda^* p_1 = 0$$
$$U_2(x_1^*, x_2^*) - \lambda^* p_2 = 0$$
$$M - p_1 x_1^* - p_2 x_2^* = 0$$

The last condition is familiar — the utility-maximizing bundle is on the budget line. It is the first statement characterizing an interior solution. Eliminating λ^* by combining the first two conditions, we get

$$\frac{U_1(x_1^*, x_2^*)}{U_2(x_1^*, x_2^*)} = \frac{p_1}{p_2}$$

But, as we saw in footnote 2 in Chapter 2, the right side of this expression is just $MRS(x_1^*, x_2^*)$. Hence, we have

$$\frac{p_1}{p_2} = MRS(x_1^*, x_2^*)$$

which is the second statement characterizing an interior solution.

FIGURE 3.3   The utility-maximizing consumption bundle

The utility-maximizing consumption bundle (x_1^*, x_2^*) at point A is the point on the budget line where an indifference curve is tangent to the budget line. That is, at the utility-maximizing bundle, the budget line and the indifference curve have the same slope.

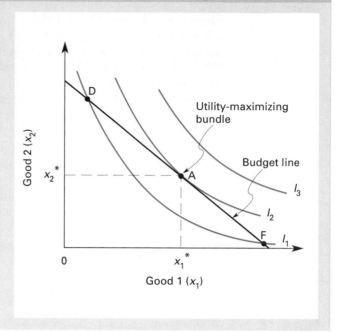

along the budget line, substituting good 2 for good 1. A corresponding argument tells us that if the consumer is considering some bundle on the budget line where *MRS* exceeds p_1/p_2 — say, bundle D in Figure 3.3 — he or she will move to the right along the budget line, substituting good 1 for good 2.

We can summarize these results in the following way: When indifference curves are smooth, an interior solution is characterized by two conditions:

$$p_1 x_1^* + p_2 x_2^* = M$$

and

$$MRS(x_1^*, x_2^*) = p_1/p_2$$

We can repeat these statements in plain English:

When indifference curves are smooth and when the quantities demanded of both goods are positive, the utility-maximizing bundle is on the budget line at the point where the budget line is tangent to an indifference curve.

Corner Solutions

The characterization above presumes that the consumer decides to buy some of both goods. It is called an *interior solution* because graphically it always lies somewhere in the space between the two axes. But this characterization does *not* apply if the consumer decides not to buy even the smallest amount of a particular good. This case is called a *corner solution*, because graphically it lies, not in the interior between the two axes, but at a corner where the budget line intersects one of the two axes.

In fact, deciding not to buy a particular good is not an unusual or perverse choice. Imagine taking a walk through several large stores that offer various kinds of merchandise

— hardware, groceries, clothing, electronic equipment, books, records, cosmetics — and tabulating the number of goods that you will never buy out of all the items for sale. Chances are that your list will be extraordinarily long. Of the vast array of available goods, most of us choose not to buy most of them.

With two goods, two kinds of corner solutions are possible. We will focus on the case in which this consumer decides not to buy any of good 1 and instead chooses to spend the entire budget on good 2. In this corner solution, the utility-maximizing bundle is bundle ($x_1 = 0$, $x_2 = M/p_2$) — the bundle where the budget line intersects the x_2 axis. (In Problem 3.3, you can explore the corner solution in which the consumer spends the entire budget on good 1.)

What types of indifference curves give rise to corner solutions, and what types do not? If indifference curves *do not* intersect the x_2 axis, then we will *never* see a corner solution. In other words, no matter how expensive good 1 becomes, the consumer will persist in buying a positive quantity of it. This case is shown in Figure 3.4. Even when the price is relatively high, as in Figure 3.4b — the steep slope of the budget line is a telltale sign that good 1 is expensive relative to good 2 — the consumer still buys some of good 1. By definition, then, it must be an essential good.

On the other hand, if the indifference curves *do* intersect the x_2 axis, then a corner solution *is* possible. This case is shown in Figure 3.5. When the price of good 1 is moderate, as in Figure 3.5a, the consumer will decide to buy some of both goods. However, in Figure 3.5b, where good 1 is relatively expensive, the consumer decides not to buy any of good 1. That is, in Figure 3.5b, this consumer's utility-maximizing

---

FIGURE 3.4 Essential goods

If indifference curves do not intersect the x_2 axis, then x_1^* is always positive, and good 1 is therefore an essential good. In both (a), where p_1 is moderate, and (b), where p_1 is high, x_1^* is positive.

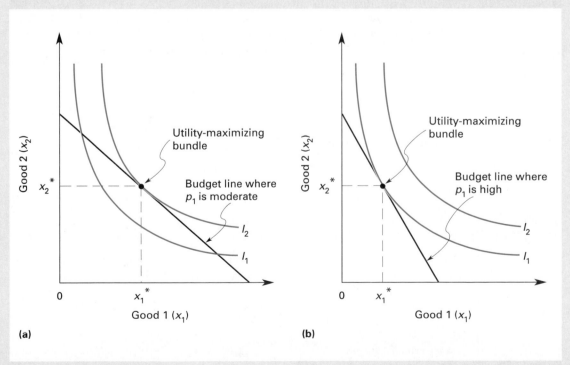

(a)

(b)

solution is this: $x_1{}^* = 0$ and $x_2{}^* = M/p_2$. In this circumstance, the consumer chooses to spend the whole budget on good 2. In the case shown in Figure 3.5, good 1 is an inessential good. If its price is too high, the consumer decides not to buy any.

When good 1 is an inessential good, what determines whether the result is an interior or a corner solution? The determining factor is the relationship between the opportunity cost of good 1, p_1/p_2, and MRS at the point where the budget line intersects the x_2 axis. If $MRS(x_1,x_2)$ at the point $x_1 = 0$ and $x_2 = M/p_2$ is greater than p_1/p_2, as in Figure 3.5a, the result is an interior solution. If it is less than p_1/p_2, as in Figure 3.5b, the result is a corner solution.

We can summarize these results as follows: If $MRS(x_1,x_2)$ at the point $x_1 = 0$ and $x_2 = M/p_2$ is less than p_1/p_2, the result is a corner solution in which the consumer buys only good 2:[4]

$$x_1{}^* = 0 \text{ and } x_2{}^* = M/p_2$$

We can repeat these results in plain English:

If, at the point where the budget line intersects the x_2 axis, the budget line is steeper than the indifference curve, the consumer buys only good 2.

If we now look at a large group of people with heterogeneous preferences, we get an interesting prediction regarding the percentage of the group who consume an inessential good. Given any arbitrary price p_1 that is neither too high nor too low, some people will find themselves in the situation shown in Figure 3.5a and will buy a positive amount of good 1 while others will find themselves in the situation shown in Figure 3.5b and will not buy any of it. Then, if we increase p_1 — the price of the inessential good — some people who were initially in the situation in Figure 3.5a will find themselves — after the price increase — in the situation in Figure 3.5b. In other words, we have derived the following prediction:

If the price of an inessential good increases, the percentage of the group who consume a positive amount of the good will decrease.

---

4 We can use calculus techniques to see when we have a corner solution. We know from footnote 2 in Chapter 2 that

$$MRS(x_1,x_2) = \frac{U_1(x_1,x_2)}{U_2(x_1,x_2)}$$

Hence, we have a corner solution if

$$\frac{U_1(0,M/p_2)}{U_2(0,M/p_2)} < \frac{p_1}{p_2}$$

For example, suppose that $U(x_1,x_2) = x_2 + x_1x_2$. Then

$$\frac{U_1(0,M/p_2)}{U_2(0,M/p_2)} = \frac{M}{p_2}$$

Hence $\quad\quad x_1{}^* = 0$ and $x_2{}^* = M/p_2 \quad$ if $M < p_1$

As you may want to verify, $\quad x_1{}^* = \frac{(M - p_1)}{2p_1} \quad$ and $\quad x_2{}^* = \frac{(M + p_1)}{2p_2} \quad$ if $M \geq p_1$

FIGURE 3.5   Inessential goods

If indifference curves intersect the x_2 axis, then there is always a p_1 large enough that $x_1^* = 0$, and good 1 is therefore an inessential good. In (b), for example, p_1 is so large that $x_1^* = 0$. In (a), p_1 is low enough that x_1^* is positive.

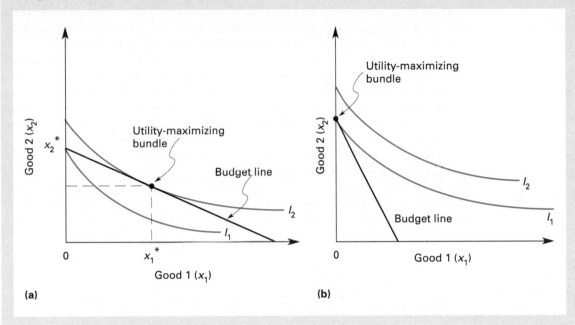

In the following problem, you can explore the case in which good 2 is an inessential good.

PROBLEM 3.3

Suppose that indifference curves intersect the x_1 axis but not the x_2 axis. Draw a figure in which the consumer chooses to buy only good 1, and describe the conditions that give rise to this corner solution.

3.5

Elasticity

At various points in the following sections, we will show precisely how quantity demanded of particular goods responds to a change in an exogenous variable, and we will compare *measures of responsiveness*. To make meaningful comparisons, however, we need a *units-free* measure of responsiveness — one that is not based on a particular measure like quarts or gallons. In this section we will develop a general units-free measure of responsiveness — known as **elasticity** — that economists use in a variety of contexts.

elasticity

Engel curve

To see why the measure must be units-free, let us look at two hypothetical Engel curves in Figure 3.6. An **Engel curve** — which we explore in detail in Section 3.7 — is just a graph of the demand function when all exogenous variables except income are held constant. Income — the exogenous variable — is plotted on the horizontal axis, and quantity demanded of a good — the endogenous variable — is plotted on the vertical axis. A hypothetical Engel curve for gasoline is shown in Figure 3.6a. Notice that the unit of measure for gasoline is the quart. A hypothetical Engel curve for electricity is shown in Figure 3.6b. Notice that the unit of measure for electricity is the kilowatt-hour. In both cases income is measured in dollars. Both of these Engel curves are upward sloping, indicating that quantity demanded increases as income increases. (As you will see below, however, Engel curves need not be upward sloping.)

In which of these two cases is the response of quantity demanded to a $1 increase in income greater? A glance at the two figures suggests that the right answer is gasoline because the Engel curve for gasoline is more steeply pitched than the Engel curve for electricity. However, if the unit of measure for gasoline is changed from the quart to the gallon, we get the much flatter, dashed Engel curve $E'E'$ in Figure 3.6, suggesting that the right answer is electricity.

The point is that we cannot compare demand responsiveness meaningfully by comparing the slopes of the Engel curves in Figure 3.6 because the units of measurement are not the same. Furthermore, we cannot make the comparison meaningful by choosing the same unit of measurement for each, because gasoline cannot be measured in kilowatt-hours or electricity in gallons. What we need is a *units-free measure of responsiveness*.

To develop such a measure, suppose we have a general functional relationship:

$$y = f(z)$$

FIGURE 3.6   The need for a units-free measure of responsiveness.

Because the Engel curve in (a) is steeper than the Engel curve in (b), the demand for gasoline appears to be more responsive to changes in income than the demand for electricity. But the appearance is deceiving. For example, when we measure gasoline in gallons instead of quarts, the Engel curve for gasoline in the line E'E', and the demand for gasoline appears to be less responsive. Meaningful comparisons require a units-free measure of responsiveness.

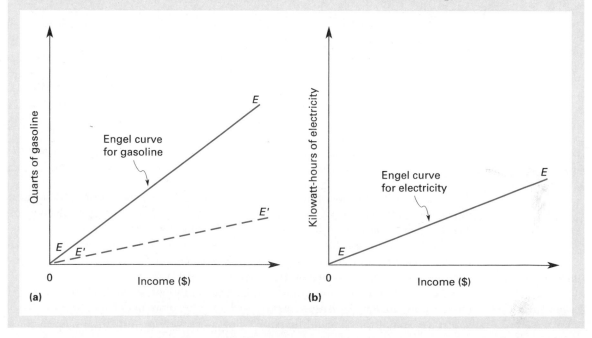

(a)

(b)

Think of y as an endogenous variable and of z as an exogenous variable. Now pick a value of the exogenous variable, say z', and evaluate the function at this point to get $y' = f(z')$. Starting at this point, we want to develop a units-free measure of the responsiveness of y to a change z. Suppose there is a change in z of magnitude Δz. Given the change in the exogenous variable, the new value of the endogenous variable is $y'' = f(z' + \Delta z)$, and the change in the endogenous variable is

$$\Delta y = y'' - y' = f(z' + \Delta z) - f(z')$$

We want a units-free measure of the change in y — Δy — induced by the change in z — Δz. If we express each of these changes as a proportionate change, $\Delta y/y'$ and $\Delta z/z'$, then the units cancel and what remain are pure numbers. Now, when we form the ratio of the proportionate change in y to the proportionate change in z, we have a units-free measure of responsiveness.

$$E = [\Delta y/y')]/[\Delta z/z']$$

Equivalently,

$$E = \frac{[f(z' + \Delta z) - f(z')]/f(z')}{\Delta z/z'}$$

arc elasticity

E is called the **arc elasticity** of y with respect to z. Notice that this is a *nonmarginal measure* of responsiveness since Δz represents a discrete, measurable change.

To get a sense of what arc elasticity is and some practice using the concept, let us look at a familiar noneconomic application: the arc elasticity of the area of a square with respect to the length of the square's side. Let y denote the area of the square and z denote the length of a square's side. Then, $f(z) = z^2$, since the area of a square is equal to the square of the length of its side. Beginning with a square with side of length 5 feet — $z' = 5$ ft and $y' = 25$ ft^2 — we want to calculate the elasticity of y (area) with respect to z (length of side). Of course, to do so we need a value for Δz. In Table 3.1, we have calculated this elasticity for various values of Δz.

From the first line of Table 3.1, we see that when the length of the square's side increases from 5 ft to 8 ft — a 60% increase — its area increases from 25 ft^2 to 64 ft^2 — a 156% increase. Consequently, the arc elasticity of area with respect to length is 1.56/.6, or 2.6. Notice that as Δz (in the first column of the table) gets smaller, the arc elasticity (in the last column) also gets smaller. From the last line of the Table 3.1, we see that a 10% increase in length results in a 21% increase in area for an arc elasticity of 2.1. Finally, looking down the last column of the table, we see that arc elasticity of area with respect to length seems to be approaching 2 as Δz approaches 0.

These calculations point to an ambiguity associated with this measure of responsiveness: it depends not just on the size of the initial square but also on the magnitude of the

TABLE 3.1	**The elasticity of a square of side 5 feet with respect to the length of its side**			
Δz	Δy	$\Delta y/y'$	$\Delta z/z'$	E
3.0 ft	39.0 ft^2	1.56	0.6	2.6
2.0 ft	24.0 ft^2	0.96	0.4	2.4
1.0 ft	11.0 ft^2	0.44	0.2	2.2
0.5 ft	5.25 ft^2	0.21	0.1	2.1

**marginal
elasticity**

increase in the square's side. To resolve this ambiguity, economists use a *marginal* measure of elasticity. To find the marginal elasticity of y with respect to z, in the arc elasticity formula we let Δz approach zero. The **marginal elasticity** ε is therefore defined as follows:[5]

$$\varepsilon = \text{limit of E as } \Delta z \to 0$$

When we discuss elasticities, we will always be talking about marginal elasticities. To keep the terminology simple, however, we will drop the adjective marginal and refer simply to the elasticity of one variable with respect to another.

PROBLEM 3.4

1. Let us find the marginal elasticity of area with respect to length when the side of the square is 5 ft. The arc elasticity of area with respect to length is then

$$E = \{[(5 + \Delta z)^2 - 25]/25\}/\{\Delta z/5\}$$

Show that this can be reduced to

$$E = 2 + \Delta z/5$$

Now let Δz approach 0 to get $\varepsilon = 2$.
2. Use the same approach to show that $\varepsilon = 2$ regardless of the length of the square's side.

Elasticity of the Number of Smokers with Respect to Price

Currently, approximately 30% of adult Americans are smokers and approximately 70% are nonsmokers. Many of these nonsmokers undoubtedly regard cigarettes as a "bad," and would never buy them. But surely at least some of these nonsmokers regard cigarettes as an inessential good and—finding themselves in the situation shown in Figure 3.5b—choose not to smoke because cigarettes are too expensive. Although some of the smokers may regard cigarettes as essential, surely for many smokers, cigarettes are an inessential good. Finding themselves in the situation shown in Figure 3.5a, these individuals choose to be smokers because cigarettes are not too expensive. If we are right in supposing that there are both smokers and nonsmokers for whom cigarettes are inessential, then our theory predicts that as the price of cigarettes increases (decreases) the

---

5 We can use basic calculus to express point elasticity in terms of the derivative of $f(z)$, $df(z)/dz$. By definition, arc elasticity at point z is

$$E = \frac{[f(z + \Delta z) - f(z)]/f(z)}{\Delta z/z}$$

Rearranging, we get

$$E = \left[\frac{f(z + \Delta z) - f(z)}{\Delta z}\right]\left[\frac{z}{f(z)}\right]$$

Notice that Δz occurs only in the first bracketed expression, and that the limit as $\Delta z \to 0$ of that expression is, by definition, the derivative of $f(z)$. Hence,

$$\varepsilon = \left[\frac{df(z)}{dz}\right]\left[\frac{z}{f(z)}\right]$$

Using this expression, it is easy to show that the marginal elasticity of the area of a square with respect to the length of its side is 2.

percentage of the population who choose to smoke will decrease (increase). Is this prediction borne out by experience? And if it is, just how responsive is smoking behavior to a change in the price of cigarettes? For example, would a $1 increase in the price of a pack result in a substantial reduction in the percentage of people who smoke?

If we let S denote the percentage of adults in the United States who smoke and p denote the price of a pack of cigarettes, we can rephrase these questions. What is the elasticity of S with respect to p? This is one of the questions that Jeffrey Wasserman (1988) addressed in his Ph.D. thesis. He estimates that in recent years in the United States, the elasticity of S with respect to p has been about $-.15$. The fact that this elasticity is negative means that S decreases as p increases, just as our theory predicts. His estimate indicates, however, that a 1% increase in p would cause S to decrease by only .15%. Since S is currently about 30%, a 1% increase in p would decrease S by roughly .045 percentage points. To put this response in perspective, let us consider a very large increase in the price of cigarettes. Wasserman's elasticity estimate indicates that if p were increased by 100%, S would decrease by 15% — that is, the percentage of American adults who smoke would drop from 30% to 25.5%. Lewit and Coate (1982) have arrived at a slightly different estimate of this elasticity. They estimate that the elasticity of S with respect to p has been about $-.26$. The evidence seems to indicate, however, that the percentage of the adult population of the United States who smoke is somewhat unresponsive to the price of cigarettes.

3.6
Comparative Statics Analysis of Demand

When we differentiated between essential and inessential goods, we were creating a *classification* or *taxonomy* based on the kind of consumption response a consumer makes to a change in the price of a good. The response in the case of an inessential good is to give it up if the price goes too high; in the case of an essential good, to continue to buy some amount regardless of price. If consumer demand theory is to be useful, it must provide a framework for asking and answering questions like these about how a consumer responds to such changes: How does an increase in a consumer's income affect his or her consumption decisions? How does an increase in the price level affect consumption decisions? What happens if the price of one good goes up and all other prices remain the same? Will consumer demand for that good necessarily decline? Will demand for all other goods necessarily increase?

We can generate a great number of such questions. There are, however, just three fundamental questions about consumption responses.

1. How will a consumer's demand for some good — say, good 1 — change in response to an increase (or decrease) in income?

2. How will a consumer's demand for good 1 change in response to an increase (or decrease) in the price of that good?

3. How will a consumer's demand for good 1 change in response to an increase (or decrease) in the price of some other good?

Notice that all three questions are about a consumer's response to a change in the value of an exogenous variable in a demand function. By altering the values of exogenous variables, we can compare solutions to the utility-maximization problem before and after the change. You were first introduced to this procedure, called **comparative statics analysis**, in Chapter 1. It is termed *statics analysis* because it is concerned with static, or stationary, equilibrium points rather than with the dynamic

comparative statics analysis

adjustments between these points. And it is termed *comparative* because it allows us to compare consumer choices in different circumstances.[6]

PROBLEM 3.5

Consider the following demand function — one that you first encountered in Problem 3.2: $x_1^* = M/(p_1 + p_2)$. Suppose that initially $M = \$120$, $p_1 = \$1$, and $p_2 = \$1$. How does x_1^* respond to a \$1 increase in p_1? To a \$1 increase in p_2? To a \$2 increase in M?

Because in Problem 3.5 you had in hand a specific demand function — one derived from a specific utility function — you were able to provide *precise answers* to the comparative statics questions posed in the problem. For example, given p_1 and p_2 equal to \$1, you discovered that whenever M increases by \$2, consumption of good 1 increases by one unit. In the following sections, we will be concerned with more general questions that presume only that a consumer maximizes his or her utility. As a result, we will not look for precise answers to comparative statics questions, but instead for *qualitative answers* that indicate the *direction* but not the magnitude of the demand response. For instance, we will ask: Does utility maximization imply that a consumer will buy less of a particular good when its price rises?

3.7

Consumption Response to a Change in Income

What will happen to the demand for good 1 as income M changes? More precisely: If the prices of both goods are held constant and if income rises, will a consumer buy more, less, or just the same amount of good 1?

Normal Goods and Inferior Goods

The answer depends on just what that good is. Casual observation suggests that as consumers become wealthier, they buy less of some goods and more of others. For example, many students eat lots of relatively inexpensive pasta for dinner before they graduate, but switch to relatively more expensive meat once they leave school and find well-paid, full-time employment. This observation provides us with a taxonomy: a good

normal good

inferior good

is a **normal good** if consumption of the good *increases* as income increases. It is an **inferior good** if consumption *decreases* as income increases.

In Figure 3.7a, good 1 is a normal good. We have constructed three dashed budget lines corresponding to income levels \$100, \$150, and \$200. Notice that the budget lines have the same slope (and are therefore parallel) since prices are held constant. Only income changes. Notice, too, that as this consumer's income increases from \$100 to \$150 to \$200, his or her consumption of good 1 increases from 6 to 9 to 12. We know, then, that for this consumer, good 1 is a normal good. The line labeled *IC* in Figure 3.7a, which passes through the utility-maximizing bundles that are generated as this consumer's income increases, is called an **income-consumption path**. In Figure 3.7a,

income-
consumption
path

---

6 These qualitative comparative statics questions are simply questions about the signs of partial derivatives of demand functions. For example, is the partial derivative of the demand function for good 1 with respect to M always positive?

FIGURE 3.7   Normal and inferior goods

In (a), as income increases, so does quantity demanded of good 1; good 1 is therefore a normal good. The income consumption path *IC* is positively sloped for a normal good. In (b), as income increases, quantity demanded of good 1 decreases; good 1 is therefore an inferior good. *IC* is negatively sloped for an inferior good.

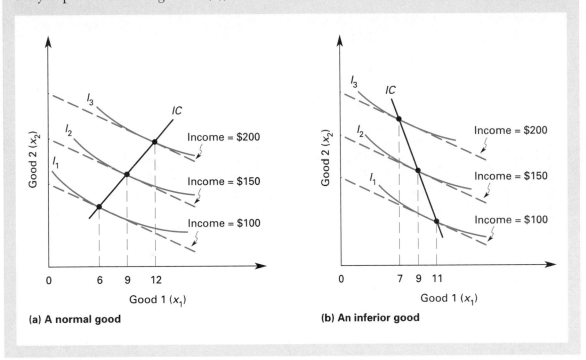

(a) A normal good

(b) An inferior good

its slope is positive because both good 1 and good 2 are normal goods. (Can you confirm that good 2 is also a normal good?)

In Figure 3.7b, good 1 is an inferior good. As this consumer's income increases from $100 to $150 to $200, his or her consumption of good 1 decreases from 11 to 9 to 7. Notice that the slope of the income-consumption path *IC* is negative in this case. (Is good 2 a normal or inferior good in Figure 3.7b?)

PROBLEM 3.6

Are the following statements true or false?
1. When *IC* is negatively sloped, good 1 is invariably inferior.
2. When *IC* is negatively sloped, one good is inferior and the other is normal.
3. Both goods cannot be inferior.
4. Both goods cannot be normal.

Engel Curves

In Figure 3.8, we have used the information from each of the cases in Figure 3.7 to construct a relationship between income and the utility-maximizing quantity of good 1. This relationship is named an *Engel curve* after the nineteenth-century Prussian statistician Ernst Engel. In effect, we have plotted the demand function for good 1 when income is

FIGURE 3.8   Engel curves

An Engel curve is a graph of a demand function, holding all prices constant and allowing income to vary. Income is plotted on the horizontal axis and quantity demanded on the vertical axis. In (a), the Engel curve for a normal good is positively sloped. In (b), the Engel curve for an inferior good is negatively sloped.

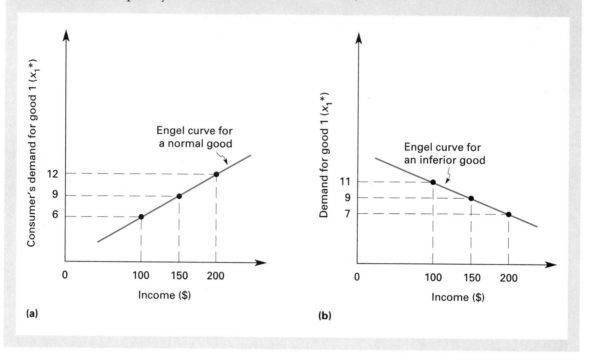

(a)   (b)

allowed to vary and prices are held constant. For a normal good, the Engel curve is positively sloped because, by definition, x_1^* increases as M increases. For an inferior good, the Engel curve is negatively sloped because, again by definition, x_1^* decreases as M increases.

PROBLEM 3.7

Suppose that *MRS* depends only on x_1. Then *MRS* is identical at all points on any vertical line in (x_1, x_2) space. Show that good 1 is neither inferior nor normal — that is, show that the utility-maximizing quantity of good 1 is independent of income. Illustrate the Engel curve for such a good.

Some Income Elasticities of Demand

Strictly speaking, we cannot say that a particular good — for example, fresh salmon — is a normal good or an inferior good without also specifying the particular consumer whose preferences we are considering. It is possible, even likely, that one person — say Janet — may respond to an increase in her income by buying more fresh salmon while another person — say Craig — may respond to an increase in his income by buying less of it. For Janet fresh salmon is a normal good, while for Craig it is an inferior good.

Nevertheless, we can get a good idea of whether, for the average consumer, a particular good is normal or inferior by using aggregate data to compute an average income

income elasticity
of demand

elasticity of demand. The **income elasticity of demand** is the elasticity of quantity consumed per capita with respect to per capita income. In empirical studies of income elasticity of demand for a good, aggregate data is used to compute an average demand function. Then, this average demand function is used to compute various average elasticities, including the income elasticity of demand.

Empirical evidence suggests that for the average consumer, fresh salmon is a normal good. Using data for North America and Europe, DeVoretz and Salvanes (1993) estimate the income elasticity of demand for fresh salmon to be 2.14. The fact that the elasticity is positive indicates that fresh salmon is a normal good. As per capita income increases, so does per capita consumption of fresh salmon. The *magnitude* of the response is also of interest. An income elasticity of demand of 2.14 indicates that a 1% increase in per capita income would result in a 2.14% increase in per capita consumption of fresh salmon. Notice just how responsive consumption of salmon is to changes in income: holding the price of salmon and other relevant variables constant, we see that per capita consumption of salmon tends to increase at more than twice the rate at which per capita income increases.

luxury

A normal good is said to be a **luxury** if consumption increases at a rate larger than the rate at which per capita income increases. Equivalently, a good is a luxury if the income elasticity of demand for the good exceeds 1. Clearly, fresh salmon is a luxury. In a now classic study of the demand for electricity in Great Britain in the 1940s, Houthakker (1951) estimated the income elasticity of demand for electricity to be 1.17. This means that in Britain in the 1940s electricity was a luxury.

necessity

On the other hand, a normal good is said to be a **necessity** if the income elasticity of demand for the good is less than 1. Baltagi and Griffin (1983) report a range of income elasticities for gasoline. A typical elasticity for gasoline is .8, indicating that a 1% increase in per capita income results in an increase in per capita consumption of gasoline equal to .8%. Therefore, gasoline is a necessity.

Of course, the income elasticity of demand for an inferior good is negative, since quantity demanded of an inferior good decreases as income increases. Wasserman (1988) finds that the income elasticity of demand for cigarettes has been declining in recent years. Up to about 1980, his estimates of the income elasticity of demand for cigarettes for American adults are positive but small. These estimates indicate that cigarettes were a necessity prior to 1980. After 1980, however, Wasserman estimates a small negative income elasticity of demand in the range of −.02 to −.2. These estimates indicate that after 1980, cigarettes were an inferior good for adults. Interestingly, when he calculates the elasticity of per capita consumption of cigarettes for teenagers with respect to average family income, he gets an estimate of −.44, indicating that a 1% increase in family income is associated with a .44% decrease in cigarette consumption by teenagers.

3.8

Consumption Response to a Change in Price

Now let us take up the second question: What will happen to the demand for a good — say, good 1 — as its own price changes, holding the price of the other good p_2 and income M constant? What happens to a particular consumer's demand for Darjeeling tea, for instance, as its price rises or falls?

In Figure 3.9a, we have drawn three budget lines and indicated the three resulting utility-maximizing bundles at points E, F, and G. (Notice that we have not included the corresponding indifference curves, which are tangent to the three budget lines at these three points.) In constructing this figure, we have held p_2 constant at $2 and M constant at $60. And we have used three different values for p_1: p_1 is $4 on the lowest budget line, $3 on the intermediate budget line, and $2 on the highest budget line.

FIGURE 3.9   **The price-consumption path and the demand function.**

In (a), the price-consumption path *PC* passes through the utility-maximizing consumption bundles that are generated as the price of good 1 changes, holding income and all other prices constant. In (b), the demand curve is the graph of the demand for good 1 as its price changes.

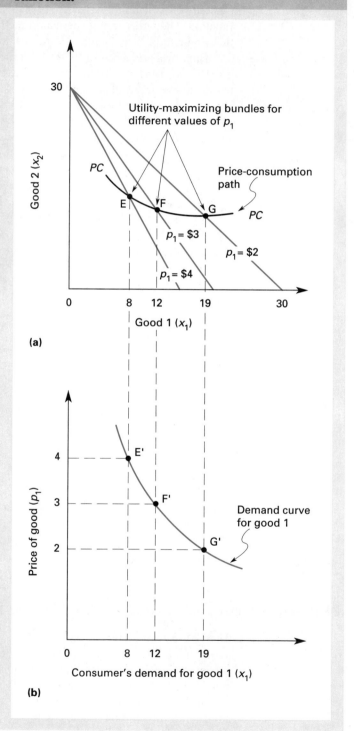

(a)

(b)

The Price-Consumption Path

price-
consumption
path

The line labeled *PC* in Figure 3.9a is called a **price-consumption path**. It connects the utility-maximizing bundles that arise as p_1 is successively decreased from $4 to $3 to $2. The price-consumption path is analogous to the income-consumption path, with this difference: in the income-consumption path, only income varied; here, only the price of good 1 varies.

The Demand Curve

ordinary
demand curve

We can use the price-consumption path to construct a relationship between the price of good 1 and the quantity demanded in much the same way that we used the income-consumption path to construct an Engel curve. This relationship — which we will call the consumer's **ordinary demand curve** for good 1 — is shown in Figure 3.9b. The three points E′, F′, and G′ on the demand curve correspond to the utility-maximizing points E, F, and G in Figure 3.9a. The demand curve is a graph of the demand function when p_1 is varied and p_2 and M are held constant. Just as common sense suggests, price and quantity demanded are negatively related in Figure 3.9b. As price increases from $2 to $3 to $4, the quantity demanded decreases from 19 to 12 to 8.[7]

Some Price Elasticities of Demand

price elasticity
of demand

Just as we can use aggregate data to compute an income elasticity of demand for the average consumer in the group, so, too, we can use aggregate data to compute a price elasticity of demand for the average consumer. The **price elasticity of demand** for a good is the elasticity of quantity consumed per capita with respect to the price of the good. (As we remarked in our discussion of income elasticities of demand, in empirical studies, aggregate data is used to compute an average demand function. Then this average demand function is used to compute various average elasticities.)

The price elasticity of demand for cigarettes has received a great deal of attention in recent years. One strategy that governments have used to reduce cigarette consumption is to raise the excise tax on cigarettes, thereby raising the price of cigarettes and — to the extent that consumption is responsive to price — decreasing consumption of cigarettes. To what extent does raising taxes on cigarettes actually reduce consumption? Lewit and Coate (1982) estimate the price elasticity of demand for cigarettes in the United States to be −.42. The fact that the elasticity is negative indicates that the demand curve for cigarettes is downward sloping: as price increases, quantity consumed decreases. This estimate indicates that a 1% increase in price would decrease cigarette consumption by .42% (and a 10% increase would decrease consumption by 4.2%). By contrast, Wasserman calculates the price elasticity of demand for cigarettes to be −.23. Wasserman's estimate indicates a smaller response of quantity consumed to a change in price. If Wasserman's estimate is accurate, a 1% increase in the price of cigarettes would decrease per capita consumption by only .23%.

---

7 It is customary in plotting this type of relationship to put the exogenous variable on the horizontal axis and the endogenous variable on the verticle axis. Although we followed this custom when we plotted the Engel curve, tradition dictates that we violate it when we plot the demand curve. The demand curve has quantity demanded (the endogenous variable) on the horizontal axis and price (the exogenous variable) on the verticle axis.

In his classic study of the demand for electricity in the United Kingdom in the 1940s, Houthakker (1951) estimated that the price elasticity of demand for electricity in Britain was −.89. Using this estimate, we see that the demand for electricity is more responsive to a change in its own price than is the demand for cigarettes. However, a 1% decrease in price produces a decrease in consumption (equal to .89%) that is still less than 1%. In this sense, both the demand for cigarettes and the demand for electricity are relatively unresponsive, or **inelastic** with respect to their own prices. More precisely: If the absolute value of the price elasticity of demand is smaller than 1, demand is said to be inelastic with respect to price. On the other hand, the demand for fresh salmon is responsive, or **elastic** with respect to price. More precisely: if the absolute value of the price elasticity of demand is larger than 1, demand is said to be elastic with respect to price. DeVoretz and Salvanes (1993) calculate the price elasticity of demand for fresh salmon to be −2.47. According to this estimate, a 1% increase in the price of salmon will decrease per capita consumption by 2.47%.

inelastic

elastic

3.9

Income and Substitution Effects

Intuition strongly suggests that the quantity demanded of any good is *negatively* related to that good's price. In other words, it seems reasonable to suppose that as the price of a good continues to drop, the consumer decides to buy more and more of it. For example, most of us would expect that as compact discs become less expensive, people who own compact disc players will buy more CDs. Graphically, the consumer's demand curve would then be downward sloping, as it is in Figure 3.9b. As Figure 3.10 reveals, however, it is possible in theory for the quantity demanded to be *positively* related to price. As p_1 increases from $2 to $3 in Figure 3.10, the quantity demanded of good 1

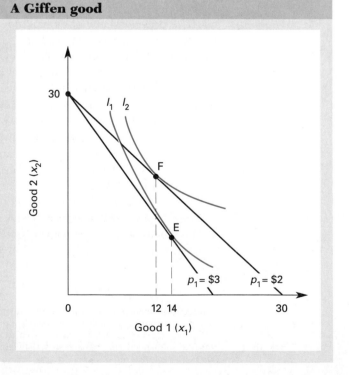

FIGURE 3.10   A Giffen good

As p_1 increases from $2 to $3, quantity demanded of good 1 increases from 12 to 14. Because quantity demanded increases as price increases, good 1 is a Giffen good.

Giffen good

substitution effect

income effect

increases from 12 to 14. When price and quantity demanded of a good are positively related, the good is called a **Giffen good**.

To understand this surprising theoretical possibility, let us look at the consumer's response to a change in the price of good 1 in more detail. We will perform a hypothetical exercise that allows us to decompose the overall response into two components, a **substitution effect** and an **income effect**. Then, using this decomposition, we can say something more definite about the consumer's response.

A change in p_1 (holding p_2 constant) changes the relative price (or opportunity cost) of good 1 in terms of good 2. If p_1 rises, good 1 is relatively more expensive and, if it drops, good 1 is relatively less expensive. The *substitution effect* of a change in p_1 is associated with the *change in the opportunity cost* of good 1.

In addition, a change in p_1 (holding p_2 and M constant) results in an equilibrium for the consumer on a different indifference curve. If p_1 goes up, the set of attainable bundles shrinks and the consumer ends up on a lower indifference curve. Therefore, we say that the increase in p_1 results in a decrease in the consumer's *real income*. Similarly, if p_1 goes down, the set of attainable consumption bundles expands and the consumer ends up on a higher indifference curve. Therefore, we say that a decrease in p_1 results in an increase in the consumer's real income. The *income effect* of a change in p_1 is associated with the change in real income, or the shift from one indifference curve to another.

Imagine, for example, the reaction of an avid New York baseball fan with $1200 per season to spend on major league ball game tickets to a drop in the price of admission to Yankee games from $20 to $10 (holding the price of admission to Mets games constant at $20). The opportunity cost of watching a Yankee game has suddenly changed from one Mets game to half a Mets game. In addition, the fan's real income has increased because he or she can now attend more of both sports events. For example, if the fan initially chose to buy tickets to 30 Yankee games and 30 Met games, after the price reduction for Yankee games, he or she can now afford to buy tickets to 40 Yankee games and 40 Met games. The substitution effect is associated with the change in the *opportunity cost* of a Yankee game, and the income effect is associated with the fact that the fan's *real income* has increased.

Income and Substitution Effects for a Price Increase

Let us look at income and substitution effects graphically. In Figure 3.11, M is held constant at $60, and p_2 is held constant at $1. When the price of good 1 is $1, the utility-maximizing bundle is bundle A — containing 30 units of good 1 — on indifference curve I_2. When the price of good 1 rises to $3, the consumer switches to bundle C — containing 12 units of good 1 — on indifference curve I_1. This consumer's response to an increase in the price of good 1 from $1 to $3 is to reduce consumption of good 1 by 18 units.

Now let us decompose this quantity response — the drop from 30 to 12 units of good 1 — into a substitution effect and an income effect. Beginning at bundle C in Figure 3.11, to isolate the substitution effect we eliminate the income effect by giving the consumer just enough additional income to allow him or her to get back to the original indifference curve, I_2. The resulting budget line is called the **compensated budget line** because it compensates for the loss in real income associated with the increase in p_1 from $1 to $3. The compensated budget line is the dashed line in Figure 3.11. It is parallel to the budget line through C because in both instances p_1 is $3. Given the compensated budget line, bundle D on indifference curve I_2 — containing 22 units of good 1 — is the utility-maximizing bundle. Having eliminated the income effect, we see that the substitution effect associated with this increase in the price of good 1 is a drop in consumption of that good from 30 to 22 units. Notice that the substitution effect associated

compensated budget line

FIGURE 3.11 Income and substitution effects for a price increase

As the price of good 1 increases from $1 to $3, quantity demanded decreases from 30 to 12. To isolate the substitution and income effects, increase income by just enough that the original indifference curve I_2 is attainable at price $p_1 = \$3$. The resulting budget line is the compensated budget line. The substitution effect is the reduction in consumption from 30 to 22, and the income effect is the reduction in consumption from 22 to 12.

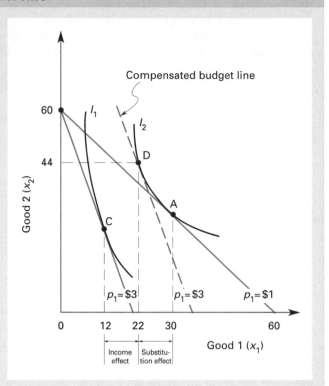

with this *increase* in p_1 from $1 to $3 is a *decrease* in consumption of good 1 from 30 to 22 units. That is, the substitution effect is *negatively related* to the price change.

To isolate the income effect, we take the added income away. As a result, the budget line shifts downward from the compensated budget line to the solid budget line through C. The consumer responds by switching from bundle D to bundle C, and consumption of good 1 drops from 22 to 12. The income effect is then a reduction in consumption of good 1 from 22 units to 12 units. Notice that the income effect associated with this *increase* in p_1 from $1 to $3 is a *decrease* in consumption of good 1 from 22 to 12 units. Therefore, in the case shown in Figure 3.11, the income effect is also *negatively related* to the price change. This reflects the fact that good 1 is a normal good in Figure 3.11. (We know that good 1 is normal, because when income decreases, the consumer buys less of it.)

PROBLEM 3.8

Using the information embodied in Figure 3.11, find an algebraic expression for the compensated budget line. What is the *added income* associated with the compensated budget line?

Income and Substitution Effects for a Price Decrease

Now let us perform the same sort of decomposition for a price reduction instead of a price rise. In Figure 3.12, when p_1 is $2, the utility-maximizing bundle is bundle A — containing 3 units of good 1 — on indifference I_1. When p_1 then drops from $2 to $1,

FIGURE 3.12 Income and substitution effects for a price decrease

As the price of good 1 decreases from $2 to $1, quantity demanded increases from 3 to 9. To isolate the substitution and income effects, decrease income by just enough so that the original indifference curve I_1 is attainable at price $p_1 = \$1$. The substitution effect is the increase in consumption from 3 to 14, and the income effect is the reduction in consumption from 14 to 9.

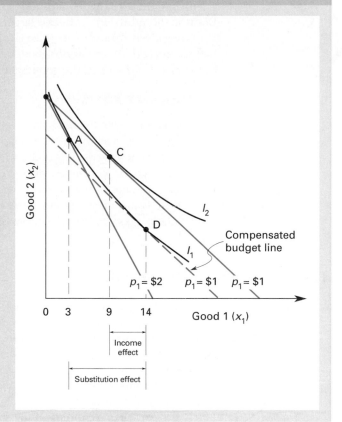

the consumer switches to bundle C — containing 9 units of good 1 — on indifference curve I_2. The consumer responds to the decrease in the price of good 1 from $2 to $1 by increasing consumption of good 1 from 3 to 9 units. Once again price and quantity demanded are negatively related. How can we decompose this increase in consumption into a substitution effect and an income effect?

First, we need to isolate the substitution effect. Beginning at bundle C in Figure 3.12, we can eliminate the income effect by changing the consumer's income just enough so that he or she can attain the initial indifference curve, I_1. Because the price of good 1 has dropped, this time we have to take income away from the consumer. The dashed line in Figure 3.12 is the compensated budget line, and the utility-maximizing bundle is bundle D, which contains 14 units of good 1. Thus, the substitution effect associated with a decrease in the price of good 1 from $2 to $1 is an increase in quantity of good 1 from 3 to 14 units. Notice, the substitution effect associated with this *decrease* in p_1 is an *increase* in consumption of good 1. Here, as in the previous case, the substitution effect is *negatively related* to the price change.

Now, beginning at bundle D, to isolate the income effect we will restore the income that we just took away. The solid line through C is the resulting budget line, and the consumer chooses bundle C, which contains 9 units of good 1. The income effect associated with this *decrease* in the price of good 1 from $2 to $1 is then a *decrease* in consumption of good 1 from 14 units to 9. In this case, the income effect is *positively related* to the price change. This positive relationship reflects the fact that good 1 is an inferior good in Figure 3.12. We know that good 1 is inferior in Figure 3.12 because in response to an increase in income, the consumer buys less of it.

In Figure 3.12 the income and substitution effects work in opposite directions. Because the substitution effect is larger than the income effect, however, the *total effect* is negatively related to the price change. In the following problem, you will discover that when good 1 is an inferior good, the income effect may be larger than the substitution effect. When it is, the good is a Giffen good.

> **PROBLEM 3.9**
>
> Consider again Figure 3.10, in which the price and quantity demanded of good 1 are positively related. Suppose that initially the price of good 1 is $3 and that it subsequently drops to $2. First, decompose the change in quantity of good 1 demanded into income and substitution effects. Then notice that the substitution effect is negatively related to the price change, that the income effect is positively related to the price change, that good 1 is an inferior good, and that the income effect is larger than the substitution effect.

The Negative Substitution Effect

In all of these decompositions, the substitution effect is negatively related to the price change. In Figure 3.11, when the price rose, the substitution effect generated a decline in the consumption of good 1. In Figure 3.12 and in your analysis of Figure 3.10, when the price dropped, the substitution effect generated an increase in consumption. The negative relationship between the substitution effect and the price change is *always* true when indifference curves are convex and smooth and when the consumer buys a positive amount of both goods.

It is easy to see why. In isolating the substitution effect we identified two points on the same indifference curve. The first was a point of tangency of the indifference curve with the original budget line — the points labeled A in Figures 3.11 and 3.12. The second was a point of tangency of the indifference curve with the compensated budget line — the points labeled D in Figures 3.11 and 3.12. If the indifference curve is convex and smooth, *MRS* diminishes from left to right along the indifference curve. Therefore, the point of tangency with the budget line that reflects the lower price of good 1 will be to the right of the other point of tangency. The result is a negative relationship between the change in price and the change in quantity demanded of good 1:

If indifference curves are smooth and convex and if the consumer buys a positive quantity of both goods, then the substitution effect is negatively related to the price change.

The Ambiguous Income Effect

Unlike the substitution effect, however, the income effect of a price change may be either negatively or positively related to the price change:

For a normal good, the income effect is negatively related to the price change; for an inferior good, the income effect is positively related to the price change.

The Slope of the Demand Curve

We can now fit these various pieces together to develop a deeper understanding of the slope of the demand curve, or the qualitative relationship between the price and the quantity demanded of a good. If the good is normal, the substitution and income effects of a price change are both negatively related to the price change and are therefore complementary:

If a good is normal, then its demand curve is downward sloping: price and quantity demanded are negatively related.

If the good is inferior, the income effect of a price change is positively related and the substitution effect is negatively related to the price change; the slope of the demand curve then depends on the relative strengths of the two effects:

If a good is inferior and if the substitution effect is larger than the income effect, then its demand curve is downward sloping: price and quantity demanded are negatively related. If a good is inferior and if the income effect is larger than the substitution effect, then its demand curve is upward sloping: price and quantity demanded are positively related.

The last result describes the Giffen good case. Although Giffen goods are theoretically possible, they are, in fact, rare. For this reason, we will set Giffen goods aside in the rest of this book and simply assume that demand curves are downward sloping.

The Compensated Demand Curve

We used the assumptions that indifference curves are smooth and convex to derive the result that the substitution effect is negatively related to the price change. In this section, we drop the assumptions of smoothness and convexity and instead use only minimal assumptions to show that the *substitution effect* is never *positively related to the price change*. We also introduce the *compensated demand curve*, which reflects only the substitution effect. Unlike the ordinary demand curve, the compensated demand curve cannot be upward sloping.

The Substitution Effect Revisited

To show that the substitution effect cannot be positively related to the price change, we need only four of the assumptions from Chapter 2 — completeness, two-term consistency, transitivity, and nonsatiation. As you know, the first three assumptions guarantee that individuals make consistent choices. The fourth assumption — nonsatiation — will also be satisfied in most choice situations. Because we are now using only minimal assumptions, essentially we are discovering an implication of the assumption that individuals are motivated by self-interest.

Recall that when we identified the substitution effect, we identified the *minimum income* that allowed the consumer to attain the original indifference curve. Let us call this minimum income the **compensatory income**. The associated budget line is, of course, the compensated budget line.

In Figure 3.13, the indifference curves have been omitted because their shapes now play no role in the analysis. In the initial situation, given the lower value of p_1 — reflected by the flatter budget line LGACON — this consumer chose the utility-maximizing

compensatory
income

FIGURE 3.13   The nonpositive substitution effect

The initial utility-maximizing bundle is at point A on the original budget line. Given the price increase (reflected in the slope of the two compensated budget lines), the compensatory income is no greater than M_1. If the compensatory income is in fact M_1, then the utility-maximizing bundle is on segment JA of the compensated budget line JAFE, and the quantity of good 1 in the utility-maximizing bundle does not exceed x_1^*. If the compensatory income is less than M_1 — say, M_2 — then the utility-maximizing bun-

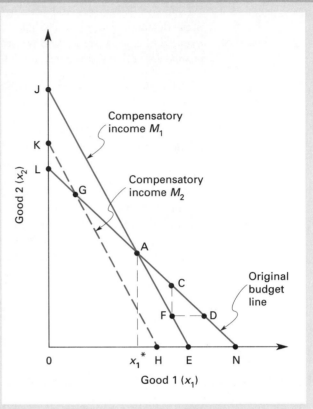

dle is on segment KG of the compensated budget line KGH, and the quantity of good 1 in the bundle is less than x_1^*. In either case, the substitution effect is nonpositively related to the price change.

bundle at A. Now suppose that p_1 goes up and let M_1 be the level of income such that the consumer could buy the original consumption bundle, given the higher price of good 1. The budget line associated with the higher price of good 1 and income M_1 is JAFE. Clearly, the compensatory income — because it is the minimum income that allows the consumer to attain the original indifference curve — can be no greater than M_1.

Suppose for the moment that the compensatory income is M_1. (It is unlikely to be this large; however, as you will see in Problem 3.10, it can be.) The compensated budget line is then JAFE in Figure 3.13. Notice that on segment AFE of the compensated budget line, only bundle A can be on the original indifference curve. Why? If another bundle on AFE were on the original indifference curve — say, the bundle at F — then, by nonsatiation, any bundle on segment CD of the original budget line would be preferred to bundle A. But this is impossible because bundle A is the original utility-maximizing bundle. Thus, we know that given the higher price of good 1 and the compensatory income M_1, this consumer will choose a bundle on segment JA of the compensated budget line. Because the quantity of good 1 in these bundles *does not exceed* x_1^*, we also know that the substitution effect in this instance is *nonpositively related* to the price change. In other words, given the compensated budget line, the quantity demanded of good 1 will not increase. Instead, it will either remain the same or decrease.

Now let us suppose that the compensatory income is something less than M_1, say M_2 in Figure 3.13. This lower compensatory income gives rise to the lower compensated budget line KGH. By simply revising the argument above, we can establish that — given the higher price of good 1 and compensatory income M_2 — the consumer will now pick a bundle on segment KG of the compensated budget line. Because the quantity of good 1 in all these bundles is *strictly less than* x_1^*, we know that the substitution effect in this instance is *negatively* related to the price change.

In sum, we now know that the substitution effect cannot be positively related to the price change:

The substitution effect is nonpositively related to the price change.

The Compensated Demand Function

In the preceding analysis, we held p_2 constant while allowing p_1 to vary. We also adjusted the consumer's income up or down so that he or she remained on the same indifference curve. And for each value of p_1, we identified the quantity of good 1 in the consumer's utility-maximizing bundle. If we now plot these price-quantity pairs, **compensated** we have what is called a **compensated demand curve**. The adjective *compensated* **demand curve** indicates that the consumer has been given the compensatory income needed to keep him or her on the original indifference curve.

In Figure 3.14a, we have held p_2 constant at \$2 and considered three different values of p_1 — \$1, \$2, and \$4. This lets us identify the corresponding points of tangency between the three compensated budget lines and the indifference curve I. These points are labelled A, B, and C in Figure 3.14a, and the corresponding points A', B', and C' on the compensated demand curve are plotted in Figure 3.14b. For instance, when p_1 is \$1 in Figure 3.14a, the compensated budget line is tangent to the indifference curve I at bundle A, which contains 16 units of good 1. Therefore, point A' in Figure 3.14b is one point on the compensated demand curve. Similarly, when p_1 is \$2 (or \$4), the compensated budget line is tangent to I at bundle B (or bundle C), which gives rise to point B' (or C') on the compensated demand curve.

Since the compensated demand curve reflects *only* the substitution effect, it cannot be upward sloping. That is, when p_1 increases, quantity demanded on the compensated demand curve will ordinarily decrease, and it cannot increase. Thus, our intuition that demand functions are downward sloping is correct for compensated demand functions.[8]

In the following problem, you will see that the substitution effect is not always negative — that it can be zero — and you will have the opportunity to construct a compensated demand curve.

---

8 Notice that to find the compensated demand function, in essence, we solved a cost-minimization problem by minimizing the cost of attaining a specified indifference curve; that is, we implicitly solved

$$\text{minimize } (p_1 x_2 + p_2 x_2) \text{ by choice of } x_1 \text{ and } x_2$$

$$\text{subject to the constraint } U(x_1, x_2) = u$$

where u is a fixed utility number. (The Lagrange multiplier method can be used to solve this problem.) The solution gives us x_1 and x_2 as functions of p_1, p_2, and u. Symbolically,

$$x_1 = H_1(p_1, p_2, u)$$

$$x_2 = H_2(p_1, p_2, u)$$

The functions H_1 and H_2 are the compensated demand functions. We have shown that the partial derivative of $H_1(p_1, p_2, u)$ with respect to p_1 is nonpositive.

FIGURE 3.14 **The compensated demand curve**

In (a), the three compensated budget lines, which are associated with three prices for good 1, are tangent to indifference curve I at points A, B, and C. These points of tangency are used to construct the compensated demand curve in (b). For example, when p_1 is \$4, the compensated budget line is tangent at bundle C, which contains 8 units of good 1; therefore, one point on the compensated demand curve is point C', where 8 units are demanded at price $p_1 = \$4$.

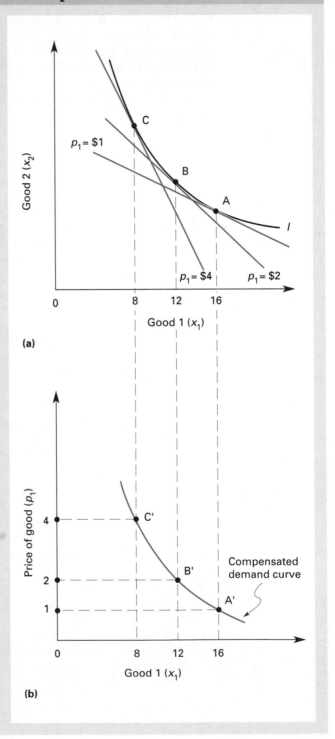

PROBLEM 3.10

Suppose we have the following utility function: $U(x_1,x_2) = \min(x_1,x_2)$. Initially, both prices are $1, and income is $30. Find the utility-maximizing bundle. Now let p_1 increase to $2. What is the compensatory income? Show that the substitution effect is zero. Construct the compensated demand curve for good 1. Now use your answer to Problem 3.2 to find the ordinary demand curve for good 1, given $p_2 = 1$ and $M = 30$, and plot both demand curves on the same diagram.

We now have two demand curves: the ordinary demand curve, which arises from the consumer's real choice problem, and the compensated demand curve, which arises from the fictional choice problem in which the consumer is given a different income — the compensatory income — every time the good's price changes. In the remainder of the book, when we use the term *demand curve*, we will mean the ordinary demand curve. When we talk about the compensated demand curve, we will always add the adjective *compensated* to distinguish it from the ordinary demand curve.

3.11

Complements and Substitutes

Now let us turn to the last comparative statics question: how will consumer demand for a good change in response to a change in the price of some other good? For example, how does a consumer's demand for Pepsi change when the price of Coke changes? More generally, how does x_1^* respond to a change in p_2, holding p_1 and M constant?

Two possibilities are shown in Figure 3.15. When p_2 is $1, the consumer chooses the bundle containing 6 units of good 1 at point A in both Figures 3.15a and 3.15b. Now, what happens when p_2 rises to $2? The higher price for good 2 causes the budget line to pivot around point F, shifting it from GAF to HCF. Because of the increase in p_2, the quantity demanded of good 1 *decreases* to 4 in Figure 3.15a, but it *increases* to 8 in Figure 3.15b. In other words, the consumer's response depends on the consumer's preferences. When p_2 increases, the consumer may decide to buy either more or less of good 1. Both possibilities are consistent with utility-maximizing behavior.

What have we learned? Although our theory gives us no qualitative result, it does provide us with a useful taxonomy. If x_1^* decreases in response to an increase in p_2 as in Figure 3.15a, we say that good 2 is a **complement** for good 1. Movies and popcorn, computers and software, and tennis balls and tennis rackets are all examples of complements. When the price of a movie goes up, a consumer might decide to go to fewer movies and therefore buy less popcorn. The utility function $U(x_1,x_2) = \min(x_1,x_2)$ — a function you explored in Problems 3.2 and 3.10 — illustrates the case of *perfect complementarity*. Right skis and left skis, for instance, are perfect complements since you do not decide to buy one ski without buying the other.

On the other hand, if x_1^* increases in response to an increase in p_2 as Figure 3.15b, we say that good 2 is a **substitute** for good 1. Coke and Pepsi, coffee and tea, or Volvos and BMWs might be thought of as substitutes. The utility function $U(x_1,x_2) = x_1 + x_2$ — the function we used in Chapter 2 to capture Amy's preferences — illustrates the case of *perfect substitutability*. As you know, when p_1 is equal to p_2, these preferences imply that any bundle on the budget line is a utility-maximizing bundle. However, if p_2 decreases ever so slightly, the consumption of good 1 goes to zero. For example, if the price of one brand of soft drink rises by just a bit, a consumer will switch to a substitute brand — if they are perfect substitutes and if the consumer is initially indifferent between them.

FIGURE 3.15 The consumption response to a change in the price of another good

In (a), the quantity demanded of good 1 decreases from 6 to 4 as the price of good 2 increases from $1 to $2. In this case, good 2 is said to be a complement for good 1. In (b), the quantity demanded of good 1 increases from 6 to 8 as the price of good 2 increases from $1 to $2. In this case, good 2 is said to be a substitute for good 1.

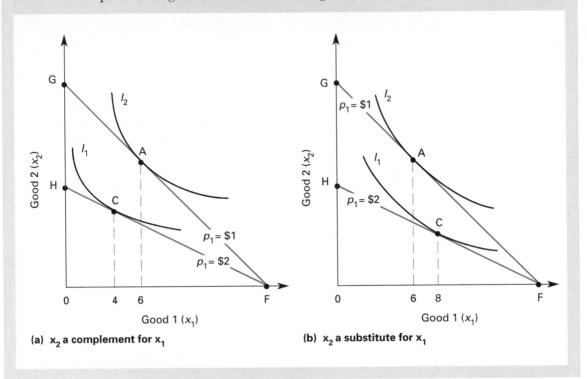

(a) x_2 a complement for x_1

(b) x_2 a substitute for x_1

Some Cross-Price Elasticities of Demand

cross-price elasticity of demand

If we want to measure the response in quantity demanded of one good with respect to a change in the price of another good, we can calculate a cross-price elasticity of demand. The **cross-price elasticity of demand** for good 1 with respect to the price of good 2 is the elasticity of per-capita consumption of good 1 with respect to p_2. Using aggregate data for North America and Europe, DeVoretz and Sylvanes (1993) calculate the cross-price elasticity of demand for fresh salmon with respect to the price of frozen salmon to be 1.12. The fact that this elasticity is positive means that frozen salmon is a substitute for fresh salmon: the higher the price of frozen salmon, the larger the quantity demanded of fresh salmon. Furthermore, a 1% increase in the price of frozen salmon will result in a 1.12% increase in the per capita demand for fresh salmon.

From time to time, cross-price elasticities of demand have played a role in anti-monopoly court cases. For example, in the 1950s Du Pont was charged with monopolizing the market for cellophane production in the United States. Du Pont countered the charge by arguing that the relevant market was not the narrowly defined market for cellophane (where it was a monopolist) but the more broadly defined market for so-called flexible packaging materials (where its market share was roughly 18%). In support of its argument it pointed to a very high cross-price elasticity of demand between cellophane and other flexible packaging materials such as waxed paper. The Supreme

Court ruled in favor of Du Pont, saying that "it seems to us that Du Pont should not be found to monopolize cellophane when that product has the competition and interchangeability with other wrappings…." (*U.S. Reports* 1956, 400)

3.12

Composite Commodities

Throughout this chapter, we have focused on consumer choice problems in which there are just *two goods*. As you have undoubtedly realized, very few real choice problems involve just two goods. In the course of a day, each of us uses dozens of different goods, and in the course of a year we buy and use hundreds or even thousands of different goods. How can the analysis of this chapter shed light on these real choice problems?

Perhaps surprisingly, for many problems the analytical tools we have developed for the two-good choice case are sufficient for analyzing much more complex choice problems. To see why, let us focus on a particular consumer's demand for just one good — Allison's demand for gasoline. Allison buys gasoline for her car, which she uses to get around town. Of course, to use the car she has to buy other complementary products like lubricating oil and tires. Her car is not, however, Allison's only available means of transportation. She often takes the bus and, less frequently, a taxi. To use the analytical tools from the two-good choice problem to analyze Allison's demand for gasoline, we will lump together all goods other than gasoline into a **composite commodity**. Lubricating oil, tires, bus and taxi rides, and all the goods other than gasoline that Allison buys are contained in this composite commodity. To analyze her demand for gasoline, we will then look at her choice of a consumption bundle composed of two goods: gasoline (good 1) and this composite commodity (good 2).

composite commodity

We can measure the quantity of gasoline in these consumption bundles in gallons. Since the composite commodity is just the amount Allison spends on all goods other than gasoline, we can measure the quantity of the composite commodity — Allison's expenditure on all other goods — in dollars. A consumption bundle is then just (x_1, x_2), where x_1 is gallons of gasoline and x_2 is expenditure on all other goods. Allison's budget line is

$$p_1 x_1 + x_2 = M$$

Here M is Allison's income and p_1 is the price of gasoline. Because the composite commodity is measured in dollars, its price is just $1 per unit. We see that, as far the budget line is concerned, the only new twist in this analysis is that the price of good 2— the composite commodity—is 1.

Similarly, as far as Allison's consumption preferences are concerned, there is also just one new twist. As you will see, however, this new element is more subtle. If Allison's preferences for these bundles composed of gallons of gasoline and expenditure on all other goods satisfy the completeness, two-term consistency, transitivity, and continuity assumptions, then we know from Chapter 2 that Allison has a well-defined preference ordering over such bundles. She has continuous indifference curves in the (x_1, x_2) space; and her preference ordering can be represented by a utility function $U(x_1, x_2)$. Clearly, then, we can use the tools developed in this chapter to analyze Allison's choice of how much gasoline to buy (that is, her demand for gasoline) and how much to spend on all other goods. The new element in this analysis concerns the prices of the goods included in the composite commodity. Because Allison's preference ordering for these bundles changes as the prices of the goods in the composite commodity change, these prices must be held constant.

To see why prices of these goods affect Allison's preference ordering, let us try a simple thought experiment. First, imagine that on Sunday evening we ask Allison to reveal her preference ordering for consumption bundles containing gallons of gasoline and expenditure on all other goods. Suppose that Allison tells us that she prefers bundle (50,1000) containing 50 gallons of gasoline and $1000 to spend on all other goods, to bundle (10,1200) containing 10 gallons of gasoline and $1200 to spend on all other goods. Now imagine that on Monday morning a series of unanticipated and radical price changes hit the headlines. The prices of lubricating oil and tires have jumped by 1900%; the price of a bus ride has fallen from $2.00 to $0; and the price of a taxi ride has dropped from $10 to $0.50. After Allison has read about these price changes on Monday evening, we once again ask her to reveal her preference ordering for bundles containing gasoline and dollars spent on all other goods. Will she still prefer bundle (50,1000) to bundle (10,1200)? More generally, will Monday evening's preference ordering be the same as Sunday evening's? Almost certainly not. After these radical price changes, it is very likely that she will prefer bundle (10,1200) to bundle (50,1000). After all, the prices of the goods that are complementary to gasoline (lubricating oil and tires) have skyrocketed and the prices of substitute means of transportation (buses and taxis) have plummeted. Therefore it is no longer attractive for Allison to use her car to get around town relative to taking a bus or a taxi. In fact, she may choose to not to drive her car at all and rely instead on buses and taxis for transportation. If she does give up driving her car, gasoline is of no use to her, and on Monday evening she will definitely prefer bundle (10,1200) to bundle (50,1000).

We see that we can legitimately use a composite commodity to reduce complex choice problems to relatively simple problems that can be solved graphically using the tools developed in this chapter for the two-good case. Indeed, we will do so repeatedly in the following chapters. We must recognize, however, that when we use a composite commodity, we are implicitly assuming that the prices of all the goods included in the composite commodity are held constant.[9]

Two General Properties of Demand Functions

It is clear that the precise form of a particular consumer's demand functions will be determined by his or her preferences. For example, regardless of the values of the exogenous variables in the utility-maximizing problem, a dedicated nonsmoker will not buy cigarettes. Yet we can easily derive two general propositions about the properties of demand functions.

No Money Illusion

no money illusion

One important property of demand functions — **no money illusion** — is easy to establish. Suppose that all the exogenous variables in a demand function change proportionately. For instance, suppose that both prices and the budget increase by a factor of 2. How will the individual consumer respond to this change in the exogenous variables? Let us consider the two budget lines

$$p_1x_1 + p_2x_2 = M$$

$$2p_1x_1 + 2p_2x_2 = 2M$$

---

9 Hicks (1939) and Leontief (1936) were the first economists to use composite commodities rigorously.

Notice that the slopes of these two budget lines are identical. This reflects the fact that when we double both prices, the opportunity cost of one good in terms of the other does not change. Notice, too, that both budget lines intersect the x_2 axis at the same point — M/p_2 — and both intersect the x_1 axis at the same point — M/p_1. This reflects the fact that when prices and income double, the consumer's purchasing power does not change. In other words, these two budget lines are coincident or identical. (You may want to choose specific values for the exogenous variables and actually plot these two budget lines.)

Because the budget lines are identical, the solutions to the utility-maximizing problems are also identical. In other words, the individual's consumption decisions *will not change* in response to a proportional increase in all prices and income because neither the opportunity cost of one good in terms of the other nor the consumer's purchasing power have changed. We can write this result more precisely:[10]

Select arbitrary values for the exogenous variables p_1, p_2, and M, and then multiply these values by some positive constant $a > 0$ to determine a new set of values $ap_1, ap_2,$ and aM. The quantities demanded of both goods at these two sets of prices and incomes are identical; that is,

$$D_1(p_1, p_2, M) = D_1(ap_1, ap_2, aM)$$

$$D_2(p_1, p_2, M) = D_2(ap_1, ap_2, aM)$$

The importance of this simple result is that it tells us the types of functions that can and cannot be demand functions. For example, the demand functions you derived in Problem 3.2,

$$x_1^* = M/(p_1 + p_2) \text{ and } x_2^* = M/(p_1 + p_2)$$

are consistent with the no-money-illusion result since

$$M/(p_1 + p_2) = aM/(ap_1 + ap_2)$$

PROBLEM 3.11

Which of the following functions are and are not consistent with no money illusion?

1. $x_1^* = M/p_1$

2. $x_1^* = Mp_2/p_1$

3. $x_2^* = M/(p_1 p_2)^{1/2}$

4. $x_2^* = 1 + p_1 - 5p_2 + M/20$

---

[10] In mathematical terminology, we have learned that demand functions are *homogeneous of degree zero* in prices and income.

Engel's Aggregation Law

The observation that a consumer will spend his or her whole budget allows us to derive another important restriction. In this case, the restriction applies not to demand functions individually but to the entire system of demand functions. We know that the utility-maximizing bundle is on the budget line, or that

$$p_1 x_1^* + p_2 x_2^* = M$$

**Engel's
Aggregation
Law**

Rewriting this expression gives us the following proposition, known as **Engel's Aggregation Law**:

A system of demand functions must satisfy the property that the sum of prices multiplied by quantities demanded equals income:

$$p_1 D_1(p_1, p_2, M) + p_2 D_2(p_1, p_2, M) = M$$

Engel's aggregation law is just a formal way of saying that people spend what they spend. Like the no-money-illusion result, it imposes a strong restriction on acceptable systems of demand functions. To see the kinds of demand systems that Engel's aggregation law does and does not permit, consider the following problem.

PROBLEM 3.12

Which of the following cannot be systems of demand functions? That is, which of these systems do not satisfy Engel's aggregation law? For each system of equations, simply ask: Does $p_1 x_1^* + p_2 x_2^*$ equal M?

1. $x_1^* = M/3p_1$, $x_2^* = 2M/3p_2$

2. $x_1^* = M/5p_1$, $x_2^* = 3M/4p_2$

3. $x_1^* = M/2 + p_2 - p_1$, $x_2^* = M/2 + p_1 - p_2$

SUMMARY

We began this chapter by considering the *constraints* — wealth, time, and human resources — on individual decision making. We also noted how complex rational decision making can be, because the individual's economic decisions are inherently intertemporal and because they inevitably involve imperfect information. To analyze decision making in this complex world, we created an ideal case; we defined a choice problem involving just *one period*, *perfect information*, and *two goods*.

We then looked at the consumer's *constrained-choice problem* in this static framework. Given the prices of consumption goods and the consumer's income, the solution — a *system of demand functions* — yields the utility-maximizing quantities of those goods.

We then graphically solved a range of choice problems, beginning with the demand for *essential* and *inessential goods*. A consumer will always buy some amount of an essential good, regardless of how high its price is. By contrast, a consumer will not necessarily buy a positive amount of an inessential good; if the price is high enough, he or she will choose not to buy any. This distinction helps us to understand why most individuals choose not to buy many — perhaps most — of the goods available in advanced economies.

Next, we characterized *normal* and *inferior goods* in terms of the consumer's demand response to a change in income. As income goes up, the consumption of a normal good also increases, but the consumption of an inferior good declines.

We then explored the relationship between a good's own price and the quantity demanded of that good, which we called the (ordinary) *demand curve*. Surprisingly, the demand curve can be upward sloping (in the theoretically possible case of Giffen goods) or downward sloping (in the standard case for all other goods). The fact that we lack a label for the standard case, in which the consumption of a good goes down when its price goes up, reflects how pervasive this case seems to be.

To understand why the *Giffen good* is theoretically possible, we decomposed the quantity response to a price change into income and substitution effects. We found — just as intuition suggests — that the substitution effect for all goods and the income effect for normal goods are negatively related to the price change. However, the income effect for inferior goods is positively related to the price change. Giffen goods are therefore inferior goods for which a positive income effect dominates a negative substitution effect. We then introduced a new demand curve, the *compensated demand curve*, which — because it incorporates only the substitution effect — can never be upward sloping.

Next we looked at how demand for one good changes in response to a change in the price of some other good. We called goods *complements* when consumption moves up or down in tandem (right shoes and left shoes) and *substitutes* when an increase in consumption of one good is paired with a decline in consumption of another (chocolate mousse and lemon meringue pie). More precisely, good 2 is a complement (or a substitute) for good 1 if quantity demanded of good 1 decreases (or increases) as the price of good 2 increases. In all of these comparative statics applications, we used the concept of *elasticity* to measure and compare the response of quantity demanded to changes in the values of exogenous variables in the demand function.

We then discussed the *composite commodity theorem*, which allows us to reduce complex choice problems with many endogenous variables to relatively simple problems that can be solved graphically.

Finally, we discovered two important general properties that act as restrictions on demand functions. First, one important property of individual demand functions is known as *no money illusion*. For instance, if all prices and income double, the consumer's real situation is unaltered. Consequently, his or her utility-maximizing choices do not change. Second, the entire system of demand functions must satisfy *Engel's aggregation law*. This law is simply a reflection of the truism, "We spend what we spend." These restrictions are of significant practical use to economists who use data to estimate demand functions.

A major thrust of this chapter has been to create a set of useful analytical tools for exploring consumer choice problems. In the next chapter, we will put these newly developed tools to work as we analyze a number of varied and interesting problems.

EXERCISES

1. A normal good at one level of income need not be a normal good for all levels of income. To see why not, draw an Engel curve that initially rises and subsequently falls as income increases. Then construct an indifference map that would generate the Engel curve you drew. Begin by constructing the income-consumption path corresponding to this Engel curve.

2. Consumption bundles (10,20) and (15,40) are both on the income-consumption path. What, if anything, can you say about the *MRS* at these two bundles? Illustrate your answer.

3. Rita's indifference curves are smooth and convex. Given prices $p_1 = \$2$ and $p_2 = \$4$, Rita buys consumption bundle (100,50).

   a. If p_1 increases to $3 and Rita's income increases by $100, can you tell if she will be better off or worse off?

   b. If p_1 increases to $3 and Rita's income increases by $97, can you tell whether she will be better off or worse off?

4. Good 1 is not a Giffen good, and bundles (10,23) and (15,40) are both on the price-consumption path that is generated by changing p_1. What, if anything, can you say about the *MRS* at these two bundles? Illustrate your answer with a carefully drawn graph.

5. Nancy spends all her income on good 1 and good 2, and her income-consumption path is downward sloping. Is it possible that both goods are normal? That both are inferior? That good 1 is normal? That good 1 is inferior? That one of these goods is inferior and the other normal?

6. Smiling Jack's utility function is

   $$U(x_1,x_2) = x_2(1 + x_1)$$

   a. Carefully plot the indifference curve that passes through the bundle (2,1).

   b. Is good 1 essential or inessential? What about good 2?

7. Ted lives in a two-good world. He always spends 40% of his income on good 1 and 60% on good 2.

   a. What are his demand functions?

   b. Suppose that both prices are $1, and construct Ted's income-consumption path and the Engel curves for both goods.

8. Suppose that the *MRS* of good 2 for good 1 depends only on the quantity of good 1. What is the relationship between quantity demanded of good 1 and income? What is the income elasticity of demand for good 1? (You may want to review your answers to Exercises 6 and 8 at the end of Chapter 2.)

9. Nancy spends all her income on good 1 and good 2. As p_1 increases while p_2 remains fixed, Nancy's price-consumption path is horizontal.

   a. How does Nancy's expenditure on good 1 respond to changes in p_1?

   b. Show that Nancy's demand for good 1 is proportional to $1/p_1$.

   c. Is good 1 a complement or a substitute for good 2?

   d. What is Nancy's price elasticity of demand for good 1?

10. It is sometimes argued that demand for medical services is perfectly inelastic with respect to the price of medical services. By considering the limitations imposed by a finite income, show that no demand curve can be perfectly inelastic for all prices.

11. Ronald spends all his income on good 1 and good 2, and good 1 is *not* a Giffen good. As p_1 increases while p_2 remains fixed, Ronald's price-consumption path is downward sloping.

    a. What can you say about the price elasticity of demand for good 1?

    b. Is good 1 a complement or a substitute for good 2?

*12. Brett's *MRS* is given by the following function:

   $$MRS = x_2/x_1$$

   What are Brett's demand functions? Is either good inferior? Is either good a Giffen good? Is either good inessential?

13. Norma spends all her income on good 1 and good 2 and her income-consumption path is upward sloping.

    a. What if anything can you say about the demand response for good 1 and good 2 to an increase in income?

    b. Is it possible that good 1 is a Giffen good?

14. Mr. Lucky intends to spend a recent inheritance of $1,000 over the next two periods. He has no other source of income. Let x_1 and x_2 be two composite commodities: expenditure on consumption in this period and in the next period. Suppose that the rate of interest that Mr. Lucky can get on his savings is 25%; that is, for every $1 invested in this period, he will have $1.25 in the next period. What is Mr. Lucky's budget line? That is, what combinations of x_1 and x_2 does his inheritance allow him to have? What is the opportunity cost of consumption in the first (second) period in terms of foregone consumption in the second (first) period?

15. Mr. Lucky's cousin Not-So is broke, but his grandmother has left him an inheritance of $1250 in trust. Let x_1 and x_2 be two composite commodities: expenditure on consumption in this and the next period. The terms of the trust specify that he cannot have the money until the

next period, but his banker will lend him money at a 25% interest rate (thereby frustrating his grandmother's intentions). For every $1 borrowed today, Not-So must pay back $1.25 tomorrow. What is Not-So's budget line? How does it compare with Mr. Lucky's?

*16. "The demand for any good tends to be more elastic with respect to price in the long run than in the short run." Explain why this statement might be true, and name some goods to which you think the statement applies.

*17. Consider the following scheme devised by the parent of an overweight child to reduce the child's consumption of candy bars. The parent offers to sell candy bars to the child at their market price of $1 plus a parental tax of $0.50 per candy bar. To induce the child to cooperate, the parent offers to increase the child's allowance by A dollars. If the child accepts the deal, he or she agrees not to buy candy from anyone else. Draw a diagram in which you identify the minimum value of A that will induce the child to cooperate. Assuming that the parent does increase the child's allowance by that amount and that the child accepts the offer, will the child's consumption of candy bars decrease? Will the amount of tax the parent collects from the child be as large as the increase in the child's allowance?

*18. Suppose that the indifference curves between x_1 and x_2 are concave (as opposed to convex) to the origin. Show that the point on the budget line where $MRS(x_1,x_2)$ is equal to p_1/p_2 is not a solution to the utility-maximizing problem. What points on the budget line are preferred to this point? Show that utility maximization implies that the consumer will spend all of his or her income on good 1 or good 2.

*19. Show that a utility-maximizing consumer will never choose a consumption bundle (in which both quantities are positive) on a nonconvex portion of an indifference curve.

*20. The following utility function, in which F is pounds of food and T is yards of textiles, is an example of *hierarchical preferences*:

$$U(F,T) = \begin{cases} F & \text{if } F \le 100 \\ T & \text{if } F > 100 \end{cases}$$

a. Suppose income M is $100 and the price of textiles p_T is $1. Find the demand functions for both goods as the price of food p_F varies. Hint: show that when p_F is larger than $1, this consumer will buy only food, and that when p_F is less than $1, he or she will buy exactly 100 pounds of food.

b. Find the two demand functions for arbitrary values of M, p_F, and p_T.

REFERENCES

Baltagi, B. H. and J. M. Griffin. 1983. "Gasoline Demand in the OECD," *European Economic Review*, 22:117–37.

DeVoretz, D. J. and K. G. Salvanes. 1993. "Market Structure for Farmed Salmon," *American Journal of Agricultural Economics*, 75:227–33.

Hicks, J. R. 1939. *Value and Capital*, London: The Clarendon Press.

Hicks, J. R., and R. G. D. Allen. 1934. "A Reconsideration of the Theory of Value: Parts I and II," *Economica*, 1:52–75, 196–219.

Houthakker, H. S. 1951. "Some Calculations on Electricity Consumption in Great Britain," *Journal of the Royal Statistical Society*, Series A, No. 114 Pt. III, 351–71.

Leonteif, W. W. 1936. "Composite Commodities and the Problem of Index Numbers," *Econometrica*, 4:39–59.

Lewit, E. M. and D. Coate 1982. "The Potential for Using Excise Taxes to Reduce Smoking," *Journal of Health Economics*, 1:545–70.

Simon, H. 1987. "Behavioral Economics" and "Bounded Rationality," in *The New Palgrave: A Dictionary of Economics*, J. Eatwell, M. Milgate, and P. Newman (eds.), London: The Macmillan Press.

Slutsky, E. 1915. "Sulla theoria del bilancio del consumatore," *Giornale degli economisti e rivista di statistica*, 51:1–26. English translation: "On the Theory of the Budget of the Consumer," in *Readings in Price Theory*, G. J. Stigler and K. E. Boulding (eds.), Homewood, Ill.: Richard D. Irwin, 27–56.

Wasserman, J. 1988. *Excise Taxes, Regulation, and the Demand for Cigarettes*, Santa Monica, California: The Rand Corporation.

CHAPTER 4

Vicarious Problem Solving: Applications of the Theory of Choice

In Chapter 3, we first defined the choice-making problem from the consumer's perspective and then tried to anticipate how each consumer would solve that problem. The analysis created in Chapter 3 is thus meant to do what Thomas Schelling calls *vicarious problem solving*:

> If we know what problem a person is trying to solve, and if we think he can actually solve it, and if we can solve it too, we can anticipate what our subject will do by putting ourself in his place and solving his problem as we think he sees it. This is the method of "vicarious problem solving" that underlies most of microeconomics. (1978, 18)

As we try our hand at vicarious problem solving in this chapter, the central question is just how much territory we can cover — that is, how wide-ranging our theory of consumer choice will prove to be. The time has come, as the Walrus said, to talk of many things. Not of shoes and ships and sealing wax, perhaps, but of Polaroid cameras and private clubs, ski holiday packages, racquetball court assignments, and more.

4.1
Lump-Sum Versus Excise Taxes

One issue that is bound to induce heated discussion anywhere is the question of taxation. Can our analytical tools help us to shed some light on this highly charged subject? The basic issue — given that governments are going to dip their hands into private pockets to pay for public services — is what sort of taxation scheme would the taxpayer prefer? In other words, given that someone must pay a particular sum of money to the government, what sort of tax institution would leave him or her better off?

Excise Tax Versus Lump-Sum Tax

excise tax

lump-sum tax

We will compare two taxes: an **excise tax** and a **lump-sum tax**. An excise tax is one in which a given tax surcharge is added to the price of each unit of a particular good. Excise taxes on gasoline, liquor, and perfume are common examples. By contrast, a lump-sum tax is a fixed tax liability. Under this scheme, a government simply demands that an individual remit a certain sum. For example, the Conservative government in Britain first introduced and then was forced to review a highly controversial tax that has many of the features of a lump-sum tax — the Community Service Tax.

Imagine, then, that a government wants to raise a specified sum of money by imposing either a lump-sum tax or an excise tax on some good — gasoline, for example. From the taxpayer's point of view, which is preferable? The first thing to notice is that an excise tax increases the *opportunity cost* of the taxed good to the consumer. By contrast, a lump-sum tax alters the *budget* available to the individual.

Let us suppose that good 1 is gasoline and that an excise tax on gasoline has been imposed. Because we will be using the composite commodity theorem to simplify the problem, good 2 will be a composite commodity or good (expenditure on all other goods). Since good 2 is expenditure, it is measured in dollars (or pounds or yen) and its price is therefore $1.

Let us begin by considering a consumer — Ms. C — before any tax is imposed. Her pretax budget line is the dashed line ACG in Figure 4.1, where x_1 is quantity of gasoline and x_2 is quantity of the composite good.

Now let us impose an excise tax t per unit of gasoline. Ms. C's budget line is now the solid line ADH. We know from Chapter 3 that the new budget line is represented graphically by a line rotated downward from the point at which the pretax budget line intersects the x_2 axis. In other words, the same budget is still available (indicated by the intersection of both budget lines at the same point on the x_2 axis), but the price (inclusive

FIGURE 4.1   Excise versus lump-sum taxes

Given the excise tax budget line ADH, the utility-maximizing bundle is point D, and the tax revenue is equal to distance DC. A lump-sum tax that yields the same tax revenue gives rise to the flatter lump-sum tax budget line BDEF. Given this budget line, the individual will choose some point on segment DE on a higher indifference curve. The lump-sum tax is therefore preferred to the excise tax even though both taxes yield the same tax revenue.

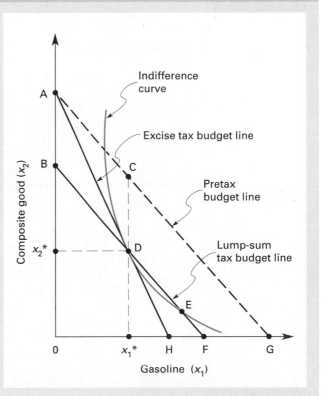

of the excise tax) of gasoline is higher once an excise tax is in effect (indicated by the steeper pitch of the new budget line).

Once the excise tax is in place, Ms. C chooses the consumption bundle at point D in Figure 4.1. The tax take, or the amount of tax the government collects, is just tx_1^* because x_1^* is the amount of gasoline Ms. C buys and t is the tax per unit of gasoline. Let us identify the tax take graphically. In the absence of the excise tax, Ms. C could have bought the bundle at point C on the pretax budget line. The tax take is therefore equal to the distance DC.

Now, what about the alternative scheme, in which a lump-sum tax yields the same revenue, distance DC in Figure 4.1? Once the lump-sum tax is imposed, Ms. C's budget constraint is the solid line BDEF in Figure 4.1. The new budget line is below, but parallel to, the pretax budget line since Ms. C's income — but not the prices she pays — has changed. Notice that the lump-sum tax budget line passes through point D. Why? In the absence of any tax, the bundle at point C is attainable and, since the lump-sum tax is equal to distance DC, the bundle at D is attainable after the lump-sum tax has been deducted from her income.

Although Ms. C could buy the bundle at D, she will choose instead some bundle on segment DE of the lump-sum budget line because this segment lies above and to the right of the indifference curve in Figure 4.1. By nonsatiation, any point on segment DE is preferred to the bundle at D. Of course, this means that Ms. C. is better off with the lump-sum tax than she is with the excise tax. In other words, a lump-sum tax is the preferable form of taxation:

Given a choice between a lump-sum tax and an excise tax that raise the same revenue, the consumer will choose the lump-sum tax.

In this analysis, we have implicitly assumed that Ms. C's indifference curves are convex and smooth and that she buys a positive amount of gasoline. For her, the substitution effect is therefore non-zero. Yet, in Section 3.10, we saw that when indifference curves are kinked, the substitution effect may be zero. Is the lump-sum tax still preferred when the substitution effect is zero? To find out, try the following problem.

> **PROBLEM 4.1**
>
> Suppose that Kinky's preferences can be represented by the following utility function: $U(x_1,x_2) = \min(x_1,x_2)$. As you discovered in Problem 3.10, the substitution effect is zero for this utility function. Show that Kinky will be indifferent between an excise tax and a lump-sum tax that raise equal revenue.

At the outset of this section, we were careful to discuss the question of the preferred form of taxation in the context of a single person, Ms. C. To extend the result directly to a larger group of taxpayers in a municipality, province, state, or nation, however, we would have to assume that the group is composed of taxpayers whose individual preferences and income are all *identical*. Yet taxpayers in any particular jurisdiction are not so much alike. We therefore must be cautious in applying these principles of taxation to real situations. Imagine, for example, the choice between a lump-sum tax and an excise tax on cigarettes that raise the same revenue in a jurisdiction where half the taxpayers are smokers and half are non-smokers. The heavy smokers will clearly prefer the lump-sum tax and the non-smokers will prefer the excise tax.

An Application to the Theory of Clubs

representative
consumer

Nevertheless, we can identify certain groups in which the assumption of a **representative consumer** — the assumption that the preferences and income of an individual randomly selected from the group will be characteristic of each person in that group — is likely to be more nearly true. Private clubs, for example, cater primarily to people who seek the same amenities and can all afford the membership fee. Because club members can, in a rough way, be viewed as self-selecting according to certain preferences and income levels, any individual club member we select is likely to be representative of the whole membership.

Let us broaden the meaning of taxation to apply to any circumstances in which sums are taken out of someone's pocket and used to fund some project of a group to which that person belongs. If the project is a private club, then what is the preferred way for such a club to assess its membership fees? Of course, this is a comparative institutional question about the taxing arrangements that are preferable from the perspective of the club members. In Problem 4.2, you can adapt what you have learned about the relative desirability of excise and lump-sum taxes to discover what that preferred arrangement will be.

PROBLEM 4.2

Suppose that a private dining club, composed of 100 members with identical preferences, incurs an overhead cost of $100,000 each year and that the cost of each meal is $50. (If the club sells one meal in a year, for example, its total costs are $100,050; if it sells five meals, its total costs are $100,250.) The club is considering two possible fee structures designed to generate just enough revenue to cover its costs. Its first option is to charge members a fixed price p_1 per meal. Let x_1^* denote the number of meals per year that each member buys at price p_1. If the club is to cover costs, it must choose p_1 so that $100x_1^*(p_1 - 50) = \$100,000$ or so that $x_1^*(p_1 - 50) = \$1,000$. The club's second option is to charge each person a membership fee equal to $1,000 and then to sell meals at a price of $50 per meal. Show that from the point of view of the club members, the second option is preferred to the first if indifference curves are smooth and convex. Hint: $p_1 - \$50$ is analogous to an excise tax on club meals, and the $1,000 membership fee is analogous to a lump-sum tax.

Many private clubs actually use fee structures like the one chosen by the hypothetical club in Problem 4.2 by selling a membership fee that just covers their overhead and then selling their services at marginal cost. That membership fee is analogous to a lump-sum tax.

Government Subsidies

Governments not only take money out of people's pockets. In some cases, they put money in through a variety of subsidy schemes. In Canada, for instance, lower-income parents are given monthly family allowance checks, the size of which depends on the number of children in the family. In the United States, many schoolchildren receive lunches subsidized by the government. So, too, in the United States, the tax deductibility of mortgage interest payments is a significant subsidy to home buyers. Welfare payments, public-housing projects, and many other programs are examples of government subsidies in North America, the U.K., Europe, Australia, and elsewhere. Any such subsidy is, in effect, just a tax whose value is negative. As you will discover in Exercise 2 at the end of this chapter, the sort of analysis we have just done for taxes also applies to subsidies — and the outcome is similar. Given a choice between a lump-sum subsidy and a per-unit subsidy on some good, which costs the government the same amount, the consumer will prefer the lump-sum subsidy.

4.2

Measuring Benefits and Costs

As we indicated in Section 1.6, cost-benefit analysis is a very important tool in any economic policy maker's tool kit. But how can we measure the benefits and costs to individuals arising from a particular policy or institution? We will begin by asking a specific question: What value does Mr. Polo, a potential member of an exclusive dining club, place on the right to be a member of the club? More precisely, what is the value to him of the right to buy meals in the club at some specified price p_1?

If we can devise adequate benefit measures for this specific problem, we can then adapt those measures to a range of similar benefit questions. In the context of a proposed rural electrification project, for instance, we could measure the value a farmer places on the right to buy electricity at some specified price. And we can adapt these measures to gauge costs as well as benefits. For example, we could measure the cost to an individual smoker of the now very large excise tax on cigarettes.

We will make the realistic assumption that "meals at the club" is an inessential good and begin the analysis by identifying Mr. Polo's equilibrium in two circumstances. In the first situation, he is not a member and therefore does not buy meals at the club. In the second situation, he is a club member and can buy meals at price p_1. In Figure 4.2, x_1 is the number of meals he eats at the club and x_2 is his expenditure on all other goods. Because in the first situation Mr. Polo is not a member, he spends his entire income M on the composite good. The initial equilibrium is therefore M units up the vertical axis at E_0 on indifference curve I_0. In the second situation, however, he can buy club meals at price p_1, and his budget line is the solid line E_0E_1 in Figure 4.2. The subsequent equilibrium is at E_1 on indifference curve I_1. In essence, our problem is to measure the value that Mr. Polo places on the move from indifference curve I_0 to indifference curve I_1. Furthermore, we want to measure this value in dollars or, equivalently, in units of the composite good.

Equivalent Variation for a New Good

equivalent
variation

By taking the subsequent indifference curve I_1 as our point of reference, we get a measure called the **equivalent variation** and labeled EV in Figure 4.2. This measure answers the following question: What is the *variation* in income that is *equivalent* to the right to buy club meals at price p_1? The answer is distance EV in Figure 4.2. Why? Because if Mr. Polo had EV of additional income instead of a club membership, he would still be on the subsequent indifference curve I_1. In other words, that additional income is *equivalent* to the right to buy club meals.

Compensating Variation for a New Good

compensating
variation

On the other hand, by taking the initial indifference curve I_0 as our point of reference, we get a measure called the **compensating variation** labeled CV in Figure 4.2.

FIGURE 4.2 Measuring the benefit of a new good

Mr. Polo's initial equilibrium, when he is not a club member, is at E_0 on indifference curve I_0. His subsequent equilibrium, when he is a member, is at E_1 on the higher indifference curve I_1. What is the value of club membership to Mr. Polo? The *variation* in income that is *equivalent* to club membership is distance EV since, given that he is not a member, this additional income would put him on indifference curve I_1. The *variation* in income that *compensates* for club membership is distance CV since, given that he is a member, if his income was reduced by CV, he would be on indifference curve I_0.

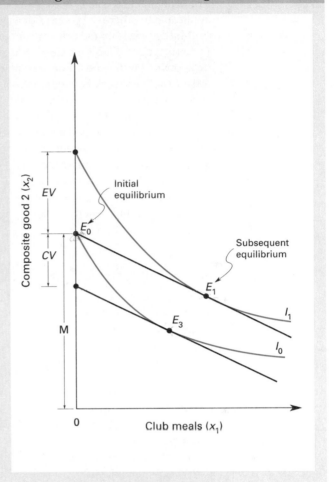

This measure answers the following question: What *variation* in income *compensates* for the right to buy club meals at price p_1? The answer is distance CV. Why? Because if Mr. Polo had a club membership but his income had been reduced by \$CV, he would still be on the initial indifference I_0 at point E_3. In other words, the reduction in income exactly *compensates* for the right to buy club meals.

Another interpretation of CV is useful. Since \$CV exactly compensates for the right to buy meals in the club, it is the *maximum price* that Mr. Polo will pay for meal privileges. Therefore, if he is offered meal privileges for any price less than \$CV, he will buy them — and end up on an indifference curve higher than I_0. We will use this interpretation in Section 4.3 where we consider the demand for consumer capital.

PROBLEM 4.3

Show that as p_1 increases, CV for a new good decreases. In other words, show that the larger is p_1, the smaller is the maximum amount a consumer will pay for the right to buy good 1 at price p_1.

So far, we have been focusing on measures of the benefit associated with the introduction of a specific new good, meals at a private club. These measures are obviously applicable to other new goods. For example, what value would someone in the town of Lethbridge place on the privilege of being able to listen to a symphony orchestra based in Lethbridge? These measures are also applicable to the costs associated with the disappearance of goods. For example, what value would a New Yorker place on the loss of the New York Yankees baseball team to Dallas, Texas? We could easily adapt these concepts to measure the resulting costs borne by a New York resident as well as the benefits enjoyed by a Dallas resident.

Many interesting policies and institutions, however, involve not the introduction of a new good, but a change in the price of some existing good. For example, every time the government raises the excise tax on cigarettes, a smoker faces a higher price for smoking. Every time your university increases tuition fees, you face a higher price for your education. Let us adapt the equivalent and compensating variations to measure the costs and benefits of such price changes.

FIGURE 4.3   Measuring the cost of a price change

The initial equilibrium, associated with the lower price of good 1, is at E_0 on indifference curve I_0. The subsequent equilibrium, associated with the higher price of good 1, is at E_1 on the lower indifference curve I_1. The *variation* in income that is *equivalent* to the price increase is distance EV since, given the lower price, this reduction in income would put the consumer on indifference curve I_1. The *variation* in income that *compensates* for the price increase is distance CV since, given the higher price, if income was increased by CV, the consumer would be on indifference curve I_0.

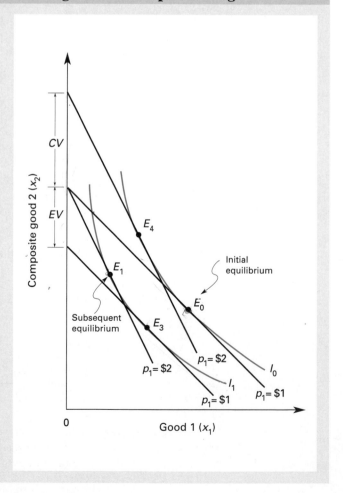

Let us begin with a price increase, and again suppose that good 2 is a composite good. In Figure 4.3, p_1 is initially \$1 and the initial equilibrium is at E_0 on indifference curve I_0. The price of good 1 then rises to \$2, and the subsequent equilibrium is at E_1 on indifference curve I_1.

Equivalent Variation for a Price Change

To identify the equivalent variation of this price change, we will use the subsequent indifference curve I_1 as a point of reference and ask: What variation in income is equivalent to the price increase? In other words, holding p_1 constant at its initial value of \$1, what variation in income is equivalent to the price increase? The answer is distance EV in Figure 4.3. If this consumer has to give up \$$EV$ of income but can still buy good 1 at the initial price of \$1, he or she will remain on indifference curve I_1. In other words, a decrease in income of \$$EV$ is equivalent to a price increase from \$1 to \$2.

Compensating Variation for a Price Change

To identify the compensating variation of this price change, we will use the initial indifference curve I_0 as a point of reference and ask: What variation in income compensates for the price increase? In other words, holding p_1 constant at its subsequent value of \$2, what variation in income compensates for the price increase? The answer is distance CV in Figure 4.3. Even though the price of good 1 has increased from \$1 to \$2, if this consumer's income is increased by \$CV, he or she will remain on indifference curve I_0 at E_4. In other words, a \$CV increase in income compensates for the price increase.

Comparing Equivalent Variation and Compensating Variation

Curiously, in Figure 4.3 the equivalent variation associated with the price increase is smaller than the compensating variation. This raises an important question: Are these two measures *ever* the same? They are when the good in question is neither normal nor inferior and the quantity demanded is therefore independent of income. (You considered preferences of this sort in Problem 3.7.) In Figure 4.4 we have repeated the exercise from Figure 4.3. The difference is that good 1 in Figure 4.4 is neither normal nor inferior. As a result, the vertical distance between the two indifference curves is constant. Therefore, distance E_3E_0 is equal to distance E_1E_4. But distance E_3E_0 is equal to EV and distance E_1E_4 is equal to CV. We see, then, that EV is equal to CV in Figure 4.4.

There is another way to look at Figure 4.4. Since the indifference curves are vertically parallel, MRS is constant along any vertical line in this figure. But this implies that quantity demanded of good 1 is independent of income. When quantity demanded of good 1 is independent of income, we say that there are *no income effects* for good 1. We can summarize these results:

When good 1 is neither normal nor inferior — that is, when there are no income effects for good 1 — EV is identical to CV.

In Problem 4.4, you can find the equivalent and compensating variations for a price decrease. However, do keep two observations in mind: 1. The indifference curve attained in the subsequent situation is the point of reference for the equivalent variation. 2. The indifference curve attained in the initial situation is the point of reference for the compensating variation.

FIGURE 4.4 The case in which *CV* equals *EV*

The initial equilibrium, associated with the lower price of good 1, is at E_0 on indifference curve I_0. The subsequent equilibrium, associated with the higher price of good 1, is at E_1 on the lower indifference curve I_1. Because good 1 in neither normal nor inferior, the vertical distance from one indifference curve to the other is always the same. Consequently, *CV* is equal to *EV*.

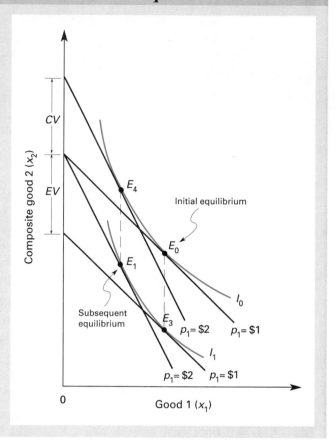

PROBLEM 4.4

In Figure 4.3, suppose that the initial price is $2 and the subsequent price is $1. The initial equilibrium is therefore at E_1 and the subsequent equilibrium at E_0. What is the equivalent variation of this price reduction? What is the compensating variation?

Consumer's Surplus

consumer's surplus

The *CV* and *EV* benefit measures share one major drawback: to use either of them, we must know what a consumer's preferences look like. A more practical measure of benefit, known as **consumer's surplus** (*CS*), can be calculated simply by observing what consumers actually buy and then estimating their demand functions from their consumption behavior.[1]

How can we use *CS* to measure the value to Mr. Polo of the privilege of buying meals at price p_1 at his private club? Mr. Polo's demand curve for club meals is shown in Figure 4.5. At price p_1, the price at which meals are actually sold in the club, Mr. Polo buys six meals per period. Now suppose that we interpret the prices along this demand curve

---

1 Hicks (1943) provides a thorough graphic analysis of consumer's surplus.

as the value Mr. Polo places on successive meals. He values the first meal at $300, the second at $280, and so on. Notice that even though Mr. Polo values the first meal at $300, he pays only p_1 for it. He therefore receives a surplus of ($300 − p_1) on that first meal. His surplus on the second meal is ($280 − p_1), and so on. Mr. Polo's total surplus on the six meals that he actually buys at p_1 — his CS — is therefore the shaded area in Figure 4.5.

We can also use CS to measure the benefit of a price reduction or the cost of a price increase. In Figure 4.6, for example, the shaded area can be interpreted either as the benefit to the consumer of a price reduction from $15 to $10 or as the cost borne by the consumer of a price increase from $10 to $15.

Because the only information needed to calculate CS is an individual's demand curve for the good in question, CS is more practical as a benefit measure. But is it a good measure compared with CV and EV, which have more solid theoretical foundations? Interestingly:

When good 1 is neither normal nor inferior,
or when there are no income effects for good 1, then

$$EV = CV = CS$$

FIGURE 4.5   Consumer's surplus for a new good

The consumer's surplus (CS) measure of the benefit of the right to buy good 1 at price p_1, instead of being unable to buy it at any price, is the shaded area.

surplus 300-p₁ on 1st meal
280-p₁ on 2nd meal

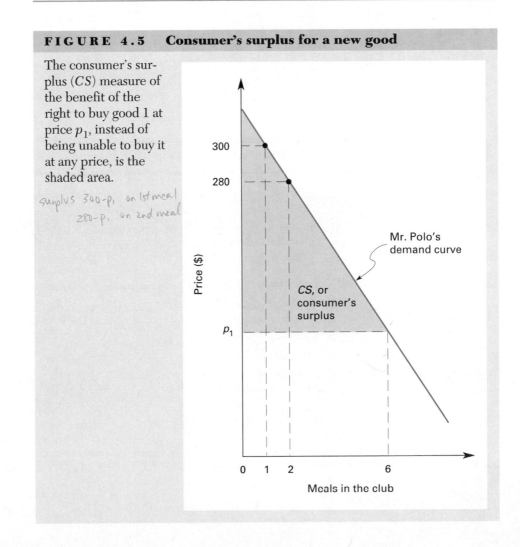

FIGURE 4.6 Consumer's surplus for a price reduction

The consumer's surplus (CS) measure of the benefit of the right to buy good 1 at price $p_1 = \$10$, instead of price $p_1 = \$15$, is the shaded area.

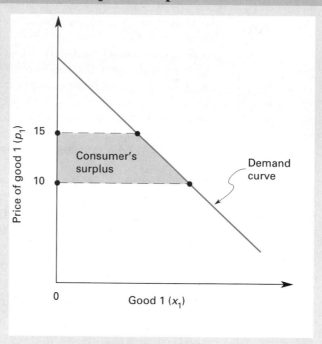

When we use the consumer's surplus measure at various points in the following chapters, we will assume that demand for the good in question is independent of income or, equivalently, that the good is neither normal nor inferior.[2]

PROBLEM 4.5

Suppose that for Ms. J the demand for good 1 is independent of income and is given by the following demand curve:

$$p_1 = 100 - 2x_1$$

What is the benefit to her of a decrease in the price of good 1 from $60 to $40? If good 1 is initially unavailable, what is the benefit to Ms. J if it is subsequently available at $p_1 = \$50$?

---

2 Although preferences do not always, or even usually, display this very convenient property, Willig (1976) provides a convincing argument that even when they do not, CS remains a useful measure of individual benefit when the portion of income spent on the good in question is small.

The Demand for Consumer Capital

consumer
capital

Let us now turn our attention to the vast array of decisions that people make about buying **consumer capital**: the very significant class of goods valued for the services they yield. We buy beds, chairs, and television sets for what they allow us to do: sit, sleep, and watch TV. We buy refrigerators to get refrigeration, telephones to get telephone service, and personal computers to do word processing and play video games.

Notice that the items themselves have only *indirect value*. Few of us find a refrigerator intrinsically appealing; we simply use it to keep our meat and milk cold. Some of us are nearly phobic about flying; nevertheless, we still buy plane tickets as a means to an end — say, a holiday in Puerta Vallarta or Cannes. Consumer capital, then, is valued only *indirectly*, as a necessary means of producing a valued service or good. Notice, too, that producing a desired service from consumer capital often means buying *complementary*, or interdependent, goods. We buy both cars and gasoline to get transportation; both televisions and electricity to get TV programming; both a printer and computer paper to get computer printouts; and both skis and lift tickets to go skiing. As economists, our problem is to determine the conditions under which a consumer will decide to buy a particular item of consumer capital. In other words, we want to analyze the demand for consumer capital.

Imagine that an economist is trying to derive the demand for cameras. The economist might begin with two observations. First, cameras are items of consumer capital because the buyer values not cameras but photographs. Second, producing photographs involves a complementary because the photographer must buy both a camera and some film.

Because our potential purchaser, whom we will call Buff, directly values photographs, but not film or cameras, we will need to write her utility function as $U(x_1, x_2)$, where x_1 is the quantity of photographs and x_2 is a composite good. We will assume for convenience that one unit of film will produce one photograph. Therefore, the number of photos produced will be equal to the quantity of film, and we can then interpret x_1 as either the number of photos or as the amount of film.

Buff's budget constraint in this consumer-capital framework is novel. It is

$$p_1 x_1 + x_2 = M - n p_c$$

where p_1 is the price of film, x_1 the quantity of film (or photographs), n the number of cameras bought, and p_c the price of a camera. The constraint simply says that expenditure on film and the composite good $(p_1 x_1 + x_2)$ is equal to Buff's total income less the expenditure on cameras $(M - n p_c)$.

To further simplify things, let us assume that Buff can produce all the photographs she wants with just one camera and that she cannot rent a camera. Then, it is clear that she will buy either one camera or none. Furthermore, if she does not buy a camera, she cannot produce any photos. Our problem is to discover when she will buy a camera and how the price of the camera, p_c, and the price of film, p_1, affect her decision making.

In Figure 4.7, we can easily deduce that if Buff does not buy a camera, she will end up at point G, with no photos and M units of the composite good, since if she has no camera, she will not buy any film, and she will therefore spend her entire income $\$M$ on the composite good. On the other hand, if she does buy a camera, she will choose the bundle on the budget line that maximizes her utility. These observations reveal the general principles that determine whether Buff will buy a camera or not. If her

FIGURE 4.7   Consumer capital and the budget line

If she has no camera, Buff will choose point G. If she has a camera, she will choose a point on the budget line.

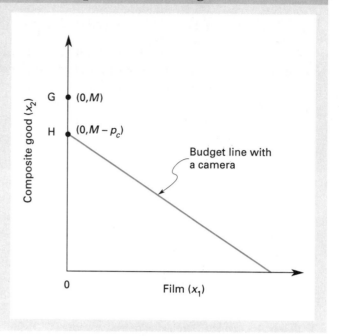

utility at point G is larger than her utility from the utility-maximizing bundle on the budget line, Buff will not buy a camera. If it is smaller, she will. If we make the seemingly reasonable assumption that photos are an inessential good, we can restate this principle: If the indifference curve through point G lies above the budget line, she will not buy a camera, but if it intersects the budget line, she will buy one.

Now we can use Figure 4.8 to discover how the price of a camera influences Buff's decision. The indifference curve is pivotal because it passes through point G. If the

FIGURE 4.8   The demand for consumer capital

If the price of a camera is low enough, p'_c in this figure, Buff will buy a camera and end up somewhere on segment DE of the "low price for camera" budget line. If the price of the camera is high enough, p''_c in this figure, she will not buy a camera and will end up at point G on indifference curve I.

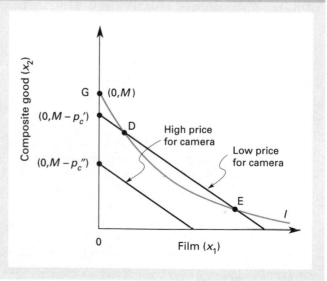

price of the camera is too high — p_c'' in Figure 4.8 — then the relevant budget line lies everywhere below the indifference curve, and Buff will choose not to buy a camera. But if the price of a camera is not too high — p_c' in Figure 4.8 — then the relevant budget line intersects the indifference curve and Buff will decide to buy a camera.

Let us be more precise about the relationship between the price of and the demand for a camera. Draw a budget line in Figure 4.8 parallel to the existing budget lines and just tangent to the indifference curve. Use p_c^r to denote the price of a camera defined by this budget line. Of course, p_c^r is equal to the distance from the point at which the budget line you drew intersects the x_2 axis to point G. We know that Buff will not buy a camera if its price is greater than p_c^r and that she will but a camera if its price is less than or equal to p_c^r. (We have arbitrarily assumed that when $p_c = p_c^r$, Buff will buy a camera, even though she is actually indifferent between buying or not buying it.) The price p_c^r — clearly the critical one — is a **reservation price**. If the price of a camera exceeds Buff's reservation price, she will not buy it. If it is less than or equal to her reservation price, she will.

Because owning a camera effectively confers the privilege of buying photographs (film) at price p_1, we see that p_c^r is the *maximum price* that Buff is willing to pay for the right to buy photographs at price p_1. In this context, you can then see that the reservation price is just our old friend CV, the compensating variation. That is, p_c^r is the reduction in income that exactly compensates for the privilege of buying photographs at price p_1.

Since p_c^r is simply Buff's CV, we know from Problem 4.3 that it is inversely related to p_1. In Figure 4.9, the line RR', which gives the reservation price for the camera associated with any price of film, is therefore downward sloping. If the market prices for film and a camera are in the green area above this downward-sloping line, Buff will not buy a camera. If prices are on or below the line in the gray area, she will buy a camera.

reservation
price

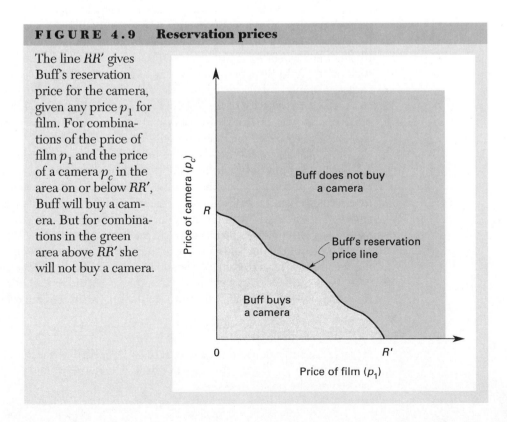

FIGURE 4.9   Reservation prices

The line RR' gives Buff's reservation price for the camera, given any price p_1 for film. For combinations of the price of film p_1 and the price of a camera p_c in the area on or below RR', Buff will buy a camera. But for combinations in the green area above RR' she will not buy a camera.

Price of camera (p_c)

Buff does not buy a camera

Buff's reservation price line

R

Buff buys a camera

0 R'

Price of film (p_1)

A great many consumer decisions conform to the structure of our camera and photographs problem. Most decisions about consumer durables — items such as VCRs, personal computers, electric crêpe makers, water beds, or backpacks — can be interpreted in this framework. Other, less obvious consumer choice decisions can also be understood in this way. For example, suppose you are considering a ski holiday in Cortina, Italy. You can interpret p_c as the cost of airfare to Italy, p_1 as the price per day of accommodation and lift tickets, and x_1 as the number of days on the mountain.

✴ 4.4

Two-Part Tariffs

two-part tariff

Knowing something about the demand for consumer capital should tell us something about the other side of the coin: the pricing policy of firms. In particular, if a firm could exploit the interdependent demand between the complementary items needed to produce a directly valued good, what pricing strategy would it follow? Walter Oi, a pioneer in the study of what are usually called **two-part tariff** questions, was curious about this pricing problem. Specifically, Oi (1971) asked how executives of Disneyland would exploit their monopoly power in setting the price of admission to the park and the prices of each of the amusements inside the gates: "If you were the owner of Disneyland, should you charge high lump-sum admission fees and give the rides away, or should you let people into the amusement park for nothing and stick them with high monopolistic prices for the rides?" (77). Insofar as the Disneyland executives want to extract the largest possible profit in choosing the two sets of tariffs, or prices, they face a fairly tricky pricing problem.

The Polaroid Land Corporation faced a similar pricing dilemma in the 1950s. The introduction of the Polaroid camera gave birth to a new commodity, the "instant photograph." At that time, the corporation had a monopoly on both the camera and the film it used. Because the demand for its camera and its film were so clearly interdependent, the Polaroid Corporation's pricing predicament was closely analogous to the pricing dilemma faced by the owners of Disneyland. Should the corporation attach a high price tag to the camera and essentially give the film away, or should it sell the camera cheaply and charge a high price for the film? Here, the Disneyland entry fee is analogous to the price of the Polaroid camera. We can think of the price of the camera as an entry fee into the world of instant photographs and the price per exposure as analogous to the price per amusement ride.

We can learn a great deal about this pricing problem by adopting three assumptions. The first assumption is quite realistic: instant photographs are inessential. And so is the second: all the photographs desired can be taken with one camera. The third is a representative-consumer assumption: Polaroid's potential customers all have preferences and income identical to Buff's in the preceding section. This last assumption allows us to focus on Polaroid's profit from just one consumer, Buff.

What combination of the price of the camera, p_c, and the price of film, p_1, will maximize the profit Polaroid Corporation can exact from Buff? Specifically, let us suppose that Polaroid's cost of producing a camera is $5 and its cost of producing a unit of film is $1. Polaroid's profit from Buff can then be written in the following way:

$$\text{profit} = x_1^*(p_1 - 1) + n^*(p_c - 5)$$

Here, n^* is Buff's demand for cameras (0 or 1), and x_1^* is her demand for film, given the two prices p_1 and p_c. Because the firm will choose p_1 and p_c so that n^* is 1, we can rewrite the profit function as

$$\text{profit} = x^*_1(p_1 - 1) + (p_c - 5)$$

If we assume for simplicity that Buff's demand for instant photos is independent of her income, we can then solve this profit-maximization problem easily. Buff's demand curve for instant photos is presented in Figure 4.10. Let us start by supposing that Polaroid charges $3 for its film. Given this price, if Buff had a camera, she would buy 5 units of film. Polaroid's profit on the film would be $10 = 5($3 − $1), or the gray area in Figure 4.10. Given p_1 = $3, Polaroid will clearly decide to price its camera at Buff's reservation price. Yet, from Section 4.2, we know that because Buff's demand for instant photos is independent of her income, her reservation price for the camera is simply the consumer surplus associated with p_1 = $3. If Polaroid decides to sell its film at $3, it will then sell its camera at price p_c^r, represented by the green area in Figure 4.10. Its profit will then be equal to the sum of the two shaded areas in Figure 4.10, minus the cost of producing the camera, $5.

But Polaroid can do better than that. As you can easily verify, as long as the price of film exceeds $1 — the cost of producing a unit of film — Polaroid can increase its profit by decreasing the price of its film and correspondingly increasing the price of its camera to reflect Buff's increasing reservation price. When p_1 is equal to $1, Polaroid's profit from its film is zero [15($1 − $1)], but the profit from its camera is the area of triangle GAF in Figure 4.10 minus the $5 cost of producing the camera. In Problem 4.6,

FIGURE 4.10   The Polaroid pricing problem

If Polaroid sells its film at price p_1 = $3, it will sell its camera at price p_c^r, equal to the green area, because Buff's reservation price for the camera is identical to her consumer surplus from instant photographs. Polaroid's total profit in this case is the green area, plus the gray area, less the $5 cost of producing the camera. As long as p_1 exceeds $1 (the cost of producing a unit of film), its profit increases as p_1 decreases. Therefore, to maximize profit,

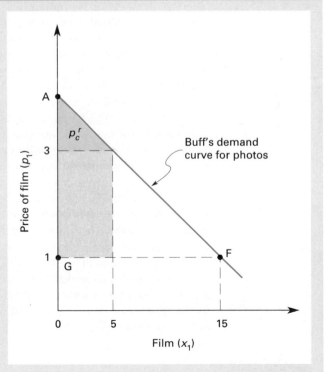

Polaroid should sell film at cost (p_1 = $1) and the camera at a price equal to the triangular area GAF.

you will see that Polaroid's profit decreases as it lowers the price of film below $1. To summarize these results:

The firm's profit-maximizing strategy is to sell film at cost and to charge the corresponding reservation price for the camera. [3]

PROBLEM 4.6

Consider any p_1 less than $1, and the associated reservation price for the camera. Show that profit is smaller than it is when Polaroid sells its film at $1 and its camera at area GAF.

We now have a positive prediction about Polaroid's profit-maximizing strategy: it will sell its film at cost and will charge the corresponding reservation price for the camera. What was the Polaroid Corporation's actual pricing policy? A Polaroid camera in 1955 cost approximately $1100 in 1990 U.S. dollars — surely an order of magnitude greater than the cost of producing the camera. Because it had a monopoly in selling instant cameras and instant film, Polaroid could exploit the obvious interdependence in the demand for cameras and film. Its dual monopoly position permitted it to extract aggregate profits in excess of the aggregate profits that independent monopolists in film and (separately) in cameras could have managed.

We cannot examine here the robustness of this pricing model with respect to the obviously restrictive assumption that consumers are identical. However, the model does seem to generate some insight into Polaroid's actual pricing behavior. By analogy, we can generalize from the model to illuminate any pricing strategy that conforms to the two-part-tariff pricing structure. For example, using the two-part-tariff model, we can analyze the pricing strategies chosen by the owners of Disneyland; by computer companies selling hardware and software; and by copy-machine companies selling machines and all the fluid, paper, and other paraphernalia that go with them. Telephone companies, cable TV companies, and utility companies all use similar pricing structures: a hook-up fee and a separate fee based on use. (If you have rented an apartment and paid for your own utilities, you have probably encountered this sort of strategy.) Unlike Polaroid, Disneyland, and copy-machine companies; telephone, cable, and utility companies are regulated, and their ability to extract profit is therefore constrained. Nevertheless, they do choose to use two-part tariffs.

Our model may also help to shed light on other pricing phenomena. For example, as we noted in the preceding section, the demand for ski holidays at Cortina, Italy, and air transport to Italy are interrelated in precisely the same way as the demand for Polaroid cameras and film. Of course, neither ski resorts nor airlines can independently exploit this interrelationship in demand. Enter travel agencies that sell package deals: one of their roles in economic life seems to be to exploit the profit potential arising from this demand interdependence. You can probably think of other firms that aim at exploiting such demand interdependency.

---

3 See Schmalensee (1982) for a more complete analysis of this type of pricing problem.

The Demand for Leisure and the Supply of Labor

Although we remarked at the outset of Chapter 3 that choosing how to distribute our time among all the available alternatives is a fundamental decision, so far we have omitted *time* from our formulation of the consumer-choice problem. Let us remedy that oversight by reformulating the choice problem to include the element of time.

Work, Leisure, and Income

As we saw in Section 2.4, one useful way of conceptualizing the problem is to imagine that we choose to divide our time between work and leisure. That is, we divide our time between activities that do and do not earn income. Let T be time available in some period, h be hours of work, and x_1 be hours of leisure. Because the hours of work and at leisure must add up to total time, the **time constraint** (analogous to the budget constraint) is

time constraint

$$h + x_1 = T$$

How we choose to divide our time between work and leisure obviously determines our work-generated income; that is, the time at work multiplied by the wage rate determines earned income. Here we are assuming (somewhat unrealistically) that a particular person — called Jan — can choose her hours of work. Letting w be the wage rate at which Jan can sell her labor and assuming that she has A dollars of income from other sources, we can write Jan's income as $A + wh$. We will assume that Jan spends her income on a composite good, x_2.

Now let us express Jan's preferences in terms of two goods, leisure x_1 and quantity of the composite good x_2. Her choice problem is then to maximize $U(x_1, x_2)$ by choice of x_1, x_2, and h, subject to the time constraint $h + x_1 = T$, and subject to the budget constraint $x_2 = A + wh$. This choice problem is more complicated than the problems we have looked at so far because Jan is faced with not two but three choices and because she is also faced with not one but two constraints.

To simplify the problem, we will combine the constraints by eliminating h. Notice that the time constraint can be rewritten as $h = T - x_1$. Combining this equation with the budget constraint yields $x_2 = A + w(T - x_1)$. In other words, Jan's expenditure on the composite good is simply her nonwork income A plus her wage rate w multiplied by her hours of work, $T - x_1$. Rearranging this combined constraint, we get

$$wx_1 + x_2 = A + wT$$

price of leisure

full income

Notice that we can interpret w as the **price of leisure** and $A + wT$ as potential or **full income**. We can think of Jan, then, as spending her full income $(A + wT)$ on leisure and consumption.

We have reduced Jan's choice problem to this: maximize $U(x_1, x_2)$ by choice of x_1 and x_2, subject to the combined constraint. Because in this problem Jan faces just two choices and one constraint, we can use familiar techniques to solve it. The solution is shown in Figure 4.11. Jan demands x_1^* hours of leisure and spends x_2^* on consumption goods.

Notice that we have also derived Jan's supply of labor. Because the time she devotes to work and leisure is equal to total time available $(h + x_1 = T)$, her supply of labor

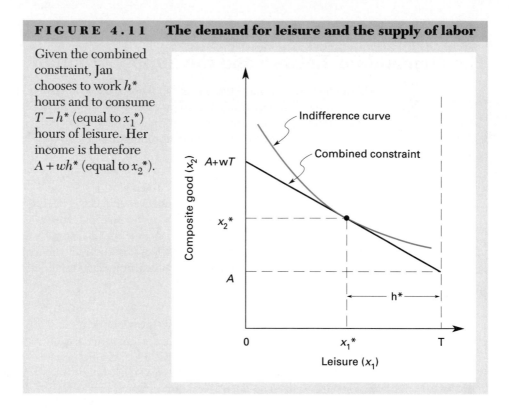

FIGURE 4.11 **The demand for leisure and the supply of labor**

Given the combined constraint, Jan chooses to work h^* hours and to consume $T - h^*$ (equal to x_1^*) hours of leisure. Her income is therefore $A + wh^*$ (equal to x_2^*).

is $h^* = T - x_1^*$. This particular view of labor supply will play a central role in analyzing labor markets in Chapter 13.

PROBLEM 4.7

Historically, as wages rates have increased in western societies, the work week has declined. A hundred years ago in the United States, for instance, the average work week was more than 70 hours. Today it is less than 40. Using the framework just developed, diagram the case in which the quantity of labor supplied decreases as the wage rate increases. In this case, is leisure a normal or an inferior good?

Time and Money Prices

Usually, consumption and leisure are interrelated activities. Leisure activities, for example, often require the expenditure of income: green fees for golfing, the cost of specialized equipment for backpacking, or the price of a ticket for a concert. Conversely, consumption requires the expenditure of time: it takes time to shop for clothes, see a movie, or buy and use a personal computer. This observation led Gary Becker (1965) to formulate the consumer choice problem in an enlightening way by including in the

full price   **full price** of a good both a *time price* and a *money price*.

Let us explore Becker's formulation by considering the case in which consumption requires both time and money. Let p_1 and p_2 be money prices and z_1 and z_2 be time prices for goods 1 and 2. Consuming one unit of good 1, for example, requires p_1 units of money and z_1 units of time. The consumer's choice problem again involves two constraints: the budget constraint,

$$p_1 x_1 + p_2 x_2 = A + wh$$

and the time constraint,

$$z_1 x_1 + z_2 x_2 + h = T$$

Once again, we can combine the two constraints. From the time constraint, we have $h = T - z_1 x_1 - z_2 x_2$. The time devoted to work is simply the total time available T minus the time devoted to consumption. When we combine this with the budget constraint, we have

$$p_1 x_1 + p_2 x_2 = A + wT - wz_1 x_1 - wz_2 x_2$$

We can rearrange this combined constraint to get

$$(p_1 + wz_1)x_1 + (p_2 + wz_2)x_2 = A + wT$$

Here too we can interpret $A + wT$ as potential or full income, and — this is the crucial point — we can interpret $p_1 + wz_1$ as the full price of good 1 and $p_2 + wz_1$ as the full price of good 2.

Let us summarize what have we learned. Because consumption takes time, the opportunity cost of time must be included in the *full price* of any good. The opportunity cost of time is the amount required to consume a unit of a good multiplied by the value of time, the wage rate w. To fully understand consumption decisions, we must take into account the opportunity cost of time. In the next section, we will see just how significant a role this insight can play.

The Tragedy of the Commons

Many interesting economic problems involve the use (and potential overuse) of a limited resource by those who have access to that resource. A limited resource is one that can accommodate only a certain level of use before its utility, or value, is effectively extinguished. Only so many swimmers can comfortably swim laps in a pool and only so many sun lovers can happily sunbathe on a beach before overcrowding takes all the fun out of these activities. And only so many drivers can converge on Manhattan before gridlock sets in.

common-property problems

As we saw in Chapter 1, economists often speak of such problems collectively under the label **common-property problems**. They sometimes call the overexploitation of a common-property resource "the tragedy of the commons," after an article of the same name by biologist Garrett Hardin (1968). In this article, Hardin compares the problem of uncontrolled population growth to the historical problem of the overgrazing of the pastures held in common by villagers in England and in colonial New England. Hardin predicted that just as individual farmers continued to add one cow and then another to the commons until the pasture land was devastated by overgrazing, human beings, too, might well produce one child and then another until the resources of the world were completely overtaxed by a population too large to be sustained by the earth's limited capacity.

Hardin mentions several other activities that could result in the tragedy of the commons: the cattle owner's overgrazing on U.S. national forestry lands; the insistence of maritime nations on upholding the so-called freedom of the seas; a New England city council's decision to provide free downtown parking during the Christmas-shopping rush; and the "fouling of our own nest [because we are putting] sewage, or chemical, radioactive, and heat wastes into water: noxious and dangerous fumes into the air: and distracting and unpleasant advertising signs into the line of sight" (1245).

Racquetball and the Tragedy of the Commons

Let us look at a familiar common-property problem. At community centers, private clubs, and universities around the world, racquetball court time is often allocated on a first come, first served basis. Sometimes the scheme works well. At Yale University a few years ago, for example, courts were usually available at any time of the day: court time was not a scarce good.

A problem arises, however, in places where there are many ardent racquetball players and limited court space. When we last visited the University of Colorado, for example, we were told to sign up in person sometime after 7 A.M. on Wednesday to reserve a court for Thursday. "Tragically," we actually had to show up considerably before 7 A.M. because a lineup began to form about 6 A.M. At the Jewish Community Centre in Vancouver, British Columbia, allocation of court time was a slightly more civilized affair. We could book a court for Thursday by phoning the center after 9 A.M. on Wednesday. Still, to guarantee ourselves a court, we had to start dialing at 9 A.M. in the expectation of getting through by 9:30 A.M. The first come, first served allocation mechanism — whatever form it might take — makes signing up for court time a common-property problem.

First Come, First Served Allocation

What can we learn about the implications of this allocation mechanism by applying the tools we have developed? Let us imagine a situation in which 200 avid players have common access to a racquetball court facility, perhaps because they are students at a particular university. We will use a representative-player assumption to simplify the analysis — that is, we will suppose that these players have identical preferences and that they value their time at $10 per hour. To make the problem very specific, we will assume that the racquetball facility has the capacity to accept 3,000 bookings a month and that the duration of a booking is one hour. The facility can therefore accommodate up to 15 bookings per player per month ($15 \times 200 = 3,000$). The value of the time spent playing racquetball by one player is then $10 per booking. Suppose, too, that the players have free access to the courts — they need not pay a fee for booking court time.

We will adapt the approach developed in the preceding section by letting x_1 be the number of bookings the player makes per month and x_2 be the now-familiar composite good, and by supposing that nonwork income is zero. If access to the courts really is free, the player's choice problem is to maximize $U(x_1, x_2)$, by choice of x_1 and x_2, subject to the constraint,

$$10x_1 + x_2 = 10T.$$

Although access may be free, we must account for the value of time spent on the court. Thus, the implicit price of each booking is the value of an hour of time, $10. The constraint then says that the value of the time spent on the court each period, $10x_1$, added to the value of the composite good, x_2, must add up to full income, $10T$.

In the solution to this problem, if each player demands a relatively small number of bookings, say 10, then the total number of bookings demanded each month,

2,000 = 10 × 200, will be less than the facility's capacity, 3,000, and everyone can be accommodated without difficulty. But what happens when the demand for court time is greater than the facility's capacity? What happens, for example, when each player demands 20 bookings per month, so that total demand, 4,000 = 20 × 200, exceeds capacity, 3,000?

Just what occurs in this circumstance will be determined by the booking scheme used by our imaginary university. If players have to show up in person to book, excess demand implies that lineups will form before the appointed hour. If players have to phone for a booking, excess demand implies that they will be forced to spend time on the telephone trying to get through. In this case, the amount of time actually spent on the phone will be random: some will be lucky and get through on the first try; others will be unlucky and spend a significant amount of time dialing.

Under either booking procedure, however, access to bookings is not really free even though the university does not charge for the use of its courts. The time required to make a booking — which we can regard as the time price of making a booking — will increase until the excess demand is eliminated; that is, until the total number of bookings demanded is just 3,000 or until each player demands exactly 15 bookings per month (since 15 × 200 = 3,000).

How do we confirm that an equilibrium will be reached when the time price is just large enough that demand for bookings is equal to the fixed supply? We need to look at the individual player's choice problem once the implicit price per booking includes both the time required to make a booking and the time actually spent on the court. Let q represent the time necessary to make a booking. The total time spent per booking is $(1 + q)$, since the game itself takes an hour to play and since it takes q hours to make a booking. The total time price per booking is then $\$10(1 + q)$, and the revised constraint for the player's choice problem is then:

$$10(1 + q)x_1 + x_2 = 10T$$

In Figure 4.12, we have illustrated the solution to the player's choice problem when q is large enough that each player demands 15 bookings. The total number of bookings demanded is therefore 3,000, and the excess demand has been eliminated. The player's equilibrium is at point A on the indifference curve. To identify graphically the value to the individual player of the time spent acquiring a booking, we have also included the constraint that would arise if q were equal to zero — the dashed line in Figure 4.12. The value of the time spent in the lineup each month is then the distance AB.

Institutional Mechanisms for Allocation

Notice that when there is excess demand, it is time in the lineup that discourages players from attempting to use the facility so frequently and thereby establishes an equilibrium between demand and supply. Yet, as we know from the foregoing section, time is a valuable resource. The "tragedy" of spending time in the lineup needlessly uses up this valuable resource. That is, spending time to acquire bookings is avoidable. It is the consequence of using a first come, first served institution for allocating bookings.

There *are* other institutional arrangements that are clearly better. For instance, imagine substituting a money price for the time price. Specifically, suppose that the university charged a dollar price equal to $10q$ for each booking. Then the player's constraint would still be $10(1 + q)x_1 + x_2 = 10T$ (since we have just substituted an equivalent money price for a time price) and the player's equilibrium would still be at point A in Figure 4.12. Notice that there would then be no excess demand for bookings since each player again demands 15 per month. This price institution produces an equilibrium

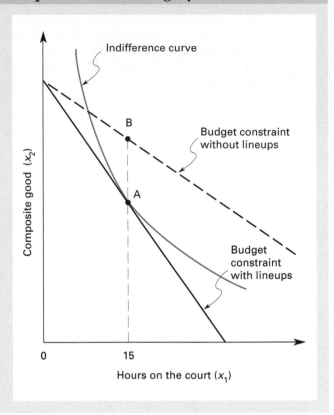

FIGURE 4.12 **Racquetball and the tragedy of the commons**

The representative player chooses to spend 15 hours on the court and 15q hours waiting in line to book courts. The value of time spent waiting in line is distance AB.

Indifference curve

B

Budget constraint without lineups

A

Budget constraint with lineups

Composite good (x_2)

0   15

Hours on the court (x_1)

in which the player is just as well off, and it completely avoids the waste of time that occurs with the first come, first served institution.

With this price institution, the time resources that would have been spent in lineups have instead been spent working, and the income generated by this work has been transferred to the university as court fees. Under one institutional arrangement, the university could earmark those revenues for acquiring more recreational facilities. Even if the university chose to put the revenues into its general fund, resources would not be needlessly used up in lineup time.

Alternatively, imagine that the racquetball players at this university are a cooperative and resourceful group. They could collectively design a system that would allow each of them to attain the more desirable point B in Figure 4.12. For instance, one very simple mechanism would be to issue individual players the right of access to 15 bookings. Each player gets the same number of bookings as under a first come, first served arrangement and avoids the time price involved in the queuing system.

The point of this exercise is to show that free access is not really free when we consider the time price of access. Relative to a price mechanism, a first come, first served institution substitutes time prices for money prices. The "tragedy" is that the time price is a real resource cost: individuals' time is needlessly wasted in lineups.

Although lineups may not be a significant problem in your own life, they certainly were a problem in the former Soviet Union prior to the move towards a market economy. Where the price mechanism is not used to allocate consumer goods, lineups are a pervasive feature of economic life. Historically, the excess demand for consumer goods at state-administered prices resulted in a colossal amount of time spent lining up to buy scarce products. In fact, in many Soviet families, the full-time "job" of the retired members was to stand in lines to buy household goods.

*4.7

Index Numbers

We are continually bombarded by index numbers. We may be told, for example, that in the third quarter of some year, real disposable income grew at $x\%$ per year or that the consumer price index has increased at $y\%$ per year. The first statement is about a

quantity index *quantity index* — an indicator of the amount of real disposable income available to consumers. Ordinarily, an increase in real disposable income is interpreted as an increase in the average consumer's economic welfare, since he or she can buy more. The sec-

price index ond statement is about a **price index** — an indicator of the price level that consumers face in the marketplace. If a consumer's income is unchanged, then an increase in the consumer price index is ordinarily interpreted as a decline in the average consumer's economic welfare, since he or she can buy less with the same income.

In this section, we will see precisely what quantity and price indexes are, and we will learn two important things about these indexes. First, given the same data, two different quantity (or price) indexes can send different qualitative messages — for example, that disposable income (or the price level) is both increasing and decreasing. Second, when two different indexes do send different messages, it may be impossible to determine which message is correct. The setting we will use to develop an understanding of index numbers is deceptively simple, but the understanding itself is profound.

Let us begin by imagining that we can observe the consumption decisions of a particular person named Norm in two different periods. Let us also assume that Norm's preferences are identical in both periods. A question naturally arises: In which period was Norm better off? If we can answer this question, a second question then arises: By how much was he better off?

Quantity Indexes

There can be no direct answer to the second question. Even if we knew Norm's utility function, we could not say how much better off he was in one period than another, because a direct answer requires cardinal information. As we saw in Chapter 2, a utility function contains only ordinal information. Nevertheless, we may be able to use the information at hand to construct an indirect answer: a quantity index that will give us some indication of how the aggregate quantity of the goods Norm consumed has changed from period to period.

Analogous questions arise at the macroeconomic level. Were U.S. citizens better off in 1994 than in 1993? If so, by how much was the average person better off? If we again adopt the assumption of a representative consumer, we can reinterpret this microeconomic exercise — which focuses on a single person, Norm — in a macroeconomic context. If we assume that the economy is composed of individuals with preferences identical to Norm's, we can then interpret the indexes discussed below as indexes of real national income per capita.

We can see the types of problems that arise with any index number by using the two-good case. The notation is necessarily a little clumsy: subscripts denote goods, and superscripts denote time periods. Thus, in period 0, Norm buys the bundle $B^0 = (x_1^0, x_2^0)$ at prices (p_1^0, p_2^0). From these quantities and prices, we can compute his income in period 0: $M^0 = p_1^0 x_1^0 + p_2^0 x_2^0$. In period 1, he buys the bundle $B^1 = (x_1^1, x_2^1)$ at prices (p_1^1, p_2^1), and his income is $M^1 = p_1^1 x_1^1 + p_2^1 x_2^1$.

If this information on prices and quantities is available, it obviously reveals something about Norm's preferences and therefore something about his well-being.[4] But exactly what does it tell us? The first step is to answer the following question: In what circumstances can we infer that either B^0 is preferred to B^1 or that B^1 is preferred to B^0? If we can infer that one or the other of these statements is true, we can develop a quantity index indicating the extent to which aggregate quantity consumed in one period exceeds aggregate quantity consumed in the other.

Let us begin by looking at the case in which Norm is definitely better off in period 1. Suppose that B^0 is inside Norm's period-1 budget constraint, as in Figure 4.13. That is, suppose that

$$p_1^1 x_1^0 + p_2^1 x_2^0 < p_1^1 x_1^1 + p_2^1 x_2^1 \qquad (= M^1)$$

The left-hand side of this inequality is the expenditure required to buy B^0 at period-1 prices, and the right-hand side is Norm's actual expenditure in period 1. Because bundle B^1 is revealed by Norm's choice to be the utility-maximizing bundle in period 1 and because bundle B^0 is attainable in period 1, we infer that B^1 is preferred to B^0:

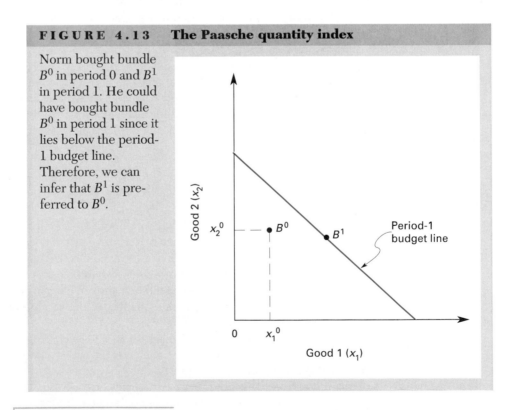

FIGURE 4.13   **The Paasche quantity index**

Norm bought bundle B^0 in period 0 and B^1 in period 1. He could have bought bundle B^0 in period 1 since it lies below the period-1 budget line. Therefore, we can infer that B^1 is preferred to B^0.

---

4 We can be more precise about the assumption that Norm's preferences are identical in the two periods. His utility function has four arguments — $x_1^0, x_2^0, x_1^1, x_2^1$ — because a good today and the same good tomorrow must be regarded as different goods. We are assuming, then, that Norm's utility function can be written in the following way:

$$U(x_1^0, x_2^0, x_1^1, x_2^1) = U'(x_1^0, x_2^0) + U'(x_1^1, x_2^1)$$

The function $U'(x_1, x_2)$ is then Norm's utility function in each period.

$$\text{If } p_1^{\ 1}x_1^{\ 0} + p_2^{\ 1}x_2^{\ 0} \ < \ p_1^{\ 1}x_1^{\ 1} + p_2^{\ 1}x_2^{\ 1} \ (=M^1), \text{ then } B^1 \text{ is preferred to } B^0.$$

Paasche quantity index

The inequality that allows us to make this inference suggests a quantity index known as the **Paasche quantity index.** If we divide Norm's actual expenditure in period 1 by the expenditure required to buy B^0 in period 1, we have an index of the extent to which Norm's aggregate consumption in period 1 exceeds his aggregate consumption in period 0. The Paasche quantity index P is defined as follows:

$$P = [p_1^{\ 1}x_1^{\ 1} + p_2^{\ 1}x_2^{\ 1}]/[p_1^{\ 1}x_1^{\ 0} + p_2^{\ 1}x_2^{\ 0}]$$

We can then restate the proposition above:

If the Paasche quantity index exceeds 1, then B^1 is preferred to B^0.

As we will see, if this index is less than 1, we cannot be sure that Norm is worse off in period 1. As a result, this quantity index is not always an accurate indicator of Norm's well-being.

Notice that the Paasche quantity index uses period-1 prices for aggregating quantities in both periods. By substituting period-0 prices for aggregating quantities in both periods, we have another quantity index, known as the **Laspeyres quantity index**, denoted by L:

Laspeyres quantity index

$$L = [p_1^{\ 0}x_1^{\ 1} + p_2^{\ 0}x_2^{\ 1}]/[p_1^{\ 0}x_1^{\ 0} + p_2^{\ 0}x_2^{\ 0}]$$

By simply reversing the argument of the previous paragraph, we arrive at an analogous proposition:

If the Laspeyres quantity index is less than 1, then B^0 is preferred to B^1.

In other words, if L is less than 1, Norm was better off in period 0 because he could have bought B^1 in period 0 but chose instead to buy B^0.

As you will discover in the following problem, P can be less than 1 and L greater than 1 at the same time. In this case, which is shown in Figure 4.14, the two indexes send conflicting messages. P indicates that Norm's consumption has fallen and L that it has risen. Furthermore, neither of these two propositions is applicable, and without more information on Norm's preferences, we cannot know in which period Norm was better off.

> **PROBLEM 4.8**
>
> Given the information in Figure 4.14, show that P is less than 1 and that L is greater than 1. In addition, draw one indifference map in Figure 4.14 such that B^1 is preferred to B^0 and another such B^0 is preferred to B^1.

Price Indexes

price indexes

We used fixed sets of prices (period-0 prices or period-1 prices) above to define two quantity indexes. In this section, we will reverse the procedure and use fixed sets of quantities to define **price indexes**. Price indexes are supposed to measure the extent to which the *price level* — as opposed to the prices of individual goods — changes from one period to another. We will discover that the commonly used price indexes, like the commonly used quantity indexes, are not entirely satisfactory.

The Paasche price index, denoted by P', uses period-1 quantities:

$$P' = [p_1^{\ 1}x_1^{\ 1} + p_2^{\ 1}x_2^{\ 1}]/[p_1^{\ 0}x_1^{\ 1} + p_2^{\ 0}x_2^{\ 1}]$$

FIGURE 4.14   An index-number puzzle

Norm bought bundle B^0 in period 0 and B^1 in period 1. In this case, P is less than 1 and L is greater than 1, and it is impossible to tell in which period Norm was better off.

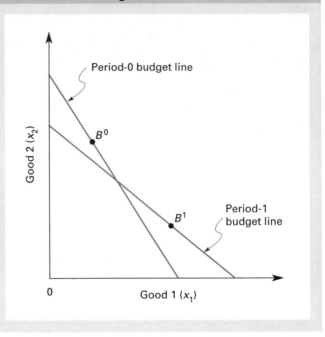

If P' is 2, for example, it takes twice as many dollars to buy B^1 at period-1 prices than at period-0 prices.

The Laspeyres price index, denoted by L', uses period-0 quantities:

$$L' = [p^1_1 x^0_1 + p^1_2 x^0_2]/[p^0_1 x^0_1 + p^0_2 x^0_2]$$

If L' is 2, for instance, it would cost twice as much to buy B^0 at period-1 prices than at period-0 prices.

It is useful to look at the case in which Norm has the same income in both periods. We can then use these price indices to restate the conditions under which we know for certain that Norm is better off in one period than in the other:

When L' is less than 1, then P' is also less than 1, and Norm is better off in period 1; when P' is greater than 1, then L' is also greater than 1, and Norm is better off in period 0.

The difficulty is that the situation is not always so clear-cut. It is entirely possible that L' is greater than 1 and, at the same time, that P' is less than 1. When this happens, the two indices convey different messages. L' indicates that the price level has risen and P' that it has fallen. Which message is correct? There is no way of knowing, given only the information we have at hand.

PROBLEM 4.9

In period 0, $p_1 = \$4$ and $p_2 = \$3$, and Norm bought the bundle (15,20). In period 1, $p_1 = \$5$ and $p_2 = \$2$, and Norm bought the bundle (10,35). Compute the two quantity indexes and the two price indexes. In which period was Norm better off?

SUMMARY

In this chapter, we wanted to see just how widely applicable the tools of Chapter 3 would prove to be. We also extended the theory of self-interest to include time prices as well as money prices. And we looked at index numbers. We can draw two important general lessons from the wide-ranging economic problems explored in this chapter.

First, the presence of a *non-zero substitution effect* is the crucial factor in a broad range of interesting theoretical problems in economics. For instance, in the absence of a substitution effect, we saw that taxpayers would be indifferent between a lump-sum tax and an excise tax that produced the same tax revenue. Similarly, it is easy to show that in the absence of a substitution effect, private club members would not care which of two arrangements they used to cover their overhead costs. And, as you will discover in Exercise 13, in the absence of a substitution effect, the economic puzzles associated with index numbers disappear. The presence of a non-zero substitution effect, then, influences in a crucial way the results in these applications.

Second, we were able to reduce very complex problems to manageable ones by employing the useful fiction of a *representative consumer*. We simplified the real diversity of individual tastes and incomes to those of a representative individual and then analyzed only this person's choice problem. This abstraction is an extremely useful one, as long as we recognize the need to reintroduce diversity when confronting real situations. The most general conclusion we can draw is that these tools can yield insights into a wide range of economic problems from everyday experience: they help us to do vicarious problem solving.

EXERCISES

1. The government wants to raise $50 a month from Joe Blow. A $1 sales tax per package of cigarettes will raise the required revenue, as will a lump-sum tax of $50 per month. Which tax would Joe prefer? Will he smoke more cigarettes under the sales tax or the lump-sum tax?

2. Suppose that the government has decided to transfer income to a particular person. Draw a graph analogous to Figure 4.1 and compare the implications of a program that subsidizes the consumption of some good — food or shelter, for example — with the implications of a lump-sum transfer of cash.

   a. Show that if the two programs involve an equal expenditure of public revenues, the recipient will never prefer the first program.

   b. Supposing that the two programs involve an equal expenditure of public revenues, illustrate the case in which the recipient would be indifferent between them.

3. The 50 students in Dunnell's Boardinghouse have formed a club to buy a coffee vending ma-

chine that costs $500. They currently pay $0.75 per cup at the cafe next door, and they figure that coffee from the machine will cost them just $0.25 per cup. The problem is that no one except Jane has $10 to pay his or her share of the $500. Jane has agreed either 1. to lend each of the other students $10, in which case they can get coffee at $0.25 per cup immediately, or 2. to buy the machine herself and charge $0.75 per cup until she recovers the $490. Only then will the price drop to $0.25 per cup. Which option would you recommend to these students?

4. Buff has an old camera that produces instant photographs. The film for this camera costs $2 per exposure. A new camera model on the market is identical to Buff's camera in every way but one: the film for the new model costs only $1 per exposure. Let p_c' denote the price of the new camera and p_c'' the price at which Buff could sell her old camera.

   a. Use a graphic argument based on indifference curves to determine the price differential $p_c' - p_c''$ at which Buff will be indifferent between keeping her old camera and selling it so that she can buy the new model.

b. Now suppose that her demand for instant photographs is independent of her income, and use a graphic argument based on her demand curve for instant photographs to determine the same price differential.

5. Jay's income elasticity of demand for garlic is zero, and his demand curve for garlic is

$$p = 150 - 2x_1$$

a. What is the maximum sum that Jay will pay in order to have 50 units of garlic rather than none?

b. If he currently cannot buy garlic at any price, what is the maximum amount that he will pay for the opportunity to buy it at a price of $30 per unit?

c. What is the maximum amount that he is willing to pay for the opportunity to buy garlic at a price of $10 rather than $30 per unit?

6. Each of the 100 kids in Ess Cee has the following demand for rides on Walt's Magic Merry-Go-Round:

$$p = 10 - x$$

where x is the number of rides per week and p is the price per ride. Demand is independent of income. What is magical about Walt's Merry-Go-Round is that it costs nothing to run and has unlimited capacity. What two-part tariff maximizes Walt's profit? How much profit does Walt earn? How many rides does each kid take in a week?

7. Unions commonly bargain for a basic wage rate w and an overtime rate. Assume that the overtime rate is $1.5w$ and that it is paid for hours worked in excess of 40 per week.

a. Construct the relevant budget line between leisure and a composite good.

b. Assuming that the union member would choose to work 40 hours per week at wage rate w, will he or she want to work overtime?

c. Assuming that members are contractually obligated to work at least 40 hours per week, illustrate the conditions under which the union member would prefer no overtime work.

8. Ralph currently has two jobs. His primary job pays well, $20 per hour, but he can work no more

than 40 hours per week at it. In fact, he always chooses to work 40 hours at this job. His secondary job pays only $15 per hour, but he can work as few or as many hours as he wants. Currently he chooses to work 10 hours at his secondary job. For Ralph, leisure is a normal good. If the wage rate for his primary job increases to $22 per hour, will Ralph increase or decrease the number of hours he works in the secondary job?

9. Helga currently gets a $1,000 weekly investment income, and she works 10 hours each week at $50 an hour, thereby earning an additional $500. Leisure is neither an inferior nor a normal good for Helga. If offered the choice between a 10% increase in her investment income and a 20% increase in her hourly wage rate, which would Helga choose? Assume that she is free to choose her hours of work.

10. At many universities, students are admitted free to football and basketball games. Because seating is on a first come, first served basis and because the number of good seats is limited, the good seats are often taken 1 to 2 hours before game time. What would happen if more good seats were made available to students? If the average quality of the seats in the student section were improved? Can you devise a better institution for allocating seats to students?

11. Buford buys consumption bundle (4,8) when the prices of good 1 and good 2 are both $1, and he buys bundle (8,2) when the price of good 1 is $1 and the price of good 2 is $2. Is it possible to infer from this information which of the two bundles Buford prefers?

12. Howard's income was $10,500 in both periods 0 and 1. For which of the following three cases was Howard better off in period 1? For which was he worse off in period 1? For which cases are you uncertain?

a. Both P' and L' exceed 1.

b. Both P' and L' are less than 1.

c. L' exceeds 1 and P' is less than 1.

Construct a diagram consistent with case a in which you indicate Howard's budget line and consumption bundle for both periods. Do the same for case c.

13. When we used Norm's consumption decisions to develop quantity indexes for him, we supposed

that we knew nothing about his preferences. Suppose now that his preferences in both periods are captured by the following perfect-complements utility function:

$$U(x_1,x_2) = \min(x_1,x_2)$$

Supposing that Norm always chooses the utility-maximizing bundle, show that 1. if one quantity index is less than 1, then so is the other; 2. if one quantity index is greater than 1, then so is the other; and 3. if one quantity index is equal to 1, then so is the other. Explain these curious results. Hint: Ask yourself why the situation shown in Figure 4.14 cannot arise with this utility function.

*14 Let us generalize the basic insight regarding lump-sum versus excise taxes. Suppose that Laura's indifference curves are smooth and convex and that both good 1 and good 2 are essential. Consider her choice between 1. a system of excise taxes, composed of separate excise taxes t_1 and t_2 on goods 1 and 2, or 2. a lump-sum tax, and suppose that both raise equal tax revenue.

a. Show that she is never better off with the system of excise taxes.
b. When will she be indifferent to the two tax regimes?
c. How would your answer to part b change if her indifference curves were not smooth?
d. How would your answer to part b change if good 1 were inessential?

*15. I buy gasoline only when my tank is virtually empty, and I always fill it up because it takes 10 minutes of my valuable time to buy 5 gallons, 10 gallons, or the full 20 gallons. Show that my behavior is utility-maximizing. Hint: Using Becker's full-income apparatus, consider my budget lines between gasoline and a composite good when I buy 5 gallons at a time, 10 gallons at a time, 20 gallons at a time.

*16. An economist decided to take the train rather than an airplane from California to a convention in Colorado. Even though the train fare was about half the airfare, most other travelers chose to fly. What factors bear on their choice of transportation? Suppose that travelers place no value on the experience of traveling by rail or by air. Develop a model that determines which passengers go by train and which by plane.

*17. The recently abandoned 55-mph speed limit in the United States was imposed to reduce the nation's fuel consumption. Because most automobiles get better gas mileage at 55 mph than at higher speeds, the idea behind the legislation was that the lower speed limit would reduce gas consumption even if drivers did not reduce the number of miles they drove. Yet the lower speed limit actually tends to reduce the number of miles driven as well. Explain why. Is this a sensible way to reduce fuel consumption? Hint: Suppose first that all consumers have identical preferences, identical nonwage incomes, and identical wage rates, and find a better institution for achieving a specified reduction in fuel consumption. What considerations arise when you drop the representative-consumer assumption?

REFERENCES

Becker, G. 1965. "A Theory of the Allocation of Time," *The Economic Journal* 75:493–517.

Hardin, G. 1968. "The Tragedy of the Commons," *Science* (Dec):1243–48.

Hicks, J. R. 1943. "The Four Consumer's Surpluses," *Review of Economic Studies* 11:31–41.

Oi, W. 1971. "A Disneyland Dilemma: Two-Part Tariffs for a Mickey Mouse Monopoly," *Quarterly Journal of Economics* 85:77–96.

Schelling, T. 1978. *Micromotives and Macrobehavior*, New York: W. W. Norton.

Schmalensee, R. 1982. "Monopolistic Two-Part Pricing Arrangements," *Bell Journal of Economics* 85:67–76.

Willig, R. 1976. "Consumer's Surplus Without Apology," *American Economic Review* 66:589–97.

CHAPTER 5

Choice Making Under Imperfect Information

In many ways, life is like a game of poker. In life, as in poker, blind chance and imperfect information play important roles. In life, as in poker, we make decisions on the basis of imperfect information. And in life, as in poker, we must assess the risks associated with alternative courses of action. Yet the theory of choice we developed and explored in Chapters 2, 3, and 4 assumes that individual economic actors live in a riskless universe and that they are perfectly informed: that is, that they know with certainty the outcome of any economic decision they make. Yet it is clear that the outcomes of everyday decision making are *risky*, or *probable* rather than riskless or certain, and are made on the basis of *imperfect information*. For example, every time I drop three quarters into a vending machine to buy some gum, there is at least some probability that I will walk away empty-handed and 75 cents poorer; some other probability that I will get both the gum and my 75 cents back; and some third, larger, probability that I will get the gum but not the 75 cents. Indeed, a whole class of economic choice questions — including problems in gambling, insurance, occupational choice, speculation, and the internal organization of firms — cannot be treated in our initial theory of consumer choice making.

risk

imperfect
information

In the first two sections of this chapter, we extend the theory of consumer choice to incorporate **risk** and **imperfect information**. Using the methodology described in Chapter 1, we first select a familiar situation with a risky outcome — a TV game show. Then we look for an initial hypothesis that explains our observations and carefully restructure the hypothesis to create an economic model, or theory, known as the theory of expected utility. In the following section, we generalize the theory of expected utility, and, in the last three sections, we apply the expanded theory to a whole range of situations involving risk or imperfect information.

5.1
Expected-Utility Theory

We will begin our exploration of the theory of expected utility with simple games of chance because they are so easy to understand. Having understood how the theory works in this elementary environment, we will then see how to elaborate the theory so that it can be applied in the more complicated environment of the real world.

Let us begin by imagining a TV game show in which a certain player — say, Chauncey — is given the choice between walking away with a fixed sum of money $M or staking it on a game called Risk. If Chauncey decides to play Risk, the game show host will toss a coin. If a head appears, Chauncey wins $200; if a tail appears, he wins nothing.

We can think of $M as the *opportunity cost* of playing Risk. Clearly, if $M is sufficiently small, Chauncey will choose to play Risk, and if $M is sufficiently large he will choose to walk away with $M. What more can we say about Chauncey's choice? What principles govern Chauncey's choice in this risky situation?

Calculating Expected Monetary Value

**expected
monetary value**

First, let us calculate the expected monetary value of the payoffs to Risk. An **expected monetary value** is simply a weighted average of the payoffs to the possible outcomes, where the weights are the probabilities of occurrence assigned to each of the possible payoffs. Because in Risk the probability of winning $200 is 1/2 and the probability of winning nothing is 1/2, the expected monetary value of the payoff to Risk is $100: $100 = (1/2)$200 + (1/2)$0. On any single play of this game, Chauncey would win either $200 or $0. However, if he played the game repeatedly, *on average* he would expect to win $100 per play, winning $200 half the time and $0 half the time. The expected monetary value of the other option facing Chauncey is, of course, $M, since if he chooses this option he gets $M with probability 1.

**expected
monetary value
hypothesis**

Having done these expected monetary value calculations, we are tempted to guess that Chauncey will play Risk in preference to taking $M if $M < $100, and will take $M in preference to playing Risk if $M > $100. That is, it is tempting to think that in choices involving risk, individuals choose the option with the largest expected monetary value. Let us call this the **expected monetary value hypothesis**. To see why this hypothesis is not necessarily correct, try the following problem.

> ### PROBLEM 5.1
>
> You now have a chance to play Risk — but the stakes are better: you can walk away with $M dollars, or you can gamble on the outcome of a coin toss. If a head appears, you get $2 million, but if a tail appears, you get nothing. Calculate the expected monetary value of the game. What value of $M would make you indifferent between taking $M or playing this version of Risk? Is it smaller than the expected monetary value of the game?

If past experience is any guide, the number you wrote down in answering Problem 5.1 is certainly less than $1 million — the expected monetary value of Risk in this problem — and it is probably less than $500,000. The expected monetary value hypothesis, then, does not seem to account for our behavior. It seems that *risk itself plays a role in shaping our behavior*. Daniel Bernoulli, a contemporary of Adam Smith, proposed the *expected-utility hypothesis* as a replacement for the expected monetary value hypothesis.[1] This hypothesis takes into account the role of risk in shaping our actions. Before you consider the theory of expected utility, however, try the following problem to reinforce your understanding of expected monetary values.

---

1 Bernoulli's version of this paradox, known as the Saint Petersburg paradox, is treated in Exercise 1 at the end of this chapter. Bernoulli's original work has been recently reprinted. See Bernoulli (1954).

The Expected-Utility Hypothesis

Bernoulli argued that in evaluating risky prospects, individuals compare — not the expected monetary values of payoffs — but the *expected utilities of payoffs*. There is something inherently attractive about this approach because it focuses not on the monetary value of a prize but on just how much the prize means to an individual — that is, on the *utility* of the prize to the individual. Expected utility is calculated in the same way as an expected monetary value, except that the utility associated with a payoff is substituted for its monetary value. To calculate an expected utility, simply compute a weighted average of the utilities associated with the payoffs, using the appropriate probabilities as weights.

What is Chauncey's expected utility for Risk? If we think of wealth (command over goods) as a composite commodity, we can write Chauncey's utility as a function of wealth:

$$u = U(w)$$

where u is Chauncey's utility, w is his wealth, and U is his utility function. For example, let us suppose that Chauncey's wealth before he makes his choice about playing Risk is $0. In other words, he is flat broke. If he decides to play, one of two possible outcomes will occur: 1. he will win $200, his wealth will then be $200, and his utility will be $U(200)$; or 2. he will win $0, his wealth will then be $0, and his utility will be $U(0)$. The probability of each of these outcomes is, of course, 1/2. Taking the probability-weighted average of these utilities gives us Chauncey's **expected utility** of playing Risk.

expected utility

Chauncey's expected utility of Risk = $(1/2)U(200) + (1/2)U(0)$

Of course, his other option is to walk away with $M. If he chooses to take $M rather than play Risk, his wealth will be $M with probability 1. The expected utility associated with this option is then $U(M)$.

expected-utility hypothesis

According to the **expected-utility hypothesis**, Chauncey will choose to play Risk in preference to taking $M if the expected utility of playing Risk is greater than the expected utility of taking $M, or if

$$(1/2)U(200) + (1/2)U(0) > U(M)$$

Of course, he will take $M if the inequality is reversed.

But how is this expected-utility function constructed? This is the question we are about to tackle.

The Expected-Utility Function

We are now about to examine in some detail how to construct an expected-utility function.[2] To keep the discussion relatively simple, we will look at a situation in which any risky prospect has at most three possible outcomes. That is, we will be talking about lotteries — or what we will call *prospects* — which offer *three different prizes*, or *outcomes*. For concreteness, the prizes themselves will be $10,000, $6,000, or $1,000. Now, suppose that some game offers $10,000 with probability p_1, $6,000 with probability p_2, and $1,000 with probability p_3. From our understanding of probability, we know that $p_1, p_2,$ and p_3 are numbers greater than or equal to 0 and less than or equal to 1. In addition, since there are only three possible outcomes, these three probabilities must add up to 1: $p_1 + p_2 + p_3 = 1$.

prospect
We will use the term **prospect** to refer to any set of three probabilities — $p_1, p_2,$ and p_3 assigned to their respective outcomes — $10,000, $6,000, and $1,000 — and we will denote a prospect by

$$(p_1, p_2, p_3: 10{,}000, 6{,}000, 1{,}000)$$

or, more simply, by

$$(p_1, p_2, p_3)$$

with the understanding that the first probability (p_1) pertains to the first prize ($10,000), the second probability (p_2) to the second prize ($6,000), and the third probability (p_3) to the third prize ($1,000). For example, the lottery that offers $10,000 with probability 1/4, $6,000 with probability 1/2, and $1,000 with probability 1/4, is denoted by (1/4, 1/2, 1/4: 10,000, 6,000, 1,000) or, equivalently, by (1/4, 1/2, 1/4). The notation can also represent riskless, or *assured,* outcomes: outcomes that occur with probability 1. For example, either (1, 0, 0: 10,000, 6,000, 1,000) or (1, 0, 0) denotes the assured outcome, $10,000. To be certain you understand this notation, try the following problem.

PROBLEM 5.4

Describe in words exactly what each of the following prospects is, and calculate its expected monetary value. (.25, .25, .50), (.2, .5, .3), (.5, .4, .1), (0, 1, 0).

Our task is to find a utility function such that whenever one prospect is preferred to another, the expected utility of the preferred prospect is larger than the expected utility of the other prospect. The utility function $U(w)$ will assign utility numbers to each of the three outcomes — $10,000, $6,000, and $1,000. The utility numbers themselves can be written as $U(10{,}000)$, $U(6{,}000)$, and $U(1{,}000)$.

---

2 See von Neumann and Morgenstern (1944) for the classic development of the theory. For a more accessible treatment, see Luce and Raiffa (1957), or the entry titled "expected-utility hypothesis" by Mark J. Machina in *The New Palgrave.*

To see just what our objective is, let us look at two specific prospects, (.2, .5, .3) and (.3, .3, .4), and suppose that the person whose preferences we are considering prefers the first prospect to the second one. That is,

(.2, .5, .3) is preferred to (.3, .3, .4)

We want to find a utility function — the three numbers $U(10{,}000)$, $U(6{,}000)$, and $U(1{,}000)$ — such that the expected utility of the first prospect is greater than the expected utility of the second prospect:

$$.2U(10{,}000) + .5U(6{,}000) + .3U(1{,}000)$$

$$> .3U(10{,}000) + .3U(6{,}000) + .4U(1{,}000)$$

To find such a function, we will use an assumption that is central to the theory of expected utility.

continuity assumption

The assumption is called the **continuity assumption**. (Notice that this assumption is different from the assumption called the continuity of preferences assumption in Chapter 2.) To see what our new continuity assumption involves, let us consider another simple game. Suppose that Chauncey is given a choice between the following prospects:

Prospect 1: (0, 1, 0)

Prospect 2: $(e, 0, 1 - e)$

Prospect 1 is the assured prospect $6,000. In Prospect 2, e is the probability of the $10,000 prize, $1 - e$ is the probability of the $1,000 prize, and the $6,000 prize is impossible (probability 0). Notice that as e increases, Prospect 2 becomes increasingly more attractive. At one extreme, when $e = 0$, both prospects are riskless, or assured. and Prospect 1 is the preferred prospect since it offers $6,000 while Prospect 2 offers only $1,000. At the other extreme, when $e = 1$, both prospects are again assured, but now Prospect 2 is the preferred prospect since it offers $10,000 while Prospect 1 offers only $6,000. Given these results — Prospect 1 is preferred to Prospect 2 when $e = 0$ and Prospect 2 is preferred to Prospect 1 when $e = 1$ — it seems plausible to assume that there is some value of e, greater than zero but less than 1, such that the individual is indifferent between the two prospects. This is the continuity assumption:

CONTINUITY ASSUMPTION

For any individual, there is a unique number e^*, $0 < e^* < 1$, such that

(0, 1, 0) is indifferent to $(e^*, 0, 1 - e^*)$

Since e^* must be greater than 0 and less than 1, this assumption guarantees that individuals are willing to make *tradeoffs* between risky and assured prospects: they are willing to bear some risk. The probability e^* plays a very significant role in our theory, so you should be certain that you understand the continuity assumption. In particular, notice that for any individual, e^* is a *number* and that *this number will vary from individual to individual*.

> **PROBLEM 5.5**
>
> Jack says that he is indifferent between $6,000 and a lottery that pays $10,000 with probability .75 and $1,000 with probability .25. His sister Jane says that she prefers $6,000 to this lottery. What can you say about the number e^* for Jack? For Jane?

We will begin to construct the utility function $U(w)$ by assigning the utility number 1 to the \$10,000 prize and the utility number 0 to the \$1,000 prize. Thus, $U(10,000)$ = 1 and $U(1,000) = 0$. (We choose utility numbers 1 and 0 as a matter of convenience. We could have assigned arbitrary utility numbers, so long as the number assigned to the \$10,000 prize is larger than the number assigned to the \$1,000 prize.) To complete the job, we need to assign a utility number to the \$6,000 prize. As you will see, only one number will do: we must choose $U(6,000) = e^*$.

From the continuity assumption, we know that in any given individual's eyes there is a risky prospect $(e^*, 0, 1 - e^*)$ that is equivalent to $(0,1,0)$, the assured prospect offering \$6,000 with probability 1. In other words, for any individual there is a number e^*, greater than 0 and less than 1, such that $(0, 1, 0)$ is indifferent to $(e^*, 0, 1 - e^*)$. If the expected-utility result is to hold, the expected utility of the assured prospect $(0, 1, 0)$ must be equal to the expected utility of the equivalent risky prospect $(e^*, 0, 1 - e^*)$. But the expected utility of the assured prospect is just $U(6,000)$. The expected utility of the equivalent risky prospect is $e^*U(10,000) + (1 - e^*)U(1,000)$, or simply e^*, because $U(10,000) = 1$ and $U(1,000) = 0$. Therefore, we must choose $U(6,000) = e^*$. The expected-utility function is then

$$U(10,000) = 1, \ U(6,000) = e^*, \ U(1,000) = 0$$

To be sure that you know how this utility function has been constructed, try the following problem.[3]

> **PROBLEM 5.6**
>
> Using the information from Problem 5.5, construct a utility function for Jack.

von Neumann-
Morgenstern
utility function

This utility function is often called a **von Neumann-Morgenstern utility function** in honor of the mathematician John von Neumann and the economist Oskar Morgenstern who developed the modern theory of expected utility in their classic book, *The Theory of Games and Economic Behavior*. Notice that this utility function is *not* an ordinal utility function like the utility functions in Chapter 2. If it were an ordinal utility function, we could assign any number larger than $U(1,000) = 0$ and smaller than $U(10,000) = 1$ to the \$6,000 prize. But, as we have seen, we cannot pick an arbitrary utility number for this prize. We must choose $U(6,000) = e^*$.

We used the continuity assumption to construct the von Neumann-Morgenstern utility function. Two additional assumptions that are considered in the appendix are also important in the theory of expected utility. When these assumptions are satisfied, and when the utility function is constructed as described above, we have the following important result:

If an individual prefers one prospect to another, then the preferred prospect will have a larger expected utility. Furthermore, if an individual is indifferent between two prospects, then the two prospects will have the same expected utility.

---

3 More generally, given any two numbers a and b with $a > b$, we could let $U(10,000) = a$ and $U(1,000) = b$. We would then have to assign a utility number to \$6,000 as follows:

$$U(6,000) = ae^* + b(1 - e^*)$$

To see just how powerful this result is, notice that if we have just *one* piece of information for any individual, we can predict that individual's choice in any situation where the prizes are $10,000, $6,000, or $1,000 — assuming, of course, that the individual's preferences satisfy our assumptions. That crucial piece of information is e^*, the probability that makes the individual indifferent between $6,000 and the risky prospect $(e^*, 0, 1 - e^*)$. The number e^* gives us this powerful predictive capacity because it allows us to construct the individual's utility function and therefore to calculate expected utilities for any prospect involving these three prizes. The following problem will help you check your understanding of this result.

PROBLEM 5.7

Use the utility function you constructed in the previous problem to find Jack's preference ordering for the following prospects: (1/2, 1/4, 1/4); (1/3, 1/3, 1/3); (0, 1, 0); (7/12, 0, 5/12); (1/4, 1/2, 1/4); (3/4, 0, 1/4).

The predictive power of the theory of expected utility means that it is relatively easy to generate experimental evidence to test the theory. In fact, a great deal of experimental testing of the theory has already been done. One of the more interesting results of this research is evidence that, in certain situations, the theory is inadequate. In fact, a great deal of recent work attempts to modify the theory so that it does work in these problematical situations. Machina's 1987 article surveys this empirical evidence and the efforts to modify the theory. Despite its inadequacy in these situations, it is fair to say that expected utility theory is by a wide margin the most often used theory of decision making in the presence of risk and/or imperfect information. Later in this chapter, we use it to address a number of questions.

5.2
Generalizing the Expected-Utility Approach

Obviously, expected-utility theory is not restricted to prospects with the three prizes of $10,000, $6,000, and $1,000. Clearly, *any* three money prizes would do. Indeed, prizes *other than* money prizes are perfectly possible. For example, the prizes might be cars, houses, training programs, consumption bundles, or virtually anything else that individuals value. As you will see, the expected-utility approach is therefore not limited to financial risk; it can be applied to a whole spectrum of individual choices involving risk.

We can easily extend the theory from the three-outcome case to prospects with any number of possible outcomes. For each additional outcome, we simply need to generate an additional utility number. Suppose, for example, that we added the possibility of a $3,000 prize to the three prizes we have been considering, and suppose, too, that Jack is indifferent between this $3,000 prize and a lottery offering $10,000 with probability .4 and $1,000 with probability .6. To extend Jack's utility function, we would assign the utility number .4 to $3,000. Jack's utility function would then be $U(10{,}000) = 1$, $U(6{,}000) = .75$, $U(3{,}000) = .4$, and $U(1{,}000) = 0$. Using this utility function, we could then predict what his choice would be in any situation in which prospects offer these four prizes. Using this procedure, we can extend the theory to encompass risky prospects with any number of outcomes.

In some important circumstances, however, the expected-utility approach cannot be applied without reinterpreting the notion of probability, and in others it is simply not applicable.

Subjective Probabilities

We have been using coin-tossing games as illustrations of risky situations for two reasons. First, these games are clearly risky because their outcomes are random events. Second, in these games, the probability of any outcome is objectively known. Yet, expected-utility theory is often applied to risky situations in which the probability of any outcome is not objectively known. And it is often applied to situations that involve not risk, but *imperfect information* — that is, to situations in which the outcome is *certain* but *unknown*. The key to applying expected-utility theory in these latter two cases is to use **subjective probabilities**.[4]

subjective probabilities

First, let us look at buying gum from a vending machine as a risky situation in which the probability of any outcome is not objectively known, and then reconsider it as a situation involving imperfect information. We will see how the expected-utility approach can be applied to both cases with the use of subjective probabilities. Each time I drop 75 cents into a vending machine to get some gum, I think that there is some probability that the gum will not drop. This is a genuinely risky event — because the outcome is genuinely random — if, for instance, the machine is built so that it releases gum with probability 19/20 and does not release it with probability 1/20. My problem is that there is an objective probability that I will not get the gum — but I do not know what it is.

How do I make rational decisions in this case? Perhaps I could attach a subjective probability to the nonappearance of the gum, based on past experience with this machine or others like it. In this case, the expected-utility approach is applicable — if probabilities are reinterpreted as subjective probabilities.

But what if the outcome is not risky but certain? In other words, what if the vending machine is in one of the two states: working order or out-of-order. In this case, the problem is an informational one: I simply do not know whether the machine is functioning or not. How do I make rational decisions under imperfect information? Perhaps by forming a subjective probability about the state of the machine, again based on past experience with this or similar machines. Here again, the expected-utility approach is applicable if probabilities are interpreted as subjective probabilities.

From the vending-machine user's point of view, then, there is no difference between genuine risk, where outcomes are random, and imperfect information, where outcomes are certain but information is lacking. The outcome is treated as probabilistic in either case.

In fact, many choices include both risk and imperfect information. Enrolling in a premed program in anticipation of being among the 3 out of every 10 applicants accepted by medical schools involves genuine risk if selection procedures by admission officers are random — that is, if candidates are chosen by throwing the names of acceptable applicants into a hat and drawing out the "winners." Enrolling in premed also involves imperfect information, however, if students who do not have the ability necessary to meet medical school admissions standards nevertheless decide to enroll in the program. In this case, the outcome is certain — these students will *not* be accepted into medical school — but the students themselves do not know it.

Whatever the nature of the choice — a genuinely risky problem, an informational problem, or both — we can still analyze it using the expected-utility approach if we are willing to reinterpret the probabilities as subjective probabilities. The real issue is whether people actually do in fact view outcomes in a particular choice situation as probabilistic.

---

4 For further information, see the entries in *The New Palgrave* titled "subjective probability" (I. J. Good) and "state-dependent preferences" (Edi Karni).

State-Dependent Preferences

The expected-utility approach cannot be directly applied when a person's preferences depend on which outcome, or "state of the world," actually turns up. We have implicitly assumed that an individual's preference ordering over prospects is independent of the outcome that actually occurs. In many cases, this assumption is appropriate. For example, if I win the Irish Sweepstakes, my preferences over consumption bundles will not change.

state-dependent   Sometimes, however, preferences are **state-dependent**. Imagine how the preferences of a childless couple hoping to adopt a baby might differ over items such as strollers, baby foods, and child-care services. In this case, preferences depend on whether an agency selects the couple to be adoptive parents. Whenever you venture out into rush-hour traffic, you risk being injured in an accident. If you were disabled, your consumption preferences would change — perhaps dramatically. When preferences are state-dependent, the expected-utility approach to risky choice making is not directly applicable. In such situations, it must be extended to incorporate state-dependent preferences.

5.3
Attitudes Towards Risk

Different people differ in their psychological attitudes towards *risk-taking*: some people are perfectly willing to invest in highly speculative penny stocks, for example, or in a resort development in the heart of the Amazon jungle, whereas others are unwilling to undertake any venture more risky than opening a savings account. A convenient way to think about this variation in attitudes towards risk is to view individual preferences as falling into one of three categories: *risk-averse, risk-neutral,* or *risk-inclined.*

Let us concentrate in this section on attitudes towards financial risk. We will express utility as a function of wealth, w, and write an individual's utility as

$$u = U(w)$$

To see exactly what these three attitudes towards risk entail, we will consider the following prospect:

$$(p, 1 - p: w_1, w_2)$$

where p is the probability of getting outcome w_1, and $1 - p$ is the probability of getting outcome w_2. In this notation for prospects, the first probability (p) pertains to the first outcome (w_1), and the second probability $(1 - p)$ to the second outcome (w_2). For convenience, we will suppose that w_1 exceeds w_2.

Let us consider one individual's attitude towards risk. Suppose that this person — let us call him Jim — has initial wealth of w_0. If Jim holds the prospect described above, his wealth will be $w_0 + w_1$ with probability p and $w_0 + w_2$ with probability $(1 - p)$, and his expected utility will be

$$pU(w_0 + w_1) + (1 - p)U(w_0 + w_2)$$

The expected monetary value of this prospect, w_e, is just

$$w_e = pw_1 + (1 - p)w_2$$

If Jim held an assured prospect that offered w_e with probability 1, his expected utility would be

$$U(w_0 + w_e)$$

Let us imagine that Jim has been offered the choice between these two prospects. Keep in mind that both prospects offer *identical expected monetary values* but one is *risky* and the other *assured*.

risk-neutral

We will call Jim **risk-neutral** if the two prospects are equally attractive to him. That is, Jim is risk-neutral if

$$pU(w_0 + w_1) + (1 - p)U(w_0 + w_2) = U(w_0 + w_e)$$

risk-averse

We will call him **risk-averse** if the assured prospect is preferred. That is, Jim is risk-averse if

$$U(w_0 + w_e) > pU(w_0 + w_1) + (1 - p)U(w_0 + w_2)$$

risk-inclined

Finally, we will call him **risk-inclined** if he prefers the risky prospect. That is, Jim is risk-inclined if

$$pU(w_0 + w_1) + (1 - p)U(w_0 + w_2) > U(w_0 + w_e)$$

The following problem will help you to understand these important distinctions.

> **PROBLEM 5.8**
>
> Melvin's utility function is $U(w) = w^{1/2}$, Jane's is $U(w) = w$, and Baby Doe's is $U(w) = w^2$. All three have the same initial wealth — $w_0 = 0$. That is, they are all penniless. Consider the risky prospect (1/4, 3/4: 100, 0) — a prospect that offers \$100 with probability 1/4 and \$0 with probability 3/4. The expected monetary value of this prospect is \$25 — that is, $w_e = 25$. Show that, if given a choice between \$25 and the risky prospect (1/4, 3/4: 100, 0), Melvin prefers the assured \$25, Jane is indifferent between the two, and Baby Doe prefers the risky prospect. Now quickly sketch these utility functions. Notice the differences in the curves associated with these risk-averse, risk-neutral, and risk-inclined preferences.

We can determine from the shape of the utility function — that is, from the way in which the slope of the function changes as wealth w increases — which of the three cases we are considering. The utility function in Figure 5.1a represents the preferences of someone who is risk-neutral. As wealth w increases, utility increases at a constant rate: the slope of the utility function is *constant*. We can interpret the slope of the

marginal utility of wealth

utility function as **marginal utility of wealth** because its slope is simply the rate at which utility increases as wealth increases. We then see that risk neutrality is associated with constant marginal utility of wealth.[5]

By comparison, in the risk-averse case in Figure 5.1b, the slope of the utility function *decreases* as wealth increases, and in the risk-inclined case in Figure 5.1c, the slope *increases* as wealth increases. Risk aversion is thus associated with diminishing marginal utility of wealth and risk inclination with increasing marginal utility of wealth.

---

5 We can use calculus to define marginal utility of wealth, $MU(w)$:

$$MU(w) = U'(w)$$

Then, $U''(w) = 0$ implies risk neutrality, $U''(w) < 0$ implies risk aversion, and $U''(w) > 0$ implies risk inclination.

FIGURE 5.1   **Preferences towards risk**

In (a), the slope of $U(w)$ is constant, reflecting constant marginal utility of wealth and risk-neutral preferences. In (b), the slope of $U(w)$ decreases as w increases, reflecting diminishing marginal utility of wealth and risk-averse preferences. In (c), the slope of $U(w)$ increases as w increases, reflecting increasing marginal utility of wealth and risk-inclined preferences.

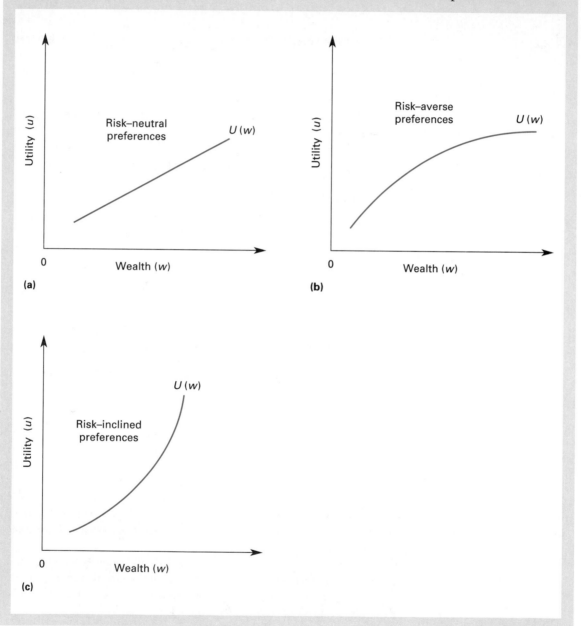

Now, let us justify these assertions about Figure 5.1 by examining in detail the risk-averse case. Jim's utility function in Figure 5.2 is like the one shown in Figure 5.1b. We will show that, given a choice between a risky prospect and an assured prospect with the same expected (monetary) value, Jim will prefer the assured prospect. That is, we will show that

$$U(w_0 + w_e) > pU(w_0 + w_1) + (1 - p)U(w_0 + w_2)$$

As we proceed, we will also be creating important tools for use in the applications that follow.

In Figure 5.2, point A on the w axis corresponds to wealth $w_0 + w_2$ and point B to wealth $w_0 + w_1$. Point E, corresponding to wealth $w_0 + w_e$, clearly lies somewhere between points A and B. Exactly where it lies depends on the value of p. As p goes from 0 to 1, $w_0 + w_e$ goes from point A to point B. If p is zero, $w_0 + w_e$ is coincident with point A. If p is 1/4, it is one-fourth of the distance between A and B, and so on. Because we have assumed in constructing Figure 5.2 that p is equal to 1/2, E is exactly half the distance from A to B. To find $U(w_0 + w_e)$ in Figure 5.2, simply move vertically up from point E to the utility function at point F. Thus, $U(w_0 + w_e)$ is the distance EF in the diagram.

Now we need to find Jim's expected utility for the risky prospect. To identify $pU(w_0 + w_1) + (1 - p)U(w_0 + w_2)$, construct the dashed line connecting points C and D in Figure 5.2, and then move vertically up from point E to point G on this dashed line. The distance EG is Jim's expected utility of this risky prospect. Why? Just as $w_0 + w_e$ moves from point A to point B as p moves from 0 to 1, so too, the expected utility of the risky prospect moves along the dashed line from point C to point D. In the case shown in this figure where p equal to 1/2, the expected utility is halfway along this dashed line, directly above point E. Notice that distance EF exceeds distance EG or, equivalently, that

$$U(w_0 + w_e) > pU(w_0 + w_1) + (1 - p)U(w_0 + w_2)$$

We have shown, then, that the preferences shown in Figure 5.2 are risk-averse.

FIGURE 5.2   Risk aversion

By construction, $w_0 + w_e = p(w_0 + w_1) + (1-p)(w_0 + w_2)$. The utility of $w_0 + w_e$ is distance EF. The expected utility of the risky project $(w_1, w_2; p_1, p_2)$ is distance EG. Since the individual is risk-averse, EF exceeds EG.

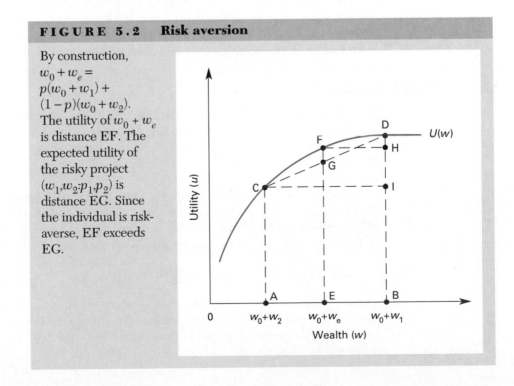

Do risk-averse preferences characterize your own behavior? Recall your answer to Problem 5.1, where you considered the choice between the risky prospect (1/2, 1/2 : 2,000,000, 0) and the assured prospect that offered $M with probability 1. We asked you to write down the value of $M that would make you indifferent between these two prospects. If the value you wrote down is less than a million dollars, you are risk-averse.

Let us now turn to the risk-neutral case. If the utility function in Figure 5.2 had been linear, the dashed line CD would have been coincident with the utility function, and the points F and G would therefore have been coincident. In this case, the individual would have been indifferent between the two prospects: he or she would be risk-neutral.

PROBLEM 5.9

Use a graphic argument similar to the one above to show that a risk-inclined person will prefer the risky prospect to the assured prospect.

5.4
Shedding Risk

risk pooling

A common institution among people who fish for sport is a share-the-bounty convention. At the end of an outing, members of a fishing party usually have a tacit understanding that anyone who catches a trophy fish will take that fish home. Otherwise, the members of the group divide the catch equally, without regard to who actually caught which fish. We can view this institution as a form of insurance against the embarrassment of being "skunked" — coming home empty-handed. Such forms of insurance are arrangements known as **risk pooling**.

Other examples of risk pooling include the understanding among nineteenth-century American pioneers that if one family lost a home to fire, the whole community would pitch in to help them rebuild and the tradition among the Inuit in the North American Arctic of sharing their food equally, even in times of famine.

Informal Risk Pooling

In this section, we use our analytical tools to develop an understanding of risk pooling and of the preferences that make such an institution attractive. We begin by considering two householders, Abe and Martha, who face identical but independent risks — the risk that their houses will burn — and ask if there is any institution they can create that will reduce the burden of risk.

Imagine that the probability that either Abe or Martha will experience a fire is p. Further, suppose that the loss associated with a fire is L dollars. (In what follows, we will concentrate on Abe, but it should be clear that the same analysis applies to Martha.) In the absence of a risk-pooling agreement, Abe's expected utility is just

$$pU(w_0 - L) + (1 - p)U(w_0)$$

where w_0 is his initial wealth. Abe's house will burn with probability p. If it does, Abe's wealth will be $w_0 - L$, and his utility will be $U(w_0 - L)$. On the other hand, the probability that his house will not burn is $1 - p$. Abe's wealth will then be w_0, and his utility will be $U(w_0)$.

Let us now suppose that Abe and Martha agree to *pool* their risks; that is, they agree to share any loss due to fire. We now have three relevant events: both houses burn; one house burns; neither house burns. Because the probabilities of fire are independent, the probability that both will burn is p^2, the product of the two independent probabilities that either house burns. If both houses do burn, Abe will incur a loss of L. Similarly, the probability that neither burns is $(1-p)^2$. In this event, Abe experiences no loss. Finally, the probability that exactly one house burns is $2p(1-p)$. In this event, Abe incurs a loss equal to $L/2$. (To calculate this probability, notice that the probability that Abe's house burns and Martha's does not is $p(1-p)$. Similarly, the probability that Martha's burns and Abe's does not is also $p(1-p)$. Thus, the probability that exactly one house burns is $2p(1-p)$.) Abe's expected utility associated with this risk-pooling agreement is then

$$p^2 U(w_0 - L) + 2p(1-p)U(w_0 - L/2) + (1-p)^2 U(w_0)$$

When does this risk-pooling agreement actually enhance Abe's expected utility? More precisely, when is

$$p^2 U(w_0 - L) + 2p(1-p)U(w_0 - L/2) + (1-p)^2 U(w_0) >$$

$$pU(w_0 - L) + (1-p)U(w_0)$$

The answer is this: The risk pooling agreement enhances Abe's utility if he is *risk-averse*. To see why, first rewrite the inequality from above as follows:

$$2p(1-p)U(w_0 - L/2) > p(1-p)U(w_0 - L) + p(1-p)U(w_0)$$

Then divide both sides of the expression by $2p(1-p)$ to get

$$U(w_0 - L/2) > (1/2)U(w_0 - L) + (1/2)U(w_0)$$

Now we can use the graphic tools from the previous section to show that this inequality holds if Abe is risk averse. In constructing Figure 5.3 we assumed that Abe is risk averse. Notice that $U(w - L/2)$ is distance EG, $U(w_0 - L)$ is distance AC, and $U(w_0)$ is distance BD. To find $(1/2)U(w_0 - L) + (1/2)U(w_0)$, draw the dashed line from C to D and move to the midpoint of this line segment. Point F directly above point E is the midpoint, and $(1/2)U(w_0 - L) + (1/2)U(w_0)$ is equal to distance EF. Since EF is less than EG, we have discovered that Abe prefers the risk-pooling agreement to going it alone, because he is risk-averse. Similarly, if Martha is risk-averse, she, too, will prefer the risk-pooling agreement.

By using the appropriately shaped utility functions, you can check to see that a risk-inclined householder prefers to go it alone and that a risk-neutral householder is indifferent between the two arrangements. An important point emerges from this exercise:

When individuals are risk-averse, they have clear incentives to create institutions allowing them to share, or pool, their risks.

Notice that the risk-pooling institution we have considered does nothing to alter the physical environment; it does nothing to reduce the incidence of fire. Yet it does increase the expected utility of the householders in the pool.

FIGURE 5.3   Risk pooling

The expected utility of the risk pooling agreement exceeds the exceeds the expected utility of bearing the risk alone if $U[w_0 - (L/2)]$ exceeds $[U(w_0 - L) + U(w_o)]/2$. But $U[w_0 - (L/2)]$ is distance EG, and $[U(w_0 - L) + U(w_0)]/2$ is distance EF. A risk-averse individual therefore prefers to pool risks.

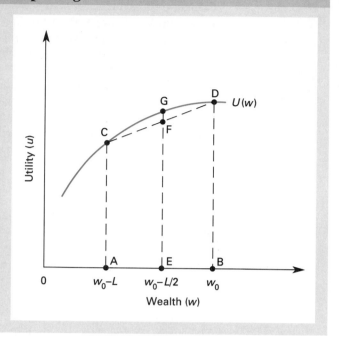

PROBLEM 5.10

Consider two identical steelhead fishers with utility functions $u = x^{1/2}$, where x is the number of fish. Graph this utility function and convince yourself that it represents risk-averse preferences. Assuming that the probability that either will catch one fish is 1/10 and that it is impossible for one fisher can catch two fish, show that if they agree to pool their risks, both will be better off than if they refuse to divide the catch.

In pioneer societies, risk-pooling arrangements such as the community agreement to rebuild homes destroyed by fire were commonly informal arrangements. Such informal risk-pooling arrangements persist today among members of extended families or close-knit communities. In most modern societies, however, the functions these informal institutions used to perform have been taken over to a large extent by insurance markets.

The Market for Insurance

Let us continue to use Abe's risk-of-fire problem as our example and to assume that Abe is risk averse as we explore insurance markets. First, we need to describe Abe's demand for fire insurance, and then we can look at the supply of insurance. Our objective is to show that in a competitive insurance market he will be able to buy fire insurance at a price that makes him better off. Not only will he be better off than if he was forced to bear the burden of risk by himself. He will also be better off than if he took part in an informal risk-pooling agreement of the kind we just described.

We will consider an insurance policy offering full coverage; that is, one that will reimburse Abe for the full amount of the loss in the event of fire. Such a policy pays

reservation
demand price

Abe L in the event of fire and, of course, nothing if there is no fire. We want to find Abe's **reservation demand price** for such a policy. In other words, we want to determine the *maximum amount* he is willing to pay for the policy rather than having to bear the risk of fire himself.

First we want to show that Abe's expected utility in the absence of fire insurance is distance EF in Figure 5.4. His expected wealth is just $w_0 - pL$. And as p ranges from 1 to 0 his expected utility moves along the dashed line CD in Figure 5.4. To find his expected utility, move vertically up from his expected wealth, $w_0 - pL$ at point E, to point F on the dashed line. Therefore, if Abe does not buy fire insurance, his expected utility is distance EF; that is,

$$EF = pU(w_0 - L) + (1 - p)U(w_0)$$

certainty
equivalent

Next, we want to identify the **certainty equivalent** of this risky prospect: the assured prospect, w_{ce}, such that Abe would be indifferent between the assured prospect and the risky one. Algebraically, the certainty equivalent w_{ce} satisfies the following equation:

$$U(w_{ce}) = pU(w_0 - L) + (1 - p)U(w_0) = EF$$

To identify w_{ce} in Figure 5.4, first move horizontally from point F to point G on the utility function and then vertically down to point H on the wealth axis. If Abe has assured prospect w_{ce}, his expected utility will be HG, equal to EF, the expected utility of the risky prospect that Abe has in the absence of insurance. (You already have some experience with certainty equivalents. In Problem 5.1, you wrote down your own certainty equivalent of the prospect $(1/2, 1/2: 2,000,000, 0)$, and in Problem 5.3, you calculated Chauncey's certainty equivalent of Risk.)

EF - if Abe does not buy fire ins. his EU is EF

FIGURE 5.4   The demand for insurance

The expected utility of the risky prospect $(p, 1 - p : w_0 - L, w_0)$ is distance EF. Wealth w_{ce} with no risk yields the same utility since HG = EF. Therefore, w_{ce} is the certainty equivalent of the risky prospect: $(p, 1 - p : w_0 - L, w_0)$. Accordingly, the individual would pay up to I_r for full insurance coverage against loss L.

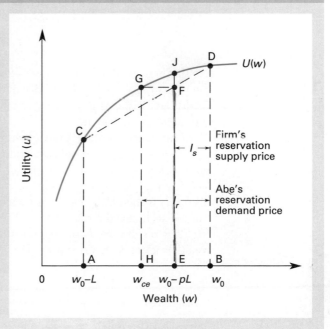

Now, if Abe buys the insurance policy at price I, his wealth level is $w_0 - I$, regardless of whether a fire does or does not occur. Since in the absence of insurance Abe's expected utility is distance EF = HG in Figure 5.4, Abe's reservation price I_r satisfies

$$U(w_0 - I_r) = \text{EF} = \text{HG} = U(w_{ce})$$

Looking at the terms on the extreme left and extreme right in this expression, we see that $w_0 - I_r$ is equal to w_{ce}, or that

$$I_r = w_0 - w_{ce} = \text{HB}$$

This result is intuitive. If Abe did pay I_r for insurance, his assured income would be w_{ce}, the certainty equivalent of personally bearing the risk of fire. If I (the actual price of the insurance) is less than I_r, then Abe's (expected) utility is larger if he buys the policy than it is if he does not. Conversely, if I is greater than I_r, his expected utility is larger if he does not buy the insurance than if he does buy it. That is, if $I < I_r$, he will buy fire insurance, and if $I > I_r$, he will not.

Now that we understand the demand for insurance, let us turn to the supply side of insurance. Will insurance firms be willing to offer full coverage on terms attractive to Abe? That is, is there a viable market for insurance? Let us begin by making the not-so-satisfactory assumption that insurance companies are risk-neutral. We will return later to a more satisfactory discussion of risk bearing by insurance companies.

On the assumption that insurance companies are risk-neutral, what is the lowest price at which a risk-neutral firm will offer full coverage? The answer to this question is an insurance firm's **reservation supply price**, denoted by I_s. Because the firm is by definition risk-neutral, it will simply compare expected monetary values in deciding whether to offer insurance. Ignoring for simplicity any costs it incurs in writing and administering a policy, the firm will pay out L with probability p and \$0 with probability $(1-p)$. Its expected costs are therefore just pL, equal to distance EB in Figure 5.4. Its revenue from selling a policy is I, and it will write the policy if I exceeds pL. The insurance firm's reservation supply price is therefore

reservation
supply price

$$I_s = pL = \text{EB}$$

In the case shown in Figure 5.4, there is a viable market for insurance because the reservation supply price I_s (distance EB) is less than the reservation demand price I_r (distance HB). At any price I greater than I_s and less than I_r, both parties to the transaction gain from it.

If we make the standard competitive assumption that many insurance firms compete to write insurance policies, and continue to ignore the costs of writing and administering policies, we can conclude that in equilibrium price will be driven down to I_s.[6] In this case, Abe trades his risky prospect for the assured prospect $w_0 - pL$, and his utility is then $U(w_0 - pL)$, or the distance EJ in Figure 5.4. Abe's utility gain from the transaction is therefore FJ.

This result is really quite interesting. In this market equilibrium, Abe's expected wealth is identical to his expected wealth in the absence of an insurance policy — yet

---

6 To find the competitive equilibrium, we have invoked the fact that profit is zero in a competitive equilibrium, a result that you probably encountered in earlier course work in economics. We will develop this result in Chapter 9.

he bears no risk. In terms of expected income forgone, the price of insurance is zero, yet Abe clearly benefits since he bears no risk at all. We have learned, then, that the simple act of risk pooling uses no real resources but creates real value.

As we noted, the analysis is based on the assumption that insurance firms are risk-neutral. There is, however, a sense in which insurance firms' attitudes towards risk are irrelevant to our analysis. If insurance companies sell a large number of such policies, effectively they are pooling a large number of independent risks of fire. A fundamental result in statistics — called the *law of large numbers* — then implies that such companies can be quite accurate in projecting their costs. The larger the number of policies they sell, the more accurate are their cost calculations. As the number of policies they sell gets very large, the risk that each firm bears gets very small. Effectively, such firms bear very little risk, and their attitudes towards risk are therefore not of material interest.

> **PROBLEM 5.11**
>
> Show that the reservation price for full coverage of a risk-inclined householder is less than pL. This result implies that, for such householders, $I_r < I_s$. Thus, there is no price at which this householder and a risk-neutral insurance company could engage in a mutually beneficial transfer of risk.

Let us summarize what we have learned:

If no resources are required to write and administer insurance policies and if individuals are risk-averse, there is a viable market for insurance.

Risk Spreading

risk spreading

We have seen that insurance is simply a market mechanism for risk pooling and that it is potentially valuable to risk-averse individuals. The other side of this coin is a phenomenon called **risk spreading**. To see what's involved, imagine that you own some indivisible and risky asset — a promising 2-year-old racehorse, for example. Clearly, risks are entailed in holding this asset. The horse's promise may not materialize: it may break a leg; it may be kidnapped for ransom and disappear; it may fail as a stud horse or brood mare. In this circumstance, someone who is risk-averse might prefer to spread the risk rather than remain the sole owner of the asset.

A prime example of such an asset is Devil's Bag. As a 2-year-old, this horse was thought to be the latest and greatest American wonder. Its owner chose to sell it to a syndicate — a group of joint shareholders, each of whom owned a fraction of the horse — for $36 million, rather than to bear the risk alone. A syndicate is therefore a risk-spreading institution. In fact, the owner was wise to think that owning Devil's Bag was a risky business and to choose to spread that risk. The racehorse did not fulfill his potential and was retired as a 3-year-old.

Syndicating a racehorse is only one example of risk spreading: the common device in which a risky, indivisible asset is spread over more than one holder. The joint-venture companies that sponsored voyages of discovery (or perhaps, plunder) by men like Sir Francis Drake are illustrations of risk spreading from an earlier time. Today, joint-stock companies spread the risks of a firm among the firm's stockholders. Problem 5.12 conveys the basic insight of risk spreading:

Risk-averse individuals may prefer holding some part of a risky asset to holding the entire asset.

> **PROBLEM 5.12**
>
> Patricia's utility function is $U(w) = w^{1/2}$, and her initial wealth is $100, $w_0 = 100$. For a price of $100, she can buy an asset that will yield $10,000 with probability 1/20 and $0 with probability 19/20. Observe that the expected monetary value of this asset is $500 while its price is just $100. Show that she will not buy this asset alone but will join a syndicate with 10 equal partners.

The Case for Risk Aversion

Risk aversion is thought to be the usual, or representative, attitude towards risk. This view is supported by abundant examples of risk-averse behavior. Most people choose to insure against various kinds of losses; even the fabulously wealthy are not the sole owners of Kentucky Derby contenders like Go For Gin and Sunday Silence; the joint-stock company is a dominant form of business enterprise. So, too, an ever-increasing number of U.S. firms are teaming up with foreign competitors in joint-venture arrangements. One of the motivating forces behind these joint ventures is that they lower the risk associated with high-tech product development, which almost invariably carries a multimillion dollar price tag. For instance, the arch rivals Texas Instruments and Hitachi joined forces to develop a 16-megabit dynamic RAM chip for the computer market because, as one TI executive put it, "We both needed a partner to minimize our risks." The ubiquity of these risk-pooling and risk-spreading arrangements is fairly convincing evidence that most individuals are risk-averse.

5.5

The Economics of Asymmetric Information

Young job seekers often complain that they could do jobs they have had no experience with, if only they were given the chance. Implicit in the statement are two presumptions: 1. that the young person in question could indeed do the job, and 2. that he or she cannot successfully convey this fact to the prospective employer. As a result, the employer — who perhaps uses on-the-job experience as the criterion for separating good prospective workers from bad ones — is unwilling to hire the inexperienced youth. The key element in this case is clearly a problem of **asymmetric information**. The young person knows that he or she is capable of doing the job, but the employer does not, and the young person may have no effective way to the communicate the relevant information to the employer.

asymmetric information

A similar phenomenon arises in the market for car insurance. If a driver is under age 25, particularly if that driver is also male and single, collision insurance rates can be astronomical. These rates reflect the fact that, on average, drivers in this category have significantly higher accident rates than do other drivers. But not all young, single males are bad drivers, and some are very good. If we presume that the good drivers know that they are good, they face a problem analogous to that of young job seekers: they cannot easily convey this information to insurance companies. Often, their options are limited to either paying extremely high rates or going without collision insurance.

hidden characteristic

In this section, we develop some simple models that let us explore problems that arise when information is asymmetric. The first model involves a particular **hidden characteristic**: the driving ability of a particular male driver under the age of 25, which is — from the perspective of an insurance company — an unknown, or hidden, factor.

Hidden Characteristics

We can extend the insurance model from the preceding section to explore problems arising from hidden characteristics. Here we will focus on collision insurance rather than fire insurance, and we will add three assumptions about hidden characteristics.

1. The relevant characteristic of any driver is the *probability of loss from a collision,* and this characteristic is *not* uniform across drivers: Some drivers are low-risk and others are high-risk.

2. Each driver is *completely informed* about his or her own characteristic: drivers know whether they are low risk or high risk.

3. Drivers cannot communicate their risk characteristic costlessly to insurance companies: The driving characteristic of an individual — high-risk or low-risk — is *hidden* from insurance companies.

We will assume that there are just two types of drivers: a low-risk group and a high-risk group. Let p^1 be the probability that a low-risk driver causes a collision, and p^2 the probability that a high-risk driver causes a collision. The loss from any collision is L, and the cost of the loss is borne by the driver responsible for the collision. Clearly, p^1 is less than p^2. We will also assume that all drivers are risk averse and that they have identical preferences and identical wealth levels, w_0. In this model, then, the two groups of drivers are differentiated *only* by the probability of collision. In all other respects, drivers in the two groups are identical.

In exploring the market for collision insurance, we will only consider policies that offer full coverage against loss L. Let us begin by deriving the reservation prices for the two groups. In Figure 5.5, the reservation price for a member of the low-risk group

FIGURE 5.5   More on the demand for insurance

Individuals in low-risk and high-risk groups incur loss L with probabilities p^1 and p^2, respectively, and they have identical utility functions and initial wealth w_0. For the low-risk group, w_{ce}^{1} is the certainty equivalent of the risky prospect and I_1^{r} the reservation price for insurance offering full coverage against loss L. Similarly, for the high-risk group, w_{ce}^{2} is the certainty equivalent and I_2^{r} the reservation price.

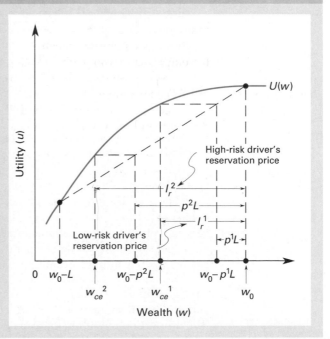

is denoted by I_r^1, and the reservation price for a member of the high-risk group is denoted by I_r^2. Since full coverage is more valuable to high-risk drivers than to low-risk drivers, I_r^2 is larger than I_r^1. If insurance companies could identify without cost every driver's risk characteristic, then in a competitive market equilibrium, insurance companies would supply two types of policies: one for low-risk drivers and the other one for high-risk drivers. If we again ignore the costs of writing insurance policies, the competitive prices of the low-risk and high-risk policies would be $p^1 L$ and $p^2 L$ as shown in Figure 5.5.

full information equilibrium

These are the prices that would emerge in a **full information equilibrium** — that is, in a situation where insurance companies were fully informed about each driver's probability of a collision. The full information equilibrium is, of course, a simple generalization of what we discovered in the preceding model of the insurance market.

In this model, however, a driver's risk characteristic is *hidden* and cannot be *costlessly identified* by insurance companies. What will the equilibrium look like in this situation? Let us begin by assuming that the cost of identifying each driver's risk characteristic is prohibitively high. In this extreme circumstance, the market will offer only one policy. Again assuming a competitive insurance market and ignoring firms' costs of writing and administering policies, the market price for this policy will be determined by the *relative sizes* of the two groups. Let s be the proportion of low-risk drivers in the population and $1 - s$ the proportion of high-risk drivers. The probability that a randomly selected driver will incur loss L is then $sp^1 + (1 - s)p^2$. If they all buy insurance, the market price I will satisfy

$$I = L[sp^1 + (1 - s)p^2]$$

From this equation, we see that

$$p^1 L < I < p^2 L$$

But, $p^1 L$ and $p^2 L$ are the equilibrium prices for low- and high-risk drivers in the full information equilibrium. These inequalities indicate that when identifying risk characteristics is prohibitively expensive, if all drivers do choose to buy insurance, low-risk drivers pay more than in the full-information equilibrium and high-risk drivers pay less:

In the equilibrium in which all drivers buy insurance, low-risk drivers subsidize the insurance purchases of high-risk drivers.

However, low-risk drivers will buy an insurance policy, *only* if I is less than (or equal to) the reservation price I_r^1. Notice that in Figure 5.5, $p^2 L$ exceeds I_r^1. Notice, too, that as the proportion of low-risk drivers in the population, s, approaches zero — or equivalently, as the proportion of high risk drivers, $(1 - s)$, approaches 1 — I approaches $p^2 L$. Therefore, I is not necessarily less than I_r^1. Indeed, if the proportion of high-risk drivers is large enough, the price I will exceed I_r^1. In this case, low-risk drivers will refuse to buy an insurance policy, and the market price for insurance will not be I. Instead, the resulting competitive equilibrium will be one in which only high-risk drivers buy insurance, and the market price will be $p^2 L$. To summarize:

If the proportion of high-risk drivers is not too high, then in equilibrium all drivers will buy insurance, and low-risk drivers will subsidize high-risk drivers. But, if the proportion of high-risk drivers is too high, then in equilibrium, only high-risk drivers will buy insurance, and low-risk drivers will be forced out of the market.

---

market failure

This is a case of **market failure**: a failure that arises because drivers' risk characteristics are hidden from insurance companies. As we saw in the previous section, insurance markets perform a valuable function: with perfect information, such markets allow individuals to shed all risk at no cost to themselves (in terms of expected monetary wealth). When drivers' risk characteristics are hidden, the insurance market may fail in the sense that low-risk drivers will personally bear the risk of loss from collision.

adverse
selection

This market failure arises from a phenomenon called **adverse selection**. When insurance companies cannot identify individual risk characteristics, they are forced to offer a single policy — one that is obviously more attractive to high-risk than to low-risk drivers. In fact, if some low-risk drivers choose not to insure, rates climb; that rate hike then drives even more low-risk drivers out of the market, causing rates to go even higher and forcing even more low-risk drivers out of the market. In our model, where there are just two types of drivers, if the proportion of high-risk drivers is large enough, all the low-risk drivers are forced out of the market — an extreme form of adverse selection.[7]

Adverse Selection: The "Lemons Principle"

The phenomenon of adverse selection has a more colorful tag, the "lemons principle," attributable to George Akerlof (1970). Akerlof was concerned with the market for lemons — the kind you drive, not the kind for making lemonade. Akerlof asked why the market price of a new car drops by $3,000 or more the instant the proud owner drives it off the lot. He answered by arguing that 1. anyone who wanted to sell the new car he or she had recently bought might very well have learned in the short period since the car was bought that it was a lemon, and 2. a wary buyer in the second-hand market could figure this out. Therefore, the buyer in the second-hand market will demand a significant discount off the new-car price to compensate for the high subjective probability that the car is a lemon. Unfortunate people who impulsively bought the wrong (for them) new car, or decided that they could not really afford a new car, will be indistinguishable from those who discovered that the car they bought really was a lemon. Those unfortunate people will also be forced to accept a discounted price if they want to sell their car in the second-hand market.

To develop a deeper understanding of the lemons problem, imagine that there are only two types of used cars: "lemons" and "jewels." Imagine, too, that ascertaining whether a particular used car is a lemon or a jewel is prohibitively costly for a potential buyer — but that car sellers do know. That is, the car's characteristic — lemon or jewel — is a hidden characteristic. And imagine that all car owners who want to sell their cars initially put them on the market. The price of used cars will then reflect the mix of lemons and jewels offered for sale.

Let us assume that buyers form subjective probabilities based on the relative proportions of lemons and jewels offered for sale. The owner of a jewel will then be unable to sell it at a price that reflects its true value, because the owner cannot effectively communicate the car's true worth. (How many lemon owners will honestly say that their car is a lemon?)

Some owners who want to sell their jewels at a "fair" price may decide not to sell at the market price. The proportion of lemons on the market then increases, further depressing the market price and perhaps inducing other owners of jewels to withdraw their

---

7 See Rothschild and Stiglitz (1976) for a more complete analysis of insurance and asymmetric information. See also the entries in *The New Palgrave* titled "asymmetric information" (A. Postlewaite), "adverse selection" (C. Wilson), and "moral hazard" (Y. Kotowitz).

cars from the market. In the eventual equilibrium, some owners of jewels — unwilling to accept significantly less than the car's true value — choose not to sell at the market price. If all such owners make this choice, there will be a market for lemons but none for jewels. Because of the problem of a hidden characteristic, in this situation lemons drive jewels (some or all of them) out of the market — a phenomenon that we might call either *adverse selection* or *the lemons principle*.

PROBLEM 5.13

Suppose that, with perfect information, the market value of a jewel is $2,400 and the market value of a lemon is $1,200. Assume that, in the absence of perfect information, the market price of a car will be $s$$2,400 + (1 − s)$1,200, where s is the proportion of jewels on the market. There are three groups of potential sellers: 200 owners of jewels whose reservation prices are $2,000; 400 owners of jewels whose reservation prices are $1,600; and 400 owners of lemons whose reservation prices are less than $1,200. Show that the cars in the last two groups — but not the cars in the first group — will be sold. What is the market failure in this case?

Signaling

signaling

The problem that has threaded its way through this section is that when relevant characteristics are hidden, people suffer real economic consequences. For example, in our model of the market for collision insurance, low-risk drivers either subsidize high-risk drivers or they are driven from the market and forced to do without insurance. Clearly, the individuals who suffer have an incentive to try to find a way out of dilemma posed by hidden characteristics. Their response is known as **signaling**.

Let us modify our model of hidden characteristics in the market for collision insurance to incorporate the possibility that low-risk drivers can signal (convincingly identify themselves) to insurance firms. What we need is some form of low-risk certification. If the certificate is to produce a signaling equilibrium, three conditions must hold. Condition 1: insurance companies must be convinced that the certificate does signal a low-risk driver. Given a convincing certificate, the competitive equilibrium price for insurance for a driver with a certificate will be p^1L. Condition 2: the cost to low-risk drivers of getting a certificate must be small enough so that they have an incentive to acquire it. Condition 3: the cost to high-risk drivers of getting a certificate must be large enough so that they have an no incentive to acquire it. If these conditions are satisfied, two policies will be offered in equilibrium, one for drivers with a certificate at price p^1L, and the other for drivers without a certificate, at price p^2L. Furthermore, all low-risk drivers — but no high-risk drivers — will present a certificate.

Differential costs of acquiring a certificate are central to this signaling model. Let C^1 and C^2 denote costs of acquiring such a certificate for low- and high-risk drivers respectively, and suppose that C^1 is less than C^2. For the moment, suppose, too, that condition 1 is satisfied: insurance firms find the certificate convincing. Then, condition 2 will be satisfied if the following inequality holds:

$$C^1 < I_r^1 - p^1L$$

Recall that in our model, low-risk drivers prefer doing without insurance to paying price p^2L for insurance; that is, I_r^1 is less than p^2L as shown in Figure 5.5. Therefore the value of a certificate to low-risk drivers is $I_r^1 - p^1L$. They will acquire a certificate if this value is larger than the cost of a certificate. Similarly, condition 3 will be satisfied if the following inequality holds:

$$p^2L - p^1L < C^2$$

The value of the certificate to high-risk drivers would be $p^2L - p^1L$, which must be smaller than C^2 to insure that high-risk drivers do not acquire the certificate. Finally, if both of these inequalities are satisfied, the credibility of the certificate as a signal, specified in condition 1, is also satisfied, and the result is a signaling equilibrium. To summarize:

> **If it is very costly for high-risk drivers to obtain the signal and not too costly for low-risk drivers, then there will be a signaling equilibrium in which low-risk drivers acquire the signal in order to get a lower insurance rate by differentiating themselves from high-risk drivers.**

It is useful to compare the properties of this signaling equilibrium relative to the equilibrium in the absence of signaling. The first point of comparison concerns the equilibrium in which all drivers buy insurance and low-risk drivers subsidize high-risk drivers. Relative to this alternative, signaling simply *redistributes wealth* from high-risk drivers to low-risk drivers. However, since low-risk drivers spend money to acquire certificates, the *gains* to low-risk drivers as a group are *smaller* that the losses for high-risk drivers as a group. The other point of comparison is the equilibrium in which low-risk drivers simply do not insure. Relative to this alternative, signaling, in effect, *creates wealth* since it facilitates the formation of a new market in which low-risk drivers shed the risk that they otherwise would have borne themselves.

Now that we understand the conditions necessary for a signaling equilibrium, let us see where we can find markets characterized by a signaling equilibrium. In some places, insurance companies offer a discount to any young driver who presents a certificate or diploma from a reputable driver education program. That is, insurance companies regard drivers with such certificates as low-risk drivers, relative to young drivers who do not have certificates. Why do they accept these certificates as a convincing signal that a young driver is a lower risk?

One possibility is that drivers with certificates are lower-risk because they learned good driving habits in the driver education program. This is what economists call a **human capital** explanation. By taking the driver education course, the young driver acquires skills — the human capital — that make him or her a better driver. Another possibility is that drivers with certificates are at lower risk because of an inherent low-risk characteristic. This explanation — which presumes that there is an *inherent difference* between young drivers — requires, first, that a high-risk driver's cost of acquiring a certificate is higher than the anticipated benefit in the form of lower insurance rates and, second, that a low-risk driver's cost of acquiring a certificate is lower than the anticipated benefits. Is it true that a significant number of young drivers — knowing that they are inherently high-risk — anticipate that they will have a hard time acquiring a certificate and therefore choose not to even try for it? If so, then this signaling model would seem to provide at least a partial explanation of why insurance companies accept driver education certificates as proof of a young driver's low-risk characteristic.

If we look a little further afield, we can find circumstances that clearly involve a signaling equilibrium. Imagine, for example, a number of firms that produce competing products, say different CD players. The hidden characteristic is the *quality* of each firm's CD player. Some produce high-quality players and others produce low-quality players, and consumers are unable to accurately assess quality prior to purchase. Firms that produce high-quality players have a real incentive to signal that high quality because

human capital

they can sell their products at a higher price. They will therefore look for some kind of "certificate of quality" that they can afford to offer—and that low-quality firms cannot afford to offer. That certificate is a sufficiently comprehensive warranty against defects. Clearly, offering a product warranty costs high-quality firms less for the simple reason that their products have fewer defects. Just consider the extreme case of a firm that produces a product of maximal quality — a product that is 100 percent defect-free. It can offer a perfectly comprehensive warranty, secure in the knowledge that the warranty will cost it nothing since its product is free of defects. Thus, the signaling model leads us to anticipate an equilibrium in which high-quality products are sold at relatively high prices with comprehensive warranties that signal their quality, and low-quality products are sold at relatively low prices with minimal warranties or no warranty at all. This is what we actually see in many markets for consumer durables.

screening

So far, we have concentrated on signaling. The other side of the coin is **screening**. In the collision insurance model, low-risk drivers acquired a certificate to signal that they were low-risk, and insurance firms used the certificate to *screen* drivers — that is, to divide drivers into different risk groups. In our discussion of warranties, high-quality firms offered comprehensive warranties to signal that their products were high quality, and customers used the warranty to screen products — that is, to sort out products by quality level. To return to our inexperienced job searcher, we see that employers sometimes use job experience (and, of course, references) to screen applicants — that is, job experience signals an applicant's capability. Frustratingly, this particular screening technique has a Catch-22. If all employers use it, inexperienced workers may find it impossible to break into the market. Particularly in times of high unemployment, employers may have no incentive to experiment with other screening techniques, and inexperienced workers may be frozen out of the market.[8]

Once we grasp the basic insights of signaling/screening equilibria, we can look at familiar events from a new perspective. For example, these ideas suggest that a major function of higher education is to provide relatively gifted individuals with a means of signaling their abilities to the world. A degree from Harvard or Stanford or Oxford or Queen's may be valuable partly because it is seen as a signal of the degree holder's ability. The following problem, adapted from Stiglitz (1975), will allow you to explore this possibility in a very simple model.

> ### PROBLEM 5.14
>
> Imagine a world peopled by superior and inferior workers: a superior worker is worth $50 per hour to any employer, and an inferior worker is worth only $20 per hour. These people work for exactly 10 hours and then retire. Let s be the proportion of superior workers, and $1 - s$ the proportion of inferior workers. What will the common wage be if the superior workers do *not* signal their ability? Assume that in the labor-market equilibrium, workers are paid their expected worth. Now suppose that a degree costs superior workers $200 and that it is simply impossible for an inferior worker to get a degree. For what values of s will superior workers acquire a degree to signal their superior productivity?

---

8 Interested readers are referred to the insightful and remarkably readable book by Spence (1974).

Moral Hazard Problems: Hidden Actions

hidden actions

moral hazard problems

The asymmetric information problems we have so far looked at involve hidden characteristics — characteristics such as quality of a product or the probability that a particular driver will cause an accident — that are known by one party to a transaction but not by the other. There is another class of asymmetric information problems that involve not hidden characteristics, but instead **hidden actions**. These hidden action problems are sometimes called **moral hazard problems**. For example, think of a student who wants to write a final examination early. Imagine that this student's last final is scheduled for December 22, and that all his or her other examinations are over by December 8. Clearly, this student would prefer to write the last final, say, on December 9 or 10 rather than December 22.

Will the instructor cooperate? You already know the answer — probably not. However, it is useful to think about why instructors are generally so reluctant to permit students to write finals early. In most cases, if the instructor could be *certain* that the student would not tell other students about the exam, he or she would be happy to accommodate this student. But there is an obvious moral hazard problem — the instructor has no reliable way of knowing whether or not the student will tell other students about the examination. In other words, the student's action is hidden from the instructor. It's not that instructors assume the worst; it's just that they generally have a *non-zero subjective probability* that the student will talk to others about the examination. It is this positive subjective probability that makes an instructor reluctant to grant a student's request to write an early final exam. Notice that the student who wants to write early is *worse off* than he or she would be if the action was *not* a hidden action. Since no one else would be worse off and this student would be better off if he or she did take the exam and did not tell other students about it, we have another failure to achieve efficiency. Again, the failure is attributable to *asymmetric information*.

We can also adapt our collision insurance model to illustrate a similar moral hazard problem. Let us suppose that all drivers are identical; they have the same wealth, the same preferences, and face the same probabilistic loss L. The new wrinkle is this: sometime prior to an accident but after the driver has bought insurance, the driver can take an action that reduces the probability of loss L. Specifically, if the driver spends C on accident prevention, the probability of loss L is reduced from p to p'. (It is convenient to think of drivers as actually spending money to reduce the probability of an accident, but it is not necessary. Instead, we might think of the driver as exerting time and effort to reduce the probability of collision — say, by driving more slowly and practicing defensive driving techniques — and therefore think of C as the value the driver places on that time and effort.) The problem is that spending C on accident prevention cannot be observed by insurance companies: it is a hidden action. To make the problem interesting, we will assume that

$$C < L(p - p')$$

If this inequality did not hold, the reduction in the expected loss, equal to $L(p - p')$, is not large enough to justify the expenditure on accident prevention, C. In Figure 5.6, if insurance companies could be sure that all their customers would actually spend C to reduce the probability of loss from p to p' once they had bought insurance, then the equilibrium price for full coverage would be $p'L$, customers would have assured wealth level $w_0 - C - p'L$, and each customer would enjoy utility level EF. But the customer — having already bought full coverage against loss L and knowing that spending C on accident prevention is a hidden action — will choose not to spend C.

FIGURE 5.6   Hidden actions in the insurance market

If insurance companies could be sure that their customers would spend C to reduce the probability of accidents from p to p', the price of insurance would be $p'L$ and customers would get expected utility EF. But since spending C is a hidden action, the price of insurance will be pL. A customer who buys insurance at this price gets expected utility GH. If this customer instead spends C to reduce the probability of accident and buys no insurance, he or she gets expected utility EJ. Since GH is less than EJ, customers choose this last option.

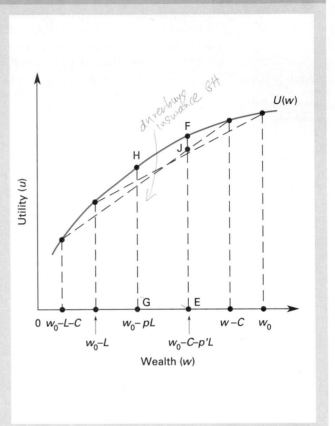

Anticipating the customer's behavior, insurance companies will not offer insurance at price $p'L$. Instead, they will offer full coverage only at the higher price pL.

Given this higher price, if a driver does buy insurance, expected utility is equal to distance GH in Figure 5.6. The driver has the option of going without insurance and spending C on accident prevention. Expected utility associated with this course of action is distance EJ. Since EJ exceeds GH, in the case shown in Figure 5.6, the driver will choose not to buy insurance. Since this driver could get expected utility EF if there was no hidden action, we again have a market failure attributable to asymmetric information. However, it is not necessarily the case that EJ exceeds GH. For example, if C was a bit larger than it is in Figure 5.6, the opposite would be true, and drivers would buy insurance. In this case, the burden of the hidden action is EF minus GH. To summarize:

> If an individual could credibly promise to spend C on accident prevention, the price of full coverage would be $p'L$, and he or she would clearly be better off. But, since the action is hidden, the promise is not credible, and insurance companies will not offer insurance at this price.

To see that hidden action problems are not uncommon, try the following problem.

PROBLEM 5.15

Explain the hidden action problem in the following situations.
a. A teenager has a drinking problem, and the parents refuse to lend the family car to the teenager.
b. Fires and, therefore, fire insurance claims, have a pronounced counter-cyclical pattern: insurance claims for fires are relatively low when times are good and relatively high when times are bad.

SUMMARY

In this chapter, we extended the theory of preferences and consumer choice to situations involving *risk* and *imperfect information* and then used this expanded theory to examine a variety of problems in which either risk or imperfect information play a central role.

We began with an empirical paradox: contrary to what one might expect, in many game situations involving a choice among risky prospects, players do not choose the prospect with the highest *expected monetary value*. Following Daniel Bernoulli's lead, we proposed the alternative hypothesis that they choose the prospect with the highest *expected utility*. A *prospect* is just a list of possible outcomes and associated probabilities. For each possible outcome there is a utility, and the expected utility of a prospect is the probability-weighted average of these utilities of outcomes. The *expected-utility theory* is often applied to situations that involve not risk, but rather imperfect information. To apply the expected-utility approach to these situations we can think of a prospect as a list of possible outcomes and associated *subjective probabilities*.

We then identified three possible attitudes towards risk — *risk aversion*, *risk neutrality*, and *risk inclination* — and we argued that the prevalence of *risk-pooling* and *risk-spreading* arrangements provides convincing evidence that in most situations, most people are risk-averse. This led us to a detailed exploration of the market for insurance — an important risk pooling arrangement.

Finally, we turned to an exploration of some intriguing problems that arise when information is asymmetric. We used a series of insurance market models to articulate both the problems associated with *assymetric information* and various partial solutions to them. We began by looking at a number of situations involving a *hidden characteristic*, and showed how hidden characteristics can give rise to market failure. For example, if young drivers' risk characteristics are hidden characteristics— known to the drivers themselves but not to insurance companies — then low-risk drivers may choose not to insure, and if they do insure they will, in effect, be subsidizing high-risk drivers. We then showed how *signaling* and *screening* might partially resolve the market failures associated with hidden characteristics. Finally, we looked at several situations involving *hidden actions* and showed how, in these *moral hazard problems*, hidden actions can also give rise to market failure.

EXERCISES

1. Consider the following game. Daniel offers to toss a coin until one head appears, and he promises to pay you 2^n dollars, where n is the toss on which the first head appears. If it appears on the first toss, you get $2; if on the second, $4; if on the third, $8; and so on. What is the maximum

amount you would pay to play the game? What is the expected monetary value of this game? This is the exercise that led Daniel Bernoulli to propose the expected-utility hypothesis.

2. Show that the expected monetary value hypothesis is a special case of the expected-utility hypothesis. Hint: what attitude towards risk makes an individual indifferent between two prospects if they have the same expected monetary value?

3. In draw poker, suppose a player is dealt four clubs and a two of hearts. The player may discard the two of hearts in the hope of getting another club to complete a club flush. Does the situation in which the player discards the two of clubs and draws another card involve risk or imperfect information?

4. Guy Rogers reveals the following piece of information regarding his preferences for risky prospects with prizes of $20, $12, and $0:

    (0, 1, 0: 20, 12, 0) is indifferent to
    (.7, 0, .3: 20, 12, 0)

    a. Explain in words the meaning of this preference statement.
    b. Assuming that Guy satisfies the expected-utility assumptions, find a utility function that represents Guy's preferences for prospects with these three prizes.
    c. Is Guy risk-averse, risk-neutral, or risk-inclined? Explain.
    d. Compute Guy's expected utility for the following prospects:

        Prospect A (.6, 0, .4: 20, 12, 0)

        Prospect B (.4, .2, .4: 20, 12, 0)

        Prospect C (0, 1, 0: 20, 12, 0)

        Prospect D (.3, .4, .3: 20, 12, 0)

        Prospect E (.5, .2, .3: 20, 12, 0)

    e. What is Guy's preference ordering for these prospects?

5. Julie says that she is indifferent between a lottery that pays either (i) $100 or $10 with equal probability and (ii) $50 with certainty. Which lottery will Julie choose in each of the following situations?

    a. (1/4, 3/4: 100, 10) or (1/2, 1/2: 50, 10)
    b. (3/4, 1/4: 100, 10) or (9/10, 1/10: 50, 10)

    c. (1/2, 1/2: 100, 10) or (2/6, 3/6, 1/6: 100, 50, 10)

6. Consider the following prospects that offer prizes $10, $5, and $1.

    Prospect A (1/3, 1/3, 1/3: 10, 5, 1)

    Prospect B (1/2, 0, 1/2: 10, 5, 1)

    Prospect C (0, 3/4, 1/4,: 10, 5, 1)

    a. Let $U(10) = 1$ and $U(1) = 0$, and then find $U(5)$ for a risk-neutral person.
    b. Show that the statement that C preferred to B preferred to A is consistent with expected-utility theory. Is this preference ordering associated with risk aversion, risk inclination, or risk neutrality?
    c. Show that the statement that B preferred to A preferred to C is consistent with expected-utility theory. Is this preference ordering associated with risk aversion, risk inclination, or risk neutrality?
    d. Show that the statement that A preferred to B preferred to C is inconsistent with expected-utility theory.

7. Farmer Jane has to decide whether or not to fertilize her field. The decision is a difficult one, because her profit depends not only on her decision with respect to fertilizer, but also on whether it rains or not. Her profit w in each of the four possible cases is given below:

	Do not fertilize	Fertilize
Rain	$w = \$16$	$w = \$25$
No rain	$w = \$9$	$w = \$0$

    Suppose that the probability of rain is 1/2. Will Jane fertilize her field if her utility function is $U(w) = w^{1/2}$? If it is $U(w) = w$? If it is $U(w) = w^2$?

8. In looking at insurance markets, we ignored the costs of writing and administering insurance policies. Once we introduce such costs, some of the lessons we learned require amendment. A friend once gave us a piece of advice: even though you are risk-averse, never buy insurance against small losses. Is this good advice?

9. Mike is going to Lake Tahoe and plans to take $2,500. With probability 1/2, he will lose $1,600 on his way to Tahoe. Thus, he will spend $2,500 in Tahoe if he is lucky and only $900 if he is unlucky. His utility from the trip is given by the following function:

$$U(E) = E^{1/2}$$

where E is the amount of money he spends in Tahoe.

a. What is Mike's expected utility from the trip?

b. Suppose Mike can buy an insurance policy that will cover the entire $1,600 loss. Will he buy it if its price is $1,000? $900? $800?

c. What is Mike's reservation price for this insurance policy?

d. What is the competitive-equilibrium price of the policy if insurance companies have perfect information and incur no transaction costs?

10. Kevin is also going to Tahoe with $2,500, has the same utility function as does Mike, but is more careful with his money than is Mike — Kevin will lose $1,600 with probability 1/4.

a. What is Kevin's reservation price for the insurance policy offering full coverage against the $1,600 loss?

b. Suppose now that there are many people like Mike, and many like Kevin, and that insurance companies cannot tell which people are careless with their money ($p = 1/2$) and which are careful with their money ($p = 1/4$). Suppose, too, that the insurance market is competitive, that insurance companies incur no transactions costs, and that the only policy offered is the full-coverage policy. Carefully describe the competitive equilibrium when half the people are like Mike ($p = 1/2$) and half like Kevin ($p = 1/4$). When one-eighth are like Mike and seven-eighths like Kevin.

11. Many people in the United States get their health insurance through a group health insurance plan. Typically, *all* employees of the same firm are insured under the group plan. It is often the case that the per-person group rate is significantly lower than the rate an individual member of the group could get if he or she bought comparable insurance on the open market. Develop an asymmetric information explanation of this phenomenon.

12. A number of serious diseases, including AIDS and hepatitis, can be transmitted via blood transfusion from a diseased person to an uninfected person. This creates a nasty hidden characteristic problem for the supply of blood for transfusions. One response to the problem is to rely on charitable blood donations instead of paying for blood. What is the advantage of this approach? Is this an example of market failure driven by asymmetric information?

13. Some states have recently made it illegal to discriminate on the basis of sex and age in the sale of automobile insurance. Insurance firms must offer the same price to all residents of these states, regardless of age or sex. (An older friend is waiting for the day when the same sort of laws prohibit such discrimination in the sale of life insurance.) Could this sort of legislation be a source of market failure?

14. Ms. Q, whose $1,000 wealth is invested in a riskless asset, has been offered the chance to buy a firm that produces snake oil. The price of the firm is $500. The Federal Drug Administration is reviewing the snake oil with an eye to banning its sale. She believes that with probability 1/2 the snake oil will be banned and the business will then be worthless and that with probability 1/2 it will be approved and the business will then be worth $2,500. Her utility function is $1n(w)$, the natural logarithm of her wealth w. Will she buy the business?

15. This problem concerns a puzzle raised by individuals who simultaneously insure and gamble. This behavior is puzzling because risk-averse preferences induce people to insure but not to gamble, and risk-inclined preferences induce them to gamble but not to insure. In this problem, you can rediscover a very famous explanation of this puzzle suggested by Friedman and Savage (1948). Mr. Inflection's utility function is

$$U(w) = w^{1/2} \qquad \text{if } w \leq 1$$

and

$$U(w) = w^2 \qquad \text{if } w > 1$$

a. What is Mr. Inflection's attitude towards risk?

b. Let Inflection's initial wealth be equal to 1, $w_0 = 1$, and suppose that he will incur a loss $L = 1/2$ with probability p = 1/20 and that he can insure against this loss for a price p times L, or 1/40. Suppose, too, that he can buy a lottery ticket that will pay $J = 1$ with probability $q = 1/1,000$ (and will otherwise pay nothing) for a price equal to q times J, or 1/1,000. Inflection has four options: to buy insurance, to buy the lottery ticket, to buy both, or to buy neither. Rank the four options. In particular, show that he will buy both.

c. In 25 words or less, what is the explanation of Mr. Inflection's curious behavior?

*16. Lucky Pierre is a risk-averse prospector who has struck it rich. He has $W worth of gold — his only wealth — safely stashed away on his claim. He wants to get his gold from his claim to the big city where he hopes to spend it. His friend Wells Fargo will transport the gold for him free of charge. With probability p, all the gold on any trip will be stolen; with probability $(1 - p)$, none of it will be stolen. Show that Lucky's expected utility is larger if half the gold is transferred in each of two trips than if all the gold is transferred in a single trip.

5A
Appendix: The Expected-Utility Theorem

In this appendix, we state and prove an expected-utility theorem for the case in which prospects have three possible outcomes. This theorem is interesting for a number of reasons. Recall that the expected-utility hypothesis is very old, dating from the late eighteenth century, the time of Adam Smith. Furthermore, risk has always been prevalent — even ubiquitous — in real choice situations. It is puzzling, then, that the expected-utility hypothesis was not turned into a theorem until the 1940s, and that the expected-utility approach was not widely used until the 1960s. It is especially puzzling because the expected-utility assumptions are so intuitively appealing and because they so easily yield a proof of the theorem.

The three prizes or outcomes are w_1, w_2, and w_3. We assume that

$$w_1 \text{ is preferred to } w_2, \text{ and } w_2 \text{ is preferred to } w_3$$

The three outcomes are fixed throughout the analysis. Only the probabilities of their occurrence change. We will denote a prospect by (p_1, p_2, p_3), where p_1 is the probability of winning prize w_1, p_2 is the probability of winning prize w_2, and p_3 is the probability of winning prize w_3. The three outcomes are exhaustive and mutually exclusive; therefore,

$$p_1 + p_2 + p_3 = 1$$

To assure a complete preference ordering over prospects we need to adapt the completeness assumption, the two-term consistency assumption, and the transitivity assumption from Chapter 2.

ASSUMPTION: COMPLETENESS

Given any two prospects, say prospect 1 and prospect 2, one of the following statements is true:

prospect 1 is preferred to prospect 2

prospect 2 is preferred to prospect 1

prospect 1 is indifferent to prospect 2

ASSUMPTION: TWO-TERM CONSISTENCY

Given any two prospects, say prospect 1 and prospect 2, only one of the following statements is true:

prospect 1 is preferred to prospect 2

prospect 2 is preferred to prospect 1

prospect 1 is indifferent to prospect 2

ASSUMPTION: TRANSITIVITY

Given any three prospects, say prospect 1, prospect 2, and prospect 3:

1. If prospect 1 is preferred to prospect 2 and prospect 2 is preferred to prospect 3, then prospect 1 is preferred to prospect 3.

2. If prospect 1 is preferred to prospect 2 and prospect 2 is indifferent to prospect 3, then prospect 1 is preferred to prospect 3.

3 If prospect 1 is indifferent to prospect 2 and prospect 2 is preferred to prospect 3, then prospect 1 is preferred to prospect 3.

4. If prospect 1 is indifferent to prospect 2 and prospect 2 is indifferent to prospect 3, then prospect 1 is indifferent to prospect 3.

These three assumptions guarantee the existence of a complete preference ordering over prospects, just as they guaranteed a complete preference ordering over consumption bundles in Chapter 2.

To prove the expected-utility theorem, we need three additional assumptions. The continuity assumption, discussed in Section 5.1, is already familiar to you:

ASSUMPTION: CONTINUITY

There is a unique number e^*, $0 < e^* < 1$, such that

$(0, 1, 0)$ is indifferent to $(e^*, 0, 1 - e^*)$

The probability e^* is, of course, person-specific. It makes the individual indifferent between a prospect that guarantees prize w_2 with certainty, prospect $(0, 1, 0)$, and a risky prospect that offers prize w_1 with probability e^* and prize w_3 with probability $1 - e^*$, prospect $(e^*, 0, 1 - e^*)$.

The Substitution Assumption

The substitution assumption concerns the ability of individuals to evaluate compound prospects. A compound prospect is one that has as one of its outcomes (or prizes) another risky prospect (or lottery). The wheels of fortune on the streets of Paris that offer as prizes lottery tickets in the French National Lottery are one example of a compound prospect. The accumulator bet in horse racing is another example. When the bettor places a "double," it means that the payout for winning one race is to be used as the stake for betting on the next race.

Let us create a compound prospect and then see how to represent it in our notation. We will call $(.35, .50, .15)$ the original prospect. Now, to create a compound prospect, let us substitute the prospect $(.75, 0, .25)$ for the prize w_2 in the original prospect, We will call $(.75, 0, .25)$ the substitute prospect. Notice that only prizes w_1 and w_3 are possible in this compound prospect. What is the probability of winning prize w_1? In the compound prospect, there are two routes to prize w_1 — the direct route described in the original prospect and the indirect route created by the substitution. The probability of getting w_1 by the direct route is just .35 — the probability of w_1 in the original prospect. The probability of getting w_1 by the indirect route is the product of two probabilities, .50 multiplied by .75: .50 is the probability of w_2 in the original prospect, or what we can regard as the probability of substitution, and .75 is the probability of w_1 in the substitute prospect. Hence, in this compound prospect, the probability of w_1 is .725 (.35 + .50 multiplied by .75). Similarly, in the compound prospect, there is a direct and an indirect route to prize w_3. By the direct route, the probability is .15. By the indirect route the probability is .50

multiplied by .25. Hence, the probability of w_3 is .275 (.15 + .5 multiplied by .25). Thus, this particular compound prospect can be written as (.725, 0, .275).

To understand the substitution assumption, let us see how Jack from Problem 5.5 would rank the original prospect and the compound prospect. (This requires that we think of the three outcomes, or prizes, as w_1 = $10,000; w_2 = $6,000; and w_3 = $1,000.) Will Jack prefer the original prospect (.35, .50, .15) or the newly created compound prospect (.725, 0, .275)? Recall that for Jack the value of e^* is .75. From the continuity assumption, we then know that Jack is indifferent between prospect (0, 1, 0) (prize w_2 with certainty) and the substitute prospect (.75, 0, .25). Because we created the compound prospect from the original prospect by substituting (.75, 0, .25) for prize w_2, it seems reasonable to assume that Jack will also be indifferent between the original prospect and the compound prospect: We can restate this more formally as the substitution assumption:

ASSUMPTION: SUBSTITUTION

Given any original prospect (p_1, p_2, p_3) and the number e^* for any individual, by substituting $(e^*, 0, 1 - e^*)$ for w_2 in the original prospect, we create the compound prospect $[p_1 + p_2 e^*, 0, p_3 + p_2(1 - e^*)]$. We assume that the individual is indifferent between the original and the compound prospects. That is,

$$(p_1, p_2, p_3) \text{ is indifferent to } [p_1 + p_2 e^*, 0, p_3 + p_2(1 - e^*)]$$

This assumption can be seen as having two parts. The first part of the assumption seems reasonable enough: if individuals can do the required compound probability calculations effortlessly, then we assume that their preferences will satisfy this assumption. The second part is that individuals can actually do the requisite calculations without great difficulty: we assume that they understand the laws of compound probability and that they can make calculations accordingly. Although some people have learned to do such calculations easily, many people have fairly limited computational abilities. This suggests that the substitution assumption is problematical. To test your facility with such calculations, try the following problem.

PROBLEM A5.1

Recall from Problem 5.5 that Jack is indifferent between prospects (0, 1, 0) and (.75, 0, .25). Show that for Jack, the following indifference statements are implied by the substitution assumption:

(1/3, 1/3, 1/3) is indifferent to (7/12, 0, 5/12)

and

(1/2, 1/4, 1/4) is indifferent to (11/16, 0, 5/16)

The Ordering Assumption

The ordering assumption concerns the way individuals order their preferences over prospects having the same two outcomes but different probabilities. Let us look at the two specific prospects, (.26, 0, .74) and (.25, 0, .75). It seems reasonable to assume that the first prospect will be preferred to the second prospect, because the probability of winning the preferred prize w_1 is higher with the first prospect. We can restate this more formally as the ordering assumption:

Assumption: Ordering
Given two prospects that involve the same two outcomes and different probabilities, the preferred prospect is the one that offers the higher probability of winning the preferred outcome.

We know from Section 5.1 how to construct the expected utility function.

$$U(w_1) = 1, \ U(w_2) = e^*, \ U(w_3) = 0$$

The expected utility of prospect (p_1, p_2, p_3) is then

$$p_1 U(w_1) + p_2 U(w_2) + p_3 U(w_3) = p_1 + p_2 e^*$$

expected utility theorem

We are now in a position to state and prove the **expected utility theorem**.

Expected Utility Theorem

Suppose that the assumptions we have made in this appendix are true. Then, given any two prospects, say (p_1', p_2', p_3') and (p_1'', p_2'', p_3''),

1. (p_1', p_2', p_3') is preferred to (p_1'', p_2'', p_3'')

   implies and is implied by

2. $p_1' + p_2' e^* > p_1'' + p_2'' e^*$

   Or, to restate 2 in words, the expected utility of prospect (p_1', p_2', p_3') exceeds the expected utility of prospect (p_1'', p_2'', p_3'').

   PROOF: We will begin by showing that statement 1 implies statement 2. So, assume that statement 1 is true. Our objective is to show that statement 2 is then also true. Using the substitution assumption, first in conjunction with prospect (p_1', p_2', p_3'), and then in conjunction with prospect (p_1'', p_2'', p_3''), we get

3. (p_1', p_2', p_3') is indifferent to $(p_1' + p_2' e^*, 0, p_2' + p_2'(1 - e^*))$

4. (p_1'', p_2'', p_3'') is indifferent to $(p_1'' + p_2'' e^*, 0, p_3'' + p_2''(1 - e^*))$

   Then, using statements 1, 3, and 4 in conjunction with the transitivity assumption, we get

5. $(p_1' + p_2' e^*, 0, p_3' + p_2'(1 - e^*))$ is preferred to $(p_1'' + p_2'' e^*, 0, p_3'' + p_2''(1 - e^*))$

   Then, using the ordering assumption in conjunction with statement 5, we get

6. $p_1' + p_2' e^* > p_1'' + p_2'' e^*$

   But, statement 6 is identical to statement 2. Hence, we have shown that statement 1 implies statement 2.

   To show that statement 2 implies statement 1, we can simply reverse the argument. Suppose that statement 6 (identical to 2) is true. Using the ordering assumption in conjunction with 6, we get statement 5. The substitution assumption gives us statements 3 and 4. Using 6, 3, and 4 in conjunction with the transitivity assumption, we get statement 1. This completes the proof of the theorem.

REFERENCES

Akerlof, G. 1970. "The Market for 'Lemons': Quality, Uncertainty and the Market Mechanisms," *Quarterly Journal of Economics* 84:488–500.

Bernoulli, D. 1954. "Exposition of a New Theory on the Measurement of Risk," *Econometrica* 22:23–36.

Friedman, M., and L. J. Savage 1948. "The Utility Analysis of Choices Involving Risk," *Journal of Political Economy* 56:279–304.

Good, I. J. 1987. "Subjective Probability," in *The New Palgrave: A Dictionary of Economics*, J. Eatwell, M. Milgate, and P. Newman (eds.), London: The Macmillan Press.

Karni, E. 1987. "State-Dependent Preferences," in *The New Palgrave: A Dictionary of Economics*, J. Eatwell, M. Milgate, and P. Newman (eds.), London: The Macmillan Press.

Kotowitz, Y. 1987. "Moral Hazard," in *The New Palgrave: A Dictionary of Economics*, J. Eatwell, M. Milgate, and P. Newman (eds.), London: Macmillan.

Luce, R., and H. Raiffa 1957. *Games and Decisions,* New York: Wiley.

Machina, M. J. 1987. "Expected-utility Hypothesis," in *The New Palgrave: A Dictionary of Economics*, J. Eatwell, M. Milgate, and P. Newman (eds.), London: Macmillan.

Postlewaite, A. 1987. "Asymmetric Information," in *The New Palgrave: A Dictionary of Economics*, J. Eatwell, M. Milgate, and P. Newman (eds.), London: Macmillan.

Rothschild, M., and J. E. Stiglitz. 1976. "Equilibrium in Competitive Insurance Markets: An Essay on the Economics of Imperfect Information," *Quarterly Journal of Economics* 90:630–49.

Spence, A. M. 1974. *Market Signaling: Information Transfer in Hiring and Related Screening Processes,* Cambridge, Mass.: Harvard University Press.

Stiglitz, J. E. 1975. "The Theory of 'Screening,' Education, and the Distribution of Income," *American Economic Review* 65:283–300.

von Neumann, J., and O. Morgenstern. 1944. *The Theory of Games and Economic Behavior,* Princeton: Princeton University Press.

Wilson, C. 1987. "Adverse Selection," in *The New Palgrave: A Dictionary of Economics*, J. Eatwell, M. Milgate, and P. Newman (eds.), London: Macmillan.

PART III

The Firm

In Part III, the focus is on the firms that transform the natural resources owned and supplied by individuals into the goods and services these individuals demand. Because these firms are entities created by and for human beings, given the infinite number of ways to organize economic activity, the natural questions are: Why do firms come into being? Why do they take the particular organizational forms that we see? We address these questions in Chapter 6. We see how firms resolve the contradiction between collective interests and individual self-interest through their organizational forms and ask why multiperson firms exist.

In Chapters 7 and 8, we take a more standard approach by viewing the firm as an organization described by its production function (by the terms on which it can transform inputs into outputs) and motivated by its desire to maximize profit. In Chapter 7, we construct the theory of production when only one input is variable, and then we build the corresponding theory of cost. In Chapter 8, we extend the theory of production and cost to the more realistic environment of many variable inputs.

CHAPTER 6

The Theory of the Firm

With this chapter, we make the leap from the theory of demand to the theory of supply. In the theory of demand, we focused on the behavior of individual consumers. In the theory of supply, we will be looking at the behavior of firms.

inputs

outputs

production function

A firm is an entity that buys factors of production, or **inputs**, and transforms them into goods or services, or **outputs**, for sale. In a sawmill, for example, logs, labor, and saws are all inputs, and lumber is the output. If we suppose that a firm makes only one product, we can describe the firm's ability to transform inputs into output by a **production function**. A production function might tell us, for example, that given 11 cubic yards of cedar, a 36-inch circular saw, and 12 hours of labor, a lumber company can produce 810 linear feet of 4-by-4 lumber. We will spend a great deal of time defining and exploring the production function in the following two chapters. For now, an intuitive notion of what the term means is sufficient.

In the theory of supply, the firm plays a role closely analogous to the role played by the individual in the theory of demand. In the theory of demand, individuals are described by utility functions; they are motivated by the desire to maximize utility; and they are constrained by the terms on which they can buy goods and services and can sell labor and other resources. Correspondingly, in the theory of supply, firms are described by production functions; they are motivated by the desire to maximize profit; and they are constrained by the terms on which they can buy inputs and can sell goods or services.

As you will see in the following chapters, this approach to the theory of supply is very powerful. Its power flows in large part from the relatively simple model of the firm it assumes. In this approach, the firm is a given, predetermined entity that can be fully described by its production function: inputs go in at one end of the production process, they are transformed by the firm, and they emerge at the other end as output. Notice, however, that firms, unlike individuals in consumer theory, are not natural entities. Instead, they are owned by individuals and are usually created to serve the interests of those owners. This suggests that it might be useful to look inside the firm to see what we can learn about the economic principles that guide the firm's organization.

Once we pause to look inside the firm rather than to view it from the outside as a predetermined entity — as a kind of black box into which we cannot see — many intriguing questions emerge. Among these are questions about the internal organization of firms and about the forces that both bring firms into existence and limit their size.

6.1

Organizational Issues

In this chapter we look inside the black box as we raise a number of questions about firms and suggest a general approach to answering them. We can begin our analysis by reexamining what the term **firm** means. Of course, a firm can range in size from a

firm

coconut-milk peddler on the beach or the family-run corner grocery store to huge firms like General Motors Corporation, Japan's Mitsubishi Corporation, or Daimler-Benz of Germany. At least as significant as the variation in the size of firms is the variation in their organizational forms. The corner grocery and GM differ not only in size but also in organizational structure.

Three Structures of the Firm

One way to get a useful overview of the diversity of organizational forms is to consider the relationship between the ownership and the management, or control, of different firms. If we isolate this aspect of the firm, we discover that firms generally take one of three possible forms: the owner-managed firm, the partnership, and the publicly held firm.

residual
claimant

owner-managed
firm

The most common form is the owner-managed firm where one person owns the firm and also makes the important managerial decisions. Economists often use the term **residual claimant** for the person (or persons) who have claim to the profit of a firm. In the **owner-managed firm**, the owner-manager is the sole residual claimant. The window cleaning company owned and operated by Will Seymore is one example of an owner-managed firm. The economics consulting firm run by Marvin Shaffer is another. Both are cases of owner-managed firms because the person who makes the managerial decisions that affect the firm's profit is the same person who lays claim to that profit. In fact, if you think of all the firms that you have contact with in a week, many or even most will be owner-managed.

partnership

The second important organizational form is the **partnership**. In this case, there is no single owner, or residual claimant, and no single manager. Instead, the ownership and management functions of the firm are jointly shared by two or more people who work in the firm. Law and accounting firms are commonly organized as partnerships. Many small businesses, such as restaurants, gas stations, meat markets, and clothing stores, are often owned and operated by two or more business partners, all of whom work in the business, share in the managerial functions, and receive some share of the firm's profits.

publicly held
firm

If we rank organizational structures by the dollar volume of business, the third organizational form — the **publicly held firm** — must be considered the predominant form. In a publicly held firm, ownership is spread over many individuals, none of whom owns a significant portion of the firm. Consequently, ownership is almost totally separated from management, or control.[1]

Most of the firms on the *Fortune 500* list fit this category. Their owners are their shareholders — all those who hold some of the firm's common stock. The firms themselves, however, are actually run by professional managers who essentially are employees (even though they, too, may hold some of their firm's common stock). These managers are supervised by a board of directors who represent the firm's many shareholders.

Although individual shareholders may lay claim to some portion of the firm's profits, they play no significant role in the day-to-day management of the firm. Conversely, the firm's managers can claim relatively little of the firm's profits, even though they are responsible for making the decisions that affect the firm's operation.[2]

---

1 There are really three types of corporations: public, private, and governmental. The common stock of public corporations — the dominant form — is traded on organized markets such as the New York Stock Exchange, whereas the common stock of private corporations is not. Because we are concerned with private economic activity, government corporations are not a subject of our analysis.

2 These distinctions concern the relationship between ownership and control in firms, not the legal status of firms. By partnerships, then, we mean firms characterized by a small number of residual claimants, each of whom exercises some managerial control. By publicly held firms, we mean not corporations but rather firms characterized by what Berle and Means (1935) call the "divorce of ownership from control," because ownership is dispersed among a large number of people.

Although we can loosely identify three basic organizational structures, the significant point is that the patterns of ownership and control — the organizational forms laid out in the firm's organization chart — are extremely diverse. Indeed, if we look more deeply into the firm, we see even more organizational diversity. For example, think of the many ways in which workers in a firm are compensated for their labor. Some get hourly wages, some get salaries, and others get piece rates. Compensation can also take other forms: for example, stock options and profit-sharing arrangements for managers and, in some cases, for all employees; Christmas bonuses or productivity-determined bonuses; and all sorts of perquisites ("perks"), ranging from a key to the executive washroom to personal use of the company car or even the corporate airplane.

For example, a rapidly expanding chain of Italian fast-food outlets, Sbarro, awards its productive managers up to 15% of a restaurant's net profits. Pepsi-Co gives its top managers perks such as first-class air travel, luxury hotels on the road, a company car, and annual salary bonuses; it gives all its employees access to a gym and a sculpture garden as well as unlimited free Pepsi at work. Genentech, the company that engineered the blood-clot-dissolving drug Activase, offered each of its employees options on 100 shares of stock when the company was given the official green light to market its new product by the Food and Drug Administration. Inco Ltd. of Sudbury, Ontario, pays its mine workers individual bonuses for increased productivity in constructing underground supports (with, as we will see, unfortunate results).

Think, too, of the diversity of institutional arrangements governing job security. In many firms, seniority determines an employee's job security. The longer an employee has been with a firm, the more secure is his or her position. In other workplaces — in the construction industry, for example — workers are typically hired on a short-term basis and have virtually no job security. In some firms, management is constrained in deciding who is to be terminated by an elaborate set of quasi-judicial procedures. In others, management has nearly a free hand in deciding who is to be dismissed and what are acceptable grounds for dismissal.

Once we think in more detail about just what a firm is, we see that the term covers a colossal variety of institutional arrangements. The task of a theory of the firm — given this perspective from within the black box — is to create a systematic way in which to understand the diversity of the entity that we call "the firm." Therefore, a theory of the firm must help us to understand why firms exist and what determines both their size and their particular organizational structures.

Cooperation from Noncooperative Behavior

At the heart of theories of the firm lies a puzzle. If we view the firm from the outside and ignore the details of its operation, we see the firm to be an enterprise fundamentally characterized by cooperation. Two lumberjacks using a double-handled saw work together to produce lumber for sale. Four employees of a small moving company cooperate to get the furniture out of the customer's apartment and into the van. Partners in a law firm specializing in criminal cases may jointly prepare and argue the cases; they may divide the cases between them, each preparing and arguing some of them; or one partner may research all the cases and the other argue them. But, whatever their arrangement, the services their firm provides depend on the partners' joint, or cooperative, effort. In short, the success of any firm ultimately depends on the cooperative efforts of its workers.

Once we abandon this external perspective and look inside the firm, however, a different picture emerges. When we venture into the firm we see only individuals: owners, managers, secretaries, supervisors, assemblers, receptionists, janitors, sales personnel, and cashiers. What motivates all these individuals? As economists, we assume that they are pursuing their own self-interest. But once we realize that the individuals who compose the firm are motivated by self-interest, a puzzle emerges. We know that the firm's success in achieving its collective objectives depends on the cooperative effort of the people involved in the productive process. Yet these people are motivated not by collective but by private objectives.

We must wonder, then, how and to what extent the self-interested individuals within the firm actually work to promote the interests of the firm as a whole. Do lumberjacks ever slack off when they are working or spend more time than necessary sharpening the saw? Do the moving company's workers ever take extended coffee breaks or pocket one of the customer's possessions? Does a lawyer ever take office supplies for private use or fail to put in the time needed to track down a key witness? Do assembly-line workers ever call in sick when they simply want a day off or deliberately assemble a product improperly?

Such common industrial ailments as slacking off at work, malingering, theft, and sabotage suggest that the behavior of individuals sometimes does frustrate and even undermine the collective interests of the firm as a whole. For example, a recent study of phone calls made by employees from the workplace found that about 33 percent of all such calls were personal rather than work-related, costing large companies as much as $1 million per year. In Britain, the former chairman of Guinness was charged with stealing Guinness funds in connection with a multimillion dollar scandal. Using this internal perspective, we can rephrase our question: How can the firm secure the cooperation of its employees? The following problems will help to get you into the spirit of this inquiry.

PROBLEM 6.1

Life insurance salespeople are sometimes paid a large bonus for selling a new policy. For example, a salesperson might receive $1,500 today for selling a new policy whose annual premium is only $1,000. Of course, the purchaser has the option of canceling the policy at the end of any year. Given this scheme, how does the self-interest of an unscrupulous salesperson diverge from the insurance company's interest?

PROBLEM 6.2

A stock option allows its holder to buy stock from the firm at a specified price during a specified time period. Suppose that company X's stock is selling today for $10 a share and that the board of directors is thinking of giving Margaret, the Chief Executive Officer (CEO), the following stock option: she can buy up to 10,000 shares at $10 per share any time during the next 3 years. If you were a shareholder of this company, would you be in favor of giving the CEO this stock option? Why or why not?

A Key to the Puzzle: Institutions

As you probably realized from Problems 6.1 and 6.2, the key to answering the question "How can the firm secure the cooperation of its employees?" lies in the amazing diversity of institutions, or organizational forms, that firms exhibit. The central hypothesis of the theory of the firm is that the institutional structure of a given firm is the structure that best harmonizes the self-interest of individuals within that firm with the wider collective interest of the firm itself. The important point is this: the way in which a firm is internally organized will depend on its objectives. For example, a garment manufacturer's institutional arrangements will be different, depending on whether its goal is to make thousands of cheap dresses or a few hundred very expensive dresses.

Think of a particular dress manufacturer's decision about whether to pay sewing-machine operators an hourly wage or a piece rate. If the company decides on a piece rate (a fixed sum for each dress), what behavior can it anticipate from its employees? Under this arrangement, operators will try to increase their rate of production by sewing more quickly and paying less attention to detail, because their take-home pay will be greater.

In this case, then, a piece rate may induce the individual workers to produce relatively low-quality dresses at a relatively high rate. Thus, if the dress manufacturer is in the low-quality, high-volume segment of the garment industry, paying by piece rate serves to harmonize the self-interest of the individual operators with the dress manufacturer's objective. However, if the manufacturer produces an expensive line of dresses in which meticulous attention to detail counts, paying individual workers by piece rate might frustrate the firm's goals. A firm that sells in the high-quality segment of the industry, then, would be working against its own best interests by choosing piece-rate payments. We would therefore expect to see such a firm pay its operators an hourly wage.

All institutional arrangements can be analyzed in terms of how nearly they achieve a congruity between individual self-interest and the collective interests of the firm. The work habits of individual sewing-machine operators will vary, for instance, depending on the circumstances in which they can be dismissed or suspended; on how often their work is monitored; and on benefit packages and bonus structures. As you saw in answering Problem 6.2, stock options encourage executives to be good managers by allowing them to capture some of the profit their good management creates.

The behavior of the individuals who make up a firm is moderated by the firm's organizational form — by its institutions:

The central hypothesis of the modern theory of the firm is that the organizational forms that we encounter every day are the ones that achieve the closest possible identity between the objectives of the individuals inside the firm and those of the firm as a whole.

Does cooperation actually arise from noncooperative behavior? We have already seen that people in the workplace sometimes frustrate the interests of the firm as a whole. Problem 6.1, for example, was inspired by a recent scandal in the sale of life insurance in Ontario. Insurance salespeople behaved in the unscrupulous way you may have imagined in answering that problem. Inco's productivity bonuses — characteristic of incentives used throughout much of the hard-rock mining industry — recently have sparked a controversy over underground safety. Some miners intentionally shorten the bolts that are critical for underground support because they can install almost three times as many shorter bolts during an 8-hour shift and thus almost triple their bonuses.

The Existence of Multiperson Firms

If we suppose that incidents of this kind are not uncommon — that institutional arrangements resolve the potential conflicts of interest within the firm only imperfectly — then another puzzle arises. If securing the cooperation of individual workers inside a firm is such a tricky business, why bother creating firms of more than one person? In the one-person, owner-managed firm, the firm is the individual; its collective goals are therefore identical to the individual's self-interested ones. Because owner-managers of one-person operations need not devise clever institutions to secure their own cooperative behavior, no organizational issues arise. Given that such difficult organizational issues inevitably crop up when more than one person works in a particular firm, why do multiperson firms exist? And what determines their size once they come into being?

6.2
Organizational Issues

A complete theory of the firm answering these organizational questions does not exist yet. However, we can set out the basic issues and illustrate some of the important research results to date as well as the method economists use to address these questions. Let us begin with a situation in which we would never expect to see more than one person in a firm. This exercise will help you to understand why multiperson firms create organizational dilemmas.

The One-Person Firm

In our neighborhood on the third Saturday of every month, the tinker's bell reminds us to bring out our knives for sharpening — at a price, of course. The tinker, whom we will call Roberta, combines her capital equipment (a cart, a foot-powered grinding wheel, and a brass bell); her skill; and, most important, her own effort, to sharpen the knives that are brought to her.

How much effort Roberta puts in — and effort is the touchstone in this analysis — is entirely up to Roberta. She can work at her wheel either quickly or slowly; she can spend time making small talk or not; she can walk along the sidewalk briskly or at a more leisurely pace; she can work from morning until night or put in only a few hours each day; she can be out on the streets seven days a week or only on weekends. In short, Roberta has a great deal of latitude in the effort she exerts.

We will limit our analysis to how much effort Roberta chooses to expend and will therefore ignore other choices she might make, such as using an electrically powered grinding wheel instead of a foot-powered one; a siren instead of a bell; or a station wagon instead of a cart. In this very simple model, then, effort alone determines the tinker's output. If we assume that the number of knives that Roberta actually sharpens in any period is proportional to the effort she expends and that she charges everyone the same price per knife, then the income her business generates in a period will be directly proportional to the effort she puts into it. For simplicity, we will assume that each unit of effort generates $1 of income. That is,

$$y_R = e_R$$

where y_R is Roberta's income and e_R is her effort. Because this income-effort relationship tells us the terms on which Roberta can convert her effort into command over goods — that is, into income — it effectively describes the technology of tinkering for Roberta.

How much effort will she actually choose to expend? To find the answer, we need to know what Roberta's preferences are. We can capture her preferences in a utility function $U(e_R, y_R)$ in which her utility is a function of the effort she expends, e_R, and the income she earns, y_R. We will assume that income is a "good": holding e_R constant, as y_R increases Roberta is better off. In contrast, we will assume that effort is a "bad": holding y_R constant, as e_R increases Roberta is worse off. Therefore, as we move upward in Figure 6.1 Roberta gets progressively better off, and as we move to the right she gets progressively worse off.

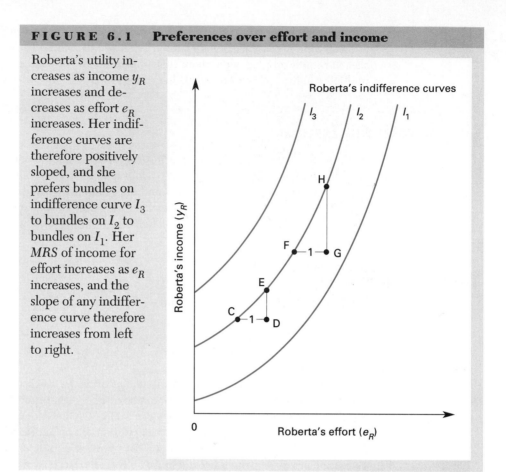

FIGURE 6.1 **Preferences over effort and income**

Roberta's utility increases as income y_R increases and decreases as effort e_R increases. Her indifference curves are therefore positively sloped, and she prefers bundles on indifference curve I_3 to bundles on I_2 to bundles on I_1. Her *MRS* of income for effort increases as e_R increases, and the slope of any indifference curve therefore increases from left to right.

Because income is a good and effort a bad, the indifference curves in Figure 6.1 are upward sloping. If Roberta increases her effort by one unit beginning at point C, for example, her utility decreases because effort is a bad. To get back to the original indifference curve, I_2, her income must be increased by DE in Figure 6.1. The first characteristic of these indifference curves, then, is that they are upward sloping.

We will also assume that the larger the initial level of effort, the greater the increase in income necessary to compensate for a unit increase in effort. In other words, the more effort that Roberta presently puts into her business, the greater must be the increase in her income to compensate for yet more effort on her part. Then, because effort at point F in Figure 6.1 exceeds effort at point C, distance GH exceeds distance DE. The second characteristic of any indifference curve, then, is that its slope increases from left to right.

Seeing how the one-person firm operates is now a simple matter. Roberta will choose the amount of effort e_R that maximizes her utility $U(e_R, y_R)$, knowing that income y_R is proportional to effort: $y_R = e_R$. She must therefore choose a point on the line $y_R = e_R$ in Figure 6.2. The solution to Roberta's choice problem, and therefore the equilibrium for the one-tinker firm, is at point W, where Roberta exerts e^* units of effort and earns income y^* — an amount equal to e^*. Given the constraint that income equals effort, the equilibrium for the one-tinker firm is (e^*, y^*) at point W, because this point is associated with the highest attainable indifference curve:

FIGURE 6.2 The one-person firm

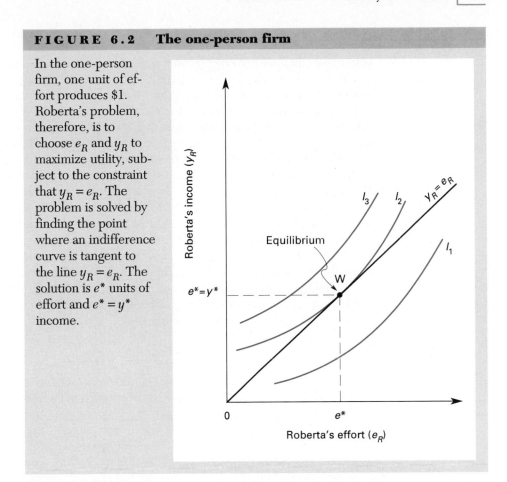

In the one-person firm, one unit of effort produces \$1. Roberta's problem, therefore, is to choose e_R and y_R to maximize utility, subject to the constraint that $y_R = e_R$. The problem is solved by finding the point where an indifference curve is tangent to the line $y_R = e_R$. The solution is e^* units of effort and $e^* = y^*$ income.

At the equilibrium of the one-person firm, the slope of the indifference curve, or the marginal rate of substitution of income for effort (*MRS*), is equal to 1, the rate at which additional effort generates additional income.

A Two-Person Alternative

What would be the comparable equilibrium if Roberta were in a partnership with another tinker? By comparing the one-tinker and two-tinker firms, we can both 1. identify an awkward organizational issue that arises in the two-tinker firm, and 2. see why the one-person firm (at least in this simple model) is the preferred organizational form and therefore the one we would expect to see.

To make these points in the simplest possible way, we will consider the case in which two tinkers with identical preferences and identical technologies — we will call them Roberta and Victor — join together to form one firm. We are therefore assuming that the indifference curves in Figures 6.1 and 6.2 describe Victor's preferences as well as Roberta's, and that a unit of his effort produces \$1 of income, just as a unit of her effort does.

The technological constraint faced by the two-tinker firm is that the sum of their incomes must equal the effort that they jointly expend:

$$y_R + y_V = e_R + e_V$$

where y_R and e_R are Roberta's income and effort, and y_V and e_V are Victor's.

We will determine these four quantities — effort and income for Roberta and for Victor— in the context of a partnership form of organization. Let us suppose that Roberta and Victor are *equal partners*: that is, that each receives exactly half of their combined earnings. Every day, Roberta and Victor make their rounds, putting their effort into sharpening knives. At the end of the day they meet, pool their earnings, and divide them in half.

What will be the equilibrium in this two-person partnership? In other words, what effort will each put into the business and how much income will each get out of it? Let us suppose that Roberta chooses her own effort to maximize her own utility, *taking Victor's effort as given*, and that Victor chooses his effort to maximize his own utility, *taking Roberta's effort as a given*. Furthermore, we will look for an equilibrium in which Roberta and Victor expend the *same effort* and enjoy the *same income*; that is, we will look for a *symmetric equilibrium*. We can easily find such an equilibrium because Roberta and Victor have identical preferences and are equally productive.

Notice that in this partnership, the aggregate income of the firm is equal to $(e_R + e_V)$, and Roberta's share is exactly half that amount. Therefore, her income is determined by the following income-effort relationship:

$$y_R = (e_R + e_V)/2$$

Notice that if Roberta increases her own effort by one unit, her own income increases by only half of a dollar. Victor's income is determined in an analogous way.

Since their preferences and technologies are identical, we know from our analysis of the single-person firm that by working alone, each partner could have achieved point W in Figure 6.2. Can they manage the same result in their partnership? To find out, let us suppose that initially both tinkers put out e^* units of effort. Assuming that Victor continues to expend e^*, let us see whether or not Roberta will continue to expend e^* as well.

When e_V is equal to e^*, Roberta's income-effort relationship is

$$y_R = (e_R + e^*)/2$$

Given this income-effort relationship, Roberta's private problem is to choose e_R so as to maximize her own utility.

In Figure 6.3, we have constructed this income-effort relationship — the solid line $y_R = (e_R + e^*)/2$. We have also included the analogous income-effort relationship for the one-tinker firm from Figure 6.2 — the dashed line $y_R = e_R$. The dashed line allows us to identify the equilibrium for the one-tinker firm, which is (e^*, y^*) at point W. Notice that the two income-effort relationships intersect at W. In other words, given that Victor puts out e^* units of effort, if Roberta also put out e^* units of effort, her income would again be y^*.

Yet we see from Figure 6.3 that Roberta will choose point D rather than point W. In other words, even if Victor puts out e^* units of effort, Roberta will decide to put out less effort. Why? Notice that as Roberta reduces her effort by one unit, the total income of the firm declines by \$1, but her personal income declines by only \$0.50. As a result, Roberta chooses the combination of effort and income at D, where her *MRS* is equal to the rate at which her own effort increases her own income (1/2).

Because Roberta and Victor have identical preferences, we also know that if for some reason Roberta were to put out e^* units of effort, Victor would decide to put out less. In sum, the partnership fails to achieve the equilibrium of the one-tinker firm.

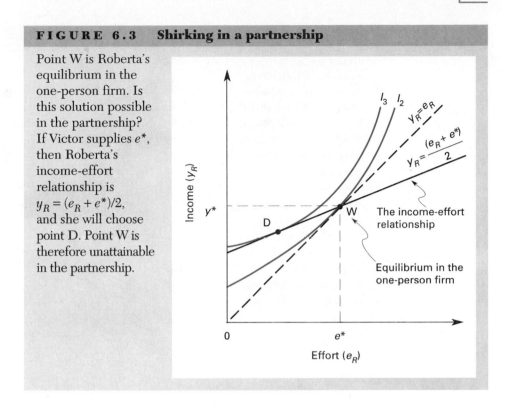

FIGURE 6.3   Shirking in a partnership

Point W is Roberta's equilibrium in the one-person firm. Is this solution possible in the partnership? If Victor supplies e^*, then Roberta's income-effort relationship is $y_R = (e_R + e^*)/2$, and she will choose point D. Point W is therefore unattainable in the partnership.

The Partnership Equilibrium

How much effort will the tinkers actually put into the partnership? In any symmetric equilibrium, both Roberta and Victor will supply the same effort and earn the same income. But this implies that at the equilibrium, Roberta's income will be equal to the effort she supplies, since one unit of effort creates $1 of income. In other words, the partnership equilibrium will lie on the dashed line $y_R = e_R$ in Figure 6.4. Furthermore, because each will choose the level of effort that maximizes private utility and because the slope of the income-effort relationship is 1/2, for each of them *MRS* at the equilibrium will be 1/2. Therefore, the equilibrium will be at point F in Figure 6.4 on the line $y_R = e_R$ where *MRS* is equal to 1/2.[3]

Point W in Figure 6.4 is the equilibrium for the one-tinker firm, and point F is the partnership equilibrium. Since W in on a higher indifference curve than F, we see that both Roberta and Victor are worse off in the partnership than if each worked in a one-person firm. Clearly, in this partnership, the pursuit of private self-interest by the two tinkers frustrates their collective interest. If, starting at the partnership equilibrium, the two partners were simultaneously to increase their effort, their personal incomes would increase by $1 for each additional unit of effort — and they would obviously be better off. For example, Roberta would move upward and to the right from F along the line $y_R = e_R$ in Figure 6.4. The difficulty with their partnership is this: at point F, neither Roberta nor Victor has a *private incentive* to put out more effort, because each receives only half the income generated by an additional unit of personal effort:

---

3 It is possible that there is more than one point on the line $y_R = e_R$ at which *MRS* is equal to 1/2. In this case, there are multiple equilibria in the partnership model. For simplicity, we ignore this possibility.

FIGURE 6.4   The partnership equilibrium

In the partnership equilibrium, Roberta (or Victor) supplies e' units of effort, earns income y', and attains indifference curve I_1. The one-person firm equilibrium, where Roberta (or Victor) supplies e^* units of effort, earns income y^*, and attains indifference curve I_2, is clearly Pareto-preferred to the partnership equilibrium.

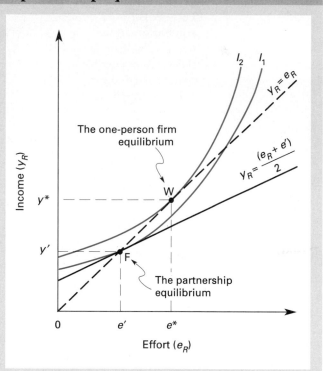

The partnership fails to create the right private incentives because neither partner can capture the whole of the added output that their personal effort creates.

residual
claimancy

Notice the key role that **residual claimancy** plays as an incentive in this analysis. In both the one and two-person firms, an added unit of effort creates an additional $1 of income. In the partnership equilibrium, however, each tinker chooses a point where *MRS* is equal to 1/2 because each claims only *half* of the added income generated by additional personal effort. By contrast, in the equilibrium of the one-person firm, each tinker chooses a point where *MRS* is equal to 1 because each claims *all* the additional income created by their own additional effort. In both cases, the tinker's right as a residual claimant dictates the choice of effort she or he puts into the firm.

We have assumed that Roberta and Victor are not honorable enough simply to agree to the equilibrium at point W in Figure 6.4 and to stick to their bargain by expending e^* effort apiece. This honorable solution is certainly a possibility, particularly in the two-partner case. In Problem 6.3, however, you will have a chance to see why honor might get stretched too thin when a larger number of partners is involved.

The fundamental point is that Roberta and Victor cannot improve on the single-person equilibrium. They have nothing to gain, and — as our analysis reveals — may well have something to lose by forming a partnership. Therefore, the partnership arrangement potentially involves a real cost to the two partners.

> ### PROBLEM 6.3
>
> Suppose that three individuals are in a partnership, that all three have identical preferences and technologies, and that each partner receives one-third of the total income from the firm. Construct a diagram analogous to Figure 6.4 and identify the equilibria for the one-person firm and for the two- and three-person partnerships. What is the fate of this type of partnership as the number of partners grows larger?

The two-tinker firm is preferable only if some real advantage is associated with it — for example, if a unit of effort produced *more income* in a partnership than it does in a one-person firm. We will extend our model to incorporate this possibility in the next section. As it stands, however, there is no such advantage in this model and therefore no reason for anything other than a one-person firm to exist. Given this model, multiperson firms offer nothing but troublesome institutional dilemmas.

Pareto Optimality and Choice of Institutions

We can use the one- and two-tinker models to articulate more clearly the basic hypothesis of modern theories of the firm — that the institutions we actually see are the ones that most nearly harmonize the private interest of individuals with the collective interest of the firm as a whole. Because our two tinkers are both better off in the one-person firm equilibrium than they are in the partnership equilibrium, the one-person firm is the Pareto-preferred organizational form.

Modern theories of the firm assume, quite reasonably, that when individuals choose between organizational forms, they choose the organization that is Pareto-preferred. For example, this assumption implies that Roberta and Victor will choose to work in one-person firms rather than in a partnership. Now let us extend the comparison to all organizational forms:

Modern theories of the firm suppose that a Pareto-optimal organizational form will be chosen. An organizational form is Pareto-optimal if there is no other organizational form that will leave all parties at least as well off and at least one party better off.

Team Production

If multiperson firms create nothing but trouble, why do we encounter so many larger firms in everyday economic life? Multiperson firms come into being only when the advantages that accrue to size outweigh the disadvantages created by organizational difficulties. One such advantage arises from the gains in productivity associated with **team production**, the arrangement in which two or more workers accomplish a productive task through their joint, or team, effort. The idea of team production is simply a variation on the old adage, "Many hands make light work." In team production, the hypothesis is that many hands do *more* work. In many circumstances, team production is potentially more productive than isolated production, in which laborers work alone. The higher productivity of team production may therefore account for the existence of multiperson firms.

We will begin this section, then, by exploring the *productivity gains* associated with team production. We will see that when these gains are large enough, the partnership form

team production (margin note)

of organization is Pareto-preferred to the one-person firm. We will then introduce and analyze another organizational form — the owner-managed team — and determine the circumstances in which each of the three organizational forms — the one-person firm, the partnership, and the owner-managed team — is Pareto-preferred to the other two.

Productivity of Teams

In their pioneering work, Alchian and Demsetz (1972) used the example of workers loading boxes onto a truck to illustrate the productive potential of teams. Imagine two identical workers — each hired for 1 day only — loading boxes. For the moment, let us fix the effort expended by each worker over the day and compare the output when each laborer works in isolation with the output when the two work as a team.

First, suppose each worker expends his or her fixed effort in loading boxes alone. Let x be the aggregate number of boxes loaded. Then, suppose they work together, lifting one box from opposite sides and expending their fixed effort as a team. Let y be the aggregate number of boxes the team loads. Alchian and Demsetz argue that if the boxes are large and awkward or if they are heavy, y will exceed x. In this case, production in teams is more productive than production in isolation. It is even possible — if the boxes are heavy enough that one worker cannot lift them but not too heavy for two to lift — that x is zero and y is positive. In this case, production in teams is infinitely more productive than production in isolation.

We can identify a whole array of jobs in which team production is economic. In a large number of construction tasks — installing siding or drywall, for example — two pairs of hands are almost essential. Surveying is another productive activity in which two people working together as a team are vastly more productive than they would be if they worked in isolation.

In creating our own model of team production, we will follow Alchain and Demsetz's lead by looking at the task of loading boxes onto a truck. We will suppose that workers receive a fixed price for each box they load and that the number of boxes loaded is proportional to effort. We can then describe the technology by a proportional relationship between income and effort. Suppose that when the task is done by individuals working in isolation, each unit of effort produces \$1 of income, and when individuals work in two-person teams, each unit of effort produces \$$B$ of income. Team production is then more productive than isolated production when B exceeds 1. In this section, we will assume that B is greater than 1 — that is, we will only look at the case in which team production is more productive than isolated production.[4]

The superior productivity of teamwork provides an incentive to organize economic activity into multiperson firms. Yet is the superior productivity of teamwork sufficient to offset the organizational costs of a two-person firm? If it is, which organizational form should we expect team production to take? To find out, let us return to our two workers, Roberta and Victor, and continue to assume that they have identical preferences.

Partnership with Team Production

We already know from the two-tinker model how to find the equilibrium if the team is organized as a partnership. Roberta's equilibrium will lie on the line $y_R = Be_R$ in

---

4 Notice that if one team worker decides not to put out any effort, a difficulty arises with this description of team technology. For example, suppose that Victor decides not to work, and that e_V is therefore equal to zero. This means that Roberta is left loading boxes by herself. In this case, Roberta's effort actually produces only \$1 rather than \$$B$ per unit. To remedy this difficulty, we assume that the factor of proportionality for team production is B if both e_R and e_V are strictly positive, but is only 1 if either e_R or e_V is zero.

Figure 6.5 since a unit of effort in the team produces B dollars of income and, at the equilibrium, MRS will be equal to $B/2$ since, in the partnership, an additional unit of effort increases Roberta's income by $B/2$. In Figure 6.5, the partnership equilibrium for Roberta is at point C. (Of course, Victor will also pick a point analogous to point C.) In Problem 6.4, you can discover a key result for yourself:

> The partnership is Pareto-preferred to the one-person firm if B is sufficiently large — that is, if the productivity gain associated with team production is sufficiently large.

PROBLEM 6.4

Begin by constructing the income-effort relationship for a worker loading boxes alone, and identify the equilibrium for the one-person firm. On the same diagram, identify the point that corresponds to the equilibrium for the partnership at point C in Figure 6.5. In doing so, choose the value of B so that the equilibria of the partnership and the one-person firm are on the same indifference curve. Which organizational form is Pareto-preferred for larger values of B? For smaller values?

FIGURE 6.5   The owner-managed firm

Both the owner-manager, Roberta, and the employee, Victor, can attain point D. If we imagine that Victor's effort is measured on the horizontal axis and his income on the vertical axis, then Victor's income-effort relationship is composed of two segments — $0e''$ and DZ. To maximize utility, Victor will supply effort e'' and earn income y''. As owner-manager, Roberta's income-effort relationship is $y_R = Be_R$. Hence, as owner-manager, Roberta also supplies effort e'' and earns income y''. In the owner-managed firm, Roberta (and Victor) attains an equilibrium that is preferred to the partnership equilibrium.

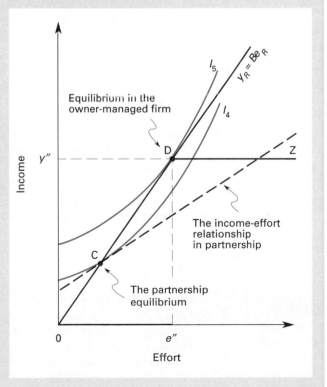

The Owner-Managed Team

If Roberta and Victor could overcome the organizational difficulty inherent in the partnership equilibrium at point C in Figure 6.5, however, they could do even better. Specifically, Roberta could attain point D in Figure 6.5, where her effort is e'' and her income y'' — a point clearly preferable to point C. Is there an organizational arrangement that would allow Roberta to attain point D (and Victor to attain the analogous point)? There is, provided that it not too costly to write contracts and to monitor — that is, to observe and verify — the effort of a teammate.

For the moment, let us assume that contracting and monitoring costs are nonexistent. (Later, we will extend the model to include these costs.) Now suppose that Roberta, as the team's owner-manager, offers to employ Victor under this contract: Victor will receive an income of y'' from Roberta if he supplies e'' or more units of effort. If he supplies less than e'' units of effort, however, he will receive no income.

If Victor agrees to these terms, the contract is enforceable, because we have assumed that his effort can be monitored without cost. There are two aspects to enforceability. First, enforceability means that if Victor fails to supply at least e'' units, Roberta can demonstrate to some court, without cost, that Victor did not meet the contractual conditions, and she will not have to pay him y''. On the other hand, it means that if Victor does supply at least e'' units of effort and Roberta fails to meet her end of the deal, then Victor can demonstrate without cost that he has met the contractual conditions, forcing Roberta to pay him y''.

Let us show that this contract allows both parties to attain (e'', y'') at point D in Figure 6.5. First, if we imagine that Victor's effort is measured on the horizontal axis and his income on the vertical axis, then Victor's income-effort relationship is composed of two horizontal line segments. The first is segment $0e''$ of the horizontal axis, because Roberta will pay him nothing if he does not supply at least e'' units of effort. The second is segment DZ of the line $y = y''$, because Roberta will pay him y'' if he supplies at least e'' units. To maximize his own utility, Victor will therefore choose point D on this income-effort relationship where he supplies e'' units of effort and receives y'' in income.

Now let us turn to Roberta. As the owner-manager, she is the exclusive residual claimant for the firm. This means that her income is the amount remaining after Victor has supplied e'' and been paid y''. Accordingly, her income-effort relationship is

$$y_R = B(e'' + e_R) - y''$$

But, because y'' is equal to Be'', Roberta's income-effort relationship can be rewritten as

$$y_R = Be_R$$

Given this income-effort relationship, we know that to maximize her own utility, Roberta will also choose point D in Figure 6.5 where she, too, supplies e'' units of effort and receives y'' as income.

The owner-managed team thus allows both team workers to attain the effort-income combination (e'', y''), a combination that is clearly Pareto-preferred to the combination attainable in a partnership at point C. In the following problem, you can show that the owner-managed team is also Pareto-preferred to the one-person firm.

PROBLEM 6.5

Draw a diagram in which you identify the point that corresponds to the equilibrium for an owner-managed team at point D in Figure 6.5. On the same diagram, construct the income-effort relationship for a one-person firm and identify the equilibrium. Notice that the owner-managed team is Pareto-preferred to the one-person firm.

To summarize what we have discovered so far:

In the absence of contracting or monitoring costs, the owner-managed team is Pareto-preferred to both the one-person firm and the partnership.

Contracting and Monitoring Costs

We have discovered that when it costs nothing for a firm to enter into contracts with its employees or to monitor their performance, the owner-managed team is Pareto-preferred to both the single-person firm and the partnership. However, entering into such contracts is seldom free of cost. Even an unwritten agreement — the proverbial handshake — costs the parties to the agreement time and effort. Written contracts are even more expensive because somebody (or several somebodies) must draw them up, type them out, duplicate copies, send the copies to the contracting parties, and so on.

Monitoring workers can also be an expensive business. For example, it costs money — sometimes a great deal of money — to take a case through the courts if an employee does not meet the terms of a contract. It often costs money, too, just to find out whether the terms of a contract have been met. Think of the problem faced by a university president in deciding if some professor has actually fulfilled his or her contractual obligations. How can the president monitor classroom performance without spending money on regular in-class supervision, student achievement tests, and other assessment methods?

Other types of employee monitoring also can be expensive. For example, more and more businesses of all sizes are investing in costly telecommunications monitoring to generate data to be used to prod workers into higher productivity and to trap workers who abuse the phone system. Depending on the design of a company's telecommunications system, it can cost up to $100,000 to install call-accounting systems used to monitor and report on workers' use of company phones. Alchian and Demsetz (1972) argue that the cost of supervision in the legal profession is also extremely high. For example, if a law firm supervisor wants to determine whether one of its lawyers has prepared a case adequately, he or she may have to replicate the whole of the employee's work. In such cases, the owner-manager's advantage in being the single residual claimant may well be outweighed by the cost disadvantage of monitoring employees.

Let us extend our model to include the costs associated with entering into contracts with employees and monitoring employee productivity. Notice that these costs arise only in the owner-managed team, since neither contracting or monitoring is necessary to enforce the equilibrium in either the partnership or the one-person firm.

What is the symmetric equilibrium of the owner-managed team in the presence of these contracting and monitoring costs? To find out, let us begin by identifying the highest indifference curve Roberta can attain if she has to pay for half the monitoring

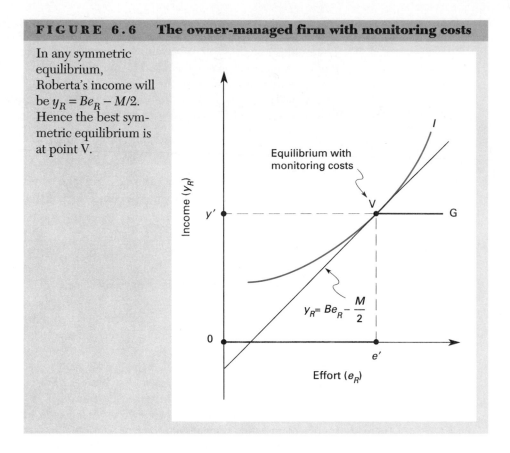

FIGURE 6.6   The owner-managed firm with monitoring costs

In any symmetric equilibrium, Roberta's income will be $y_R = Be_R - M/2$. Hence the best symmetric equilibrium is at point V.

costs, denoted by M, but can keep all the income generated by her own effort. Her income-effort relationship is then

$$y_R = Be_R - M/2$$

Given this relationship, the highest indifference curve that Roberta can attain is the combination of e' units of effort and an income of y' at point V in Figure 6.6.

The following contract will allow both Roberta and Victor to attain the income-effort combination at point V in Figure 6.6: Victor will receive an income of y' from Roberta if he supplies e' or more units of effort. But, if he supplies less than e' units of effort, he will receive no income. To see why, simply adapt the argument used to find the initial equilibrium for the owner-managed team. The following problem will get you started.

> **PROBLEM 6.6**
>
> Given this contract, what is Victor's income-effort relationship? What is Roberta's?

To reinforce your understanding of the role of monitoring costs, try the following problem.

PROBLEM 6.7

a. First construct a diagram in which you identify the equilibrium of the one-person firm. Then find values for *B* and *M* such that the one-person firm and the owner-managed team are equally attractive.
b. Beginning at this position, if you increase *M* by a small amount, which of the two organizational forms is now Pareto-preferred?
c. Beginning again at the initial position, if you now increase *B* by a small amount, which is Pareto-preferred?

The Pareto-Preferred Organizational Forms

We now have a moderately complex model with three possible organizational forms: 1. the single-person firm using the isolated technology and 2. the partnership, or 3. the owner-managed team using the team technology. Because each organizational form has its advantages and disadvantages, choosing the right one can be a complicated and interesting problem. Depending on the circumstances, any one of the three organizational forms we have considered can be Pareto-preferred to the other two forms.

A single-person firm cannot take advantage of the potentially greater productivity associated with team production, but it can make the best of its less productive technology because there is no problem harmonizing the self-interest of its single worker and the interest of the firm as a whole. They are one and the same. A partnership can take advantage of the productivity gains associated with team production, but it cannot make the best use of its more productive technology because the private self-interest of the partners is at odds with the collective interest of the partnership as a whole. Which of these two firms is preferable? It all depends on whether, in a given industry, the productivity advantage associated with teamwork, *B*, is large or small. If *B* is small, then a single-person firm will be Pareto-preferred. If *B* is large, then a partnership will be Pareto-preferred. This is, in essence, what you learned in answering Problem 6.4.

What about an owner-managed team? Like a partnership, it can take advantage of the greater productivity associated with team production. In fact, if monitoring costs, *M*, are small, it can take much better advantage of those productivity gains than the partnership can and will be Pareto-preferred to both a partnership and a single-person firm. If *M* is large, however, a partnership or a single-person firm — or both — will be Pareto-preferred to an owner-managed team.

Clearly, which organizational form will be Pareto-preferred in any given circumstance will depend on the specific values of the parameters *B* and *M*. In Figure 6.7, we have indicated the portions of the parameter space in which each of the three organizational forms is Pareto-preferred. Notice that for the sake of completeness, we have also allowed *B* to be less than 1 in Figure 6.7. (When *B* is less than 1, team production is less productive than is production in isolation.) To summarize these results:

In the green area, where both *B* and *M* are large, the partnership is Pareto-preferred to the other organizational forms. In the gray area, where *B* is large and *M* is small, the owner-managed firm is Pareto-preferred. And in the

unshaded area, where *B* is small and *M* large, the single-person
firm is Pareto-preferred.[5]

Figure 6.7 is essentially a metaphor for the theory of the firm: it conveys both
how complex the problem of choosing an appropriate organizational form can be and
how economists approach that problem. That approach is to assume that in any particular
circumstance, the *Pareto-preferred organizational form* will be chosen. For example,
the one-person firm is attractive because the owner of the one-person firm does not have
to ask: How can I secure my own cooperation? But it is also unattractive because the
firm size is limited to a single person — and therefore it cannot tap into any productivity
gains associated with team production. As a result, we would expect to see single-
person firms in circumstances where gains from team production are small or nonexistent and where achieving cooperation is difficult.

FIGURE 6.7   Pareto-preferred organizational forms

In the green portion
of the figure, where
both *M* and *B* are
large, the partnership
is the Pareto-pre-
ferred form of orga-
nization. In the gray
portion of the figure,
where *B* is large and
M is small, the
owner-managed team
is the Pareto-pre-
ferred form of orga-
nization. In the
unshaded portion of
the figure, where *B* is
small and *M* is large,
the one-person firm
is the Pareto-pre-
ferred form of orga-
nization.

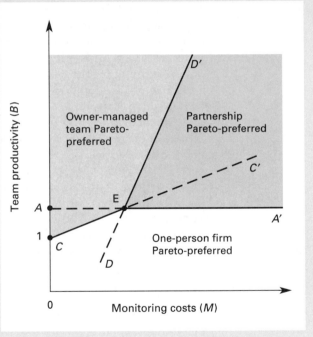

---

5 We can examine Figure 6.7 more closely. Lines *CC′* and *DD′* are not necessarily straight, but it is convenient to assume that they are. On the horizontal line *AA′*, the partnership and the one-person firm are
equally attractive; above *AA′* the partnership is Pareto-preferred and below it the one-person firm is Pareto-
preferred. On the line *CC′*, the one-person firm and the owner-managed team are equally attractive; above
CC′ the owner-managed team is Pareto-preferred and below it the one-person firm is Pareto-preferred.
Line *CC′* has two special features: first, the point $M = 0$ and $B = 1$ is on *CC′*; second, *CC′* is upward sloping.
Notice that all three organizational forms are equally attractive at E, the point where lines *AA′* and *CC′* intersect. On the line *DD′*, the partnership and the owner-managed teams are equally attractive; above *DD′*,
the owner-managed team is Pareto-preferred and below it the partnership is Pareto-preferred. Line *DD′* has
two special features: first, it passes through point E; second, it is positively sloped and steeper than *CC′*.

6.5

Specialization and the Division of Labor

specialization

division of labor

We have seen how team production is a potential source of productive advantages. In this section, we will explore **specialization** and the **division of labor**. Adam Smith was the first to identify these twin phenomena as important sources of the productivity advantages that give rise to the "wealth of nations." (Indeed, most economists date the year of birth of economics as 1776 — the year in which Smith's *Inquiry Into the Nature and Causes of the Wealth of Nations* was first published.) In the opening few pages of *Wealth of Nations*, Smith argues that the greatest improvement in the productive powers of labor stems from the effects of the division of labor: the breaking up of the productive process into a series of smaller specialized tasks, each performed again and again by a single person.

Smith's fundamental insight is that a group of workers is potentially more productive when an entire production process is *divided* into a series of separate tasks so that individual workers can *specialize* in one or a few of those tasks. In Smith's illustration — the eighteenth-century pin factory — labor is vastly more productive in the presence of division of labor and specialization.

We find a modern counterpart of the pin factory under any of the golden arches spread around the globe: in any McDonald's restaurant, the task of making and selling a Big Mac is divided into a number of separate operations. Among these tasks are taking the customer's order; cooking the meat patty; putting it in a bun; adding the lettuce, onion, cheese, pickle, and special sauce; wrapping it up; conveying it to the front counter; bagging it; handing it to the customer; pushing the Big Mac button on the cash register; taking the customer's cash; making change; and trying to sell an apple pie as well. No single person ever does all or even most of these jobs. Instead, each McDonald's employee specializes in just one or a few of them. In some outlets, specialization is so extreme that the person who rings up an order is different from the one who takes the customer's money and counts out the change.

According to Smith, three factors explain the increased productivity that arises from specialization and the division of labor. First, specialized workers become more productive simply as a result of practice and repetition. With practice, McDonald's employees who wrap the burgers get to be very fast at it. The longer people spend at one task — *learning by doing* — the more proficient they become.

Second, by specializing in one or a few tasks, workers do not lose time moving from one task to another. A firm can therefore economize on *aggregate setup costs* — the costs of getting ready to do each task — by having each worker perform one or a few rather than all jobs. Think how much time would be lost if each McDonald's order-taker had to walk into the kitchen first to place and then to pick up each order.

Third, Smith argued that specialization encourages *technical progress*. People who concentrate on a small number of tasks are likely to discover more efficient ways to perform them. For example, workers who specialize in a task may be able to design tools and machines to make the work even more efficient. In many McDonald's outlets, for instance, standard cash registers have been replaced by simpler, more specialized ones, in which each key is a pictograph representing one of the items for sale. (Could it be that some clever employee devised this labor-saving cash register?) To see the productivity implications of setup costs, try the following problem.

> ### PROBLEM 6.8
>
> Suppose some manufacturing process involves two separate stages and that the setup times for each stage are 60 and 120 minutes, respectively. It takes 60 minutes for a worker to get ready for stage 1 and 120 minutes to get ready for stage 2. Suppose that the worker, having expended the setup time, takes 10 minutes in each stage to process 1 unit of output. Show that 1 worker could produce 15 units in 8 hours; that 2 workers, each working for 8 hours, could produce 36 units; and that 13 workers, each working for 8 hours, could produce 252 units. Given 13 workers, how many should specialize in stage 1 and how many in stage 2? Notice that the productivity per worker increases from 15 to 18 to 19.4 units per worker as the number of workers increases from 1 to 2 to 13.

Team production and specialized production share one important feature: because both are potentially more productive, both may account for the existence of firms. (Whether the full potential of that specialization is realized, however, depends once again on how successfully a firm's organizational arrangements harmonize the self-interest of individual workers with the firm's collective goals.) However, team production and specialization differ in one crucial respect: the team-production process does not take place as a series of specialized activities, each carried out by a single worker. Two important observations follow from this difference.

First, in specialized production, the task of determining whether a worker is carrying his or her own load is usually fairly simple. In a sequential production process, we can watch the semifinished good as it passes from hand to hand: we can inspect the frozen hamburger patties before they are put on the grill and after they have been cooked, check the Big Macs in their buns for the seven essential ingredients, and watch as they are placed on the racks by the checkout area. As a result, if something goes amiss, we can assess fairly accurately and relatively costlessly just which worker has let the firm down.

In team production, however, it may be harder to assess how much effort an individual worker puts into the job. Alchian and Demsetz have suggested that in team production, clues to each worker's effort are sometimes available. These might include how rapidly a person loading boxes moves to the next piece to be loaded, how many coffee breaks are taken. Such clues notwithstanding, all that we can observe for certain is the output produced by the team as a whole. We cannot see the number of boxes that I lifted, or that you lifted, but only the number that we lifted together.

Second, in specialized production, all stages of the production process need not be carried out by a single firm. For instance, McDonald's frozen hamburger patties and its sesame-seed buns are both made by other firms; the sesame seeds on top of the buns and the beef that goes into making the meat patties are produced by still other firms. Thus, some segments of the Big Mac production process are carried out in-house and others are carried out in other firms. By contrast, team production must always be carried out within the confines of a single firm because it cannot be divided into a series of segmented tasks. A large, heavy box is indivisible: I cannot first lift and load "my half" of it and then move on while you lift and load "your half."

Specialized production — because it differs in essential ways from team production — raises distinctive issues. In particular, specialization permits the choice between coordinating all stages of the process in-house or coordinating some stages in-house and others through markets. We can see both arrangements in the world around us. For instance, the Croissant Palace bakes and sells its croissants on the premises, but it relies on another firm to produce its dough. A canola oil refinery may buy its canola seeds in the marketplace and have the seed oil extracted by another firm specializing in crushing and extraction, but may carry out the oil refining and product packaging processes in-house. Campbell Soup Company in Canada gets its mushrooms and poultry from its own farms, but it buys the English muffins and precooked fried eggs for its frozen breakfasts from outside suppliers. And Toyota recently ran magazine advertisements with the caption, "We buy the best parts in the world, no matter which state they're from." The ad listed 44 components for Camrys manufactured in its Georgetown, Kentucky, plant — including engine mounts from Ohio, airbags from Mississippi, audio systems from Indiana, steering columns from Vermount, and fuel pumps from South Carolina — that were bought from 174 of Toyota's more than 390 U.S. suppliers.

Transactions Costs

What determines whether all stages of specialized production will take place within a single firm or will be coordinated by markets? The answer is actually a theory of firm size. It tells us, for example, what factors encourage Pillsbury to buy raw wheat and process its own flour or to buy flour from another firm; or it tells us what factors encourage Campbell Soup Company to produce and process its own fried eggs or to buy precooked fried eggs from another firm.

We already know that coordinating production inside a multiperson firm presents problems that can be difficult and expensive to resolve. If there were no costs associated with coordinating production through markets, we would expect to see a series of small firms interacting in markets for semifinished goods. However, market transactions do entail costs. The transaction costs of coordinating production through markets include the costs of writing and enforcing contracts between firms, the costs of keeping accurate records of transactions, and the time cost of exchanging money for goods.

Ronald Coase (1937) pioneered a general approach that has been used to determine whether specific production activities will take place inside a multiperson firm or through markets. Coase argued that the choice will depend on the relative costs of the two options. To summarize his argument:

A firm will expand to the point at which the organizational cost of adding another function in-house is just equal to the transaction cost of coordinating that function through the marketplace.

Although we cannot set out Coase's analysis in detail, we will draw a fundamental distinction between two kinds of partly finished goods — *generic* and *specific* — that serve as inputs in other production processes, and we will examine the *transactions costs* associated with each.[6]

Generic Inputs

Think of the relationship between a baking company that makes bread from flour (and other essential ingredients) and a flour manufacturer that makes flour from wheat. We can imagine that a particular baking company might mill its own flour. If the flour it produces in-house is identical to the flour produced elsewhere, the company will be indifferent between using its own flour and using flour produced by a dozen other millers.

---

6 Williamson (1985) is the most comprehensive guide to literature on transactions-costs economics.

generic input

As Gertrude Stein might have said, "Flour is flour is flour." Because flour is a **generic input** — different sources of it are interchangeable — we can imagine a flour market composed of many suppliers (millers) and many demanders (a multitude of other baking companies, large and small, for example). In such a market, we can use Coase's hypothesis to separate the activities coordinated in-house from those coordinated through markets by comparing their respective costs.

Specific Inputs

specific inputs

In some production processes, however, inputs are not generic but specific. For example, N C Machine, a tool-and-die shop in Wichita, has manufactured a styrofoam container for a McDonald's hamburger, the handle for a Sears Craftsman wrench, and the plastic holder for a Toyota auto seat belt. Dowty Canada Ltd. builds the nose-wheel and main landing gear for Lockheed's P-7A airplane. Johnson Controls of Milwakee makes seats for Chrysler's Grand Cherokee. A small Toronto supplier makes Campbell's fried eggs. These are **specific inputs** because they are of no (or limited) use to any firm except the firm for which one they are intended. The plastic holder for a Toyota auto seat belt, for instance, is of no use to anyone but Toyota.

When an input is highly specific, then, there cannot be a market for that input in the ordinary sense of the word. There might be more than one supplier, but there will be precisely one demander. (More than one firm might make the K-car chassis, for example, but only Chrysler Corporation will buy it.) Furthermore, no supplier will produce firm-specific, partly finished goods simply on speculation that the lone demander will buy them. The demander and its supplier(s) will invariably come to a detailed contractual agreement before any partly finished goods are produced. For example, Campbell Soup Company went through long, delicate negotiations before its fried-egg supplier agreed to buy the equipment it needed to begin producing fried eggs. And such agreements are costly.

Let us see what sort of issues specific inputs raise and why costly agreements are necessary if one firm is to produce a specific input for another. Specifically, let us suppose that I want to manufacture a one-of-a-kind customized car for someone whose tastes are so peculiar that the car will be worthless to anyone else. Suppose, too, that we have a verbal agreement in which you agree to make the auto body for me and I agree to pay you $100,000 for it. If you do produce the body to my specifications, will I actually pay you the promised price on delivery day? If I am honest and if I can, I will. But if I am less than honest, I may try to take advantage of you. Ignoring the scrap value of the body, you are now holding an auto body that has value to me alone. Suppose I offered you half the amount we had agreed upon? If I could convince you that I would not offer more, you would accept. In fact, you would accept any positive price rather than keep the body yourself. By producing a highly specific input, then, you have put yourself into a very shaky bargaining position.

On the other hand, I may have put myself into an equally awkward position. If I do not have time to get the auto body elsewhere, you may be able to extract more than $100,000 from me. Suppose that I have incurred $100,000 in additional costs and that using the body you have made, I can immediately sell the car for $250,000. Suppose, too, that if I do not deliver the finished product immediately, the deal is off and I will be left with an unmarketable car. What is the maximum I would pay for the body? It is virtually $250,000 — and if you were unscrupulous, you would ask for that amount. Clearly, if you and I are to make a transaction, we must have some form of contractual protection. And that protection will be costly. If it is too costly, our market arrangement simply will not be viable — and all production will be done in-house.

Any specific input raises this sort of issue. The consequence is that costly contractual arrangements must be entered into whenever one firm acquires a specific input from another. There is therefore a bias toward in-house production of specific inputs.

An equally important problem for suppliers of specialized parts is that they must often buy expensive single-purpose equipment. The dies used to stamp a specific auto body, for example, are extremely expensive and have only one use. Campbell's fried-egg supplier invested in expensive equipment to produce an input that only Campbell demands — fried eggs of very specific color, shape, and thickness. Again, suppliers will need to protect themselves against the potential for unscrupulous dealing created by these specific capital assets, and such protection may be expensive.

The problems associated with specific inputs and specific capital assets are common in all kinds of production processes. They almost invariably arise whenever one firm subcontracts work to another. A drywaller who subcontracts with a general contractor, for example, clearly faces these problems because the finished walls are specific to the building. An accounting firm may have difficulties if it puts effort and money into designing a specific bookkeeping system for a particular firm. A computer-parts manufacturing company may have problems if it produces components specific to a particular firm's computer. These transactions almost invariably mean that the demander and the supplier must agree to mutually protective measures — and these measures cost something.

> **PROBLEM 6.9**
>
> The law sometimes attempts to facilitate contracting in the presence of specificity. For example, a Mechanic's Lien Act, on the books in virtually all jurisdictions in North America, permits building tradespeople to register a lien against the real property they are working on. The lien prevents the sale of the property until the tradesperson's bill has been paid. Is such legislation in the self-interest of property owners as well as tradespeople?

Let us summarize the implications of input specificity:

On one hand, firms have an incentive to decentralize their activity; that is, to buy partly finished goods as inputs, because they can thereby avoid the difficulties associated with harmonizing the interests of individuals within the firm. On the other hand, firms have a disincentive to buy specific inputs from other firms, because these inputs are associated with what we might call contracting costs. Whether we will find decentralization (that is, coordination of economic activity by markets) or centralization (that is, coordination of economic activity within firms) depends on whether or not the advantages of decentralization outweigh the resulting contracting costs.

Remember, too, that even when the activity is coordinated in the marketplace, a market for a specific input is not a "market" in the ordinary sense of the word. It is instead a hybrid of the in-house and market systems of coordination.

SUMMARY

This exploration of the organization of the firm has been tentative rather than definitive. We wanted to provide you with a sampling of the kinds of intriguing (and sometimes difficult) questions that arise once we look inside the firm itself and to suggest how economists are attempting to analyze these questions.

We began with the observation that coordinating economic activity within firms is problematical. The basic problem — from the firm's point of view — is how to secure the cooperation of its workers in achieving the firm's collective objectives. (How can a Macy's department store, for instance, control theft by its employees?) Broadly speaking, the answer lies in designing organizational forms that harmonize or identify as closely as possible the collective interests of the firm with the self-interest of the individuals within it.

We then developed a model in which we could explore this problem more fully. We looked at three organizational forms — a *one-person firm* using isolated production, a *partnership* using team production, and an *owner-managed team* using team production — in a range of environments described by two parameters — the cost of monitoring, M, and the productivity of effort in team production, B. To illustrate the economist's approach to the theory of the firm, we used the *Pareto criterion* to choose among the three forms. If B is large and M is small, the owner-managed team is Pareto-preferred. If B is small and M is large, the one-person firm is Pareto-preferred. And if both B and M are large, the partnership is Pareto-preferred.

When we considered *specialized production*, we saw that the problem of harmonizing incentives also determines whether certain productive activities will be coordinated *in-house* or in the *marketplace* by means of transactions among vertically interrelated firms, or by a hybrid of the two. The theory of the firm is thus a part of a more general theory of the organization of economic activity as a whole.

We discovered, too, that incentive problems are extraordinarily diverse: different problems require different solutions. Given so many different incentive problems and so many different solutions in terms of organizational form, the range of economic questions yet unexplored is enormous. The theory of the firm and the broader theory of economic organization are both wide open to further analysis.

EXERCISES

1. In this problem, we will use the following utility function to illustrate the possible equilibrium organizational structures explored in Sections 6.2 through 6.4.

$$U(e,y) = 8(y - e^2/2)$$

With this utility function, MRS (or the slope of an indifference curve) is equal to e:

$$MRS = e$$

In the two-person team, each unit of effort produces $\$B$ of income, and in the one-person firm, each unit of effort produces $\$1$ of income.

a. Draw two indifference curves.

b. Derive the following results for the one-person firm:

utility-maximizing quantity of effort = 1

utility-maximizing income = 1

maximized utility = 4

Hints: At the utility-maximizing equilibrium,

the slope of the income-effort relationship is equal to MRS; to compute maximized utility, evaluate $U(e,y)$ at the utility-maximizing values of effort and income.

c. Derive the following results for the two-person partnership:

utility-maximizing quantity of effort = $B/2$

utility-maximizing income = $B^2/2$

maximized utility = $3B^2$

Hint: The slope of the income-effort relationship for the partnership is $B/2$.

d. Derive the following results for the owner-managed team:

utility-maximizing quantity of effort = B

utility-maximizing income = $B^2 - M/2$

maximized utility = $4B^2 - 4M$

Hint: In effect, the manager and the employee each pay half of the monitoring cost, M.

e. Use the maximized-utility results from above to construct a diagram with M on the horizontal axis and B^2 on the vertical axis, in which you identify values of M and B^2 such that 1. the one-person firm is Pareto-preferred to the other firms, 2. the owner-managed firm is Pareto-preferred, and 3. the partnership is Pareto-preferred. Hint: Begin by finding values of M and B^2 such that maximized utility is the same for the one-person firm and the partnership, for the one-person firm and the owner-managed firm, and for the partnership and the owner-managed firm.

2. Brothers Brett and Bart had a very peculiar argument — each claimed that his horse was slower than his brother's. To resolve their argument, they agreed to bet $100 on the outcome of a quarter-mile race. At the appointed hour, Brett and Bart mounted their horses and, when the starter's gun fired, nothing happened — whereupon a bystander, wise in the ways of economic incentives, whispered something to the brothers. In a matter of seconds, the question of which horse was the slower was resolved to the satisfaction of Brett and Bart. What did the wise bystander suggest?

3. Any homeowner will tell you that getting home repairs done satisfactorily by outside tradespeople can be a struggle. The problem is one of *asymmetric information*: although individual tradespeople know whether they are skilled and reliable, it is difficult for the homeowner to know. We pay $50 per year to belong to a homeowners' club that 1. refers us to tradespeople, and 2. checks back to see that we are happy with their work. Our checks for repairs are written to the homeowners' club, which then pays the tradesperson a specified percentage of the total bill. Is this sort of organization likely to solve the homeowner's asymmetric information problem? If you were the manager of the homeowners' club, how would you operate the club? In particular, how would you use the information provided by the club members? If you were a homeowner, what sort of management scheme would induce you to join the club? If you were a competent tradesperson, would you work for the club? What quality of work would you provide for club members?

4. Restaurants such as McDonald's and Burger King typically are run as franchises. The parent company (McDonald's of America, for example) teaches the franchisee how to run the establishment (in the case of McDonald's, at an institution called "Hamburger University") and then allows the franchisee to use the product trademark (the golden arches, for example) and to buy specialized packaging materials and ingredients. The terms of the typical franchise contract require the franchisee to pay an initial lump sum and a percentage of its gross revenues to the parent firm. The parent company can and does inspect the franchisee's operation and records from time to time. If the operation is not up to the standards of cleanliness and product quality specified in the contract, the parent company can unilaterally revoke the franchise. In addition, the franchisee must be the exclusive or sole owner of the restaurant and must agree to work full-time in the restaurant. The parent company typically agrees not to franchise another restaurant within a specified radius, say 10 miles. This type of contract raises a number of interesting questions. Why does the parent company choose to sell franchises instead of hamburgers? Why does the parent company insist on exclusive ownership of the franchised restaurant? Why does the parent company inspect the operations of its franchisees? Claim: a sensible franchisee would refuse to buy a franchise unless it knew that all other franchise contracts could and would be revoked if the franchisees failed to meet the parent company's standards. Do you agree? Why or why not? Why does one franchisee care about the way in which others run their restaurants? Why does the parent firm agree to the restriction that it cannot sell other franchises within a specified radius of existing franchises?

5. Success in the textbook market requires three things: a good book, the author's responsibility; an attractive book, the designer's responsibility; and an effective sales effort, the responsibility of the sales staff. The author typically is paid a royalty for each book sold, equal to something like 15% of the wholesale price of the book; the designer typically is a salaried member of the publisher's staff; and individual salespeople often receive a percentage commission on the sales they make. How do these compensation arrangements influence the incentives of the affected parties? Why are designers paid a salary instead of a commission? Why do publishers not pay authors a fixed sum to produce books? Why are

commissions so often used in sales in preference to, or in addition to, salaries?

6. A home computer called the Orange is produced by combining a 512K chip with specialized equipment designed exclusively for it. Many firms produce identical chips, but only Firm O produces the specialized equipment. The market price for a chip is $X; the cost to Firm O of producing the specialized equipment is $Y; and the market price for the Orange computer is $Z, which exceeds $X + $Y. The Orange computer can be produced and marketed in one of three possible ways. Firm O can buy the chips and then assemble and sell Oranges. Some chip manufacturer can buy the specialized equipment from Firm O and assemble and sell Oranges. Some third firm can buy both the chips and the specialized equipment produced by Firm O and assemble and sell Oranges. Which of these organizational forms would you expect to see and why?

7. IBM buys many of the specialized parts for its IBM computers from other firms. So, too, General Motors buys many of the specialized parts for its cars and trucks from other companies. Buying a particular specialized part from two or more different firms is common practice for the purchasing firm. Why would a firm like IBM or GM insist on having multiple suppliers for each of its specialized parts?

8. In jobs characterized by a considerable amount of learning by doing, a long-time employee is more valuable to the firm simply because he or she is familiar with the in's and out's of the firm's operation. We can think of this learning as *firm-specific human capital*: "firm-specific" because the learning is valuable only to the particular firm and "human capital" because it is embedded in individual people. For example, a student who works in a summer resort may take anywhere from a day to a week to be able to do the job without asking a lot of questions that use up both the student's and the supervisor's time. A common practice in the resort business is to pay a substantial bonus to students who stay for the entire season and to refuse to rehire students who quit before the end of the season. Why do resorts use these compensation and hiring schemes? More generally, in occupations characterized by considerable firm-specific human capital, wages tend to increase with seniority, and firms sometimes establish nonvested pension plans that pay the employee a pension only if he or she stays with the firm for some specified length of time. What purpose do such compensation schemes serve for the firm?

9. Imagine an extreme case of firm-specific human capital. It takes a new employee one period to learn a job. During that period, he or she is completely unproductive. Having mastered the job in the first period, the employee is productive in the second period. There are only two periods. All potential employees can earn wage w' in some other job in each period. Assuming that the rate of interest is zero, the firm must choose a wage rate for period 1, w_1, and for period 2, w_2, such that

$$w_1 + w_2 \geq 2w'$$

It could choose $w_1 + w_2 > 2w'$ of course, but will not do so. Why not? Will it ever choose $w_1 > w'$ and $w_2 < w'$? Is there any advantage to the firm in choosing $w_2 > w'$ and $w_1 < w'$? Suppose that there are two types of potential employees: the first type is going off to college after one period and the second type is not. Assuming that the firm cannot identify who is college-bound and who is not, show that it should choose $w_1 < w'$ and $w_2 > w'$.

REFERENCES

Alchian, A., and H. Demsetz. 1972. "Production, Information Costs, and Economic Organization," *American Economic Review* 62:777–95.

Berle, A., and G. C. Means. 1935. *The Modern Corporation and Private Property*, New York: Macmillan.

Coase, R. 1937. "The Nature of the Firm," *Economica* 4:386–405.

Smith, A. 1937. *The Wealth of Nations*, The Cannan Ed., New York: Random House, The Modern Library.

Williamson, O. 1985. *The Economic Institutions of Capitalism: Firms, Markets, Relational Contracting*, New York: Free Press.

CHAPTER 7

Production and Cost: One Variable Input

Consumer theory, which helped us to understand the decisions of individual consumers in the marketplace, is complemented by another branch of microeconomics, the *theory of the firm*. We are now setting out on an extended journey as we create the tools needed to analyze the decisions of individual firms.[1] We can use these tools to answer several important questions: How will a firm decide which industry to enter in the first place? How does a firm decide how much to produce of whatever goods and services it sells? What inputs will a firm buy to make its products and how much of each will it buy? How much will it charge for its products? Finding ways to answer these questions will occupy us in Chapters 7 through 12. Along the way, we will see that these tools can be applied to a number of interesting problems outside the confines of the theory of the firm.

The material is arranged in a series of steps, with each section building on the foundations laid in its predecessors. If you follow through the next few chapters slowly and carefully, checking your understanding at each step, you will arrive at the end with a solid grounding in production, cost, and supply analysis — a grounding that will allow you to think clearly about a whole range of important and interesting economic problems.

We begin by defining and illustrating the concept of a production function. We then define a number of cost-minimization problems, ranging from the long run down to the shortest possible short run, and we explore the production function when quantities of all inputs but one are held constant. Next, we turn from production to cost considerations as we develop the theory of cost when only one input is variable. Finally, we apply the tools of short-run production and cost to an all-too-familiar traffic congestion problem and to multiplant firms.

7.1

The Production Function

Economists think of the firm as an organization that buys inputs and then transforms them into marketable goods or services. This abstraction allows us to see the features common to all firms — from coconut-milk peddlers to IT&T. Imagine a Popsicle manufacturing

[1] The classic presentations of most of the material in the next two chapters are in Hicks (1939) and Samuelson (1947). See also these entries in *The New Palgrave*: "production: neoclassical theories" (M. I. Nadin), "production and cost" (M. A. Fuss), and "production functions" (D. W. Jorgenson).

company that buys inputs such as sugar, sticks, packaging materials, natural and artificial flavoring, molds, labor, and refrigeration and then processes them to make Popsicles of various flavors. If we suppose for simplicity that each firm produces only one good (say, grape Popsicles), we can imagine a function that tells us what quantity of that good the firm can produce from any bundle of inputs. Thus, a grape-Popsicle production function might tell us that if we had 24 hours of labor, 50 pounds of sugar, 1 gallon of grape flavoring, 20 gallons of water, 2 kilowatt-hours of electricity, and 10 standard Popsicle molds, we could produce 500 dozen grape Popsicles.

Defining the Production Function

In Chapter 6, we promised to expand on this intuitive definition of a *production function*. Let us begin by considering some product, which we will call good Y, made from two inputs, which we will call input 1 and input 2. We will denote the quantity of good Y by y, the quantities of inputs 1 and 2 by z_1 and z_2, and an **input bundle** by (z_1, z_2). Thus, the input bundle $(10, 97)$ is composed of 10 units of input 1 and 97 units of input 2. For simplicity, we will be concentrating on the two-input case.

input bundle

Imagine combining the two inputs to produce good Y. Of course, these inputs can be combined by using any of a number of technologies, some of which may be more productive than others. For example, if the input bundle is composed of 1 acre of wheatland (input 1) and 100 pounds of wheat seed (input 2), these inputs can be combined in many different ways to produce wheat (good Y). The entire acre can be uniformly seeded at a rate of 100 pounds of seed per acre; 1/3 of an acre can be seeded at a rate of 300 pounds of seed per acre; and the seed can be sown at any depth. We will assume that among these possible technologies, one is **technically efficient**; that is, it maximizes the quantity of output that can be produced from a particular bundle of inputs. The technically efficient technology is used to define the production function, $F(z_1, z_2)$. Thus, the **production function**

technically efficient

production function

$$y = F(z_1, z_2)$$

tells us the *maximum quantity* of good Y that can be produced from any input bundle (z_1, z_2).

We can describe a firm by this production function if we assume that the technically efficient production process is both known and used. In so doing, we are making the sweeping assumption that the firm has resolved complex informational, organizational, incentive, and engineering problems. For example, we are assuming that the Kansas farmer knows the technology that will yield the most wheat from 1 acre of land and 100 pounds of seed. Yet this is not always the case. For instance, when Millar Western Pulp Ltd. decided to go into pulp and paper production, it opted for the environmentally cleaner but more energy-intensive chemothermomechanical pulp mill technology used extensively in Europe rather than the standard chemical technology common in North American pulp mills. Yet the company made its decision without knowing for certain just what this unfamiliar technology involved. To help you understand just what a production function is, we will begin by looking at two types of production functions — fixed and variable proportions — and by illustrating both types with examples drawn from everyday life.

A Fixed-Proportions Production Function

fixed-proportions production function

In a **fixed-proportions production function**, the ratio in which the inputs are used never varies. We need one nut and one bolt to make one fastener; one right shoe and one left shoe to make a pair of shoes; one piano and one pianist to make music.

However, the fixed proportion need not be a one-to-one ratio. For example, 6 ounces of apple juice and 4 ounces of cranberry juice are needed to make the perfect cranapple drink. This recipe gives rise to the following fixed-proportions production function:

$$y = \min(z_1/6, z_2/4)$$

where y is the number of cranapple drinks, z_1 is ounces of apple juice, and z_2 is ounces of cranberry juice. If you had 24 ounces of apple juice and 20 ounces of cranberry juice, how many cranapple drinks could you make? There is enough apple juice for 4 drinks (4 = 24/6) and enough cranberry juice for 5 drinks (5 = 20/4), so you could make just 4 drinks (4 = min(5,4)), and you would have 4 ounces of cranberry juice left over. In fact, as you will see in the following problem, the recipe for any food or drink gives rise to a fixed-proportions production function.

> **PROBLEM 7.1**
>
> A good recipe for seviche calls for 16 ounces of red snapper fillet, 3 ounces of lime juice, 1 ounce of coriander, and 8 ounces of Bermuda onion.
> a. If a restaurant has 32 ounces of snapper, 9 ounces of lime juice, 5 ounces of coriander, and 48 ounces of onion, what is the maximum quantity of seviche the restaurant can make?
> b. What is the production function for seviche?

Leontief production functions

These production functions are useful as illustrations not only because they are so simple, but also because they are economically important. For example, fixed-proportions production functions (also known as **Leontief production functions** in this context) are the basis of *input-output analysis*, a tool widely used for economic planning.

Variable-Proportions Production Functions

variable-proportions production functions

In most production functions, however, the proportions of the inputs can be varied. In **variable-proportions production functions**, increased amounts of one input can be substituted for decreased amounts of another. For example, let us imagine a fictional firm — Mr. Tipple's Courier Service — that produces the output courier services, measured in miles. Tipple owns a truck around which he has built his courier service. In addition to the truck itself, he uses two inputs: a driver's time (input 1) and gasoline (input 2). Tipple can combine time and gasoline in varying proportions to produce the courier services he provides. For example, if he tells his employee to drive at 70 mph, he uses less time and more gas to produce each mile of courier services than if he tells his employee to drive at 40 mph.

Let us suppose that Tipple has an input bundle composed of z_1 hours of a driver's time and z_2 gallons of gasoline. The maximum number of miles of courier services, y, that he can produce given z_1 hours of time is determined by how fast the truck is driven. Letting s denote speed in mph, we see that

$$y \leq sz_1$$

For example, if z_1 is 10 and s is 50, a driver cannot drive more than 500 miles.

To determine how many miles z_2 gallons of gas will produce at speed s, we need the technological relationship between miles per gallon (mpg) and speed. For Tipple's truck, mpg is inversely proportional to s, and the factor of proportionality is 1200. That is,

$$\text{mpg} = 1,200/s$$

For example, if the truck is driven at 40 mph, it gets 30 mpg, and if it is driven at 60 mph, it gets 20 mpg. This relationship between mpg and s tells us that

$$y \leq 1200z_2/s$$

For instance, if the truck is driven at 60 mph, it is impossible to go more than 100 miles on 5 gallons of gas.

Given the constraints embodied in these two inequalities, we can find the production function for Tipple's Courier Service by choosing speed s to maximize distance y. The two inequalities are plotted in Figure 7.1 for fixed values of z_1 and z_2. The solution to this maximization problem must be *on* or *below* both of these lines. The green area represents all combinations of s and y that satisfy both constraints by requiring no more than z_1 hours of time or z_2 gallons of gas. In this green area, s^* — the speed that maximizes distance y — is determined by the point at which the two constraints intersect. As you can easily determine, the speed that maximizes y is just

$$s^* = (1200z_2/z_1)^{1/2}$$

and the distance traveled y^* is

$$y^* = (1200z_1z_2)^{1/2}$$

To underscore the fact that this is the production function, we can rewrite this result as

$$F(z_1, z_2) = (1200z_1z_2)^{1/2}$$

How do we know that this is the production function? Because it tells us the *maximum* number of miles that any input bundle composed of time and gasoline will produce. Furthermore, we have also identified the technologically efficient method for

FIGURE 7.1   Finding a production function

Given z_1 hours of a driver's time, the truck cannot be driven more than sz_1 miles. Hence, $y \leq sz_1$. Given z_2 gallons of gasoline, the truck cannot be driven more than $1200z_2/s$ miles. Hence, $y \leq 1200z_2/s$. To find the production function, choose s to maximize y, subject to these two constraints. Both

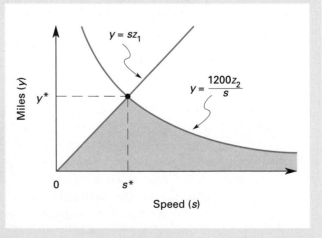

constraints are satisfied only in the green area. The solution is to drive at speed s^*, which means that the truck can be driven y^* miles.

combining any bundle of time and gasoline. Driving the truck at speed s^* will make the most of any such input bundle.

> **PROBLEM 7.2**
>
> Suppose that Tipple has an input bundle composed of 10 hours and 30 gallons of gas. What is the maximum number of miles his truck can be driven? What speed is required to achieve this result? Given the same input bundle, how far can the truck be driven at 40 mph? At 80 mph?

Cobb Douglas production function

This production function is an illustration of the historically important **Cobb Douglas production function**. The general form of this function in the two-input case is

$$y = Az_1{}^u z_2{}^v$$

where A, u, and v are positive constants. Cobb and Douglas (who later became a U.S. senator from Illinois) used this form to estimate a relationship between national product and the aggregate inputs of labor and capital (1948).

7.2
The Short- and Long-Run Cost-Minimization Problems

Before we explore the production function, we will put it in perspective by seeing just how it fits into the standard theory of the firm. We will assume that the firm's objective is to maximize its profit. A firm's profit is simply its revenue from selling its product minus the cost of producing that product. We begin that analysis with an important result:

Profit maximization implies cost minimization.

That is, a profit-maximizing firm will produce its output at minimum cost. We will defer analysis of the firm's revenue until later chapters. In this chapter and the next we will focus on the firm's costs.

The Long-Run Cost-Minimization Problem

long-run cost minimization

Let us begin with the problem of **long-run cost minimization**. By the long run, we mean a planning horizon long enough that a firm can vary all its inputs. In the two-input case, the long run is the planning horizon in which the firm can choose quantities of both inputs 1 and 2. Let us suppose that a particular firm wants to produce y units of output per period. It will minimize its cost by finding the least expensive input bundle that will produce y units of output. If the prices of its inputs are w_1 and w_2, then the cost of any input bundle the firm buys is simply the sum of the amounts spent on inputs 1 and 2, or

$$w_1 z_1 + w_2 z_2$$

The firm's long-run cost-minimizing problem, then, is to choose the input quantities z_1 and z_2 that will minimize its total costs, subject to the constraint that it can actually produce y units of output. Symbolically, we can write the long-run cost-minimization problem as

$$\text{minimize } w_1 z_1 + w_2 z_2$$
$$\text{by choice of } z_1 \text{ and } z_2$$
$$\text{subject to the constraint } y = F(z_1, z_2)$$

Input Prices

Remember that the cost-minimization problem is formulated in terms of *one period*. Therefore, we are considering input quantities and prices in terms of one period — and this can be a subtle qualifier. We must be careful to measure quantities of all inputs and all input prices in terms of the same period. No real problem is associated with *hired inputs*, such as labor, or *rented inputs*, such as temporary office space. If the period is a year and if input 1 is labor, for instance, then the unit of measure for input 1 is one worker for one year, and the price of input 1 — w_1 — is a worker's annual wage. In contrast, if the period is instead a week and if input 1 is once again labor, then the unit of measure for input 1 is one worker for one week, and the price of input 1 — w_1 — is a worker's weekly wage.

But some confusion is possible if *capital inputs* such as trucks or buildings are *bought* rather than rented. Let us suppose, for example, that a firm that hires labor (input 1) and buys trucks (input 2) to produce transportation services. If the firm buys trucks that last for five years, it is convenient to take the unit of time, or the period, to be five years. The unit of measure for input 2 is then *a truck*, the price of input 2 is the price of a truck, and quantity of input 2 is number of trucks bought. The unit of measure for input 1 (labor) is then one worker for five years, the price of input 1 is a worker's earnings over a five-year period, and quantity of input 1 is number of workers hired for five years.

Short-Run Cost-Minimization Problems

As we have seen, a firm's long-run planning horizon is long enough that it can vary the quantities of all its inputs. Yet firms are not always in this fortunate position of complete flexibility. If Ford Motor Company wants to produce more Mustangs this year, its options are distinctly limited. It can run its assembly lines around the clock by hiring and training more workers, and it may be able to accelerate the assembly process itself, provided that its body-stamping plants, engine plants, and other facilities can produce enough parts. However, it does not have the necessary lead time in the space of a year to create new assembly lines (or body-stamping or engine plants).

If the firm's planning horizon is such that the firm can vary *some*, but not all, of its inputs, it faces the problem of **short-run cost minimization**. There are many short runs corresponding to planning horizons in which the firm can vary the quantity of just one, just two, or just three inputs, and so on. Each of these planning horizons defines its own short-run cost-minimization problem.

short-run cost
minimization

In the two-input case, if the quantity of input 2 is fixed, we have a short run in which input 1 is the only variable input. The short-run cost-minimization problem is then to choose z_1 to minimize the cost of producing y units of output. We consider this short-run cost-minimization problem later in this chapter, and we take up long-run cost minimization in the next chapter. But first we must see what the production function looks like when the quantity of one input is fixed.

7.3

Production: One Variable Input

We know what a production function is, what two simple production functions look like, and where the production function fits into the firm's profit and cost calculations. The next step is to ask: What happens to output as we vary the quantity of one input, holding the quantities of all other inputs fixed? For example, how does a wheat farmer's harvest change if the quantity of wheat seed is varied, holding the quantities of land and all other inputs fixed?

Total Product

total product function

By fixing, or holding constant, the quantity of all inputs except one, we can write the production function as a function of one variable — the quantity of the single variable input. Written this way, the production function is called the **total product function**. It tells us what the output — or *total product* — will be for any quantity of the variable input (given the fixed quantities of the other inputs). To see how a total product function is derived from a production function, let us look at the case in which there are only two inputs. If we fix z_2 at 105 units, then the total product function, denoted by $TP(z_1)$, is defined as follows:

$$TP(z_1) = F(z_1, 105)$$

In other words, the total product function $TP(z_1)$ is derived from the production function simply by fixing the value of z_2 in the production function $F(z_1, z_2)$.

PROBLEM 7.3

We have already derived the following production function for Tipple's Courier Service:

$$F(z_1, z_2) = (1{,}200 z_1 z_2)^{1/2}$$

Find the total product function when z_2 is 12; when z_2 is 27. Graph these total product functions with z_1 on the horizontal axis and y on the vertical axis.

In Figure 7.2, we have constructed the typical, or standard, total product function. The quantity of the variable input z_1 is plotted on the horizontal axis, and output y is on the vertical axis. Notice that the slope of this total product function — which indicates the

FIGURE 7.2   A total product function

The curve 0GCE is the standard stylization of a total product function. It gives us the maximum quantity of output y that can be produced for any given quantity of input 1.

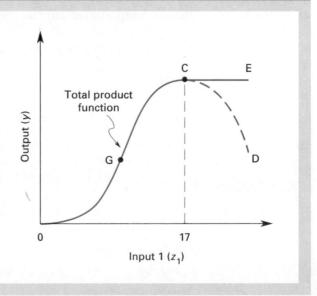

rate at which output changes as z_1 increases — is different at different values of z_1. For instance, the slope is steep near point G, while it is not so steep near the origin and near point C. This rate of change has a special name and a special role in the theory of the firm.

Marginal Product

marginal product

The rate at which output changes as the quantity of the variable input increases (given fixed quantities of all other inputs) is called the **marginal product** of the input and is denoted by $MP(z_1)$.[2] Because this rate of change is just the slope of the total product function, we see that

$$MP(z_1) = \text{slope of } TP(z_1)$$

In Figure 7.2, if you consider the curve that includes the dashed segment CD rather than the solid segment CE, perhaps you will recognize it from an introductory economics course. You have probably noticed, too, that the general shape of this curve is different from the total product functions you graphed in Problem 7.3. In a moment, we will look more closely at the reasons for constructing the standard total product function in this way and consider, too, alternative stylized functions.

Notice that because the slope of the dashed segment CD in Figure 7.2 is negative, marginal product is also negative when z_1 exceeds 17. In this region, more of the variable input actually reduces the total product. Cows and common pasture can be combined to produce milk, but too many cows on the pasture land can cause milk production to decrease. (In fact, most of the common-property problems listed in Section 4.6 illustrate this problem.)

Although these possibilities are real, they are *not* consistent with our definition of a production function — if we assume that firms have the option of using all or part of any input bundle. Because a production function gives the maximum output producible from any bundle of inputs, if the firm in Figure 7.2 has more than 17 units of input 1, it will decide to use precisely 17 units of input 1 and no more. In other words, if too many cooks spoil the broth, some of the cooks will be kept out of the kitchen.

free-disposal assumption

This is sometimes called the **free-disposal assumption**. In the common-property problem, there is no central authority — that is, no firm — to keep the counterproductive cows off the common pasture. Taken together, the definitions of the production function and the free-disposal assumption imply that marginal product cannot be negative — that is, CE rather than CD is the relevant total product function when z_1 exceeds 17.

Now let us consider a related question: Can the marginal products of all inputs simultaneously be zero? Imagine that input 1 is farm labor (measured in worker-hours), input 2 is a strawberry patch (measured in acres), and good Y is strawberries (measured in pints). If the input of land is fixed at 1 acre and if units of farm labor are continually added to it, eventually the point of maximum total product, corresponding to point C in Figure 7.2, will be reached. As more labor is added to the one-acre patch beyond that point, an excess of farm labor will occur, and its marginal product will be zero.

---

2 In mathematical terms,

$$MP(z_1, z_2) = F_1(z_1, z_2)$$

where $F_1(\cdot)$ is the partial derivative of $F(\cdot)$ with respect to z_1.

What is the marginal product of land when the marginal product of labor is zero? Notice that in posing this question, we are assuming that farm labor is now the fixed input and the size of the strawberry patch is the variable input. If another acre of land is brought into production and the excess farm labor is used to cultivate it, more pints of strawberries will be produced. In other words, when the marginal product of farm labor is zero, the marginal product of land is positive. More generally, although the marginal product of one input may be zero, the marginal products of all inputs cannot simultaneously be zero:

> **Given the free-disposal assumption, the marginal product of any input is always greater than or equal to zero; furthermore, for any input bundle, the marginal product of at least one input is positive.**

The total product function from Figure 7.2 is plotted in Figure 7.3a. The associated marginal product function $MP(z_1)$ is plotted in Figure 7.3b. Notice that as z_1 increases, the slope of $TP(z_1)$, and therefore marginal product, increases until z_1 is equal to 10. The slope of $TP(z_1)$ and therefore marginal product, then decreases until z_1 is equal to 17. Finally, both the slope of $TP(z_1)$ and marginal product are zero when z_1 exceeds 17. Because marginal product begins to decline at 10, this point is called the point of *diminishing marginal productivity*. The fundamental assumption in production theory is that such a point of diminishing marginal productivity always exists.

Diminishing Marginal Productivity

diminishing marginal productivity assumption

The idea of diminishing marginal productivity is not only significant in the theory of production but also fundamental to the history of economic thought. Reverend Thomas Malthus, a prominent English economist of the early nineteenth century, was the first to formulate the hypothesis of diminishing marginal productivity. He observed that in response to population pressure, new land was continually being opened for cultivation. He argued that if the converse of diminishing marginal productivity — increasing marginal productivity — were true, added labor would be more productive on cultivated than on virgin land. If that were the case, we would have no economic incentive to bring raw land under cultivation. From this argument and from the fact that new land was brought under the plow as the population grew, he concluded that labor devoted to food production necessarily brings diminishing marginal product. The **assumption of diminishing marginal product**, linked historically with Malthus's name, reflects his argument that at some point marginal product will begin to diminish:

ASSUMPTION: DIMINISHING MARGINAL PRODUCT

Suppose that the quantities of all inputs except one — say, input 1 — are fixed. There is a quantity of input 1 — say, z_1'' — such that whenever z_1 exceeds z_1'', the marginal product of input 1 decreases as z_1 increases.[3]

---

3 Diminishing marginal product is an assumption about a second partial derivative of the production function. For $z_1 > z_1''$, we assume that the partial derivative of marginal product with respect to z_1 is negative. That is,

$$MP'(z_1) = F_{11}(z_1, z_2) < 0 \qquad \text{for } z_1 > z_1''$$

where $F_{11}(\cdot)$ is the second partial derivative of $F(\cdot)$ with respect to z_1.

FIGURE 7.3   From total product to marginal product

The marginal product associated with any value of z_1 is the slope of the total product function at that value of z_1. For $z_1 < 10$, marginal product increases as z_1 increases because the total product function gets steeper as z_1 gets larger. For $z_1 > 10$, marginal product decreases as z_1 increases because the total product function gets flatter as z_1 gets larger. For $z_1 > 17$, marginal product is zero because the slope of the total product function is zero.

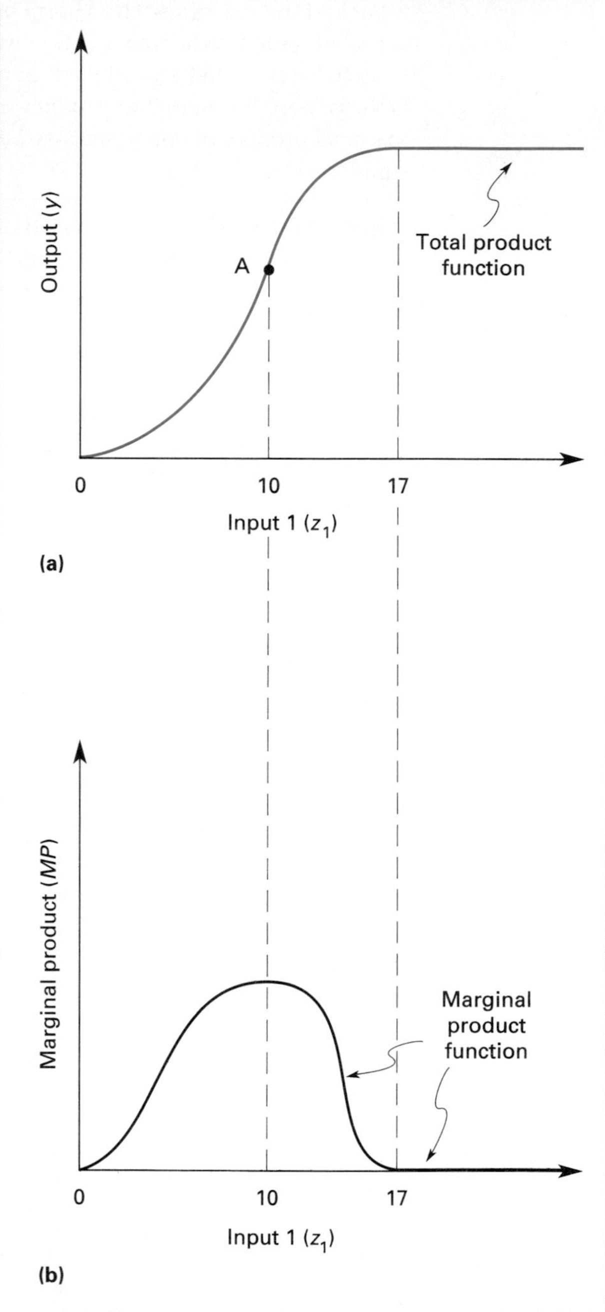

Notice that in Figure 7.3b, marginal product not only diminishes when z_1 exceeds 10 but also increases when z_1 is less than 10. The Malthusian hypothesis of a declining marginal product is a fundamental assumption in production theory, and the empirical evidence that supports it is strong. But an initially increasing marginal product is neither an inevitable feature of the world nor guaranteed by our assumptions. Whether marginal product does or does not initially increase in a particular production process is an empirical question. The stylized total product function in Figure 7.3 therefore represents only one possibility.

At least two alternative stylizations of the total product function are useful and interesting. One such possibility, shown in Figure 7.4, is that marginal productivity may be initially constant rather than increasing. (Notice that the linear segment of $TP(z_1)$ in Figure 7.4a is associated with a constant marginal product in Figure 7.4b.)

In the third stylization, the total product function exhibits diminishing marginal productivity from the outset. In this case, the first unit of the variable input contributes most to total product, and each successive unit contributes less than the one preceding it. A

FIGURE 7.4   **From total product to marginal product: another illustration**

The slope of the total product function in (a) is constant for $z_1 < 29$; marginal product in (b) is therefore constant for $z_1 < 29$. For $z_1 > 29$, the slope of the total product function gets smaller as z_1 gets larger; marginal product therefore decreases as z_1 increases for $z_1 > 29$.

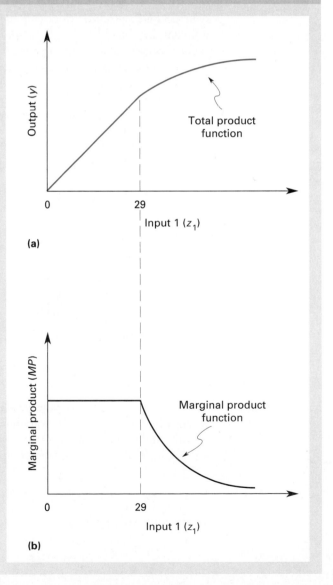

total product function exhibiting diminishing marginal product throughout looks like those you constructed in answering Problem 7.3. The slopes of those total product functions became progressively less steep as z_1 increased, reflecting diminishing marginal productivity of the variable input for all values of z_1.

These alternative stylizations of the total product function are conceivable and relevant. However, $TP(z_1)$ is usually drawn to indicate that as the quantity of the variable input increases, the marginal product rises at first and only later begins to diminish. The rationale is that increasing the amount of the variable input at first increases the productivity of all the units of that input. Imagine the kitchen of a major downtown hotel. The dinner shift begins with only a few kitchen workers, but as more and more help is added, the number of dinners the kitchen can produce increases at a rapid rate. Why? One reason is that the workers can specialize. Some only prepare vegetables; others only make sauces; still others wash dishes. Another reason is that the kitchen can be organized more efficiently. For example, the workers can all save steps (and thereby spend more time at their individual tasks) by preparing food at more compact and specialized work stations. At some point, however, the gains from a more efficient division of labor and organizational structure begin to diminish. Beyond this point of diminishing marginal product, $TP(z_1)$ gets progressively flatter as z_1 increases. As even more help is added to the hotel kitchen, food production continues to increase, but at a declining rate until, perhaps, marginal product finally reaches zero.

Although this rationale seems most convincing when the variable input is labor, whether any particular production process does or does not exhibit initially increasing marginal product is a question we can answer only by empirical investigation. It is therefore useful to have all three of the stylized total product functions at your fingertips. In the following problem, you can discover yet another possibility.

PROBLEM 7.4

We can think of producing fasteners (good Y) by combining nuts (input 1) and bolts (input 2). If z_2 is fixed at 10 units ($z_2 = 10$), the total product function is

$$TP(z_1) = \begin{cases} z_1 \text{ if } z_1 \leq 10 \\ 10 \text{ if } z_1 > 10 \end{cases}$$

In one diagram, carefully graph this total product function. In another diagram directly below the first, graph the associated marginal product function.

Average Product

average product

Like marginal product, **average product** is a way of looking at how output varies with changes in the quantity of the variable input. It is just the total product divided by the quantity of the variable input; that is, average product is the product per unit of the variable input. The average product of input 1, $AP(z_1)$, is therefore

$$AP(z_1) = TP(z_1)/z_1$$

To reinforce your understanding of average product, try the following problem.

PROBLEM 7.5

In the production function for Tipple's Courier Service, suppose that z_2 is 12. Then, from Problem 7.3, the total product function is

$$TP(z_1) = 120(z_1)^{1/2}$$

Find the average product function.

Let us see how to derive the average product function from the total product function in Figure 7.5. First, choose any point on the total product function and, from the origin, draw a ray that passes through that point. The slope of this ray is equal to average product at the point at which the ray intersects the total product function. At point A, for instance, the average product is the slope of the ray 0A. Why? The slope of the ray is equal to distance DA divided by distance 0D. But DA is the total product at point A, and 0D is equal to quantity of input 1 at point A. Therefore, the slope of the ray 0A is the total product divided by the quantity of input 1, or the average product. Similarly, the slope of the ray 0B is the average product at point B.

Let us now compare $MP(z_1)$ and $AP(z_1)$. At point A in Figure 7.5, for instance, $MP(z_1)$ exceeds $AP(z_1)$. At point H, however, $AP(z_1)$ exceeds $MP(z_1)$. To see why, simply construct the line tangent to the total product function at point A and notice that the slope of the tangent line, which is marginal product at point A, exceeds the slope of the ray through point A. The opposite is true at point H.

Point B is of special interest. At this point, average product and marginal product are identical because the ray through the origin to point B is tangent to $TP(z_1)$ at B. It is also a point of special interest for another reason: average product is at a maximum

FIGURE 7.5   From total product to average product

Average product at point A is the slope of the dashed line 0A because DA is total product and 0D is quantity of input 1. Similarly, average product at point B is the slope of the dashed line 0B. Notice that at point B average product is a maximum, and average product is equal to marginal product.

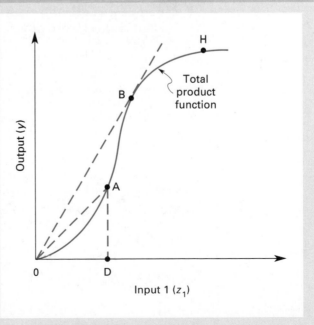

at B. To see why B is the point of maximum average product, try drawing another ray through the origin that intersects or is tangent to the total product function and that is steeper than 0B. It cannot be done.

In Figure 7.6a, we have constructed the standard stylization of the total product function and in Figure 7.6b, we have derived both measures of productivity — average and marginal product. This figure presents some important qualitative relationships between marginal product and average product. Although these relationships can be expressed in a variety of ways, the following observations offer perhaps the most insight: [4]

---

1. When marginal product is greater than average product,
average product is increasing.
2. When marginal product is less than average product,
average product is decreasing.
3. When marginal product is equal to average product, average product
is neither increasing nor decreasing; it is constant.

A simple analogy may help you to see the common sense of these relationships. Imagine a kindergarten room. If the average weight of the assembled children is a (for average pounds) and if another small person whose weight is m (for marginal pounds) joins the group, what will happen to the average weight of any child now in the schoolroom? If m exceeds a, the average weight of a child in the now larger group will rise; if m is less than a, it will fall; if m is equal to a, it will not change.

As you will discover in Problem 7.6, these curves will be different for different stylizations of the total product function.

> **PROBLEM 7.6**
>
> Construct a total product function like the one shown in Figure 7.4a. Below the graph of the total product function, derive the corresponding average and marginal product functions. Compare these curves with those in Figures 7.6a and 7.6b. Check to see that the curves you have drawn are consistent with the three observations above concerning the relationships between average and marginal products.

---

4 Because we will encounter these sorts of relationships at several points in this and the following chapters, it is useful to explore them more carefully. Consider any function $f(x)$ with domain $x > 0$ and the implied "marginal" function

$$M(x) = f'(x)$$

and "average" function

$$A(x) = \frac{f(x)}{x}$$

Differentiating $A(x)$, we have

$$A'(x) = \frac{xf'(x) - f(x)}{x^2}$$

or, equivalently,

$$A'(x) = \frac{f'(x) - f(x)/x}{x}$$

But this can be written as

$$A'(x) = \frac{M(x) - A(x)}{x}$$

Therefore $A(x)$ is increasing, decreasing, or stationary as $M(x)$ is greater than, less than, or equal to $A(x)$.

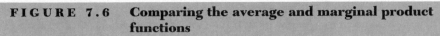

FIGURE 7.6   **Comparing the average and marginal product functions**

In (b), we have derived *AP* and *MP* associated with *TP* in (a). Three values of z_1 — 23, 38, and 67 — are noteworthy: 1. *MP* is rising or falling as z_1 is less than or greater than 23, and *MP* attains its maximum value at $z_1 = 23$; 2. *AP* is rising or falling as z_1 is less or greater than 38, *AP* attains its maximum value at $z_1 = 38$, *MP* is equal to *AP* at $z_1 = 38$, and *MP* is greater or less than *AP* as z_1 is less or greater than 38; 3. *MP* is zero when z_1 exceeds 67.

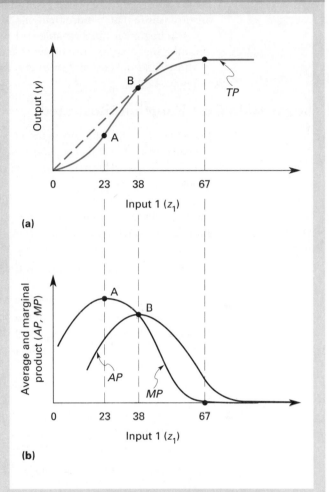

7.4

Costs of Production: One Variable Input

Now let us consider the short-run cost-minimization problem that arises when just one input is allowed to vary. If input 2 is the fixed input and input 1 the variable input, then the cost-minimization problem can be stated as

$$\text{minimize } w_1 z_1 \text{ by choice of } z_1$$

$$\text{subject to the constraint } y = TP(z_1)$$

That is, choose z_1 to minimize the expenditure on the variable input ($w_1 z_1$), subject to the constraint that the firm produces y units of output [$y = TP(z_1)$].

Because this problem is so simple, in the space of a few pages we can learn everything there is to know about how various cost functions inherit the properties of their corresponding total product functions. This elementary grounding in the relationship between production functions and the cost of production will be very useful in the next chapter, where we will reconsider production and cost in the more complex, realistic cases in which more than one input is variable.

We begin with the variable cost function, define average variable cost and short-run marginal cost, explore the fixed cost of production, and conclude with definitions of short-run total cost and short-run average cost.

The Variable Cost Function Illustrated

Once we know what quantity of output a particular firm wants to produce, we can discover from the total product function the minimum quantity of the variable input required to produce that output. This minimum quantity is the solution to our simple cost-minimization problem. We can then determine what the *minimum variable cost* of the output will be by multiplying this quantity by the price of the input w_1. We will assume throughout that the firm can buy any amount of the variable input at a fixed price w_1 per unit. We can thus derive from the total product function the **variable cost function**, written as $VC(y)$:

variable cost
function

$$VC(y) = \text{the minimum variable cost of producing } y \text{ units of output}$$

Let us use Tipple's Courier Service to develop an algebraic illustration. Suppose that Tipple has just 12 gallons of gas on hand and that he cannot buy any more in this period. In this case, gasoline is the fixed input and his driver's time is the variable input. From Problem 7.3, the total product function is

$$TP(z_1) = 120(z_1)^{1/2}$$

where z_1 is hours of time. Since this function describes the relationship between miles driven (y) and time (z_1), we have

$$y = 120(z_1)^{1/2}$$

For example, if Tipple wants the truck driven 240 miles, the minimum amount of a driver's time that he needs is 4 hours. Although a driver could take more than 4 hours to drive 240 miles on 12 gallons of gas, 4 hours is the minimum time required. Letting w_1 denote the hourly wage of Tipple's driver, we see that $4w_1$ is the variable cost of driving 240 miles, or $VC(240) = 4w_1$. Similarly, if Tipple wants the truck driven 360 miles, he needs 9 hours. In this case, we see that $VC(360) = 9w_1$.

More generally, if we invert the total product function by solving for z_1 in terms of y, we have the minimum time needed to drive the truck y miles. If we let z_1^* represent this minimum time, we have

$$z_1^* = y^2/(14{,}400)$$

Now, simply by multiplying by w_1 we have the variable cost function for Tipple's Courier Service when he has 12 gallons of gas:

$$VC(y) = w_1 y^2/(14{,}400)$$

This gives us the minimum cost of driving the truck y miles when Tipple pays his driver w_1 per hour and has just 12 gallons of gas on hand.

> **PROBLEM 7.7**
>
> Suppose that Tipple has 27 gallons of gasoline on hand. First find z_1^*, the minimum number of hours needed to drive y miles. Then find the corresponding variable cost function, $VC(y)$.

Deriving the Variable Cost Function

To this point, we have explored two variable cost functions for Tipple's Courier Service. Now we will develop a graphic technique that can be applied to any cost-minimization problem when only one input is variable. The series of four interlinked diagrams in Figure 7.7 shows just how the variable cost function $VC(y)$ can be derived from the total product function $TP(z_1)$ and the cost of input 1, w_1. We have plotted the standard total product function in Figure 7.7a, and we have then used the diagrams in Figure 7.7b and 7.7c to derive the variable cost function in Figure 7.7d.

Let us see how that derivation is accomplished. Suppose that the firm wanted to produce 768 units of good Y. Consulting $TP(z_1)$ in Figure 7.7a, we see that 16 units of input 1 is the least costly way of doing so because 16 is the smallest quantity of input 1 that will produce 768 units. From the ray in Figure 7.7b, we see that 16 units of input 1 will cost $16w_1$. Because the minimum cost of producing 768 units of Y is $16w_1$, $(768, 16w_1)$ is one point on the variable cost function $VC(y)$ in Figure 7.7d.

To identify this point in Figure 7.7d, we have (horizontally) projected the cost $16w_1$ from Figure 7.7b into Figure 7.7d. Using the 45-degree line in Figure 7.7c, we have also projected output 768 from Figure 7.7a into Figure 7.7d. The intersection of these two projections at $(768, 16w_1)$ in Figure 7.7d is one point on $VC(y)$. All other points on $VC(y)$ have been constructed in the corresponding way. For example, 22 units of input 1 are needed to produce 2971 units of good Y, and $(2971, 22w_1)$ is therefore another point on $VC(y)$.[5]

Average Variable Cost and Short-Run Marginal Cost

We defined the concepts of average product and marginal product when we looked at the total product function. Now we will define the corresponding concepts of average variable cost and short-run marginal cost in relation to the variable cost function. Although their labels are a bit of a mouthful, the concepts themselves are straightforward. As you might have guessed, **average variable cost**, written $AVC(y)$, is just the variable cost per unit of output:

average variable
cost

$$AVC(y) = VC(y)/y$$

short-run
marginal cost

The **short-run marginal cost**, $SMC(y)$, as you might also have guessed, is the rate at which cost increases in the short run as output increases. Because the only variable cost

---

5 What we accomplish in Figure 7.7 is, in essence, the inversion of the function $y = TP(z_1)$. Write the inverse of this function as $z_1 = H(y)$. This function tells how much z_1 is required to produce any given y. The variable cost function is then just w_1 multiplied by $H(y)$:

$$VC(y) = w_1 H(y)$$

FIGURE 7.7 **Deriving the variable cost function**

VC in (d) is derived from *TP* in (a). From (a), we see that $z_1 = 16$ is necessary to produce output $y = 768$; from (b), we see that 16 units of input 1 cost $16w_1$. Projecting $y = 768$ into (d), through the 45 degree line in (c), and projecting $16w_1$ into (d), we have one point on VC, the point $(768, 16w_1)$.

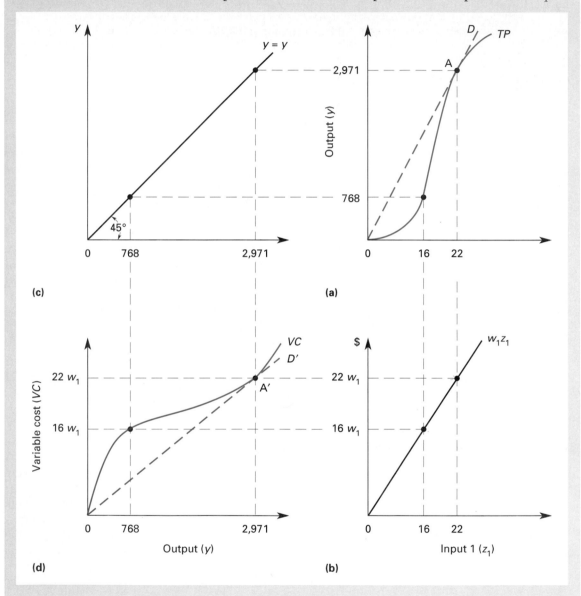

in the short run is the cost associated with the variable input, the short-run marginal cost of output is simply the slope of the variable cost function:[6]

$$SMC(y) = \text{slope of } VC(y)$$

6 Mathematically, we see that $SMC(y)$ is simply the derivative of $VC(y)$:
$$SMC(y) = VC'(y)$$

In Figure 7.8, we have illustrated the graphic techniques used to derive the average variable cost and the short-run marginal cost. We have constructed the ray through the origin to point A on $VC(y)$ and the line TT that is tangent to $VC(y)$ at point A. Because the slope of the ray is average variable cost at A and the slope of the tangent line is marginal cost at A, we see that $AVC(y)$ is less than $MC(y)$ at point A.

We can use these graphic techniques to derive and compare the average variable cost and short-run marginal cost functions implied by any variable cost function. The variable cost function $VC(y)$ from Figure 7.7d is reproduced in Figure 7.9a. The average variable cost function $AVC(y)$ and the short-run marginal cost function $SMC(y)$ derived from $VC(y)$ are shown in Figure 7.9b. You need to understand why both curves in Figure 7.9b are U-shaped and why they intersect at output level 2971. If you are unsure, pick up a pencil and paper and derive $SMC(y)$ and $AVC(y)$ from $VC(y)$, using the technique described in Figure 7.8.

What does Figure 7.9 tell us about the relationship between average variable cost and short-run marginal cost? We see three perhaps familiar relationships:

1. When SMC lies below AVC, AVC decreases as y increases.
2. When SMC is equal to AVC, AVC is neither increasing nor decreasing: its slope is zero.
3. When SMC lies above AVC, AVC increases as y increases.[7]

FIGURE 7.8   Deriving average variable cost and short-run marginal cost

AVC at point A is equal to the slope of the dashed line 0A. SMC at point A is the slope of the tangent line TT. At point A, AVC is less than SMC.

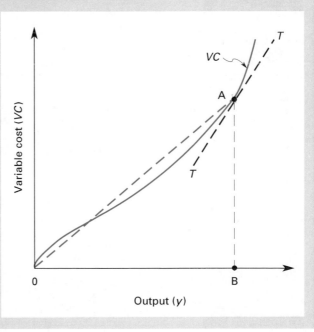

---

7 These results are another application of the general relationship between averages and marginals developed in footnote 4.

These relationships follow from the same arithmetic truisms that predict your grade point average: if your grades this term are lower than your previous average, your average will fall; if they are the same, your average will remain the same; if they are higher, your average will go up.

In Figure 7.9c, we have reproduced the standard total product function $TP(z_1)$ from Figure 7.7a, and in Figure 7.9d, we have derived the related marginal product and

---

FIGURE 7.9   Comparing cost and product functions

In (b), we have derived *SMC* and *AVC* from *VC* in (a). The slope of *VC* is smallest at $y = 768$; therefore, *SMC* attains its minimum value at $y = 768$. At $y = 2971$, the ray 0A is tangent to *VC*; therefore, *SMC* is equal to *AVC*, and *AVC*

attains its minimum value at $y = 2971$. Similarly, in (d), we have derived *MP* and *AP* from *TP* in (c). In comparing (b) and (d), notice that *SMC* and *AVC* are inverted images of *MP* and *AP*.

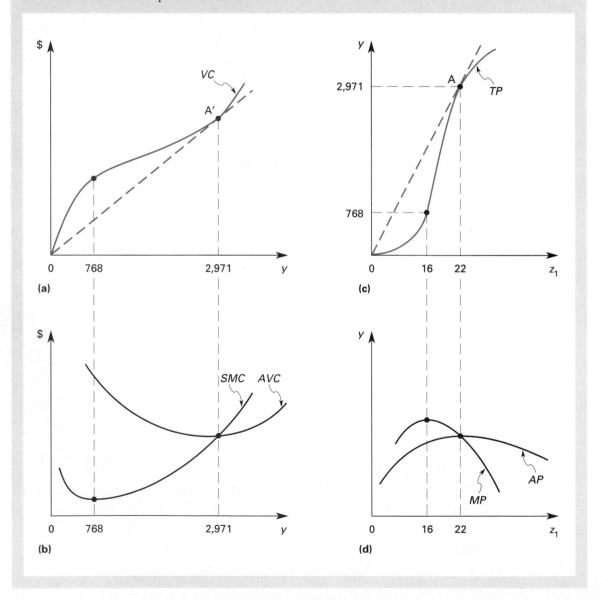

average product functions $MP(z_1)$ and $AP(z_1)$. In Figure 7.9d, marginal product is at its peak when the quantity of the variable input is 16 or when the output is 768, and it diminishes thereafter. Correspondingly, in Figure 7.9b, short-run marginal cost is at its lowest point when the output is 768, and it increases thereafter. Increasing short-run marginal cost, then, seems to be a direct implication of diminishing marginal product. Similarly, decreasing short-run marginal cost seems to be a direct implication of increasing marginal product. It is almost as if we could generate the marginal cost curve in Figure 7.9b by inverting the image of the marginal product curve in Figure 7.9d.

The average product and average variable cost curves in Figures 7.9b and 7.9d show the same kind of strikingly similar, but inverse, relationship. At input levels below 22 (or output levels below 2971), average product is increasing, and average variable cost is decreasing. At input levels above 22 (or output levels above 2971), average product is falling, and average variable cost is rising. Once again, we could almost generate the average variable cost function by inverting the image of the average product function.

Average Product and Average Cost

Doing two simple algebraic exercises will help you to see why these relationships hold. We will look at an arbitrary point on the total product function:

$$y' = TP(z_1')$$

Average product at this point is just the output $TP(z_1')$ divided by the quantity of the variable input z_1':

$$AP(z_1') = TP(z_1')/z_1'$$

Average variable cost at this point is just the expenditure on input 1 divided by the output:

$$AVC(y') = w_1 z_1'/TP(z_1')$$

We can rewrite this expression as

$$AVC(y') = w_1/[TP(z_1')/z_1']$$

But the denominator here is just average product. Thus, average variable cost is equal to the price of the variable input divided by average product:

$$AVC(y') = w_1/AP(z_1')$$

In this sense, the average variable cost function is the inverted image of the average product function.

Marginal Product and Marginal Cost

Let us turn now to the relationship between the marginal product function and the short-run marginal cost function. Again, imagine choosing some arbitrary level of the variable input z_1' and then increasing that level by some very small amount Δz_1. The corresponding increase in the variable cost Δc will be just the additional quantity of the input multiplied by the price of the input:

$$\Delta c = w_1 \Delta z_1$$

The amount by which output increases, Δy, will be (approximately) the marginal product of the variable input at level z_1' multiplied by the additional quantity of the variable input:

$$\Delta y = MP(z_1')\Delta z_1$$

By definition, short-run marginal cost is simply the rate of increase of variable cost as output increases; that is, it is approximately $\Delta c/\Delta y$. Substituting the results from above,

$$SMC(y') = w_1\Delta z_1/MP(z_1')\Delta z_1$$

Canceling Δz_1, we see that the short-run marginal cost at output y' is simply the price of the variable input divided by the marginal product of the variable input at level z_1':

$$SMC(y') = w_1/MP(z_1')$$

In this sense, the short-run marginal cost function is the inverted image of the marginal product function.[8]

Fixed Cost

fixed cost

By specifying the price of the variable input w_1, we have been able to derive from the total product function the associated variable cost function. But what about the cost associated with the fixed input? The cost of the fixed input, which is called a **fixed cost**, is simply the price of the input multiplied by its quantity:

$$FC = w_2 z_2$$

where z_2 is quantity of the fixed input.

average fixed cost

We can express fixed costs on a per-unit basis by dividing the fixed cost by output. This is called the **average fixed cost** of production, denoted by $AFC(y)$:

$$AFC(y) = FC/y$$

To understand the relationship implied by this statement, try the following problem.

PROBLEM 7.8

Plot the horizontal line FC on a graph in which y is on the horizontal axis and dollars are on the vertical axis. Now graph $AFC(y)$. What happens to $AFC(y)$ as y gets arbitrarily large? As y gets arbitrarily small?

Short-Run Total Cost and Short-Run Average Cost

short-run total cost

The **short-run total cost** of output, written $STC(y)$, can be calculated simply by adding up the variable cost and the fixed cost:

$$STC(y) = VC(y) + FC$$

---

8 We noted in footnote 5 that
$$VC(y) = w_1 H(y)$$
where $H(y)$ is the inverse of $y = TP(z_1)$. Differentiating this expression, we see that
$$SMC(y) = w_1 H'(y)$$
But $H'(y)$ is $1/[TP'(z_1)]$, or $1/[MP(z_1)]$. Hence,
$$SMC(y) = \frac{w_1}{MP(z_1)}$$

short-run
average cost

Short-run total cost can also be expressed on a per-unit basis, called **short-run average cost** and written $SAC(y)$, by dividing the short-run cost by the number of units of output:

$$SAC(y) = STC(y)/y$$

PROBLEM 7.9

$SMC(y)$ is defined as the slope of $VC(y)$. Show that $SMC(y)$ is also equal to the slope of $STC(y)$. In other words, show that for any value of y, the slope of $STC(y)$ is equal to the slope of $VC(y)$.

FIGURE 7.10   Seven cost functions

In (a), STC is derived from VC by adding FC. Each of the cost functions in (b) can be derived from the cost functions in (a): $AFC = FC/y$, $AVC = VC/y$, and $SAC = STC/y$. Finally, SMC = slope of VC, and SMC slope of STC.

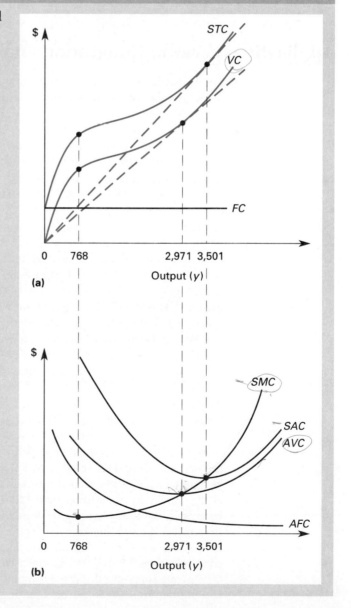

Or, equivalently, short-run average cost can be calculated by adding up the average variable cost and the average fixed cost:

$$SAC(y) = AVC(y) + AFC(y)$$

Figure 7.10 shows all of these cost functions. FC, $STC(y)$, and $VC(y)$ are in Figure 7.10a, and $AFC(y)$, $AVC(y)$, $SAC(y)$, and $SMC(y)$ are in Figure 7.10b. Because $SMC(y)$ is the marginal function associated with $STC(y)$ and because $SAC(y)$ is the average function associated with $STC(y)$, we immediately know a great deal about the relationship between $SMC(y)$ and $SAC(y)$:

SAC is increasing or decreasing as *SMC* lies above or below it, and the slope of *SAC* is zero when *SMC* is equal to *SAC*.

Applications: Traffic Congestion and Multiplant Firms

Let us use these tools to do some vicarious problem solving, just as we did in Chapter 4. The number of cars entering and leaving any major city in the world has grown dramatically over the past three decades. Bumper-to-bumper traffic at the start of a working day is a frustrating fact of everyday life for millions of commuters. Although the problem of traffic congestion does not involve a firm, we will see that the production and cost concepts developed in this chapter allow us to generate some interesting insights into this troubling problem. Conversely, in the last section of the chapter, you will see that much of what we learn about the congestion problem can easily be applied to firms.

Imagine a suburb called Surrey that is connected to the nearby city of Wetvan by two roads — Route 1 and Route 2. Imagine, too, that every weekday morning 5,000 residents of Surrey hop into their cars and drive to work in Wetvan. We want answers to these questions: What principles determine how many commuters will choose each route? What are the costs of commuting for the Surrey commuters? Do these commuters make the most effective use of the two roads that connect their town to the big city? Throughout the analysis we will ignore the money that these commuters spend on gasoline and automobiles so that we can isolate the *time costs* of commuting.

We can begin by looking at the technology on Route 1 from the commuter's perspective. As you undoubtedly know, commuting time on most roads depends on traffic density. If the number of commuters who pick a particular road is small, the trip takes a relatively short time. As more and more cars converge on a road, however, traffic builds up until, beyond some point, the larger the number of commuters, the longer it takes each commuter to get to work.

The precise relationship between average commuting time and numbers of commuters on Route 1 is presented in Figure 7.11. The time per commuter is measured on the vertical axis and the number of commuters using Route 1, N_1, is measured on the horizontal axis. Notice that Route 1 is congestion-free when N_1 is less than 1,200. Notice, too, that when fewer than 1,200 commuters take this route, each commuter spends 18 minutes traveling from Surrey to Wetvan. When more than 1,200 commuters use Route 1, however, each commuter spends more than 18 minutes traveling to Wetvan, and the commuting time increases as N_1 increases. For example, if 3,600 commuters use Route 1, the time per commuter rises to 30 minutes.

We are supposing that every commuter on Route 1 spends the same amount of time commuting. In doing so, we are ignoring a number of the features of real commuting

FIGURE 7.11   The costs of commuting

If fewer than 1,200 commuters use Route 1, commuting time per commuter is 18 minutes and there is no congestion. In contrast, if more than 1,200 commuters use Route 1, time per commuter increases as the number of commuters increases, reflecting increasing congestion on the route. Since com-

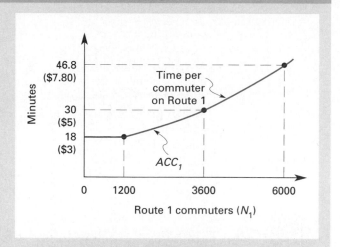

muters value their time at $10 per hour, we can translate the time costs of commuting into money costs. For example, if 3,600 commuters use the route, the money cost is $5 per commuter, equal to half an hour (30 minutes) times $10 per hour. ACC_1 gives the average cost per commuter on Route 1.

situations to concentrate on the relationship between traffic density and commuting time. For example, the very real possibility that a commuter who gets up early can reduce his or her commuting time by hitting the road while most other commuters are still in bed does not arise in this model.

Figure 7.11 presents the time cost per commuter on Route 1 as a function of the number of commuters using the route, N_1. For many purposes, it is useful to express this time cost in monetary terms. We will assume that the hourly wage rate of these commuters is $10, and we will value their time at this rate. An 18-minute commute then costs $3 — since 18 minutes is three-tenths of an hour — and a 60-minute commute costs $10. On the vertical axis in Figure 7.11, we have attached alternative labels to convert the time cost per commuter into a dollar cost per commuter.

Notice that the dollar cost per commuter is, in effect, an average cost function, where the output is the number of trips to Wetvan from Surrey N_1, and the total cost is the total value of the time spent by the N_1 Surrey commuters in traveling to Wetvan. To reflect this fact, we have used the label ACC_1 in Figure 7.11 for *average commuting cost* on Route 1. What are the corresponding total and marginal cost functions?

To derive the total cost function, we just need to observe that the total commuting cost is equal to the number of commuters N_1 multiplied by the average commuting cost ACC_1. In Figure 7.12, we have constructed the *total commuting cost* function for Route 1 and labeled it TCC_1. When N_1 is less than 1,200, TCC_1 rises at a constant rate because Route 1 is congestion-free. When N_1 exceeds 1,200, however, the ever-increasing congestion from that point on means that TCC_1 rises at an ever-increasing rate. For any point such as point A on TCC_1, the average commuter cost ACC_1 is equal to the slope of the ray from the origin to A, and what we will call the *marginal commuter cost* — or MCC_1 — is equal to the slope of TCC_1. Notice that MCC_1 exceeds ACC_1 when N_1 exceeds 1,200.

Because it is not subject to congestion, commuting on Route 2 is easy to model. A Surrey commuter on Route 2 will arrive in Wetvan in 30 minutes, *regardless* of

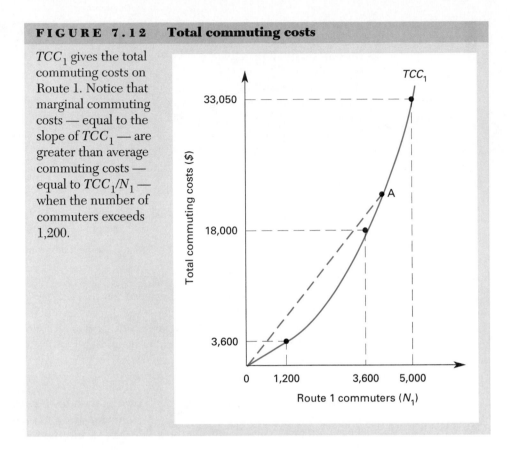

FIGURE 7.12   Total commuting costs

TCC_1 gives the total commuting costs on Route 1. Notice that marginal commuting costs — equal to the slope of TCC_1 — are greater than average commuting costs — equal to TCC_1/N_1 — when the number of commuters exceeds 1,200.

how many other commuters are also using this route. In other words, Route 2 is slow but sure. The average cost of the 30-minute commute on Route 2 is $5 since the hourly wage rate is $10 and the trip takes half an hour, or $ACC_2 = \$5$. The total commuting cost on Route 2 is then $TCC_2 = 5N_2$. And finally, the marginal commuting cost is also $5, or $MCC_2 = 5$.

Now let us see what determines how many of Surrey's commuters will choose Route 1 and how many will choose Route 2. We will assume that every commuter in this model wants to minimize the time spent commuting — or, equivalently, the cost of commuting. Because each commuter is free to choose either route, the average commuting cost in equilibrium must be the same on both routes. Why? Suppose that on Monday, 1,200 commuters choose Route 1 and 3,800 choose Route 2. Then the average commuting cost on Route 1 is only $3 but the average commuting costs on Route 2 is $5. Some of the commuters who took Route 2 on Monday will then decide to switch to Route 1 on Tuesday. As a result, ACC_1 will increase on Tuesday. This process will end only when enough commuters have switched from Route 2 to Route 1 so that ACC_1 is equal to ACC_2. Therefore, in equilibrium, 3,600 commuters will use Route 1, and the remainder of the 5,000 commuters, or 1,400 commuters, will use Route 2.

PROBLEM 7.10

What will the equilibrium allocation be if there are 6,000 commuters? If there are 4,000 commuters? If there are 3,000 commuters?

Are these Surrey commuters making effective use of their roads? To find out, let us turn to Figure 7.13a, where we have plotted both TCC_1 and TCC_2. Notice that TCC_1 has been plotted relative to 0_1 in the standard way, and the values for N_1, which are set out just below the horizontal axis, increase from left to right beginning at 0_1. However, TCC_2 has been plotted relative to the second origin at 0_2, and the values for N_2, which are set out just above the horizontal axis, increase from right to left, beginning at 0_2. The distance from 0_1 to 0_2 is exactly 5,000, reflecting the fact that 5,000 Surrey commuters travel to Wetvan. Therefore, any point along the horizontal axis in Figure 7.13a corresponds to an allocation of commuters to the two routes. For example, at the equilibrium allocation, 3,600 commuters take Route 1 and 1,400 take Route 2.

Now consider the allocation at point A. Distance AC is the total cost of commuting on Route 1, TCC_1, and distance AB is the total cost of commuting on Route 2, TCC_2. Adding up the two distances gives us distance AD, the total cost of commuting for this al-

---

FIGURE 7.13   The allocation of commuters to routes

In (a), total commuting costs on Route 1 and Route 2, TCC_1 and TCC_2, are plotted relative to 0_1 and 0_2, respectively. Since any point on the horizontal axis corresponds to an allocation of commuters to routes, we get total commuting costs for any allocation by vertically summing TCC_1 and TCC_2 to get TCC. Total commuting costs TCC are minimized when 2,000 commuters are allocated to Route 1 and 3,000 to Route 2. In (b), we see that marginal commuting costs on the two routes — MCC_1 and MCC_2 — are equal when TCC is a minimum. Further, if commuters have common access to the two routes, average commuting costs on the two routes — ACC_1 and ACC_2 — are equalized in the equilibrium at E. The equilibrium allocation is 3,600 commuters to Route 1 and 1,400 to Route 2.

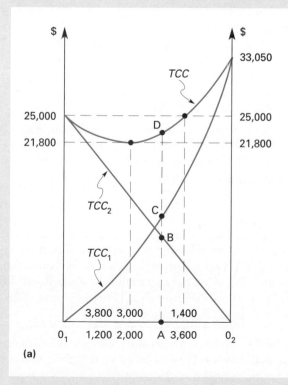

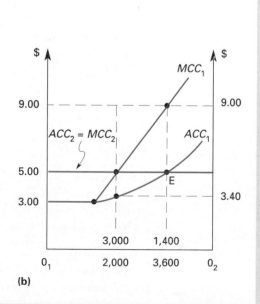

(a)

(b)

location. Using this method, we have computed the total commuting cost for all possible allocations and have labeled the resulting curve *TCC*. Notice that *TCC* is smallest when 2,000 commuters take Route 1 and 3,000 take Route 2. The total commuting costs associated with this allocation are just $21,800. By contrast, at the equilibrium allocation (where 3,600 take Route 1 and 1,400 take Route 2), the total commuting costs are $25,000. Notice that if all 5,000 commuters traveled along Route 2, the total commuting costs would likewise be $25,000. In this equilibrium, then, it is as if Route 1 simply did not exist.

Using the cost-benefit criterion, we then see that the Surrey commuters are not making effective use of their roads. According to the cost-benefit criterion, one allocation is preferred to another if it is associated with smaller total commuting costs. Because the total commuting costs are smallest when 2,000 commuters use Route 1 and 3,000 use Route 2, this allocation is cost-benefit-optimal.

To better understand these results, let us turn to Figure 7.13b. We have drawn the two sets of average and marginal cost curves and identified the equilibrium at point E at the intersection of ACC_1 and ACC_2. Notice that to the right of point E the average cost of commuting is higher on Route 1 and that to the left it is higher on Route 2. Therefore, if the allocation of commuters was at any point other than E, some commuters would have a private incentive to switch routes.

The marginal commuting cost curves reveal why the equilibrium is suboptimal and why total commuting costs are minimized when 2,000 commuters use Route 1 and 3,000 use Route 2. On either route, the marginal commuting cost is the rate at which total commuting costs on that route increase as the number of commuters increases. Beginning at the equilibrium allocation, let us ask: What happens to the total commuting costs if we force one commuter off Route 1 and onto Route 2? Since MCC_1 is $9, TCC_1 will decrease by (approximately) $9, and since MCC_2 is $5, TCC_2 will increase by $5. Thus, total commuting costs *TCC* will decrease by approximately $4. More generally, beginning at any point where MCC_1 is not equal to MCC_2, *TCC* can be reduced by shifting a commuter from the route where marginal cost is larger to the route where marginal cost is smaller. Therefore, we know that total commuting costs are smallest at the allocation where the marginal costs of commuting on the two routes are identical. The allocation where $MCC_1 = MCC_2$ in Figure 7.13a (and where *TCC* is lowest in Figure 7.13a) is at $N_1 = 2,000$ and $N_2 = 3,000$. More generally, to minimize total commuting costs *TCC*, allocate commuters to the two routes so that $MCC_1 = MCC_2$.

PROBLEM 7.11

What is the optimal allocation if there are 6,000 commuters? If there are 3,000 commuters? If there are 1,000 commuters?

Let us summarize what we have learned:

In equilibrium, commuters allocate themselves to routes so as to equalize the average commuting cost on the two routes. Yet optimality demands that the commuters are allocated so as to equalize marginal costs on the two routes. Because Route 1 is subject to congestion, marginal cost exceeds average cost. Therefore, in equilibrium, too many commuters use Route 1.

The suboptimal equilibrium in this model arises because commuters have unrestricted, or common, access to a road that is subject to congestion. Taking this perspective, you can see that the traffic congestion problem is yet another type of *common-property problem*. Like some of the other common-property problems you already encountered, solutions are possible. For example, one solution is to charge a *toll* on Route 1. What toll can be levied on Route 1 that will be large enough that commuters on Route 2 have no incentive to switch to Route 1 at the optimal allocation, when 3,000 commuters use Route 2 and 2,000 commuters use Route 1? From Figure 7.13b, we see that the optimal toll is $1.60 ($5.00 − $3.40).

This toll will raise $3,200 per day — $1.60 from each of the 2,000 commuters using Route 1. If this toll revenue was distributed to the 5,000 commuters, each commuter would receive $.64 per day. The net effect of this optimal toll is then to make each commuter better off by $.64 per day than in the initial, common property equilibrium.

On Route 1, the input called "commuters' time" is used to produce an output called "trips to Wetvan." Notice from this perspective that TCC_1 is just a variable cost function. What is the associated total product function that translates the input "commuters' time" into the output "trips to Wetvan"? To find out, we could begin with the variable cost function TCC_1 and derive the total product function by reversing the procedure used in Figure 7.7. Yet without doing so, we can readily see two important properties of that total product function. First, it exhibits a constant marginal product for any amount of time less than 18 minutes per commuter. Second, it exhibits a diminishing marginal product for any amount of time greater than 18 minutes per commuter. Therefore, it has the same general shape as the total product function in Figure 7.4a. Of course, the point at which marginal product begins to diminish is just the point at which additional commuters begin to create congestion. In other words, *congestion* is a specialized name for *diminishing marginal product* on a road. Although Malthus never encountered this sort of congestion problem, he certainly would have recognized it as a case of diminishing marginal product.

The Allocation of Output Among Different Plants

multiplant firms

Now let us reinterpret what we learned about congestion to solve an interesting problem that all **multiplant firms** face. A multiplant firm is one that has more than one production facility or plant, and the problem it faces is how to allocate its output to its various plants. For example, if a firm wants to produce 5,000 units of output and if its objective is to minimize cost, what principles govern the amount that is produced in each of its plants? To answer this question, all we need to do is to reinterpret Figure 7.13.

Let us suppose for the moment that the firm has just two plants. We can then think of TCC_1 and TCC_2 in Figure 7.13a as the variable cost functions associated with the two plants, and MCC_1 and MCC_2 in Figure 7.13b as the corresponding short-run marginal cost functions. In both parts of the figure, the length of the axis connecting 0_1 and 0_2 can be reinterpreted as the output of 5,000 units that this particular firm wants to produce. The firm's problem is to allocate the 5,000 units of output to its two plants so as to minimize its total variable cost.

Given this reinterpretation, the curve TCC in Figure 7.13a tells us the firm's total variable cost for any allocation of the 5,000 units of output to the two plants. We can see that the firm's cost-minimization problem is solved by allocating 2,000 units to the first plant and 3,000 to the second plant. More important, using the logic of Figure 7.13b, we can derive the general rule that governs the cost-minimizing allocation of *any* quantity of output to *any* number of plants. Consider any allocation of output to plants in which short-run marginal cost is not the same for two plants. Total cost can be reduced by allocating output from the high marginal cost plant to the low marginal cost plant:

To minimize the total variable cost of producing a given output in two or more plants, a firm allocates output to the plants so that short-run marginal cost is the same in all plants.

SUMMARY

We began this chapter by defining a *production function* and providing illustrations of it. Next, we defined the *long-run cost-minimization problem* and then observed that there are many *short-run cost-minimization problems*, depending on the firm's time horizon and the number of variable inputs over that time horizon. The simplest of these is the time horizon in which only one input is variable.

Then, we began our exploration of the production function by fixing the quantity of all inputs but one, input 1, thereby defining the *total product function* $TP(z_1)$. We then defined the concepts of *marginal product* and *average product*:

$$MP(z_1) = \text{slope of } TP(z_1)$$
$$AP(z_1) = TP(z_1)/z_1$$

The most important assumption regarding $TP(z_1)$ is the *assumption of diminishing marginal product*: beyond some quantity of input 1, the slope of $TP(z_1)$ begins to get flatter, or marginal product diminishes. We then discovered some important interrelations between $MP(z_1)$ and $AP(z_1)$: $AP(z_1)$ is rising or falling as $MP(z_1)$ is greater or less than $AP(z_1)$.

We then learned virtually everything there is to know about costs in the simple one-variable-input case. Indeed, we developed a total of seven cost concepts, beginning with the variable cost function $VC(y)$:

$$VC(y) = \text{minimum expenditure on the variable input necessary}$$
$$\text{to produce } y \text{ units of output}$$

The expenditure on the fixed input, or the fixed cost FC, is held constant by definition and is therefore unrelated to the quantity of output.

All the other cost functions can be constructed from these two. First, by adding them up, we can define the *short-run total cost function*, $STC(y)$:

$$STC(y) = VC(y) + FC$$

Associated with each of these is an *average function*, which is derived simply by dividing by the quantity of output:

$$AVC(y) = VC(y)/y$$
$$SAC(y) = STC(y)/y$$
$$AFC(y) = FC/y$$

The *average fixed cost function* $AFC(y)$ is negatively sloped and asymptotic to both axes (that is, as y goes to zero, $AFC(y)$ goes to infinity, and as y goes to infinity, $AFC(y)$ goes to zero). In the standard case, both *average variable cost* $AVC(y)$ and *short-run average cost* $SAC(y)$ are U-shaped, and $SAC(y)$ lies above $AVC(y)$. Indeed, we can generate $SAC(y)$ from $AVC(y)$ by adding (vertically) $AFC(y)$ to $AVC(y)$:

$$SAC(y) = AVC(y) + AFC(y)$$

The most interesting cost concept is *short-run marginal cost*: the rate at which cost increases as output increases, or the added cost required to produce an additional unit of output. $SMC(y)$ can be derived from either $VC(y)$ or $STC(y)$ as follows:

$$SMC(y) = \text{slope of } VC(y) = \text{slope of } STC(y)$$

We also developed some important interrelationships: $SMC(y)$ intersects $AVC(y)$ at the point where $AVC(y)$ attains its minimum value. To the left of this point, where $SMC(y)$ is less than $AVC(y)$, $AVC(y)$ is falling; to the right of this point, where $SMC(y)$ exceeds $AVC(y)$, $AVC(y)$ is rising. The interrelationships between $SMC(y)$ and $SAC(y)$ are qualitatively the same as those between $SMC(y)$ and $AVC(y)$.

Finally, we considered a *traffic congestion problem*. We discovered that to minimize total commuting costs, commuters traveling on two different routes should be allocated so that the marginal commuting costs on the two routes are identical. We also discovered that when commuters have unrestricted access to all routes, the equilibrium will be suboptimal because average commuting costs are equalized in equilibrium. We then saw how to find a toll that would shift the equilibrium to the optimum. Finally, we reinterpreted these results in the context of a *multiplant firm* that wanted to produce a fixed output at minimum variable cost. We saw that to minimize its variable cost, the firm must allocate its output so that the short-run marginal costs in all its plants are identical.

EXERCISES

In Exercises 1, 2, and 3, y is quantity of output and z is quantity of the variable input. In all three exercises, the total product function has the standard shape shown in Figure 7.3.

1. Suppose that the following statement is true: "When z increases from 10 to 11, average product increases from 45 to 48." Indicate whether each of the following statements is true, false, or uncertain; explain your answers.

   a. Output y is 450 when z is 10.
   b. When y is 450, SMC is upward sloping.
   c. When y is 450, AVC is downward sloping.
   d. When y is 450, SAC is downward sloping.
   e. When z is 10, MP is upward sloping.
   f. When z is 10, MP exceeds 45.
   g. When y is 450, SMC is less than AVC.
   h. When y is 450, SMC is less than SAC.
   i. SAC is greater when y is 450 than it is when y is 528.

2. Suppose that the following statement is true: "When y is 300, SMC is \$75, SAC is \$65, and AP is 30." Indicate whether each of the following statements is true, false, or uncertain; explain your answers.

   a. When y is 300, z is 10.
   b. When z is 10, MP is less than 30.
   c. When y is 300, AVC exceeds SMC.
   d. The point of diminishing returns to the variable input occurs where z is greater than 10.
   e. The price of the variable input is less than \$2,000.

   f. The price of the variable input is greater than \$500.
   g. VC at y equal to 300 is less than \$20,000.

3. Suppose that the following statement is true: "When y is 100 units, SMC is \$100, SMC is upward sloping, MP is 10, and AP is 20." Indicate whether each of the following statements is true, false, or uncertain; explain your answers.

   a. The price of the variable input is \$1,000.
   b. The price of the fixed input is \$1,000.
   c. When z is 10, MP is downward sloping.
   d. When y is 100, AVC is less than SMC.
   e. When y is 100, AVC is \$50.
   f. When y is 100, SAC is upward sloping.
   g. When y is 100, SAC is greater than \$49.

4. We all know that the more insulation a building has, the less it costs to cool or heat the building. Let T' denote the ambient temperature inside a building and T'' the ambient temperature outside. Suppose that the fuel consumption z_1 necessary to maintain a constant temperature differential D is inversely proportional to the amount of insulation z_2 and directly proportional to the square of the temperature differential. That is, suppose that

$$z_1 = D^2/z_2$$

a. What is the good that is being produced, and what is its production function?

b. Suppose that $z_2 = 1$, T'' is $50°F$ and $w_1 = \$2$. What expenditure on fuel is necessary to maintain a temperature of $70°F$ inside the building? How much more would it cost to maintain this temperature if T'' was $30°$?

c. Now suppose that $z_2 = 2$ and repeat these calculations.

5. Given the production function

$$y = \min(z_1, z_2)$$

First, supposing that the quantity of input 2 is fixed at 100 units, derive and plot $TP(z_1)$, $MP(z_1)$, and $AP(z_1)$. Then, supposing that w_1 and w_2 are both \$1, derive all seven cost functions and plot them in a graph analogous to Figure 7.10.

6. Consider the following production function:

$$y = (z_1)^{1/3}(z_2)^{2/3}$$

Input prices are $w_1 = \$2$ and $w_2 = \$3$.

a. Suppose that z_2 is fixed at 1 unit: $z_2 = 1$. Derive the total product function, the variable cost function, the average variable cost function, and the short-run total cost function. Hint: To find the variable cost function, first observe that y^3 units of z_1 are needed to produce y units of output when $z_2 = 1$, and then compute the cost of y^3 units of input 1.

b. Now suppose that z_2 is fixed at 8 units and repeat the same exercises.

c. Using the cost functions from a and b, compute and compare the variable and short-run total cost of producing 1, 2, 3, and 4 units of output.

7. A firm owns two plants that produce the same good. The marginal cost functions for the two plants are

$$SMC_1 = 10y_1$$

$$SMC_2 = 5y_2$$

where y_1 and y_2 are quantities of output produced in each plant.

a. If the firm wants to produce 15 units of output at minimum cost, how much should it produce in each plant?

b. Now consider an arbitrary quantity of output y. To minimize costs, what fraction of

the total output should the firm produce in each plant?

8. If a firm has two plants and can vary just one input, to minimize cost it should allocate output to the plants so that the marginal product of the variable input is the same in the two plants. Explain.

9. Examination writing poses an interesting economic problem. For simplicity, think of a three-hour final examination with two 50-point essay questions. The student then has 180 minutes to allocate to the two questions. What principles should guide the student's allocation of time if the student's objective is to maximize the mark received on the examination.

*10. Hank works for his dad, producing widgets by tending his dad's magic widget maker. (His dad does not allow anyone else to even touch the magic machine.) For every hour he tends the machine, Hank produces 10 widgets. His dad pays Hank \$10 per hour for the first 8 hours in any day, \$20 per hour for the next 8 hours, and \$40 per hour for the last 8 hours of the day.

a. Find VC, AVC, and SMC.

b. Now suppose that Hank's dad can sell each widget for \$2.50 and that he wants to maximize his profit. How many widgets should he ask Hank to produce, and how many hours per day will Hank have to work?

*11. On the island of Molo there is a lovely lake that produces fish according to the following total product function:

$$y = 1{,}000z^{1/2}$$

where y is the daily fish take and z is the number of fishers on the lake. The corresponding marginal and average product functions are

$$MP(z) = 500/z^{1/2}$$

$$AP(z) = 1{,}000/z^{1/2}$$

At the end of the day, each fisher on the lake has caught the average product, $1{,}000/z^{1/2}$ fish, and the harvest of fish from the lake is therefore equitably distributed among the fishers. Molo fishers can also fish in the ocean, where they catch 100 fish per fisher, regardless of the number of fishers. There are 150 fishers on the island.

a. What are the total, marginal, and average product functions for the ocean fishery?

b. Currently, 100 fishers fish on the lake and 50 in the ocean. Verify that all 150 fishers have 100 fish at the end of each day and that the total harvest is 15,000 fish per day.

c. If all 150 fishers fished in the ocean, what would the total harvest be? Given the allocation in b, what is the net value of the lake fishery to the fishers of Molo?

d. What allocation of fishers maximizes the total harvest?

e. Given the optimal allocation from d, what is the total harvest of the fishers of Molo? What is the net value of the lake fishery with this allocation?

f. Can you devise an institution that would produce the optimal allocation of fishers? Is there a property-rights solution to this problem?

g. You have encountered these kinds of problems in Chapters 1 and 4. What is the generic name for these problems?

REFERENCES

Douglas, P. H. 1948. "Are There Laws of Production?" *American Economic Review* 67:297–308.

Fuss, M.A. 1987. "Production and Cost," in *The New Palgrave: A Dictionary of Economics*, J. Eatwell, M. Milgate, and P. Newman (eds.), London: Macmillan.

Hicks, J. R. 1939. *Value and Capital*, London: The Clarendon Press.

Nadin, M.I. 1987. "Production: Neoclassical Theories," in *The New Palgrave: A Dictionary of Economics*, J. Eatwell, M. Milgate, and P. Newman (eds.), London: Macmillan.

Jorgenson, W.W. 1987. "Production Functions," in *The New Palgrave: A Dictionary of Economics*, J. Eatwell, M. Milgate, and P. Newman (eds.), London: Macmillan.

Samuelson, P. A. 1947. *Foundations of Economic Analysis*, Cambridge, Mass.: Harvard University Press.

CHAPTER 8

Production and Cost: Many Variable Inputs

In Chapter 7, we concentrated on the simple case in which only one input in a production process was variable. In this chapter, we use the understanding developed in Chapter 7 to explore cost and production in the more complicated, realistic environment in which more than one input is variable. In most real situations, firms do have the flexibility to vary more than one input during the relevant period. For example, if the Denver and Rio Grande Western Railroad wants to increase the amount of coal it hauls out of western Colorado, it can usually acquire new rolling stock and hire more train crews within a 6-month time frame. If it wants to double its existing track, it can acquire the additional quantities of inputs such as tracks, ties, and signaling equipment, but it needs a lead time significantly longer than 6 months. If it wants to add whole new lines, it can again alter the quantities of the inputs it uses, but it needs an even longer lead time. You will have a good understanding of these more realistic cases once we extend our original theory of cost and production to the case in which two inputs can be varied.

8.1
Isoquants and Input Substitution

In Chapter 7, we defined the production function, $y = F(z_1, z_2)$, and began to explore it by fixing the quantity of one input to define the total product function. This allowed us to see how output changed as quantity of the variable input changed. In this section, we resume our exploration of the production function by fixing the quantity of output. This procedure allows us to investigate **input substitution** — that is, how one input can be substituted for another. Our goal is to understand the many ways in which a fixed quantity of output can be produced.

input substitution

An **isoquant** is a curve composed of all the input bundles that will produce some fixed quantity of output. Isoquants are to production theory what indifference curves are to consumer theory. Just as indifference curves in consumer theory represent all the consumption bundles that a person ranks as equally attractive, an isoquant in production theory represents all the input bundles that can produce the same quantity of output.

isoquant

To get a sense of what isoquants are, let us return to Tipple's production function for courier services,

$$y = (1{,}200z_1z_2)^{1/2}$$

Recall that y is the quantity of courier services measured in miles, z_1 is hours of a driver's time, and z_2 is gallons of gas. By fixing y, we define an isoquant. For example, suppose we fix y at 120 miles. Then, setting y equal to 120 in the expression above gives us the following algebraic description of the isoquant:

$$120 = (1{,}200z_1z_2)^{1/2}$$

Now, squaring both sides of this expression and dividing by 1,200 gives us a simpler expression for the isoquant:

$$12 = z_1z_2$$

This expression tells us that any input bundle such that the product of z_1 and z_2 is 12 will produce 120 miles of courier services. For example, the input bundle might be composed of 2 hours of a driver's time and 6 gallons of gasoline, or 3 hours of a driver's time and 4 gallons of gasoline, or 4 hours of a driver's time and 3 gallons of gasoline. In Figure 8.1, we have constructed both this isoquant and the isoquant for 240 miles. As you can verify, the 240-mile isoquant can be described by the following equation: $48 = z_1z_2$.

Just as any indifference map is filled with indifference curves, any isoquant map is filled with isoquants. And just as the farther an indifference curve is from the origin, the higher its utility number, so, too, the farther an isoquant is from the origin, the higher the level of output associated with it.

The Shape of Isoquants

Notice that both isoquants in Figure 8.1 are smooth and that their slopes decrease from left to right. But do all isoquants look like this? Are other general shapes possible? Try the following problem to find out.

FIGURE 8.1   Isoquants for courier services

All the bundles of hours and time on the 120-mile isoquant will produce 120 miles of courier services, and all the bundles on the 240-mile isoquant will produce 240 miles of courier services.

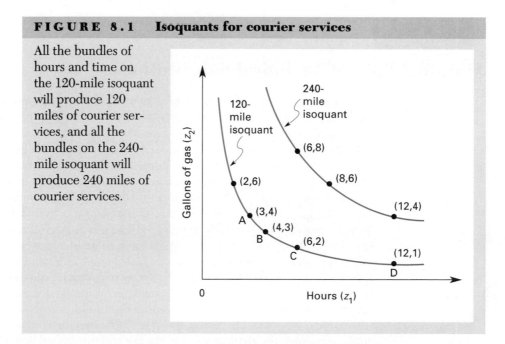

PROBLEM 8.1

1. John Henry uses a furnace and fuel to produce heat. The furnace can use either coal or wood for fuel. One ton of coal produces 5 thermal units (TU) of heat and one ton of wood produces 2 TUs. Given the furnace, the production function for heat is

$$y = 5z_1 + 2z_2$$

where y is TUs of heat, z_1 is tons of coal, and z_2 is tons of wood. Construct the isoquant for 20 TUs.

2. The standard bartender's recipe for rum-and-Coke calls for 2 ounces of rum and 6 ounces of Coke. The implied production function is

$$y = \min(z_1/2, z_2/6)$$

where y is number of drinks, z_1 is ounces of rum, and z_2 is ounces of Coke. Construct the isoquant for two drinks.

As you discovered in Problem 8.1, isoquants may take different forms. But what can we learn from the shapes of isoquants? For example, what is the economic meaning of the differences between the isoquants in Figures 8.2a and 8.2b? (These are the isoquants you constructed in Problem 8.1.) Notice that the shape of each is distinctive. In Figure 8.2a, the slope of the isoquant is constant throughout. In Figure 8.2b the slope of the isoquant is infinite above the kink and zero to the right of the kink. At the kink itself, the isoquant has no well-defined slope. What does the slope of an isoquant tell us? And what is the significance of the fact that the isoquant in Figure 8.2b is kinked? Before we can answer these questions, we need a new tool — a measure called the marginal rate of technical substitution.

Marginal Rate of Technical Substitution

The term *marginal rate of technical substitution* deliberately echoes another familiar one from consumer theory, the marginal rate of substitution (*MRS*). In consumption theory, we used *MRS* to measure the rate at which one good could be substituted for another, holding utility constant. The marginal rate of technical substitution (*MRTS*) measures the rate at which one input can be substituted for the other, holding output constant. In this section we first define *MRTS* and then explore the concept in some detail.

To begin, we will pick an arbitrary input bundle — say, bundle A in Figure 8.3 — on the isoquant for 100 units of output. Our objective is to find *MRTS* at bundle A. Imagine that the firm is initially at A and consider a nonmarginal reduction in the quantity of input 1 by 5 units — $\Delta z_1 = 5$. What increase in the quantity of input 2 — Δz_2 — will compensate for the reduction in quantity of input 1? From Figure 8.3 we see that quantity of input 2 must be increased by 3 units to get back to the isoquant for 100 units of output. That is, the increase $\Delta z_2 = 3$ compensates for the decrease $\Delta z_1 = 5$. The ratio $\Delta z_2/\Delta z_1$ is the nonmarginal rate of substitution. In the case shown in Figure 8.3, the nonmarginal rate of substitution is 3/5 or .6. Notice that the nonmarginal rate of substitution is equal to the absolute value of the slope of the dashed line *AB* in Figure 8.3.

FIGURE 8.2   Some illustrative isoquants

In (a), where inputs 1 and 2 are perfect substitutes, any bundle on the isoquant will produce 20 TUs (thermal units) of heat. In (b), where inputs 1 and 2 are perfect complements, any bundle on the isoquant will produce two drinks.

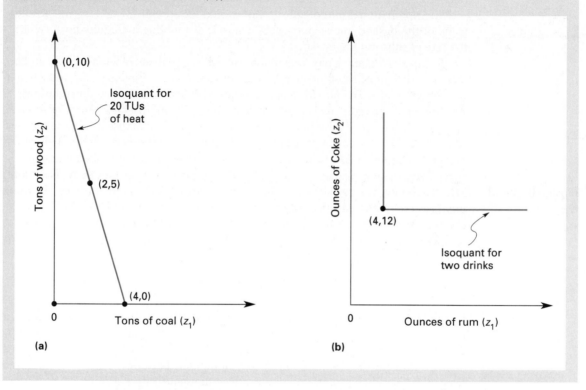

FIGURE 8.3   The marginal rate of technical substitution *MRTS*

The marginal rate of technical substitution, *MRTS* at point A is the absolute value of the slope of the line *TT*, which is tangent to the isoquant at A.

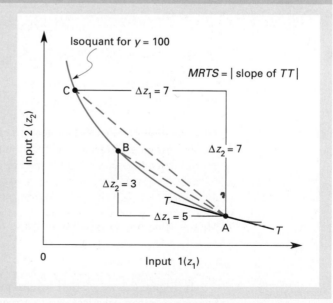

The ratio $\Delta x_2/\Delta x_1$ is called a *rate of substitution* because it tells us the rate at which we must increase quantity of input 2 per unit reduction in quantity of input 1. It is *nonmarginal* because the initial reduction in quantity of input 1 is a *measurable change*. The ratio $\Delta x_2/\Delta x_1$ is an ambiguous and therefore an unsatisfactory measure because it depends on the magnitude of Δz_1. As you can see from Figure 8.3, had we chosen $\Delta z_1 = 7$, the nonmarginal rate of substitution would have been 7/7 or 1 — the absolute value of the dashed line segment AC. There is a troubling ambiguity here. What is the rate of substitution — .6 or 1?

To resolve this ambiguity, economists use the marginal rate of technical substitution, *MRTS* — the rate of substitution associated with a marginal, or infinitesimal, reduction in quantity of input 1. To find *MRTS* , just imagine what happens to the nonmarginal rate of substitution as Δz_1 gets smaller and smaller, eventually approaching zero. For $\Delta z_1 = 7$, the nonmarginal rate of substitution is determined by the slope of the dashed line segment AC. For $\Delta z_1 = 5$, the nonmarginal rate of substitution is determined by the slope of the dashed line segment AB. Notice that as Δz_1 approaches zero, the dashed line segment approaches the line labeled *TT* tangent to the isoquant at input bundle A. Therefore, *MRTS* at bundle A is the absolute value of the slope of *TT*. Or, more formally: the **marginal rate of technical substitution** of input 2 for input 1 at any input bundle (z_1,z_2), denoted by $MRTS(z_1,z_2)$, is the absolute value of the slope of the isoquant at that point.

marginal rate of technical substitution

To get a better working knowledge of *MRTS*, let us find out what *MRTS* is for Tipple's Courier Service. The production function is

$$y = (1{,}200z_1z_2)^{1/2}$$

Our objective is to find *MRTS* at an arbitrary bundle (z_1,z_2). If we reduce quantity of input 1 by Δz_1 and compensate for the reduction by increasing quantity of input 2 by Δz_2, we get input bundle: $(z_1 - \Delta z_1, z_2 + \Delta z_2)$. Since the increase in quantity of input 2 compensates for the decrease in quantity of input 1, both bundles are on the same isoquant. Alternatively, both bundles produce the same output y. This last statement gives us the following equations:

$$y = (1{,}200z_1z_2)^{1/2}$$
$$y = [1{,}200(z_1 - \Delta z_1)(z_2 + \Delta z_2)]^{1/2}$$

Setting the right sides of these equations equal to each other and solving explicitly for Δz_2, we get

$$\Delta z_2 = (z_2\Delta z_1)/(z_1 - \Delta z_1)$$

This equation gives us the increase in quantity of input 2 — Δz_2 — needed to compensate for an arbitrary decrease in quantity if input 1 — Δz_1. Using this result, we get the following expression for the nonmarginal rate of substitution:

$$\Delta z_2/\Delta z_1 = z_2/(z_1 - \Delta z_1)$$

Then, letting Δz_1 approach 0 we get

$$MRTS = z_2/z_1$$

In Figure 8.1 we plotted two isoquants for Tipple's Courier service. Using this formula, you can calculate *MRTS* for any point on these isoquant. At input bundle

(2,6) for example, *MRTS* is 3. Notice that as we move from left to right along either of these isoquants, *MRTS* continually decreases.

PROBLEM 8.2

The following isoquant for heat produced from coal (input 1) and wood (input 2) as fuels is plotted in Figure 8.2a:

$$20 = 5z_1 + 2z_2$$

Determine the *MRTS* of wood for coal for all points along this isoquant.

Perfect Substitutes and Perfect Complements

perfect substitutes

There are two extreme cases of input substitutability — *perfect substitutes* and *perfect complements*. You saw in Problem 8.2 that wood can be substituted for coal in the production of heat at a constant rate of 5/2. If the quantity of coal is reduced by 2 tons, for example, then the quantity of wood must be increased by 5 tons (2 tons times 5/2) to maintain heat output. Or, if the product is denim jeans, and if input 1 is cotton thread and input 2 is polyester thread, polyester thread can be substituted for cotton thread at the constant rate 1/1. When inputs are **perfect substitutes**, one input can always be substituted for the other on fixed terms and *MRTS* is constant.

PROBLEM 8.3

The following isoquant for 2 rum-and-Coke cocktails is plotted in Figure 8.2b.

$$2 = \min(z_1/2, z_2/6)$$

Now determine the *MRTS* of Coke for rum for all points along the horizontal and vertical segments of the isoquant. Is *MRTS* defined at input bundle (4,12)?

---

perfect complements

As you saw in answering Problem 8.3, when mixing standard rum-and-Cokes, more Coke is *not* a substitute for less rum: a bartender who has only 4 ounces of rum cannot make more than 2 rum-and-Cokes no matter how much Coke is on hand. So, too, in producing fasteners from nuts and bolts, more bolts cannot be substituted for fewer nuts. When inputs are **perfect complements**, substitution is impossible, and *MRTS* cannot be defined for the bundle at the kink in the isoquant.

Diminishing Marginal Rate of Technical Substitution

Most interesting economic cases fall somewhere in between perfect substitutes and perfect complements: one input can be substituted for the other, but the *MRTS* is not a constant. This intermediate case is represented by the isoquants for Tipple's Courier Service in Figure 8.1. In such intermediate cases, it becomes progressively more difficult to substitute one input for the other. To see why, let us substitute input 1 for input 2 on the 120-mile isoquant in Figure 8.1. In the move from A to B, 1 added hour of time substitutes for 1 less gallon of gas, while in the move from B to C, 2 added hours are needed to substitute for 1 less gallon, and in the move from C to D, 6 added hours are needed to substitute for 1 less gallon. This diminishing capacity to substitute one input seems to make intuitively good sense. Notice, too, that it means that *MRTS* gets smaller and smaller, or diminishes, from left to right along an isoquant. A diminishing *MRTS* is an assumption that is commonly adopted in production theory.

MRTS as a Ratio of Marginal Products

Now we want to establish an important relationship between *MRTS* and the *marginal products* of the two inputs. The marginal rate of technical substitution of input 2 for input 1 is equal to the marginal product of input 1 divided by the marginal product of input 2.

To understand why this is true, notice first that when the quantity of input 1 is decreased by Δz_1, the change in total output y is (approximately) the marginal product of input 1 multiplied by the change in quantity of input 1:

$$\Delta y = MP_1 \Delta z_1$$

Since Δz_2 compensates for this reduction in z_1, it must produce an identical change in output, Δy. Thus,

$$\Delta y = MP_2 \Delta z_2$$

Of course, when Δz_1 is very small, *MRTS* is approximately $\Delta z_2 / \Delta z_1$. Solving the first of these approximations for Δz_1 and the second for Δz_2 and then forming the substitution ratio $\Delta z_2 / \Delta z_1$ yields

$$MRTS = (\Delta y / MP_2) / (\Delta y / MP_1)$$

But this expression reduces to

$$MRTS = MP_1 / MP_2$$

Or, to restate this expression in words:

MRTS is equal to the marginal product of input 1 divided by the marginal product of input 2.[1]

---

1 We can use the implicit function theorem to express *MRTS* in terms of the partial derivatives of $F(\cdot)$. The isoquant for y' units of output can be written as

$$y' = F(z_1, z_2)$$

where y' is fixed and z_1 and z_2 are free to vary. Since the isoquant defines z_2 as an implicit function of z_1, we can use the implicit function theorem to express this isoquant as

$$z_2 = g(z_1)$$

MRTS is, of course, just $-g'(z_1)$, where $g'(z_1)$ is the derivative of $g(z_1)$. Combining these equations, we have the following identity

$$y' = F[z_1, g(z_1)]$$

Differentiating the identity with respect to z_1 gives us

$$F_1[z_1, g(z_1)] + g'(z_1) F_2[z_1, g(z_1)] = 0$$

Returns to Scale

So far we have used two strategies to explore the production function. In the last chapter we held quantity of one input constant so that we could look at the relationship between quantity of the variable input and quantity of output. In the preceding two sections of this chapter, we held output constant so that we could look at the way in which one input can be substituted for another. In this section, we will hold the *input mix* constant so that we can look at the relationship between the *scale of production* and *quantity of output*.

scale of production

Once again Tipple's Courier Service provides a convenient example. Notice that input mix is *constant* along any ray through the origin in Figure 8.4. For all input bundles on ray 0A in Figure 8.4, for example, the ratio of z_1 to z_2 is 3. Therefore, as we move along the ray, the **scale of production** — but not the input mix — changes. How does output responds to a change in scale of production along ray 0A? Suppose we start at bundle (6,2) on the 120 mile isoquant. If we were to double the scale of production, we would get input bundle (12,4) on the 240-mile isoquant. If we were to triple the scale of production, we would get input bundle (18,6) on the 360-mile isoquant. And, finally, if we were to quadruple the scale of production, we would get input bundle (24,8) on the 480-mile isoquant. Notice that when we doubled the scale of production, output doubled; when we tripled the scale of production, output tripled; when we quadrupled the scale of production, output quadrupled. Notice also that there is nothing special about ray 0A. Had we chosen ray 0B instead, we would have arrived at the same conclusion: when we increase the scale of production by some factor a, output increases by the same factor a. These observations reflect the fact that Tipple's production function exhibits *constant returns to scale*.

constant returns to scale

It is useful to define constant returns to scale more carefully. Beginning at bundle (z_1, z_2), if we increase the scale of production by factor $a > 1$, we get bundle (az_1, az_2). Of course, output at the initial bundle is $F(z_1, z_2)$, and output at the scaled-up bundle is $F(az_1, az_2)$. A firm experiences **constant returns to scale** if

$$F(az_1, az_2) = aF(z_1, z_2)$$
$$\text{for } a > 1$$

To get a better understanding of this definition, let us use it to verify what we learned for Figure 8.4 — that Tipple's production function has constant returns to

---

where $F_1(\cdot)$ and $F_2(\cdot)$ denote the partial derivatives of $F(\cdot)$ with respect to z_1 and z_2. The partial derivative $F_i(\cdot)$ is, of course, the marginal product of input i. Rearranging this equation, we get

$$-g'(z_1) = \frac{F_1(z_1, z_2)}{F_2(z_1, z_2)}$$

But the left side of this equation is just *MRTS*. Hence,

$$MRTS(z_1, z_2) = \frac{F_1(z_1, z_2)}{F_2(z_1, z_2)}$$

Thus, for example, for the production function $F(z_1, z_2) = z_1 z_2$, $MRTS(z_1, z_2) = z_2/z_1$.

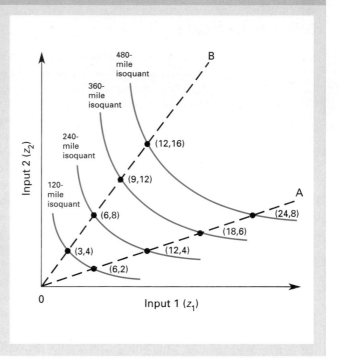

FIGURE 8.4   Constant returns to scale

As we move out from the origin along any ray, we are holding the input mix constant while varying the scale of production. Starting at bundle (3,4) on ray 0B (or at bundle (6,2) on ray 0A), notice that output doubles when the scale of production doubles, output triples when the scale of production triples, and output quadruples when the scale of production quadruples. Thus, this production function exhibits constant returns to scale.

scale. For Tipple, $F(z_1,z_2)$ is $(1{,}200z_1z_2)^{1/2}$. To get an expression for $F(az_1,az_2)$, simply substitute az_1 for z_1 and az_2 for z_2 in this production function to get $(1{,}200az_1az_2)^{1/2}$. But this can be rewritten as $a(1{,}200z_1z_2)^{1/2}$, which is just $aF(z_1,z_2)$. And we see that Tipple's production does exhibit constant returns to scale.

Constant returns to scale is thought by many economists to characterize many actual production processes, but it is definitely not the only possible case. In particular, increasing returns to scale is important in many production processes. A firm experiences **increasing returns to scale** if

increasing returns to scale

$$F(az_1,az_2) > aF(z_1,z_2)$$
$$\text{for } a > 1$$

For example, if a firm doubles its scale of production and its output triples, then this is a case of increasing returns to scale. The following problem allows you to begin the exploration of the geometric foundations of increasing returns to scale.

PROBLEM 8.4

Harriet's product is "fenced pasture land," measured in square feet. She produces it with 2 inputs. Input 1 is land (measured in square feet) and input 2 is barbed wire (measured in feet). The barbed wire is used to fence the land. Harriet's pastures are square, and she needs a foot of barbed wire to produce a foot of fencing. Her production function is

$$y = \min[z_1, (z_2/4)^2]$$

That is, given z_1 square feet of land, Harriet can produce a pasture no larger than z_1 square feet, and given z_2 feet of barbed wire, she can fence a pasture no larger than $(z_2/4)^2$ square feet since each side uses $z_2/4$ feet of barbed wire.

a. Suppose that Harriet's initial input bundle is (20,8). She can then produce just 4 square feet of fenced pasture. Show that her output more than doubles as she doubles the scale of production, or that there are increasing returns to scale.

b. Suppose that Harriet's initial bundle is (120,48). She can then produce 120 square feet of fenced pasture. Show that her output doubles as she doubles the scale of production, or that there are constant returns to scale.

decreasing
returns to scale

We can complete this classification of returns to scale by defining decreasing returns to scale. A firm experiences **decreasing returns to scale** if

$$F(az_1, az_2) < aF(z_1, z_2)$$
$$\text{for } a > 1$$

With decreasing returns to scale, if a firm doubles its scale of production, its output increases by less than double. If the production function includes all relevant inputs, it is difficult to imagine decreasing returns to scale. After all, by exactly replicating what was done with the initial input bundle, a firm can double output when the scale of production is doubled. For this reason, decreasing returns to scale are usually attributed to unmeasured or hidden inputs.[2]

From Problem 8.4 it is clear that mixed cases of returns to scale are possible. It is perfectly possible, for example, that there are initial increasing returns to scale and eventual decreasing returns to scale.

PROBLEM 8.5

Consider the following general form of the Cobb Douglas production function:

$$y = Az_1{}^u z_2{}^v$$

where A, u, and v are positive constants. Show that there are increasing, constant, or decreasing returns to scale as $u + v$ exceeds, is equal to, or is less than 1.

---

2 Returns to scale for homogeneous production functions deserve special attention. A production function is homogeneous of degree $h > 0$ if

$$F(az_1, az_2) = a^h F(z_1, z_2) \text{ for all } a > 0$$

As you can easily show, for a homogeneous production function there are decreasing, constant, or increasing returns to scale as the degree of homogeneity h is less than, equal to, or greater than 1.

8.4

The Cost-Minimization Problem: A Perspective

Now, we are ready to define the long-run cost-minimization problem and to use the solution — a system of input demand functions that identifies the least costly input bundle for any level of output — to form the cost function. The *cost function* tells us the minimum cost of producing any level of output in the long run. Before plunging into a detailed analysis of cost minimization, however, let us put the **long-run cost-minimization problem** and its solution into perspective. From Section 7.4, we know that the long-run cost-minimization problem will take this form:

long-run cost-minimization problem

$$\text{minimize } w_1 z_1 + w_2 z_2$$

by choice of z_1 and z_2

subject to the constraint $y = F(z_1, z_2)$

Before we can think of solving this problem, we must distinguish between the variables that are being chosen, or determined (the endogenous variables), and the variables that are givens (the exogenous variables).

In this problem, the endogenous variables are the quantities of the two inputs z_1 and z_2. The exogenous variables are the prices of the two inputs w_1 and w_2 and the level of output y. The input prices are, we assume, genuinely outside the firm's control; from the firm's point of view, they are fixed. The fact that output is exogenous in this problem simply reflects the fact that we are analyzing the firm's problem in stages. In the next stage (considered in later chapters), we will combine the cost function developed in this chapter with revenue considerations to analyze the firm's choice of output. For now, however, we will assume that the level of output is fixed.

The solution to the cost-minimization problem gives us the cost-minimizing values of the endogenous variables, written as $z_1{}^*$ and $z_2{}^*$, as functions of the exogenous variables y, w_1, and w_2. These functions are simply the rules prescribing the quantity of each input that minimizes the cost of producing y units of output when the prices of the inputs are w_1 and w_2. Because the quantity demanded of each input is so clearly dependent, or *conditional*, on the level of output y, these input demand functions are usually called **conditional input demand functions**.

conditional input demand functions

long-run cost function

Once we know these demand functions, determining the **long-run cost function** is a simple accounting step. This function — written $TC(y, w_1, w_2)$ to remind you that the total cost of production depends on the quantity of output and on the prices of the inputs — is just the sum of the quantities demanded of the inputs multiplied by the respective prices of those inputs:

$$TC(y, w_1, w_2) = w_1 z_1{}^* + w_2 z_2{}^*$$

To help you understand just what the terms *conditional input demand function* and *long-run cost function* mean, we will derive these functions for the standard rum-and-Coke production function introduced in Problem 8.1. We have chosen this simple example because we can readily identify the cost-minimizing input bundles. The production function is

$$y = \min(z_1/2, z_2/6)$$

where y is number of drinks, z_1 is ounces of rum, and z_2 is ounces of Coke.

To minimize costs for this fixed-proportions production function, for every drink, simply use 2 ounces of rum and 6 ounces of Coke. If y is 2, use exactly 4 ounces of rum and 12 ounces of Coke; if y is 7, use exactly 14 ounces of rum and 42 ounces of Coke; and so on. More generally, the following rules tell us how much rum and how much Coke a bartender needs to mix y standard rum-and-Cokes:

$$z_1^* = 2y$$
$$z_2^* = 6y$$

These are the conditional input demand functions for this production function. Because the input proportions are fixed in this production function, the conditional input demand functions do not depend on prices of the inputs: if we want 5 standard rum-and-Cokes, we need 10 ounces of rum regardless of how expensive rum may be or how inexpensive Coke may be.

When we move from the conditional input demand functions to the long-run cost function, however, input prices necessarily enter the picture because the total cost is calculated by multiplying the price of each input by quantity demanded and then totaling the results. The long-run cost function for rum-and-Cokes is

$$TC(y, z_1, z_2) = 2yw_1 + 6yw_2$$

where w_1 is the price of an ounce of rum and w_2 is the price of an ounce of Coke.

In the following problem, you can find conditional input demand functions and a long-run cost function for another simple case.

PROBLEM 8.6

From Problem 8.1, we know that John Henry produces heat from coal and wood according to the following production function:

$$y = 5z_1 + 2z_2$$

where z_1 is tons of coal and z_2 is tons of wood. Find the conditional input demand functions and the long-run cost function for this production function. Begin by assuming that $2w_1 < 5w_2$ and show that John Henry should buy only coal to minimize his costs; then show that he needs $y/5$ tons of coal to produce y TUs of heat; then calculate the cost of producing y TUs of heat using coal as the only input. Now suppose that $2w_1 > 5w_2$. Which input should John Henry use? How much of it does he need to produce y TUs of heat? How much must he spend to produce y TUs of heat?

8.5
Solving Cost-Minimization Problems

To solve more complex cost-minimization problems, we can use graphic techniques like those we used to solve the consumer's utility-maximization problem in Chapter 3. Here we limit our attention to cases where there is a diminishing *MRTS* and where the quantity of both inputs in the cost-minimizing input bundle is positive. As you know from Chapter 3, this type of solution is called an *interior solution*.

For any level of output y, the set of feasible input bundles is composed of all the input bundles that will produce at least y units of output. In Figure 8.5, we have used Tipple's Courier Service to illustrate the feasible input bundles for 120 miles of courier

FIGURE 8.5   The cost-minimizing bundle

Bundles in the green area on and above the isoquant are feasible bundles for 120 miles of output because they will produce 120 miles of courier services. All bundles on the lowest isocost line cost $18, all bundles on the intermediate isocost line cost $24, and all bundles on the highest isocost line cost $30. The least expensive bundle that will produce 120 miles is bundle (2,6) which costs $24. Notice that the $24 isocost line is tangent to the isoquant at the cost-minimizing bundle (2,6). Alternatively, *MRTS* is equal to w_1/w_2 at the cost-minimizing bundle.

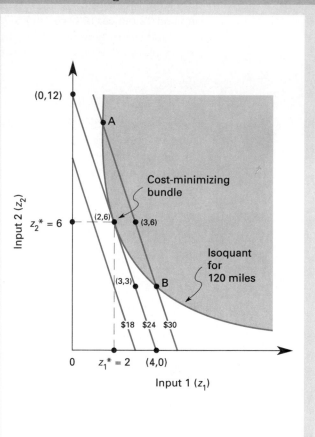

service. The green area is the set of bundles of time and gasoline that will allow Tipple to produce at least 120 miles of courier service. More generally, the set of **feasible input bundles** for y units of output is composed of all the input bundles on or above the isoquant for y units of output.

feasible input bundles

To solve the cost-minimization problem, we must find the cheapest, or least costly, feasible input bundle. But how can we represent the cost of various input bundles in Figure 8.5? Let us look first at an example. Suppose an hour of a driver's time costs $6 ($w_1 = 6$) and a gallon of gas costs $2 ($w_2 = 2$), Then, as you can easily verify, all the following input bundles cost $24: (4,0), (0,12), (2,6), (3,3). Indeed, any input bundle on the line

$$24 = 6z_1 + 2z_2$$

costs exactly $24. This line is an *isocost line* because all the input bundles on it cost the same amount, namely $24. In Figure 8.5, we have constructed this isocost line and two other isocost lines associated with $18 and $30. Notice that the isocost line for $30 is further from the origin than the isocost line for $24, which in turn is further from the origin than the isocost line for $18.

isocost line

More generally, an **isocost line** is defined in this way. Input bundles that lie on the following line all cost c, and the line itself is called an isocost line:

$$c = w_1z_1 + w_2z_2$$

Notice that the absolute value of the slope of the isocost line is w_1/w_2. This slope reflects the fact that a firm must give up w_1/w_2 units of input 2 to get an additional unit of input 1. In other words, the *opportunity cost* of input 1 in terms of input 2 is w_1/w_2.

> **PROBLEM 8.7**
>
> What is the opportunity cost of input 2 in terms of input 1? Where does the isocost line intersect the z_1 axis? The z_2 axis? What happens to the isocost line as w_1 approaches 0. As w_2 approaches 0? As c approaches 0? As c gets arbitrarily large?

We now have the tools necessary to solve the cost-minimization problem. Figure 8.5 shows the solution to Tipple's cost-minimizing problem — assuming that he wants to produce 120 miles of courier services, that the price of a driver's time is $6 per hour, and that the price of gas is $2 per gallon. Because Tipple wants to minimize his costs, his goal is to be on the isocost line associated with the smallest possible total expenditure. In other words, he wants to be on the isocost line closest to the origin. But, because he wants to produce 120 miles of service, he is constrained to choose a feasible input bundle — an input bundle in the shaded area on or above the isoquant for 120 miles. Of the three isocost lines in Figure 8.5, the $18 line is obviously the most preferred. However, no input bundles on the $18 isocost line are feasible because none of these bundles will actually produce an output of 120 miles.

From Figure 8.5, we see that the input bundle (2,6) — a combination of 2 hours of time and 6 gallons of gas — is the least costly input bundle that will produce 120 miles when w_1 is $6 and w_2 is $2. To minimize costs, then, Tipple should buy input bundle (2,6), which costs him $24. In this case, the minimum cost of producing 120 miles of courier services is $24. Of course, Tipple's cost-minimization problem is interesting only in that it illustrates the two general principles of cost minimization.

The First Principle of Cost Minimization

first principle of cost minimization

We can deduce the **first principle of cost minimization** from Tipple's problem, where you saw that the cost-minimizing input bundle $(z_1{}^*, z_2{}^*)$ for y units of output lies on or above the isoquant. That is, the cost-minimizing bundle is a feasible input bundle. But as long as input prices are not zero the cost-minimizing bundle lies on the isoquant, not above it. Why? Because for any bundle above the isoquant, there are cheaper bundles on the isoquant. Consider, for example, input bundle (3,6) in Figure 8.5 which lies above the isoquant for 120 miles. Any bundle between points A and B on that isoquant is cheaper.

The first principle of cost minimization, then, is that the cost-minimizing input bundle is on the isoquant:

$$y = F(z_1{}^*, z_2{}^*)$$

The Second Principle of Cost Minimization

second principle of cost minimization

We can also deduce the **second principle of cost minimization** from Tipple's problem in Figure 8.5. Since the cost-minimizing bundle must be *feasible*, it cannot be on an isocost line that lies below the isoquant for 120 miles. And since it must be the *cheapest* feasible bundle, it cannot be on an isocost line that intersects the isoquant. We know, then, that the cost-minimizing bundle must be at the point where the isocost line is tangent to the isoquant in Figure 8.5. Recall that absolute value of the slope of the isoquant is *MRTS* and that the absolute value of the slope of the isocost line w_1/w_2.

The second principle of cost minimization, then, is that *MRTS* is equal to w_1/w_2 at the cost-minimizing bundle:

$$MRTS(z_1^*, z_2^*) = w_1/w_2$$

We can provide a more intuitive understanding of the second principle by making use of the fact that *MRTS* is the ratio of MP_1 to MP_2.[3] The second principle can then be written as

$$MP_1/MP_2 = w_1/w_2$$

Manipulating this expression yields

$$MP_1/w_1 = MP_2/w_2$$

In other words, at the cost-minimizing input bundle, the marginal product per dollar for input 1, MP_1/w_1, is equal to the marginal product per dollar for input 2, MP_2/w_2. To see the why, let us consider some other input bundle on the isoquant where the marginal product per dollar of input 1 is less than the marginal product per dollar of input 2. Let us suppose, for example, that MP_2 is 6 and w_2 is \$2 and that MP_1 is 2 and w_1 is \$1. Then

$$MP_1/w_1 = 2/1 < 6/2 = MP_2/w_2$$

Because at the margin, a dollar spent on input 1 is less productive than a dollar spent on input 2, the firm ought to be able to reduce its costs by substituting input 2 for input 1. To see why, suppose that the firm reduces the quantity of input 1 by 1 unit. Its output will fall by approximately 2 units since MP_1 is 2. To compensate for this decrease in output, the firm must increase the quantity of input 2 by approximately 1/3 of a unit since MP_2 is 6. Has the firm succeeded in reducing costs? The answer is yes. Since w_1 is \$1, as the firm reduces the quantity of input 1 by 1 unit, its costs dropped by \$1. Since w_2 is \$2, as the firm increases the quantity of input 2 by 1/3 of a unit, its costs rise by \$2/3 (1/3 multiplied by \$2). The reduction in costs is (\$1 − \$2/3) or \$1/3.

---

3 We can use the method of Lagrange to obtain these two principles. The Lagrange function is

$$L(z_1, z_2, \lambda) = w_1 z_1 + w_1 z_2 + \lambda[y - F(z_1, z_2)]$$

Setting the partial derivatives of L($\cdot$) with respect to z_1, z_2, and λ equal to zero, we obtain

$$w_1 - \lambda^* F_1(z_1^*, z_2^*) = 0$$
$$w_2 - \lambda^* F_2(z_1^*, z_2^*) = 0$$
$$y - F(z_1^*, z_2^*) = 0$$

The third condition is, of course, the first principle of cost minimization. Combining the first two conditions to eliminate λ^* yields.

$$\frac{F_1(z_1^*, z_2^*)}{F_2(z_1^*, z_2^*)} = \frac{w_1}{w_2}$$

But from footnote 1, the left side is $MRTS(z_1^*, z_2^*)$, and we then have the second principle of cost minimization:

$$MRTS(z_1^*, z_2^*) = \frac{w_1}{w_2}$$

Thus, by substituting input 2 for input 1, the firm is able to reduce costs by one-third of a dollar, while maintaining its output. More generally, if MP_1/w_1 is less than MP_2/w_2, the input bundle cannot be the cost-minimizing input bundle because cost can be reduced and output maintained by substituting input 2 for input 1.

Using this line of reasoning, we can easily generalize the second principle of cost minimization to the case in which there are many inputs:

To minimize costs, the marginal product per dollar must be identical for all inputs.

Now let us use the production function for Tipple's Courier Service to provide a concrete example. The first principle of cost minimization in the context of Tipple's Courier Service is

$$y = (1{,}200 z_1^* z_2^*)^{1/2}$$

Above we showed that *MRTS* for Tipple's Courier Service is z_2/z_1. The second principle of cost minimization then gives us

$$z_2^*/z_1^* = w_1/w_2$$

We now have two equations in two unknowns, z_1^* and z_2^*. We can solve these equations for the conditional input demand functions

$$z_1^* = y[w_2/1{,}200 w_1]^{1/2}$$
$$z_2^* = y[w_1/1{,}200 w_2]^{1/2}$$

Notice that z_1^* increases as w_2 increases and decreases as w_1 increases, and that z_2^* increases as w_1 increases and decreases as w_2 increases. That is, as our intuition suggests, the cost-minimizing quantity of either input is positively related to the price of the other input and negatively related to its own price. Notice, too, that *both* z_1^* and z_2^* increase as y increases — that is, the cost-minimizing quantities of both inputs increase as the quantity of output increases. This result also makes sense intuitively.

If we now multiply z_1^* by w_1 and z_2^* by w_2 and add the results, we will have the long-run cost function for Tipple's Courier Service:

$$TC(y,w_1,w_2) = y(w_1 w_2/300)^{1/2}$$

Notice that cost increases as output increases and as either input price increases. Like the other comparative statics results we have seen, these, too, are intuitive. In subsequent sections, we will see which of these are and are not general results. But first, try the following problem.

PROBLEM 8.8

1. First solve the two simultaneous equations above to verify that the expressions we have written down are indeed the conditional input demand functions for this production function.
2. If $w_1 = \$6$ and $w_2 = \$2$, what is the cost-minimizing input bundle for 120 miles and what is the total cost? For 240 miles? For 360 miles?
3. Now suppose that input prices double so that $w_1 = \$12$ and $w_2 = \$4$. Show that the cost-minimizing input bundle for 120 miles is the same as it was in 2 and that total cost is double what it was in 2.

8.6

Comparative Statics for Input Prices

In this section, we will look at some comparative statics properties of the conditional input demand functions and the long-run cost function. First we will look at the effects of a uniform percentage change in the prices of *all* inputs. Then we will look at the effects of a change in the price of just *one* input.

Suppose Tipple initially has to pay $6 per hour for labor and $2 per gallon for gas, and subsequently that both input prices double to $12 per hour for labor and $4 per gallon for gas. What effects do these price changes have on the amount of labor and gas Tipple will use and on the cost of producing a given quantity of courier services? First, by looking at Tipple's conditional input demand functions, we see that the cost-minimizing input bundle does not change: for each mile of service produced, Tipple will use 1/60 of an hour of labor and 1/20 of a gallon of gas. Then, by looking at the long-run cost function, we see that long-run costs double. At the initial prices, Tipple's costs are $.20 per mile and, at the higher prices, his costs are $.40 per mile.

We can show that these are very general results. Suppose that for output y we have one set of input prices, (w_1, w_2), and the corresponding cost-minimizing input bundle (z_1^*, z_2^*). We will denote the cost of this bundle by c^*. Given these input prices, we know that there is an isocost curve tangent to the isoquant for y units of output at bundle (z_1^*, z_2^*). Now let us generate another set of input prices by multiplying the original prices by a positive number a, to get prices (aw_1, aw_2). Since both input prices have changed by the same factor of proportionality, the slope of the isocost lines has not changed. Therefore, given the new input prices, it is still true that an isocost curve is tangent to the isoquant for y units of output at bundle (z_1^*, z_2^*). This means that the cost-minimizing input bundle has not changed. What *has* changed is the cost of that bundle. At the original prices, its cost was c^*; at the new prices, its cost is ac^*.

If all prices change by the same factor of proportionality a, (i) the cost-minimizing input bundle for y units of output does not change, and (ii) the minimum cost of producing y units of output changes by the factor of proportionality a.

Next let us look at the effects of an increase in the price of one input, holding the price of the other input and the level of output constant at y. Suppose that Tipple initially has to pay $6 per hour for labor and $2 per gallon for gas, and then suppose that the price of labor subsequently quadruples, so that he has to pay $24 per hour for labor. What effects does this change in the price of labor have on the amount of labor and gas Tipple will use and on the cost of producing a given quantity of courier services? First, by looking at Tipple's conditional input demand functions, we see that the cost-minimizing quantity of labor drops from 1/60 to 1/120 of an hour for each mile of service produced and that the cost-minimizing quantity of gas rises from 1/20 to 1/10 of a gallon for each mile of service produced. Then, looking at the long-run cost function we see that long-run costs increase from $.20 per mile to $.40 per mile.

Now we will show that these are also very general results. We will assume that there is a diminishing *MRTS* and that a positive quantity of both inputs is demanded prior to an increase in the price of input 1. The initial equilibrium in Figure 8.6 is at bundle (z_1', z_2'). The increase in the price of input 1 means that isocost curves necessarily get steeper since the slope of an isocost line is the absolute value of w_1/w_2. Then, given a diminishing *MRTS*, the second principle of cost minimization dictates that the new cost-minimizing bundle (z_1'', z_2'') is on the steeper portion of the isoquant above and to the left of

FIGURE 8.6   Costs and input prices

Given initial input prices, the cost-minimizing bundle is (z_1', z_2'). After the price of input 1 increases, the subsequent cost-minimizing bundle is (z_1'', z_2''). At both the initial and the subsequent prices, the cost of (z_1'', z_2'') exceeds the cost of (z_1', z_2') at the initial input prices. This reflects the fact that when the price of an input increases, the minimum cost of producing a given level of output increases (assuming, of course, that the firm actually buys some of the input).

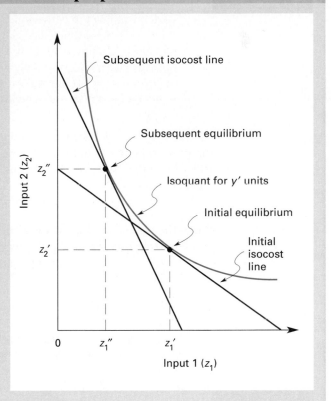

the initial equilibrium as shown in Figure 8.6. Notice that quantity of input 1 necessarily decreases and quantity of input 2 necessarily increases. To summarize this result:

Supposing that the cost-minimizing quantity of both inputs is positive and that there is a diminishing *MRTS*, if the price of input *i* increases and the price of input *j* does not change, the cost-minimizing quantity of input *i* decreases and the cost-minimizing quantity of input *j* increases.

Now let us show that in response to the increase in the price of input 1 in Figure 8.6, the cost of producing y' units of output necessarily increases. The key is to notice that — even before the increase in the price of input 1 — bundle (z_1'', z_2''), which is the cost-minimizing bundle *after* the price of input 1 increases, is more expensive than bundle (z_1', z_2'), the cost-minimizing bundle *before* the price of input 1 increases. To see why, try drawing an isocost line through bundle (z_1'', z_2'') in Figure 8.6 that is parallel to the initial isocost line. It will be further from the origin than the initial isocost line, indicating that at the initial prices bundle (z_1'', z_2'') is more expensive than bundle (z_1', z_2'). To summarize this result:

If the price of an input increases and if the quantity demanded of that input is positive, then the minimum cost of producing any given level of output increases.

To see why the *opportunity cost of an input* is key in determining which combination of inputs minimizes costs, try the following problem.

PROBLEM 8.9

In determining the cost-minimizing input bundle, it is really the opportunity cost of an input that matters. The opportunity cost of input 1 is just w_1/w_2. Suppose there is a diminishing *MRTS* and that a positive quantity of input 1 is initially demanded. Show that an increase in the opportunity cost of input 1 leads to a decrease in quantity demanded of input 1 and an increase in quantity demanded of input 2.

Now let us look briefly at the implications of an increase in the price of just one input — say input i — in the more general context in which there are many inputs. We will assume that there is a diminishing *MRTS* between input i and every other input, and that quantity demanded of input i is initially positive. In response to an increase in w_i, two things necessarily occur:

First, the cost of producing any given level of output increases. Second, the cost-minimizing quantity of input i decreases. In other words, the firm substitutes away from an input when its price increases.

The seemingly obvious insight that a firm substitutes away from an input when it becomes relatively more expensive is an important one for the simple reason that many noneconomists overlook or underestimate this substitution response.

The input substitution in the cod fishery off Newfoundland and in the shrimp-packing industry on the Gulf of Mexico discussed in Chapter 1 were just two examples of international cases of input substitution. Many other examples of input substitution also appear regularly in the headlines. For instance, increases in the price of oil in the 1970s resulted in a massive, economy-wide substitution away from oil and from energy use in general. So, too, sudden spirals in metal prices can also trigger input substitution. For example, when aluminum-can sheet prices jumped in the late 1980s, U.S. beverage-can makers started a serious search for alternative materials. Most manufacturers picked sheet steel because it was selling at 15 percent less per pound than sheet aluminum.

PROBLEM 8.10

Above we derived the following conditional input demand functions for the rum-and-Coke production function:

$$z_1{}^* = 2y \qquad z_2{}^* = 6y$$

Notice that when the price of input 1 increases, the bartender does not substitute away from input 1. Yet we just argued that firms substitute away from inputs when their price increases. Explain this discrepancy.

8.7

Comparative Statics for the Level of Output

In this section, we want explore two questions. First, how does quantity demanded of an input respond to a change in the level of output? Does quantity demanded necessarily increase when the level of output increases? Second, what happens to long-run total cost as output increases? Does long-run cost necessarily increase linearly with output?

Normal and Inferior Inputs

output expansion path

To explore the first of these questions we have constructed an output expansion path in Figure 8.7. Notice that line EE in Figure 8.7 runs through each of the three isoquants at the cost-minimizing input bundle. The path is called an **output expansion path** because it connects the cost-minimizing input bundles that are generated as output is increased, or expanded. Because input prices are held constant in this comparative exercise — w_1 is $10 and w_2 is $20 — the isocost lines in Figure 8.7 are parallel.

normal input

inferior input

The output expansion path in the theory of the firm is analogous to the income-consumption path in consumer theory. We can therefore draw on consumer theory for analogies as we classify and compare types of inputs. An input is said to be a **normal input** if the quantity demanded increases as output increases; it is an **inferior input** if quantity demanded decreases as output increases. In Figure 8.7, input 2 is a normal input — at least in the range of output levels represented in the figure — because as output increases, so does the quantity demanded of input 2. On the other hand, input 1 is a normal input at output levels up to 100. At levels beyond 100, however, input 1 is an inferior input because as output increases beyond 100, the quantity demanded of input 1 decreases. It is clear that as output increases, quantity demanded of an input may increase or decrease. Just as normal and inferior goods were possible in consumer theory, so, too, normal and inferior inputs are possible in production theory.

We can easily derive the output expansion path for Tipple's Courier service. From the second principle of cost minimization we know that along the output expansion path $MRTS$ is equal to w_1/w_2. In other words, along the output expansion path an isoquant is

---

FIGURE 8.7 **The output-expansion path**

The line EE is called an output expansion path because it passes through the cost-minimizing bundles that are generated as output increases, holding input prices constant. Input 2 is a normal input for all values of y, whereas input 1 is an inferior input for output levels greater than 100 and a normal input for output levels less than 100.

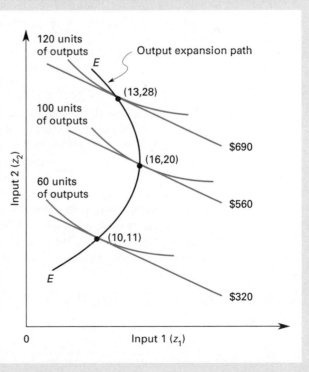

tangent to an isocost line. Recall that $MRTS$ for the courier service is just z_2/z_1. We then see that along Tipple's output expansion path

$$z_2^*/z_1^* = w_1/w_2$$

But this can be rewritten as

$$z_2^* = (w_1/w_2)z_1^*$$

So, Tipple's output expansion path is just a ray through the origin with slope w_1/w_2. When w_1 is \$6 and w_2 is \$2, for example, the output expansion path is just $z_2 = 3z_1$.

homothetic production functions

Tipple's production function is one member of an important class of production functions that have expansion paths that are rays through the origin. These production functions are called **homothetic production functions**. For a homothetic production function, $MRTS$ is constant along any ray through the origin in (z_1,z_2) space, and the output expansion path of a homothetic production function is therefore a ray through the origin.[4] Keep in mind, however, that not all production functions are homothetic. For example, because its output expansion path in not a ray through the origin, the production function shown in Figure 8.7 is not homothetic.

PROBLEM 8.11

Can either input 1 or input 2 be an inferior input when the production function is homothetic?

Long-Run Costs and Output

long-run average cost

By focusing on homothetic production functions it is easy to develop some important relationships between long-run costs and returns to scale. Let us begin with long-run average cost, which we will denote by LAC. It is defined in the predictable way: **long-run average cost** LAC is equal to total cost of output divided by quantity of output:

$$LAC(y) = TC(y)/y$$

We want to show that as output y increases, LAC is constant, decreasing, or increasing as there are constant, increasing, or decreasing returns to scale. These results are intuitive. When all quantities in the input bundle double, costs double. In the case of constant returns to scale, output also doubles, and, as a result, average cost does not change. In contrast, in the case of increasing (decreasing) returns to scale, output more (less) than doubles, and, as a result, average cost falls (rises).

To begin, let us pick an input bundle on the output expansion path — say, bundle (z_1',z_2') on the isoquant for y' units of output in Figure 8.8. Because this bundle is on the expansion path, an isocost curve is tangent to the isoquant at this initial bundle. Let c' denote the cost of this bundle. Clearly,

$$c' = w_1 z_1' + w_2 z_2'$$

---

4 A differentiable production function is homothetic if $MRTS(z_1,z_2)$ can be written as a function of z_2/z_1. This property ensures that $MRTS(z_1,z_2)$ is constant along any ray through the origin and therefore that expansion paths are rays through the origin.

FIGURE 8.8   Costs and returns to scale

Notice first that $LAC(y') = c'/y'$ and $LAC(y'') = ac'/y''$. Now suppose that this production function exhibits increasing to scale. Then $y'' > ay'$. But this implies that $LAC(y'') < LAC(y')$. Hence, increasing returns to scale implies that long-run average cost decreases as output increases. Similarly, decreasing returns to scale implies that long-run average cost increases as output increases. Finally, constant returns to scale implies that long-run average cost does not change as output increases.

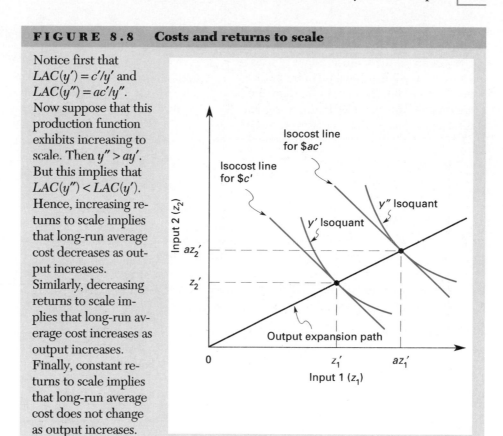

Then, the long-run average cost of y' units of output is just

$$LAC(y') = c'/y'$$

Now let us increase both inputs by factor $a > 1$ to get input bundle (az_1', az_2'). Because the production function is homothetic, this new bundle is also on the output expansion path, and it is associated with y'' units of output. Since this new bundle contains a times as much of each input, its cost is ac'. The long-run average cost of y'' units of output is then just

$$LAC(y'') = ac'/y''$$

Now, suppose that the production function exhibits constant returns to scale. Then y'' is equal to ay'; that is, increasing quantities of all inputs by factor of proportionality a results in an increase in output by factor of proportionality a as well. Using this result, we see that $LAC(y'')$ is equal to $LAC(y')$. When there are *constant returns to scale*, average cost remains constant as output increases.

Next, suppose that the production function exhibits increasing returns to scale. Then y'' exceeds ay', and we see that $LAC(y'')$ is less than $LAC(y')$. When there are *increasing returns to scale*, average cost decreases as output increases.

Finally, suppose that the production function exhibits decreasing returns to scale. Then y'' is less than ay', and we see that $LAC(y'')$ exceeds $LAC(y')$. When there are *decreasing returns to scale*, average cost increases as output increases.

FIGURE 8.9   More on costs and returns to scale

Because in (a) there are constant returns to scale, *TC* is a linear function of output, and *LAC* is constant. Because in (b) there are increasing returns to scale, *TC* increases at a decreasing rate as output increases, and *LAC* decreases as output increases. And because in (c) there are decreasing returns to scale, *TC* increases at an increasing rate as output increases, and *LAC* increases as output increases.

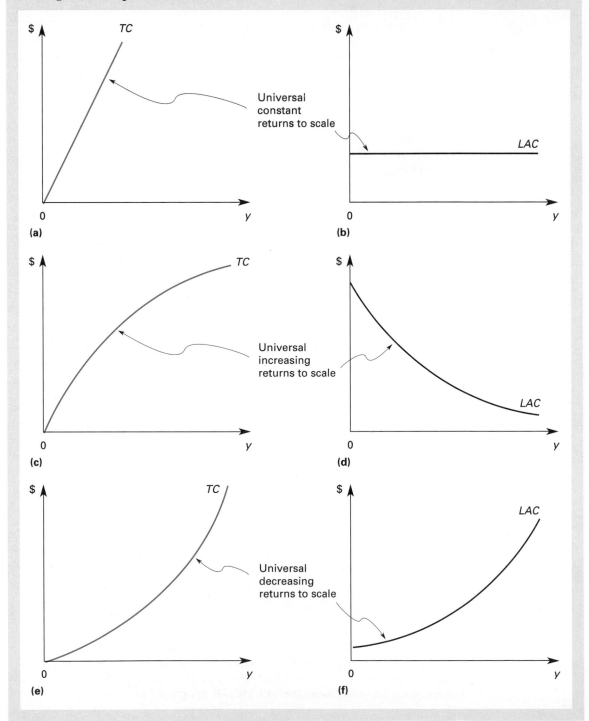

> **PROBLEM 8.12**
>
> As you know, Tipple's production function exhibits constant returns to scale. Find Tipple's $LAC(y)$ and verify that long-run average cost does not change as output changes.

In Figure 8.9, we have shown TC and LAC for the three pure cases. In Figure 8.9a, there are constant returns to scale at all levels of output; in Figure 8.9b, there are increasing returns to scale; and in Figure 8.9c, decreasing returns to scale.

In Figure 8.10a, we have shown a mixed case. Up to 19 units of output, there are increasing returns to scale and LAC is therefore decreasing. Beyond 19 units of output, however, there are decreasing returns to scale and LAC is therefore increasing. At 19 units of output there are constant returns to scale and LAC is neither increasing nor decreasing at this point.

long-run marginal cost

In Figure 8.10b, we have used the techniques developed in Chapter 7 to derive long-run marginal cost LMC from the long-run cost function TC. Of course, **long-run marginal cost** LMC is just the rate at which cost increases as output increases, or the slope of the long-run cost function:

$$LMC(y) = \text{slope of } TC(y)$$

Figure 8.10 shows what are by now familiar relationships between average and marginal curves:

> When LMC lies below LAC, LAC is decreasing; when LMC lies above LAC, LAC is increasing; LMC intersects LAC where LAC is a minimum.

And we can interpret these relationships in a different way:

> With increasing returns to scale, long-run marginal cost is less than long-run average cost; with decreasing returns to scale, long-run marginal cost exceeds long-run average cost; and with constant returns to scale, long-run marginal cost equals long-run average cost.

8.8

Comparing Long-Run and Short-Run Costs

One final topic remains: identifying the relationships between long-run and short-run costs of production. Although only one long run exists, many short runs are possible, depending on the number of inputs that are variable. To further complicate matters, each of these short runs can have any number of cost functions, depending on the quantities of the fixed inputs. We can learn most of what there is to know about the relationship between short- and long-run costs, however, by limiting our discussion to the two-input case.

All the relationships between long-run and short-run costs spring from two basic relationships between the single long-run cost function and any of the short-run cost functions:

> The long-run cost of production is less than or equal to the short-run cost of production for all levels of output:
>
> $$TC(y) \le STC(y) \text{ for all values of } y$$

In addition, the long-run and short-run costs of production are identical at one level of output:

$$TC(y) = STC(y) \text{ for one value of } y$$

These two assertions are illustrated in Figure 8.11. $STC(y)$ lies above $TC(y)$ at all values of y other than $y = 100$, where $TC(y) = STC(y)$. How do we know that these assertions are true? Suppose, for example, that the input bundle (10,35) is cost-minimizing for 100 units of output. Then the long-run minimum cost of 100 units of output can be easily calculated:

$$TC(100) = 10w_1 + 35w_2$$

FIGURE 8.10   Deriving *LAC* and *LMC* from *TC*

At $y = 19$, the ray 0AD is tangent to TC; therefore, LMC is equal to LAC when $y = 19$. Further, LAC attains its minimum value at $y = 19$. The slope of TC is smallest at $y = 10$, and LMC therefore attains its minimum value at $y = 10$.

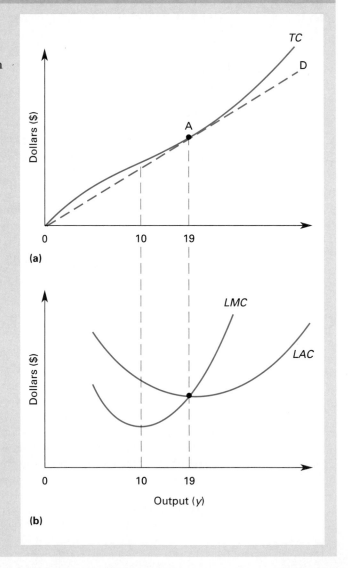

Now let us fix the quantity of input 2 at 35, thereby defining a total product function. What will be the minimum cost of producing 100 units of output in this particular short run with this total product function? Clearly, 10 units of input 1 are cost-minimizing in this short run. In turn, this implies that

$$STC(100) = 10w_1 + 35w_2$$

In other words, the minimum cost of producing 100 units of output is identical in this particular short run and in the long run. Thus, the two cost functions have one point in common. For any other level of output, the cost of production in the short run cannot be less than in the long run. Why not? Because the firm has more flexibility in the long run, it can choose the quantities of all its inputs in the long run, but it cannot do so in the short run. And, except in very odd cases, the short-run cost of production will exceed the long-run cost of production for any output level other than 100. This standard case is presented in Figure 8.11.

We can draw a number of implications from this standard case. The long-run cost function in Figure 8.12a is derived from a production function characterized by increasing returns to scale up to 78 units of output and by decreasing returns to scale thereafter. Figure 8.12a also includes two short-run cost functions STC_1 and STC_2. STC_1 is tangent to TC at 45 units of output where there are increasing returns to scale. And STC_2 is tangent to TC at 93 units of output where there are decreasing returns to scale. The corresponding average and marginal cost functions are presented in Figure 8.12b.

Let us concentrate first on the relationship between the two short-run average cost functions and the long-run average cost function. SAC_1 is tangent to LAC when y is equal to 45, the output at which STC_1 is tangent to TC. At all other output levels, SAC_1 lies above LAC. Similarly, SAC_2 is tangent to LAC at 93 units of output and lies above it elsewhere.

Now let us turn to the relationships between the two short-run marginal cost functions and the long-run marginal cost function. Notice that at output 45, SMC_1 is equal to LMC and that at output 93, SMC_2 is equal to LMC. To understand why these

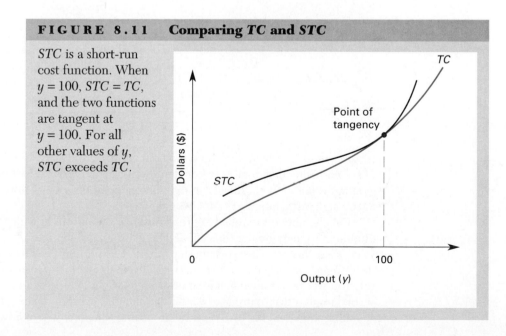

FIGURE 8.11   Comparing *TC* and *STC*

STC is a short-run cost function. When $y = 100$, $STC = TC$, and the two functions are tangent at $y = 100$. For all other values of y, *STC* exceeds *TC*.

FIGURE 8.12 Relationships between long-run and short-run cost functions

Here we see the relationships between various long- and short-run cost functions. STC_1 is tangent to TC at $y = 45$. Hence, at $y = 45$, SMC_1 is equal to LMC, and SAC_1 is tangent to LAC. Similarly, STC_2 is tangent to TC at $y = 93$. Hence, at $y = 93$, SMC_2 is equal to LMC, and SAC_2 is tangent to LAC.

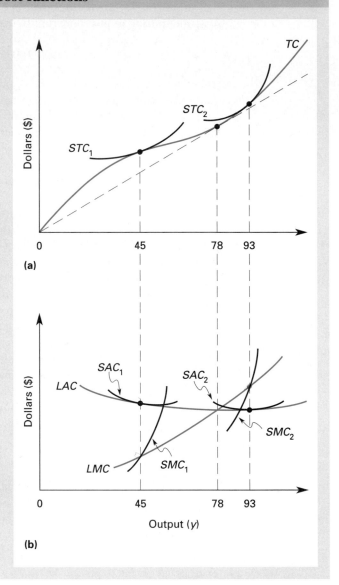

(a)

(b)

relationships must hold, look for a moment at SMC_1 and LMC. Each is just the slope of the corresponding total cost function. Because the two total cost functions are tangent at output level 45, they have the same slope at this point. Notice, too, that both SMC_1 and SMC_2 intersect LMC from below.

Finally, notice the following relationships: the output at which SAC_1 attains its minimum value is greater than 45, and the output at which SAC_2 attains its minimum value is less than 93. These relationships are a bit surprising. The first implies that to produce 45 units of output at minimum cost in the long run, in the corresponding short run, the firm will be producing at a point where SAC_1 is still decreasing. Conversely, the second implies that to produce 93 units at minimum cost in the long run, in the corresponding short run, the firm must be producing at a point where SAC_2 is increasing.

How can we understand these results? Let us look more closely at 45 units of output. LMC is less than LAC at this level of output, and LAC therefore must be falling at 45. Since STC_1 is tangent to TC at 45, SMC_1 must also be less than SAC_1 at 45. Therefore, SAC_1 must also be falling at 45 units. You may want to construct an analogous argument to explain why SAC_2 must be increasing at 93 units.

Because these relationships can be slippery and practice is needed to master them, try your hand at the following problem.

PROBLEM 8.13

Consider a cost function like the one shown in Figure 8.9a, which has been derived from a production function characterized by constant returns to scale throughout. Construct a diagram analogous to Figure 8.12.

A Theory of Market Structure

theory of market structure

In Chapter 6, we posed a fundamental economic question: Why do firms exist at all? We approached this question from an organizational point of view. We can now use the insights from this chapter to tackle that question from another perspective. Using the different average cost functions that we have encountered in this chapter, we can sketch out a very basic but insightful **theory of market structure**: a theory we can use to predict whether or not firms come into existence and how many firms will establish themselves in a particular market.

To articulate this cost-based theory of market structure, we will use the four stylized long-run average cost functions in Figure 8.13. Let us begin with the case of *universal decreasing returns to scale* in Figure 8.13a. Because long-run average cost is everywhere increasing, size is obviously associated with a cost penalty. The bigger the output of a firm, the more costly the good or service is to produce. In fact, goods and services will not be supplied in this case by firms at all — at least not by firms as we know them. Why? Suppose a firm tries to serve more than one buyer. To cover its costs, its price will have to be no smaller than its average cost. But because potential buyers can produce the good or service for themselves at a lower average cost, they will not pay the higher price needed to cover the firm's costs. We do not know of any firms selling tooth brushing services, for example, because it is cheaper for us to brush our own teeth. We can think of the case of decreasing returns to scale as a case where a market will be characterized by *household production*: production will be conducted on the smallest possible scale.

What about the case of *universal constant returns to scale* in Figure 8.13b? When returns to scale are constant throughout, size is not associated with a cost penalty; however, nothing is gained by being large. If a firm were to come into existence, it could not sell its output at a price greater than its average cost of production. If it tried to sell at a higher price, its potential customers would simply make the good in their own backyards. When returns to scale are everywhere constant, firms have no compelling reason to exist.

In the remaining two cases in Figure 8.13, firms will come into being. Because both cases are characterized by ranges of output over which there are *increasing returns to scale*, the potential do-it-yourselfer in these cases must labor under the cost disadvantage associated with a relatively small scale of production.

Only in these two cases, then, do firms serve an economic purpose. When long-run average cost of production is everywhere downward-sloping, as in Figure 8.13c, there

FIGURE 8.13   A cost-based theory of market structure

With decreasing returns to scale, as in (a), *LAC* is everywhere upward-sloping. Thus, a cost penalty is associated with large size, and we expect this sort of good to be produced on the smallest possible scale. With constant returns to scale, as in (b), neither a cost penalty nor a cost advantage is associated with size, and this sort of good could be produced on any scale. With increasing returns to scale, as in (c), a cost advantage is associated with size, and this sort of good will be produced by one or a few firms. In the mixed case, as in (d), the initial increasing returns to scale guarantee that production will be done by firms. Whether it will be done by a few relatively large firms or by many relatively small firms depends on the output level at which *LAC* attains its minimum value.

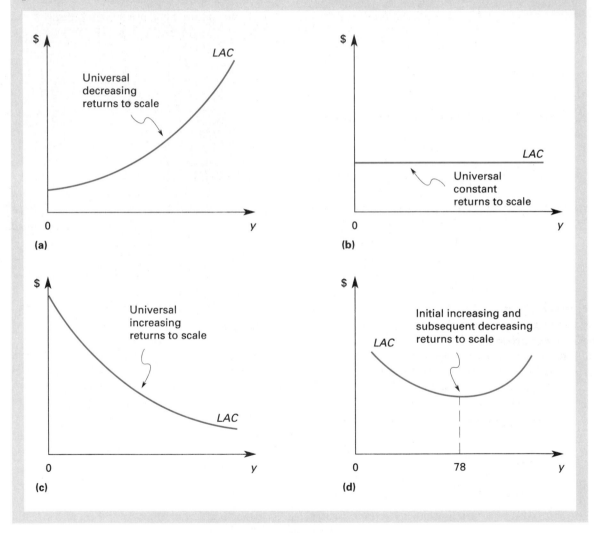

are *universal increasing returns to scale*, and a cost advantage is always associated with a still larger output. As we will discover in Chapter 10, in this circumstance, a small number of relatively large firms will supply the good or service in question. Public utilities such as electricity and telephone service are industries in which being big pays off. We have an important understanding, then, of the elementary force that generates markets characterized by *monopolies* or *oligopolies*.

We know that a U-shaped average cost curve reflects *initial increasing and subsequent decreasing returns to scale*, as in Figure 8.13d. Broadly speaking, *two possible market structures* arise in this case. If the output level at which $LAC(y)$ attains its minimum value (78 units in Figure 8.12d) is relatively large we again expect to see a market characterized by *monopoly* or *oligopoly*. On the other hand, if the output level at which the long-run average cost curve attains its minimum value is relatively small, then a large number of relatively small firms will supply the good or service. The initial increasing returns to scale guarantee that production will be done by firms, and the subsequent decreasing returns to scale guarantee that a large number of firms will do the job. Since there will be a large number of competing firms in this case, we will have a market that is a *competitive market*.

In this section, we have laid the groundwork for understanding market structure. The chapter as a whole has extended our understanding of how production functions — and their offspring, cost functions — provide the foundation for a theory of economic behavior of firms in Part IV. In Chapter 9, we take a closer look at competitive markets typified by a relatively large number of firms. And in Chapters 10, 11, and 12, we turn to markets typified by relatively few firms.

SUMMARY

This chapter continued the exploration of a firm's production function begun in Chapter 7 by extending the analysis to cases in which more than one input is variable. We drew on correspondences between consumer theory and the theory of the firm as we looked at *isoquants* (analogous to indifference curves), defined the marginal rate of technical substitution *MRTS* (analogous to the marginal rate of substitution in consumption), and discussed the *assumption of a diminishing marginal rate of technical substitution*.

We then defined the important concept of returns to scale. Suppose we double the quantities of all inputs. We have *constant returns to scale* if output also doubles, *increasing returns to scale* if output more than doubles, and *decreasing returns to scale* if output less than doubles.

Turning from the theory of production to the theory of cost, we solved the firm's *cost-minimization problem* for y units of output by identifying the input bundle on the isoquant for y units of output where *MRTS* is equal to w_1/w_2, or where the marginal product per dollar is identical for all the inputs in the input bundle.

We then took up several comparative statics exercises. One of the resulting propositions — that firms substitute away from inputs as those inputs become relatively more expensive — is extremely useful in understanding economic reality. For instance, it explains why a car that gets 50 mpg was not on the market until the Organization of Petroleum Exporting Countries (OPEC) engineered worldwide increases in the price of oil, and why gold and silver are never used in household wiring even though they are both superior electrical conductors to copper.

We then turned to the important relationship between returns to scale and costs of production. We saw that as output increased, the average cost of production increased, decreased, or remained unchanged as returns to scale were decreasing, increasing, or constant.

We then compared costs in the short run and the long run. All the comparisons were driven by two fundamental points: the short-run cost function *STC* is tangent to the long-run cost function *TC* at one point, and *STC* lies above *TC* at all other points. Finally, we presented a cost-based *theory of market structure* that prepares the way for the analysis in Part IV.

EXERCISES

1. Suppose that the following is true:

   A cost-minimizing firm, faced with constant input prices, recently increased the quantity of each of its inputs by 10%. As a result, its output increased from 100 units to 120 units.

   Indicate whether each of the following statements is true, false, or uncertain, and explain your answer.

   a. When y is 100, there are increasing returns to scale.
   b. The firm's production function is not homothetic.
   c. When y is 100, *LAC* is downward sloping.
   d. When y is 100, *LMC* exceeds *LAC*.
   e. When y is 100, *LMC* is downward sloping.
   f. If the firm had increased the quantity of each input by 5%, output would increase from 100 to 110 units.

2. Suppose that the following is true:

   "When $w_1 = w_2 = \$10$, the cost-minimizing bundle for 100 units of output is $z_1 = z_2 = 20$. When $w_1 = \$8$ and $w_2 = \$10$, the cost-minimizing bundle for 110 units of output is $z_1 = 28$ and $z_2 = 19$."

   Indicate whether each of the following statements is true, false, or uncertain, and explain your answer.

   a. When $w_1 = w_2 = \$10$, *LAC* for $y = 100$ is $4.
   b. Input 2 is an inferior input.
   c. Input 1 is a normal input.
   d. The firm's output expansion path is downward sloping.
   e. The production function is not homothetic.
   f. When $w_1 = w_2 = \$5$, *LAC* for $y = 100$ is $2.
   g. When $w_1 = \$16$ and $w_2 = \$20$, the minimum cost of producing $y = 110$ is $828.
   h. When $w_1 = \$8$ and $w_2 = \$10$, the minimum cost of producing $y = 100$ is no greater than $360.
   i. The bundle with 22 units of both inputs will not produce $y = 110$.
   j. When $w_1 = \$20$ and $w_2 = \$20$, the minimum cost of producing $y = 110$ is no greater than $940.

3. Indicate whether the following statements are true, false, or uncertain, and explain your answer.

   a. Increasing returns to scale and diminishing marginal product are incompatible.

   b. When the firm's output expansion path has a negative slope, input 2 is inferior.
   c. When the firm's output expansion path has a negative slope, both inputs are inferior.
   d. A cost-minimizing firm would never use an input bundle where the isoquant was upward sloping.
   e. At Fomoco, the marginal products of inputs 1 and 2 are 5 and 10, respectively, and their prices are $30 and $15; hence, Fomoco is using a cost-minimizing input bundle.
   f. The production function $F(z_1, z_2) = \min(z_1, 2z_2)$ is homothetic.

4. Indicate whether each of the following statements is "possibly true" or "certainly false," and explain your answer.

   a. The cost-minimizing bundle for $y = 50$ is $z_1 = 10$ and $z_2 = 40$ when $w_1 = w_2$, and it is $z_1 = 12$ and $z_2 = 37$ when $w_1 = \$20$ and $w_2 = \$15$.
   b. The cost-minimizing bundle for $y = 50$ is $z_1 = 10$ and $z_2 = 40$ when $w_1 = w_2$, and it is $z_1 = 7$ and $z_2 = 42$ when $w_1 = \$20$ and $w_2 = \$15$.
   c. The cost-minimizing bundle for $y = 50$ is $z_1 = 10$ and $z_2 = 40$ when $w_1 = w_2$, and it is $z_1 = 6$ and $z_2 = 45$ when $w_1 = \$20$ and $w_2 = \$15$.

5. Kim runs a very interesting business. She buys pizzas from one of two pizza parlors in her town and then delivers them. It takes her 20 minutes to deliver one pizza. If she buys pizzas from Sorrento's Pizza Parlor, she pays w_1 for a box with one pizza in it, and if she buys them from Pizza 222, she pays w_2 for a box with two pizzas in it. Show that her cost function is

   $$TC(y, w_1, w_2, w_3) = y\,[w_3/3 + \min(w_1, w_2/2)]$$

   where w_3 is the value of an hour of Kim's time.

6. Jeff runs a roadside stand where he sells soft drinks. One of his creations, Razapple Juice, is concocted by mixing raspberry juice with apple juice. Long experience has taught Jeff that he must use at least 30% apple juice and at least 30% raspberry juice when mixing a batch of Razapple. If he does not, his customers demand a refund, claiming that the mix is not Razapple, and if he does, they are perfectly satisfied with the product.

a. Considering only the costs associated with buying apple and raspberry juice, what is the minimum cost of producing a gallon of Razapple Juice when raspberry juice costs $10 per gallon and apple juice costs $20 per gallon? When raspberry juice costs $20 per gallon and apple juice costs $10 per gallon? When raspberry juice costs $10 per gallon and apple juice costs $10 per gallon?

b. Construct the isoquant for 1 gallon of Razapple Juice. For y gallons of Razapple Juice.

c. Find the cost-minimizing bundle for y gallons of Razapple Juice when the price of a gallon of apple juice is less than the price of a gallon of raspberry juice. When the price of a gallon of apple juice is greater than the price of a gallon of raspberry juice.

d. Find the cost function for Razapple Juice.

7. A young entrepreneur, Liz, is considering going into the lawn-mowing business for the summer. Since she can work as many hours as she chooses in the family business at w_1 per hour, her time is worth w_1 per hour. The price per gallon of the gasoline that she needs to buy for her lawn mower is w_2. She can rent a mower that cuts a 12-inch swath and uses 1/3 of a gallon of gas per hour for w_3 per hour. Using this mower, she can cut 10,000 square feet of lawn in an hour. For convenience, let 10,000 square feet be the unit in which output is measured. She can rent a larger mower, for w_4 per hour, that uses 1 gallon of gas per hour and cuts 3 units of lawn per hour.

a. Find the production functions for the smaller and the larger mowers. Note that each production function has three inputs: hours of Liz's time, gallons of gas, and hours of the smaller or the larger mower.

b. Derive the conditional input demand functions and the cost functions.

c. Show that using the smaller mower is a cheaper way to cut grass if $2w_1 < w_4 - 3w_3$. Why is this result independent of the price of gasoline?

d. How large must be the price she gets for cutting a unit of lawn to induce her to choose to cut grass rather than to work in the family business?

8. In Problem 8.4 we found the following production function for producing "fenced pasture land" using input 1 (land measured in square feet) and input 2 (barbed wire fence measured in lineal feet).

$$y = \min[z_1, (z_2/4)^2]$$

a. Find the output expansion path.

b. Now find the conditional input demand functions, and the long-run cost function.

9. The following is a general case of the Cobb Douglas production function:

$$F(z_1, z_2) = z_1{}^u z_2{}^v$$

where u and v are positive constants. The marginal rate of technical substitution for this production function is

$$MRTS(z_1, z_2) = (uz_2/vz_1)$$

a. What do the first and second principles of cost minimization imply about the cost-minimizing input bundle for this production function?

b. Let $u = 1/3$ and $v = 2/3$, and then find the conditional input demand functions, the cost function, and the average cost function.

c. Let u = 3/4 and v = 3/4, and repeat these exercises.

*10. Draw an isoquant that is concave (as opposed to convex) to the origin. Show that a cost-minimizing firm will never choose an input bundle with a positive quantity of both inputs. More generally, show that a cost-minimizing firm will never choose an input bundle with a positive quantity of both inputs on a concave portion of an isoquant.

*11. Consider the following production functions:

$$F(z_1, z_2) = [(z_1)^2 + (z_2)^2]^{1/2}$$
$$F(z_1, z_2) = z_1 + z_2$$

a. On one diagram, draw the isoquants associated with one unit of output, paying special attention to the points where the isoquants intersect the axes.

b. Now suppose that $w_1 < w_2$, and find the cost-minimizing bundles on each isoquant. Then find the cost-minimizing bundles when $w_1 > w_2$.

c. Find the cost functions associated with these production functions.

d. "The concave portion of any isoquant is economically irrelevant." Do you agree?

PART IV

Goods Markets

In Part IV, we combine the theories of consumer choice and of the firm into a larger picture of the interaction of consumers and firms in markets for goods. Our objective is to learn about the forces that determine equilibrium price and quantity in any goods market and about the properties of equilibrium in goods markets. We take up competitive markets in Chapter 9, monopoly in Chapter 10, oligopoly in markets for homogeneous goods in Chapter 11, and oligopoly in markets for differentiated goods in Chapter 12.

In Chapters 9 and 10, we focus on efficiency. We see that competitive markets are efficient while monopoly markets are not, and we explore a number of institutions designed to rectify the inefficiency of monopoly. In Chapter 11, we grapple with one of the toughest questions in economics: What is the appropriate model of oligopoly? In Chapter 12, we turn our attention to product design and niche marketing as the key decisions of the modern firm.

CHAPTER 9

The Theory of Perfect Competition

At the end of the last chapter, we noted that one type of market structure — perfect competition — is characterized by a large number of relatively small firms. In this chapter, we explore *perfect competition* in detail and define the kinds of markets to which the model of perfect competition applies. Much of the theory of perfect competition was developed by Alfred Marshall, a turn-of-the-century British economist. The classic reference is Book V of Marshall's *Principles of Economics* (1920).

The questions we will be asking fall into two categories: conceptual and technical. In the first two sections, we focus on conceptual issues: What is a competitive equilibrium? What are its properties? In what circumstances is the model of perfect competition appropriate? To isolate these conceptual issues from technical ones, we take them up in the restricted context of a simple exchange economy in which goods are exchanged, but not produced.

In the remainder of the chapter, we look at technical issues: Where do the demand and supply functions used to identify a competitive equilibrium come from? How does short-run equilibrium differ from long-run equilibrium? We raise these issues in the wider context of an economy characterized by both production and exchange.

Finally, in the last section, we discuss rent control and consider what happens when voluntary exchange in competitive markets is impeded by such price controls.

9.1

A Competitive Model of Exchange

By creating an extremely simple competitive model, we can highlight the essential features of competitive market transactions in the ordinary world. For simplicity, we will set aside production questions until Section 9.3 and focus on a simple **exchange economy**. In this very basic market, goods are exchanged but not produced.

exchange economy

The goods in our simple competitive model are five tickets to a rock concert and the participants are ten students. Assuming that each student wants only one ticket to the concert, we can completely describe the preferences of a student by a **reservation price**. If the student does not have a ticket, what is the maximum price he or she will pay to buy one? Or, if the student does have a ticket, what is the minimum price he or she will accept to sell it?

reservation price

In either case, the answer is the student's reservation price. Again for simplicity, we will suppose that potential buyers are male and potential sellers are female. On the buyer's side, we will assume that a male student will buy a ticket at his reservation price. If a male student is offered one at a price greater than his reservation price, he will not buy it. But if the price is less than or equal to his reservation price, he will. On the seller's side, if a female student is offered a price higher than her reservation price, she will sell her ticket. But if the price is less than or equal to her reservation price, she will not sell it.

We can then describe the preferences of these ten students by ten reservation prices, R_A through R_J, which we will list in descending order. Let us suppose that the highest reservation price is \$100 and that reservation prices fall by \$10 increments as we move down the list. Thus,

$$R_A = \$100, R_B = \$90, \ldots, R_J = \$10$$

Imagine that each of the five female students has a ticket and that none of the five male students can buy a ticket elsewhere. Because all ten students would like to see the concert and only five tickets are available, they potentially can enter into market exchanges among themselves. Which five students will ultimately hold the concert tickets and at what price will the tickets be exchanged?

Suppose that the five tickets are initially allocated to the five students whose reservation prices are $R_B = \$90$, $R_C = \$80$, $R_F = \$50$, $R_H = \$30$, and $R_I = \$20$. We will give these students feminine names that begin with the identifying reservation price subscript. Betty is the student whose reservation price is R_B, Cathy is the one whose reservation price is R_C, and so on. These students are the *potential suppliers* of tickets. The male students without tickets — the *potential demanders* — are those whose reservation prices are $R_A = \$100$, $R_D = \$70$, $R_E = \$60$, $R_G = \$40$, and $R_J = \$10$. We will give these students masculine names.

Market Demand

market demand function

We know the individual demand functions of each male student. For example, Dan is willing to buy one ticket at any price less than or equal to \$70, but he will not buy one at any higher price. We can use individual demand information of this kind to construct a **market demand function** that gives the total number of tickets demanded by the five male students at any given price. First, let us consider relatively high prices. Because Alan's reservation price, $R_A = \$100$, is the highest of the five demanders, we know that if the price of a ticket exceeds \$100, the demand for tickets will be zero. At slightly lower prices — prices below $R_A = \$100$ but above $R_D = \$70$ — Alan is willing to buy a ticket, but Dan and the other three demanders are not. At such moderately high prices, the market demand is one ticket. At any price less than $R_D = \$70$ but greater than $R_E = \$60$, Alan and Dan are willing to buy tickets, but Earl and the remaining two demanders are not. At any price in this range, the market demand is two tickets. By simply repeating this procedure, we can construct the entire market demand function for the group of five demanders.

That market demand function is plotted in Figure 9.1a, where p is price and y is quantity. The six vertical line segments labeled *dd* represent the market demand function. (The horizontal dashed lines have been added to give the demand function visual integration.) To read the quantity demanded at any given price from Figure 9.1a, first locate the price on the vertical axis, move horizontally to the demand function, and then move vertically downward to identify quantity demanded on the horizontal axis. For instance, at a price of \$25, the quantity demanded is four.

FIGURE 9.1   Demand and supply

In (a), we have constructed the market demand function implied by the five reservation prices of students without tickets: $100, $70, $60, $40, and $10. In (b), we have constructed the market supply function implied by the five reservation prices of students with tickets: $20, $30, $50, $80, and $90.

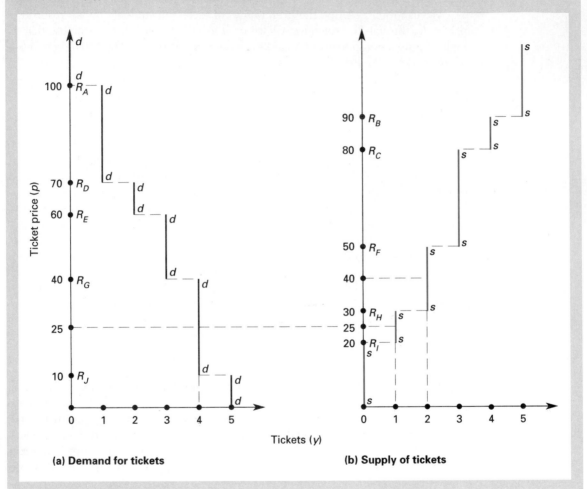

(a) Demand for tickets

(b) Supply of tickets

Market Supply

market supply function

Now let us construct a **market supply function**. Whether or not the suppliers — the five female students who have tickets — will be willing to sell their tickets is determined by their individual reservation prices. For instance, Cathy will offer her ticket for sale at any price greater than $R_C = \$80$, but she will keep it at any price less than or equal to $80. Using this kind of information, we can construct the market supply function just as we constructed the market demand function by asking who will and who will not supply a ticket at any given price.

The market supply function in Figure 9.1b is composed of six vertical segments labeled ss and connected by dashed lines. Figure 9.1b is read in exactly the same way as Figure 9.1a. If the price of a ticket exceeds the highest reservation price among the suppliers, R_B = $90, for instance, all five ticket holders will offer a ticket for sale. At prices above $90, five tickets will be supplied. If the price is $40 in Figure 9.1b, Helen and Irene will each offer a ticket for sale because $40 exceeds their reservation prices ($30 and $20), but the remaining three suppliers will not because $40 is less than their reservation prices ($50, $80, and $90). At the $40 price, two tickets will be supplied.

The Walrasian Auctioneer

Now that both the market supply and the market demand functions are in place, how many tickets will ultimately be exchanged and at what price? In other words, what will be the equilibrium in this market for concert tickets? To find out, we will imagine that there is an auctioneer who acts as a *price setter* in the market. The auctioneer is called the **Walrasian auctioneer** after the nineteenth-century French economist, Leon Walras, who invented this process to study competitive equilibrium.

Walrasian auctioneer

As you know, most real markets do not have price-setting auctioneers. In order to study competitive equilibrium, however, we need an imaginary auctioneer who sets prices because (as you will see later) all participants in competitive markets are assumed to take price as given. In other words, they are assumed to be price takers, not price setters. You should think of the imaginary price-setting Walrasian auctioneer, then, as simply a useful analytical device for studying competitive equilibrium.

Let us imagine that the Walrasian auctioneer begins by announcing a price for a ticket. Each demander then writes "X" on a slip of paper if he is willing to buy a ticket at that price and "O" if he is not. At the same time, each supplier writes down "Y" if she is willing to sell a ticket at that price and "O" if she is not.

The auctioneer then collects the slips from all ten students and compares the number of *X*'s — quantity demanded at the announced price — and the number of *Y*'s — quantity supplied at the announced price. If quantity demanded at the announced price exceeds quantity supplied — that is, if there is **excess demand** — then the auctioneer announces a higher price and repeats the procedure. If, instead, quantity supplied exceeds quantity demanded — that is, if there is **excess supply** — then the auctioneer announces a lower price and repeats the procedure.

excess demand

excess supply

If the auctioneer announces the price $25 in Figure 9.1, for example, Alan, Dan, Earl, and George will mark down *X*'s, but only Irene will write down a *Y*. Because there is excess demand, the auctioneer will announce a higher price and then tabulate the results at that new and higher price. If the auctioneer announces the price $95 in Figure 9.1, for example, only Alan will be willing to buy a ticket, but all five ticket holders will be willing to sell their tickets. Because there is excess supply, the auctioneer will announce a new, lower price and again tabulate the results.

The auction ends — and the market is in *competitive equilibrium* — only when quantity demanded is equal to quantity supplied. When this happens, the auctioneer collects money from each demander willing to buy at the announced price, gives the appropriate amount of money to each of the sellers, and transfers the tickets from sellers to buyers.

Competitive Equilibrium

How many tickets will be exchanged once this point of equilibrium has been reached, and what will the competitive equilibrium price be? In Figure 9.2, both the demand and supply functions have been plotted in one diagram. The demand function is labeled *DD* and the supply function *SS*. From Figure 9.2, we see that the auction will end only when the auctioneer announces a price that lies somewhere in the interval $50 to $60.

FIGURE 9.2   Competitive equilibrium in an exchange economy

The functions labeled *SS* and *DD* are the supply and demand functions from Figure 9.1. Any price p^e greater than $50 and less than or equal to $60 is a competitive equilibrium price. The competitive equilibrium quantity is $y^e = 3$.

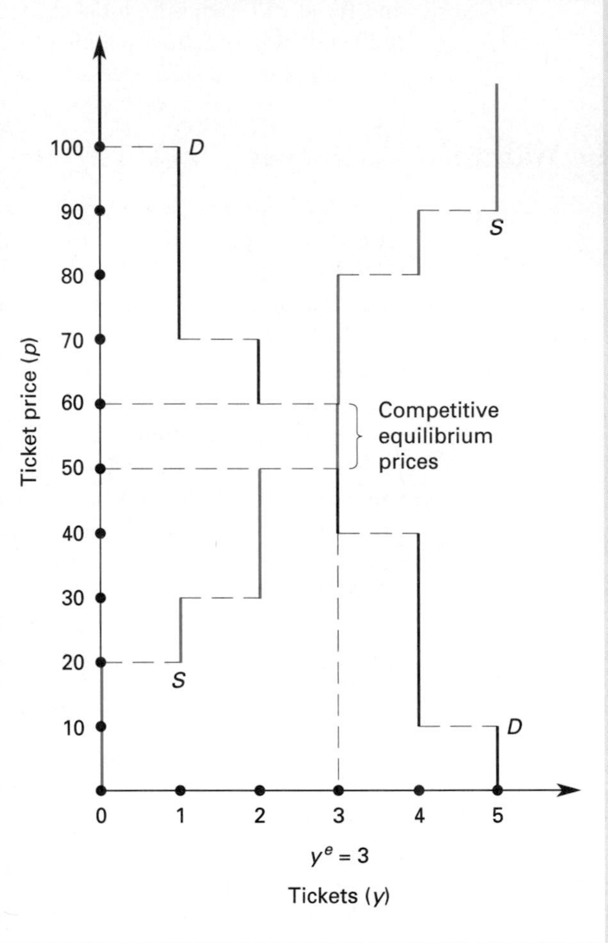

At higher prices, there is excess supply; at lower prices, excess demand. At any price in this interval, however, three tickets will be demanded and three supplied.

competitive
equilibrium

Any point at which quantity demanded is equal to quantity supplied is a **competitive equilibrium**. In this case, there are many competitive equilibrium prices. Denoting an equilibrium price by p^e, we see that $\$50 < p^e \leq \$60$. (We have included the weak inequality sign because we have assumed that at a price equal to $60, Earl — whose reservation price is $60 — will buy a ticket.) Denoting an equilibrium quantity by y^e, we see that in each of these competitive equilibria $y^e = 3$; that is, three tickets are exchanged.

This market-clearing process thus determines both equilibrium price and equilibrium quantity. In our ticket model, although the equilibrium quantity is unique, the equilibrium price is not: the auction will stop when the auctioneer announces any price between $50 and $60. The equilibrium price that actually emerges from the auction will depend on the precise rules used by the auctioneer. Yet, equilibrium price and quantity are simply by-products of a more fundamental process in this competitive market: the allocation of tickets and of wealth to students. By allocation, we mean two things: 1. which students finally do and do not have a ticket to the concert, and 2. how much money is in each student's pocket at the end of the process. The competitive equilibrium therefore determines how both tickets and wealth (or command over all other goods) are allocated to students.

Pareto Optimality, or Efficiency

One feature of the *competitive equilibrium allocation* in this market deserves careful attention. The students with the five highest reservation prices, R_A through R_E, have tickets, and the five students with the lower reservation prices, R_F through R_J, do not; that is, the five students who value the tickets most highly are the ones who have them. An implication of this feature is that no further exchange of tickets for money between any two of the ten students can keep both students as well off and make at least one of them better off. Why is this true?

The highest reservation price among those without tickets is Fran's, $R_F = \$50$, and the lowest among those with tickets is Earl's, $R_E = \$60$. Since R_E exceeds R_F, there is no sum of money that Fran will be willing to offer Earl for a ticket and that Earl will also be willing to accept. We have then established an important result: the competitive equilibrium allocation is Pareto-optimal, since no student can be made better off while leaving the other students at least as well off. This illustrates an important, even fundamental, result:

Provided that certain conditions are met, a competitive equilibrium allocation is Pareto-optimal, or efficient.

We will consider the conditions under which competitive equilibrium is Pareto-optimal at various points in this and later chapters.

The Role of Initial Allocation

What would happen with a different initial allocation of tickets to students? Would the equilibrium price and quantity also be different? Would the tickets still be allocated to those with the highest reservation prices? Would the equilibrium allocation again be Pareto-optimal? To find out, try the following problem.

> **PROBLEM 9.1**
>
> Suppose that the students who were given the tickets in the initial allocation were those with the reservation prices $100, $90, $70, $40, and $10. Construct a diagram analogous to Figure 9.2. What is the range of equilibrium prices and the equilibrium quantity in this case? What is the allocation of tickets in this competitive equilibrium? Identify the students who are better off and those who are worse off in the new equilibrium than in the original equilibrium.

This problem illustrates some important points about this particular economy. First, the competitive equilibrium quantity depends on the *initial allocation*. In the case analyzed in the text, the quantity exchanged in the competitive equilibrium was 3. However, in Problem 9.1 — where the initial allocation of tickets to students was different — the quantity exchanged was 2. To cite another example of the dependence of equilibrium quantity on the initial allocation: first, if tickets were initially given to the students with the five highest reservation prices, equilibrium quantity would be zero. Second, a student is better off when he or she initially has a ticket. Third, although equilibrium quantity and the welfare of individual students depend on the initial allocation, the competitive equilibrium allocation is always the same. In the competitive equilibrium, the tickets go to the five students, male or female, with the five highest reservation prices.

The Function of Price

Finally, notice that the range of competitive equilibrium prices does not depend on the initial allocation in this model. This reflects the fact that price is a signal that serves to allocate tickets to the students who place the highest value on them. The imaginary device of a Walrasian auctioneer highlights the allocational role of price, since each demander responds to the announced price by indicating whether he wants to buy a ticket at that price and each supplier responds by indicating whether she wants to sell her ticket at that price. Thus, we see the fundamental role that price plays in an unfettered market economy — that is, in an economy free of impediments to the voluntary exchange of goods or services between suppliers and demanders:

In a market economy, prices are the signals that guide and direct allocation.

In our ticket model, price performs this allocative function well, since the equilibrium is Pareto-optimal. As we will see in subsequent chapters, however, the Pareto optimality of competitive equilibrium is a result that requires careful qualification and interpretation. For example, in Chapter 17, we will look at some important qualifications under the general heading of *externalities*. In the meantime, you can discover the general nature of such qualifications in the following problem.

> ### PROBLEM 9.2
>
> Consider a ticket model with just four people and two tickets. Harry and Sarah have ordinary reservation prices, each equal to $10. However, because Jane and Bob are dating, their reservation prices are more complex. If Jane has a ticket, then Bob's reservation price is $20; if she does not, his reservation price is $0. Similarly, if Bob has a ticket, Jane's reservation price is $20; if he does not, her reservation price is $0. Show that there are two competitive equilibrium allocations. In one allocation, the price is less than or equal to $10, and Harry and Sarah have the tickets. In the other, the price is greater than $10 and less than $20, and Jane and Bob have the tickets. Show that the first of these allocations is not Pareto-optimal.

A competitive market system of allocation is appealing to many economists (and noneconomists) because the gains from trade are fully realized in competitive equilibrium. In our ticket model, for example, the potential gains from trade in the initial allocation of tickets were fully realized in the competitive equilibrium allocation.

Notice, however, that the initial allocation is not unlike the distribution of inherited wealth and abilities in the real world. Each of us must play life's game with the 'tickets' allocated at birth, including inherited wealth and talent. Some of us are lucky and others unlucky, just as five of the students were fortunate and five unfortunate in the initial allocation of concert tickets. And what someone ends up with in the competitive equilibrium depends on what he or she starts with. In Problem 9.1, you discovered the unsurprising but important result that students were better off when they were given tickets in the initial allocation than when they were not.

The larger implication is that a competitive equilibrium is incapable of redressing initial inequalities. It merely provides a means for realizing the full potential of gains from trade — *given the initial allocation*. As you will see in the last section of this chapter, on rent control, impediments are sometimes placed on the market system of allocation in order to redistribute income. Not surprisingly, the consequences for allocation are adverse. Rent control thus illustrates the potential for conflict between equity and allocational efficiency.

9.2
Potential Difficulties with the Competitive Model

Our ticket model is founded on two crucial assumptions that are analytical trouble spots. Because these two troublesome assumptions are at the core of all models of perfect competition, we will look at both very carefully. Later in the chapter, we will consider the additional assumptions that come into play in a competitive model once production is introduced.

Price Taking or Price Manipulating

First, let us consider the assumption, implicit in these models, that all the students behaved as if they were price takers. We assumed that in responding to the auctioneer's announced price, the students simply consulted their preferences and honestly reported the action that was in their own self-interest at the announced price.

Yet any of these students might have *misrepresented* their preferences in an attempt to influence the market-clearing price in a personally favorable direction. Indeed, we can easily identify real-world situations in which demanders or suppliers intentionally misrepresent their positions. In the residential real estate market, for instance, homeowners regularly quote a selling price higher than their real reservation price to agents or to prospective buyers in an attempt to increase the price at which the house is finally sold. Their behavior indicates that they do not see themselves as mere price takers, unable to affect the market price of a good. On the other side of the real estate coin, potential home buyers typically negotiate by underrepresenting their real reservation price for buying a home in an attempt to lower the price at which the house is sold. Again, these potential home buyers do not see themselves as price takers.

Individuals do have the incentive and, as we will see, some power to manipulate prices. Suppose that nine students in our ticket model are ingenuous souls who view themselves as price takers but that one student is a fox among the chickens: a price manipulator. Now, suppose that the manipulator is a supplier, Fran. How can she increase the market-clearing price? By responding to the auctioneer's announced prices as if her reservation price were higher than $R_F = \$50$, or, loosely speaking, by reporting a false reservation price R_F' higher than $50. Will her manipulative behavior pay off? Suppose that her false reservation price R_F' is $55, which is less than Earl's reservation price, $R_E = \$60$, but greater than her true reservation price, $R_F = \$50$. Fran's price manipulation in this case gives rise to a (false) supply function that shifts from two to three tickets at $55 rather than at $50. As you can easily verify, the range of market-clearing prices is now reduced from the interval $50 to $60 to the interval $55 to $60. In this instance, Fran's deliberate misrepresentation works to her advantage (and, incidentally, to the advantage of Helen and Irene as well) because the market-clearing price may increase but will not decrease as a result of her manipulations.

What will happen if Fran decides to report an even higher false reservation price, $65, which is larger than $R_E = \$60$ but less than $R_D = \$70$? Now the (false) supply function, $S'S'$ in Figure 9.3, shifts from two to three tickets at $65. In this situation, the auction will not close at a competitive equilibrium price. Instead, as Figure 9.3 reveals, the market-clearing price will be in the interval $60 to $65, and only two units will

FIGURE 9.3   **Price manipulation**

Fran's reservation price is $50. If she attempts to manipulate price by acting as if her reservation price were $65, and if no one else attempts to manipulate price, the market-clearing price will lie between $60 and $65, and Fran's price manipulation will have worked to her own disadvantage since she will not sell her ticket.

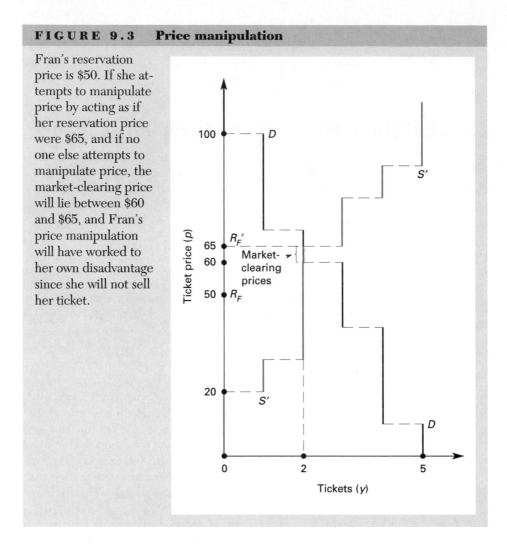

be traded. Alan and Dan will each buy a ticket, and Helen and Irene will each sell one. In this case, Fran's misrepresentation works to her disadvantage, since she ends up keeping a ticket she otherwise would have sold.

If she does not overdo it, then, Fran can manipulate the price of the tickets to her own advantage by misrepresenting her true position — and she may be tempted to do so. Of course, any of the demanders or suppliers could choose to play the role of the fox among the chickens. If one of the demanders — Earl, for example — is the price manipulator instead of Fran, and if the nine other students all represent their positions honestly, he could reduce the range of market-clearing prices from the interval $50 to $60 to the interval $50 to $52 by reporting the false reservation price $R_E' = \$52$. If Earl is the only price manipulator, reporting $R_E' = \$52$ would clearly be in his own best interest.

PROBLEM 9.3

Suppose that Earl chooses to report an even lower false reservation price, $R_E' = \$45$. What would be the range of market-clearing prices? How many tickets would be traded? Who would gain and who would lose as a result of this misrepresentation?

Why would any of the students then choose to be chickens (or price takers) rather than foxes (or price manipulators)? By misrepresenting their true reservation prices rather than reporting them honestly, all the students could potentially manipulate the market-clearing price to their own advantage. Yet if any of them chose to do so, the result might or might not be a competitive equilibrium. And, of course, the manipulator might or might not gain from the misrepresentation. The assumption of price-taking behavior is necessary because if students reported false reservation prices, the outcome might not be a competitive equilibrium.

Large Numbers and Price-Taking Behavior

One way out of this dilemma is to restrict our model to situations in which there are large numbers of both demanders and suppliers, none of whom demands or supplies a significant percentage of the quantity traded in a competitive equilibrium. In this case, it is reasonable to suppose that the gaps between reservation prices will be small. As a result, since no individual can significantly affect the market-clearing price by misrepresenting his or her true position, no individual has any incentive to try to manipulate price. If, for instance, out of 100,000 wheat farmers, one farmer chooses to report a false reservation price, the likely consequences are that price will not be significantly affected, and the lone manipulator will end up holding wheat that he or she would have preferred to sell at the equilibrium price.

Given large numbers of insignificant buyers and sellers, the competitive model is appropriate because all potential participants in the process of market exchange will see themselves as price takers rather than price manipulators. For this reason, economists typically assume large numbers of insignificant buyers and sellers in setting out a model of perfect competition.

Price Making: The Walrasian Auctioneer

We have now come to acceptable terms with one problematic assumption only to be confronted by another, more difficult one. In our simple model, we invoked the convenient artifice of a Walrasian auctioneer, who announced a price, adjusted the price up or down in response to excess demand or to excess supply, and cleared the market only at the equilibrium price, where quantity demanded was equal to quantity supplied. This artifice functions like the dramatic device of the *deus ex machina*, the god who brings a play to a harmonious conclusion by sorting out the muddled affairs of mere human beings.

Yet in the real world, there are only a few markets — the London Bullion Exchange is one — with an auctioneer who follows market-clearing rules such as those outlined in the ticket model. If we drop this assumption of a godlike auctioneer who brings about the competitive equilibrium, what is left? Where does the competitive equilibrium price come from?

In most real transactions, the price maker is the supplier or the demander (or both). In the market for groceries, for example, a Safeway outlet sets the prices, and grocery shoppers take them (or leave them). A tuna cannery sets the price it will pay for tuna, and a tuna fisher either sells the catch to the cannery or goes elsewhere. A ticket scalper at a major league ballpark quotes a price; a potential ticket buyer rejects it and offers another; the scalper rejects the buyer's price and makes another. The process continues until either the two strike a bargain or the potential buyer goes off to find another scalper.

In all these cases, price makers are constrained by the prices their competitors offer, because their potential customers (or suppliers) typically have the option of approaching someone else. Safeway cannot set prices higher than those their customers think they can get at the A&P, for example, without losing potential buyers to the A&P. The point remains, however, the individual suppliers or demanders are the price makers in most actual market transactions, transactions that are characterized by the process of offer and counter-offer.

Once we eliminate the assumption of the auctioneer, does any other assumption guarantee that a competitive equilibrium will result from the more characteristic real-world process of offer and counter-offer?

Perfect Information

Economists sometimes invoke the assumption of perfect information to fill the void created by the exodus of the auctioneer. The argument is that if all buyers and sellers are sufficiently well informed, then the process of offer and counter-offer will result in a competitive equilibrium price. Suppose that all the participants in the process of exchange set prices: buyers make bids to buy and sellers make offers to sell. Suppose, too, that every buyer knows the offer prices of all sellers and that every seller knows the bid prices of all buyers. All the buyers will approach the seller with the lowest offer price; the seller then raises it. Conversely, all the sellers will approach the buyer with the highest bid price; the buyer then lowers it. This process continues until all the bid and offer prices converge to the same price.

Will that common price — the price at the point of convergence — necessarily be a competitive equilibrium price? If it were not, there would be either excess demand or excess supply. If there were excess demand, some buyer or buyers, unable to buy anything at the common price, would raise their bid prices, and sellers would respond by raising their offer prices. At a common price, then, there can be neither excess demand nor excess supply. But this means that the common price that emerges from this process of offer and counter-offer in the presence of perfect information is necessarily a competitive equilibrium price.

The bedrock assumptions of the theory of competitive markets are thus the assumptions of large numbers (or of price taking) and of perfect information. Nevertheless, economists have achieved no unanimous agreement about whether either or both assumptions are necessary. The debate centers on whether or not a competitive equilibrium will result from voluntary market exchange even in the absence of large numbers of inconsequential buyers and sellers or of perfect information.

Robustness of the Competitive Model

Essentially, the issue is one of how well the model stands up — that is, how *robust* it is — when either one or both of these assumptions is not satisfied. Testing the robustness of an economic model can be very difficult because economics is not a laboratory science. Nevertheless, within the last three decades, some economists have conducted laboratory experiments that do bear directly on these two assumptions.

In the laboratory design, experimenters induce real people to exhibit specified reservation demand and supply prices for some artificial commodity chosen by the researchers. These kinds of experiments test the robustness of the competitive model. First, the typically small number of suppliers and demanders in the laboratory fails to meet the criterion of large numbers (or price taking). Second, the very limited information made available to each of these suppliers and demanders fails to satisfy the criterion of perfect information. Because the demand and supply functions are known to the experimenter, the equilibrium price and quantity predicted by a competitive model can be calculated and then compared with the results from the laboratory market. Furthermore, by using alternative trading institutions — the sets of rules governing the trading activity of the subjects — experimental economists can examine the robustness of the competitive model under a range of such institutions.

To what extent are the experimental results consistent with the predictions of the model of perfect competition? In summarizing the results from approximately 175 experiments, Vernon Smith (1982) concludes that they converge with astonishing speed to the competitive equilibrium. These experiments and others like them suggest that neither of the two assumptions is necessary for the model of perfect competition to provide a close approximation of what takes place in many real markets.

9.3
The Assumptions of Perfect Competition

Having looked at perfect competition in a simple exchange economy, we can now present a comparatively more complex treatment of the theory in markets where firms produce the goods demanded by consumers. We will begin by setting out the traditional assumptions on which the theory is built. The first two assumptions are now familiar, and the other two assumptions are new.

ASSUMPTION: LARGE NUMBERS
No individual demander buys and no individual supplier produces a significant proportion of the total output.

As we have seen, this assumption implies that all demanders and suppliers will be price takers.

We have already considered the role of perfect information in a simplified market environment in which goods are bought and sold but not produced Here, we will broaden the assumption somewhat to apply to more complex market environments in which goods are also produced.

ASSUMPTION: PERFECT INFORMATION
All participants have perfect knowledge of all relevant prices and of all relevant technological information.

This assumption means, on one hand, that firms know the prices of all the goods they could possibly produce, the technology for producing those goods, and the prices at which they could buy the required inputs. It means, on the other hand, that all individuals know both the prices at which they can buy all goods and the prices at which they can sell their resources in general and their labor in particular.

The third assumption concerns the nature of the products made for sale in a competitive market.

ASSUMPTION: PRODUCT HOMOGENEITY
In any given market, the products of all firms are identical.

This assumption limits the applicability of the competitive model to markets in which the products made by competing firms are virtually the same, or *homogeneous*. It rules out the application of the model to markets in which products are significantly differentiated, or *heterogeneous*. The model applies to the market for corn, for instance, because the corn produced by thousands of farmers in the American Midwest is virtually indistinguishable. But it does not apply to the automotive industry, for example, because no two firms make cars or trucks that are identical.

The fourth assumption concerns the possibility of switching resources from one use to another.

ASSUMPTION: PERFECT MOBILITY OF RESOURCES
All inputs are perfectly mobile.

If firms can freely allocate resources to different uses, they are then able both to expand (or to contract) their scale of production in a particular market and to enter (or to leave) the industry itself. As we will see later on in the chapter, this flexibility, or *mobility*, plays an important role in the theory of perfect competition.

The fifth assumption rules out a variety of externalities. It rules out, for example, the interdependent preferences you encountered in Problem 9.2.

ASSUMPTION: INDEPENDENCE
The preferences of each individual are independent of the consumption decisions of other individuals and the production decisions of firms. The production functions of all firms are independent of the consumption decisions of individuals and the production decisions of other firms.

Instances of interdependent preferences abound in everyday life. For example, people who are sensitive to second-hand smoke often base their own decisions about where to work or sit in a restaurant on the behavior of smokers in their vicinity. Rush-hour travellers typically make decisions about when and how to commute based on the behavior of other commuters in their area who drive to work, or take the bus, or walk, or stay at home. These are examples of interdependent preferences that are ruled out by the independence assumption. You have also encountered examples of interdependent technologies. In Chapter 1, for example, you saw that how much oil a particular oil company could pump from a common pool depended on the decisions of other oil companies with wells in the same reservoir: the more oil that other firms pumped from the common pool, the less a particular firm could pump out of it. This and related common property problems are examples of interdependent technologies that are likewise ruled out by the independence assumption. In Chapter 17, we consider the vexing problems — known as externality problems — that are raised by such interdependent preferences and technologies.

These five assumptions are the foundation on which we build the theory of perfect competition in the short run and in the long run.

The Firm's Short-Run Supply Decision

As we saw in the ticket exchange model, competitive equilibrium price and quantity are determined by the intersection of a demand and a supply function. Before we can implement this approach in a situation where firms supply goods and consumers demand them, we need the firm's short-run supply function.

What exactly is a short-run supply function? Just as an individual consumer's demand function for good Y tells us how much the consumer will demand at any given price p, so the individual firm's short-run supply function for good Y tells us how much the firm will supply at any given price p. Just as we found the consumer's demand function by solving the consumer's utility-maximizing problem, we can find the firm's short-run supply function by solving its profit-maximizing problem.

A firm's profit is simply the firm's revenue minus its cost:

$$\text{profit} = \text{revenue} - \text{cost}$$

total revenue function

Since the competitive firm is a price taker, its revenue is just price multiplied by the quantity produced, or py. It is convenient to call this expression the competitive firm's **total revenue function**, $TR(y)$. Thus,

$$TR(y) = py$$

In the short run, the competitive firm's cost is given by the short-run cost function $STC(y)$ from Chapter 7. We can therefore express the firm's profit as a function of its output y in the following way:

$$\pi(y) = TR(y) - STC(y)$$

profit function

We will call $\pi(y)$ the firm's **profit function** because this function gives us the firm's profit as a function of its output y.

Notice that profit depends on both price p and output y. But, since the competitive firm is a price taker, price is an exogenous variable — one that the firm cannot choose. It can choose its own output, however, and y is therefore the endogenous variable in this profit-maximizing problem. The problem we want to solve is then

$$\text{maximize profit } \pi(y) \text{ by choice of output } y$$

short-run supply function

The solution to this problem will give us the profit-maximizing output, which we will denote by y^*, as a function of the exogenous variable p. This function is called the firm's **short-run supply function**. Keep in mind that all relevant prices are held constant in this exercise — the price of the firm's output p is constant, and the prices of all the inputs the firm uses are also held constant.

In Figure 9.4a, the firm's total revenue function is the line py, and its short-run cost function is the curve STC. Because p is fixed, the total revenue function is a straight line whose slope is p: each additional unit of output adds p to the firm's total revenue. The short-run cost function is the standard stylization from Section 7.4.

The profit function $\pi(y)$ in Figure 9.4b is derived from the two functions in Figure 9.4a by subtracting cost $STC(y)$ from revenue py for every value of y. For example, when output is 33, profit is the distance CD in Figure 9.4a. Therefore, the distance C′D′ in Figure 9.4b is equal to the distance CD in Figure 9.4a. Notice, too, that in Figure 9.4a, revenue is equal to cost at two levels of output — at 25 and at 56. Therefore, in Figure 9.4b, profit is equal to zero at these output levels. Finally, notice that profit is negative when output is less than 25 or when it is greater than 56.

The profit-maximizing output in Figure 9.4 is clearly $y^* = 44$. What can we say about this level of output that will help us to identify the firm's profit-maximizing rule and, therefore, its supply function? The crucial observation is that the slope of the profit function is zero at $y^* = 44$ or, putting the same observation differently, that the rate of change of profit with respect to output is zero at the point where profit is a maximum. To see why, notice that if the slope of the profit function is positive (as it is to the left of 44 units of output in Figure 9.4b), the firm can increase profit by increasing output. Conversely, if the slope of $\pi(y)$ is negative (as it is to the right of 44 units of output), the firm can increase profit by decreasing output. We can summarize this result :

FIGURE 9.4   **Profit maximization**

In (a), we have drawn the short-run total cost function *STC* and the total revenue function *TR*. Subtracting *STC* from *TR*, we derive the profit function $\pi(y)$ in (b). Profit is maximized at $y^* = 44$, where the slope of the profit function is zero.

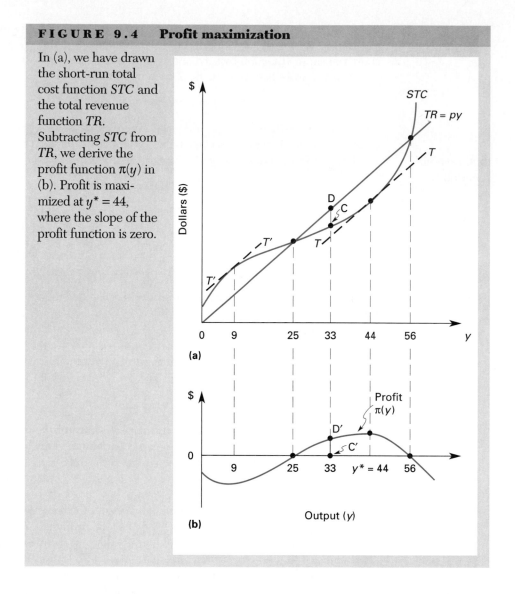

The rate of change of profit with respect to output is zero at the point where profit is a maximum.

marginal
revenue

short-run
marginal cost

But the rate of change of profit with respect to output is simply the rate of change of total revenue with respect to output — **marginal revenue** *MR* — minus the rate of change of cost with respect to output — **short-run marginal cost** *SMC*. So, to maximize profit, the firm chooses the quantity of output where *MR* minus *SMC* is equal to zero, or where *SMC* is equal to *MR*. For a price-taking firm, *MR* is constant and equal to price p, since each unit of output contributes p to the firm's revenue. To maximize profit, therefore, the firm will choose the level of output y^* at which $SMC(y^*)$ is equal to *MR*, which itself is equal to price p. That is,

$$SMC(y^*) = MR = p$$

To understand this result, let us return to Figure 9.4a. Line TT, which is tangent to $SC(y)$ at $y^* = 44$, has the same slope as the total revenue function. This means that SMC is equal to MR at 44 units of output. As a result, the slope of the profit function is zero at $y^* = 44$.

We seem to have found a simple rule of thumb for the profit-maximizing firm:

**Produce the level of output at which marginal revenue (or price)
is equal to marginal cost.**

This rule requires qualification, however, because SMC is equal to MR at two levels of output in Figure 9.4 — at 44 units, where profit is a maximum, and at 9 units, where profit is a minimum. And as we will see, the firm's profit-maximizing rule requires yet another qualification.

Although the diagram in Figure 9.4 is fine for finding the profit-maximizing output for one price, it is not useful for finding the profit-maximizing output for many different prices. The "marginal revenue equals marginal cost" rule suggests that to find the firm's supply function, we need a diagram that includes MR and SMC. In Figure 9.5, we also included the average variable cost function $AVC(y)$ to illustrate an additional qualification. We will show that the firm's short-run supply function is composed of the two segments labeled ss in Figure 9.5.

FIGURE 9.5   The competitive firm's supply function

The competitive firm's supply function is composed of the two segments labeled ss. When p is less than \$23, the firm supplies nothing because it cannot cover the variable costs associated with any positive quantity. When p exceeds \$23, the firm chooses the level of output where $p = SMC$. Thus, the second segment of the firm's supply function is SMC above the point where SMC intersects AVC.

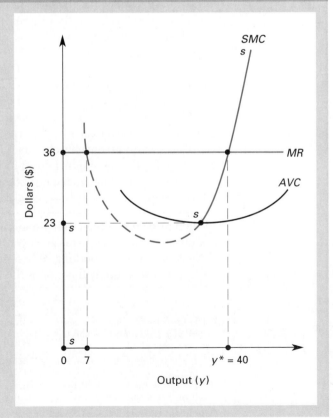

Let us begin by identifying the profit-maximizing output when price is $36 in Figure 9.5. We know that the horizontal line running through $36 and labeled *MR* is marginal revenue when price is $36, since marginal revenue is equal to price. Notice that marginal cost is equal to marginal revenue, or *SMC* = *MR*, at two levels of output: 7 and 40. From Figure 9.4 we know that one of these levels of output maximizes profit and the other minimizes it. Which is which?

Profit is a maximum at 40 units because $SMC(y)$ intersects *MR* from below. To see why, suppose that the firm is producing 40 units. What will happen to its profit if the firm produces an additional unit? The added cost of the extra unit is given by *SMC* and the added revenue by *MR*. Because *SMC* exceeds *MR* to the right of 40 units, the added unit of output adds more to cost than to revenue, and profit falls. Beginning again at 40, what will happen to the firm's profit if it produces one less unit of output? The reduction in revenue is given by *MR* and the reduction in cost by *SMC*. Since *MR* exceeds *SMC* to the left of 40 units, the decrease in revenue exceeds the decrease in cost, and profit falls once again. Profit is therefore a maximum at 40 units.

On the other hand, profit is a minimum at 7 units because *SMC* intersects *MR* from above. To see why, let us suppose that the firm is producing 7 units. What will happen to its profit if the firm produces an additional unit? The added cost of the extra unit is given by *SMC*, and the added revenue by *MR*. Because *SMC* is less than *MR* to the right of 7 units, the increase in cost resulting from an additional unit of output is less than the increase in revenue, and profit rises. Beginning again at 7 units, what will happen to the firm's profit if it produces one less unit of output? The reduction in revenue is given by *MR* and the reduction in cost by *SMC*. Since *MR* is less than *SMC* to the left of 7 units, the decrease in revenue is less than the decrease in cost, and profit rises once again. Profit is therefore a minimum at 7 units.

These results suggest a rule that can be used to identify the profit-maximizing output for any price: move horizontally from price to the rising portion of *SMC* and then vertically down to the quantity axis. The firm's supply function therefore seems to be the rising, or positively sloped, portion of *SMC*.

This rule, however, needs a final qualification. Notice that in Figure 9.5, average variable cost is never less than $23 since the minimum value of *AVC* is $23. This means that at any price less than $23, the firm cannot cover its variable costs of production if it produces a positive quantity of output. Because it can avoid these variable costs of production altogether by shutting down production, when price is less than $23, the firm will maximize profit by producing nothing at all. The firm's supply curve in Figure 9.5 is then composed of the two segments labeled *ss*. These results are easily generalized:

> When price is less than the minimum value of *AVC*, there is no positive level of output at which the firm can cover its variable costs of production, and it will therefore produce nothing. When price is greater than the minimum value of *AVC*, the firm's supply function is the rising portion of *SMC* that lies above *AVC*.[1]

---

1 The firm's supply function is derived by solving its profit-maximization problem: maximize $\pi(y)$ by choice of y. Differential calculus tells us two useful things about the profit-maximizing value of y, y^*, in the event that $y^* > 0$.

1. If $\pi(y)$ is differentiable, then $\pi'(y^*) = 0$. That is, a necessary condition for $y^* > 0$ to be the profit-maximizing value of y is that $\pi'(y)$ be equal to zero at y^*.
2. If $\pi'(y^*) = 0$ and $\pi''(y^*) < 0$, then $\pi(y)$ attains a (local) maximum at y^*. That is, $\pi'(y^*) = 0$ and $\pi''(y^*) < 0$ are sufficient conditions for $\pi(y)$ to attain a (local) maximum at y^*.

These two statements allow us to find the firm's supply function. Application of the first yields

$$p - STC'(y^*) = 0$$

FIGURE 9.6   The profit rectangle

When $p = \$36$, the firm supplies $y^* = 40$. Its profit is 40 multiplied by [$\$36\,(p) - \$26\,(AVC)$], or the area of the profit rectangle.

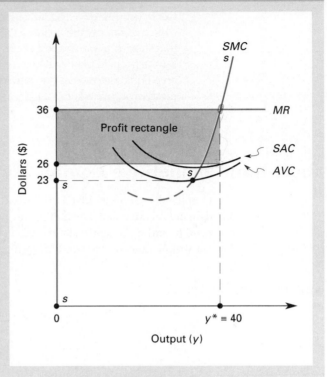

Now let us find a way to represent the firm's profit using a similar diagram. Profit is simply total revenue py^* minus short-run total cost $STC\,(y^*)$. $STC(y^*)$ is equal to output multiplied by short-run average cost, or $y^*SAC(y^*)$. The firm's profit can therefore be expressed as

$$\pi(y^*) = y^*[p - SAC(y^*)]$$

By adding SAC to the diagram, we can identify the firm's profit as well as its supply function. In Figure 9.6, the firm's profit when p is \$36 can be identified by area labeled profit rectangle. The vertical side of the profit rectangle is price minus short-run average cost, $p - SAC$. The horizontal side is the profit-maximizing output y^*. The area of the profit rectangle is then $y^*(p - SAC)$, or the firm's profit.

---

or

$$p = MC(y^*)$$

because $STC'(y)$ is $MC(y)$. The second statement is satisfied at y^* if $STC''(y^*) > 0$ or, equivalently, if $MC'(y^*) > 0$. $MC'(y^*) > 0$ simply means that the marginal cost function is rising at y^*. That is, $\pi''(y^*) < 0$ tells us that only the rising portion of the marginal cost function is relevant. Of course, y^* will be zero if p is less than the minimum value of $AVC(y)$, because in this case there is no positive output that will allow the firm to recover its variable costs.

PROBLEM 9.4

Construct your own diagram of Figure 9.6, and suppose that p is $24. In your diagram, identify the quantity that the firm will supply at this price. Notice that short-run average cost at this level of output is greater than $p = $24, so the firm's profit is negative. Construct a rectangle in your diagram with area equal to the firm's negative profit. Why would a firm ever produce a positive output when it makes a negative profit by doing so?

Short-Run Competitive Equilibrium

Graphically, a competitive equilibrium is determined by the intersection of a market demand function and a market supply function. To get the market demand function we need to add up or aggregate demand over individual demanders, and to get the market supply function we need to aggregate supply over individual firms.

Aggregating Demand

First, we will examine the *market demand function*. We have assumed that all demanders are price takers, and in Chapter 3 we used the same price-taking assumption to derive individual demand functions. To find the market demand function for any particular good, we need a way to aggregate individual demand functions. Figure 9.7 illustrates the process of aggregation for two demanders. The individual demand functions for good Y are labeled AA' and BB', and the line labeled BCD represents the aggregation of these two individual demand functions, or the market demand curve when there are just two consumers in the market. This market demand curve is constructed by choosing a price, finding the quantities of good Y demanded by each of the individuals at that price, summing the quantities to locate one point on the aggregate demand function, and then repeating the process for all other possible prices. When the price is $4, for instance, the buyer whose demand function is AA' will demand 5 units; the buyer whose demand function is BB' will demand 11 units; and their aggregate demand is 16 units. The point (16,4), is therefore one point on the market demand function. [2]

Implicit in this aggregation procedure is the assumption that quantity demanded by one individual is independent of quantity demanded by other individuals. This indepen-

---

2 Let us consider an algebraic example. Suppose the two individual demand functions are

$$p_1 = \frac{1}{y_1} \qquad \text{for the first individual}$$

$$p_2 = \frac{10}{y_2} \qquad \text{for the second individual}$$

The aggregation question is this: Given a common price, say $p = p_1 = p_2$, what is the aggregate quantity demanded? To answer the question, we first write y_1 and y_2 as functions of the common price p (that is, $y_1 = 1/p$, $y_2 = 10/p$) and then add to obtain

$$y_1 + y_2 = \frac{1}{p} + \frac{10}{p} = \frac{11}{p}$$

In aggregating the supply functions of individual firms, the same procedure is necessary. Since we are interested in obtaining the aggregate quantity supplied at any price, we must write the quantity supplied by any firm as a function of the common price before adding.

FIGURE 9.7   Aggregating demand

The individual demand functions are AA' and BB', and the aggregate demand function is BCD. When price is $4, one person demands 5 units and the other 11 units. Together they demand 16 units, and (16,4) is therefore one point on the market demand function.

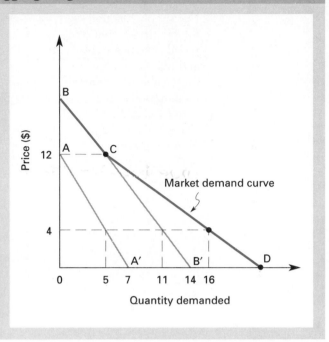

dence follows from the independence assumption — which guarantees that the preferences of any individual are independent of the consumption decisons of other individuals.

PROBLEM 9.5

Why is the aggregate demand function coincident with BB' when price exceeds $12 in Figure 9.7? What is distance 0D in Figure 9.7?

PROBLEM 9.6

Suppose there are 1,000 individuals with the following demand function for good Y:

$$\text{Quantity demanded} = 1 - .001p$$

Show that the market demand function is $y = 1,000 - p$, or that the market demand curve is $p = 1,000 - y$.

Aggregating Short-Run Supply

It is now a simple matter to calculate the short-run market supply function by aggregating the short-run supply functions of all firms in the market. To illustrate the aggregation procedure, we have constructed the market supply function in Figure 9.8 for a case in which there are two firms in a market. One firm's supply function is represented by the two segments 0A and BC, and the other firm's by the two segments 0A' and B'C'. The aggregate, or market supply function, is composed of the three segments labeled SS in Figure 9.8.

FIGURE 9.8 Aggregating supply

The supply function for one firm is composed of segments 0A and BC; the supply function for the other is composed of segments 0A′ and B′C′. The aggregate supply function is composed of the three segments labeled SS.

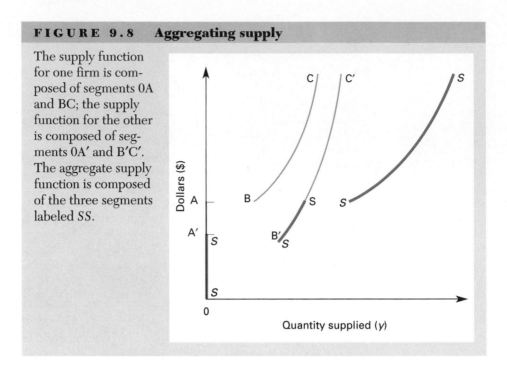

Like the demand aggregation procedure, the supply aggregation procedure is based on an implicit assumption — that the quantity supplied by any firm is independent of quantity supplied by others firms. The independence assumption guarantees that the production function of any firm, and therefore its short-run marginal cost function, is independent of the production decisions of other firms. In the following problem, you can check your understanding of this aggregation procedure.

PROBLEM 9.7

Suppose that 100 firms — each with the following short-run supply function for good Y — are in a particular market:

$$\text{quantity supplied} = .01p$$

Show that the market supply function is

$$y = p$$

Short-Run Competitive Equilibrium

We can now identify the short-run competitive equilibrium by finding the price at which quantity demanded equals quantity supplied. This equilibrium is represented in Figure 9.9b by the intersection of the market supply and market demand functions at point (y^e, p^e). The competitive equilibrium price is p^e, and the quantity exchanged at this price is y^e. The position of a representative firm in this market is illustrated in Figure 9.9a.

Because the scales on the two (vertical) price axes are identical, we can project the market price p^e from Figure 9.9b into Figure 9.9a. Notice, however, that the scales on the two (horizontal) quantity axes are not the same because the representative firm's output, 15 units, is only a small fraction of the total market output y^e.

Notice that once again the independence assumption plays a role in the analysis. The equilibrium in Figure 9.9b makes sense only if 1. the market demand function is independent of quantity supplied and 2. the market supply function is independent of quantity demanded. The first assumption is satisfied if the preferences of individuals are independent of the production decisions of firms, and the second is satisfied if the production functions (and therefore supply functions) of firms are independent of the consumption decisions of individuals. The independence assumption guarantees that these conditions are met. To get some practice with short-run competitive equilibrium, try the following comparative statics exercise.[3]

PROBLEM 9.8

Suppose that firms are forced to pay an excise tax of $10 per unit on every unit of output they sell. Show that this tax shifts each firm's supply curve vertically upward by $10. What happens to the market supply curve? If the demand curve is vertical — that is, if demand is perfectly price inelastic — what happens to equilibrium price when this tax is imposed? If the demand curve is not perfectly price inelastic, show that the price increases will be less than $10.

---

3 We can use differential calculus to see the precise nature of this sort of comparative statics question. For example, suppose that we are interested in the effect that a change in the price of mangoes p_M will have on the equilibrium price of apples p_A. Write the demand for apples as

$$y = D(p_A, p_M)$$

to reflect the possibility that the demand for apples is affected by the price of mangoes. Because different soil conditions and climates are needed to produce mangoes and apples, the supply of apples will not depend on the price of mangoes; so we write the supply of apples as

$$y = S(p_A)$$

In equilibrium, we have

$$D(p_A{}^e, p_M) = S(p_A{}^e)$$

where $p_A{}^e$ is the equilibrium price of apples. Now, totally differentiate this equilibrium condition to obtain

$$D_2(p_A{}^e, p_M)dp_M = [S'(p_A{}^e) - D_1(p_A{}^e, p_M)]dp_A{}^e$$

and solve for $dp_A{}^e/dp_M$: the rate of change of the equilibrium price of apples with respect to the price of mangoes:

$$\frac{dp_A{}^e}{dp_M} = \frac{D_2(p_A{}^e, p_M)}{[S'(p_A{}^e) - D_1(p_A{}^e, p_M)]}$$

The denominator on the right is ordinarily positive since $S'(p_A)$ is likely to be positive and $D_1(p_A, p_M)$ negative. Therefore, the sign of $dp_A{}^e/dp_M$ turns on the sign of $D_2(p_A, p_M)$. For example, if apples and mangoes are substitutes, then $D_2(p_A, p_M) > 0$ and therefore $dp_A{}^e/dp_M > 0$. Chapters 9 and 10 of Samuelson (1947) are devoted to the method of comparative statics analysis in economics.

FIGURE 9.9 **Short-run competitive equilibrium**

In (b), the competitive equilibrium price is p^e and quantity is y^e. In (a), the representative firm supplies 15 units at the equilibrium price p^e. The light green area in (b) is aggregate consumers' surplus, and the dark green area is aggregate producers' surplus.

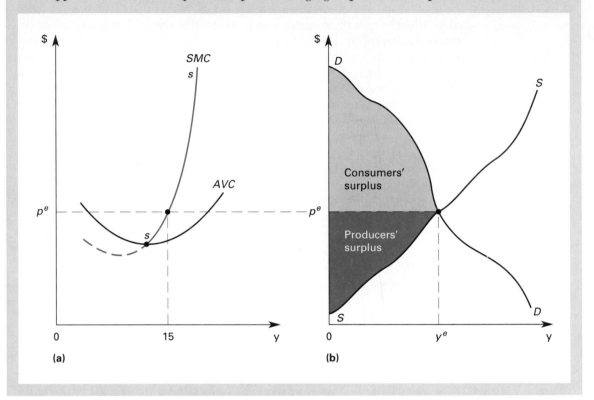

(a)

(b)

9.6

Efficiency of the Short-Run Competitive Equilibirum

At the beginning of this chapter, we saw that the competitive equilibrium of the exchange economy model was Pareto-optimal, or efficient. Is the equilibrium in Figure 9.9 similarly efficient? Because every firm in this competitive equilibrium is producing at the point where price equals short-run marginal cost, no firm can sell an additional unit of output at a price that will cover its short-run marginal cost of producing that additional unit. Remember, too, that the short-run marginal cost of a unit of output is just the market value of the variable inputs needed to produce the unit. If we think of firms in the short run as trading variable inputs (processed into good Y) for consumers' dollars, we recognize that the potential gains from trade are fully realized in this equilibrium. Once the competitive equilibrium is attained, it is impossible to sell an additional unit of output at a price that will cover the market value of the added resources needed to produce it. In this sense, the short-run competitive equilibrium is efficient.

Having an economic measure of the gains from trade is useful in many circumstances. (We will be using such a measure in this and subsequent chapters.) In Figure 9.9,

consumers'
surplus

we can identify gains to both consumers and firms. The aggregate measures of these gains are known, respectively, as **consumers' surplus** — indicated by the light green area of Figure 9.9b — and producers' surplus — indicated by the dark green area. But where do these measures come from and what do they mean?

We introduced the notion of one consumer's surplus in Section 4.2. (You may want to review that discussion briefly.) Consumers' surplus in competitive equilibrium is just the sum of the surplus enjoyed by all consumers at the competitive equilibrium price. As we noted in Section 4.2, however, consumers' surplus is a theoretically well-grounded benefit measure only in the special case in which the consumer's indifference curves are vertically parallel — the case in which quantity demanded of Y is unresponsive to the consumer's income. If the indifference maps of all consumers are characterized by such parallel indifference curves, then CS can be used without hesitation as a measure of aggregate consumers' benefit. If consumer demand for Y is responsive to income, however, we can use CS as long as we recognize that it is just a rough-and-ready approximation of consumers' benefits.

producers'
surplus

Producers' surplus is a measure of benefits to the owners of firms. The measure of benefit to any one owner would seem to be a profit measure. In the short run, the appropriate measure is revenue minus variable cost since the firm's fixed cost is just that — fixed. **Producers' surplus** is calculated by subtracting aggregate variable cost from aggregate revenue. Aggregate revenue is the rectangle in Figure 9.9b with sides p^e and y^e. Since the supply curve is the marginal cost of output, aggregate variable cost is the area under the supply curve SS from the origin to y^e. Thus, producers' surplus, calculated by subtracting aggregate variable cost from aggregate revenue, is indicated by the dark green area in

total surplus

Figure 9.9b.[4] The sum of consumers' surplus and producer's surplus — called **total surplus** — is a measure of the aggregate gains from trade realized in this market.

PROBLEM 9.9

In Problems 9.6 and 9.7, you found the following market demand and supply functions

$$\text{market demand} = 1,000 - p$$

$$\text{market supply} = p$$

First, find the competitive equilibrium and draw a diagram to illustrate it. Then compute consumers' and producers' surplus in this equilibrium. (Remember that the area of a triangle is 1/2 its base multiplied by its height.)

Because the aggregation procedures used to define these measures of benefit are simply to add up the benefits accruing to all individuals without any regard to the distribution of those benefits, they are *cost-benefit measures* of benefit. Wherever we use them, we are implicitly invoking the controversial assumption discussed in Section 1.6 that a dollar of benefit is a dollar of benefit — regardless of who gets it.

---

4 It is important to keep in mind that the calculation of producers' surplus is based on the assumption that input prices are constant. If there are substantial changes in input prices as industry output expands, then the producers' surplus calculation is misleading.

9.7

Long-Run Competitive Equilibrium

Although new firms cannot enter or leave the industry in the short run, they can *enter* or *exit* in the long run. Therefore, in the long-run analysis we need to distinguish between established firms (those already in the market) and potential firms or entrants (those not yet in existence). If, for instance, the market is house painting, the established firms are the commercial house painters currently in business. The potential entrants are house-painting firms that have not yet been established, firms, for example, that are just twinkles in some entrepreneurial student's eye.

No-Exit, No-Entry, and Long-Run Equilibrium

There are two obvious requirements, or conditions, of long-run equilibrium:

1. No-exit condition: In long-run equilibrium, no established firm wants to exit the industry.
2. No-entry condition: In long-run equilibrium, no potential firm wants to enter the industry.

The no-exit condition implies that the long-run equilibrium price p^e must be high enough that each established firm makes at least zero profit. The no-entry condition implies that p^e must be low enough that no potential entrant could earn positive profit.

Notice the economic role of profit as a signal guiding the allocation of resources in the long run.

> Positive profit is a signal that induces entry, or the allocation of additional resources to the industry. On the other hand, negative profit is a signal that induces exit, or the allocation of fewer resources to the industry.

To put the role of profit as signal guiding the allocation of resources in proper perspective, it is important to bear in mind that profit and cost — as we use the terms — are economic, not accounting, concepts. In the economic calculation of cost, all inputs that are used by the firm are valued at their opportunity cost. To produce its output in any period, say a year, a firm uses variable inputs, like labor and electricity, and capital inputs, like buildings and machines. The opportunity cost calculation for variable inputs is straightforward — they are valued at market prices. If the market wage of a tool-and-die maker is $40 per hour, this price is used to value the labor services of tool-and-die makers used by the firm during the year. For capital inputs, however, the opportunity cost calculation is more subtle. Capital inputs are valued at the maximum price they would fetch in some other use. Consider a firm's warehouse, for example. The opportunity cost of the warehouse is the maximum amount that another user would pay to rent the warehouse for the year. In contrast, accountants value capital inputs based on their historical cost and on somewhat arbitrary rates of depreciation. Thus the economist's conception of cost is an economic conception based on the opportunity cost of inputs, not an accounting conception. Similarly, the economist's conception of profit — revenues minus economic costs — is an economic, not an accounting concept.

Two factors determine the menu of long-run production choices open to established firms: the long-run average cost function *LAC* and the possibility of exiting the industry. (We will use the U-shaped stylization of *LAC* in Figure 9.10 throughout the analysis, even though other stylizations are possible.) Established firms can decide to pro-

FIGURE 9.10   Exit, entry, and long-run competitive equilibrium

The no-exit condition is violated for any price less than c', the minimum average cost. And the no-entry condition is violated for any price larger than c'. The only price that satisfies both conditions is c'. Therefore, the long-run competitive equilibrium price p^e is equal to the minimum average cost c'.

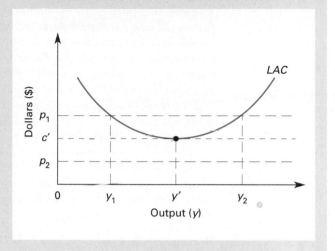

duce at any point on *LAC* in Figure 9.10, or they can decide to exit — to buy no inputs. The choices open to entrants are much the same. They can enter the market by producing at some point on *LAC*, or they can stay out of the industry.

To talk more easily about the position of any particular firm in the long-run competitive equilibrium, we need some terminological shorthand. We will call the level of output at which long-run average cost attains its minimum value the **efficient scale of production**. In Figure 9.10, the efficient scale of production is y' units of output. And we will call the average cost at the efficient scale of production the **minimum average cost**. In Figure 9.10, minimum average cost is c'.

efficient scale of production

minimum average cost

Price Equal to Minimum Average Cost

The no-exit and no-entry conditions imply that the long-run competitive equilibrium price is equal to the minimum average cost. To see why, suppose the price were higher than c' — say, p_1 in Figure 9.10. Because p_1 exceeds *LAC* for any level of output larger than y_1 but smaller than y_2, potential entrants anticipate making a positive profit at any such level of output. In the long run, then, new firms will enter the industry when price is p_1. That is, because the no-entry condition is not satisfied, price p_1 cannot be the long-run equilibrium price. Because an analogous argument applies to any other price higher than c', we see that the no-entry condition implies that the long-run equilibrium price cannot exceed the minimum average cost.

Now suppose that the price were less than c' — say, p_2 — in Figure 9.10. Because *LAC* now exceeds p_2 at all levels of output, all established firms will incur losses. In the long run, profit-maximizing firms will leave the industry. That is, because the no-exit condition is not satisfied, p_2 cannot be the long-run equilibrium price. Because an analogous argument applies to any other price less than c', we see that the no-exit condition implies that the long-run equilibrium price cannot be less than the minimum average cost.

Since p^e cannot exceed c' and cannot be less than c', it must equal c'. That is:

In long-run equilibrium, price is equal to the minimum average cost.

The Individual Firm in Long-Run Equilibrium

Knowing that price equals minimum average cost, we also know the position of every firm in the long-run equilibrium. In Figure 9.11, y' is the only output level at which an established firm can cover its cost of production when price is equal to c'. To avoid losses at the equilibrium price, each must be producing at the efficient scale of production y'. This, in turn, means that each firm will be on the short-run average cost function SAC tangent to LAC at y' in Figure 9.11. From the relationship between marginals and averages developed in Chapters 7 and 8, we also know that both long-run and short-run marginal cost functions will pass through the point (y', c'). We can summarize these results by the following series of equalities:

In long-run equilibrium, marginal revenue is equal to price, which is equal to the minimum average cost of production, which in turn is equal to long-run average cost, short-run average cost, long-run marginal cost, and short-run marginal cost:

$$MR = p^e = LAC(y') = SAC(y')$$
$$= LMC(y') = SMC(y')$$

Long-Run Supply Function

long-run supply function

We can use the properties of equilibrium to develop what is called the **long-run supply function** (*LRS*). The long-run competitive equilibrium is then determined by the intersection of *LRS* and the demand function. We will consider three cases: industries characterized by constant costs, by increasing costs, and by decreasing costs. In the short run, we assumed that all input prices were constant. As we derive *LRS*, we will incorporate changes in input prices that arise as industry-wide output expands or contracts. These changes in input prices determine whether any particular industry is a constant-cost, increasing-cost, or decreasing-cost industry.

FIGURE 9.11   The firm in long-run competitive equilibrium

In long-run competitive equilibrium, each firm produces at the efficient scale of production y', and price is equal to the minimum average cost c'. As a consequence, $p^e = c' = LAC = LMC = SMC = SAC$.

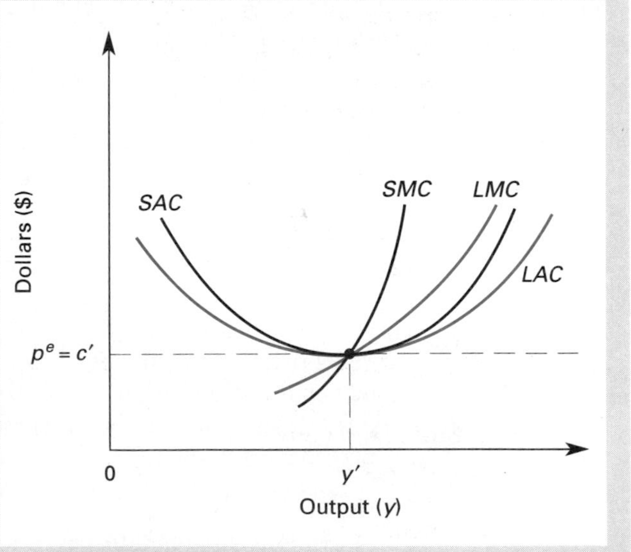

As the aggregate output of a certain industry expands or contracts, the aggregate quantities of the inputs used in that industry will correspondingly expand or contract. If egg production goes up, for instance, the amounts of hens, chicken coops, and chicken feed required by egg producers will also go up. And as input requirements increase, the price of any particular input will either remain constant, increase, or decrease. These three possibilities determine the three cases of constant-cost, increasing-cost, and decreasing-cost industries.

The Constant-Cost Case

In the constant-cost case, as the aggregate quantity of output produced changes, the prices of all inputs remain constant. Because in the constant-cost case the prices of all inputs are independent of aggregate industry output, the various cost functions for individual firms will not change as industry output changes. In particular, neither the efficient scale of production nor the minimum average cost will change as aggregate industry output expands or contracts. The position of a representative firm in long-run equilibrium will always be exactly as shown in Figure 9.11, and the long-run competitive equilibrium price will always be c'. This means that LRS must be a horizontal line through c', as in Figure 9.12, because this is the only possible shape such that any market demand function will intersect LRS at price c'. If the market demand function in Figure 9.12 is DD, for instance, the long-run equilibrium quantity will be y_1; if it is $D'D'$, the long-run equilibrium quantity will be y_2. In both cases, the long-run equilibrium price is c'.

A Dynamic Story

If market demand changes, how will an industry characterized by constant costs move from one long-run equilibrium to another in response to that change? Let us suppose

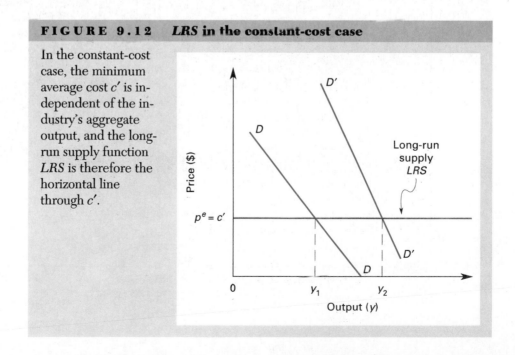

FIGURE 9.12 **LRS in the constant-cost case**

In the constant-cost case, the minimum average cost c' is independent of the industry's aggregate output, and the long-run supply function LRS is therefore the horizontal line through c'.

that the industry initially is in the long-run equilibrium at point E in Figure 9.13b. The representative firm in Figure 9.13a is producing y' units of output in response to the initial long-run equilibrium price of c'.

In Figure 9.13b, the short-run supply function SS is the aggregation of SMC over all firms in the industry; that is, SS is the short-run supply function in the initial equilibrium. Then for n identical firms, the aggregate output in the initial equilibrium at point E is ny'.

Suppose that the demand function now shifts from DD to $D'D'$ in Figure 9.13b because one of the exogenous variables has changed. For example, it might shift because the price of a substitute has risen or because the price of a complement has fallen. In the short run, the price of the good will increase to p'', and each established firm will expand its output to the point where short-run marginal cost equals price p''. In other words, each firm will produce y'' in Figure 9.13a, and their aggregate output will be ny'' in Figure 9.13b. Because in the short run p'' exceeds SAC, each firm will be earning a profit. Furthermore, because p'' exceeds LMC, established firms have a long-run incentive to further expand their output. Given the price p'', in the long run they would

FIGURE 9.13   Pseudodynamics in the constant-cost case

The initial demand and supply functions in (b) are DD and SS, and the the initial equilibrium is at E. The representative firm in (a) produces y', and the n firms in the industry produce aggregate output equal to ny'. The demand function now shifts to $D'D'$, producing the short-run equilibrium price p''. At this price, each firm produces y'', and

aggregate output is ny'' in the short-run equilibrium. Because p'' exceeds c', new firms will enter the industry. This process of long-run adjustment through entry will continue until there are n' firms each producing y', so that price is driven back down to c'. In the new long-run equilibrium at E', the short-run supply function is $S'S'$.

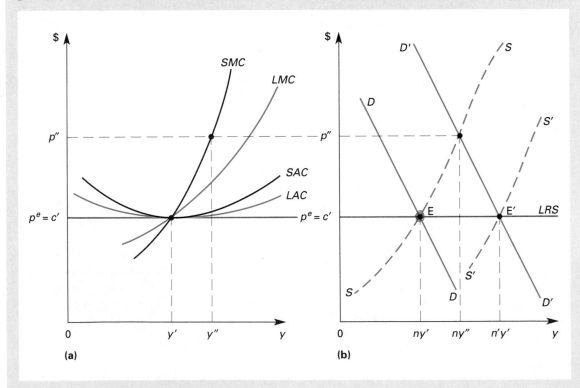

(a)   (b)

choose the output level where long-run marginal cost equals p''. More important, because p'' exceeds c', the shift in demand will also spur new firms to enter the industry.

The supply response to this shift in demand is then twofold: established firms expand their production, and new firms enter the industry. However, as established firms expand and as new firms enter, the short-run supply function shifts to the right, and the short-run equilibrium price drops. We have not shown this short-run market supply function or the short-run equilibrium associated with it because as long as the price exceeds minimum average cost c', new entrants can still earn a profit and will therefore enter the industry. This entry will continue until the price is driven back down to c'.

When price is again equal to c', the only level of output that does not create losses for the representative firm is, once again, y'. In the new long-run equilibrium, each firm will again produce output y' at long-run average cost equal to c'. If n' is the new and larger number of firms in the new long-run equilibrium at E', the aggregate output will be $n'y'$. The short-run supply function at the new long-run equilibrium, labeled $S'S'$ in Figure 9.13b, will then be the aggregation over n' firms of the short-run marginal cost function SMC in Figure 9.13a.

Our account of the adjustment from one long-run equilibrium to another contains some serious deficiencies. In both the initial and the subsequent long-run equilibria, each firm is in the position shown in Figure 9.11. Yet during the adjustment process, price is obviously not equal to c'. If firms took these transient nonequilibrium prices as given and if they expected them to be maintained, their long-run decisions would lead them to produce at a point where long-run marginal cost is equal to the nonequilibrium price. Of course, as the price changes, these firms would discover that they had made the wrong long-run decision.

This scenario suggests that if firms have any foresight, they will realize that these nonequilibrium prices will not be maintained indefinitely and therefore will decide against basing their long-run decisions on these prices. To analyze their decisions in this case, we would need a theory of how firms form their expectations about the path of future prices when the industry is in disequilibrium. But since we have no such theory, we have no adequate theory of decision making in disequilibrium. We have only a theory of equilibrium, not a theory of the dynamics of market adjustment as an industry shifts from one long-run equilibrium to another.[5]

The Increasing-Cost Case

In many industries, as the industry-wide output expands and as the quantities of inputs demanded therefore increase, the prices of some or all of those inputs will also increase. Where inputs are natural resources, this input-price response is almost universally true. Mining firms that supply ore, for example, naturally exploit the richest and most accessible ore bodies first. As more ore is demanded, they move on to poorer, less accessible ore bodies. As they do so, the cost per unit of ore rises.

In industries where inputs are characterized by increasing costs, what will the long-run supply curve look like? As aggregate industry output increases and as the prices of at least some inputs also increase, the minimum average cost of production must rise. Therefore, as industry-wide output increases, the long-run equilibrium price — which is equal to the minimum average cost of production — must also increase. This

---

5 Frisch (1936) provides an interesting discussion of the very troublesome problem of choice in disequilibrium.

means that the *LRS* must be upward sloping. The increasing-cost case is illustrated in Figure 9.14. Given the demand function *DD*, the long-run equilibrium price is p_1 and quantity is y_1. Given $D'D'$, the long-run equilibrium price is p_2 and quantity is y_2.

Although we cannot discuss the process of adjustment rigorously, we can consider a mock dynamic exercise similar to the one for the constant-cost case. The exercise allows us to identify some of the forces at play in the adjustment process and to compare the size of a representative firm in the initial and the subsequent equilibria.

Suppose that at an initial equilibrium, each of *n* firms supplies y' units of output at a long-run equilibrium price equal to the initial minimum average cost of production c'. The position of a typical firm is presented in Figure 9.15a. The aggregate quantity ny' supplied by these *n* firms at price c' is one point on the long-run market supply function, and *SS* is the initial short-run supply function. What will happen if demand now shifts from *DD* to $D'D'$? The price of the good will initially rise and — just as in the constant-cost case — the firms in the market will earn profit. In the short run, established firms will again respond by expanding output. This profit also acts as a spur to potential entrants, and new firms will enter the market.

As a result, the industry as a whole will demand more inputs and, by definition, the price of some inputs will increase. As input prices increase, each firm's cost of production will also increase. In particular, the efficient cost of production will increase, and each firm's long-run average cost function will therefore shift upward. Suppose for the moment that in the long run the efficient scale of production does not change. That is, suppose that *LAC* shifts directly upward, as shown in Figure 9.15a, rather than upward and to the

FIGURE 9.14 *LRS* **in the increasing-cost case**

In the increasing-cost case, efficient average cost increases as industry output increases. Thus, *LRS* is upward sloping. In response to a shift of the demand function from *DD* to $D'D'$, output in long-run equilibrium increases from y_1 to y_2, and equilibrium price increases from p_1 (the minimum average cost in the initial equilibrium) to p_2 (the minimum average cost in the subsequent equilibrium).

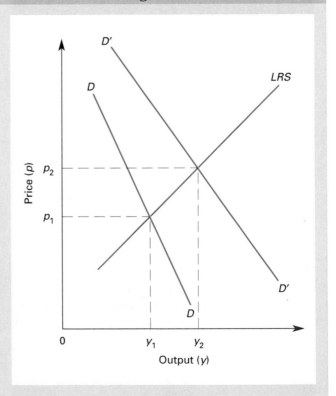

left or to the right. Because of the upward shift in each firm's *LAC*, the quantity of output produced by each firm in the new long-run equilibrium will still be equal to y', but the equilibrium price will equal the new — and higher — minimum average cost c''.

In response to this shift in demand, the number of firms increases from n to n', short-run supply shifts to $S'S'$, the long-run equilibrium price of the good increases from c' to c'', and the marketwide output increases from ny' to $n'y'$. The quantity $n'y'$ at price c'' in Figure 9.15b, is therefore another point on the long-run market supply function, labeled *LRS*.

Because we assumed that the efficient scale of production y' did not change, the increase in industry-wide output in the long run was necessarily achieved by new firms entering the industry. But if the efficient scale of production had increased — if *LAC* had shifted up and to the right — the story would have been different. For example, the increase in efficient scale might have been so large that no new entry was required. Indeed, the number of firms actually might have decreased as industry output expanded. On the other hand, if the efficient scale had decreased — that is, if *LAC* had shifted up and to the left — the number of firms required in the new equilibrium would be larger than n'.

FIGURE 9.15   Pseudodynamics in the increasing-cost case

Given the demand function *DD*, price in the initial equilibrium is c', each firm produces y', and aggregate output is ny'. When demand shifts to $D'D'$, the short-run equilibrium price is p'. At this price, new firms will enter and established firms may expand. As this process of industry expansion occurs, input prices are pushed up, shifting up the long-run average cost function. In the new long-run equilibrium, the long-run average cost function has shifted up to *LAC'*, and price has been driven up to c'', the minimum average cost in this long-run equilibrium.

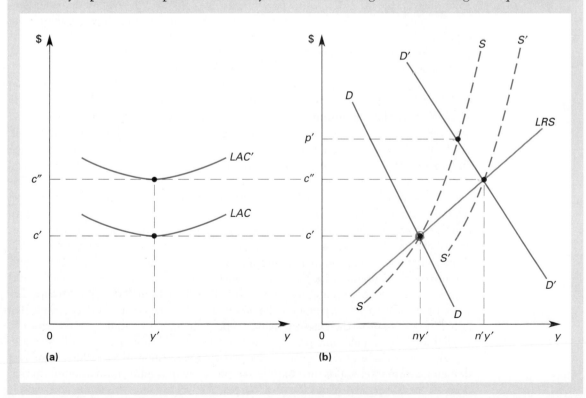

(a)

(b)

The Decreasing-Cost Case

It is also possible that the prices of some inputs might decrease as industry demand for them increases. Although examples of such inputs are not easy to find and the decreasing-cost case is rare, we will summarize this possibility quickly. As you can verify easily, if the prices of some or all inputs decrease (and if the prices of the remaining inputs are constant) as the aggregate quantity of inputs demanded increases, the *LRS* will be downward sloping.

9.8

Comparative Statics

When we characterized industries as belonging to one of three categories — constant costs, increasing costs, or decreasing costs — and saw how firms in each category moved from one long-run equilibrium to another in response to shifts in market demand, we accomplished two related tasks. We created a theory of equilibrium price and quantity and a theory of the allocation of resources to markets. Let us take some time to put these results into perspective by considering some comparative statics exercises. Let us consider what happens to equilibrium price and quantity when market demand shifts and when market supply shifts. (You should be able to verify the following results by constructing the relevant demand and supply diagrams.)

The market demand function for a good can shift for any number of reasons. Tastes may change, causing a shift in market demand. For example, in the 1980s, there was apparently no demand for "grunge" clothing or the "stair-climber" exercise machines that became popular in the early 1990s. So, too, the price of either a substitute or a complement for the good may change, causing the market demand for that good to shift accordingly. If the price of a substitute for good *Y* goes up, then the market demand function for good *Y* will shift upward and to the right. For example, if coffee becomes more expensive, the demand for tea will shift upward and to the right. If the price of a complement goes up, the opposite will occur. For example, if a ski-lift ticket becomes more expensive, the demand for ski-equipment rentals will shift down and to the left.

Suppose that for some reason the demand function for good *Y* does shift up and to the right. In all three cases — constant costs, increasing costs, and decreasing costs — both short-run equilibrium price and quantity will increase. In the constant-cost case, however, the long-run equilibrium quantity will increase, but long-run equilibrium price will remain unchanged. In the increasing-cost case, both long-run equilibrium price and quantity will increase. In the decreasing-cost case, long-run equilibrium price will decrease, but long-run equilibrium quantity will increase.

Let us turn now to changes in market supply. Again, a number of factors can cause a shift in the market supply function. Technological change — the development of more efficient production processes, for example — can cause shifts in market supply functions. So can changes in the prices of inputs. If the price of a variable input goes up, both the short-run and the long-run market supply functions will shift upward and to the left. For instance, the dramatic increases in the price of crude oil in the 1970s caused a shift in the supply functions for a whole range of plastic products, including plastic cups, because crude oil is an essential input in the production of many plastics. Suppose, then, that either the short-run or the long-run market supply function does shift up and to the left. In all three cases, equilibrium price will increase and equilibrium quantity will decrease.

As we saw earlier, these kinds of price and quantity responses to changes in market demand and market supply are merely symptomatic of a more fundamental market process: the competitive allocation of resources. We will examine this topic more closely in Chapter 16. For now, we will simply highlight the role that competitive markets play by contrasting the competitive equilibrium to the outcome that results when an impediment to market exchange is imposed. By a market impediment, we mean anything that alters the ability of suppliers and demanders to voluntarily exchange goods or services free of institutional interference. The classic example of such an impediment is rent control.

*9.9
Rent Control

We began this chapter with a model in which goods were exchanged, but not produced. The central message to emerge from that model was that prices serve as signals to guide the allocation of goods to their most productive uses. Specifically, we saw that the allocation of goods associated with the competitive equilibrium price is Pareto-optimal. We will close the chapter by viewing allocation from a different perspective, as we explore a case in which prices are *not* allowed to perform their allocative function.

price ceiling

We will look at a case in which a **price ceiling** is imposed in a competitive market. Specifically, we will think in terms of a particular market for rental housing in which the price ceiling is popularly known as rent control. Our model will capture important features of actual rental housing markets where there are government-imposed rent controls. It will not be directly applicable to any of them, however, because any real market is characterized by significant variation among rental units. For example, some units are detached houses, others are duplexes, and still others are apartments in very large apartment complexes. Some units have a superb view or access to recreational facilities, and others offer almost no amenities. By contrast, in this model, we will assume that all rental units are *identical*.

In addition, real rent-control laws vary widely from one jurisdiction to another. In some jurisdictions, rent-control legislation has almost no real impact on rental prices, while in others the ceiling on rental prices is substantially below the competitive equilibrium price and is strictly enforced. In some jurisdictions, rent control applies to all rental units, while in others it applies only to older units. Rent-control laws are often complex and sometimes involve an elaborate enforcement mechanism. In some locales, controls are placed on the rental price itself while in other places, controls are placed on the rate of increase in rental prices.[6] By contrast, in this model, rent control is just a rent ceiling, and — although we will consider some enforcement issues — the model itself does *not* provide for an enforcement mechanism.

The Rent Control Model

Let us imagine that in any month there are 1,000 demanders of rental housing units. We will call all these people renters, the rental units apartments, the renters who are looking for an apartment searchers, and the renters who occupy an apartment tenants. Each renter's demand can be described by a *reservation price*, and, as we learned in Section 9.1, the market demand curve is then composed of 1,000 vertical segments. For simplicity, we have approximated this segmented curve in Figure 9.16 by a smooth market demand curve.

Because real rental markets cater to the housing needs of people such as students who move frequently, *rental turnover* is an important feature of any such market. To capture turnover in this model, we will assume that each month 2% of the 1,000 renters

---

6 For a more detailed discussion, see "rent control" by Kurt Klapholtz in *The New Palgrave*.

leave this market and are replaced by other renters with identical reservation prices. As a result, the market demand curve remains the same, but the population of renters changes from month to month as renters enter and leave the market.

Like the market demand curve, the long-run supply curve is composed of a large number of vertical segments reflecting a reservation supply price for each apartment. (Below we will consider more carefully the factors that determine reservation supply price.) Once again, we have approximated this segmented curve in Figure 9.16 by a smooth long-run supply curve.

Since the decisions to replace and maintain rental units are important in real rental markets, we will assume that apartments last for a finite period of time and that they require periodic maintenance. Specifically, we will adopt the following assumptions. Each apartment is owned by one landlord and accommodates one renter. Maintenance entails the expenditure of $50 per month. Each new apartment lasts for 120 months (10 years) if it is maintained every month. If maintenance is not done in a given month, the apartment becomes uninhabitable. In any event, it becomes uninhabitable after 120 months.

In a competitive equilibrium, it makes no difference who actually pays the monthly maintenance. If the tenant pays the maintenance cost, the equilibrium rental price for an apartment is lower by $50 than if the landlord pays. For simplicity, we will assume that the landlord pays for maintenance.

FIGURE 9.16   **The economics of rent control**

In the absence of rent control, the equilibrium price and quantity would be $p^e = \$500$ and $y^e = 600$ apartments. Relative to this competitive equilibrium, the rent-control equilibrium — in which the price ceiling is $400 and quantity of rental housing supplied is 450 apartments — has several properties. The dark green area represents surplus that is apparently transferred from landlords to tenants. The light green area represents the surplus that is de-

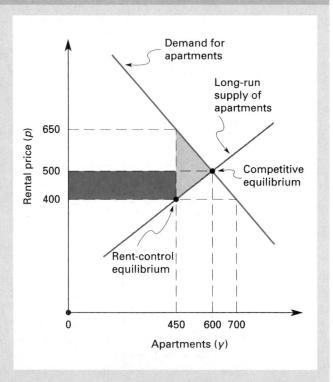

stroyed (or the potential gains from trade that are not realized). At the $400 price ceiling, there is excess demand for 250 apartments (700 − 450). Because this rental price cannot increase, this excess demand will result in phenomena such as excessive search costs and under-the-table deals.

Let us suppose that this market is initially in the long-run equilibrium shown in Figure 9.16, where the rental rate is $500 per month and 600 apartments are supplied. Now suppose that a rent ceiling of $400 per month is imposed in this market. What are the effects of this rental ceiling in the short run? In the long run? Who gains and who loses from rent control?

Apparent Effects of Rent Control

Assuming that this price ceiling is enforced, its impact seems to be straightforward. There is an apparent distributional effect, since each tenant seems to be better off by $100 per month and the owner of each apartment seems to be worse off by $100. When the $400 ceiling is imposed, income or surplus is then transferred from landlords to tenants. There are apparently no *short-run* allocational effects, since the initial allocation is Pareto-optimal, and no tenant has an incentive to move once the rental price falls to $400 per month. Yet the actual distributional and allocational effects may not be so clear-cut as the model initially suggests. Let us see what we might be overlooking.

Short-Run Effects

We can begin by looking at the allocation of the 600 existing apartments. To capture one important feature of real rental markets, we assumed a 2% turnover rate in this market. As some renters move on and others replace them, an average of 12 apartments are vacated and reallocated to new tenants in each month. The question we want to answer is this: What principles govern this reallocation of apartments? If the landlord gets only $400 per month, then price no longer guides allocation because from Figure 9.16 we know that there is excess demand at the $400 rental rate. Seven hundred renters want an apartment, but only 600 can be accommodated in the 600 existing apartments. If price does not perform the allocational role, what does?

Let us suppose for a moment that the addresses of all vacant apartments are published in the local newspaper and that the first searcher to get to a vacant apartment rents it. On average, 12 apartments will be vacated in each month, and a large number of searchers will be trying to rent them. If the effective price of an apartment averages only $400 per month, more than 100 searchers would be apartment hunting; however, as we will see, the effective price will actually be more than $400. Rent control thus creates a game, apartment hunting, played each month by a large number of searchers trying to rent just 12 apartments. It is this game that replaces price as the allocative mechanism.

If you have ever hunted for an apartment in a tight rental market, you will know how this game is played. The minute the local paper hits the streets, searchers thumb through the "for rent" section of the classified ads and then speed off to the closest advertised vacancy, hoping to be the first on the scene. Any more leisurely strategy is bound to fail when excess demand is significant at the rent-controlled price. Of course, the success rate will be small, meaning that a searcher who is new to the market must expect to spend a great deal of time and energy before finally finding an apartment. The costs of this search activity — gas, time, and wear and tear on the car and nerves — mean that the effective price of an apartment will be considerably more than the $400 paid to the landlord each month.

Viewed from another perspective, these search costs mean that some of the surplus available from the original 600 apartments is destroyed in the game of apartment hunting, which replaces price as the allocative mechanism under rent control. That is, attempting to use a rent ceiling to transfer surplus from landlords to tenants creates forces that tend to destroy some of that surplus. Because effective rent control confers a valuable monthly bonus on tenants, searchers willingly expend time, energy, and money to get access to this bonus, thereby dissipating its value.

The situation is closely analogous to the problem of allocating racquetball courts on a first come, first served basis in Section 4.6. In both cases, real resources are used to achieve an allocation that could have been achieved at lower cost by a price mechanism. We can draw a general conclusion:

> **The real costs of allocating a fixed quantity of some good or service are higher when a non-price allocative mechanism is substituted for a price mechanism.**

The next question is this: Who gets the vacant apartments? We cannot be exactly sure, since blind chance plays an important role in determining who gets to a vacant apartment first. But we can be sure about one thing: almost certainly, some renters with reservation prices lower than $500 will be lucky enough to get apartments. For example, in the very first month after rent control comes into force, most of the searchers will have reservation prices lower than $500. Therefore, we must expect these searchers to get most of the vacant apartments in that first month.

So far we have assumed that landlords advertise vacant apartments and rent to the first searcher who shows up. In reality, the landlord may not be willing to rent to the first searcher. Because there is excess demand, the landlord can afford to pick and choose among searchers based on his or her personal likes and dislikes. It is also possible, and even likely, that if excess demand is large enough, vacant apartments won't be advertised at all. The landlord (or the last tenant) may already know one or more searchers and may find it attractive to rely on these informal contacts rather than to deal with the large numbers of searchers who will respond to a formal ad.

Thus blind chance, the personal preferences of landlords, and personal contacts will all play some role in reallocating apartments as they become vacant. As a consequence, the allocation of apartments will not be Pareto-optimal because the 600 available apartments will not be allocated to the 600 renters with reservation prices greater than or equal to the long-run equilibrium price of $500. Instead, some of the 100 renters with reservation prices between $400 and $500 will inevitably manage to rent apartments because they are lucky enough to spot an ad first, or because some landlord likes their looks, or because they know the vacating tenant. Again, we can draw a general conclusion:

> **When the allocation of a fixed quantity of some good or service is not guided by price signals, the allocation need not be Pareto-optimal.**

To this point, we have assumed implicitly that the tenant pays and the landlord receives just $400 per month for any apartment. Even the most casual observation of real markets with rent control reveals that more money is likely to change hands. In New York City, "key money" means a bribe that a searcher pays a landlord for the privilege of signing an initial lease. In Toronto, a "sublet fee" means a bribe that a searcher pays a tenant to sublet a rent-controlled apartment. These bribes are so much a part of apartment hunting that often no attempt is made to be discreet about them. For example, the following advertisement appeared on a bulletin board in a convenience store located in a large rent-controlled apartment complex: "Wanted: one-bedroom apartment. Willing to pay $500 sublet fee."

Rent control can also be circumvented in more subtle ways. In this model, maintenance is the landlord's responsibility. Given the excess demand caused by rent control, the landlord has an incentive to pass the $50 per month maintenance cost to the tenant, while maintaining the rent-controlled price of $400. And the landlord can always find a tenant willing to pay the additional $50. If it is possible to do so, then, landlords will shift maintenance responsibilities to tenants. Alternatively, the landlord may be able to tie the lease of the apartment to the lease of furniture — charging just $400 to rent the apartment while overcharging for the furniture — thereby increasing the effective rental rate for the apartment.

These are just a few of the many possibilities for circumventing the intent of rent control. These can be thought of as informal and incomplete price mechanisms that emerge to fill the void created when the real price mechanism is suspended. They clearly work to reduce the extent of income redistribution and to increase the price of rent-controlled accommodations. The final conclusion to be drawn from the analysis of the short run is:

The actual extent of redistribution of income from landlords to tenants will be less than it initially appears to be.

Long-Run Effects

Before we can consider the effects of rent control in the long run, we need to think about what the *long-run reservation supply price* for an apartment actually means. Once an apartment becomes uninhabitable at the end of 120 months, the landlord faces a long-run investment decision: whether to build a new apartment or to convert the land to its next best use. For example, let us suppose that it will cost some landlord $60,000 to rebuild the apartment and that the landlord's next best option is to sell the land to a 7-Eleven convenience store for $50,000. The landlord's reservation supply price is a monthly rental price for the apartment such that he or she is indifferent between rebuilding the apartment and selling the land to 7-Eleven. If the rental price is p per month, the landlord's net monthly return is $\$(p - 50)$, since maintenance is the landlord's responsibility. The reservation supply price is then the value of $\$p$ such that the discounted present value of the net monthly return over 120 months, less the $60,000 rebuilding cost, is just equal to the $50,000 that 7-Eleven is willing to pay for the property. If the real rental rate is larger than this value, then the landlord will rebuild the apartment; if it is less than this value, he or she will sell the land to 7-Eleven.

To the extent that rent control reduces the net monthly return of landlords, the supply of apartments in the long run will diminish as some landlords decide to convert their land to alternative uses at the end of the 120 months. If we suppose for purposes of illustration that the $400 rent ceiling is effective, then we see from Figure 9.16 that just 450 apartments will be supplied in the long run. Thus, 150 potential landlords and potential tenants will be frozen out of the market by rent control. The surplus that is destroyed as a result is represented by the triangular shaded area in Figure 9.16. Notice, too, that in the long run, apartment hunting becomes a grim affair. Again assuming a turnover rate of 2% per month, many searchers will be looking and only nine apartments will be vacant each month.

Although we have learned that in the long run, the supply of rental housing will shrink under rent-control legislation, it is entirely possible that a significant drop in the supply might take place within a much shorter time span. For instance, one obvious response that landlords can and do make to rent control is to convert their rental units to owner-occupied units, which they then sell off to individual buyers. Renters in apartments and townhouses sometimes are evicted; their vacated apartments are then converted into condominium units and sold within a matter of months. Not surprisingly, in many rent-controlled jurisdictions, it is illegal to convert apartments into condominiums. Indeed, in some places it is illegal to demolish rental accommodation.

Let us briefly summarize what we have learned about the potential effects of rent control in this model. Some tenants will clearly be better off under rent control. In particular, tenants who occupy apartments when rent-control legislation is imposed will benefit. All landlords will be worse off, and some will be induced to convert their land to alternative uses, thereby reducing the supply of apartments. As a consequence of that reduced supply, some renters will be worse off. Under rent control, the ways in which available apartments are allocated both impose costs on searchers — thereby increasing the effective price of rental housing — and produce an allocation that is not Pareto-optimal.

Rent control is just one example of a market impediment. In the following problem, you can explore some implications of another market impediment — a **price floor**.

price floor

> ### PROBLEM 9.10
>
> In Section 1.3, we briefly considered two schemes for supporting the price of agricultural goods, the *price subsidy program* and the *buy-and-store program*. Identify the surplus destroyed and the implications for the public purse for each of these programs.

SUMMARY

A *market demand function* tells us the aggregate quantity of a good demanded by all consumers at any given price, and a *market supply function* tells us the aggregate quantity supplied by all suppliers at any given price. A *competitive equilibrium price* — determined by the intersection of market demand and market supply functions — is the price at which the quantity demanded exactly equals the quantity supplied. Although both a price and a quantity are determined in any competitive equilibrium, both are symptomatic of the more fundamental function served by any market: the *allocation of goods* to individual consumers.

We began the chapter with an elementary exchange-economy model that allowed us to concentrate on the properties of a competitive market allocation and examine two crucial (and problematical) assumptions of the competitive model. The most important property is that the allocation of goods in competitive equilibrium is Pareto-optimal: all the gains from trade are realized in the competitive equilibrium. However, this result requires careful qualification — a task we will take up in Chapters 16 and 17.

We used the device of the *Walrasian auctioneer* to find the competitive equilibrium in this exchange economy. In so doing, we implicitly assumed that all the economic actors behaved as price takers in responding to the prices announced by the auctioneer. This *price-taking assumption* raised an important conceptual difficulty: In what circumstances will individuals act as price takers rather than price manipulators? We found that individuals act as price takers when there are large numbers of insignificant buyers and sellers. This is the basis of the large-numbers, or price-taking, assumption, which is included in most models of perfect competition.

The presence of the Walrasian auctioneer raises yet another conceptual problem: In the absence of this device, is the competitive model still applicable? We found that it does apply if all buyers and sellers are perfectly informed. This is the basis of the *perfect-information assumption*, which models of perfect competition also include. These two conditions are really sufficient conditions for the applicability of the competitive model: if a market is characterized by large numbers and by perfect information, then the competitive model is applicable.

Because the world so rarely conforms to these two conditions, we naturally are led to ask if something less will do. This is the question at the heart of a great deal of recent work in experimental economics. The results to date suggest that less may well do: the competitive model seems to yield fairly good predictions even when numbers are small and information quite imperfect.

When we replaced the exchange model with a more complex competitive model incorporating both production and exchange, the supply function became more complicated. We discovered that (with suitable qualifications) a firm's *marginal cost function* is its *short-run supply function*. Then, by aggregating short-run supply functions over firms and demand functions over individuals, we were able to identify the *short-run competitive equilibrium*.

In the long run, the competitive model is driven by *exit* and *entry*. Taken together, these two processes imply that in long-run equilibrium, each firm will operate at the minimum point on its long-run average cost function and that price, marginal revenue, long-run average cost, short-run average cost, long-run marginal cost, and short-run marginal cost will be identical.

The *long-run competitive equilibrium* is determined by the intersection of the *long-run supply function* and the market demand function. The slope of a long-run supply function, *LRS*, depends on the nature of the response of input prices to an industry's demand for those inputs. *LRS* may be upward sloping, horizontal, or downward sloping, depending on whether the industry is characterized by increasing costs, constant costs, or decreasing costs.

Because in any competitive equilibrium with production, the competitive price is equal to the short-run marginal cost of each firm (and in any long-run equilibrium, price is equal to long-run marginal cost), no further gains from trade are possible. No customer is willing to pay what it costs any firm to produce an additional unit of output. This result, which we will examine in more depth in Chapter 16, is a reflection of the *Pareto optimality or efficiency of competitive equilibrium*.

We closed the chapter by considering a model of *rent control* — a common institution that results in a noncompetitive equilibrium. The detailed analysis of this noncompetitive equilibrium allowed us to put the allocative function of competitive prices in perspective. Of course, allocation is not the only function served by prices. They also determine the distribution of income. And rent control is just one of many noncompetitive institutions — including agricultural price supports, quotas, and minimum wages — that are intended to redistribute income or wealth. The appeal of all such institutions lies largely in their redistributionary impact. Yet they all result in an equilibrium that is not Pareto-optimal. The rent-control case thus serves to highlight a troubling issue in economics: the tension that often arises between the objectives of economic efficiency, or Pareto optimality, and distributional equity. In Chapter 14, we will analyze this problem of efficiency versus equity in more detail.

EXERCISES

1. Indicate whether each of the following statements is true, false, or uncertain, and explain your answer.

   a. In the short run, a competitive firm would never produce where *AVC* is downward sloping.

b. A competitive firm in long-run equilibrium in an increasing-cost industry will produce at a point where *LAC* is rising.

c. If *LAC* is U-shaped, the number of firms in a constant-cost industry will decrease in response to a decrease in demand.

d. In the short run, a competitive firm would never produce where *SAC* is downward sloping and *AVC* is upward sloping.

e. If a competitive firm is currently producing where *SAC* is upward sloping, then other firms will enter the industry.

f. If *LAC* is U-shaped, the number of firms in an increasing-cost industry will increase in response to an increase in demand.

g. A competitive firm in long-run equilibrium in a constant-cost industry will produce at a point where *LAC* is a minimum.

h. In the short run, a competitive firm would never produce where *SMC* is downward sloping.

i. A competitive firm in long-run equilibrium in a decreasing-cost industry will produce at a point where *SMC* exceeds *LMC*.

j. If a competitive firm is currently producing where *SAC* is downward sloping, then no other firms will enter the industry.

k. In long-run competitive equilibrium, all firms produce at a point where there are constant returns to scale in production.

l. If a competitive firm in short-run equilibrium is currently making zero profit, then no other firms will enter the industry.

2. Gismos are produced in a constant-cost industry by firms that have a U-shaped *LAC*. Minimum average cost is $2 and the efficient scale of production is 50 gismos. The demand for gismos is

$$p = 12 - .001y$$

where *p* is price and *y* is quantity of gismos.

a. In the long run, what are the equilibrium price and quantity of gismos? How many firms will produce gismos, and how much will each produce in equilibrium? What profit will each firm earn in equilibrium?

b. Now suppose the demand for gismos changes to

$$p = 16 - .001y$$

What are the equilibrium price and quantity of gismos? How many firms will produce gismos, and how much will each produce in equilibrium?

c. Suppose now that the government imposes an excise tax equal to $1 per gismo and that demand is as specified in b. What effect will this tax have on long-run equilibrium price and quantity? What can you say about the short-run effects of this tax, relative to its long-run effects?

d. Suppose now that the market for gismos is initially in the long-run equilibrium you described in a and that demand again shifts as in b. What could you say about the new long-run equilibrium if the gismo industry is an increasing-cost industry instead of a constant-cost industry?

3. The government of Tasmann is thinking about paying every milk producer a $100,000 annual subsidy. Supposing that milk production is a constant-cost industry in Tasmann and that milk producers have U-shaped average cost curves, what effect will this subsidy have on: 1. the long-run equilibrium price and quantity of milk, 2. the quantity of milk produced by each firm, and 3. the number of firms producing milk?

4. The government of Xanadu is going to impose one of two taxes on the widgit industry, which is a perfectly competitive, constant-cost industry in which firms have U-shaped average cost curves. One tax is a $2 per unit excise tax on widgits, and the other is a $1,000 lump-sum tax on each firm in the industry. The Secretary of Commerce has determined that the two taxes will raise the same tax revenue from each firm in the long-run equilibrium associated with each tax.

a. Which tax will widget consumers prefer?

b. What effect will the excise tax have on output per firm? What effect will the lump-sum tax have on output per firm?

5. The strawberry industry is perfectly competitive, and the cost function of a typical firm is

$$TC(y) = 100 + y^2$$

where *y* is crates of strawberries per day. The corresponding marginal cost function is

$$LMC(y) = 2y$$

What is $LAC(y)$? What is the efficient scale of production? Hint: LMC intersects LAC at the efficient scale of production. What is the minimum average cost? What is the long-run equilibrium price of strawberries?

6. In Chapter 8 we derived the following cost function for Tipple's Courier Service

$$TC(y,w_1,w_2) = y(w_1w_2 / 300)^{1/2}$$

This cost function is associated with the following constant-returns-to-scale production function,

$$y = (1{,}200z_1z_2)^{1/2}$$

The associated average and marginal cost functions are

$$LMC(y) = LAC(y) = (w_1w_2/300)^{1/2}$$

Given these cost functions, what is the long-run competitive equilibrium price? Claim: The number and sizes of firms in long-run competitive equilibrium are indeterminate even though long-run equilibrium price and quantity are perfectly well defined. Explain. What accounts for these curious results?

7. Firm F's short-run cost function is

$$STC(y) = 30y + y^2 + 400$$

and its short-run marginal cost function is

$$SMC(y) = 30 + 2y$$

a. If $p = \$50$, how much will this firm produce? What will its profit be? Is $p = \$50$ a long-run equilibrium price?
b. What is this firm's short-run supply function? Graph the supply function.
c. Find the price at which this firm would earn zero profit in the short run. Is this price a long-run equilibrium price?

8. Consider an industry in which there are 10 identical firms and 1,000 identical demanders. Each demander has the following demand function:

$$y = 1 - .005p$$

Each firm has the following short-run cost function:

$$STC(y) = 10y + y^2$$

The associated marginal cost function is

$$SMC(y) = 10 + 2y$$

a. What is the market demand function?
b. What is one firm's supply function?
c. What is the market supply function?
d. Construct a graph illustrating one firm's supply function, the market supply function, and the market demand function. What are short-run equilibrium price and quantity?
e. Suppose that firms must pay an excise tax equal to $10 per unit of output. Show that a firm's marginal cost function inclusive of the excise tax is

$$SMC(y) = 20 + 2y$$

Given the $10 excise tax, what is the market supply function, and what is the equilibrium price?
f. Compare the price increase associated with the excise tax with the tax itself. Why did price rise by less than the $10 tax?

*9. Governmentally imposed output restrictions of one form or another are notoriously popular with farmers. In Canada, for example, egg producers have lobbied successfully for quotas on egg production. Suppose that egg production is a constant-cost industry initially in long-run competitive equilibrium, that LAC is U-shaped, and that each farmer currently produces 5,000 eggs per day. Now suppose that each farmer is given a quota allowing the farmer to produce up to 4,000 eggs per day and the quotas can be bought and sold.

a. What impact will this quota system have on the price of eggs in the short run and in the long run?
b. What impact will it have on the number of eggs produced by a typical firm in the short run and the long run?
c. What impact will it have on the number of firms in the long run?
d. Who benefits and who is harmed by this quota system? In particular, do future egg farmers benefit from this quota system?
e. What sort of enforcement problems do you think the quota system might raise?
f. Will this quota system be more attractive to established egg farmers when the demand for eggs is inelastic with respect to price or when the demand is elastic with respect to price?

*10. The production of gasoline in the United States is an increasing-cost industry because the price of crude oil increases as gasoline producers demand more crude oil. Suppose that the supply of crude oil to the United States from the Middle East is cut off. What impact will this have on *LRS* for gasoline? On the equilibrium price and quantity of gasoline in the U.S. market? In response to this disruption in the supply of crude oil, imagine that an effective ceiling is imposed on the price of gasoline. Write a short essay on the probable impacts of the price ceiling. Address the following questions. How will the available supply of gasoline be allocated? Will the allocation be Pareto-optimal? Will the allocation process needlessly use real resources? Will a black market for gasoline emerge? Relative to the free-market equilibrium, who will benefit from the price ceiling and who will be hurt by it? What sorts of enforcement issues are likely to arise?

REFERENCES

Frisch, R. 1936. "On the Notion of Equilibrium and Disequilibrium," *Review of Economic Studies,* 3:100–5.

Joyce, P. 1984. "The Walrasian Tatônnement Mechanism and Information," *Rand Journal,* 15:416–25.

Klapholtz, K. 1987. "Rent Control," in *The New Palgrave: A Dictionary of Economics*, J. Eatwell, M. Milgate, and P. Newman (eds.), London: The Macmillan Press.

Marshall, A. 1920. *Principles of Economics*, 8th ed., New York: Macmillan.

Samuelson, P. A. 1947. *Foundations of Economic Analysis*, Cambridge, Mass.: Harvard University Press.

Smith, V. 1982. "Markets as Economizers of Information: Experimental Examination of the 'Hayek Hypothesis,'" *Economic Inquiry*, 20:165–79.

CHAPTER 10

Monopoly

Now we turn from the competitive market to its extreme opposite: monopoly. Imaginatively, this is a shift from the New York Stock Exchange (a market characterized by many buyers and sellers) to local telephone service (a market served by a single firm). We begin by defining monopoly and analyzing how a monopolist chooses price and quantity, and we discover that the monopoly equilibrium is not Pareto-optimal. Next, we identify the sources of monopoly power and consider a number of public policy responses to monopoly. Then, we look at several kinds of price discrimination — the extremely clever pricing strategies monopolists can and do use.[1]

10.1

Monopoly Defined

monopoly

A firm is a **monopoly** if no other firm produces either the same good or a close substitute for it. This definition of monopoly is unavoidably ambiguous because we cannot define "close substitute" with perfect precision. For example, we might decide to call General Motors (GM) a monopolist in Corvettes because only GM makes Chevrolet Corvettes. But are any (or all) of the sports cars produced by Jaguar, BMW, Mercedes-Benz, or Nissan close substitutes for a Corvette? So, too, the Detroit Tigers are the only major-league baseball team in Detroit. But are the Tigers a monopolist in the Detroit market? Or are either (or both) of Detroit's major-league football or basketball teams — the Lions or the Pistons — close substitutes? Or is a television all-sports network a close substitute? Whether either GM or the Detroit Tigers is technically a monopolist is unclear.

Telephone service is a less ambiguous case. In most communities, only one firm provides local service. We can imagine substitutes for the telephone service — carrier pigeons, smoke signals, or the government mail service, but none of these seems similar enough to phone service to be a close substitute.

How can we be certain that a conceivable substitute is a close substitute? One way to systematically distinguish substitutes that are "close" enough is to ask whether a change in the price of any substitute substantially changes the demand for the good or service in question. This is simply a *cross-price elasticity measure* of the demand for one good (steel or cellophane, for example) to a change in the price of another good (aluminum or

---

1 For an overview of the material in this chapter, see "monopoly" (Edwin G. West) and "natural monopoly" (William W. Sharkey) in *The New Palgrave*.

waxed paper, for example.)[2] If none of the cross-price elasticities is large, then none of the potential substitutes is close enough. The firm can then be regarded as a monopoly.

Why is this qualification about close substitutes so important? Suppose that two firms produce two distinct products but that these products are close substitutes. For example, the New York City Opera and the Metropolitan Opera Company offer similar kinds of musical entertainment to New Yorkers. How much profit each company makes depends both on its own pricing decisions and on its competitor's pricing decisions. When the Met thinks about cutting the price of a season ticket, for example, it must also anticipate the New York City Opera's reaction to the price cut. The Met's profit from any price cut depends on whether or not the New York City Opera decides to lower its own season-ticket price in response. In considering the pricing decisions of firms such as the Met or the New York City Opera, the presence of close substitutes necessarily muddies the waters because pricing decisions are *interdependent*. We will look further at these complex pricing scenarios in the following two chapters on oligopoly. By contrast, a monopolist does not need to concern itself with how other firms will react to its decision. As a result, the theory of monopoly is considerably simpler than the theory of oligopoly.

In the last chapter, we thought of the competitive firm as choosing quantity to maximize profit, which is total revenue minus total cost. Once again in this chapter we will think of the firm — in this case, a monopolist — as choosing quantity to maximize profit. The analysis is similar in important respects. In particular, in both cases the profit-maximizing problem is solved by finding the output where marginal revenue MR is equal to marginal cost MC. Nevertheless, the monopolist's problem is more complex because, for a monopolist, price and marginal revenue are endogenous variables — chosen by the monopolist — while, for the competitive firm they are exogenous variables — determined by impersonal market forces. Before turning to the monopolist's profit-maximizing decision we must sort out the relationships among a number of revenue concepts.

The Monopolist's Revenue Functions

market demand curve

For the monopolist, the relationship between price p and output y is determined by the **market demand curve**; that is,

$$p = D(y)$$

Thus, given any quantity y, price p is determined by the demand curve $D(y)$. This market demand curve is the aggregation of quantity demanded over all the monopolist's consumers. We will suppose that the market demand curve is downward sloping — the more the monopolist wants to sell, the lower its price must be.

average revenue

We assume that the monopolist sells all the units it produces at the same price. Price can then be interpreted as **average revenue** AR. Since all units are sold at the same price, the average amount any unit contributes to the firm's revenue is the price at which it is sold. Then, for any quantity of output y the market demand curve $D(y)$ de-

total revenue

termines both price p and average revenue AR. **Total revenue** $TR(y)$ is then just quantity y multiplied by average revenue or price $D(y)$.

$$TR(y) = yD(y)$$

---

2 You may want to review the definition of cross-price elasticity in Section 3.11.

Marginal Revenue

Recall that for a competitive firm both price and marginal revenue are exogenous variables. Indeed, because a competitive firm has no control over price, marginal revenue is equal to price. For the monopolist, both price and marginal revenue are endogenous variables, determined by the monopolist's choice of output. This is the fundamental difference between a monopolist and a competitive firm.

marginal revenue

Marginal revenue $MR(y)$ is, of course, the rate at which total revenue $TR(y)$ changes as output y changes. What is the relationship between price (or average revenue) and marginal revenue for a monopolist? When the monopolist's output is *positive*, marginal revenue is *less than price*.

To understand this important result, keep in mind that the monopolist sells all units at the same price and has a downward sloping demand curve. Because the demand curve is downward sloping, to sell an additional unit the monopolist must lower price. Therefore, its marginal revenue is less than the price at which the additional unit is sold by an amount equal to the quantity originally sold multiplied by the price reduction. Suppose that the monopolist in Figure 10.1 is initially at point A, where it is selling 3 units at price $82. To sell one additional unit — or 4 units in total — it must reduce its price by $6 from $82 to $76. The resulting change in total revenue, approximately equal to marginal revenue, is $58 — or $304 (4 multiplied by $76) minus $246 (3 multiplied by $82). This change is $18 less than $76, the price at which the fourth unit sold. The $18 difference between price and marginal revenue is equal to the original 3 units sold multiplied by the $6 price reduction. In Figure 10.1, the shaded area represents the revenue

FIGURE 10.1 The monopolist's marginal revenue

Beginning at point A, suppose that the monopolist drops price by just enough to sell one additional unit of output. The change in total revenue, which approximates marginal revenue, is the area of the shaded rectangle ($76) minus the area of the cross-hatched rectangle ($18).

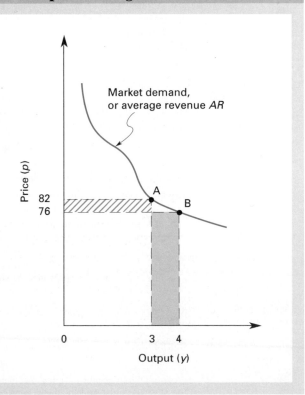

generated by selling the fourth unit at $76, and the cross-hatched area represents the revenue lost by reducing the price on the original three units by $6.

For a more precise understanding of the relationship between marginal revenue and price or average revenue, let us consider a more general experiment. Suppose initially that the monopolist is on its market demand curve, selling y units at price p and generating total revenue equal to py. Now suppose it reduces price by amount Δp and that quantity demanded increases by amount Δy, generating total revenue $(p - \Delta p)(y + \Delta y)$. The resulting change in total revenue is then

$$p\Delta y - y\Delta p - \Delta p\Delta y = (p - \Delta p)(y + \Delta y) - py$$

Now divide the left-hand side of this expression by Δy to express this relationship as a rate of change with respect to output:

$$[p - \Delta p] + y[-\Delta p/\Delta y]$$

To find marginal revenue, we let Δp approach zero. As Δp approaches zero, the first term in square brackets approaches p. The second term in brackets — $[-\Delta p/\Delta y]$ — is approximately the slope of the demand curve at the initial point. As the price change Δp gets smaller and smaller, the approximation gets better and better, and in the limit as Δp approaches zero, the approximation is perfect. Thus, as Δp approach zero, we get the following expression for marginal revenue:

$$MR(y) = p + y(\text{slope of the demand curve})$$

In other words:

Marginal revenue MR is equal to price p plus quantity y multiplied by the slope of the demand curve.

In this expression, p captures the rate at which revenue increases as an infinitesimal additional amount is sold at price p. This term is analogous to the added revenue generated in Figure 10.1 when a fourth unit is sold at a price of $76. The rate at which price must be decreased in order to sell an infinitesimal additional amount is given by the slope of the demand curve. Of course, it is negative because the demand curve is downward sloping. Therefore, the second term — $y(\text{slope of the demand curve})$ — captures the rate at which revenue on the original y units drops as price is decreased to sell an infinitesimal additional amount. This second term is analogous to the reduction in the revenue from the original three units in Figure 10.1 when price is reduced from $82 to $76 to sell a fourth unit.

Since the slope of the demand curve is negative, we get an important relationship between price and marginal revenue for a monopolist:

For any positive output, the monopolist's marginal revenue is less than its price.[3]

---

3 Letting $D(y)$ be the demand function, we have
$$TR(y) = yD(y)$$
Marginal revenue is, of course, just the derivative of $TR(y)$. Differentiating $TR(y)$, we have
$$MR(y) = D(y) + yD'(y)$$
which is clearly less than price as long as y is positive; that is,
$$D(y) + yD'(y) < D(y)$$
because $D'(y)$ is negative. Notice, too, that the demand and marginal revenue functions must intersect the price axis at the same point since, when y is zero, marginal revenue is equal to price.

Marginal Revenue and the Price Elasticity of Demand

Economists sometimes find it convenient to express marginal revenue in terms of the *price elasticity of demand,* introduced in Section 3.8. Price elasticity of demand at a point (y, p) on the demand curve can be written as

$$\eta(y) = p/[y(\text{slope of the demand curve})]$$

Combining this expression with the earlier expression for marginal revenue yields

$$MR(y) = p[1 + 1/\eta(y)]$$

Price elasticity $\eta(y)$ is, of course, a negative number since the slope of the demand curve is negative. It is instructive to rewrite the relationship between marginal revenue and the price elasticity of demand in terms of the absolute value of price elasticity — $|\eta(y)|$.

$$MR(y) = p[1 - 1/|\eta(y)|]$$

Notice that marginal revenue is positive if $|\eta(y)|$ exceeds 1 and negative if $|\eta(y)|$ is less than 1. In other words:

Marginal revenue is positive if demand is elastic with respect to price, and it is negative if demand is inelastic with respect to price.

These results are intuitive. Suppose, for example, that demand is elastic with respect to price. Then, for a marginal decrease in price, the proportionate increase in quantity is larger than the proportionate decrease in price, and total revenue increases or, equivalently, marginal revenue is positive. In contrast, if demand is inelastic with respect to price, for a marginal decrease in price, the proportionate increase in quantity is smaller than the proportionate decrease in price, and total revenue decreases or, equivalently, marginal revenue is negative.

Linear Demand Curve

So far, we have formed the total revenue function, defined marginal and average revenue, and discovered that marginal revenue is less than price, or average revenue, for any positive quantity of output. To give you a better sense of what these relationships mean, we will explore in some detail the special (and simpler) case in which the demand curve is a straight line. We will be using such linear demand curves at several points in this and subsequent chapters.

The linear demand curve in Figure 10.2a can be written algebraically as

$$p = a - by$$

where a and b are positive constants. The total revenue function for this market demand function is y multiplied by $a - by$, or

$$TR(y) = ay - by^2$$

This total revenue function is plotted in Figure 10.2b and labeled *TR.*

Two features of this *TR* function are immediately apparent. First, when output is zero, total revenue must also be zero. Second, when output is equal to a/b, total revenue must

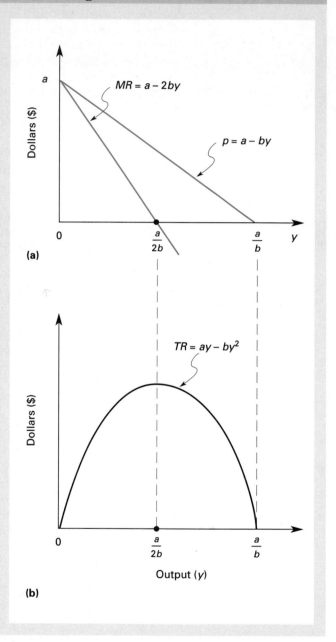

FIGURE 10.2   A linear demand function and the associated total and marginal revenue functions

The linear demand function $p = a - by$ intersects the price axis in (a) at a and the quantity axis at a/b. The associated marginal revenue function MR is also linear. It, too, intersects the price axis at a, but it is twice as steep as the demand function and therefore intersects the quantity axis at $a/2b$. Comparing TR and MR, we see that when marginal revenue is positive (negative), total revenue increases (decreases) as more output is sold and that when marginal revenue is zero, total revenue is at a maximum.

again be zero because the quantity a/b can be sold only at a price equal to zero. Of course, for any quantity of output greater than zero and less than a/b, total revenue will be positive because price exceeds zero for any such quantity. In Figure 10.2b, total revenue increases as y increases until it reaches a maximum when y is $a/2b$. Thereafter, as y increases, total revenue decreases until it is again zero when y is a/b.

Now let us find the marginal revenue function $MR(y)$. We know that marginal revenue is equal to price p plus quantity y multiplied by the slope of the demand curve. But, for this linear demand curve, p is equal to $a - by$ and the slope of the demand curve is equal to $-b$, so marginal revenue is equal to $a - by - by$, or

$$MR(y) = a - 2by$$

This marginal revenue function is also plotted in Figure 10.2a. It intersects the vertical axis at a, just as the market demand curve does, but it is twice as steep as the market demand curve. The demand curve intersects the quantity axis at a/b. Because the marginal revenue function is twice as steep, it intersects the quantity axis at $a/2b$.

Notice especially the following relationships between $TR(y)$ and $MR(y)$:

---

1. When the total revenue function is positively sloped, marginal revenue is positive; 2. when total revenue is a maximum, marginal revenue is zero; and 3. when the total revenue function is negatively sloped, marginal revenue is negative.

These relationships are obvious once we translate the original definition of marginal revenue. Above we said that marginal revenue $MR(y)$ is the rate at which total revenue $TR(y)$ changes as output y changes. Equivalently, we could have said that $MR(y)$ is the slope of $TR(y)$. In the following problem, you can establish similar relationships between marginal revenue and the price elasticity of demand.

> **PROBLEM 10.1**
>
> First show that for a linear demand curve
>
> $$|\eta(y)| = (a - by)/(by) = a/(by) - 1$$
>
> Then establish the following relationships: 1. when marginal revenue is positive, demand is elastic with respect to price; 2. when marginal revenue is negative, demand is inelastic with respect to price; 3. when marginal revenue is zero, the price elasticity of demand is 1.

10.3
Maximizing Profit

Let us turn now to the monopolist's profit-maximizing decision. Because the principles that guide the monopolist's choice in the short run and in the long run are virtually identical, we will consider them together. The monopolist's cost function $TC(y)$ can therefore be interpreted as either the long-run cost function or the short-run variable cost function. (We will see below why we use the variable cost function in the short run.)

We can then write profit $\neq(y)$ as a function of output y as follows:

$$\neq(y) = TR(y) - TC(y)$$

Alternatively, we can write profit in terms of average revenue $AR(y)$ and average cost $AC(y)$:

$$\neq(y) = y[AR(y) - AC(y)]$$

 monopolist's profit-maximizing problem

The **monopolist's profit-maximizing problem** is then to *maximize profit $\neq(y)$ by choice of output y*.

In Figure 10.3 we have plotted the average and marginal revenue curves, *AR* and *MR*, and the average and marginal cost curves, *AC* and *MC*. First, notice that average revenue *AR* is equal to average cost *AC* at two levels of output: $y = 30$, and $y = 95$. Consequently, profit π is equal to zero at these output levels. Profit π is positive in the range of output between 30 and 95 because *AR* exceeds *AC*. Conversely, it is negative at output levels less than 30 and greater than 95 because *AC* exceeds *AR*.

Notice, too, that marginal revenue *MR* is equal to marginal cost *MC* at two levels of output: $y = 8$, and $y = 58$. Because *MC* intersects *MR* from above at 8 units of output, profit is a minimum at 8 units of output. In contrast, because *MC* intersects *MR* from below at 58 units of output, profit is a maximum at 58 units of output. That is, the profit-maximizing quantity y^* is 58.

To show that profit is maximized at $y^* = 58$, let us suppose that the monopolist is initially producing $y^* = 58$ and ask: What will happen to its profit if it produces one more unit of output? The addition to its revenue is given by *MR* and the addition to its cost by *MC*. Because *MC* exceeds *MR* to the right of $y^* = 58$, the increase in its cost exceeds the increase in its revenue, and profit therefore falls as the monopolist produces one more unit. Now, beginning again at $y^* = 58$, let us ask: What will happen to its profit if the monopolist produces one less unit? The reduction in its revenue is given by *MR* and the reduction in its cost by *MC*. Because *MR* exceeds *MC* to the left of $y^* = 58$, the reduction in revenue exceeds the reduction in cost, and profit therefore falls as the monopolist produces one less unit. Since profit falls as the monopolist produces either more than or less than $y^* = 58$, profit is a maximum at $y^* = 58$.[4]

profit rectangle

The cross-hatched rectangular area in Figure 10.3 is the monopolist's **profit rectangle**: its vertical side is profit per unit sold, equal to price ($82) minus average cost ($60); its horizontal side is the profit-maximizing output (58 units); the area of the rectangle is the monopolist's profit.

In the following problem, you can show that profit is at a minimum when marginal cost intersects marginal revenue from above, as it does at 8 units of output in Figure 10.3.

> **PROBLEM 10.2**
>
> Show that profit is at a minimum when *MR* = *MC* and *MC* intersects *MR* from above.

One last detail requires attention. If the average cost function *AC* lies above the average revenue function *AR* at all levels of output, there is no positive output level at

---

4 All this can be said more simply using a little calculus. We know (1) that $\pi'(y^*) = 0$ is necessary for $y^* > 0$ to be a profit-maximizing level of y and (2) that $\pi(y)$ attains a (local) maximum at y^* if, in addition, $\pi''(y^*) < 0$. By definition,

$$\pi(y) = TR(y) - TC(y)$$

Differentiating with respect to y and setting the result equal to zero, we obtain the following first-order condition for profit maximization:

$$MR(y^*) = MC(y^*)$$

The second-order condition, $\pi''(y^*) < 0$, is just

$$MR'(y^*) < MC'(y^*)$$

That is, the slope of the marginal revenue function is less than the slope of the marginal cost function at the profit-maximizing quantity.

FIGURE 10.3   Maximizing monopoly profit

To maximize profit find the point where *MC* intersects *MR* from below. Then, starting from this point of intersection, (i) to find the profit maximizing output (58) move vertically down to the quantity axis, and (ii) to find the profit maximizing price ($82) move vertically up to the demand curve and then horizontally over to the price axis.

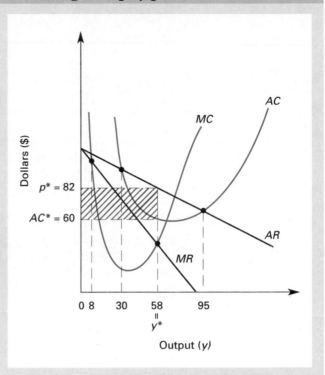

which the monopolist can cover its costs. However, it can achieve zero profit by producing nothing, incurring no costs and receiving no revenue. Therefore, if *AC* lies everywhere above *AR*, the monopolist will shut down production. Because the monopolist's profit is *zero* if it produces nothing but is *negative* if it produces some output, it will produce nothing. This line of reasoning is obviously true in the long run, when *AC* is the long-run average cost function. It is also true in the short run — if *AC* is the short-run average variable cost function. It is for this reason that we defined $TC(y)$ at the outset of this section as either the long-run cost function or the short-run variable cost function.

Let us summarize what we have learned about the monopolist's profit-maximizing problem in the case where *AC* intersects *AR*:

First find the point where *MC* intersects *MR* from below. Then, to identify the profit-maximizing level of output, move vertically downward from the point of intersection to the horizontal axis. To identify the profit-maximizing price p^*, move vertically upward from the point of intersection to the average revenue *AR* curve and then horizontally over to the price axis. Finally, to identify the monopolist's profit, construct the profit rectangle with horizontal side equal to y^* and vertical side equal to $p^* - AC^*$.

In the following problems, you will have the chance to practice finding the graphic solution to the monopolist's profit-maximizing problem and to review the crucial relationship between the *MR* and *MC* curves in determining the profit-maximizing output.

PROBLEM 10.3

Suppose that the average revenue function is

$$p = 100 - y$$

and that the cost function is

$$TC(y) = 40y$$

On one diagram, carefully construct the average revenue, marginal revenue, average cost, and marginal cost functions. Then show that y^* is 30 and p^* is \$70. Construct the profit rectangle and show that profit is equal to \$900.

PROBLEM 10.4

First, draw a linear AR curve, like the one in Problem 10.3, and the associated MR curve. Then draw a U-shaped MC curve that is tangent to the MR curve at one point and lies above it at all other levels of output. Beginning at the point where $MR = MC$, what happens to profit as the monopolist produces one more unit? One less unit? What is the profit-maximizing level of output? What can you say about the relationship between the AC and AR curves?

10.4

The Inefficiency of Monopoly

As we saw in the last chapter, in a competitive equilibrium all the gains from trade are realized. Recall that in a competitive equilibrium, each competitor chooses a level of output such that marginal cost is equal to price. Furthermore, if any firm were to produce a bit more output, marginal cost would exceed price. Therefore, in a competitive equilibrium, it is impossible to sell an additional unit of a good at a price that covers the marginal cost of producing the extra unit.

By contrast, the gains from trade are *not* fully realized in the monopoly equilibrium. In the monopoly equilibrium, marginal cost — which is equal to marginal revenue — is less than price. Therefore, beginning at the profit-maximizing output, an additional unit could possibly be sold at a price that covers its marginal cost. (We will soon see why a monopolist may not be able to take advantage of this opportunity.) Consequently, the gains from trade are not fully exploited in monopoly equilibrium. For example, the profit-maximizing output in Figure 10.4 is $y^* = 6$, and the profit-maximizing price is $p^* = \$50$, which is greater than $MC^* = \$25$.

Because p^* exceeds MC in the monopoly equilibrium, some potential gains from trade are not realized.

To better understand this result, we can perform a thought experiment. Let us begin by reinterpreting the average revenue, or market demand, function as the aggregation of individual reservation prices for one unit of the monopolist's good. (You encountered this type of demand curve in the discussion of the exchange model in Section 9.1.)

FIGURE 10.4   The inefficiency of monopoly

Suppose the monopolist initially sells $y^* = 6$ at the profit-maximizing price $p^* = \$50$ and then decides to sell one more unit at a price greater than distance AB and less than distance AG. The buyer, who is willing to pay AG, and the monopolist, whose marginal cost is AB, are both better off, and none of the original buyers is worse off. Therefore, the monopoly equilibrium is not Pareto-optimal. The green area is a measure of the burden of monopoly.

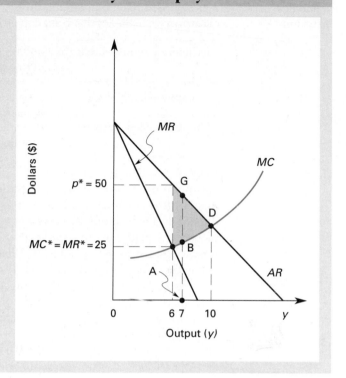

Although such a market demand curve is actually a series of descending vertical segments rather than a smooth line, if the number of individual demanders is large enough, their aggregated demand function can be approximated by a smooth market demand function. Imagine that a monopolist first announces a "take-it-or-leave-it" price of $p^* = \$50$ and that all potential buyers take the monopolist's announcement at face value. The result is just the standard monopoly equilibrium in Figure 10.4: the six buyers with reservation prices greater than $50 buy the good and buyers with lower reservation prices do not. Now suppose the clever monopolist considers making and selling one additional unit. If it sells that unit at any price greater than distance AB but less than distance AG, both the monopolist and the purchaser of that additional unit will be better off — and no purchaser who bought the good at price $p^* = \$50$ will be worse off. Therefore, beginning at the monopoly equilibrium, the sale of the additional unit is Pareto-improving. That is:

The monopoly equilibrium is not Pareto-optimal.

If we pursue this thought experiment to its logical conclusion by imagining that the monopolist continues to sell additional output one unit at a time — at a price greater than or equal to its marginal cost and less than or equal to the corresponding reservation price on the demand function — we see from Figure 10.4 that eventually 10 units will be sold. Relative to the monopoly equilibrium, the additional total surplus realized is indicated by the green area in Figure 10.4. This is a measure of the **burden of monopoly** — that is, the potential surplus that is unrealized at the monopoly equilibrium. Because these gains are not fully realized, monopoly is said to represent a **market failure**.

burden of monopoly

market failure

efficiency
criterion

This thought experiment also reveals that the gains from trade in Figure 10.4 are fully realized when 10 units are produced and sold. More generally, it reveals the **efficiency criterion** for a market that is monopolized and, indeed, for markets in general:

Efficiency requires that the good be produced up to the point where price p is equal to marginal cost MC.

One final, important message comes out of this thought experiment:

The unrealized gains from trade in the monopoly equilibrium signal unrealized monopoly profit.

In other words, at the monopoly equilibrium, the monopolist has failed to extract the maximum profit possible. Indeed, the monopolist's strategy in this thought experiment of first announcing a take-it-or-leave-it price and later announcing a price reduction is a wily attempt to extract a profit greater than the profit it makes in the monopoly equilibrium. In a market characterized by repeated sales over many periods, however, this strategy will not work. What eventually occurs is a slightly altered version of the story of the boy who cried wolf. The buyers with the higher reservation prices soon catch on to the monopolist's stratagem and withhold their demand at the original price in anticipation of being able to buy the good at a lower price in the future. Even though this particular pricing strategy cannot succeed for long, we should nevertheless recognize that a monopolist has a clear incentive to devise strategies that are more profitable and more complex than the simple MR equals MC strategy.

We will look at such strategies in Section 10.7, under the general rubric of *price discrimination*. In the meantime, the following problem will help you to review the important points arising out of our thought experiment. Because we will be returning to this problem at crucial points later in the chapter, it deserves your careful attention.

PROBLEM 10.5

Suppose that some book vendor can produce a book at a constant marginal cost of $8 and that 11 potential buyers have the following reservation prices: $55, $50, $45, ... , $10, $5. Each will buy the book at any price less than or equal to his or her reservation price.

1. If the book vendor must announce a take it-or-leave-it price, what price maximizes profit? What quantity will be sold, and what are the book vendor's profits? Are there unrealized gains from trade? Hint: The only prices you need to consider are the 11 reservation prices, and you can calculate profit for each of these reservation prices.

2. Suppose that the book vendor knows what each potential buyer's reservation price actually is and that those buyers are completely isolated from each other. The vendor can then set an individual price for each buyer. How many books will it sell? At what price will it sell each book? What are its profits? Show that this solution is Pareto-optimal, or efficient.

10.5

Sources of Monopoly

By now, you know what a monopoly is, how the profit-maximizing monopolist chooses price and quantity, and in what sense the monopoly equilibrium represents a market failure. But what forces bring a monopoly into being in the first place? And what are the possible policy responses to the market failure associated with monopoly? Let us examine each question in turn.

Although the sources of monopoly power are many and varied, we can classify monopolies under six categories: the franchise monopoly; the resource-based monopoly; the patent monopoly; the technological, or natural, monopoly; what we might call the monopoly by good management.

Government Franchise Monopoly

franchise
monopoly

One historic and contemporary source of monopoly power is the franchise. A **franchise monopoly** arises when a government grants the exclusive right to do business in a specified market to some individual or firm. A historic example is King Charles II's granting of the exclusive rights to the North American fur trade to the Hudson's Bay Company in 1670. A contemporary example is the granting of exclusive rights to broadcast at specified frequencies to radio and television stations. Broadcast franchises sometimes give rise to monopoly and more frequently to oligopoly.

Patent Monopoly

patent
monopoly

Another form of monopoly arising from governmental action in many countries is the **patent monopoly**, secured by either patent or copyright. For example, in the United States, authors and inventors are granted "the exclusive right to their respective writings and discoveries" under the U.S. Constitution. Patents in the United States are granted in most cases for a period of 17 years. Patent monopoly is a pervasive phenomenon in the prescription drug trade and has played a central role in a wide range of other industries as well, including the photocopying, computer, and telecommunications industries. Even the shoe machinery industry was at one time significantly affected by patent monopoly.

Resource-Based Monopoly

resource-based
monopoly

Another source of monopoly power is the exclusive ownership of a natural resource essential in a particular production process. For example, owning one of the various hot springs scattered throughout Europe and North America conveys monopoly power to its owners in the local or regional markets for water spas. The Aluminum Company of America offered a more powerful example of a **resource-based monopoly** prior to the end of World War II. Alcoa was a virtual monopolist in primary aluminum production from its inception in the late nineteenth century until 1945; its monopoly position arose in part from its control of virtually all domestic sources of bauxite ore.

Technological (or Natural) Monopoly

In Section 8.9, we discussed market structure and argued that if the efficient scale of production in a given industry is large enough, we expect to see only one firm in the market. The source of monopolistic power in this case is technological, the by-product of

natural
monopoly

significant economies of scale. A firm in this category is therefore called a technological or **natural monopoly**. Because these firms experience declining average cost over a significant range of output, rival firms are unable to produce at these low costs and will fail.

Public utilities such as natural gas, electricity, and telephone services are classic illustrations of technological, or natural, monopolies. In all three cases, the economies of scale are driven by the distribution networks needed to deliver the good or the service to the point of use. We find other, less conspicuous natural monopolies in the many small towns of rural North America that have only one movie theater. Although the economies of scale in absolute terms are not large in this industry, they are nevertheless large relative to the demand generated by a population of 5000 or fewer. The local movie theater is to a small town what the Tigers baseball club is to Detroit.

Let us be more precise about what we mean by the term natural monopoly. We say that a firm is a natural monopolist if no other firm will enter the market when the monopolist produces the standard profit-maximizing output.[5] To use this definition, we need a theory of entry, since a firm is a natural monopolist *only* if no other firm will enter its market when it pursues the profit-maximizing strategy outlined in the previous section. We will use a very simple theory of entry driven by one assumption — often called the **Sylos postulate**, after the Italian economist Paulo Sylos-Labini:

Sylos postulate

THE SYLOS POSTULATE

In deciding whether to enter a market, a potential entrant takes the output of existing firms as given.

Figure 10.5a presents the standard production and pricing decisions of a monopolist. It chooses to produce $y^* = 410$ and to sell each unit of output at a price of $p^* = \$48$. First, we will examine the case in which the firm presented in Figure 10.5a is a natural monopolist. Assuming that the potential entrant regards the monopolist's current output $y^* = 410$ as fixed, it will consult its own **residual demand function** in Figure 10.5b to see if it can expect to cover its costs if it does enter. The market demand function faced by the potential entrant is called *residual* because it represents that portion of the market demand that remains unsupplied by the monopolist. Thus, the origin of the residual demand function in Figure 10.5b, labeled 0_E, corresponds to the output level $y^* = 410$ in Figure 10.5a. The entrant's residual demand function intersects the entrant's price axis at $p^* = \$48$, which means that price will be no higher than \$48 even if the entrant produces nothing. The entrant's average cost curve AC in Figure 10.5b is plotted relative to the entrant's origin 0_E.

residual demand
function

In general, whether the potential entrant can find a level of output that allows it to cover its costs will depend on the relationship between its average cost function and the residual demand function. Because AC lies everywhere above the residual demand function in the case shown in Figure 10.5b, the potential entrant will recognize that it cannot cover its production costs at any level of output, and it will decide against entry. The firm presented in Figure 10.5a is therefore a natural monopoly. Interestingly, it is entirely possible that the entrant in Figure 10.5 is more efficient than the established firm (in the sense of having lower AC for any level of output). In the following problem, you can construct the case in which there is no natural monopoly in the industry because the potential entrant does see a chance of becoming a viable competitor.

---

5 The term *natural monopoly* is sometimes used in another way by economists. If AC is everywhere downward sloping, then to minimize the total cost of industry output, all the output should be produced by just one firm. Therefore, industries in which AC is everywhere downward sloping are sometimes called natural monopolies.

PROBLEM 10.6

In Figure 10.5a, the average revenue function intersects the price axis at $70. Construct a diagram identical to Figure 10.5a in all respects except one. Shift the average and marginal revenue functions up by $30. Then show that there is no natural monopoly in this case.

FIGURE 10.5   Natural monopoly

In (a), the monopoly equilibrium is price $p^* = 48$ and quantity $y^* = 410$. If an entrant took the monopolists output $y^* = 410$ as fixed, it would perceive the residual demand function in (b). Since AC lies above the residual demand function, there is no quantity at which the entrant could make a profit, and this is therefore a case of natural monopoly.

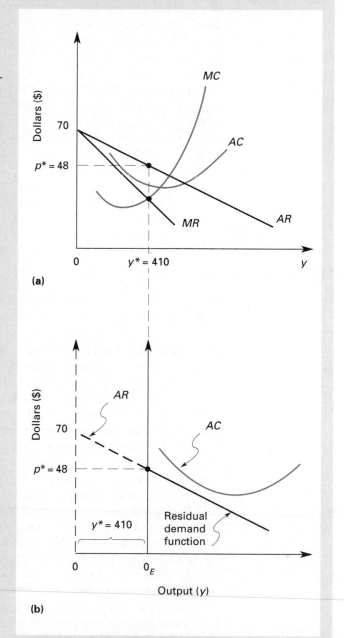

(a)

(b)

Monopoly by Good Management

Suppose that a monopolist finds itself in the position you considered in Problem 10.6. If it chooses price and quantity in the ordinary way, a second firm will enter — and the first firm therefore will *not* be a natural monopolist. Some obvious and intriguing questions beg to be answered in this case.

First, is there anything the monopolist could do to deter entry of a second firm? If so, would the monopolist find it profitable to deter entry? These are really oligopoly rather than monopoly questions because they involve the interaction between two firms: the established monopolist and a potential entrant. Although we will not consider them until the next chapter, we can preview the results by noting that in certain circumstances, the answer to both questions is yes. In these circumstances, there will be just one firm in the market, but that firm will not be a natural monopolist. Rather, this is a case of **monopoly by good management**: the firm is a monopolist because it manages its affairs with an eye to deterring entry.

monopoly by good management

In these circumstances, the monopolist will not simply produce the output where marginal revenue is equal to marginal cost. It will instead take a larger view of the profit-maximizing problem, by essentially redefining it as the problem of maximizing profit subject to the constraint that there be no entry. Ordinarily, to deter entry, the solution is to produce an output larger than the standard monopoly output. It is important to realize that this behavior can result in significantly less unrealized surplus than occurs in the ordinary monopoly equilibrium. That is, this behavior can dramatically reduce the burden of monopoly. Monopoly by good management is thus quite a different phenomenon from natural monopoly.

*10.6
Regulatory Responses to Monopoly

From whatever sources monopoly power may spring, its very existence poses two closely related problems that seem to demand some kind of governmental regulatory response. The first problem is that the potential gains from trade are not fully realized because price exceeds marginal cost. The problem for governments is that in monopolized industries, the goods or services are *underproduced*. Governments then face an *efficiency dilemma*: Should they step in and attempt to induce greater production?

The second problem stems from the fact that price ordinarily exceeds average cost at the monopoly solution. As a result, monopolists may be able to make a supra-normal profit — one above the normal or "fair" return on capital investment included among the costs in the cost function. Governments then face a *distributional dilemma*. Who should be the ultimate recipients of the supra-normal profit — the owners of the monopoly or someone else? To complicate matters, the current owners of a monopoly may not be earning a supra-normal profit. Suppose that the present owners bought the monopoly from its original owners. The selling price of such a firm will have included a "goodwill" element, which is, in effect, the discounted present value at the time of sale of all future monopoly profits. In this case, the current owners will be earning only a normal return on their investment. In this section, we will largely ignore the distributional questions raised by monopoly and concentrate on the efficiency issue.

The particular governmental responses that will be effective depend on the source of the monopoly power. In resource-based monopolies, regulatory measures that promote competition as an alternative to monopoly are sometimes possible. In the other monopolies, however, competition is not a feasible alternative, and governments must look elsewhere for remedial measures.

Divestiture in a Resource-Based Monopoly

From an economic standpoint, regulating resource-based monopolies is a relatively easy task because eliminating monopoly power is both feasible and sensible. If exclusive ownership of a resource is the only source of monopoly power, a regulatory body can simply force the monopolist to sell off, or divest itself of, some portion of the essential resource. Such *divestiture* then makes competition a feasible market alternative to monopoly.

Responses to Patent Monopoly

Governments could apply a similar regulatory remedy to patent monopolies and simply wipe the right to patent inventions off the books; the monopoly power that patents convey would then be disposed of neatly. Yet patents serve a potentially useful economic purpose by stimulating the invention and development of new products and processes. From this perspective, eliminating patenting rights might not be sensible, because the economic benefit to customers of patented products might well outweigh the economic cost of monopolistically exploited innovations. As these observations suggest, patent policy is not a simple matter. Because the issues raised by patent policy are interesting and important, we consider them at length at the end of this chapter.

Responses to Natural Monopoly

Patent monopoly poses one set of issues for regulatory agencies. Natural monopoly presents quite a different set. Because a natural monopoly arises in response to a technological phenomenon — an efficient scale of production that is large relative to market demand — the industry simply cannot support a large number of competing firms: competition is not a feasible alternative to natural monopoly.

Governments have recognized that some industries — local telephone services, electricity, and other public utilities, for instance — are natural monopolies. They typically permit such industries to be monopolized but attempt to limit the monopolist to a "fair" rate of return on its investment. Fixing a precise dollar value on a fair rate of return is a serious accounting problem, and debate on this question periodically flares up between public utilities and regulatory agencies. Nevertheless, a fair rate of return is easy enough to define theoretically as a zero profit. (Remember that a normal rate of return on investment forms a part of the costs included in the cost functions.) We will look at two regulatory mechanisms aimed at achieving a fair rate-of-return, average cost pricing and rate-of-return regulation. And we will discover why each fails to achieve efficiency. We will close this discussion of the regulation of natural monopoly by considering an efficient regulatory mechanism.

Average Cost Pricing

average-cost-pricing policy

In keeping with their objective of limiting monopolies to a fair, or normal, rate of return, regulatory agencies sometimes attempt to implement an **average-cost-pricing policy**. One major problem with this policy is that even though average cost pricing (if successful) does eliminate monopoly profit, it does not induce the monopolist to produce the efficient level of output. Figure 10.6a presents one such average-cost-pricing regulatory solution. In this case, the monopoly will, in effect, be ordered to produce 47 units of output and to set price equal to its average cost of $20. Yet, like the monopoly solution it is intended to replace, the regulatory solution at point A is inefficient. At point A, marginal cost of $30 exceeds price of $20. From the perspective of efficiency, the monopolist produces too

FIGURE 10.6 Average cost pricing

In both (a) and (b), the monopolist is forced to operate where it makes no profit — where *AC* is equal to price. In (a), the resulting output *y* = 47 is larger than the output *y* = 42 where price is equal to *MC*, and average cost pricing induces

the monopolist to produce too much output. In (b), the resulting output *y* = 35 is less than the output *y* = 41 where price is equal to *MC*, and average cost pricing induces the monopolist to produce too little output.

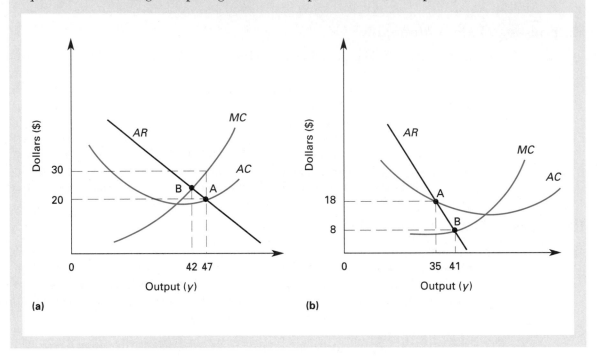

(a)

(b)

much. In this case, the efficient solution is instead at point B, where price equals marginal cost and output is 42 units. In the case shown in Figure 10.6a, then, an average-cost-pricing regulatory scheme induces the monopolist to produce too much output.

Figure 10.6b presents another possibility. Although the regulatory solution is at point A, where price equals average cost, the efficient solution is instead at point B, where price equals marginal cost. In this case, the regulatory solution induces the monopolist to produce too little output relative to the efficient solution. Average cost pricing not only fails to induce the monopolist to produce the efficient level of output. It also fails to provide the monopolist with an incentive to minimize its costs of production. This is an even more serious drawback. If the regulatory authority allows the monopoly to recover all its costs but never permits it to make a profit, why should the firm worry about keeping its costs as low as possible? The monopolist lacks any incentive to minimize costs.

Rate-of-Return Regulation

rate-of-return regulation

Closely related to average cost pricing is the predominant form of regulation in the United States, **rate-of-return regulation**, which is aimed at limiting the rate of return a regulated natural monopoly can earn on its invested capital. Unfortunately, under this type of regulation, a natural monopolist will again fail to minimize its costs of production — in this instance, by choosing to use too much capital relative to the cost-minimizing input bundle.

(See Averch and Johnson, 1961, on this point.) To understand why this distortion arises, let us consider a natural monopolist that is using just two inputs: capital owned by the firm, input 2, and some other input hired by the firm (labor), input 1. The monopolist's return on its capital is then its total revenue $TR(y)$ minus its expenditure on input 1, $w_1 z_1$:

$$\text{Return on capital} = TR(y) - w_1 z_1$$

Rate-of-return regulation imposes the following constraint on the firm's behavior: it must choose output y and an input bundle (z_1, z_2) such that

$$TR(y) - w_1 z_1 \leq r z_2$$

where r is the *allowed rate of return* on capital and z_2 is the quantity of capital. Averch and Johnson argue that the sensible regulatory agency will choose an allowed rate of return r greater than the price of capital w_2, because if r is less than w_2, the monopolist will be forced out of business. When r is equal to w_2, rate of return regulation is equivalent to average cost pricing. Therefore, we will assume that the allowed rate of return r is greater than the price of capital w_2.

Why will the monopolist use too much capital? We can develop an intuitive understanding by starting with an entirely imaginary form of regulation analogous to rate-of-return regulation. If the monopolist is told that its profit cannot exceed $1 per pound of jelly beans held in the firm's vault, then the firm will fill a huge vault with useless jelly beans because the amount of profit it can earn is constrained by the weight of the jelly beans in its vault. Under rate-of-return regulation, it is the quantity of capital instead of pounds of jelly beans that constrains the firm's ability to earn profit. We can see why by subtracting $w_2 z_2$ from both sides of the rate-of-return constraint:

$$TR(y) - w_1 z_1 - w_2 z_2 \leq (r - w_2) z_2$$

The expression on the left is just the firm's profit, and the entire inequality then means that the profit the firm is allowed to earn is constrained by the quantity of capital it has. As a result, rate-of-return regulation induces the regulated firm to use *too much capital* and *too little labor*.

Let us be more precise about the distortionary effect of rate-of-return regulation on the monopolist's choice of an input bundle. Suppose that the quantity of output produced by the monopolist, the prices of the two inputs, and the allowed rate of return on capital are all fixed. Specifically, suppose that output is 100, that the prices w_1 and w_2 are both $5, and that r is $8. We will show that if the rate-of-return regulation is effective, the monopolist will produce 100 units of output using an input bundle that has too much capital and too little labor relative to the cost-minimizing input bundle.

Because output is fixed, price and therefore total revenue are also fixed. Again for convenience, suppose that price per unit of output is $1.85 when the firm sells 100 units. Its total revenue is then $185. Since output and revenue are fixed, the monopolist's profit-maximizing problem is now reduced to choosing an input bundle that minimizes the cost of producing the fixed level of output, subject to the regulatory constraint:

$$\text{minimize } 5z_1 + 5z_2 \text{ by choice of } z_1 \text{ and } z_2$$

$$\text{subject to the constraint } 100 = F(z_1, z_2)$$

$$\text{subject to the constraint } 185 - 5z_1 < 8z_2$$

The first constraint, $100 = F(z_1, z_2)$, is that the chosen input bundle be on the isoquant for 100 units of output. This is the standard constraint in cost minimization problems. The second constraint is the regulatory constraint. Thus, the monopolist faces the standard cost-minimization problem from Section 8.5 — with the additional twist of a regulatory constraint.

If the allowed rate of return is large enough, the regulatory constraint is ineffective, and the solution to the problem is the standard cost-minimizing input bundle for 100 units of output. This case is uninteresting because rate-of-return regulation then has no effect: it fails to alter the monopolist's behavior.

The interesting case occurs when the regulatory constraint is effective or binding. In Figure 10.7, the standard cost-minimizing input bundle is (10,10) at point E, where the 100-unit isoquant is tangent to the dashed $100 isocost line. If the firm were to choose this input bundle, its profit would then be $85 ($185 − $100). The rub is that this input bundle fails to satisfy the regulatory constraint because 135 — that is, 185 − (5 × 10) — is greater than 80 — that is, (8 × 10). To satisfy the rate-of-return constraint, the monopolist will instead choose an input bundle on or above the regulatory constraint. As Figure 10.7 reveals, the cheapest input bundle on the 100-unit isoquant that satisfies that constraint is (5,20) at point E′. It is this input bundle that the monopolist will choose. Since this bundle is on the $125 isocost line, the monopolist's profit under rate-of-return regulation is $60 instead of $85, and its costs are $125 instead of $100. More generally:

The rate-of-return-regulated firm chooses an input bundle that is not cost minimizing, and it uses too much capital and too little labor relative to the cost-minimizing bundle.

Why is it a matter of social concern that the monopolist chooses an input bundle that is not cost minimizing? Suppose that demand for the monopolist's good is independent of income. Suppose, too, that the prices of the inputs are independent of the monopolist's demand for them. That is, regardless of how much or little the monopolist buys, the prices for the two inputs are always $5. In this case, point E is clearly Pareto-preferred to point E′. The monopolist's customers are indifferent between the two points because they buy 100 units at $1.85 per unit in either case. The owners of the inputs are also indifferent because they sell their inputs for $5 in either case. But the monopolist is better off at point E because its profit is larger by $25. Thus, rate-of-return regulation creates a social problem because it induces an inefficient equilibrium.

Efficient Regulatory Mechanisms

Given the difficulties with traditional regulatory policies, can we imagine other regulatory schemes that might work better? The answer depends on how much information a regulating agency has at hand. For example, if it knows the relevant cost and demand functions in Figure 10.6a, it can simply order the monopolist to produce the efficient level of output at point B. If the relevant cost and demand functions are instead those in Figure 10.6b, the regulatory agency can also order the monopolist to produce the efficient level of output at point B. However, in this case, the monopolist will incur a loss because price is less than average cost at point B — and the agency must therefore provide a subsidy equivalent to the monopolist's loss.

Yet regulatory agencies are not likely to be so well informed about the relevant cost and demand functions. In particular, collecting all the necessary detail about a monopolist's costs of production might well be far too expensive an undertaking. Nevertheless, if a regulatory agency knows only the market demand function and nothing more, it can

FIGURE 10.7   Rate-of-return regulation

Suppose the monopolist wants to produce 100 units of output. Under rate of return regulation, it will minimize cost, subject to two constraints: that it is on or above the isoquant for 100 units and on or above the regulatory constraint. In the solution to this problem, the regulated monopolist chooses the input bundle at E′, which costs \$125. In the absence of regulation, the monopolist would choose the input bundle at E, which costs only \$100.

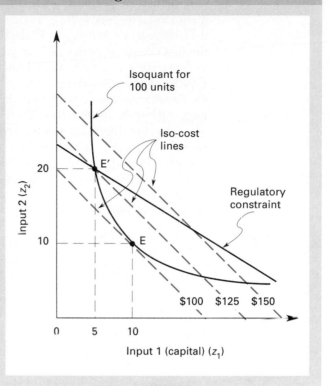

apply one regulatory mechanism (formulated by Loeb and Magat, 1979) that will induce a monopolist both to minimize costs and to produce the efficient level of output.

You actually discovered the crucial insight in Problem 10.5, where you found that if a monopolist can pick a unique price for each demander, it will choose a price equal to each demander's reservation price — as long as that reservation price exceeds the monopolist's marginal cost of production. To see how this insight can be translated into an efficient regulatory mechanism, let us return to the reservation-price demand function with n demanders and array the reservation prices of demanders from highest to lowest:

$$R_1 > R_2 > \ldots > R_n > 0$$

Suppose that the regulatory authority — knowing these reservation prices — imposes the following *subsidy scheme* on the monopolist. If the monopolist sells m units at some price p, it will be given a subsidy equal to

$$R_1 + R_2 + \ldots + R_m - mp$$

The monopolist's total revenue from the sale of m units is now the sum of the revenue generated from sales and the subsidy paid by the regulatory authority. The sum is

$$R_1 + R_2 + \ldots + R_m$$

For example, suppose that the monopolist sells two units at a price equal to 48. The subsidy will be $R_1 + R_2 - 96$, and the revenue generated by the sale of two units will be 96. The sum of the subsidy and the sales revenue will then be $R_1 + R_2$.

Given this subsidy scheme, what will the monopolist decide to do? Suppose that it is currently selling m units at price R_m. Will it choose to sell one additional unit? If so, it must lower its price to R_{m+1} and incur an additional cost equal to the marginal cost of the additional unit, $MC(m + 1)$. Under the subsidy scheme, the monopolist's revenue from the first m units is unchanged (despite the price drop) because the reduction in the sales revenue is exactly balanced by an increase in the subsidy. For instance, if the monopolist must cut its price by \$1 to sell an additional unit, the revenue from the sale of the first m units will decrease by m dollars, but the revenue from the subsidy on these units will increase by m dollars. Therefore, in deciding whether it should sell the additional unit, the monopolist will simply compare the price at which the additional unit can be sold, R_{m+1}, with the marginal cost of the additional unit, $MC(m + 1)$. If the reservation price exceeds (is less than) the marginal cost, it will decide in favor of (against) making and selling the additional unit.

If the profit-maximizing output under this subsidy scheme is m^*, then m^* will satisfy the following conditions:

$$MC(m^*) \le R_{m^*}$$

and

$$MC(m^* + 1) > R_{m^*+1}$$

You discovered this type of solution when you answered Problem 10.5. You also found that this type of solution is efficient because all the gains from trade are realized as profit to the monopolist.

The regulatory agency might regard the outcome as unfortunate because it is the monopolist who receives all the gains from trade as profit. Yet, as you will see in the following problem, the agency could recover virtually all the monopolist's profit by coupling the subsidy scheme with an appropriate proportional tax on profit. As long as the monopolist is left with *some* profit, it will produce the efficient output.

> **PROBLEM 10.7**
>
> Suppose that a 10% tax is imposed on the monopolist's profit. Then the monopolist will choose output to maximize $.9\ne(y)$ instead of $\ne(y)$. Show that the profit-maximizing output is the same for both profit-maximizing problems.

Even though the regulatory agency has no information about the monopolist's costs, it still manages to provide the monopolist with an incentive both to minimize costs and to produce the efficient output. Can this subsidy scheme be applied to other demand conditions as well? Consider the demand curve in Figure 10.8. If the monopolist sells quantity y' at price p', its revenue is $p'y'$, or the gray area of Figure 10.8. What happens if the regulatory agency tells the monopolist it will be given a subsidy equal to the green area in Figure 10.8 if it produces output y' and sells it at price p'? First, the introduction of the subsidy means that the monopolist's total revenue — which now includes both the revenue from sales and the subsidy from the government — is equal to the area under the demand curve from 0 to y' units of output. More to the point, when the monopolist now sells an additional unit under the subsidy regulation, the revenue from the original quantity sold remains unchanged. Thus, the price of that additional unit is now the monopolist's marginal revenue, and the market

FIGURE 10.8 **An efficient regulatory mechanism**

The regulator tells the monopolist that if the monopolist sells quantity y' at price p', the regulator will pay it a subsidy equal to the consumers' surplus. The monopolist's total revenue is then the gray area, equal to $p'y'$, plus the green area, equal to the subsidy promised by the regulator. As a result, the monopolist's marginal revenue function is coincident with the demand curve. Under this subsidy scheme, a profit-maximizing monopolist will produce the output where its marginal cost function intersects the demand/marginal revenue function.

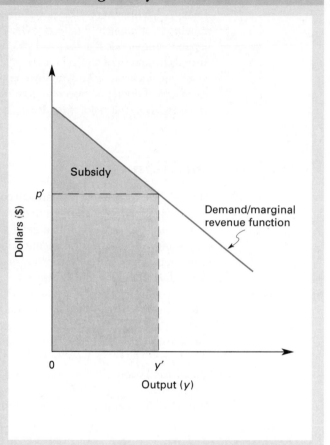

demand curve is then its marginal revenue curve. To maximize its profit, the monopolist will simply move to the point at which its marginal cost curve intersects the demand/marginal revenue curve. In other words, the monopolist will choose to produce the efficient level of output.[6]

---

6 Given this sort of subsidy scheme, the firm's total revenue function is just

$$TR(y) = \int_0^y D(y)dy$$

or

$$TR(y) = H(y) - H(0)$$

where $H(\cdot)$ is the indefinite integral of $D(\cdot)$. Its profit function is then

$$\neq(y) = H(y) - H(0) - TC(y)$$

Differentiating with respect to y, we see that profit maximization requires that

$$H'(y^*) = TC'(y^*)$$

But $H'(y)$ is just $D(y)$, and $TC'(y)$ is just $MC(y)$. Therefore, at the profit-maximizing quantity,

$$D(y^*) = MC(y^*)$$

That is, the firm produces where the marginal cost function intersects the demand function. Notice, too, that virtually all the profit can be taxed away without reintroducing inefficiency, because the quantity that maximizes $\neq(y)$ also maximizes $(1-t)\neq(y)$, where t is a tax rate greater than 0 and less than 1.

Franchise Monopoly

Finally, what are the possible government responses to franchise monopolies, such as the franchises for municipal garbage collection or city bus services? When such franchise monopolies are put out at tender and awarded to the highest bidder, we can often treat these cases as instances of natural monopoly. However, when political patronage rather than economic decision making determines the award of such franchises — be it the historical award of dominion over chunks of the New World or the more contemporary award of the rights to television broadcasting — economists have little to say.

10.7

Price Discrimination

The fact that price exceeds marginal cost at the standard monopoly solution is a symptom of the monopolist's failure to extract the maximum possible profit. An imaginative monopolist therefore will take dead aim on the as-yet-unrealized profit by trying to devise more sophisticated pricing schemes. Although sophisticated strategies aimed at extracting that unrealized profit may take many forms, the encompassing term for them all is **price discrimination**.[7]

price discrimination

As you take a closer look at price discrimination, you will recognize that this behavior is too pervasive to apply only to monopolists, given our restrictive definition of monopoly. Price-discriminating activities are attractive to any firm with some degree of market power — that is, to any firm with some ability to set its own price. What we say here about price discrimination will also apply to *oligopolies*, or markets dominated by a few firms. As you will discover in the following two chapters, the theory of oligopoly is complicated enough in the absence of price discrimination. We will therefore take up price discrimination in the relatively simpler context of monopoly.

Market Segmentation

market segmentation

All price discrimination schemes share an underlying strategy: to segment the market and to charge each segment a different price. You discovered the monopolist's ideal **market segmentation** scheme in the book vendor's pricing strategy in Problem 10.5. There, the monopolist appropriated all the surplus as profit by extracting from every consumer the largest sum of money each was willing to pay. Recall the conditions that made this most profitable strategy possible: the monopolist was able to isolate its potential customers from one another, and it knew the individual reservation prices of each customer. These conditions will rarely, if ever, be satisfied. Nevertheless, the market segmentation that makes this scheme effective can be realized and exploited to a lesser extent by other means.

perfect price discrimination

Economists usually view cases of price discrimination as falling into three broad theoretical categories. The first category is **perfect price discrimination**, the "ideal" but effectively unrealizable case exemplified by the book vendor. The monopolist successfully extracts the maximum possible profit from each customer and therefore from the whole market.

ordinary price discrimination

The second category is **ordinary price discrimination**. This is the familiar case in which the monopolist identifies potential customers by groups and charges each

---

7 For an introduction to the vast literature on price discrimination, see "discriminating monopoly" (John Hartwick) and "price discrimination" (Louis Phlips) in *The New Palgrave*.

group a separate price. For example, the pervasive phenomenon of charging different admission prices for groups called "seniors," "adults," "students," and "children" is one instance of ordinary price discrimination.

block pricing

multipart pricing

The third category, **block** or **multipart pricing**, is the case in which the monopolist charges different rates for different amounts, or "blocks," of a good or service. For instance, it is common practice to charge one rate for the first block of so many kilowatt-hours of electricity in a period and lower rates for subsequent blocks.

Perfect Price Discrimination

As you already know, perfect price discrimination means that the monopolist extracts the maximum possible profit from its market. The book vendor's problem illustrates the simplest type of perfect price discrimination because each customer demands only one unit of the product. In Section 4.4., which treated two-part tariffs, we outlined a general strategy for extracting maximum possible profit from one consumer when the monopolist knows that consumer's preferences. That strategy is to price the good at marginal cost and then charge an "entry fee" to extract maximum profit. We can view the solution to the book vendor's problem as an application of this more general result. The firm sells its book at marginal cost but adds to the price an "entry fee" equal to the customer's reservation price minus the marginal cost.

Although this theoretical case may have no precise real-world counterparts, it nevertheless throws light on the pricing strategies of firms such as Disneyland and Polaroid, which you encountered in Chapter 4. Other examples include golf courses that charge a membership fee and green fees, car rental firms that charge a daily fee and a charge per mile, and telephone and cable TV companies that charge a hookup fee and a monthly rental fee. In the pure case (not necessarily found in these examples), the solution is efficient because the product is sold at marginal cost, and all the potential gains from trade are therefore realized.

Ordinary Price Discrimination

Now let us look at ordinary price discrimination by considering first the theory and then the circumstances in which this strategy is feasible. To keep matters simple, we will ask how a monopolist sets price in a market divided into just two segments.

Let us begin with a simplifying assumption, which we will later change: the monopolist has produced a certain quantity of output — say, 44 units — and wants to maximize the profit from selling it. Its problem is to decide how much of the output to sell in each market segment and at what prices. Since the monopolist has 44 units to sell, we have assumed away all production questions and reduced the problem to one of maximizing revenue.

The two panels in Figure 10.9 represent the two market segments. Suppose that the monopolist begins by considering selling 21 units in the first market segment and 23 in the second. At this allocation, the marginal revenue of $5 in the first market segment is less than the marginal revenue of $34 in the second segment. Beginning at this allocation, if the monopolist transfers 1 unit from the first market segment to the second, the reduction in revenue in the first segment (a drop of approximately $5) will be more than compensated by the increase in revenue in the second (an increase of approximately $34). More generally, the firm's revenue will increase as it transfers output from the market segment with the lower marginal revenue to the market segment with the higher marginal revenue. From this exercise, we have discovered the solution to the monopolist's revenue-maximization problem:

FIGURE 10.9 Price discrimination: equality of marginal revenue

The monopolist has 44 units of output that it wants to allocate to the two market segments so as to maximize its revenue. To do so, it allocates the fixed quantity to the two market segments

so that marginal revenue is identical in the two segments. The optimal allocation is 14 units to segment 1 and 30 units to segment 2.

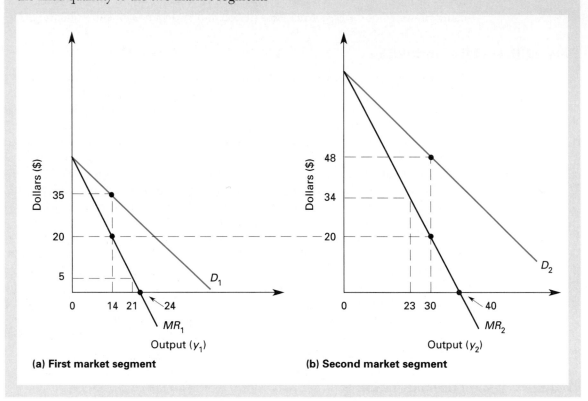

(a) First market segment

(b) Second market segment

To maximize revenue from the sale of a fixed quantity of output, allocate output so that marginal revenue is identical in all market segments.

In Figure 10.9, revenue is maximized when the monopolist allocates 14 units to the first market segment and 30 to the second market segment, since marginal revenue is then $20 in each segment.

PROBLEM 10.8

As you know, if the monopolist presented in Figure 10.9 has 44 units of output, it will sell all 44 units. Suppose that it has 100 units. Will it sell all 100 units? How many units will it sell in each market segment? Is this result consistent with the rule for maximizing revenue?

Let us expand the problem to include production. Now the monopolist's profit is

$$\neq(y_1, y_2) = TR_1(y_1) + TR_2(y_2) - TC(y_1 + y_2)$$

Here $TR_1(y_1)$ is total revenue from market segment 1, $TR_2(y_2)$ is total revenue from market segment 2, and $TC(y_1 + y_2)$ is the total cost of producing y_1 units for market segment 1 and y_2 units for market segment 2. The monopolist's problem is to choose the two outputs y_1 and y_2 so as to maximize its profit $\neq(y_1, y_2)$.

This problem is more complex than the standard monopoly problem. However, if we think of it in a different way, we can easily use familiar concepts to solve it. Think of the monopolist's decision as occurring in two stages. First, it chooses an aggregate output; then it allocates that aggregate output to the two market segments. From what you just learned, you know that in the second stage the aggregate output will be allocated so that *marginal revenue is identical in the two market segments*. And from what you know from your initial encounter with monopoly, it makes sense that in the first stage, the monopolist will choose aggregate output so that *marginal cost is equal to aggregate marginal revenue*. But exactly what is aggregate marginal revenue?

To find out, let us turn to the aggregate marginal revenue curve presented in Figure 10.10c. It has been constructed by horizontally summing MR_1 and MR_2 from Figures 10.10a and 10.10b. To see its significance, suppose that the monopolist produces 46 units and that it allocates 17 units to the first market segment and 29 to the second. As Figures 10.10a and 10.10b reveal, marginal revenue in each market segment is then $4. Therefore, this allocation — 17 units to the first market segment and 29 to the second — maximizes the monopolist's revenue from the 46 units. As Figure 10.10c reveals, the monopolist's marginal revenue is also $4. That is, the aggregate marginal revenue curve in Figure 10.10c gives us the monopolist's marginal revenue when it allocates output to market segments so as to maximize revenue. We can therefore use this curve — in conjunction with the marginal cost curve — to determine the monopolist's profit-maximizing aggregate output.

The profit-maximizing aggregate output is determined by the intersection of the aggregate marginal revenue and marginal cost curves at $y^* = 31$ units in Figure 10.10c. At this output level, aggregate marginal revenue and marginal cost are each $20. As Figure 10.10 reveals, the monopolist will then allocate $y_1^* = 10$ units to the first market segment and $y_2^* = 21$ to the second, and the corresponding profit-maximizing prices will be $p_1^* = \$30$ and $p_2^* = \$40$. We have learned the following:[8]

A profit-maximizing monopolist who is able to engage in ordinary price discrimination will choose an aggregate output where aggregate marginal revenue is equal to marginal cost, and it will allocate the profit-maximizing output so that marginal revenue is identical in all market segments.

---

8 We can use calculus to solve this profit-maximizing problem. The firm will choose y_1 and y_2 to maximize profit. Hence, the partial derivatives of the firm's profit function with respect to y_1 and y_2 must both be zero at the profit-maximizing solution. Differentiating the profit function first with respect to y_1 and then y_2 and setting results equal to zero yields

$$MR_1(y_1^*) - TC'(y_1^* + y_2^*) = 0$$
$$MR_2(y_1^*) - TC'(y_1^* + y_2^*) = 0$$

But $TC'(\cdot)$ is just $MC(\cdot)$. Thus,

$$MR_1(y_1^*) = MR_2(y_2^*) = MC(y_1^* + y_2^*)$$

FIGURE 10.10 **Price discrimination: profit maximization**

To find the profit-maximizing set of prices and quantities, first horizontally aggregate the marginal revenue functions in (a) and (b) to obtain the aggregate marginal revenue function in (c). Then find the aggregate profit-maximizing quantity, $y^* = 31$, where aggregate marginal revenue is equal to marginal cost. Finally, allocate the 31 units to the two market segments so as to equalize marginal revenue; that is, sell 10 units at price \$30 in segment 1, and 21 units at price \$40 in segment 2.

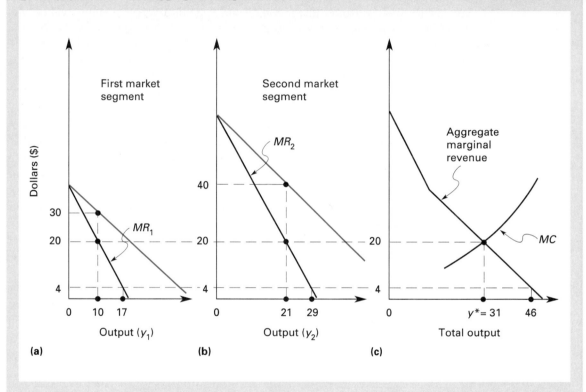

(a)   (b)   (c)

To get a better sense of what actually determines relative prices in the two market segments, it is useful to characterize the solution in terms of the price elasticities of demand in the two market segments. As we saw in Section 10.2, marginal revenue at a point on any demand curve can be expressed in terms of the absolute value of the price elasticity of demand

$$MR(y) = p[1 - 1/|\eta(y)|]$$

Using this expression for marginal revenue — and keeping in mind that equilibrium marginal revenue is the same in both segments — we see the following:

$$p_1^*[1 - 1/|\eta_1(y_1^*)|] = p_2^*[1 - 1/|\eta_2(y_2^*)|]$$

Now let us ask: When will p_2^* exceed p_1^*? Working with this equality, we see that if p_2^* exceeds p_1^*, then

$$[1 - 1/|\eta_1(y_1^*)|] > [1 - 1/|\eta_2(y_2^*)|]$$

This inequality can be rewritten as

$$|\eta_1(y_1{}^*)| > |\eta_2(y_2{}^*)|$$

Therefore, $p_2{}^*$ will exceed $p_1{}^*$ if — at the equilibrium — price elasticity of demand in the second market segment is less than price elasticity of demand in the first. Or, putting the result differently:

Price is higher in the market segment with the lower price elasticity of demand.

This result makes good sense of ordinary observations. If one of your parents falls desperately ill in Orlando or if your branch plant in London is threatening to close, you will catch the next flight out almost regardless of the fare. Your demand for airline travel is relatively price inelastic. By contrast, if you have decided to treat yourself to a holiday next spring but do not care if you go to Orlando or Mazatlan or London or Zermatt, you can pick and choose. Accordingly, your demand on any of these routes is relatively price elastic. Airline companies respond to these differing elasticities by discriminating — by charging the traveler who wants to depart tomorrow one price and the traveler who wants to depart sometime in the next month or two another, much lower price.

> **PROBLEM 10.9**
>
> The firm in Figure 10.11 has monopoly power in the first market segment but none in the second. First, find the aggregate marginal revenue curve. Then solve the monopolist's profit-maximizing problem for the conditions presented in Figure 10.11.

FIGURE 10.11   A price-discrimination problem

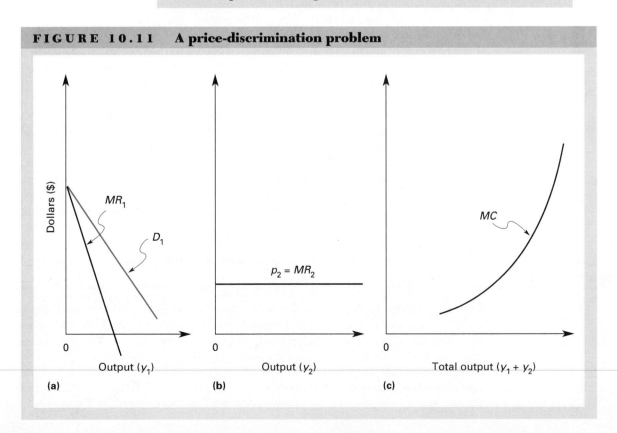

Market Segmentation Revisited

arbitrage

To establish a successful scheme of ordinary price discrimination, the monopolist must be able to *identify different price elasticities of demand* and to *segment its market accordingly* by isolating one portion of the market from the other. One entrepreneurial activity, called **arbitrage**, can undermine the monopolist's objective of market segmentation. Arbitrage is buying a good in a low-priced market and reselling it in a high-priced market. Where arbitrage can occur, market segmentation cannot be achieved effectively.

In other markets, however, arbitrage is impossible, and, in yet other markets, it is unprofitable. For example, in a wide range of cases characterized by what we might call personal services, arbitrage is impossible. Although "seniors" get a discount on movie admission prices, for example, they cannot arbitrage in this market because they cannot transfer the good — a movie they have seen — to someone else. Similarly, children cannot arbitrage in the market for haircuts — even though they can buy them more cheaply than adults — because haircuts are not transferable. All sorts of personal services from massage therapy and fitness classes to dental and medical services are markets in which arbitrage cannot occur.

In other cases, arbitrage is possible but unprofitable. For example, the retail price of a new car in Detroit, Michigan, is sometimes lower than the price of the identical model in Provo, Utah. But, relative to the price differential, the cost of transporting a car from Detroit to Provo is high enough to discourage significant arbitrage. If a price differential is large enough, however, arbitrage will occur. Thus, the possibility of arbitrage limits the degree to which prices can diverge in the two markets. In general, where transaction costs — the costs of buying, selling, and transporting — are significant, arbitrage will be unprofitable.

In still other cases, arbitrage may be both possible and potentially profitable, but the price discriminator may be able to subvert it effectively. A classic example is the case in which the duopolists Du Pont and Rohm and Haas sold the plastic molding powder methyl methacrylate to general industrial users for $0.85 per pound and to dental manufacturers for $22 per pound. When arbitragers began buying methyl methacrylate at the industrial price and reselling it to denture manufacturers at a price below $22 per pound, Rohm and Haas considered cutting the ground out from under the arbitragers by mixing arsenic with the plastic powder sold for industrial use so that it could not be used for denture work. Although the firm ultimately rejected the idea, it did circulate rumors suggesting that the industrial methyl methacrylate had been adulterated (Stocking and Watkins, 1946, 402–4).

In cases where arbitrage is either impossible or not profitable, how can the monopolist achieve market segmentation? One method is to sort the individuals in different segments of the market by requiring them to identify themselves. For example, for "seniors" to receive lower prices on prescription drugs or movie tickets, they must somehow certify their age. Requiring **direct identification** is the most obvious way to isolate market segments from one another.

direct
identification

self-selection

Another method is to rely on **self-selection**; that is, to induce individuals to sort themselves into the appropriate market niche voluntarily. The most conspicuous example is the two-segment market for airline travel. In the business travel segment of the market, demand is likely to arise on relatively short notice and to be relatively price inelastic. In the holiday travel segment, demand is usually anticipated well in advance and is likely to be relatively price elastic. A standard discriminatory mechanism is the "advanced booking discount," often hedged by such other restrictions as requiring the traveler to stay at least a week or to stay over at least one Saturday night. Because only holiday travelers are able to plan well ahead and stay for at least a week — and are therefore able to take advantage of the discount, the airline's customers reveal their identity as business people or vacationers simply by their response to its price structure.

Annual or semiannual department store sales are another rather puzzling feature of economic life that we can better understand in the context of price discrimination through self-selection. In these sales, the items are sold at prices substantially below their everyday prices, and the sales are often predictable events. The January white sales are a regular feature of the North American department store landscape, for example. What is puzzling is how stores can still manage to sell a good portion of their merchandise at everyday prices. A form of market segmentation through self-selection is part of the answer. Going to these sales usually means putting up with crowds and long lines at the cash register. To some shoppers, the package of crowds and lower prices is preferred to more elbow room and regular prices. To other shoppers, the opposite is true. Because the two kinds of shoppers select themselves by going to sales or staying away, the retailing strategy effectively segments the market. We cannot regard this strategy as a pure form of ordinary price discrimination, however, because the cost of retailing during such sales, in which volume is considerably heavier, is lower than usual.

PROBLEM 10.10

Canadian Tire offers a 4% discount for cash payments. Instead of taking 4% off the total bill, however, the firm gives customers the equivalent in Canadian Tire money. This "money" then can be presented in lieu of cash the next time customers make a purchase at a Canadian Tire store. Can you identify the two forms of price discrimination through self-selection at work here?

Multipart or Block Pricing

Finally, let us consider *multipart* or *block pricing*. We will not attempt a complete or rigorous analysis of multipart pricing. Rather, we will concentrate on understanding what it is, the circumstances in which it is feasible, and why it is even more profitable than ordinary price discrimination.

price schedule

To understand multipart pricing we need the concept of a **price schedule**. You are already familiar with a one-part price schedule. When your grocer posts a sign indicating that the (single) price of mushrooms is $3 per pound, the price schedule that you face is a one-part price schedule since you can buy any quantity you want at a single price. A multipart price schedule associates different prices with different quantity blocks. For example, your grocer might post the following two-part price schedule for mushrooms: $3 per pound for the first 5 pounds and $2 per pound for each pound in excess of 5 pounds. In this case, if you buy 8 pounds, you will pay $3 per pound for the first 5 pounds and $2 per pound for the next 3 pounds, for a total expenditure of $21. The following is a three-part price schedule: $3 per pound for the first 5 pounds, $2 per pound for the next 5 pounds, and $1 per pound for any amount greater than 10 pounds.

Now that you understand what a multipart price schedule is, let us see why it is more profitable than ordinary price discrimination. Figure 10.12 presents two individual demand curves. The demand curve for Betty is on the right. The demand curve for Sam is on the left. For reasons that will soon be apparent, we will assume that Sam's demand curve is independent of his income. And to keep the analysis simple, we will also assume that the monopoly supplier of this good incurs no costs in producing it and that Betty and Sam are

FIGURE 10.12 Multipart pricing

With the multipart pricing scheme, the firm charges any consumer $12 for the first 18 units and $8 for any units in excess of 18. Betty buys 5 units at $12 and none at $8, while Sam buys 18 units at $12 and 6 units at $8.

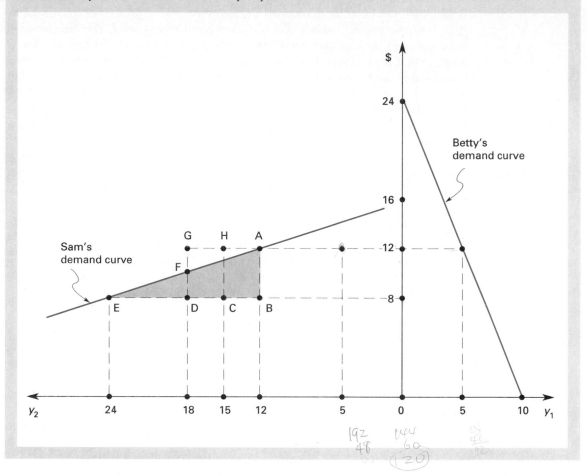

its only customers. As a point of reference, we can identify what the monopolist's pricing strategy will be if it engages in ordinary price discrimination. Since the monopolist's marginal cost is 0, it will choose the point on each demand curve where marginal revenue is equal to 0. As you can easily verify, it will charge $12 per unit in the first market segment, and Betty will buy 5 units; it will charge $8 per unit in the second market segment, and Sam will buy 24 units. The monopolist's profit and revenue will then be $252.

To show that multipart pricing can be more profitable than ordinary price discrimination, let us consider a two-part price schedule in which the monopolist charges a price of $12 per unit for the initial quantity block and a lower price of $8 per unit for each unit in excess of the initial block limit. The monopolist's problem is then to choose the block limit in the two-part price schedule — but not the two prices — that maximizes its profit. Clearly, the monopolist will choose a block limit of at least 12. What will happen if the monopolist actually sets a block limit of 12 units? Both Betty and Sam would face this two-part price schedule: a price of $12 per unit for the first 12 units and a price of $8 for every unit in excess of 12. Given this price schedule, Betty will again buy 5 units at $12 per unit. On the other hand, Sam will again buy 24 units, but he will pay $12 instead of $8 for the first 12 units. Relative to the ordinary price discrimination case, then, the monopolist will sell exactly the same amount. Yet its revenue will rise by $48 since Sam will have paid an extra $4 per unit on the first 12 units. The monopolist's profit under this two-part price schedule is $300 rather than $252. Clearly, multipart pricing is more profitable than ordinary price discrimination.

Yet the monopolist can do even better by choosing a *larger* block limit. Suppose, for example, that it increases its block limit to 15. Once again, Betty will buy 5 units at $12 per unit. The interesting question concerns Sam, who has two courses of action open to him. He will either buy just 12 units at $12 per unit, ending up at point A on his demand curve, or he will buy the entire 15-unit block at the $12 price and an additional 9 units at the $8 price, ending up at point E on his demand curve.

To see which course of action Sam will choose, suppose that he is at point A in Figure 10.12, where he has bought just 12 units at $12 apiece. First, what would Sam be willing to pay for the privilege of buying additional units at the $8 price? Second, what is the *implicit price* of this privilege under the 15-unit block limit?

To answer the first question, note that Sam's demand curve is independent of his income; therefore, we can use the concept of consumer surplus to measure his willingness to pay for this privilege. Beginning at point A, if he could buy additional units at the $8 price, he would buy 12 more units (moving from point A to point E on his demand curve). The added consumer surplus would then be $24, equal to the area of shaded triangle EBA in Figure 10.12. Therefore, Sam would be willing to pay up to $24 for this privilege.

Now for the second question. Under the 15-unit block limit, he must pay not $8 but $12 for the first three additional units (units 13, 14, and 15). The implicit price of the privilege is therefore $12. Because $12 is less than $24, he will choose the option represented by point E, where he buys 15 units at $12 per unit and 9 more units at $8 per unit — and the monopolist's profit will therefore rise by an additional $12 to $312.

Which block limit *maximizes* the monopolist's profit? The monopolist will continue to increase the block limit until the implicit price of the privilege of buying additional units at the $8 price is equal to the $24 maximum price Sam is willing to pay for that privilege. The block limit that maximizes the firm's profit is therefore 18 units since the implicit price of the privilege is then $24, equal to $4 per unit multiplied by 6 units. Under this 18-unit block limit, the monopolist's profit is $324.

Our purpose is not to present a complete analysis of the monopolist's choice of a multipart price schedule, but to indicate how this pricing strategy works. As you have seen, a multipart pricing strategy can be significantly more profitable than ordinary price discrimination. And as you will discover in the following problem, the monopolist who institutes such a strategy will not simply mimic the prices it would otherwise have charged under ordinary price discrimination, as we have so far assumed.

PROBLEM 10.11

Notice that for every $1 drop in the price per unit, Sam buys 3 more units.

a. Consider a two-part price schedule with prices of $12 and $6. What block limit maximizes profit? Is the monopolist's profit larger than it is with the $12 and $8 prices and the 18-unit block limit? Is Sam any better off?

b. Consider a two-part price schedule with prices of $12 and $0. What block limit now maximizes profit? Is the monopolist's profit now larger than in 1? Is Sam any better off?

You may be wondering why ordinary discrimination exists if multipart pricing is so much more profitable. The answer is that the monopolist must be able to meter or otherwise monitor the consumption of specific consumers like Betty and Sam. The reason your grocer does not post a multipart pricing schedule for mushrooms, for example, is that it can neither prevent arbitrage nor monitor the consumption of individual consumers. However, this kind of pricing scheme is common in the sale of electricity, natural gas, and water, because consumption literally is metered and arbitrage is costly. Cable television service is another, less obvious example of a market in which multipart pricing schemes are used. For example, Shaw Cable Company offers a limited number of television channels for $13.97 per month; a full range of television channels for $17.44; a full range of television channels plus one pay movie channel for $35.03; and a full range of television channels plus one pay movie and one pay family channel for $38.71. Another example is the common banking practice of charging a higher rate for cashing the first block of so many checks, a lower rate for the next block, and so on. Whenever it is feasible, then, monopolists do appear to use multipart pricing.

* 10.10
Patent Policy

Seen in the framework of the static, unchanging economic world we have modeled so far in this chapter, monopoly is most striking for its allocative inefficiency. Yet the real economic world is not static and unchanging, but dynamic and ever-changing. As we now place monopoly within the very different framework of a dynamic model, it will undergo a striking metamorphosis. The lure of monopoly profit becomes the magnet that attracts new and better products into being, and monopolists become the providers of products of the future.

Step back from monopoly for a moment to appreciate just how rapidly the economic world is changing. First, try to think of 10 products available at the turn of the century that are still on the shelves today. (Once past Arm and Hammer baking soda, we found that it was no easy task.) Now try to list some of the products that are a familiar part of your landscape but that were unavailable, and perhaps even unimaginable, to a college student at the turn of the century. Your list can legitimately include almost any product in transportation or communication; any article of clothing made from a synthetic fabric; any item of frozen food in your local supermarket; all of your audio equipment, tapes, records, and compact discs; almost all prescription drugs; all computer products; and on and on. Now try to imagine the thousands of new products that are just coming onto the market: *National Geographic*'s CD-ROM mammals' encyclopedia, complete with film clips and sound; a lobster trap with a biodegradable door made of plastics, cobalt, starch, and a fatty acid that rots away, allowing the lobster to escape if the trap is lost; Fuji's palm-sized video projector, which weighs only one pound and fits easily into a camcorder bag; and a miniature sewing machine that can be swallowed by patients and used to stitch internal tissues together without surgery.

In this dynamic context, monopoly is no longer just the source of a static inefficiency problem. In addition, it plays an important role in ensuring that bright, new ideas about potential goods and services are actually transformed into bright, new goods and services. For this reason, patent and copyright protection, which provide monopoly power over a specified period of time, play critical roles in promoting these transformations from idea to actuality.

As you know, patents provide exclusive rights to a new product, invention, or process for a specified period of time. Similarly, copyrights provide exclusive rights to art, music, or written material for a specified period of time. (We will use the word *patent* to refer to both.) These exclusive, or monopoly, rights are an important policy tool for governments in virtually all market economies. (The framers of the U.S. Constitution thought patent policy important enough to enshrine it in that document.) In this section, we will develop a model that will let you see why granting patents can make economic good sense — and see, too, some of the economic pitfalls associated with patents.

The Appropriability Problem

Let us begin by asking: What economic problems do patents solve? When Jonas Salk created the Salk vaccine, his invention conferred real benefits to society at large. Polio was virtually eliminated in developed countries by the early 1960s. So, too, thousands of other inventions — Bell's telephone, Land's camera, Mozart's music, Jobs' and Wosniack's computer, Virginia Woolf's novels, Lear's jet, and so on — have created what we will call social value. We will see below how to use the cost-benefit criterion to attach a dollar figure to the social value of an invention. For now, we can simply note that according to this criterion, a bright idea should be developed into a new product if the social value of the new product is greater than the development cost. But will a socially valuable invention always come into being? It is easy to see that if inventors were to bear all the development costs and reap all the benefits thereby personally capturing, or *appropriating,* all the excess of social value over the cost of development associated with their inventions — every socially useful invention would be produced. Yet inventors are not able to appropriate all the social value created by their inventions. As a result, many potentially valuable ideas never appear as products on market shelves, because their inventors simply do not have the private incentive to pursue them. This is the **appropriability problem**.

appropriability problem

A number of responses to the appropriability problem are possible. One response is to provide governmental assistance to alleviate the sometimes massive costs of product research and development (R&D). For example, to develop a new microeconomics textbook — to write and edit it, to have it reviewed and to respond to the reviews, to design the book and the graphs, to set the type — costs approximately $500,000. To put a new prescription drug on the market is significantly more expensive. According to the Pharmaceutical Manufacturers Association, R&D costs — the key to success in the drug industry — have jumped from an average of $54 million for each new medication in the 1970s to $231 million in 1990. Governments can and do subsidize new product development by providing a variety of support measures. For instance, scattered across the United States are more than 75 joint industry–government research consortiums that are developing generic technologies in everything from cement to semiconductors. Member companies can then hone those technologies for their own specific needs.

We will be focusing instead on another possible response: granting patents that confer monopoly power and, therefore, monopoly profit — to inventors, thereby increasing their private incentive to create new products. For example, the copyright on "Happy Birthday to You" — the four-line verse written by two Louisville teachers as a classroom greeting — generates about $1 million in royalties annually.

A Model of Inventions

Let us begin by supposing that a vast number of individuals or firms — for convenience, we will call them all "developers" — have an equally vast stock of innovative ideas that can be developed into marketable products. Let us suppose, too, that it costs money — a good deal of money — to transform innovative ideas into marketable

FIGURE 10.13 **The inducement to develop**

Will this firm incur the costs necessary to develop its product? If it anticipates a period of monopoly power — either because it will have patent protection or because other firms cannot imitate its product — it will earn annual profit equal to the area of the green rectangle. Annual profit multiplied by the anticipated length of the monopoly period is the inducement for the firm to develop its product. If, instead, other firms can imitate its product

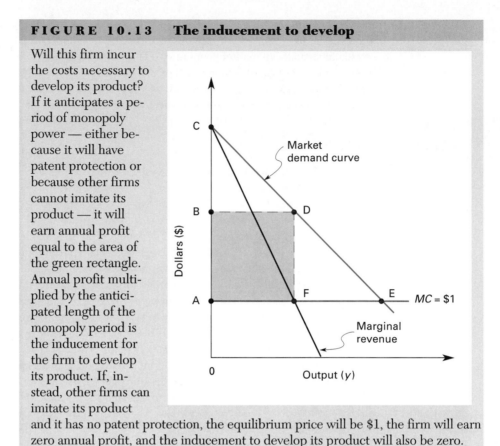

and it has no patent protection, the equilibrium price will be $1, the firm will earn zero annual profit, and the inducement to develop its product will also be zero.

products. Of course, the magnitude of this product development cost, denoted by $D, will vary from one innovation to another.

Suppose, too, that the developer — once having invested in the R&D necessary to create a marketable product — can produce it at a constant marginal cost of $1 per unit, and that in each of a number of years, the market demand for its product is given by a linear market demand function like the one presented in Figure 10.13.[9] The green area in Figure 10.13 is the annual profit $M that a monopolist in this market could earn. (We will consider only innovations for which $M is positive.) Like the development cost $D, the annual monopoly profit $M and the precise shape of the demand curve will vary from one innovation to another.

Initially, the developer of this new product will be a monopolist, and the period over which it will remain the sole firm in its industry will be determined by what we will call an *imitation lag L*. For example, when the IBM personal computer hit the market in 1981, its rival clone manufacturers were in hot pursuit less than a year later. In this case, then, the imitation lag *L* is a year. The imitation lag for a book is even shorter. Using modern reproduction techniques, book bootleggers can begin to market duplications

9 Throughout our discussion, we will assume that the demand functions for different products are independent of each other; that is, new products are neither substitutes nor complements for each other. Without this assumption, we could not use consumer surplus to measure the social value of a new product.

of a newly released book in a matter of days. And as any experienced software pirate knows, the imitation lag for much computer software can be a matter of minutes.

In other cases, the lag time is apparently large. Thus, we will assume that the developer is the sole manufacturer of its product for a lag period of L, but that once the lag period L has elapsed, anyone else can also manufacture the developer's product at a marginal cost of \$1. (Notice that we are implicitly supposing that imitators incur no development costs.) In the absence of patent protection, then, the developer is a monopolist until L has elapsed — at which point it becomes just another perfectly competitive producer. Clearly, if patent protection is to mean anything, it must extend this monopoly period beyond the L time periods attributable to imitation lag.

Finally, because patents obviously raise intertemporal issues, time considerations must be introduced. For simplicity, let us suppose that every product has a 40-year product cycle. Specifically, suppose that the market demand curve (shown in Figure 10.13) will be stable for 40 years, and thereafter it will, as it were, evaporate overnight. In addition, suppose that the entire stock of innovative ideas is in place at time-zero, that all decisions about product development are made at time-zero, and that product development itself requires no time. A patent policy will then shape developers' incentives at time-zero, thereby indirectly determining the products that will be marketed in this miniature economy across the whole 40-year time span.

In this model, each of the multitude of innovative ideas in the minds of developers can be described by its demand curve and three numbers: D, the sum of money needed to develop the idea into a marketable product; M the profit per year that a monopolist could earn by marketing the product; and L, the number of years before other firms can imitate the developed product.

We will assume that each developer knows what these three numbers are and that no one else does. In what circumstances will a developer choose to transform an innovative idea into a marketable new product?

Product Development in the Absence of Patents

If no patent protection is in place, the developer will be a monopolist for L years — and will therefore earn monopoly profits of M per year for L years. Once L years have elapsed, the developer's monopoly power will vanish. It will become just one more perfect competitor, selling its product at a price equal to the marginal cost of \$1 and earning no profit.

In deciding whether to go ahead with its product development and marketing plans, a profit-maximizing developer will compare the present value of its monopoly profits with the development cost D. The present value of monopoly profit M over L periods is just the sum of money PV that would make the monopolist indifferent between receiving PV today and M in each of the next L periods. For simplicity in calculating present values, let us suppose that the rate of interest is 0%. With this simplification, the present value of its annual monopoly profit M over L years is just L multiplied by M, or LM. (See Section 15.1 for an in-depth treatment of present value.) A profit-maximizing developer will proceed with its plans only if LM exceeds D. Thus, if L is greater than D/M, the new product will be marketed, and if L is less than D/M, it will not.

We see, then, that in the absence of patents, some innovative ideas will be transformed into marketable goods and others will not. In particular, if the imitation lag period L is small enough, no matter how socially valuable an idea might be, the developer has no private incentive to market it. For example, imagine that you have thought up a new computer game. You realize that once you have invested in the R&D necessary to develop a marketable product, your potential competitors can immediately copy and produce it at a constant marginal cost of $1. In this situation, L will certainly be less than D/M — and neither you nor anyone else will bother to invest in developing the computer game. In such cases, the appropriability problem becomes a serious consideration.

Since patents operate by extending the period of monopoly beyond the L years attributable to the imitation lag, the next question is this: What is the number of years of monopoly profit J such that the present value of the annual monopoly profit M is just equal to the development cost D? Since J satisfies $JM = D$, we see that

$$J = D/M$$

If a developer could count on being a monopolist for J years, then it could just recover its R&D costs. Therefore, if its actual monopoly period exceeds J, the developer will opt for creating its new product. We will call J the just-sufficient monopoly period. For simplicity, we will suppose that J is a shorter period than a 40-year product cycle. (If it were a longer period, the product would never come into being, because it would be obsolete before the developer could recover its R&D costs.)

The Effects of Patents

How will patent protection alter a developer's decision making? A patent law can be described by T, the time period over which patent (or monopoly) rights are granted. For example, in the United States, the copyright period for works of art extends 50 years beyond the artist's death, and the standard patent period is 17 years. How any particular patent law will affect a developer's decision depends on the nature of the relationships among the patent period T, the imitation lag L, and the just-sufficient monopoly period J. Let us look at these relationships systematically:

1. If $T > J > L$, in the absence of patent protection, the potential new product will not be marketed because the just-sufficient period J is longer than the imitation lag period L. Under patent protection, however, it will be marketed, because the patent period T is longer than the just-sufficient period J. In this case, then, a patent law solves the appropriability problem.

2. If $T > L > J$, the new product will be marketed even in the absence of patent protection because the imitation lag time L is longer than the just-sufficient period J. The patent period T simply extends the monopoly period from L years to T years. In this case, a patent law is not required to solve the appropriability problem, yet it does increase the developer's monopoly profit.

3. If $L > T > J$, the new product will be marketed because the imitation lag time L is longer than both the patent period T and the just-sufficient time J. In this case, the patent law is irrelevant.

4. If $J > T$ and $J > L$, the potential new product will not be developed and marketed because the just-sufficient period J is longer than both the patent period T and the imitation lag time L. Once again, the patent law is irrelevant.

Optimal Patent Policy

Now that we understand the possible effects of a patent in this model, let us turn to patent policy. Our first problem is to define the social value of a new product. If we suppose that the demand for these new products is independent of income, we can use the concepts of consumers' and producers' surplus to define social value.

For any new product in the marketplace, the equilibrium will be in one of two phases: either a monopoly equilibrium (where its developer is still protected from competition by imitation lag or by a patent) or a competitive equilibrium (where neither imitation lag nor a patent remains operative). In the monopoly phase, total surplus in each period is the trapezoidal area $ACDF$ in Figure 10.13. It is composed of producer's surplus (that is, the monopolist's profit), an amount equal to the area of rectangle $ABDF$, and consumers' surplus, an amount equal to the area of triangle BCD. In the competitive phase, total surplus in each period is the area of the triangle ACE. It is composed entirely of consumers' surplus. Notice that total annual surplus is thus larger in the competitive phase than in the monopoly phase by an amount equal to area of triangle DEF in Figure 10.13. This triangle simply reflects the static burden of monopoly. Of course, if the product is not developed and marketed, then total surplus is zero in each period.

In general, the cost-benefit criterion defines the social value of a new product as the discounted present value of the total annual surplus over the product's life. In the present context, the **social value** of any new product is then just the sum of total surplus in each period over all 40 periods.[10] In this model, the **social cost** of any new product is its R&D cost $D.

social value

social cost

We will consider two cases in analyzing optimal patent policy and begin by making the unrealistic assumption that a product-specific patent law can be devised for each possible new product. Then we will drop this assumption as we take up the more realistic and challenging case in which one patent law applies across the board to all new products.

Given our assumptions, we know that each of the multitude of innovative ideas described in this model is socially desirable. Why? Recall that the just-sufficient time period J for each product is less than 40 years. The social value of each product therefore exceeds its social cost even when its developer is a monopolist over the entire 40-year product cycle. This means that if the patent period T is 40 years, every innovative idea will actually be translated into a marketable product, and both the developer and all the product's consumers will be better off. Of course, this does not mean that the optimal patent period is 40 years. It simply indicates that all the products in this model are socially desirable.

What is an optimal patent policy in this circumstance? It is one that maximizes a new product's social value less its social (or R&D) cost. Let us identify that optimal patent policy. First, consider a potential new product that will not come into existence unless it is patent-protected — that is, a potential product for which the just-sufficient period J is longer than the imitation lag time L. The patent period we choose must be long enough that its developer will have a profit incentive to bring the product to market — that is, the patent period T must be longer than or identical to the just-sufficient period J. Once we have hit this target, our objective then will be to minimize the length of the monopoly phase. Why? Because total surplus in each period in the monopoly phase is smaller than it is in the competitive phase. Therefore, when J is greater than L, the optimal patent period is $T^* = J$. Any shorter patent period would fail to provide the developer with a profit incentive. Any longer patent period would extend the monopoly period needlessly, thereby reducing total surplus for each additional year of monopoly by an amount equal to the area of triangle DEF in Figure 10.13.

Now let us take up the case of a product that will come into being even though it is not patent-protected — that is, a product for which the lag time L is longer than the just-sufficient period J. In this case, no patent is required. The developer already

10 Here we are ignoring an important question: What is the appropriate social discount rate? This is an important and complex issue that we will not address.

has all the profit incentive it needs to bring the product to market. And that is all there is to optimal patent-policy making — when we can tailor a product-specific patent period for each new product.

This seemingly easy answer has a fatal drawback. The policy maker does not have the information necessary to compute the just-sufficient monopoly period J for each product — information that is crucial in identifying the optimal patent period for that particular new product. This means that policy makers are inevitably forced to apply a single patent period to a whole host of products.

Assuming that a single patent period covers all products, what is the optimal patent policy? To answer that question, we need to aggregate social value and social (or product development) costs over all products. We will call the sum of social value over all products the **aggregate social value** and the sum of social cost over all products **aggregate social cost**. The optimal patent policy maximizes aggregate social value less aggregate social cost.

Unfortunately, when one patent period applies to a multitude of innovations, policy makers are forced to confront a trade-off between creating the necessary incentives to encourage new product development and minimizing the static inefficiency of monopoly. Suppose, for example, that a policy maker is trying to choose between patent periods T of 10 or 15 years. If the policy maker opts for the shorter, 10-year period, some innovative ideas will be transformed into marketable products and others will not. Among the products that will remain undeveloped are some that would have come into being if T had been 15 years long instead. These would-be products are composed of all the innovative ideas for which the imitation lag L is shorter than the just-sufficient time period J and for which J is between 10 and 15 years. If the policy maker had chosen the longer, 15-year patent period, these innovations would have come into being — and aggregate social value less aggregate social cost would have risen accordingly. The resulting influx of new products onto the market is directly attributable to the more attractive profit incentives stemming from the now-longer patent period.

Yet this gain is offset by a loss. If the policy maker settles on the longer, 15-year patent period, the monopoly period of some — but not all — of the products that would have been developed under the shorter patent period is needlessly extended. (If the imitation lag L is shorter than 10 years, then the needless extension of the monopoly period is 5 full years; if L is between 10 and 15 years, then the extension is 15 minus L years; and if L exceeds 15 years, then the monopoly period is unaffected by the increase in T.) The total social value from these products therefore drops under the longer patent period because, for each product, annual surplus in the now-extended monopoly phase is less than it is in the now-shortened competitive phase. This is the nature of the trade-off that policy makers must confront. How can they decide on the optimal patent policy?

To find out, let us consider a small, or marginal, increase in the patent period. A marginal increase in T will have two effects. On the one hand, because it will stimulate the development of additional new products, it will tend to increase aggregate social value less aggregate social cost. On the other hand, because it needlessly increases the monopoly period of some products that would have been brought to market in any case, it will tend to decrease aggregate social value less aggregate social cost. If we call the first effect the **marginal social benefit** of increasing the patent period, and the second effect the **marginal social cost** of increasing the patent period, we can neatly characterize the optimal patent policy:

aggregate social value

aggregate social cost

marginal social benefit

marginal social cost

At the optimal patent period, the marginal social benefit of increasing the patent period is equal to the marginal social cost.

Application of this rule is more difficult than our simple model suggests because policy makers will have a hard time obtaining all the necessary information. What is that information? It is a list of all the possible products and — for each product — the annual total surplus associated with that new product in both its monopoly and its competitive phases, the product developer's R&D costs and annual monopoly profit, and the imitation lag time. To even begin to approximate this type of information is a major undertaking. As a result, policy makers typically are forced to set patent policy under conditions of very imperfect information.

What have we learned? That monopoly profit — and therefore monopoly itself — can play a beneficial role in a dynamic economy by providing an incentive to new product development. We also learned that in creating patent law, the patent policy makers invariably are caught between a rock and a hard place. They must try to find the right balance in the inevitable trade-off between creating incentives for new product development and minimizing the static inefficiency associated with monopoly.

The policy makers' balancing act is made even trickier because it takes place in an environment characterized by very imperfect information. Trying to find the delicate balance between such trade-offs under conditions of imperfect information is a difficulty that policy makers in general confront time and again. Thus, the principles and problems that arise in trying to set an optimal patent policy can serve as a metaphor for the more general principles and problems encountered in a wide spectrum of policy issues.

SUMMARY

From a formal standpoint, what differentiates the monopolist's profit-maximizing problem from the perfect competitor's is that its revenue function is more complex because the monopolist is a price setter. Its *marginal revenue function* lies *below* the demand, or average revenue, function. As a result, at the monopolist's profit-maximizing solution, the output level where marginal revenue equals marginal cost, price exceeds marginal cost.

Two important implications follow from this result. First, the monopoly solution is not Pareto-optimal; it is inefficient. Second, at the monopoly solution, the monopolist fails to extract the maximum possible profit. The first implication raises a normative question: What, if anything, should be done about monopoly? The second stimulates the monopolist to search for clever pricing strategies to extract more profit than under the ordinary, or "unimaginative," monopoly solution.

In considering the normative question, we argued that the proper policy response to monopoly depends on the source of monopoly power. If monopoly power springs from the monopoly ownership of some scarce resource, then competition — created by a governmental policy of divestiture — is a feasible alternative. If monopoly power comes from economies of scale — and the monopoly is therefore a natural monopoly — the ideal regulatory response is to induce the monopolist (whether public or private) to behave efficiently. Unfortunately, neither *average-cost pricing* nor *rate-of-return regulations* — both standard governmental responses — is entirely satisfactory because neither regulatory mechanism induces the monopolist to behave efficiently. As we saw, however, if the regulatory agency knows the monopolist's demand curve, it can devise an *efficient regulatory mechanism*.

In considering the monopolist's response to the "unimaginative" monopoly solution, we analyzed the more sophisticated strategies of *price discrimination* that are based on the monopolist's ability to segment its market. Two types of such market segmentation are common: *direct identification* (as in various discounts for senior citizens and students, for example) and *self-selection* (as in different fares for airline tickets, for example).

We considered three types of price discrimination: *perfect price discrimination*, *ordinary price discrimination*, and *multipart pricing*. Perfect price discrimination is not something we expect to see in the real world; however, this ideal case does let us see just how strong a monopolist's incentive to devise clever pricing strategies can be. Ordinary price discrimination is something we encounter almost every day of our lives, and it can take very subtle forms. Multipart pricing is more profitable than ordinary price discrimination, but, because it requires the monopolist to monitor the customer's consumption, it is not as common as ordinary price discrimination.

Finally, in our discussion of *patents* we looked at monopoly as a possible solution to an important social problem, the *appropriability problem*. Because innovators bear most of the development costs of their new ideas, but cannot appropriate most or even a significant portion of the benefits, innovators have no economic incentive to develop many socially valuable ideas. One way to enhance the innovator's economic incentive is to grant the inventor a patent monopoly — the exclusive right to use the new idea for a specified period of time. As we saw, the design of an optimal patent policy involves a troublesome trade-off between stimulating product development and reducing the inefficiency of monopoly.

EXERCISES

1. The demand function for a very famous introductory economics textbook is

$$p = 100 - .005y$$

The publisher must pay $20 per book in printing and distribution costs and, in addition, it must pay the author a $20 royalty for each book sold.

   a. Your job is to advise the publisher. What price will maximize the publisher's profit? How much profit will the publisher earn? How large will the author's royalty check be?

   b. A consultant says that the publisher and the author have the wrong sort of agreement. He says that the author and the publisher should tear up their original agreement, in which the author gets $20 per book sold, and enter a profit-sharing agreement. He recommends that the author get 40% of the profit and the publisher 60%. What price should the publisher set with this profit-sharing agreement? Hint: Is marginal cost $40 or only $20? Will both the author and the publisher prefer the profit-sharing agreement to their original agreement? Which agreement will the students who buy the textbook prefer?

   c. Can you explain why the original royalty agreement is not economically sound?

2. There is just one movie theater in Montrose. The price elasticity of demand for movies is −2 for adults, −4 for students, and −6 for children. Who will pay the highest price, and who will pay the lowest? If the children's price is $2, what are the other prices? What is the monopolist's marginal cost?

3. The demand for Wayless, a dietary supplement, is

$$p = 110 - y$$

and the cost function for any firm producing Wayless is

$$C(y) = 10y + F$$

where F is a fixed cost.

   a. What is marginal cost? How much Wayless would a monopolist produce? What price would it charge? How much profit would it earn?

   b. If the monopolist did produce the profit-maximizing quantity you found in a, show that an entrant's residual demand function would be

$$p_E = 60 - y_E$$

c. What quantity would maximize an entrant's profit, given this residual demand function? What would the price be? What would the entrant's profit be?

d. For which of the following values of F is the market for Wayless a natural monopoly? $F = \$200$, $F = \$400$, $F = \$600$, $F = \$800$.

4. When Warner-Lambert Company's patent on its anticholesterol drug Lopid was about to expire, it lobbied the U.S. Congress to extend its patent for 5 more years. If you had been an economic advisor to Congress, what advice would you have offered? What are the implications for the price of Lopid? Is there an economic case for extending this patent? If there is an economic case for offering a patent before the drug is invented, is there a case for extending the patent period after it is invented?

5. Suppose a monopolist must pay an excise tax equal to t per unit sold — if it produces y units, it must pay ty in taxes. To the monopolist, these taxes are just another cost of production, so we can write the monopolist's profit function as

$$\neq(y) = yD(y) - ty - TC(y)$$

The monopolist's profit-maximizing rule is then

$$MR(y^*) = MC(y^*) + t$$

a. Explain this rule.

b. Now, suppose that the monopolist's demand curve is

$$p = 200 - 5y$$

and that the monopolist's marginal cost is $10 per unit. What are the profit-maximizing price and quantity and the monopolist's profit when t is $10? When t is $20? When t is $30? When t is $0?

6. The managers of Vancouver's international exposition, Expo '86, considered selling two types of admission tickets: one for $20 and another for $100. The more expensive ticket would have allowed its holder to move to the head of the line into the Expo grounds. The Monterey Bay Aquarium in California uses a similar strategy. Customers who take out a year's membership are allowed to enter the aquarium at any time. Nonmembers must buy day passes good for the next available time slot — ordinarily an hour or two after they buy their tickets. Explain the con-

ditions necessary for this sort of pricing strategy to be profitable.

7. In the book trade, it is common practice to publish a novel in hardcover and sell it for $30 and then to bring out a paperback edition about 6 months later and sell it for $10. The motion picture industry uses a similar strategy. A good, new movie might be screened at first-run movie theaters for about 3 months. About the time the first run closes, the movie becomes available on videocassette. Explain these curious practices.

8. Price ceilings offer some interesting possibilities in monopoly markets. Consider the following demand function of some monopolist:

$$p = 200 - 2y$$

The monopolist's marginal cost is $80.

a. What is MR? Carefully draw both the demand curve and the marginal revenue curve. What is the profit-maximizing price and quantity?

b. Now suppose a price ceiling equal to $100 is imposed on the monopolist. Show that the monopolist's MR curve is now composed of two segments: MR is $100 for the first 50 units and is given by the original MR function for larger outputs. Draw this revised MR curve. Notice the gap or discontinuity in MR at $y = 50$.

c. What is the profit-maximizing price and quantity when a $100 price ceiling is imposed? When a $160 price ceiling is imposed?

d. What is the efficient level of output? Is there a price ceiling that will induce the monopolist to produce the efficient output?

9. Firm A has no costs of production and sells its product to just two buyers. Buyer 1's demand function is

$$p_1 = 90 - 10y_1$$

and Buyer 2's demand function is

$$p_2 = 60 - 5y_2$$

a. Assuming that the firm can engage in ordinary price discrimination, find the profit-maximizing prices. What is firm A's profit?

b. Now, suppose that the monopolist can engage in multipart pricing. Find a two-part price schedule that generates more profit than the firm gets in a. How much additional profit does it earn?

c. Finally, suppose that the firm cannot price-discriminate. First find the firm's aggregate demand function. (It is composed of two linear segments, like the demand function in Figure 9.7.) Then find its marginal revenue function. (It is composed of two linear segments, with a gap or discontinuity.) Find its profit-maximizing price, and compute its profit.

*10. Suppose that the Nickel Company is the sole producer of nickel in a "small" country such as Canada. The demand function for nickel in Canada is

$$p = 100 - y$$

where y is tons of nickel sold in Canada. Outside Canada, the market for nickel is perfectly competitive and nickel is priced at $60 per ton. Canada sets a tariff on imported nickel equal to $30 per ton. Show that Nickel Company's aggregate marginal revenue function is

$$MR(y) = 90 \qquad \text{if } y \le 10$$

$$MR(y) = 100 - 2y \qquad \text{if } 10 < y \le 20$$

$$MR(y) = 60 \qquad \text{if } y > 20$$

Nickel Company's marginal cost function is

$$MC(y) = ay$$

a. Suppose that $a = 2$. How much nickel will the company produce? How much will it sell in Canada and at what price? How much will it sell in the international market? What profit will Nickel Company earn?

b. Now, suppose that $a = 14/3$ and repeat these exercises.

c. Finally, suppose that $a = 30$ and repeat these exercises.

*11. Let us reconsider one aspect of the efficient regulatory solution in Section 10.6. We will use the following demand function:

$$p = 160 - y$$

Recall that the subsidy associated with any quantity y was identical to consumers' surplus at y, which implies that the firm's marginal revenue function is identical to its demand function. First, compute the subsidy paid for an arbitrary quantity of output y. (Remember that the area of a triangle is 1/2 its base multiplied by its height.) Then compute the firm's total revenue — including the subsidy — as a function of y. Finally, divide total revenue by y to get the average revenue function associated with this subsidy scheme. Then construct a diagram in which you identify the regulated firm's profit-maximizing output and use the average revenue function to identify its profit.

REFERENCES

Averch, H., and L. L. Johnson. 1961. "Behavior of the Firm Under Regulatory Constraint," *American Economic Review*, 52:1052–69.

Hansen, R. 1979. "The Pharmaceutical Development Process: Estimates of Development Times and the Effects of Proposed Regulatory Changes," in *Pharmaceutical Economics,* R. I. Chien (ed.), Lexington, Mass.: Lexington Books.

Hartwick, J. 1987. "Discriminating Monopoly, " in *The New Palgrave: A Dictionary of Economics*, J. Eatwell, M. Milgate, and P. Newman (eds.), London: The Macmillan Press.

Loeb, M., and W. A. Magat. 1979. "A Decentralized Method for Utility Regulation," *The Journal of Law and Economics*, 22:339–404.

Phlips, L. 1987. "Price Discrimination," in *The New Palgrave: A Dictionary of Economics*, J. Eatwell, M. Milgate, and P. Newman (eds.), London: The Macmillan Press.

Sharkey, W. W. 1987. "Natural Monopoly," in *The New Palgrave: A Dictionary of Economics*, J. Eatwell, M. Milgate, and P. Newman (eds.), London: The Macmillan Press.

Stocking, G. W., and W. R. Mueller. 1955. "The Cellophane Case and the New Competition," *American Economic Review*, 45:29–63.

Stocking, G. W. and M. W. Watkins. 1946. *Cartels in Action*, New York: Twentieth Century Fund.

West, E. 1987. "Monopoly," in *The New Palgrave: A Dictionary of Economics*, J. Eatwell, M. Milgate, and P. Newman (eds.), London: The Macmillan Press.

CHAPTER 11

Game Theory and Oligopoly

oligopoly

Two pieces of the theory of market structure are now in place: perfect competition and monopoly. What remains — the theory of **oligopoly** or competition among the few — fits less neatly into an overall picture of market structure. Indeed, to speak of *the* theory of oligopoly, as if only one existed, is misleading. Unlike monopoly and perfect competition, oligopoly has no single theory. Instead, a variety of models yield different insights into the conduct of real oligopolies.

This chapter has two purposes. In it, we develop some important tools of *game theory*, and we use those tools to explore a number of models of oligopoly. Each of the models we will consider reveals an important facet of oligopolistic behavior. For example, the Cournot model provides a solid understanding of how the number of firms in the market affects the price and the aggregate quantity of output in an oligopolistic setting. The Bertrand model helps to explain the factors that can lead to the price wars that sometimes break out between gas stations, grocery stores, and cigarette manufacturers — to name just a few. The collusive model both highlights the incentive that motivates firms to collude and underscores the difficult problems that a successful collusive agreement must overcome. For example, it helps to explain the existence of the OPEC cartel of petroleum-producing nations as well as the recurrent problems OPEC has had in trying to enforce its collusive strategy. The collusive model accounts for the collusive activities occasionally encountered in a wide range of other industries, including ocean shipping; cigarette manufacturers; baby-formula makers; ready-mix concrete suppliers; moving companies; meat packers; the potash, titanium, uranium, gypsum, cardboard, and paper bag industries; and even private colleges.

Our underlying aim is to give you an understanding of the game theoretic problems that oligopoly poses and a sampling of the tactics oligopolists use to secure market power. In fact, strategic maneuvering is the name of the oligopolistic game. In an oligopolistic industry, the number of firms — two or more — is small enough that each has some, but not complete, market power. Oligopoly thus occupies a middle ground between perfect competition and monopoly: an oligopolist neither takes price as given nor independently sets industry price and quantity. Instead, an oligopolist's decisions are always made with one eye fixed on its competitors — either anticipating or responding to moves by its rivals in the industry as they all maneuver for a bigger chunk of the profit.

In this chapter, we will look at oligopolistic industries in which products are undifferentiated, or *homogeneous* and in Chapter 12, we will look at those oligopolistic industries in which products are *differentiated*, or heterogeneous. Some of the more notable oligopolistic industries characterized by **homogeneous products** are steel, crude oil, plywood, sugar, aluminum, and uranium. Ready-mix concrete in a regional market and pulp and paper products — including the paper in this book — are yet other examples of undifferentiated products.

homogeneous
products

11.1

Game Theory

players

strategies

strategy combination

game theory

payoff

best response function

equilibrium strategy combination

Nash equilibrium

Cournot-Nash equilibrium

Before plunging into oligopoly theory, we need to look quickly at some important concepts from game theory. These concepts will have become old friends by the time you have worked through the entire chapter. The actors or "choosers" in games are usually called **players**: they are the entities like firms or individuals or governments that make choices in the game. In this chapter all the players in any game are firms, and we will often call them firms.

The things that players choose — like quantity of output or price — are called **strategies**. If firms choose quantity of output, for example, then a strategy for a firm is just a quantity of output for that firm. If instead firms choose price, then a strategy for a firm is just a price for that firm's product. A list of strategies, one for each player in the game, is called a **strategy combination**. The central problem in game theory is to predict the choices that players make. Or, using game theoretic terminology, the central problem of **game theory** is to predict the strategy combination that will be chosen.

In the eyes of a player, what distinguishes one strategy combination from another? If the player is a firm, and if the firm is a profit maximizer, then strategy combination A is preferred to strategy combination B if the firm's *profit* or **payoff** from strategy combination A is larger than its profit or payoff from strategy combination B. Payoff is the technical term that game theorists use, but in this chapter we will use the terms profit and payoff interchangeably.

The distinguishing feature of choice problems in game theory is that a player's payoff depends — not just on his or her own strategy — but also on the strategies of other players in the game. That is, each player's payoff is determined by the entire strategy combination. In this situation, each player must be concerned with the strategy choices made by other players in the game.

How do players go about choosing a strategy in this awkward situation where their payoff is determined jointly by their own choice of a strategy and by the choices of all other players? To many game theorists, the natural answer is that *each player chooses his or her own strategy to maximize his or her own payoff, given the strategies chosen by the other players*. The mapping from the strategies of other players to the strategy that maximizes the player's own payoff is called the player's **best response function**: it specifies the player's best response to the given strategies of the other players.

A strategy combination is an **equilibrium strategy combination** if every player's strategy is a best response to the strategies of all other players. Given such a strategy combination, there is nothing any individual player can independently do that will increase that player's payoff. In this equilibrium, each player's own strategy maximizes that player's own payoff. This is the notion of **Nash equilibrium** formulated by the American game theorist John Nash in 1950. It is really a generalization of ideas developed more than a century earlier by the French economist August Cournot, and for this reason a Nash equilibrium is often called a **Cournot-Nash equilibrium**. We have already used this notion of equilibrium at a number of points in the book — for example, in our discussion of common property problems in Chapters 1 and 4, in finding the equilibrium of two-person firms in Chapter 6, and in our discussion of traffic congestion in Chapter 7.[1]

---

1 For a more detailed discussion, see David Kreps' entry on "Nash equilibrium" in *The New Palgrave*.

11.2

Monopoly Equilibrium

We will develop and examine a number of oligopoly models in this chapter. Because we want to compare the equilibrium of each of these models of oligopoly with the monopoly equilibrium, we will be using a single set of demand and cost conditions throughout. Let us begin by setting out those demand and cost conditions and by computing the monopoly equilibrium.

We will use the following linear market demand function throughout the chapter:

$$p = 100 - y$$

where p is price and y is aggregate, or industry-wide, output. We will also assume that each firm in the industry can make the product at a constant cost of $40 per unit. Then $40 is the firm's marginal cost, its average cost, and what we will call its *unit cost of production*. In the first half of the chapter, we will also assume that no additional costs of production are relevant and that the oligopolists are existing, or *established* firms. In the second half, we will add the product development, or **setup costs** that a potential firm will incur if it decides to enter an industry.

We can begin by computing the standard monopoly solution that will serve as our benchmark throughout the chapter. The standard graphic solution to the monopoly problem is shown in Figure 11.1. The monopolist will produce 30 units, sell them at a price of $70 per unit, and earn a profit equal to $900. (Recall that in answering Problem 10.3 you computed this monopoly equilibrium.)

It is useful to find the solution to the monopolist's problem using algebraic techniques as well. Recall that for linear market demand functions, the marginal revenue

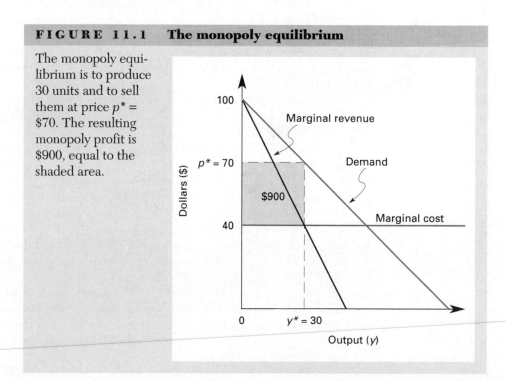

FIGURE 11.1 The monopoly equilibrium

The monopoly equilibrium is to produce 30 units and to sell them at price $p^* = $70. The resulting monopoly profit is $900, equal to the shaded area.

function and the market demand function intersect the price axis at the same point and that the marginal revenue function is twice as steep. Therefore,

$$MR = 100 - 2y$$

To find the profit-maximizing output, simply identify the value of y, written as y^*, at which marginal revenue $(100 - 2y)$ equals marginal cost (40): y^* is equal to 30. Next, using the demand function $(100 - y)$, we can compute price at the profit-maximizing output level (30): p^* is equal to 70. The monopolist's profit is then simply total revenue $(p^*y^* = 2100)$ minus total cost $(40y^* = 1200)$: p^* is equal to 900. The $900 profit is represented graphically by the shaded area in Figure 11.1

11.3

Duopoly as a Prisonner's Dilemma

duopoly

To understand the puzzles that arise in oligopolistic settings, we will begin by considering a **duopoly** — an oligopoly in which just two firms are in an industry — and we will suppose that the firms choose quantities. To further simplify the problem, we will artificially restrict the set of strategies to two elements. Specifically, we will suppose that each firm chooses to produce either a small quantity of output S equal to 15 units — or a large quantity of output L equal to 20 units. Notice that 15 units is exactly half the monopoly output of 30 units. Thus, if each firm chose strategy S, their joint output would replicate the monopoly output of 30 units. If they did so, they would also maximize their joint, or total profit. Will the firms actually choose the individual strategies that maximize their joint profit? Or will their rivalry lead them to choose individual strategies that result in a joint profit smaller than the monopoly profit?

To answer this question, we must compute the payoff, or profit functions for the two firms, identify the best response functions, and then look for an equilibrium strategy combination — a strategy combination in which each firm's strategy is a best response to the other firm's strategy. Because each firm will choose either S or L, four strategy combinations are possible in this duopoly game: (S,S) in which both firms choose S; (L,L) in which both firms choose L; (S,L) in which the first firm chooses S, and the second, L; (L,S) in which the first firm chooses L, and the second, S.

Now let us compute each firm's profit or payoff for each of these strategy combinations. If both choose S, price will be $70 $(100 - 15 - 15)$, and profit per unit produced will be $30 $(70 - 40)$. As a result, each firm's profit will be $450 (15×30) or exactly half the monopoly profit. By contrast, if both choose L, price will be $60 $(100 - 20 - 20)$, and profit per unit produced will be $20 $(60 - 40)$. As a result, each firm's profit will be $400 (20×20) or less than half the monopoly profit. If the first firm chooses S and the rival firm chooses L, price will be $65 $(100 - 15 - 20)$, and profit per unit produced will be $25 $(65 - 40)$. As a result, the first firm's profit will be $375 (15×25) and the second firm's will be $500 (20×25). Conversely, if the first firm chooses L and the rival firm chooses S, the first firm's profit will be $500 and the second's $375.

We have used these profit functions to construct the profit matrix presented in Table 11.1. The first firm's strategies are represented along the left side of the matrix, and the second firm's along the top of the matrix. Each of the four cells in the matrix corresponds to one of the four possible strategy combinations. In any cell, the entry to the left is the first firm's profit; the entry to the right, the second firm's. The payoffs for strategy combination (S,S) are $450/$450; the payoffs for strategy combination (S,L) are $375/$500; and so on.

TABLE 11.1   DUOPOLY PROFIT MATRIX

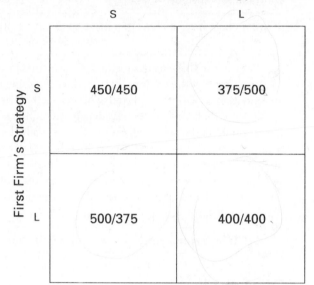

Second Firm's Strategy

	S	L
S	450/450	375/500
L	500/375	400/400

First Firm's Strategy

dominant strategy

Now let us find the best response functions. Looking at the first column of the profit matrix, we see that if the second firm chooses S, the first firm's best response is to choose L. Why? Because it earns $500 if it chooses L and only $450 if it chooses S. Looking at the second column of the profit matrix, we see that if the second firm chooses L, the first firm's best response is again to choose L because it earns $400 if it chooses L and only $375 if it chooses S. Thus, no matter which strategy the second firm pursues, the first firm's best response is to choose L. For this reason, L is said to be a **dominant strategy** for the first firm.

Because the second firm's options are exactly those of the first, its best response is likewise to choose L — regardless of what the first firm chooses. That is, L is a dominant strategy for the second firm as well as for the first. Thus, the Nash-equilibrium strategy combination is (L,L) in which each firm produces 20 units and realizes a profit of $400. Yet, if they could only agree to restrict their individual outputs to 15 units apiece, each could earn $450.

The Oligopoly Problem

This simplified version of the duopoly game illustrates the fundamental quandary encountered by economic theorists in trying to model oligopoly — and by real oligopolists in trying to play real oligopoly games. As we just saw, the blind pursuit of self-interest leads to an equilibrium in which both oligopolists are worse off than they might otherwise be. This leads us to one important insight:

Oligopolists have a clear incentive to collude or cooperate.

Yet we also discovered that if one firm were to cooperate by producing just 15 units, its rival's best response would be to produce 20 units. This leads us to the second, contradictory insight:

> Oligopolists have a clear incentive to cheat on any simple collusive, or cooperative, agreement.

self-enforcing agreement

We can use these results to put the Nash-equilibrium concept in perspective. Suppose the firms get together before they produce anything and attempt to agree on a strategy combination. A desirable property of any such agreement is that it be **self-enforcing** in the sense that, having reached an agreement, the players have a clear incentive to follow through on the agreement when they actually decide how much output to produce. Strategy combination (S,S) is attractive because it maximizes joint profit, but a joint agreement to pursue this strategy combination is not self-enforcing. To see why not, notice that when the time comes to actually choose output, each firm will be tempted to choose L not S, because by choosing L the firm maximizes its own payoff. In contrast, the Nash-equilibrium strategy combination (L,L) is clearly self-enforcing. More generally:

> If an agreement is not a Nash equilibrium, it is not self-enforcing.

The Prisoners' Dilemma

prisoners' dilemma

The matrix game in Table 11.1 is an illustration of one of the most studied games in the entire field of game theory. The game and its title — the **prisoners' dilemma** — were invented by A. W. Tucker.[2] In Tucker's original game, two partners in crime — whom we will call Bonnie and Clyde — have been arrested, but the district attorney does not have enough evidence to convict them. The district attorney offers the following deal to Bonnie. If she will provide evidence against Clyde, and if Clyde does not incriminate her, she will get a one-year prison sentence and Clyde will get a ten-year sentence. If both provide evidence against each other, however, both will receive a five-year sentence. If neither partner provides evidence, each will be convicted on a lesser charge and will get a two-year sentence. The district attorney offers the corresponding deal to Clyde.

This game has the same qualitative structure as the game in Table 11.1. Regardless of what the other partner does, the dominant strategy for Bonnie and for Clyde is to provide evidence. In the Nash equilibrium of the game, each testifies against the other and both receive five-year sentences. Yet, if they had instead managed to collude successfully, both would have been sentenced to the lesser, two-year jail terms.

> ### PROBLEM 11.1
>
> Construct the payoff matrix for this game and verify that regardless of what the other partner does, "provide evidence" is a dominant strategy.

The Cournot Duopoly Model

Now that you have some feeling for the oligopoly problem, let us drop the simplifying assumption that the firms have a choice of only two levels of output and replace it with the

---

2 See Luce and Raiffa (1957, 94).

assumption that they have a free choice of any level of output. In this game, any quantity of output that is positive or zero is a possible strategy for a firm. The resulting game is the oldest and in many ways the most interesting oligopoly model, attributable to the French economist Auguste Cournot and dating from 1838. Cournot noticed that only two French firms were producing mineral water for sale. He was intrigued by how these two firms would decide just how much of the water that flowed from their mineral springs to sell. In developing his model, he argued that each firm would choose the quantity that would maximize profit, taking the quantity marketed by its competitor as a given. Suppose that the second firm intended to sell 30 bottles of water. Cournot assumed that the first firm would take this quantity as given in deciding how many bottles it should sell.

Cournot model of duopoly

The central features of the **Cournot model** are that 1. *each firm chooses a quantity of output instead of a price* and 2. *in choosing its output, each firm takes its rival's output as a given*. In Cournot's model, then, strategies are *quantities of output*. We will denote the first firm's strategy by y_1 and the second's strategy by y_2. A strategy combination is then (y_1, y_2). To find the equilibrium strategy combination, we first need to find the firms' payoff, or profit functions. Then we need to find the best response functions, and, finally, to look for a strategy combination in which each firm's strategy is a best response to the other's strategy.

The first firm's demand function is just

$$p_1 = (100 - y_2) - y_1$$

If the first firm produces nothing, the price will be $100 - y_2$; therefore, the intercept for the first firm's demand function is $100 - y_2$. The first firm's demand function intersects the price axis in Figure 11.2 at $100 - y_2$ and, for every unit the first firm puts on the market, price drops by \$1. (This is another example of a residual demand function, introduced in Section 10.5.) The first firm's payoff function is then

$$\neq_1(y_1, y_2) = y_1(100 - y_2 - y_1) - 40y_1$$

Notice that the larger is y_2, the smaller is the first firm's profit.

If, for each value of y_2, we can find the value of y_1 that maximizes $\neq_1(y_1, y_2)$, we will have found the first firm's best response function. To solve this profit-maximizing problem, we will adapt the techniques used to solve the monopolist's profit-maximizing problem. In Figure 11.2, notice that the first firm's marginal revenue function intersects the price axis at $100 - y_2$ and that, as usual, it is twice as steep as the demand function:

$$MR_1 = (100 - y_2) - 2y_1$$

To maximize its profit, the first firm will choose the output level y_1^* at which marginal revenue equals marginal cost. In other words, y_1^* satisfies

$$(100 - y_2) - 2y_1^* = 40$$

or, solving this expression for y_1^*,

$$y_1^* = 30 - y_2/2$$

This equation is the first firm's best response function: for any value of y_2, it gives the value of y_1 that maximizes $\neq_1(y_1, y_2)$. For example, if y_2 is zero, the first firm's best response is to produce the monopoly output of 30 units $[30 - (0/2)]$. If y_2 is 10, the first firm's best response is to produce 25 units $[30 - (10/2)]$, and so on.

Because these two firms produce an undifferentiated product and have the same \$40 unit cost of production, the second firm's best response function is a twin to the first firm's:

FIGURE 11.2 **Finding a Cournot best-response function**

Given y_2, the first firm's demand function is $p_1 = (100 - y_2) - y_1$, and its marginal revenue function is $MR_1 = (100 - y_2) - 2y_1$. Its best response, or its profit-maximizing output, is $y_1^* = 30 - y_2/2$, since MR is equal to MC at this level of output.

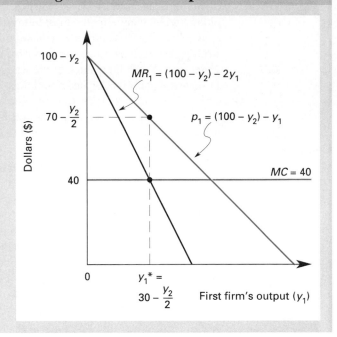

Taken together, these two best response functions can be used to find the *equilibrium strategy combination* for Cournot's model. Both firms' best response functions are shown in Figure 11.3. The equilibrium is at the point where the best response functions intersect: the equilibrium strategy combination is (20,20). In this equilibrium, each firm produces 20 units, price is \$60 $(100 - 20 - 20)$, profit per unit is \$20 $(60 - 40)$, and each firm's profit is \$400 (20×20).[3]

In what sense is this strategy combination an equilibrium? From the first firm's best response function in Figure 11.3, we see that when its rival produces 20 units, the output that maximizes the first firm's profit is likewise 20 units. Similarly, from the

$$y_2^* = 30 - y_1/2$$

---

3 More generally, we can write the duopolists' profit function as

$$\neq_1(y_1, y_2) = y_1 D(y_1 + y_2) - TC(y_1)$$
$$\neq_2(y_1, y_2) = y_2 D(y_1 + y_2) - TC(y_2)$$

where $D(\cdot)$ is the demand function and $TC(\cdot)$ the cost function. The first firm chooses a quantity y_1^*, where the partial derivative of $\neq_1(\cdot)$ with respect to y_1 is equal to zero:

$$\frac{\partial \neq_1(y_1^*, y_2)}{\partial y_1} = 0$$

Of course, this is an implicit expression for the first firm's best-response function because it determines the profit-maximizing quantity of y_1, y_1^* for any value of y_2. Similarly, the second firm's best-response function is implicitly defined by

$$\frac{\partial \neq_2(y_1, y_2^*)}{\partial y2} = 0$$

The Cournot equilibrium is then a pair of quantities (y_1^c, y_2^c) that satisfies both best-response functions.

FIGURE 11.3 **The Cournot equilibrium**

The Cournot equilibrium, in which each firm produces 20 units, is determined by the intersection of the two best-response functions.

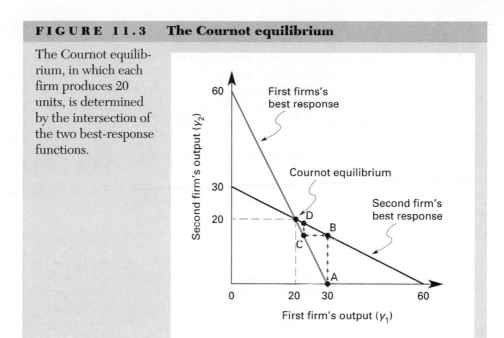

second firm's best response function, we see that when its rival produces 20 units, the output that maximizes the second firm's profit is also 20 units. At the equilibrium, then, neither firm can increase its profit by choosing some other output.

To find the Cournot-Nash equilibrium algebraically, we could solve the two best response functions for the equilibrium values of y_1 and y_2. However, we can take an even simpler approach. Because the two best response functions are *symmetric*, we know that both firms will produce the same quantity in equilibrium. This means that we can compute the equilibrium by setting both y_1^* and y_2 equal to y' in the first firm's best-response function, reflecting the fact that both will produce the same quantity y' in equilibrium. Then we can simply solve for y'. The resulting number $y' = 20$ is the quantity each will produce in the equilibrium of Cournot's model.[4]

Mock Dynamics in the Cournot Model

To understand more about the Cournot model, let us perform a somewhat artificial dynamic exercise. Imagine that in odd-numbered periods, the first firm chooses the quantity it will produce in that period and in the following period. For example, the first firm chooses the output for periods 1 and 2 in period 1; for periods 3 and 4 in period 3; and so on. In even-numbered periods the second firm chooses the quantity it will produce in that period and the following period. For example, the second firm chooses its output for periods 2 and 3 in period 2; for periods 4 and 5 in period 4; and so on. If the firms choose output by consulting their best response functions, will this dynamic model converge to the Cournot-Nash equilibrium?

---

4 If the two firms had different marginal costs, the equilibrium would not be symmetric, and we could not use this approach to find equilibrium quantities.

Suppose that in period 1, the second firm is not yet in the market. The first firm — at this point a monopolist — will choose y_1 based on y_2 equal to zero. That is, it will produce the monopoly output of 30 units in period 1, and the duopoly will therefore be at point A in Figure 11.3. In the next period, the second firm will base its own production decision on a fixed output of 30 units for its rival when it enters the market in period 2. The second firm will then produce 15 units [30 − (30/2)] in period 2, and the duopoly will be at point B on the second firm's best response function. In period 3, the first firm will now base its production decision on a fixed output of 15 units for its rival. It will produce 22.5 units [30 − (15/2)], and the duopoly will be at point C on the first firm's best response function. In period 4, the second firm will produce 18.75 [30 − (22.5/2)], and the duopoly will be at point D. As you can see from Figure 11.3, the dynamic exercise is rapidly converging to the Cournot-Nash equilibrium.

Generalizing Results

Using specific demand and cost functions, we found that (i) in the Nash equilibrium, these two firms failed to maximize their joint profit, and (ii) relative to joint profit-maximization, they produced too much output. Just how general are these results? To answer this question we will adapt techniques we used to study the consumer's utility-maximization problem. We will draw curves that are analogous to indifference curves and we will think of these two firms as maximizing profit subject to a constraint, just as we thought of consumers as maximizing utility subject to a budget constraint.

Instead of working with specific payoff functions derived from specific assumptions about market demand and the costs of the firms, we will work with general payoff or profit functions. We will denote these general profit functions by $\neq_1(y_1,y_2)$ for the first firm and $\neq_2(y_1,y_2)$ for the second firm. What should we assume about these general payoff functions? In the specific model above, we saw that the larger is y_2, the smaller is $\neq_1(y_1,y_2)$. This property reflects the fact that in Cournot's model the firms are vying to serve the same market. Since price falls as aggregate quantity increases, it follows naturally and quite generally that the profit of one firm decreases as the output of the other firm increases. This is the crucial feature of the Cournot model that leads to an equilibrium in which each firm produces more output than it would if the firms were to maximize joint profit. To highlight its importance, we will write this out as the *key assumption* of the Cournot model:

ASSUMPTION
The profit of one firm decreases as the output of the other firm increases.

We will also assume that the Nash equilibrium output of each firm is positive.

Isoprofit Curves

isoprofit curves

By choosing the level of profit for one firm in the Cournot model — say, the first firm — and then plotting all the strategy combinations that give the first firm the chosen level of profit, we have an *indifference curve* for that firm. These indifference curves are usually called **isoprofit curves**, but we will use the terms interchangeably. The thing to keep in mind is that the firm is *indifferent* between any two strategy combinations on the same indifference, or isoprofit curve *because profit is constant on the curve*.

Now let us see what we can learn about a specific indifference curve for the first firm — the isoprofit curve that passes through the Nash equilibrium strategy combination. We will denote the equilibrium strategy combination by $(y_1{}^*,y_2{}^*)$. We know that $y_1{}^*$ is the best response to $y_2{}^*$ — or that $y_1{}^*$ maximizes the first firm's profit given that the second firm's output is y_2^*. But this suggests that we think of y_1^* as the solution to the following constrained maximization problem:

$$\text{maximize } \neq_1(y_1, y_2) \text{ by choice of } y_1$$

$$\text{subject to the constraint that } y_2 = y_2^*$$

Previous experience with this type of maximization problem helps us here. In solving the consumer's constrained maximization problem, we found that the indifference curve passing through the utility-maximizing bundle was tangent to the budget constraint at the utility-maximizing bundle. Here an indifference (or isoprofit) curve is tangent to the constraint at the solution to the firm's constrained maximization problem.

Figure 11.4 shows the isoprofit curve for the first firm which passes through the Nash equilibrium. Notice that this isoprofit curve is tangent to the constraint at the Nash equilibrium. Notice, too, that it is shaped like an inverted U. To see why, begin at the Nash equilibrium and increase y_1 by a small amount $\varnothing y_1$, holding the second firm's output constant at y_2^*. As a result, the first firm's profit decreases because y_1^* maximizes the first firm's profit (given that the second firm's output is y_2^*). To compensate the first firm for this decrease in profit (that is, to get it back to the isoprofit curve), we must decrease y_2 because — given our key assumption in the Cournot model — the first firm's profit increases as the second firm's output decreases. In Figure 11.4 the required decrease in y_2 is $\varnothing y_2$. Similarly, starting again at the Nash equilibrium, if we decrease y_1 by a small amount, the first firm's profit will again fall. To compensate it for the loss of profit, we will again have to decrease y_2. Therefore, the first firm's isoprofit curve through the Nash equilibrium has an inverted U shape as shown in Figure 11.4. The arrows in the figure indicate the direction in which the first firm's profit increases. Any strategy combination below the indifference curve gives the first firm more profit than in the Nash equilibrium: this too follows from the key assumption of the Cournot model.

FIGURE 11.4 **Isoprofit or indifference curves**

At the Nash equilibrium, the first firm's isoprofit curve is tangent to the horizontal line through y_2^*. Since the first firm's profit increases as the second firm's output decreases, the isoprofit curve has the shape of an inverted U. Strategy combinations preferred by the first firm lie below the isoprofit line as indicated by the arrows.

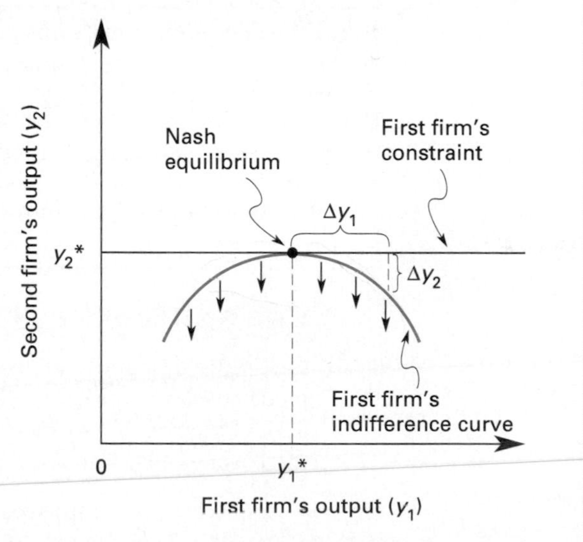

FIGURE 11.5 **Joint profit not maximized in Nash equilibrium**

Strategy combinations preferred by the first firm lie below its indifference curve and strategy combinations preferred by the second firm lie to the left of its indifference curve.

Consequently, in the shaded area both firms make more profit than they do in the Nash equilibrium. Furthermore, relative to joint maximization, the firms produce too much output in the Nash equilibrium.

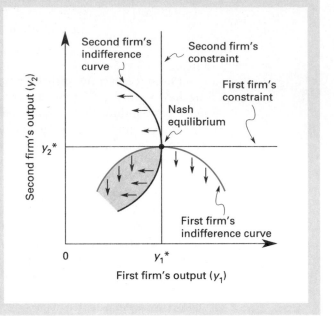

In Figure 11.5 we have introduced the second firm into the picture. The second firm's indifference curve is tangent to its constraint ($y_1 = y_1^*$) at the Nash equilibrium and has the shape of a backward **C**. As the arrows indicate, any strategy combination to the left of the second firm's indifference curve gives the second firm more profit than it makes in the Nash equilibrium.

Notice that any strategy combination in the shaded area of Figure 11.5 is both below the first firm's indifference curve and to the left of the second firm's indifference curve. Therefore, strategy combinations in this shaded area offer both firms more profit than they make in the Nash equilibrium. In other words:

In the Nash equilibrium of this general version of Cournot's model, the firms fail to maximize their joint profit.

Furthermore, the output of each firm is smaller for any strategy combination in the shaded area than it is in the Nash equilibrium. In other words:

Relative to joint profit maximization, the firms produce too much output in the Nash equilibrium.

PROBLEM 11.2

Given the demand and cost conditions used in our specific Cournot model, each firm produces 40 units and gets \$400 profit in the Nash equilibrium. First verify that the first and second firms' isoprofit curves through the Nash equilibrium are

$$400 = y_1(100 - y_2 - y_1) - 40y_1$$
$$400 = y_2(100 - y_2 - y_1) - 40y_2$$

Then carefully construct a diagram analogous to Figure 11.5 for the specific Cournot model. In your diagram, identify the set of strategy combinations that both firms prefer to the Nash equilibrium.

The Cournot Model with Many Firms

What happens to the Cournot-Nash equilibrium as the number of firms in an industry expands? You can find the answer in the case of three firms in Problem 11.3.

PROBLEM 11.3

Assuming that three firms are in the industry, first show that the first firm's marginal revenue function is

$$MR_1 = (100 - y_2 - y_3) - 2y_1$$

Then show that its best response function is

$$y_1{}^* = 30 - (y_2 + y_3)/2$$

Finally, show that each of the three firms will produce 15 units in the Cournot-Nash equilibrium and calculate each firm's profit in the three-firm Cournot-Nash equilibrium.

Let us quickly generalize what you discovered in this problem. If n firms are in the market, the demand, marginal revenue and profit functions of the first firm will be

$$p_1 = (100 - y_2 - y_3 - \dots - y_n) - y_1$$
$$MR_1 = (100 - y_2 - y_3 - \dots - y_n) - 2y_1$$
$$\neq_1(y_1, y_2, \dots, y_n) = y_1(100 - y_1 - y_2 - \dots - y_n) - 40y_1$$

Because the first firm will choose y_1 so that marginal revenue is equal to marginal cost, its best response function is

$$y_1{}^* = 30 - (y_2 + y_3 + \dots + y_n)/2$$

But because all other best response functions are symmetric to this one, all n firms will produce the same output in the Cournot-Nash equilibrium. To discover the output of one firm in this equilibrium, set $y_1{}^*$, y_2, y_3, $\dots$, y_n all equal to y' in the first firm's best response function. Then solve for y' to obtain

$$y' = 60/(n + 1)$$

This is the output of one firm in the Cournot-Nash equilibrium when there are n firms in the market.

It is useful to compute the aggregate equilibrium output and price in the Cournot model with n firms.

$$\text{aggregate equilibrium output} = 60[n/(n + 1)]$$

$$\text{equilibrium price} = 100/(n + 1) + 40[n/(n + 1)]$$

These formulas yield a number of interesting insights into the Cournot model. First, as n increases, aggregate output increases and equilibrium price decreases. When n is 1, the aggregate output is the monopoly output of 30 units and price is $70; when n is 2, aggregate output is 40 units and price is $60; when n is 3, output is 45 and price is $55; and so on. Second, as n increases without bound, the aggregate output approaches the competitive output, and the price approaches the competitive price. As you can verify, the competitive output is 60 units and the competitive price is $40. Notice that as n gets arbitrarily large, $n/(n + 1)$ approaches 1. Therefore, in the Cournot-Nash equilibrium, aggregate output approaches 60 units and equilibrium price approaches $40.

Finally, notice that the Cournot model is appealing because it spans a wide range of market structures. When only one firm is in a market, the Cournot-Nash equilibrium is the monopoly equilibrium. As the number of firms increases, output likewise increases. As a result, price and aggregate oligopoly profit decrease. In the limit, when there are infinitely many firms, the Cournot model is, in effect, a perfectly competitive model, since price is equal to the $40 marginal/average cost and aggregate profit vanishes. None of the other models we will consider has these intuitively appealing properties.

11.6

The Bertrand Model

Bertrand model

Responding to Cournot's analysis of the duopoly problem, Joseph Bertrand argued that firms choose — not quantity of output — but *price* of output. The **Bertrand model** substitutes prices p_1 and p_2 for quantities y_1 and y_2 as the variables to be chosen. Thus, the Cournot and Bertrand equilibria are logical first cousins. Cournot identified the Nash equilibrium when the firms' strategic decisions centered on a choice of quantities, and Bertrand identified the Nash equilibrium when their strategic decisions centered instead on a choice of prices. We want to find the Nash equilibrium strategy combination — or, more simply, the Bertrand-Nash equilibrium *when the firms choose prices instead of quantities.*

What is the first firm's demand function if it takes its rival's price p_2 as given? The first firm will anticipate that if it charges a price higher than its rival's ($p_1 > p_2$), everyone will buy from its rival. If the first firm charges a price lower than its rival's ($p_1 < p_2$), however, everyone will buy from it. And if it charges a price equal to its rival's ($p_1 = p_2$), the firms will split the market. For convenience, let us assume that they split the market in half. The resulting — and somewhat peculiar — market demand function is

$$y_1 = 0 \qquad\qquad\qquad \text{if } p_1 > p_2$$
$$y_1 = 100 - p_1 \qquad\qquad \text{if } p_1 < p_2$$
$$y_1 = (100 - p_1)/2 \qquad\quad \text{if } p_1 = p_2$$

(Notice that in these equations, the roles of price and quantity have been inverted: quantity is now on the left and price on the right.)

Given this demand function, what will the first firm's profit function look like? If p_1 is greater than p_2, the first firm attracts no business. That is, y_1 is equal to zero, and its profit is also zero:

$$\neq_1(p_1, p_2) = 0 \qquad\qquad\qquad \text{if } p_1 > p_2$$

On the other hand, if p_1 is less than p_2, the first firm captures the whole market. That is, y_1 is $100 - p_1$, and its profit per unit is $p_1 - 40$. Therefore, its total profit is

$$\neq_1(p_1, p_2) = (p_1 - 40)(100 - p_1) \qquad\qquad \text{if } p_1 < p_2$$

If p_1 is equal to p_2, however, the two firms evenly split the market; that is, y_1 is $(100 - p_1)/2$, and profit per unit is $p_1 - 40$. Therefore, the first firm's total profit is

$$\pi_1(p_1, p_2) = (p_1 - 40)(100 - p_1)/2 \qquad \text{if } p_1 = p_2$$

To find the first firm's best response function, we need to answer the following question: Given p_2, what value of p_1 maximizes the first firm's profit? There are four possible cases to consider. Let us begin with the two easy cases. First, if its rival charges a price greater than the monopoly price of $70, the first firm can capture the whole market with a lower price, and its best response is obviously to charge the monopoly price of $70. Second, if its rival charges a price that is less than the $40 cost per unit produced, the first firm's best response is to charge any price greater than p_2. Why? Because by choosing this price, the first firm will attract no business and will therefore incur a zero profit — an outcome that is clearly better than incurring a negative profit by matching or undercutting its rival's price.

Now let us turn to the more interesting third case, where the second firm's price is greater than the $40 cost per unit produced and less than or equal to the monopoly price of $70. The diagram of the profit function for this case is shown in Figure 11.6. The first firm's price is on the horizontal axis and its profit on the vertical axis. The profit function is composed of three segments. First, if the first firm chooses a price lower than its rival's $(p_1 < p_2)$, as the first firm's price increases, its profit likewise increases. In this segment of the profit function, the profit-maximizing price is arbitrarily close to — but less than — p_2. Thus, when p_1 is less than p_2, the first firm's maximum profit is distance CA,

FIGURE 11.6   Finding a Bertrand best-response function

The second firm's price is p_2 and is less than the monopoly price. The first firm's profit function is composed of three segments. When $p_1 < p_2$, the first firm captures the entire market, and its profit increases as its price increases. When $p_1 = p_2$, the two firms split the total profit, equal to distance CA, and each makes a profit equal to CB. When $p_1 > p_2$, the first firm's profit is zero because it sells nothing when its price exceeds the second firm's price.

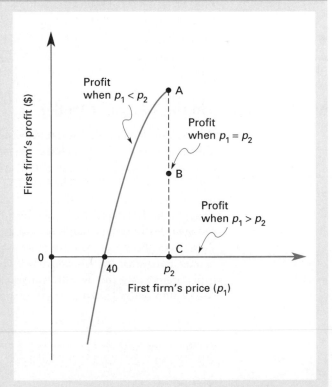

and its best price is a price just less than p_2.[5] Second, if the first firm chooses a price equal to its rival's price ($p_1 = p_2$), its profit drops by a factor of one-half because it now evenly splits the profit with the rival firm. The first firm's profit is therefore just half of the distance CA, or the distance CB. Third, if the first firm chooses a price greater than its rival's price ($p_1 > p_2$), its profit is zero. Graphically, the firm's zero profit is represented by the horizontal axis from point C onward to the right. What have we learned? When its rival's price is greater than the marginal cost of $40 and less than or equal to the monopoly price of $70, the firm's best response is to undercut its rival's price by just a hair's breadth.

Finally, let us take up the fourth case, where the second firm sets a price that is exactly equal to the marginal cost of $40 per unit. If the first firm sets a price lower than $40, it will incur a loss on every unit it sells, and its profit therefore will be negative. On the other hand, if it sets a price greater than or equal to $40, its profit will be equal to zero. Why? If it chooses any price above $40, its profit will be zero because it will attract no business. And if it chooses a price equal to $40, its profit will be zero because it will break even on every unit it sells. Because making a zero profit is better than making a negative profit, the first firm's best response is to charge any price greater than or equal to $40.

Let us summarize the results with respect to the first firm's best response to its rival's price. (The second firm's best-response function is obviously symmetric.)

1. p_1^* is $70 if $p_2 > 70$
2. p_1^* is any price greater than p_2 if $p_2 < 40$
3. p_1^* is just less than p_2 if $40 < p_2 \leq 70$
4. p_1^* is any price greater than or equal to p_2 if $p_2 = 40$

What is the Bertrand-Nash equilibrium — that is, what is the equilibrium strategy combination when firms choose prices? From 4, we see that in equilibrium each firm chooses a price equal to $40. Why? If the second firm sets a price of $40, then 4 tells us that the first firm's best response is also to set a price of $40. (Do notice, however, that $p_1 = 40$ is not the only best response, since charging any price higher than $40 also results in zero profit.) Similarly, if the first firm sets a price of $40, then the second firm's best response is to set a price of $40. Therefore, the equilibrium strategy combination is $p_1 = 40$ and $p_2 = 40$. Notice that in this equilibrium, each firm's profit is exactly zero.

Mock Dynamics in the Bertrand Model

We can also see how the Bertrand-Nash equilibrium might come about by considering a dynamic exercise in which the firms alternately choose prices. The first firm will choose the monopoly price of $70. Its rival will then undercut the first firm by setting a price just less than $70. The first firm will respond with a still lower price. This pattern of successive price undercutting will stop only when both prices have been driven down to the Bertrand-Nash equilibrium price of $40.

As this dynamic scenario reveals, the Bertrand-Nash equilibrium is not altogether satisfactory. First one firm shaves its price ever so slightly to undercut its rival, fully expecting to capture the whole market. Then its rival retaliates by shaving its price, again expecting to capture the entire market. They seesaw back and forth, each progressively undercutting the other in the expectation of capturing the entire market until, in

---

5 Strictly speaking, the best price for the first firm is not well defined here since there is no largest price less than p_2. We will, however, ignore this point.

the equilibrium, price is so low that each firm is indifferent between serving the market or abandoning it since its profit is zero in either case.

Even though the Bertrand and Cournot models differ in just one respect — strategies are prices in Bertrand's model and strategies are quantities in Cournot's — the equilibria are strikingly different. In contrast to the Cournot-Nash equilibrium, *the Bertrand-Nash equilibrium does not change as the number of firms increases*. As long as at least two firms are in a particular industry, the Bertrand-Nash equilibrium is a price equal to marginal cost, and aggregate oligopoly profit is zero.

11.7 The Collusive Model of Oligopoly

Although intuitively appealing, the Cournot model may seem a bit naive. Its central assumption, after all, is that oligopolists choose their outputs independently, taking the output of rivals as given. And if the Cournot model is a bit naive, the Bertrand model seems extraordinarily so, in that by setting price independently, the oligopolists arrive at an equilibrium in which no one makes any profit whatsoever in a potentially lucrative market. Indeed, in a number of industries dominated by a few firms, *collusive* rather than *independent* behavior seems to be a fact of economic life. For example, the two U.S. companies that control 90% of the infant formula market, Ross Laboratories and Mead Johnson, have nearly always raised prices by about the same amounts and at about the same times. The four ready-mix concrete firms in Toronto that control 92% of the industry set uniform prices for concrete products for at least 5 years. Such uniform pricing in concrete products is also the norm for many other cities across North America. Even private colleges have come under investigation by the U. S. Justice Department because within groupings — the Ivy League schools and the Seven Sisters, for instance — yearly tuitions tend to be quite similar. In this section, we will set out a **collusive model** of oligopoly to see what happens when oligopolists do decide to collude on a joint strategy. Then we will compare the outcome, or equilibrium, in the collusive model with the monopoly equilibrium on the one hand and with the Cournot and Bertrand equilibria on the other.

collusive model

We can begin with the simplest case of a duopoly. The best equilibrium that the duopolists can jointly come up with is one in which joint output, $y_1 + y_2$, is equal to the monopoly output of 30 units. That is, since each firm's marginal cost is $40, the two can jointly do no better than the monopoly equilibrium. They might agree, for example, to produce half the monopoly output (15 units) apiece. The price per unit will then be $70, and each will earn half the monopoly profit, or $450.

By contrast, each duopolist in the Cournot equilibrium earns only $400, or $50 less than in the collusive equilibrium. This means that the Cournot equilibrium, although individually rational, is collectively irrational because each firm earns less profit than it could have earned in the collusive equilibrium. The primary objection to the Cournot model is that if firms do find themselves at the Cournot equilibrium, they have a clear incentive to attempt to form a collusive agreement.

These remarks are even more appropriate to the Bertrand model. Each duopolist in the Bertrand equilibrium earns exactly $0 profit, or $450 less than in the collusive equilibrium. Like the Cournot equilibrium, the Bertrand equilibrium is individually rational, but collectively irrational. As with the Cournot model, the primary objection to the Bertrand model is that if firms do find themselves at the Bertrand equilibrium, they have a clear incentive to collude. Does this mean that the collusive model makes better sense of oligopoly than do the Cournot and Bertrand models?

Not necessarily. To see why not, we will focus on the Cournot model. Suppose that the two rivals agree to split the monopoly output evenly by producing 15 units apiece. Is this agreement self-enforcing? Suppose that the first firm is convinced that its rival will abide by the agreement to produce just 15 units. By consulting the first firm's best-response function, we can infer that its private incentive is to respond by producing 22.5 units [30 − (15/2)]. If it actually were to break the agreement by producing 22.5 units — and if its rival kept to the agreement by producing only 15 units — then the total industry output would be 37.5 (22.5 + 15), and price would be $62.5 (100 − 37.5). The first firm's profit would be $506.25 [22.5 × (62.5 − 40)], and its rival's would be $337.50 [15 × (62.5 − 40)].

If the first firm could get away with this deceptive strategy, it would earn an additional $56.25 in profit (506.25 − 450) relative to the collusive equilibrium. Again relative to the collusive equilibrium, its rival would lose $82.50 (450 − 337.50) — a loss that exceeds the first firm's gain. Therefore, the collusive strategy is collectively rational because it maximizes joint profit. But, it is individually irrational because each firm's private profit incentive urges it to depart from the collusive equilibrium; that is, the collusive agreement to produce 15 units of output apiece is *not* self-enforcing.

We have once again encountered what we called the *oligopoly problem* in Section 11.3 On the one hand, if firms find themselves at a Cournot or a Bertrand equilibrium, they have a clear incentive to collude. On the other hand, if firms manage to forge a collusive agreement, there is a clear private incentive for each party to cheat on the collusive agreement.

The history of the OPEC cartel illustrates both sides of the problem. OPEC is a cartel of oil-exporting countries that operates by assigning export quotas to individual member countries in an attempt to reduce the supply of crude oil to the world market. At various times, particularly during the mid-1970s, the cartel has been successful in restricting supply and thereby raising prices. At other times, however, many OPEC member countries have cheated on their collusive agreement by exporting more than their allotted quotas. For instance, in the late 1980s and early 1990s, newspapers often carried reports about individual OPEC countries that were "keeping their spigots wide open" — that is, exceeding their quotas on the sale of crude oil in the international oil market. As you will discover in the following problem, in the Cournot model, the individual incentive to cheat on a collusive agreement increases as the number of parties to the agreement increases, which means that the larger the number of firms in an industry, the less likely is a collusive equilibrium. If the number of firms is large enough, some firm or firms will succumb to the temptation to cheat, thereby destroying the collusive agreement.

> ### PROBLEM 11.4
>
> If three parties form a collusive agreement, the equilibrium is to allocate 10 units to each member at a profit of $300 per member. Show that if one party decides to cheat and the other two do not, the cheater will produce 20 units and enjoy a profit of $400. Therefore, the inducement to cheat is $100 when three firms form a collusive agreement, but only $56.25 when just two firms form the agreement. Now suppose that four firms are party to the agreement and that each firm is allocated 7.5 units. What is the inducement to cheat in this case?

11.8
Experimental Evidence

What are professional economists — and economics students — to make of such a profusion of oligopoly models, all yielding different equilibria? There is no answer that all or even most economists can agree on. Indeed, some evidence from experimental economics suggest that there can be *no* general oligopoly model applicable to all situations — at least, not unless the model takes into account the inclinations of the individual economic players.[6]

Let us look briefly at a series of experiments that Fouraker and Siegal (1963) conducted to test the duopoly equilibrium when two subjects, like the firms in the Cournot model, chose quantities. In the first set of 14 experiments, each subject was given a table specifying his or her individual payoffs (or profits) as functions of the quantities provided by the two players. The two subjects then played the "duopoly game" a number of times. In these experiments, each subject knew only the quantities that the other player had chosen in all previous periods — and, of course, his or her own quantities and profits. The equilibrium in the last period of this set of experiments closely approximated the Cournot equilibrium.

In a second set of 14 experiments, both subjects knew their own quantities and profits in all previous periods and those of the other player. Relative to the first set of experiments, they had additional information regarding the other player's profits. In about one-half of these experiments, the equilibrium in the last period closely approximated the Cournot equilibrium; in about one-third, it approximated the collusive equilibrium; and in about one-sixth, it approximated the competitive equilibrium.

In another series of experiments, the subjects were asked to choose price, not quantity. When both subjects knew only the price charged by the other subject in all previous periods, the best approximation was almost invariably the Bertrand equilibrium. When both subjects knew the other subject's profits in all periods as well, in nine cases the best approximation was the Bertrand equilibrium; in four, it was the collusive equilibrium; and in four, it was an intermediate equilibrium.

Taken together, these experiments suggest that no single model is applicable to all oligopoly situations. Perhaps the most economists can hope for is a selection of oligopoly models, each applicable to a particular range of economic circumstances.

11.9
Repeated Play, Supergames, and Richer Strategies

The oligopoly models we have been looking at do not capture one very important aspect of real-world oligopolies. Because the models are essentially static, or concerned with strategies and payoffs in just one period, they fail to capture the long-term dynamic interplay that characterizes most real-world oligopoly relationships. We have no adequate way to capture in these one-period models the phenomenon of what we might call "repeated play" of similar oligopoly games.

Once we recognize that oligopolists repeatedly play games of strategy and counterstrategy as they jockey for market power — often for extended periods of time — we

---

6 See Plott (1982) for a careful and thorough review of experimental evidence on oligopoly problems.

can imagine that the strategies available to them are potentially far richer than our simpler static models suggest. We will do an intuitive treatment of one strategic possibility developed by James Friedman (1971) that arises under repeated play.[7]

As you know, although collusive agreements are collectively more beneficial to oligopolists, the individual firms nevertheless have strong private incentives to try to grab a larger share of the market for themselves by cheating on the agreement. To induce all members of a collusive agreement to stick to the bargain, Friedman considered **punishment strategies** that oligopolists can devise for breaches of the collusive agreement.

punishment strategies

These punishments must be both *severe* and *credible*. It is obvious that not all punishments satisfy both these criteria. Suppose, for example, that each duopolist threatens to murder the other duopolist for a breach of their agreement. In this case, the punishment is severe enough to deter breach, but it is not credible because carrying it out would surely result in imprisonment or worse for the punisher. We will say that a punishment strategy is credible if it is in the punisher's self-interest to carry out the punishment, once a breach of the agreement occurs.

supergame

Suppose that two firms play their duopoly game an infinite number of times, in what is sometimes called a **supergame**. Remember that in any particular period, the collusive solution for each is to produce 15 units, and the Cournot solution is for each to produce 20 units. The objective is to devise punishment strategies that will make the collusive solution of 15 units in each period not only the collectively rational but also the individually rational, or profit-maximizing solution.

For a possible set of strategies, we will consider the following variant on the fable of the donkey and the carrot and stick. The first firm's carrot is its promise to produce 15 units in any given period, provided that its rival has produced 15 units in all previous periods. Its stick is its threat to provide 20 units in all subsequent periods if it ever discovers that its rival has cheated on the agreement by producing more than 15 units. The second firm's strategy precisely parallels the first firm's. Having devised and announced these carrot-and-stick strategies to each other, the duopolists break off communication and go their separate ways.

Is the threatened punishment severe enough to encourage each duopolist to produce just 15 units in each period? Is it credible? To answer the first question, we need to compare a firm's maximum profit if it abides by the collusive agreement with its maximum profit if it breaches the agreement. Let us focus on the second firm's decision. Given the first firm's announced strategy, if the second firm produces 15 units in all periods, it will earn $450 in each period. As we saw in Section 11.7, if it cheats on the agreement, the best it can do in the present period is to produce 22.5 units (the profit-maximizing quantity, given that the first firm produces 15 units). Its profit is then $506.25 in the present period. If the first firm then carries out its threat by raising its own output to 20 units in all subsequent periods, the best that the second firm can do thereafter is to produce 20 units in each period — thereby inducing the Cournot equilibrium — and its profit will then be $400 in every subsequent period. In contrast to the collusive solution, then, if the second firm breaches the collusive agreement, it gains $56.25 in the present period but loses $50 in all future periods. Whether the punishment is severe enough to be a deterrent then depends on the rate of interest. If a dollar today is not worth significantly more than a dollar tomorrow, then the punishment of losing $50 per period forever will be large enough to offset the temptation of gaining $56.25 today. In other words:

---

7 See the entry by Kevin Roberts on "collusion" in *The New Palgrave* for a more detailed treatment of the material in this section.

Unless the interest rate is extremely high, the punishment is severe enough to deter cheating.

The other question is whether the punishment is credible. That is, will it be in the first firm's self-interest to carry out its threat by actually producing 20 units in each future period if its rival breaches the collusive agreement? Let us begin with the second firm's strategy. Once it has cheated on the agreement, it will expect the first firm to carry out its threat to produce 20 units. In response, it will decide to produce 20 units as well. Let us see what the first firm's response will be in this situation. Because it will expect the second firm to produce 20 units, the first firm will serve its own self-interest best by producing 20 units as well — thereby producing the Cournot equilibrium in all future periods. The punishment is therefore credible because the first firm will actually make good on its threat to up its own production when it discovers that its rival has cheated:

If the collusive agreement is breached in some period, the announced punishment strategy will produce the Cournot equilibrium in every subsequent period.

We now know that if either firm breaches the collusive agreement to produce 15 units in each period, the duopolists will be locked into the Cournot solution for all future periods. If the interest rate is not too high, neither firm will ever breach the agreement, and the punishment strategy does make the collectively rational solution individually rational as well.

Repeated oligopoly games open up many more questions and possibilities than our example suggests. We implicitly assumed, for example, that each firm could detect cheating by its rival(s). In an industry in which market demand is subject to significant random variation or in which the number of firms is comparatively large, detection will be a harder task. If detection is too difficult, the punishment strategy simply will not do the job.[8]

> **PROBLEM 11.5**
>
> Salop (1986) has identified an interesting punishment strategy in observing that in some industries, all the firms in the market agree to include in their contracts with buyers a *most-favored-customer clause*. The clause stipulates that if a firm sells the same product to another customer at a lower price within some specified period of time, then the original customer can claim a rebate equal to the price differential multiplied by the quantity purchased. Explain how such clauses — which are apparently in the individual customer's interest — can be used to support a collusive pricing agreement that is clearly not in the interest of consumers.

The Limit-Output Model

Because the number of firms has been exogenous, the models we have explored to this point have served only as an introduction to the important and intriguing topic of

---

8 Stigler (1969) presents a good discussion of the conditions that are and are not conducive to collusion. Axelrod's *The Evolution of Cooperation* is a fascinating account of how people often manage to cooperate in repeated games in a variety of economic and noneconomic contexts.

oligopoly. In the rest of this chapter, we focus on the theory of oligopoly in the long run. In these models, the number of firms — or the market structure — is *endogenous*. The number of firms in any industry is determined by economic considerations, and, in oligopolistic industries, as in competitive industries, the key process in determining the long-run equilibrium is the *possibility of entry*.

We will explore the approach to endogenous market structure pioneered by Joe Bain (1956) and Paolo Sylos-Labini (1961), and we will explore more recent extensions of their approach. Bain and Sylos-Labini were the first to recognize the critical role that entry plays in determining the structure of an oligopolistic industry. In particular, they addressed the key question: under what conditions will a potential firm find it *unprofitable* to enter an oligopolistic market? The answer to this question is what we will call a *no-entry condition* — a condition that obviously must be satisfied in any long-run oligopoly equilibrium.

Modigliani (1958) formalized some of Bain's and Sylos-Labini's insights into the **limit-output model**, more commonly called the **limit-price model**. In presenting the limit-output model in this section and recent refinements of it in the next section, our objective is not to produce a general model, but to introduce you to useful ways of thinking about endogenous market structure in oligopolistic industries.

limit-output model

limit-price model

Barriers to Entry

We will continue to use the market demand and cost functions from the first half of the chapter, with one important exception. Given the cost function we have been using, entry will continue until the competitive equilibrium prevails — that is, until price is driven down to marginal cost, or $40. Therefore, the theory of market structure is interesting only when there is some *barrier* to the entry of new firms.

barrier to entry

A natural **barrier to entry** — and the one that we will be using — is a *setup cost* (or product development cost). Such costs are ubiquitous and can be very large indeed. It costs $500,000 to $1,000,000 to develop a new textbook on the principles of economics. Bringing a new prescription drug to the market now costs an average of $125 million for R&D. Polaroid spent $500 million on R&D to produce its SX-70 camera and film. And the Airbus has chewed up $15 billion in development costs. Clearly, the need to incur such sizable setup costs can and does deter potential entrants.

In fact, deliberately incurring whopping setup costs can be seen as a strategic move to deter entry. For example, a public relations officer of Apple Inc., the maker of the Macintosh family of computers, commented in *The Financial Post* on Apple's decision to invest heavily in R&D as a means of discouraging cloning by rival manufacturers: "We've built a lot of custom chips, designed for us to specifically enhance the operation and function of [our] computers. That, in itself, creates a tremendous barrier to anyone who wants to copy the hardware because the investment in research, development and custom manufacturing is in the millions and millions of dollars" (May 29, 1989, S3).

Let us suppose that all firms must incur a setup, or product development, cost equal to $S. In any one period, the rate of interest will determine the fixed cost associated with the setup cost. Denoting the rate of interest by i, the fixed cost is

$$K = iS$$

Adding this fixed cost to previous costs yields the following cost function:

$$C(y) = K + 40y$$

The fixed cost associated with product development — or the barrier to entry — is captured in the first term on the right, K, and what we can now call the variable costs of production are captured in the second term, $40y$.

The key assumption in the limit-output model of market structure — which we introduced as the *Sylos postulate* in Chapter 10 — is that any potential entrant takes the current industry-wide output as a given. For example, if the industry is producing 30 units at present, a potential entrant assumes that if it actually enters the industry, the established firms will continue to produce 30 units. This model is then an extension of the Cournot model, and we can use what we know about that model to develop the limit-output model.

The Inducement to Entry

inducement to entry

If the fixed cost K is the barrier to entry in this model, what is the **inducement to entry** in this market? It is the *excess of revenue over variable costs*. To see what is involved in calculating the inducement to entry, let us suppose that the established firm or firms are currently producing 30 units, and then compute the excess of revenue over variable costs the entrant would earn if it were to enter the market. Figure 11.7 shows the market demand function, the entrant's residual demand function ($p_E = 70 - y_E$), and the entrant's marginal revenue function ($MR_E = 70 - 2y_E$) for this case. The entrant's demand and marginal revenue functions are plotted relative to the origin

FIGURE 11.7   The inducement to entry

Since the monopolist produces 30 units, the entrant anticipates the residual demand curve in this figure. If it were to enter, it would maximize profit by producing 15 units, and it would anticipate profit per period equal to the shaded area, which is the inducement to entry.

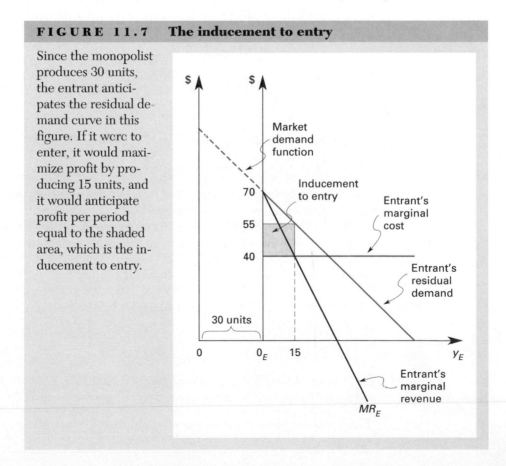

labeled 0_E, which is 30 units to the right of the origin labeled 0. If the entrant were to enter this market, it would produce 15 units, since its marginal revenue is equal to its marginal cost at this output level. If it did produce 15 units, price would be $55, its revenue would be $825 ($55 \times 15$), and its variable costs would be $600 ($40 \times 15$). In this case, the inducement to entry is $225 ($825 - 600$), equal to the shaded area in Figure 11.8. Will a potential entrant actually enter this market or will it stay out? If the barrier to entry K is less than the inducement to entry — that is, if K is less than $225 — it will enter. If K is greater than or equal to $225, it will stay out. (For simplicity, we are assuming that a potential entrant will not enter if it anticipates zero profit.)

What is the inducement to entry when established firms produce no output? Or 60 units? Or, more generally, y units? The first two questions are easily answered. If established firms produce nothing, the inducement to entry is $900 — the excess of revenue over variable costs for a monopolist. If the established firms produce 60 units, the inducement is $0 because the entrant's residual demand curve is then $p_E = 40 - y_E$. As you can see, the inducement to entry shrinks as the output of established firms grows. The third question is harder and more interesting. From the Cournot model, we see that when established firms produce y units, the entrant's best response is

$$y_E{}^* = 30 - y/2$$

The entrant's residual demand function is just

$$p_E = (100 - y) - y_E$$

Using this demand function, we can compute the price that will prevail if the entrant produces $y_E{}^*$ units:

$$p_E{}^* = 70 - y/2$$

We can compute $p_E{}^*$ minus the $40 marginal cost, or profit per unit:

$$p_E{}^* - 40 = 30 - y/2$$

The inducement to entry, $y_E{}^*$ multiplied by $(p_E{}^* - 40)$, is then

$$\text{inducement to entry} = (30 - y/2)^2$$

This expression gives us the excess of revenue over variable costs that an entrant would earn if established firms continued to produce y units after entry.

limit output

Entry will occur if the inducement to entry exceeds K, but will not occur if it is less than or equal to K. We will call the smallest value of y such that no entry occurs the **limit output**. Alternatively, we can think of the limit output as the value of y such that the inducement to entry is equal to the barrier to entry. Letting y_L denote the limit output, we have

$$(30 - y_L/2)^2 = K$$

Or, solving for y_L

$$y_L = 60 - 2K^{1/2}$$

no-entry condition

For instance, if K is $100, the limit output is 40 units; if K is $225, the limit output is 30; and so on. We can use the limit output to write the **no-entry condition** in a different way:

Entry will not occur if the output of established firms is greater than or equal to the limit output, y_L.

limit price

The **limit price** is just the price associated with the limit output, $100 - y_L$, or

$$p_L = 40 + 2K^{1/2}$$

The limit output and the limit price when K is 400 are presented in Figure 11.8. The limit output is 20, and the limit price $80. When established firms produce 20 units, the inducement to entry of $400 is identical to the barrier to entry K. Therefore, the entrant's average cost function is tangent to its residual demand function at point E. To check your understanding of the limit output, try the following problem.

> **PROBLEM 11.6**
>
> Construct a diagram analogous to Figure 11.8 for the case in which K is $196.

Strategic Choice of Industry Output

Now let us shift our attention away from entrants and think about the no-entry condition from the perspective of established firms. First, how does the possibility of entry constrain established firms in their ability to earn profit? And how does the possibility of entry affect their strategic decision making — assuming that established firms know that a limit quantity and a limit price will effectively deter such entry? To simplify matters, let us suppose that there is just one established firm, or a sitting monopolist.

We already know precisely how the entrant will behave. If y is less than the limit output y_L, it will enter the industry; if y is greater than or equal to y_L, it will stay out.

FIGURE 11.8   Identifying the limit price and the limit output

If established firms produce 20 units, the inducement to entry is $400, which is identical to the $K = \$400$ barrier to entry. Therefore, when $K = \$400$, the limit output y_L is equal to 20 units, and the limit price p_L is equal to ($100 - 20$) or $80.

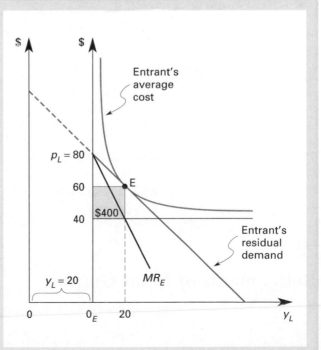

If we presume that the sitting monopolist can also calculate the limit output, how will it make use of this piece of information? We have calculated that if K is \$225, then y_L is 30 units — and 30 units is the monopoly output. Thus, if the setup costs in this industry, K, are \$225 or higher, the monopoly output of 30 units will successfully deter entry — and the sitting monopolist will remain the only firm in the market. Given the Sylos postulate, if the sitting monopolist is already producing 30 units, an entrant has no profit incentive to enter. When K is \$225 or more, then the industry is the case called *natural monopoly* in Chapter 10.

On the other hand, if K is less than \$225, the ordinary monopoly output will not deter entry because the limit output y_L is then larger than 30 units. What action will the sitting monopolist take in this case? It will produce exactly y_L units of output. Why? Because it has already incurred the setup cost, its objective now is to maximize the excess of its revenues over its variable costs or what we will call **gross profit**; that is, it wants to maximize $y(p - 40)$. If it deters entry by producing the limit output, its gross profit will be $y_L(p_L - 40)$. What would happen to the sitting monopolist's profit if it were to allow entry by producing less than the limit output y_L — say, y'? Because entry would continue until price p' was less than or equal to p_L, its gross profit would then fall to $y'(p' - 40)$ — a sum obviously less than $y_L(p_L - 40)$ because y' is less than y_L and p' is no larger than p_L. Thus, the sitting monopolist will always choose to protect its own profitability by deterring entry in this model.

gross profit

Notice that when K is less than \$225, we have the case called *monopoly by good management* in Chapter 10. The efficiency implications of this kind of monopoly are very different from those we encountered in Chapter 10. First, to deter entry, the sitting monopolist produces more than the ordinary monopoly output. Second, because entry is costly — it uses real resources — other things being equal, it is socially wasteful to have more than one firm serving this market. Of course, other things are not necessarily equal. In particular, two firms might produce even more than y_L units of output. Whether the added output is worth the additional expense of the second firm's setup cost, however, is an open question. Indeed, it is entirely possible that the monopoly by good management equilibrium is the best of the free-market alternatives.

Critique of the Model

The Sylos postulate — that entrants take the current industry output as given — is the Achilles heel of the limit-output model. A potential entrant's real concern is not with the present but with the *future output* of a sitting monopolist. When a sitting monopolist produces the limit output, its decision is intended as a credible warning to potential entrants that it will continue to produce the limit output in future periods. If entrants take the warning seriously, they will stay out of the market.

But is the threat credible? If entry does occur, will a sitting monopolist respond by continuing to produce the limit output? The following approach to answering the credibility question raised by the limit-output model was pioneered by Michael Spence (1977).

11.11

Refinements of Limit Output

Let us suppose that the appropriate model of oligopoly is the Cournot model and that every potential entrant knows that the Cournot model is appropriate. Given n established firms, the entrant can now actually calculate what the industry equilibrium would be if it were to enter and, more to the point, what its own profit would be in that equilibrium.

Notice that this approach neatly finesses the credibility question. Since the entrant knows that the Cournot model is appropriate and can calculate the Cournot equilibrium that will prevail after entry, it knows exactly how much output established firms will actually produce if it does enter. As a result, the credibility question never arises. If established firms are going to produce *more* than the limit output if entry occurs, then the entrant can anticipate that maneuver correctly, and it will stay out. On the other hand, if established firms are going to produce *less* than the limit output, the entrant will once again anticipate that maneuver correctly, and it will enter. The potential weakness of this approach is that the Cournot model may not be appropriate. As long as it is, however, the entrant will be able to make the right calculations concerning the post-entry output. Furthermore, as you will see in answering the problems at the end of this section, if a different oligopoly model is appropriate, the same general method can be used to model the resulting market structure.

To see how this approach works, suppose that the industry is currently a monopoly. If entry occurs, the industry will then be a duopoly. Reinterpreting what we learned in Section 11.10, the excess of revenue over variable cost for the entrant — or the inducement to entry — is $400. Entry will therefore occur if this $400 inducement exceeds the fixed cost K — or the barrier to entry — but it will not occur if K exceeds $400.

This raises another question: How large must the fixed cost K be so that a third firm will not enter the market? In Problem 11.3, you identified the Cournot equilibrium with three firms: each firm produces 15 units and realizes a gross profit of $225. If at present only two firms are in the market, the inducement to entry is $225, and entry will therefore not occur if K is larger than $225. Thus, if K exceeds $225 and is less than $400, only two firms will be in this market. On the other hand, if K is less than $225, a third firm will enter. This raises yet another question: How large must K be so that a fourth firm will not enter? The answer to this question raises yet another, and so on.

We can answer this unending string of questions by performing a single general calculation. Suppose that n established firms are currently in the industry. What is the inducement to entry? Because the entrant will increase the number of firms to $n + 1$, we can simply reinterpret what we already know about the Cournot model to discover the answer. Each of the $n + 1$ firms will produce $60/(n + 2)$ units in the Cournot equilibrium. As you can easily verify, the price in this equilibrium minus the marginal cost of $40 is also $60/(n + 2)$. Therefore, when n firms are in the market, the inducement to entry is

$$\text{inducement to entry} = [60/(n + 2)]^2$$

The generalized no-entry condition for the Cournot model is then
$$[60/(n + 2)]^2 \leq K$$

Given K, this condition determines the minimum number of firms that must serve this market if entry is to be unprofitable.

If we now suppose that firms enter the industry sequentially, we have a theory of market structure for this example. Given K, the number of firms in the industry will be the smallest value of n such that the generalized no-entry condition is satisfied. These results are presented in Figure 11.9, where K is measured along the horizontal axis. If K is greater than the gross profit of $900 earned by a monopolist, the market is not a viable one: no firms will serve it. If K is greater than $400 but less than $900, the industry is a natural monopoly. A single firm will produce 30 units, sell them at a price equal to $70, and earn $900 minus K in profit. If K is greater than $225 but less than $400, a duopoly will serve the market. Aggregate output will be 40 units, price will be $60, and

FIGURE 11.9   Cournot oligopoly and entry equilibrium

The number of firms in entry equilibrium is inversely related to the magnitude of the set-up cost, or the barrier to entry K. As K decreases, the number of firms and aggregate output increase, while price and profit decrease. When K is more than \$225 and less than \$400, for example, there are two firms, aggregate output is 40 units, price is \$60, and aggregate profit is $800 - 2K$.

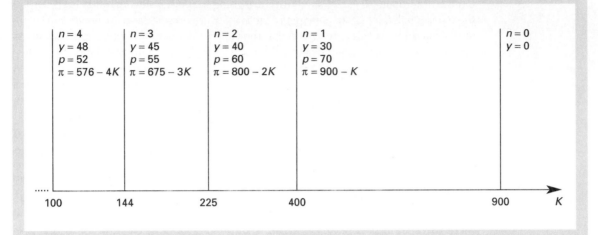

aggregate profit will be \$800 minus $2K$. If K is greater than \$144 but less than \$225, three firms will be in the industry, and so on.

In this model, setup or product development costs K can be interpreted as a barrier to entry; K is the only factor that differentiates established firms from potential entrants. Because established firms have already incurred this cost, they view it as a **sunk cost** — a cost that has no bearing on their profit-maximizing decisions. Because potential entrants have not incurred this cost, however, they see it instead as an *avoidable cost* of production — a cost they will incur only if they opt for entry. When K is large, few firms will opt for entry; when it is small, many firms will opt for entry. Thus:

sunk cost

The magnitude of the barrier to entry determines the market structure in this model.

In a more elaborate model, however, *demand conditions* will also be factors in determining market structure. For example, if the market demand function is $p = 200 - y$ instead of the demand function used throughout this chapter, $p = 100 - y$, we would expect to see more firms in the industry for any given value of K. Furthermore, as you will soon see, a setup or product development cost is not the *only* barrier to entry. We have used it simply to suggest the role that such barriers play in determining market structure. The precise effect of any particular entry barrier will vary.

As you will discover in the following problems, once the possibility of entry is introduced into the simple oligopoly models of the first half of this chapter, these models appear in a new light. Recall that in the context of a fixed number of firms, the Bertrand model seemed absurd because the cutthroat competition that drives that model ensured that the outcome would be prices equal to marginal cost. When we couple the Bertrand model with entry, however, the result is instead universal monopoly. As long as K is positive, a second firm will never enter the market. By contrast, in the collusive model at the beginning of the chapter, gross profit was maximal for a fixed number of firms. When we couple the collusive model with entry, however, potential entrants find entry enticing. As a result, in the long run, firms continue to enter the market until, in equilibrium, gross profit is minimal.

> **PROBLEM 11.7**
>
> Suppose that cost and demand conditions are identical to those used throughout this chapter. Suppose, too, that the underlying oligopoly model is the Bertrand model and that, at present, a single established firm is in the market. This sitting monopolist is producing the monopoly output and earning the full monopoly profit. Show that as long as K is positive, an entrant who understands oligopoly pricing behavior in the Bertrand model will never enter.

> **PROBLEM 11.8**
>
> Now suppose that the underlying oligopoly model is the collusive model. In the collusive equilibrium with n firms, each firm makes a gross profit equal to $\$900/n$ in each period. Suppose, too, that the entrant sees that it will be admitted to the collusive club once it incurs the setup cost, thereby becoming an established firm. Show that the no-entry condition is
>
> $$900/(n + 1) \leq K$$
>
> Compare industry-wide profit in this model with industry-wide profit in the Cournot and Bertrand models when K is 400; when K is 100.

As you have just discovered, if a sitting monopolist in the Bertrand model can credibly threaten to pursue the post-entry strategy of cutthroat competition implicit in that model, it can continue to monopolize its market regardless of how small K is. By contrast, if the established oligopolists in the collusive model anticipate that their collusive behavior will simply entice potential entrants to join the collusive club, their pre-entry incentive to act collusively will be seriously eroded. What have we learned?

First, setup costs differentiate the real economic position of established firms from the position of potential entrants. Therefore, such costs act as a barrier to entry. Second, the precise way in which this differentiation affects an entrant's anticipated profit — or the inducement to entry — depends on the nature of the oligopoly behavior subsequent to entry. Roughly speaking, the more aggressive oligopoly behavior is subsequent to entry, the more effective setup costs are as a barrier to entry. Conversely, the more cooperative oligopoly behavior is subsequent to entry, the less effective setup costs are as a barrier to entry.

Any firm's decision to incur the setup cost can be seen as a strategic decision to position itself as an established firm. It is strategic because it affects the incentives of other firms. In particular, if the firm does choose to position itself as an established firm, it effectively reduces the profit that subsequent firms can anticipate from the market.

This view of the decision to incur setup costs as a positioning strategy raises an important question. In what other ways can established firms position themselves relative to potential entrants to manipulate those entrants' incentives? The recent literature on long-run equilibrium in oligopolies has examined a whole arsenal of such positioning strategies, including moves to acquire specialized and durable capital equipment, to create patents, to stockpile essential raw materials, to hold extensive inventory, and to spend large sums of money on advertising and product development.

11.12
Positioning and Reacting

Because the subject of oligopoly is complex and sometimes confusing, in closing we will attempt to draw together insights from the entire chapter. In doing so, we will be drawing heavily on Spence (1981) — a source that provides an accessible, wide-ranging discussion of the issues raised in this chapter.[9]

Any firm able to earn consistently high profit over a long period of time requires some form of protection from potential entrants. Yet the existence of such profit is clearly an enticement to potential entrants, which raises the question: What can protect a firm's profit from entry? The answer is a combination of *structural features*, such as economies of scale and product development or setup costs, and of *actions designed to inhibit entry*. We have highlighted setup costs as a structural feature in this chapter. Their role in entry deterrence is straightforward: to entice entry, the potential entrant's market share must be large enough that the firm at least recovers its setup costs. The larger such setup costs are, the less attractive is the opportunity to enter. Thus, setup costs are one important barrier to entry and are therefore an important determinant of market structure. More generally, economies of scale are a barrier to entry.

Turning to the actions that established firms undertake in an attempt to inhibit entry, Spence distinguishes two separate but strategically interrelated sets of activities: positioning and reacting. **Positioning** is concerned with actions taken prior to entry. Accumulating inventory is one possible positioning strategy. Others include advertising, acquiring capital or production capacity, and choosing product durability. (Selling durable products today, for example, allows an established firm to capture today's and tomorrow's market today — a strategy that will materially affect a potential entrant's profitability.) **Reacting** refers to the actions of established firms subsequent to entry. An entry-deterring reaction discussed in this chapter is the threat to market a quantity at least as large as the limit output subsequent to entry.

positioning

reacting

Reacting and positioning are clearly substitutes in the sense that if the established firm can credibly threaten to be sufficiently aggressive subsequent to entry, it need not pursue any clever positioning strategy prior to entry. Recall, for example, what you learned from Problem 11.7. If firms behave in accordance with the Bertrand model, as long as K is positive, entry will never occur. Therefore, an established firm might try to substitute the post-entry threat of the ruthless price cutting imagined by Bertrand for the pre-entry positioning strategy of holding inventory. The difficulty is that this post-entry threat may not be credible, because once entry does occur, the established firm would be cutting its own throat (as well as the entrant's) by driving price down to marginal cost.

Where reactive threats may not seem credible in themselves, they sometimes can be made more believable when coupled with a positioning strategy. By actually producing output prior to entry and holding it in inventory, for example, an established firm makes its threat to market that output more credible. By actually acquiring production

---

9 You may also want to consult Dixit (1980) and Eaton and Lipsey (1980).

capacity prior to entry, an established firm makes the threat to use that capacity subsequent to entry more believable, and so on.

Indeed, in a famous antitrust case, Alcoa was accused of effectively deterring competition by using excess capacity to make more credible its implicit threat to market the limit output if entry occurred. In making a judgment against Alcoa (United States 1945), Judge Hand pointed to Alcoa's deliberate decisions to repeatedly build up its capacity as the market for aluminum expanded:

> It was not inevitable that it should always anticipate increases in the demand for ingot and be prepared to supply them. Nothing compelled it to keep doubling and redoubling its capacity before others entered the field. It insists that it never excluded rivals; but we can think of no more effective exclusion than progressively to embrace each new opportunity as it opened and to face every newcomer with new capacity already geared into a great organization, having the advantage of experience, trade connections and the elite of personnel.

In the so-called Cheerios case, the leading ready-to-eat cereal makers Kellogg, General Mills, and Post — were similarly accused of strategically deterring entry, in their case by a strategy of brand proliferation. (We will look at the Cheerios case in the next chapter.)

SUMMARY

We began the chapter by introducing the basic concepts and tools of *game theory*. We then used these tools to explore oligopoly when the number of firms is fixed. From the *Cournot* and *Bertrand models*, we learned one very basic lesson about oligopolistic interactions: there is a fundamental contradiction between what is privately rational (or profit-maximizing) and what is collectively rational. In any simple Nash equilibrium, firms have a clear incentive to collude. Yet in exploring the *collusive model* of oligopoly, we discovered that each party to a collusive agreement also has a private incentive to cheat by producing more than the agreed-upon output or by charging less than the agreed-upon price. The *prisoners' dilemma* is the game that illustrates these conflicting forces most clearly. This contradiction arises in Cournot's model of oligopoly, where firms independently choose quantities, and in Bertrand's model, where firms independently choose prices. Evidence from experimental economics and from the history of real collusive agreements supports the view that oligopolists do recognize and act on these conflicting incentives at different times.

We saw, too, that Cournot's model responds in an appealing way to changes in the number of firms. When there is only one firm. Cournot's model is identical to the standard monopoly model. As the number of firms increases, aggregate output increases, and aggregate profit and price decrease. As the number of firms approaches infinity, Cournot's model converges to the competitive equilibrium. Thus, Cournot's model captures a wide range of market structures, from monopoly to perfect competition. Bertrand's model has none these appealing properties. In that model, price is equal to marginal cost whenever there are two or more firms.

In the second part of the chapter, we arrived at several additional insights as we explored the theory of oligopoly in the long run, when firms are allowed to enter a market. We began with the *limit-output model*, in which established firms produce enough output (the limit output) that an entrant who takes the output of established firms as given will not enter. As we saw, the weakness of this model lies in the question of credibility: How believable is the threat by established firms to actually produce the limit output after entry occurs? In answering this question, we produced a *theory of market structure* based on Cournot's model.

We closed the chapter by summing up the insights to be drawn from our foray into the fascinating but complicated world of oligopolistic decision making. It is fascinating because it is at heart a game of strategic maneuvering: a game of *positioning* and *reacting*. Yet it is precisely the business of anticipating and responding to strategic moves of rivals (present and potential) that makes oligopoly so difficult to model.

EXERCISES

1. You can adapt much of the analysis in this chapter to a model with different cost and demand conditions. The market demand function is

$$p = 460 - .5y$$

The constant marginal cost for all firms is $100.

  a. Find the monopoly output and price, and compute the monopolist's profit.

  b. Find the Cournot equilibrium output for each firm and the aggregate output and price in the Cournot equilibrium, and compute the equilibrium profit of a representative firm when there are two firms in the market. When there are three firms in the market. When there are four firms in the market.

  c. Suppose that there are two firms in the market. What is the symmetric collusive equilibrium? How much profit does each firm earn in this equilibrium? If one firm honors the collusive agreement, and the other violates the agreement, how much should the violator produce to maximize its profit? What is the magnitude of the inducement to violate the collusive agreement?

  d. Now suppose that there is a fixed cost in addition to the $100 marginal cost. If the fixed cost K is $3200, what is the limit output y_L? What is the limit price p_L? Supposing that the limit output effectively deters entry, what profit would a monopolist earn by using the limit-output strategy?

  e. Now suppose that K is $20,000, that all firms regard the Cournot model as the correct oligopoly model, and that entry is sequential. How many firms will enter the market? What profit will each firm earn?

  f. Now suppose that K is $20,000, that all firms regard the collusive model as the correct oligopoly model, and that entry is sequential. How many firms will enter the market? What profit will each firm earn?

  g. Finally, suppose that K is $20,000, that all firms regard the Bertrand model as the correct oligopoly model, and that entry is sequential. How many firms will enter the market? What profit will each firm earn?

2. In this problem, you can see that common property creates a prisoner's dilemma. Harry and Sally each have 90 fish in their pens, and their preferences are such that for bundles composed of fish consumed today and fish consumed tomorrow, they prefer the bundle with more total fish. That is, the total number of fish Harry (Sally) consumes over the two periods is what matters to him (her). Each can choose one of the following two strategies: E denotes the strategy of eating all 90 fish today, and R denotes the strategy of returning all 90 fish to the river. Each fish returned to the river today results in 5/3 fish for consumption tomorrow. Under the common-property institution, Harry and Sally each take half of tomorrow's fish harvest. Construct a matrix analogous to Table 11.1 in which the entries are the total numbers of fish consumed by Harry and by Sally, and show that E is a dominant strategy for both Harry and Sally. Show, too, that they would have been better off had they both chosen R instead of E. Suppose that they are operating under a private-property institution; repeat the exercise.

3. The daily demand for round-trip air travel between cities A and B is

$$p = 2,000 - y$$

where y is the number of passengers. There is no demand for one-way travel. Each plane can carry up to 1,000 passengers. The cost of flying a plane from

A to B and back again is $K, regardless of the number of passengers on the plane. Each firm owns only one plane. Suppose that there are a number of firms in this market and that they can collusively choose and enforce one price. What price will they choose? Now suppose that the price-setting club cannot keep other firms from entering the market; that is, free entry into the market (and the club) prevails. Find the number of firms and the number of seats that will be occupied in each plane in free-entry equilibrium when K is $600,000. When K is $300,000. When K is $150,000.

4. Two courier firms serve a market with the following demand function

$$p = 100 - y$$

where y is aggregate quantity, $y_1 + y_2$. Each firm has the following cost function:

$$C(y_i) = y_i^2/2$$

where y_i is firm i's output. The marginal cost function is

$$MC(y_i) = y_i$$

a. Given y_2, what is the first firm's demand function, and what is its marginal revenue function? Draw the first firm's demand, marginal revenue, and marginal cost functions on the same diagram. What is the first firm's best-response function? What is the second firm's best-response function?

b. How much does each firm produce in the Cournot equilibrium? What is price in the Cournot equilibrium? How much profit does each firm earn in the Cournot equilibrium?

5. It is sometimes argued that advertising is a barrier to entry. Explain the circumstances in which a large expenditure on advertising by some firm this year may be a barrier to entry for another firm next year.

6. At various times in its history, Dow Chemical, the dominant producer of magnesium in the United States, has held an entire year's production in inventory. Since it is costly to hold such inventories, the interesting question is: Why do it? Some economists have claimed that large inventories create a barrier to entry, and Dow may have held them to discourage entry. Explain how inventories might serve as a barrier to entry.

7. Firms 1 and 2 both produce gismos, but firm 1 does it at a lower cost than firm 2. Firm 1 has a constant marginal cost of $15, and firm 2 has a constant marginal cost of $30. The demand for gismos is

$$p = 120 - y$$

where y is aggregate output.

a. Suppose that the firms choose quantities. Find both best-response functions. Remember, marginal costs are different, so the best-response functions will *not* be symmetric. Find the Cournot equilibrium quantities. Hint: Treat the best-response functions as two equations in two unknowns — the Cournot equilibrium quantities — and solve the equations for the unknown quantities. Compute each firm's profit in the Cournot equilibrium.

b. Suppose that the firms choose prices instead of quantities and that prices must be announced in dollars and cents. Then $15.71, $45.95, and $39.00 are permissible prices, but $45.975 and $57.0067 are not. What are the Bertrand equilibrium prices? How much does each firm earn in the Bertrand equilibrium?

8. In many high-tech industries, there is considerable "learning by doing." In particular, in these industries, the marginal cost of production appears to be strongly influenced by cumulative past output — the more the firm has produced in the past, the lower its marginal cost of production in the present. Discuss the possible effects of learning by doing on market structure.

*9. In Section 11.4 we presented a general argument showing that in the Nash equilibrium, the duopolists (i) failed to maximize joint profit and (ii) that they produced too much output, relative to joint profit maximization. The key assumption we used was that the profit of one firm decreases as the output of the other firm increases. Notice that this assumption is not appropriate when the duopolists produce goods that are complementary. If one duopolist produces skis and the other ski boots, for example, it is appropriate to assume that the profit of one firm *increases* as the output of the other firm increases. Using this assumption, show that in the Nash equilibrium duopolists that produce complementary goods (i) fail to maximize joint profit and (ii) produce too little output, relative to joint profit maximization.

11A
Collusion in Supergames

In the static models we looked at in Sections 11.3 through 11.7, collusive profit maximization is inconsistent with Nash equilibrium. In the Cournot model, for example, if the firms get together and agree to produce only 15 units apiece — half of the monopoly output — the agreement is not self-enforcing. That is, when it comes time to actually make production decisions, each firm has a clear incentive to produce more than 15 units, and each will recognize that the other has the same incentive to violate the agreement.

However, the Cournot and Bertrand models fail to capture a very important aspect of real-world oligopolies. Because these models are concerned with strategies and payoffs in just one period, they do not capture the long-term dynamic interplay that characterizes most oligopoly relationships. Because, as we have said earlier, oligopolists repeatedly play games of strategy and counter-strategy as they jockey for market power — often over extended time periods — we also see that there are actually far more potential strategies available to them than in the static models of Cournot and Bertrand.

Specifically, we will look at collusive strategies that incorporate punishments for defection from the collusive output. We will ask if this type of strategy can support collusive joint profit-maximizing behavior as a Nash equilibrium. We will discover that it quite easy — in fact, too easy — to support collusion as a Nash equilibrium; there are many Nash equilibrium strategy combinations that produce joint profit-maximizing behavior that are quite unsatisfactory because they rely on punishments that are not credible. This discovery will lead us to an important refinement of the concept of Nash equilibrium in dynamic games.[10]

stage game

supergame

We will concentrate on a very special repeated game in which two firms play the same **stage game** in each of an infinite number of periods. The stage game is the familiar Cournot duopoly game in Section 11.4. This type of game, in which the same stage game is played in each of an infinite number of periods, is called a **supergame**. We will call the first period of the supergame period 1, the second period 2, and so on.

actions

strategies

In a supergame it is important to distinguish between **actions** and **strategies**. Actions pertain to the stage games that are played in different periods. In the supergame we are considering, a player's *action* in any period is just the quantity of output that the player produces in that period. By contrast, a player's *strategy* specifies an action for each period, for each possible history of actions in the supergame up to that period. Clearly, supergame strategies can be very complex.

Trigger Strategies

trigger strategy

However, one simple type of strategy, called a **trigger strategy**, has dominated the literature on supergames. In constructing a trigger strategy, the players first collusively

---

10 Stigler (1969) presents the basic ideas on collusive oligopoly and gives a thorough discussion of the conditions that are and are not conducive to effective collusion. See Friedman (1971) for an excellent treatment of the material developed in this appendix. Robert Axelrod's book *The Evolution of Cooperation* is a fascinating and very readable account of how people often manage to cooperate in playing repeated games.

target output

punishment
output

choose the level of output to be produced in each period. We will call this the **target output**. We will take the target output to be 15 units since, if each produces 15 units, the players maximize their joint profit. The players then choose a **punishment output**. The punishment output comes into play only if some player has defected from the collusive agreement by not producing the target output. It is intended to induce the opposing player to produce the target output. This strategy is called a trigger strategy because defection of the other player in any period *triggers* the punishment output in all subsequent periods. In effect, a trigger strategy is a *promise* to produce the target output as long as the other player also produces it combined with a *threat* to produce the punishment output forever if the other player defects.

To begin the analysis, let us pick a really severe punishment output. If a firm produces and sells 100 units in any period, then from the demand function $(p = 100 - y)$ we see that price is \$0. If in any period, one player produces the punishment output, the best the other player can do is to produce nothing, thereby generating zero profit. This severe punishment output completely eliminates any possibility of profit for the opposing player in any period after he or she defects. We have called this trigger strategy *killer* because the punishment output is so severe:

Killer: (i) produce 15 units in period 1; (ii) in period t $(t \geq 2)$, produce 15 units if in all previous period the other player produced 15 units; (iii) in period t $(t \geq 2)$, produce 100 units if in any previous period the other player failed to produce 15 units.

Suppose then that these two firms get together, design and agree to *killer* as their mutual strategy, and then go their separate ways. Is their announced strategy combination (*killer, killer*) a Nash equilibrium strategy combination? Let us take the perspective of the first firm. Given that the strategy of the second firm is *killer*, is *killer* a best response for the first firm? If the answer is yes, then (*killer, killer*) is Nash equilibrium strategy combination because the positions of the two firms are symmetric.

First we must calculate the first firm's profit if it also adopts *killer*. From (i) we see that both firms start out by producing 15 units in period 1. Then, from (ii) we see that each firm will produce 15 units in period 2 because the other firm produced 15 units in period 1. Looking again at (ii) we see that each firm will produce 15 units in period 3 because the other firm produced 15 units in both period 1 and 2, and so on, for period after

equilibrium
path

period. We see that strategy combination (*killer, killer*) produces an **equilibrium path** along which each firm produces the joint-maximizing quantity of 15 units in each period. In each period, then, the first firm's profit is \$450 — exactly half the monopoly profit.

Of course, the first firm is interested in the discounted present value of this profit stream. Letting i denote the interest or discount rate, the present value of the first firm's profit is

$$\$450 + \$450/(1 + i) + \$450/(1 + i)^2 + \$450/(1 + i)^3 + \ldots$$

We have been looking at the game from the vantage point of period 1. However, the expression we derived is more general — it gives us the discounted present value of profit from current and future play of the game, not just for the first period, but for all periods. That is, at any point in time t, the value of current and future profit along the equilibrium path, discounted to time t, is given by this expression. (See Section 15.1 if you need to refresh your understanding of discounted present values.)

If the first firm does anything other than produce 15 units in period 1, from (iii) we see that it must anticipate that the second firm will produce 100 units in all subsequent periods. Given this response, the best the first firm can do is to produce nothing in all periods after period 1, since 100 units of output drives price down to \$0. The best alternative strategy therefore generates \$0 in profit in all periods after the defection period. We can use the best response function from Section 11.4 to find the profit-maximizing output for the first firm in the defection period. Given that the second firm produces 15 units in period 1, the first firm's best response is to produce 22.5 units (30 − 15/2). Aggregate output is then 37.5 units (15 + 22.5), price is $62.5 (100 − 37.5), and profit per unit is $22.5 (62.5 − 40). The first firm's defection profit in period 1 is then $506.25 (22.5 units produced × $22.5 profit per unit). We see, then, that the maximum discounted present value of profit the first firm can make if it defects is

$$\$506.25 + \$0/(1+i) + \$0/(1+i)^2 + \$0/(1+i)^3 + \ldots$$

In other words, it makes $506.25 in the defection period and $0 in all subsequent periods. Even though we have looked at defection only from the vantage point of period 1, the analysis is applicable to *any* period. Supposing that time t has arrived and that neither player has yet defected, this expression gives the discounted present value of defection at time t.

Now let us draw together what we just learned about killer strategy. Given that the second firm's strategy is *killer*, the first firm will never defect if

$$\$450 + \$450/(1+i) + \$450/(1+i)^2 + \ldots$$

$$> \$506.25 + \$0/(1+i) + \$0/(1+i)^2 + \ldots$$

If this inequality is satisfied, the first firm will not defect in period 1, nor in period 2, nor in any period. That is, when this inequality is satisfied, *killer* is a best response for the first firm, and (*killer, killer*) is a Nash equilibrium.

Let us rewrite this inequality to highlight the *inducement to defect* and the *punishment for defection*:

$$\$450/(1+i) + \$450/(1+i)^2 + \ldots > \$56.25$$

The $56.25 inducement to defect on the right side of the inequality is equal to the difference between the $506.25 profit the first firm makes in the first period if it defects and the $450 profit it makes if it does not defect. The punishment for defection is the expression on the left side of the inequality. If the first firm does not defect, its profit is $450 in each period, and, if it does defect, its profit is $0. Therefore, the punishment for defection is the discounted present value of $450 in each period after a defection.

The expression on the left side the inequality is equal to $450/$i$. Using this result, the inequality reduces to

$$\$450/i > \$56.25$$

This inequality is satisfied for any rate of interest less than 800% per period:

We conclude that (*killer, killer*) is a Nash equilibrium strategy combination for any reasonable rate of interest.

We can easily see why this is the case. The severe punishment output we used to construct *killer* translates into a $450/$i$ punishment for defection. Unless the interest rate is extraordinarily high, this punishment easily dominates the $56.25 inducement to defect.

The Credibility Problem

However, there is a major problem with *killer* — the punishment output is simply not credible. Suppose that the first firm actually defects by producing 22.5 units in some period. The second firm incurs a loss of $4,000 in any period in which it produces the punishment output since the unit cost of production is $40 and selling 100 units drives price all the way down to $0. Even though we do not know *exactly* what the second firm will do in the event of defection, we can be quite sure that it will not produce the punishment output. Since the first firm can also anticipate this response, it will not believe what amounts to an idle punishment threat:

Even though (*killer, killer*) is a Nash equilibrium strategy combination, it will not support collusion because the punishment for defection is not credible.

Killer's lack of credibility points to a serious inadequacy of unrefined Nash equilibrium in dynamic games. How can we eliminate equilibria based on non-credible threats? Alternatively, how can we refine the concept of Nash equilibrium to eliminate non-credible threats? *By insisting that the strategies pursued in the punishment phase of the supergame are Nash equilibrium strategies.*

Think of the two firms as proposing to pursue a joint-maximizing strategy supported by punishment that calls for reversion to the Cournot-Nash equilibrium of the stage game in the event of defection. We will call this trigger strategy **Cournot reversion**.

Cournot reversion

Cournot reversion: (i) produce 15 units in period 1; (ii) in period t ($t \geq 2$), produce 15 units if in all previous periods both players produced 15 units; (iii) in period t ($t \geq 2$), produce 20 units if in any previous period either player failed to produce 15 units.

Given strategy combination (*Cournot reversion, Cournot reversion*), if either player defects, the strategies that are played in the resulting punishment phase of the supergame are Nash equilibrium strategies. To see why, suppose one player has defected. Then, from (iii) we see that for the rest of time each player's strategy is to produce 20 units in each period. In other words, strategy combination (*Cournot reversion, Cournot reversion*) *induces* strategy combination (*produce 20 units in all periods, produce 20 units in all periods*) for the punishment phase of the game. Given that one firm's strategy is to produce 20 units in each period, it is clearly payoff-maximizing for the other to produce 20 units in each period. In this sense, the punishment for defection built into *Cournot reversion* is credible.

Is the resulting punishment for defection large enough to dominate the inducement to defect? Notice that the inducement to defect is still $56.25, while the punishment for defection is now only $50/i$. On the equilibrium path in this case, each firm makes $450 per period while, if it defects, it gets $400 per period in the punishment phase of the game. We see, then, that neither firm will defect if the following inequality is satisfied:

$$\$50/i > \$56.25$$

Thus:

If the interest rate is no larger that approximately 88% per period, *Cournot reversion* supports collusive joint profit maximization based on a credible punishment for defection.

> ### PROBLEM 11A.1
>
> If the target output is more than 15 units and less than 20 units we have *partial collusion* — a firm's profit per period is more than $400 but less than $450. First, suppose the interest rate is 95%, $i = .95$. This means that full collusion is not supportable. Show that it is possible to support partial collusion. Now suppose the interest rate is 100% or larger, $i = 1$. Is it still possible to support partial collusion?

Subgame Perfection

subgame
perfection

subgame perfect
Nash
equilibrium

The refinement of Nash equilibrium that we used in constructing *Cournot reversion* is called **subgame perfection**. To see what it involves we need just one more concept — the notion of a subgame. At any time t there are as many subgames as there are possible histories of play up to time t; in other words, each history of play up to time t defines a subgame. And each of these subgames encompasses the entire future play of the game. As we have seen, a player's strategy for the entire game induces a strategy for each subgame. Subgame perfection requires that, for all subgames, the induced strategy combinations are Nash equilibrium strategy combinations. A strategy combination is a **subgame perfect Nash equilibrium** strategy combination if, for all subgames, the induced strategy combination is a Nash equilibrium strategy combination.

Let us look again at our supergame to verify that (*Cournot reversion, Cournot reversion*) is a subgame perfect Nash equilibrium when the interest rate is not too high. All subgames can be divided into one of two categories: subgames that are and are not on the intended equilibrium path. For any subgame on the intended equilibrium path, the induced strategy combination is for each player is to continue to produce 15 units as long as there is no defection. As we saw, this is a Nash equilibrium when the interest rate is no larger than 88%. For any subgame that is off the equilibrium path, the induced strategy combination calls for each player is to produce 20 units in all future periods. This, too, is a Nash equilibrium.

Critique of the Collusive Model

There are two serious problems with this model of collusion. First, the assumption that the players are locked into a game with an infinite time horizon is crucial. If the players anticipate repeated play of the stage game for a known, finite number of periods, it is impossible to support collusive behavior as a subgame perfect Nash equilibrium. It is easy to see why. In the last period of play, neither player will produce the collusive output because there is no future period in which a defector can be punished. In that very last period, the players will therefore choose to produce not 15 but 20 units of output. Now, in thinking back to the next to last period and anticipating that each will produce 20 units in the last period, each will recognize that there will be no punishment in the last period for defection in the next to last period. Both will therefore produce 20 units in the next to last period. In this way the collusive behavior that can be credibly supported where there are an infinite number of periods completely unravels when there is a finite number of periods.

Second, there is a renegotiation problem. If one player defects, thereby triggering the punishment phase of the game, a situation is created in which the players have a clear incentive to try to hammer out another collusive agreement. The trouble is that if the possibility of renegotiation is anticipated, the punishment phase of the game is no longer credible: a player may be tempted to defect from the current agreement, hoping to renegotiate another after it has captured the $56.25 inducement to defect. Thus, we are left with a theory of collusive behavior that is very suggestive, but is not entirely satisfactory.

REFERENCES

Axelrod, R. 1984. *The Evolution of Cooperation*, New York: Basic Books.

Bain, J. S. 1956. *Barriers to New Competition*, Cambridge, Mass.: Harvard University Press.

Dixit, A. 1980. "The Role of Investment in Entry-Deterrence," *Economic Journal*, 90:95–106.

Eaton, B. C., and R. G. Lipsey. 1980. "Exit Barriers Are Entry Barriers: The Durability of Capital as a Barrier to Entry," *Bell Journal of Economics*, 11:721–29.

Fouraker, L., and S. Siegal. 1963. *Bargaining Behavior*, New York: McGraw-Hill.

Friedman, J. 1971. "A Non-Cooperative Equilibrium for Supergames," *Review of Economic Studies*, 38: 1–12.

Kreps, D. 1987. "Nash Eqilibrium," in *The New Palgrave: A Dictionary of Economics*, J. Eatwell, M. Milgate, and P. Newman (eds.), London: The Macmillan Press.

Luce, R. D., and H. Raiffa. 1957. *Games and Decisions*, New York: Wiley.

Modigliani, F. 1958. "New Developments on the Oligopoly Front," *Journal of Political Economy*, 66:215–32.

Plott, C. R. 1982. "Industrial Organization Theory and Experimental Economics," *Journal of Economic Literature*, 22:1485–527.

Roberts, K. 1987. "Collusion," in *The New Palgrave: A Dictionary of Economics*, J. Eatwell, M. Milgate, and P. Newman (eds.), London: The Macmillan Press.

Salop, S. C. 1986. "Practices That (Credibly) Facilitate Oligopoly Co-ordination," in *New Developments in the Analysis of Market Structure*, J. E. Stiglitz and G. F. Mathewson (eds.), Cambridge, Mass.: MIT Press.

Spence, A. M. 1977. "Entry, Capacity, Investment, and Oligopolistic Pricing," *Bell Journal of Economics*, 8:534–44.

———. 1981. "Competition, Entry and Antitrust Policy," in *Strategy, Predation and Antitrust Analysis*, S. Salop (ed.), Washington, D.C.: Federal Trade Commission.

Stigler, G. 1969. "A Theory of Oligopoly," *Journal of Political Economy*, 72:44–61.

Sylos-Labini, P. 1962. *Oligopoly and Technical Progress*, Cambridge, Mass.: Harvard University Press.

United States v. Aluminum Company of America et al. (1945), 145 F.2d 416, 424.

CHAPTER 12

Product Differentiation

The homogeneous, or undifferentiated, goods discussed in Chapter 12 — for example, magnesium, coal, ready-mix concrete, plywood, petroleum, and paper — are typically used as inputs in making finished consumer goods. As we turn our attention to such consumer goods, we will confront markets that are startlingly different: in place of the earlier homogeneity is a sometimes overwhelming diversity. The products available to consumers in any product group — for example, VCRs or microeconomic textbooks — are almost invariably heterogeneous, or differentiated.

differentiated products

Differentiated products are goods that, as a group, satisfy a particular need but differ in their individual specifications. For example, some 40 different brands of VCRs are available in about 150 models, at prices ranging from as little as $200 to as much as $1,500. The array of what advertisers call "features" and economists call "product specifications," or "characteristics," is staggering and continues to grow. Prospective buyers of VCRs can select from very basic models to VCRs sporting a whole range of options including remote controls, multi-event programmability, and stereo sound, or they can buy combinations of VCRs and video cameras or TVs with built-in VCRs. Although every model is a VCR, each is differentiated from other products in the same group by a distinguishing set of characteristics. Firms can also differentiate their products by variations in packaging, in servicing, and in warranty arrangements. Everywhere we look, from answering services to zippers, we see product differentiation.

The fact of such heterogeneity in consumer goods arises in response to significant differences in consumer preferences — the basic stuff of consumer choice making, which we explored in Chapter 2. If individual consumers did not differ markedly in their tastes, firms would have no reason to differentiate products. In the absence of such variations in personal preferences, for instance, we might all choose exactly the same model of Kodak video camera with a VCR. However, potential VCR buyers who do not see themselves as budding filmmakers welcome the range of alternative choices.

The same range of product choices, however, is not available to all consumers. As we might expect, the availability of products differs markedly among economies. For example, an emigré Polish actor living in Sweden described how a newly arrived Polish friend burst into tears when she saw all the different things for sale in an ordinary Swedish supermarket — things that were unavailable in her homeland. However, even within an advanced technological society such as Sweden or the United States, the diversity of products or services available to particular consumers can still vary markedly. For example, one of the features that distinguishes life in large cities such as New York from life in small towns such as Montrose, Colorado, is the difference in the range of products and services available. On any given night, New Yorkers can choose to eat almost any cuisine known to humankind and can pick an evening's entertainment from any number of plays, movies, or dance productions. Montrosers have only a handful of restaurants, one movie theater, and no resident drama or dance companies. This suggests that within a society, the greater the number of people who live in proximity, the larger the diversity of products in that locale.

This difference in the range of product diversity suggests that producers do encounter certain factors that limit product diversity. Those limits are product development or setup costs and increasing returns to scale. Setup costs can be sizable. For instance, Walt Disney Studios spends approximately $1.5 million every time it develops a new television show. These costs can be high enough to prohibit the development of a new product. So, too, the presence of economies of scale means that producers face a cost penalty for being small. A designer-label clothing store in Montrose, for instance, may not have a large enough clientele to make it a paying proposition. Two questions come naturally to mind: How many products will be available in a particular product group? What are the implications for individual consumers of such differences in availability?

If we choose to look at the flip side of product diversity — to see things from the entrepreneur's rather than the consumer's perspective — the question that arises is a separate but related one: What product (or line of products) should an entrepreneur produce? The answer is often some yet-unknown product. Indeed, the classic way for an entrepreneur to seize a share of a market is to introduce an innovative product. For example, the Filofax is a big, bulky address book, diary, and loose-leaf personal organizing system that has become an instant status symbol for globetrotting executives. A new disposable diaper, which takes only two years to disintegrate in landfills, has been brought to market under a mouthful of a name: Chemical-Free TenderCare Biodegradable. And Lick Your Chops is a new line of dog food that contains no preservatives, additives, salt, sugar, or artificial colors. Each of these products is carefully differentiated from other products in the same group.

Once we begin to talk about the development of newly differentiated products, we have crossed over from an economy characterized by a finite number of goods whose exact number and characteristics are *exogenous*, or given, to an economy in which the number and the characteristics of goods are instead *endogenous*, or to be determined. As we make this shift in our analysis, we see that the economy is now quite different, and we must therefore recreate the models we use to analyze it.

In this chapter, we introduce two models, each intended to determine both the number of products available in a particular product group and the prices at which those differentiated products will be marketed. The second model also determines the characteristics of these products. Several features are common to both models: product differentiation is taken to be a response to the diversity of individual tastes, the amount of product diversity is limited by product development costs or by increasing returns to scale, and new and important normative issues concerning the efficient amount of product diversity are raised.[1]

12.1

Chamberlin's Symmetrically Differentiated Products

Chamberlin model of monopolistic competition

The first model, the **Chamberlin model of monopolistic competition**, may already be familiar. This model focuses on product groups with a multiplicity of actual and potential

---

1 For an overview of the material in this chapter, see the entries by K. J. Lancaster in *The New Palgrave* entitled "non-price competition" and "product differentiation."

products. For example, the product group of ready-to-eat breakfast cereals includes all the cereals presently marketed, such as Cheerios, Team, Crispix, Grapenuts Flakes, Spoon Size Shredded Wheat, Alpha Bits, and Fruit & Fiber. The product group also includes all the unnamed, undeveloped, and unproduced cereals that have not yet appeared on supermarket shelves. The Chamberlin model is intended to determine how many of the products in this group will ultimately be produced and what the price of each product will be. We will use this model to analyze the equilibrium that results both when the number of differentiated products in the market is small and when the number is large.

Before we move to the equilibrium analysis, let us scrutinize the crucial, simplifying assumption of Chamberlin's model: given any subset of products actually produced, *all demand functions are symmetric*. This **symmetry assumption** is the hallmark of the Chamberlin view of product differentiation. As you will discover later on, this assumption may not be appropriate for many product groups. Its limitations, in fact, motivated the development of the second model we will explore in this chapter, which does not make the assumption of symmetry.

symmetry
assumption

Symmetric Preferences

To help you understand what the symmetry assumption means, we will lay out a simple example inspired by Perloff and Salop (1985). To keep the example within manageable bounds, we will assume that only four different products, labeled A, B, C, and D, are technically possible in this particular product group. Notice that when there are four products, precisely 24 unique rankings of the four products are possible. Hence, we will assume that there are 24 different types of consumers. For simplicity, we will also assume that there is just one consumer of each type (our analysis will require only that there be the same number of consumers of each type) and that the consumer buys just one unit of his or her most-favored product in the group of products actually on the market. If only two of the four products are actually available, for example, each consumer will buy one unit of the more-preferred product at the current prices.

When product prices are identical, each of the 24 consumers has a unique ranking (from most preferred to least preferred) of the four products. These 24 rankings are presented in Table 12.1. Consumer 1, for example, prefers A to B, B to C, and C to D. One part of the symmetry assumption concerns consumers' first choices — symmetry requires that each good is the first choices of an equal number of consumers. In Table 12.1, for example, each good is the first choice of six consumers.

An equally important part of the symmetry assumption concerns each consumer's second choice. The first six consumers in Table 12.1, for instance, all agree that A is the most preferred product, but they systematically disagree about which product is the best substitute for A. The second choice of consumers 1 and 2 is good B, the second choice of consumers 3 and 4 is good C, and the second choice of consumers 5 and 6 is good D. In other words, the second choices of these six consumers are evenly distributed over the other three products B, C, and D. In the same way, the second choices of those consumers whose first choices are B (or C or D) are evenly distributed over the remaining three products.

What spurs individual consumers to switch from their favorite product to one of the other three is a price differential that is "large enough." Let us assume that the consumer will decide to change from one brand to the next-preferred brand only if the price differential between adjacent products in a consumer's preference ordering is larger than e. Consumer 1 will buy B in preference to A, for instance, only if the difference between the two prices, $p_A - p_B$, is greater than e. He or she will buy C in preference to A if the difference between the two prices, $p_A - p_C$, is greater than $2e$. And he or she will buy D in preference to A if $p_A - p_D$ is greater than $3e$.

TABLE 12.1	Consumers' preferences when all products are available at a common price		
Consumer	Preference ordering	Consumer	Preference ordering
1	ABCD	13	CABD
2	ABDC	14	CADB
3	ACBD	15	CBAD
4	ACDB	16	CBDA
5	ADBC	17	CDAB
6	ADCB	18	CDBA
7	BACD	19	DABC
8	BADC	20	DACB
9	BCAD	21	DBAC
10	BCDA	22	DBCA
11	BDAC	23	DCAB
12	BDCA	24	DCBA

Symmetric Demand Functions

Given these consumers' preferences, what will the product demand functions be like with one, two, three, or four products on the market? First, suppose that only product A is actually for sale. In this case, each of the 24 consumers will demand one unit of A regardless of its price tag. In other words, the demand function for A will be perfectly price-inelastic, or graphically vertical, at 24 units. The same result holds if the single available product is instead B or C or D.

What if two products are on the market? If the two available products are A and B and if the price of B is p', or $p_B = p'$, what is the demand function for A? As you can deduce from Table 12.1, when the price of A, p_A, is within e of p', then exactly half of the 24 consumers (those numbered 1, 2, 3, 4, 5, 6, 13, 14, 17, 19, 20, and 23) prefer A, and the quantity demanded of A at any price greater than $p' - e$ and less than $p' + e$ will be 12 units. In Figure 12.1a, then, one segment of the demand function for A is the vertical line segment labeled d directly above 12 units on the horizontal axis.

When p_A is greater than $p' + e$ (but less than $p' + 2e$), however, six customers (1, 2, 13, 17, 19, and 23 in Table 12.1) will switch from A to B. In Figure 12.1a, then, a second segment of the demand function for A is the vertical line segment labeled d immediately above 6 units. When p_A exceeds $p' + 2e$ (but is less than $p' + 3e$), four more customers (3, 5, 14, and 20) will switch from A to B, and a third segment of the demand function for A is then the vertical segment labeled d above 2 units. And when the price of A exceeds $p' + 3e$, the remaining two customers (4 and 6) will switch from A to B.

If we now decrease rather than increase p_A by increments of e, the pattern is reversed: as p_A drops below $p' - e$, six customers (7, 8, 15, 18, 21, and 24) switch from B to A; as p_A drops below $p' - 2e$, four more customers (9, 11, 16, and 22) switch to A; and as p_A drops below $p' - 3e$, the remaining two customers (10 and 12) switch to A.

Although we could derive the demand function for B in just the same way, we would be wasting our time. We can simply replace the label y_A by y_B in Figure 12.1a and the label p_A by p_B — and voilà, the figure illustrates the demand function for B when the price of A is p'. Although the customers who switch as the price increases or decreases by increments of e are different, the resulting demand functions are nevertheless symmetric. Indeed, we could pick any pair of products, and the product names

FIGURE 12.1   Chamberlin demand functions

There are two products in (a) and three in (b). The line segments labeled *d* comprise the demand function for product A when the prices of the other products are held constant at *p′*. The line labeled *DD* gives the quantity demanded of any product when all prices are identical.

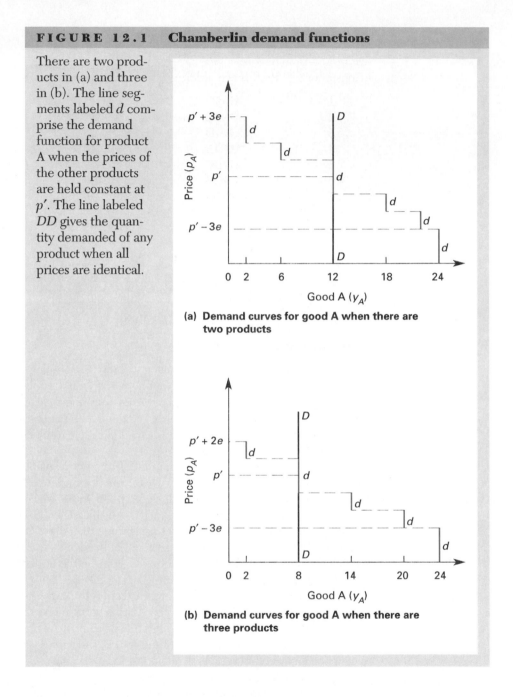

(a) Demand curves for good A when there are two products

(b) Demand curves for good A when there are three products

(and therefore the labels in Figure 12.1a) would change, but the resulting demand functions would not. This property is what we mean by symmetric demand functions.

In deriving the demand functions in Figure 12.1a, we held the price of product B constant and allowed the price of A to vary. We can also derive the demand functions for A and B when their prices move up and down in unison. If the prices of A and B are initially the same, and if these prices are increased or decreased in unison, customers will not switch brands. At any common price, 12 units of A and 12 of B will be demanded. The resulting demand function for A, for instance, is the function labeled

DD in Figure 12.1a. More generally, the demand functions for any pair of products when their prices are identical are just like the *DD* function for A in Figure 12.1a.

What happens when not two, but three products are on the market — say A, B, and C? If these three products have a common price, they will split the market evenly, and the quantity demanded of each will therefore be 8. If their prices are then allowed to move up and down in unison, the demand function for each will be completely price inelastic at 8 units. For example, the demand function for A in this case is the function labeled *DD* in Figure 12.1b. What happens if the prices of two of the products — say, B and C — are fixed at a common value p', but the price of the third — say, A — is allowed to vary? The resulting demand function for A is composed of the vertical segments again labeled *d* in Figure 12.1b, and the demand functions for B and C are symmetric to it. You can discover how these demand functions have been generated in the following problem.

> ### PROBLEM 12.1
>
> First, use Table 12.1 to identify which eight customers prefer good A when all three prices are identical — say, p'. Holding p_B and p_C equal to p', as p_A rises above $p' + e$, A loses six customers. Which six customers? Which three customers go to B and which three to C? As p_A drops below $p' - e$, A gains six customers. Which three does it gain from B and which three from C? Now fix p_A and p_C at p'. Identify the eight customers B attracts if p_B is also p'. As p_B drops below $p' - e$, which six customers does it gain?

If we take a slightly wider perspective and compare the demand functions in Figure 12.1a and 12.1b, we see that as the number of products in the market grows, the *dd* demand function for a representative product shifts down and to the left, and the *DD* function shifts to the left. Another thing we learn from these exercises is that if a new product, the *n*th product, is introduced — and if the new and the previously available products all sell at the same price — then the *n*th product will attract $1/n$ of all the customers from the product group. These customers will be drawn evenly from each of the products previously available. Entry of the new product thus diminishes demand equally for each of the goods already in the marketplace. In other words:

A new product is equally differentiated from all previously available products.

This result is clearly generated by the simplifying assumption of symmetry. Underlying this simplification is the notion that new goods compete with and are equally differentiated from all other goods currently available in the same product group. If the context is breakfast cereals, for example, it means that when Sugar Sweeties, a new breakfast cereal, hits the shelves, it draws an equal number of customers from former buyers of Cheerios, Fruit Loops, Cocoa Puffs, All-Bran, and all the other brands currently available — if their prices are all the same. If we blindly apply the assumption to movie theaters, we conclude that if a new movie theater opens in the Bronx, it will draw away customers equally from other theaters in the Bronx, in Manhattan, in Westchester County, on Long Island, and even in Montrose, Colorado — if all charge the same admission price. You can see from this example that the symmetry assumption is not always applicable. We will take a closer look at the limits of applicability of Chamberlin's model when we introduce the second model of product differentiation.

Before we use these kinds of symmetric demand functions to analyze the resulting short- and long-run equilibria, we need to make them both more realistic and more manageable. For the sake of realism, we will assume that a consumer's demand for

FIGURE 12.2   Smoothing the Chamberlin demand functions

The demand function labeled *dd* gives the quantity demanded of a representative product as its price p_R changes, holding the prices of all other products fixed at p'. The function labeled *DD* gives quantity demanded of a representative product when the prices of all products move up or down in unison. The two demand functions intersect at price p'.

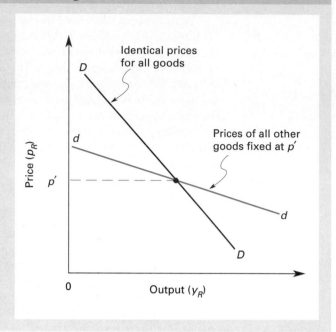

the chosen product is responsive to price: the higher the product's price, the smaller the quantity demanded. This means that the functions labeled *DD* in Figure 12.1 — those generated by changing all product prices in unison — will not be perfectly inelastic. Instead the functions will be downward sloping. For the sake of manageability, we will also smooth out the discontinuities in the functions labeled *dd* in Figure 12.1 — discontinuities that arise as customers switch from one product to another.

These modifications are shown in Figure 12.2. The function labeled *DD* gives the quantity demanded of a representative product at any price common to all goods in the product group. We have denoted the price of the representative product by p_R. The function labeled *dd* gives the quantity demanded of the representative product when the prices of all other products in the product group are equal to p'.

Notice that the function *dd* is flatter, or more elastic, than *DD* and that it intersects *DD* at the common price for all other products p'. It is more elastic because as the price of the representative product changes, while the prices of all other products remain constant, consumers switch brands. Consumers switch away from the representative product as p_R rises above p', and they switch to it as p_R drops below p'. It intersects *DD* when p_R is equal to p' because — as the symmetry assumption guarantees — when the prices of all the products are the same, the quantity demanded of each product will also be the same.

12.2
Chamberlin's Small-Numbers Case

small-numbers case

In the **small-numbers case**, there are few differentiated products. We will focus on the case in which there are just two products, the duopoly case. Back in the 1950s, North American teenagers seemed to belong either to "Ford" or to "Chevy" families, and they regularly amused themselves by arguing about the relative merits of Chevys and Fords. For illustrative purposes, let us think of the differentiated-product duopoly problem as the pricing problem Ford and Chevrolet face as each firm attempts to pry dedicated customers away from its competitor.

We will assume that the costs of production for Ford and for Chevrolet are identical and that their total cost $TC(y)$ is the sum of a fixed cost K and a constant marginal cost of production c multiplied by output y:

$$TC(y) = K + cy$$

Because product-development costs loom large in the automobile industry — for instance, GM spent \$5 billion to develop its Saturn subcompact — it is natural to think of K as a fixed cost associated with product development. For simplicity, we will call K a product development cost.

The Nash Price Equilibrium

The first equilibrium we will take up corresponds to the Bertrand equilibrium in Chapter 11, in which each firm chooses its price to maximize its own profit, taking the other firm's price as given. Because each firm acts independently rather than collusively in choosing its price, the equilibrium will be a Nash equilibrium.

Because both firms' demand conditions and cost conditions are symmetric, we know that in equilibrium, the two will charge exactly the same price. What will that equilibrium price p^e be? The function labeled DD in Figure 12.3a is the demand function for the first firm when the prices of the two firms are identical; the function labeled dd is its demand function when the second firm's price is p_2'. The DD and dd demand functions therefore intersect where p_1 is equal to p_2'. Given that the second firm's price is p_2', we can find the profit-maximizing price for the first firm, or the first firm's best price response, by finding the point where mr, the marginal revenue function associated with dd, intersects the marginal cost line MC in Figure 12.3a. This intersection determines price p_1^*, the first firm's best price response given that the second firm's price is p_2'.

Notice that p_1^* cannot be the Nash equilibrium price p^e because in equilibrium, both firms will charge the same price. Since p_1^* is not equal to p_2', it cannot be the Nash equilibrium price. The Nash equilibrium price is the price identified as p^e in Figure 12.3b. Suppose that the second firm is charging p^e. In this case, dd must intersect DD at p^e. Furthermore, mr is equal to MC when the first firm's price is p^e. Therefore, when the second firm charges p^e, the profit-maximizing price for the first firm is also p^e. This price is therefore the Nash equilibrium price.

The Collusive Price

What happens if the duopolists get together to establish price collusively instead of setting price independently? The collusive price, which maximizes the joint profit of the two firms, is p_1^* in Figure 12.4. To identify the collusive price p_1^*, we first construct the marginal revenue function associated with DD, labeled MR. This function gives the marginal revenue for both firms as their prices move up and down in unison. Because MR is equal to MC at y_1^*, the collusive price is p_1^*.

For the sake of comparison, the Nash equilibrium price p^e is also illustrated in Figure 12.4. Notice that in the Nash price equilibrium, MR is less than MC. Beginning at the Nash equilibrium at point E in Figure 12.4, imagine that both firms simultaneously increase price (and therefore decrease quantity). As they do so, traveling up DD from point E towards point E*, the profit for each increases because MR is less

FIGURE 12.3   Finging the duopoly price equilibrium

In (a), the second firm is charging price p_2'. But the profit-maximizing price for the first firm is the higher price p_1^*. Since the two prices are not equal, they are not Nash equilibrium prices. In (b), the second firm's price is p^e. Given this price, the profit-maximizing price for the first firm is $p_1^* = p^e$. Since the two prices are identical, they are the Nash equilibrium prices for this symmetric duopoly.

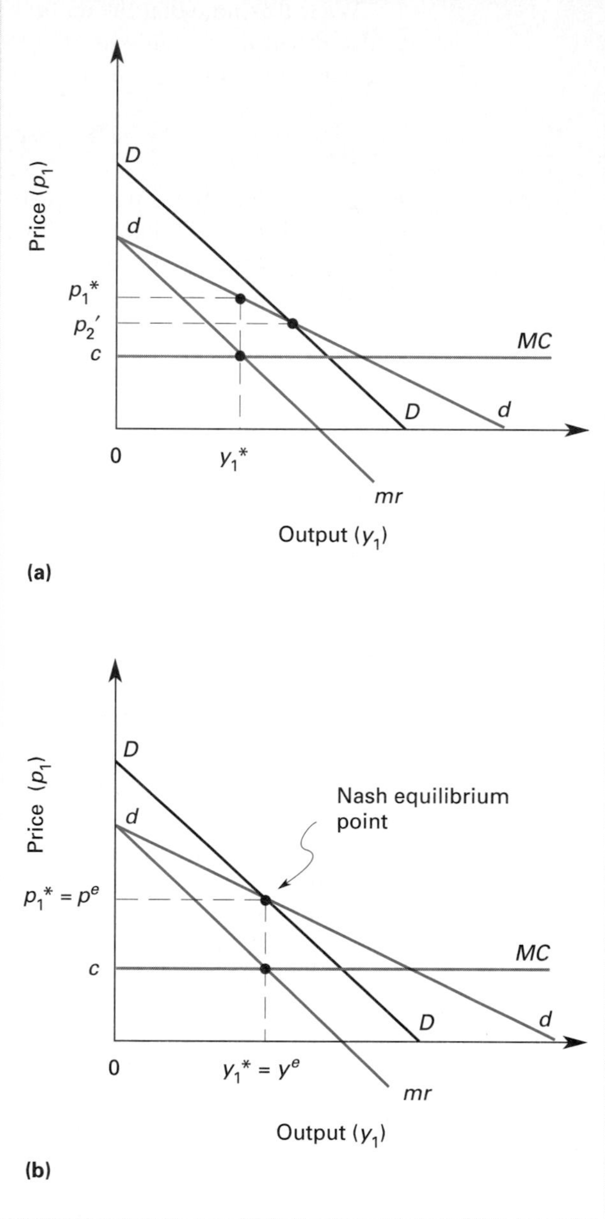

(a)

(b)

than MC. This implies that the individually rational, or Nash equilibrium, price p^e is not collectively rational. We again have encountered one half of what we called the oligopoly problem in Chapter 11.

However, as you will see in Problem 12.2, if the two firms somehow manage to reach the collusive solution at point E*, each has a private incentive to cheat on the collusive agreement by independently lowering the price of its product. This is the other half of the oligopoly problem: the collusive agreement is not self-enforcing.

FIGURE 12.4   The oligopoly problem revisited

The collusive price is p_1^* (because $MR = MC$ at y_1^*), and the Nash equilibrium price is p^e (because $mr = MC$ at y^e). Beginning at the Nash equilibrium point E, if both firms simultaneously increased their prices, they would move along DD towards E*. As they did so, their profit would increase because $MC > MR$ to the right of y_1^*. Therefore, the Nash equilibrium price, which is individually rational, is not collectively rational.

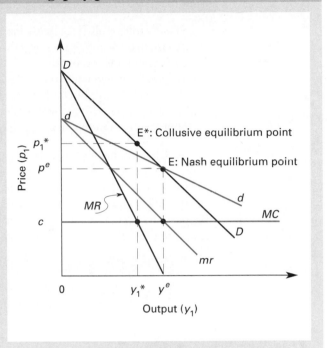

E*: Collusive equilibrium point

E: Nash equilibrium point

PROBLEM 12.2

You will need to construct the appropriate diagram very carefully. First, draw a linear DD function and its associated marginal revenue function. Remember that MR will be exactly twice as steep as DD. Then identify the collusive equilibrium point E*. Now draw through point E* a linear dd function that is flatter than DD, and construct the associated mr function, again remembering that it is twice as steep as its demand function. Using these tools, find the price that maximizes one firm's profit when the other charges the collusive price. Show that it is lower than the collusive price.

The Oligopoly Problem Again

Once again, we are faced with the oligopoly problem — this time in the context of differentiated products:

> At the independently rational, or Nash equilibrium price, the duopolists have a profit incentive to collude. However, at the collectively rational, or collusive price, each duopolist has a profit incentive to cheat on the collusive agreement by independently lowering price; that is, the collusive agreement is not self-enforcing.

Thus, in the cases of differentiated as well as undifferentiated products, punishment strategies (of the sort considered in Section 11.9) that eliminate the incentive to cheat on a collusive agreement may be attractive. Chamberlin argued, however, that such formal punishment strategies are not necessary when the number of firms is small enough. In fact, he even argued that explicit collusive agreements among oligopolists are superfluous:

> If each [oligopolist] seeks his maximum profit rationally and intelligently, he will realize that when there are only two or a few sellers his own move has a considerable effect upon his competitors, and that this makes it idle to suppose that they will accept without retaliation the losses he forces upon them. Since the result of a cut by any one is inevitably to decrease his own profits, no one will cut, and although the sellers are entirely independent, the equilibrium result is the same as though there were a monopolistic agreement between them. (1933, 48)

As Chamberlin suggests, the very structure of the problem forces competitors to realize just how interdependent their fortunes are. If one firm cuts its price, another firm will follow suit. All parties will recognize that such a short-sighted pursuit of self-interest will drive down the price in Figure 12.4 from p_1^* to p^e, an outcome that benefits no one. Because they do recognize their interdependence, Chamberlin suggested competing firms are inevitably led to practice *tacit collusion*.

PROBLEM 12.3

You can adapt the model of oligopoly pricing, taken from Sweezy (1939), to develop Chamberlin's insight more formally. First, construct a diagram in which you identify the collusive price; then construct *dd* through the collusive solution; then construct *mr*, and suppose that all firms are charging the collusive price. To capture the spirit of Chamberlin's argument, suppose that each firm believes that all other firms will match any price reduction it initiates and will not respond to any price increase. Given these beliefs about the price responses of other firms, *MR* is the appropriate marginal revenue function for price reductions, and *mr* is the appropriate one for price increases. Show that with these beliefs about the responses of competitors, no firm has a private incentive to change price.

Sweezy proposed this model as an explanation of observed price rigidity in actual oligopolized industries. For instance, until recent developments created a much more hostile economic environment, the major U.S. cigarette companies coexisted in a cozily oligopolistic relationship, free of price wars.

Entry

Is either of the two solutions we have identified a long-run equilibrium? That is, will any other firm enter this product group? The answer depends once again on the magnitude of the product development cost K. If product development costs are large enough, they will act as a barrier to entry too formidable for an entrant to surmount profitably. In this case, the duopoly will be protected from competition by further rivals. For example, so far only NASA and Europe's Arianespace are competing in carrying commercial satellite payloads into space because developing the necessary facilities is a very expensive proposition.

If such development costs are too small to deter entry, however, we can expect to find large numbers of differentiated products in a given product group. One result of the U.S. court order that forced the break-up of American Telephone and Telegraph, for instance, is that its previously monopolized book of classified advertisements telephone directory known as the *Yellow Pages* came up for grabs. In this case the barrier to entry was low because, in some states at least, telephone companies are required to sell listings at a nominal price and because establishing the requisite advertising network and printing facilities is not prohibitively expensive. Even the classifed pages slogan "Let your fingers do the walking" is not copyrighted. As a result, regional telephone companies, established publishing houses, and newly formed companies all scrambled to enter products in the telephone directories market. In the next section, we look at this large-numbers case.

12.3

Chamberlin's Large-Numbers Case

large-numbers
case

In the **large-numbers case**, where product groups are characterized by large numbers of symmetrically differentiated products, what will the resulting equilibrium look like? We can start by analyzing the price equilibrium when the number of products on the market is fixed. If we assume that each of these symmetrically differentiated products is made by a separate firm, then each firm will take the price of all other products as given when it decides on its own price. Because a price change by one firm will have an insignificant effect on the demand for any other product in the group, the rival firms will not think of their individual pricing decisions as obviously interdependent, in the way that Chamberlin argued they were in the small-numbers case.

Short-Run Equilibrium

Given that each firm regards the prices of all other products as fixed, the equilibrium price p^e must have the property that any one firm finds it profit maximizing to charge p^e if all other firms are charging p^e. To find the price equilibrium in this large-numbers case, we can simply adapt the argument used to find the Nash price equilibrium in the duopoly case. Let us see why the price p^e identified in Figure 12.5 is the equilibrium price. Because costs and demand functions are symmetric for all firms in the group, we can pick a representative firm, and then suppose that all other firms are charging p^e. The representative firm, whose price and quantity are denoted by p_R and y_R, will consider its demand function to be the one labeled dd in Figure 12.5. Given this demand function, the profit-maximizing price p_R^* is equal to p^e. Because all the other firms are in the identical position, they too will choose price p^e, and p^e is therefore the Nash equilibrium price.

Long-Run Equilibrium

To find the long-run equilibrium with large numbers of differentiated products, we need to identify the condition that deters entry. The symmetry and large-numbers assumptions imply that an entrant will make a profit slightly smaller than the profit of a representative firm prior to its entry. This suggests that in the long-run equilibrium, firms will earn approximately zero profit. If existing firms are earning a sizable profit, an entrant will anticipate making a healthy profit itself. Entry will therefore continue until profit is driven down to approximately zero. The no-entry condition, then, is that each firm earns zero profit. This long-run equilibrium is shown in Figure 12.6. At the long-run equilibrium, the average cost function is tangent to the dd function. This means that price is equal to average cost at the equilibrium output — and the representative firm is earning zero profit.

Efficiency and the Chamberlin Model

In Chapter 10, you discovered that monopolies are inefficient because price exceeds marginal cost at the monopoly equilibrium. The same sort of inefficiency arises in the

FIGURE 12.5 **Price equilibrium in the large-numbers case**

All firms other than the representative firm, whose price and quantity are denoted by p_R and y_R, are charging price p^e. Therefore, DD and dd intersect at price p^e. The representative firm's profit-maximizing price is p^e (because $mr = MC$ at this price). Thus, p^e is the equilibrium price for all firms, and each sells y^e at this price.

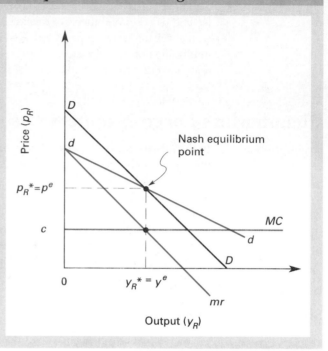

FIGURE 12.6 **Long-run equilibrium in Chamberlin's large-numbers case**

Since AC is tangent to dd at the price equilibrium, each firm is earning zero profit. The no-entry condition is then satisfied, and we have a long-run equilibrium.

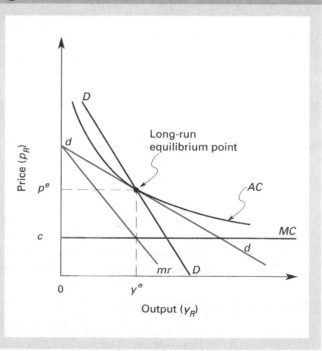

Chamberlin model of differentiated products: as Figure 12.6 reveals, the equilibrium price of each product inevitably exceeds marginal cost at the equilibrium quantity.

Yet another sort of efficiency question — this one concerning the degree of product diversity — emerges from the Chamberlin model: How can we determine the efficient number of products? We can provide a quick intuitive understanding of how this question is tackled by returning to the example of four possible products and 24 consumers. Using the cost-benefit criterion, we will say that the amount of product diversity that maximizes total surplus is **cost-benefit efficient**.

cost-benefit efficient

Suppose that only products A and B are actually on the market. Should a third product be introduced? To limit the issue to the amount of product diversity, we will assume that 1. whether there are two products or three, the price of each product is nevertheless p', and that 2. p' is not smaller than marginal cost c. If the third product, C, is put on the market, we know from Table 12.1 that it will attract the six buyers (13 through 18) who place C first in their preference rankings and also the two buyers (23 and 24) who rank the unavailable product D first and C second.

How much is it worth to each of these eight potential buyers to have the opportunity to buy C rather than A or B? In the absence of products C and D, consumer 13, whose preference ordering is CABD, buys A at price p'. We know, however, that because A is adjacent to C in that particular preference ordering, consumer 13 is actually willing to pay any sum up to $p' + e$ for product C. The opportunity to buy C at price p' is therefore worth e to consumer 13. In the absence of products C and D, consumer 17, whose preference ordering is CDAB, will also buy A at price p'. Yet consumer 17 is actually willing to pay up to $p' + 2e$ for C; the opportunity to buy C at price p' is therefore worth $2e$ to this particular buyer.

You can check to see that the result of aggregating all eight consumers' evaluations of the opportunity to buy C at price p' is $10e$. This sum is just another kind of consumers' surplus measure. What is the corresponding change in producers' surplus associated with the introduction of product C? Producers' surplus drops by K when the third product is introduced, because total revenues are unchanged but total costs are increased by K. Does the increase in consumers' surplus exceed the decrease in producers' surplus? That is, does $10e$ exceed K? If it does, then a third product increases total surplus and should be introduced according to this cost-benefit criterion.

PROBLEM 12.4

Suppose that only one product is available. Show that the consumers' surplus associated with a second product in the example above is $20e$. Then show that if three products are available, the consumers' surplus associated with the fourth product is only $6e$. Next, suppose that K is equal to $8e$. What is the cost-benefit efficient degree of product diversity?

Although determining the cost-benefit efficient amount of product diversity can be a tough analytical nut to crack, this example gives you a sense of how economists approach it. A related question concerns the relationship between the number of products produced in the long-run equilibrium and the cost-benefit efficient number of products. Are there too many, too few, or just the right number of products in the long-run equilibrium? These issues are considered at length in Spence (1976) and in Dixit and Stiglitz (1977). They show that the number of products in the long-run equilibrium can be larger than, smaller than, or equal to the cost-benefit efficient number of products. Therefore, in the Chamberlin model it is not necessarily the case that the number of products offered in equilibrium is the cost-benefit efficient number.

12.4

Address Models of Monopolistic Competition

The linchpin of the Chamberlin model — the assumption of symmetry — implies that a product newly on the market will draw an equal number of buyers from all previously available products in its group. By this implication, competition is generalized: each product competes directly and equally with every other product. In many product groups, however, the assumption that competition is *localized* rather than *generalized* seems more nearly appropriate. If competition is localized, each product competes directly only with its "neighboring" products rather than with all other products in the same group. Competitors in the luxury car market, for instance, see themselves as positioning against specific neighboring competitors rather than against every product in the market. For example, Saab, Volvo, Audi, and a middle-of-the-line Mercedes-Benz go head-to-head in the $30,000 to $40,000 sticker-price range; Jaguar and Mercedes-Benz are mutual targets in the $40,000 to $75,000 range; and Ferrari, Aston Martin, and Rolls-Royce fight it out at price tags above $75,000. Coca-Cola is planning the international launch of a new carbonated drink, aimed at the teen market, called OK to compete against Pepsi Max, Pepsi's increasingly popular lowered-sugar drink. Ford's new Windstar minivan with its car-like performance and handling is targetted to challenge Chrysler Corporation's hugely successful minivans, the Dodge Caravan and the Plymouth Voyager. And in the frozen foods industry, Campbell Soup Company pegged McCain's Foods Limited as the competitor to beat in its bid for market share in microwavable breakfast foods. The Chamberlin model cannot accommodate such positioning strategies, which are aimed at capturing *specific portions of a market* rather than drawing equal portions from all competitors.

We will create a model of localized rather than generalized competition by developing a model of geographic, or spatial, product differentiation. As you will see, the presence of significant transportation costs for potential customers in this model implies that competition within the product group is localized. The model that captures such spatially localized competition is called an **address model** because products can be described by their locations or addresses in the space.

address model

We can reinterpret this model as a more general model of product differentiation by thinking in terms of characteristics rather than geographical space. For example, if the amount of sugar is a crucial characteristic to breakfast-food buyers, the hypothetical new product Sugar Sweeties is not likely to draw the same number of customers from devotees of a sugar-free cereal, such as Shredded Wheat, as it draws from lovers of a cereal chockfull of sugar, such as Marshmallow Krispies. Instead, Sugar Sweeties is likely to compete locally with the cereals that have just slightly more and slightly less sugar content. Below we will indicate more carefully how to reinterpret the model of spatial competition as a model of characteristic competition. Either way we interpret the model, the product's address, or location, vis-à-vis its competitors is the factor that determines for any specified product which other products are and are not effective competitors.

A Model of Spatial Competition

To emphasize how this approach differs from Chamberlin's, we will resort to another illustrative exercise. Because this is a model of spatial competition, we must naturally begin by choosing a geographical space. We will imagine a large number of customers spread out evenly around the circumference of a circle, perhaps that of a volcanic island on which travel overland is impossible.

Suppose that we have eight firms spaced at equal intervals around the circle, each retailing the same product — say, hamburgers — and each charging the same price for their burgers. Their locations are indicated by the Roman numerals I through VIII in Figure 12.7. Since self-interested customers will choose to buy their burgers at the nearest stand, each firm will attract the one-eighth of the customers who live closest to it. Once again, the crucial element here is not the first choice, but the second.

What will the island customers' second choices be? Each customer's second choice will be the stand immediately to the right or to the left of that consumer's first choice. Half the customers whose first choice is I will pick II as a second choice, for instance; half will pick VIII; and none will pick III, IV, V, VI, or VII. (Identify the half whose second choice is II and the half whose second choice is VIII.) Their second choices are clearly not evenly distributed over all the other firms. The same is true of those customers whose first choice is II. Half select I as a second choice, and half III. This view of differentiated products as competing locally rather than generally — a view that is reflected in the failure of second choices to be evenly distributed over all other firms — distinguishes the address model from the Chamberlin model. As you will see, it also means that an entrant's demand function is not symmetric to the demand functions of established firms. In terms of our example, it means that an entrant who sets up between any two of the eight hamburger stands will not draw customers equally from all eight stands. Instead, it will draw only from its two neighboring stands, to the right and to the left.

Short-Run Price Equilibrium

Let us analyze the equilibrium that results from our alternative assumption about competition between differentiated products. We can begin by finding the price equilibrium

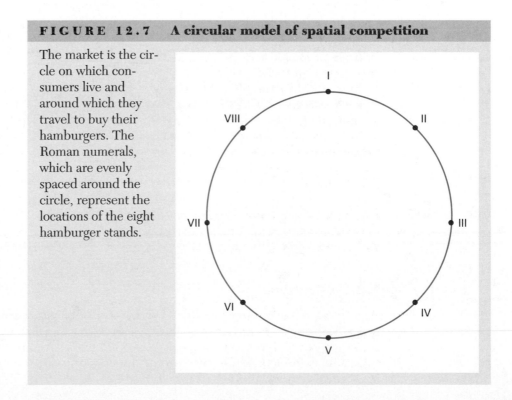

FIGURE 12.7   A circular model of spatial competition

The market is the circle on which consumers live and around which they travel to buy their hamburgers. The Roman numerals, which are evenly spaced around the circle, represent the locations of the eight hamburger stands.

when the number of firms is fixed. To simplify the analysis, we will think of the customers as distributed evenly around the circumference of the circle at a density equal to one: there is one customer per unit of market length. We will assume, too, that each customer demands one unit of the product, regardless of its price.

Because equilibrium prices depend on where each of the n firms is located, we need to specify their locations. If we assume that firms are evenly spaced throughout the market, we can then determine the short-run price equilibrium, as we did in the Chamberlin model, by examining the profit-maximizing decision of a representative firm. (Be aware, though, that firms need not be evenly spaced. Given different assumptions about the firms' locations, equilibria other than the one considered here are possible in this model.)

The length of the interval between any two of the firms, denoted by L, is just the circumference of the circle C divided by the number of firms n. Figure 12.8 shows the configuration of locations we have in mind: F denotes the location of a firm and L the distance between any pair of adjacent firms.

What will be the demand function for a representative firm? In Figure 12.9 a segment of the circumference has been removed from the circle in Figure 12.8 and straightened out. The representative firm is located at 0, and its neighboring firms are each located at a distance L from it: one to the left at $-L$ and one to the right at L. As in the Chamberlin model, we will assume that all firms except the representative firm charge a common price p'. The price p' charged by each of the two neighboring firms and the price p_R charged by the representative firm are measured vertically in Figure 12.9.

delivered price schedules

Because the diagonal lines emanating from these prices represent the total price that the consumer must pay, including transportation costs, they can be regarded as **delivered price schedules**. Assuming that the cost of transportation is just 1 per unit of distance, the consumer's delivered price of buying the product from the representative

FIGURE 12.8 **Locations on a circle**

Firms are located at equal intervals along the circle. The Fs denote the locations of firms, and L is the distance between any pair of adjacent firms.

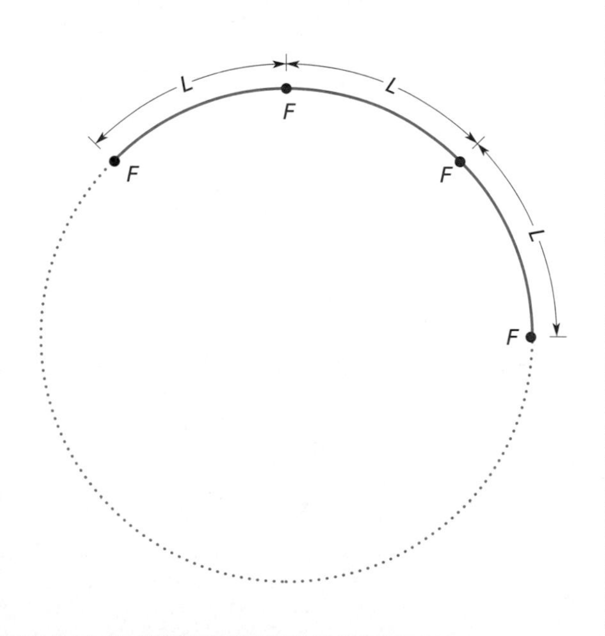

FIGURE 12.9   Market boundaries of a representative firm

The representative firm is located at 0, and the two neighboring firms are located at L and $-L$. The representative firm's market boundaries are at x' and x''.

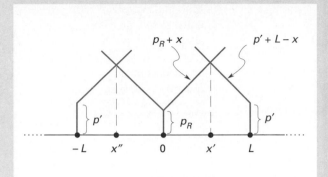

firm and transporting it to point x', for instance, is just the price of the product plus x', or $p_R + x'$. The delivered price of buying it instead from the firm located at L and carrying it to point x' is $p' + L - x'$. Point x' is important because it is the **market boundary** between the representative firm and the firm located at L. Customers to the left of x' will patronize the representative firm at 0, and those to the right will patronize the firm at L. In other words, x' satisfies the following equation:

$$p_R + x' = p' + L - x'$$

or, solving for x',

$$x' = (p' + L - p_R)/2$$

As the representative firm lowers its price p_R, the market boundary x' moves to the right. As it increases p_R, the market boundary x' moves to the left.

The point x'' is the representative firm's market boundary on the other side. Because the firm at $-L$, like the firm at L, is L units from the representative firm and charges price p', the intervals between 0 and x' and between 0 and x'' are necessarily the same length. The length of the representative firm's total market is therefore just $2x'$. Because we have assumed one customer per unit along the length of the market and because each customer buys only one unit of the product per period, the quantity demanded of the representative firm's product must also be $2x'$.[2] In other words, the representative firm's demand function is

$$y_R = p' + L - p_R$$

We can rewrite this demand function with price on the left and quantity on the right:

$$p_R = p' + L - y_R$$

---

2 Notice that if p_R is sufficiently small, the representative firm's delivered price at L (and at $-L$) will be less than p'. In this case, the representative firm would wipe out its competitors. However, those competitors will not continue to charge price p'; they will lower their prices rather than sell nothing at all. For this reason, we will assume that no firm entertains the possibility that it can charge a price so low that its neighbors sell nothing. Eaton and Lipsey (1978) discuss this problem in some detail.

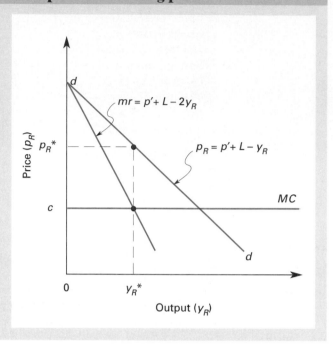

FIGURE 12.10 **The profit-maximizing price**

Marginal revenue is equal to marginal cost at $y_R{}^*$, which is the representatives firm's profit-maximizing quantity. The corresponding price is $p_R{}^*$.

This function, labeled dd, and its associated marginal revenue function, labeled mr, are shown in Figure 12.10. Assuming that both neighboring firms charge p', we can now find the profit-maximizing output level and price for the representative firm. Because it will choose a point where marginal revenue is equal to marginal cost — and assuming once again a constant marginal cost equal to c — the profit-maximizing output level $y_R{}^*$ will satisfy

$$p' + L - 2y_R{}^* = c$$

or, solving for $y_R{}^*$,

$$y_R{}^* = (p' + L - c)/2$$

By combining this result and the demand function, we discover the profit-maximizing price:

$$p_R{}^* = (p' + L + c)/2$$

Knowing how the representative firm chooses price and quantity (given p') allows us to determine the equilibrium price. Because each firm is essentially in the same boat — each has the same marginal cost, and each has rival firms at a distance of L on either side — we know that in the equilibrium, all firms will charge the same price. Therefore, in this equation, if we set $p_R{}^*$ and p' equal to p^e and then solve for p^e, we will have the Nash equilibrium price when firms are located L units apart:[3]

$$p^e = L + c$$

---

3 As in the models of oligopoly considered earlier, other types of pricing behavior are possible. Collusive pricing is one such possibility. To keep the analysis simple, we have chosen to ignore alternative strategies in this section.

We can combine this equation with the equation for the profit-maximizing quantity to find the equilibrium quantity y^e:

$$y^e = L$$

We can calculate the profit for a representative firm in this Nash equilibrium, π^e, by multiplying the equilibrium price less marginal cost by the equilibrium quantity and subtracting the product development cost K:

$$\pi^e = L^2 - K.$$

Given the initial assumption that firms are evenly distributed, we have found the short-run equilibrium in this address model of spatially differentiated products. Notice that the profit of any firm increases as the distance L between firms increases. In the short run, then, the fewer the firms, the higher the profits.

Long-Run Equilibrium

What will the long-run equilibrium be in this model? That is, under what conditions will entrants decide not to enter the market? We can discover this no-entry condition by putting ourselves into the shoes of a potential entrant. What does this entrant see when it scans the market? It sees established firms that are located L units of distance from one another and are charging the same price, $p^e = L + c$.

Should we suppose that the entrant will take these locations and prices as given? The assumption of fixed locations seems reasonable enough: established firms have incurred a product development cost K by developing a specialized outlet for retailing a certain product (or products). They cannot change sites without incurring the product development cost anew. Because these product development costs are specific to a particular location, the assumption that the entrant takes established firms' locations as given seems reasonable enough.

The assumption that it also takes their prices as fixed seems less reasonable because established firms will respond to entry by lowering their prices. When the Utah Pie Company began marketing frozen pies in the Salt Lake City area in 1957, for instance, its three principal rivals — the Carnation Company, Pet Milk, and Continental Baking — all responded by significantly lowering their prices. Although we will make use of the price-taking assumption because it simplifies the analysis, be aware that the entrant will be overestimating the size of its potential profit by taking the prices of the established firms as given.

Once the entrant has surveyed the market, it must pick a spot for itself somewhere between two established firms. It can do no better than to choose a point midway between the two. The entrant, whose location is at 0 in Figure 12.11, therefore has a neighboring firm a distance $L/2$ to the right of it, and another a distance $L/2$ to the left of it. (Here we are arbitrarily choosing an origin to coincide with the entrant's location, just as we chose an origin in Figure 12.9 to coincide with the location of a representative firm.) As you will find in the following problem, the entrant's demand function is

$$y_E = p^e + L/2 - p_E$$

where y_E is the quantity demanded from the entrant and p_E is the entrant's price. Since p^e is equal to $L + c$, the entrant's demand function can be written as

$$y_E = 3L/2 + c - p_E$$

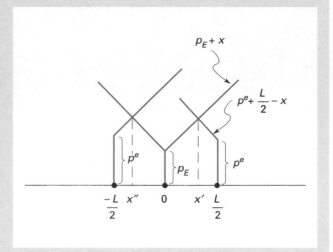

FIGURE 12.11   Entry in a spatial market

Two established firms are located at $-L/2$ and $L/2$ each charging the equilibrium price p^e. The market boundaries between the entrant, who is located at 0 and charges p_E, and the established firms at $-L/2$ and $L/2$ are at x'' and x', respectively.

Its profit-maximizing quantity and price are

$$y_E{}^* = 3L/4$$

$$p_E{}^* = c + 3L/4$$

and its anticipated profit is

$$\neq_E{}^* = 9L^2/16 - K$$

PROBLEM 12.5

Verify these results. You will need to adapt the procedures used to find the corresponding magnitudes for the representative firm in the short-run price equilibrium.

no-entry
condition

Whether the entrant actually enters hinges on the length of the interval L between the two established firms. The **no-entry condition** is that the potential entrant's profit $\neq_E{}^*$ must be less than or equal to zero or, to put it in terms of L,

$$L \leq (4K^{1/2})/3$$

If L satisfies this inequality, entry will not occur. This no-entry condition therefore determines the long-run equilibrium.

Profit in Long-Run Equilibrium

Notice that firms in the address model of product differentiation, unlike firms in the Chamberlin model, potentially can earn supranormal profit in the long-run equilibrium. To see how large that profit might be, suppose that L is as large as possible while still meeting the no-entry condition; that is, let L be equal to $(4K^{1/2})/3$. As we saw earlier, the profit of a representative firm in equilibrium is

$$\pi^e = L^2 - K$$

With L equal to $(4K^{1/2})/3$, its profit is

$$\pi^e = 7K/9$$

This is a significant profit. If a potential entrant made the more realistic forecast that the established firms would respond to entry by lowering price, the no-entry condition would permit even larger values of L — and correspondingly higher profits for the established firms.

We can extend our understanding of the relationship between the no-entry condition and established firms' profit potential in the long run by seeing what happens in this model when prices are fixed rather than determined by choice. For example, think in terms of the sale of lottery tickets in our model. The growth of lotteries has been phenomenal because they offer governments a booming source of revenue. Lottery ticket agents must pay certain setup costs (including buying a license and, often, a specialized computer terminal), and all agents must sell the lottery tickets at the same price. In a given market for lottery tickets, what will the no-entry condition be, and what is the maximum profit an established lottery ticket agent can earn?

> ### PROBLEM 12.6
>
> Suppose that all lottery ticket agents — established firms and entrants alike — must charge $5, a fixed price that exceeds their $4 marginal cost. Show first that the resulting no-entry condition is
>
> $$L \leq 2K$$
>
> and second that the maximum profit an established ticket agent can earn is therefore K.

An important lesson emerges from this address model of spatially differentiated products:

In the long run, established firms can earn supranormal profits.

This possibility arises because the demand conditions faced by an entrant in this model are very different from those that confront an entrant in the Chamberlin model. In Chamberlin's model, a direct result of the symmetry assumption is that an entrant (who charges the same price that established firms charge) will sell a quantity equal to $n/(n + 1)$ multiplied by the quantity sold by an established firm prior to entry. This means that when n is large, the entrant — simply by attracting a proportionate share of the total market — can sell a quantity virtually identical to that sold by an established firm prior to entry. The net effect is that each firm's profit in the long run is approximately zero.

In the address model, however, the entrant's position is markedly different from that of the established firms. Prior to entry, each established firm sells L units of output at the equilibrium price p^e. If an entrant chooses to market its product at the same price p^e, it will sell exactly half the amount sold by the established firms prior to entry. Why? Because the entrant entices away customers only from its two nearest rivals, not from the full spectrum of firms.

Where competition is localized, it is necessarily oligopolistic because any given firm competes only with two others. Yet as we move around the circular market, the identities of the oligopolists change. In this sense, the address model is characterized by what Kaldor (1935) called a series of "overlapping oligopolies."

Product Proliferation

product
proliferation

Because garnering supranormal profit is a distinct possibility in address models of location and of product characteristics, established firms may be tempted to stake out a greater share of the market for themselves. One of the preemptive positioning strategies they might use is **product proliferation**.

In the spatially differentiated address model, the strategy might be to establish outlets at a number of locations to ward off potentially threatening competition by entrants. For instance, a local suntanning salon in Toronto has recently opened four new outlets within a radius of 2 miles. This proliferation of shops is a preemptive move to deflect other suntanning retailers from entering. McDonald's Restaurants seems to have pursued a similar strategy worldwide to deter entrance by other fast-food chains. McDonald's is now selling food and drink in universities, airports, theaters, schools, and even on some airplane flights. Sam Walton, who was alleged to be the richest man in America, amassed a huge fortune by proliferating Walmart outlets throughout the southeastern portion of the United States, and his company is now expanding its business across the United States and into Canada.

In the model of products differentiated by characteristics other than physical location, a firm might produce a range of differentiated products within a particular group, once again to lay claim to product "territory" that potential entrants might otherwise seize. In 1972 the U.S. Federal Trade Commission accused Kellogg, General Mills, General Foods, and Quaker Oats of producing a whole battery of differentiated breakfast cereals to preempt potential competition.[4] In a similar preemptive strategy of product proliferation, Star Micronics marketed a range of ImagePower Printers, each specifically designed with an intended user in mind — banker, executive, student, editor, accountant, lawyer, engineer, and retailer. In the following problem, you have a chance to explore the basic relationship between strategic preemption and product proliferation.

> **PROBLEM 12.7**
>
> From Problem 12.6, you are familiar with the features of a long-run equilibrium in our circular model when price is fixed. Suppose that you are the first to have stumbled onto this market with very lucrative potential. Suppose, too, that you realize that soon the rest of the world will find out about this market. What strategy would you pursue to maximize your profit?

Generalizing the Model

The address model of spatial competition captures an essential element of competition in many industries. Three crucial features characterize the model: 1. consumers of the industry's product are spread out over some physical space; 2. because transporting

---

4 See Schmalensee (1978) for a discussion of the breakfast cereals case and an economic model of product proliferation.

the product is costly, other things being equal, the consumer prefers the closest product; and 3. because of product development costs, the number of products is small relative to the number of consumers. Virtually all retail and service industries share these features, as do many markets for intermediate products. Thus, the address model can make sense of a range of products differentiated by their geographical locations.

The address model can also serve as a metaphor for differentiation among products that can be meaningfully described by their characteristics along some continuum other than geographical space. In our geographical example, each product was described by a single characteristic: its location along a one-dimensional continuum. We suggested earlier that breakfast cereals might possibly be described by another kind of characteristic: their locations along some one-dimensional "sugar-content" continuum. It is more likely, however, that breakfast cereals — and most other differentiated products — are more meaningfully described by a number of such characteristics.

To describe a product group meaningfully means to write down all the characteristics that matter to consumers. Underlying this view of product differentiation, of course, is the idea that consumers' tastes are diverse. For example, think of the differences in taste among buyers of home computers. Many people are interested in home computers exclusively for their video-game capabilities; others for their word-processing capabilities; others for their accounting capabilities; others for their mathematical capabilities; and still others for some combination of two or more of these characteristics. To locate products in this group implies using not one but a number of characteristics in the address model. Lancaster (1979) presents the most thorough treatment of an address model in which goods are differentiated by characteristics.

Efficiency

In address models, as in the Chamberlin model, equilibrium price exceeds marginal cost. The result is once again the classic inefficiency that we associated earlier with monopoly. With address models, however, the issue of the efficient number of products arises as well.

Again using cost-benefit analysis, the cost-benefit efficient number of differentiated products in our circular model is fairly easy to identify: we want to choose L to maximize total surplus. However, this is equivalent to choosing L to minimize the total cost of supplying the demand generated as each consumer buys one unit of the product per period.[5] The total cost of supplying the consumer demand is threefold: the marginal cost per unit of product c, the transportation costs borne by consumers, and the product development costs K borne by firms.

What value of the interval between firms L will minimize these costs? We can leave the question of marginal cost aside because regardless of the size of L, the marginal cost required to produce each unit is inevitably incurred. Yet the other two costs — transportation costs and product development costs — do vary as L varies. As L increases, the average distance between each consumer and the nearest firm increases,

---

5 To understand this equivalence, first notice that the only effect of a price increase is to transfer surplus from consumers to firms because each consumer buys one unit regardless of price. We can therefore fix price and turn our attention to producers' and consumers' surplus. Producers' surplus at the fixed price is total revenue (a constant) less the total costs incurred by firms. Consumers' surplus at the fixed price increases or decreases as consumers' transportation costs decrease or increase. By adding up producers' and consumers' surplus, we find that total surplus is maximized by minimizing the total costs incurred by all producers and consumers.

and consumers' transportation costs therefore rise. Yet as L increases, the number of spatially differentiated products (or firms) decreases, and the product development costs of all firms taken together therefore drop.

The value of L that minimizes the cost of meeting each consumer's demand, therefore, is the value that meets the following criterion: the decrease in (total) product development costs (arising from a small increase in L) just balances the increase in (total) consumer transportation costs (arising from the same small increase in L). The precise value is $2K^{1/2}$.[6]

Product Diversity: Equilibrium Versus Cost-Benefit Efficiency

In this very simple address model, it is easy to compare the cost-benefit efficient amount of product diversity with the amount of product diversity in the long-run equilibrium. Cost-benefit efficiency demands that the spacing between firms be $2K^{1/2}$, and long-run equilibrium demands that the spacing be less than or equal to $(4K^{1/2})/3$. Because the former spacing exceeds the latter, there is too much product diversity in long-run equilibrium. In other words, if the cost-benefit efficient spacing were imposed initially, entry would inevitably follow.

Given that there is always too much product diversity in the long-run equilibrium, which of the long-run equilibria is the most cost-benefit efficient? The one that maximizes the distance between firms. In other words, the most cost-benefit efficient of the long-run equilibria in this model is the one in which L is equal to $(4K^{1/2})/3$. Notice, too, that this equilibrium is also the one in which the profits of established firms are maximized.

However, the particular cost-benefit efficiency result in this model — too much product diversity in the long-run equilibrium — is *not* a general result. We find some address models with *too little* and others with *just the right amount* of product diversity in the long-run equilibrium.[7]

SUMMARY

In this chapter, we introduced two approaches to *product differentiation*. The first is the *Chamberlin model*, in which products are symmetric and the competition among them is generalized — each product competes with every other in the product group. The second is the *address model*, in which competition is localized: each product competes only with neighboring products in its product group.

A simple conceptual experiment is useful to identify the circumstances in which one or the other model is applicable. Pick any product on the market and then imagine lowering its price. How will this price drop affect the demand for other products in the

---

6 We need to use some calculus to derive this result. If C is the circumference of our circle, then C/L is the number of firms, and total product development costs are then just CK/L. Transport costs for one firm serving a market L units long are $L^2/4$, or the integral of transport costs over the firm's market. Total transport costs are then $L^2/4$ multiplied by the number of firms C/L, or $CL/4$. We then want to choose L to minimize

$$CK/L + CL/4$$

Differentiating with respect to L, setting the derivative equal to zero, and solving for L gives the cost-minimizing value of L: $2K^{1/2}$.

7 See Eaton and Wooders (1985), for example.

group? If the price reduction decreases the quantity demanded of all other products in the group, then competition is generalized — and the Chamberlin model apparently applies. On the other hand, if the price cut reduces the quantity demanded of only a small subset of products in the group, then competition is localized — and the address model appears to be the right model.

The major analytical distinction between the two models is in how the *no-entry condition* is formulated. Because competition is generalized in the Chamberlin model, the no-entry condition is that established firms must earn zero profit. Consider the fortune of an entrant — say, firm $n + 1$. Suppose it charges the same price that established firms charged prior to its entry. Because competition is generalized, the entrant will sell $n/(n + 1)$ times the quantity sold by each established firm prior to entry. If n is large, then $n/(n + 1)$ is approximately 1, and the entrant will anticipate earning the same profit that each established firm earned prior to entry. Long-run equilibrium requires, then, that the established firms earn zero profit.

By contrast, because competition is localized in the address model, the no-entry condition is not that established firms earn zero profit. Again, consider the fortune of an entrant — firm $n + 1$ — that charges the same price as established firms prior to entry. In the one-dimensional product continuum used as an example in this chapter, the entrant will anticipate selling substantially less than the quantity sold by established firms prior to entry because it will be competing with only two established firms — that is, competition is localized. In fact, if the demand of individual consumers is perfectly price inelastic, the entrant will sell only half the quantity sold by established firms prior to its entry. Therefore, zero profit is not a condition of long-run equilibrium in address models.

In address models, the possibility of profit in long-run equilibrium suggests that *product proliferation* will be a profitable positioning strategy. In other words, by marketing a range of different products throughout the product spectrum, established firms will be able to capture this profit for themselves. Casual empiricism is certainly consistent with this insight. The Safeway grocery store chain, Walmart and McDonald's Restaurants are conspicuous examples of firms that appear to have pursued a strategy of product proliferation very successfully.[8] You can undoubtedly identify other firms that are engaged in the same sort of behavior.

In both of these models, price exceeds marginal cost in equilibrium. This implies that the kind of *inefficiency* associated earlier with monopoly exists in markets for differentiated products as well. An additional interesting issue arises in these models concerning the cost-benefit-efficient number of differentiated products in a product group. One interesting question is whether there is an invisible hand at work in markets for differentiated goods: Does the long-run equilibrium actually provide the cost-benefit-efficient number of differentiated products? Unfortunately, the answer is no, or at least, not always. We found that we could not even determine in general whether there are too many, too few, or just the right number of products in long-run equilibrium.

Clearly, we have raised more questions in this chapter than we have answered: What is the appropriate model of product differentiation in any particular application? How can we tinker with the incentives of private firms to induce them to produce the cost-benefit-efficient solutions? For that matter, how can we recognize a cost-benefit-efficient number of differentiated products if we see it? By articulating these issues, we hope to put them on your agenda of interesting problems that need answers.

---

8 See West (1982), for example, for a careful empirical analysis of this type of strategy in the supermarket industry.

EXERCISES

1. In Myrtha Tidvale, everyone lives on Main Street, which is 10 miles long. There are 1,000 people in this hamlet, uniformly spread up and down Main Street, and they each buy one ice cream cone every day from one of two stores located at either end of Main Street. These ice cream junkies ride their motor scooters to and from the store, and the motor scooters use $0.10 worth of gas per mile. Customers buy their cones from the store offering them the lowest delivered price (delivered price is the store's price plus the customer's expenditure on gas getting to and from the store). Jones owns the store at the west end of Main Street, and Smith owns the store at the east end of Main Street.

   a. If both Jones and Smith charge $1 per cone, how many will each of them sell in a day? If Jones charges $1 per cone and Smith charges $1.40, how many cones will each sell in a day?

   b. If Jones charges $3 per cone, what price would enable Smith to sell 250 cones per day? 500 cones per day? 750 cones per day? 1,000 cones per day?

   c. If Jones charges p_1 and Smith charges p_2, what is the location of the customer who is indifferent between going to Smith's or Jones' store? How many customers go to Smith's

   store and how many go to Jones' store? What are the two demand functions? Notice that they are symmetric: if you replace p_1 by p_2 and p_2 by p_1 in one demand function, you get the other demand function.

   d. Rewrite Jones' demand function, isolating p_1 on the left side of the equal sign. What is Jones' marginal revenue function?

   e. The marginal cost of an ice cream cone to Smith and to Jones is $1. In addition, each of them pays the hamlet $800 per day for the right to sell ice cream to the citizens of Myrtha Tidvale. Adapt the method illustrated in Figure 12.10 to find equilibrium prices, quantities sold, and profits.

   f. Llewelyn wants to open an ice cream store at the midpoint of Main Street. He, too, is willing to pay the hamlet $800 a day for the privilege. If Jones and Smith did not change their prices, what is the best price for Llewelyn to charge? How much profit would he earn?

   g. What do you think would happen if Llewelyn did open another store at the middle of Main Street? Would Jones or Smith change their prices or their locations? Would one or both leave the market?

REFERENCES

Chamberlin, E. 1933. *The Theory of Monopolistic Competition*, Cambridge, Mass.: Harvard University Press.

Dixit, A., and J. Stiglitz. 1977. "Monopolistic Competition and Optimum Product Diversity," *American Economic Review*, 67:297–308.

Eaton, B. C., and R. G. Lipsey. 1978. "Freedom of Entry and the Existence of Pure Profit," *Economic Journal*, 88:455–69.

Eaton, B. C., and M. H. Wooders. 1985. "Sophisticated Entry in a Model of Spatial Competition," *The Rand Journal of Economics*, 16:282–97.

Kaldor, N. 1935. "Market Imperfection and Excess Capacity," *Economica*, 2:35–50.

Lancaster, K. 1979. *Variety, Equity, and Efficiency: Product Variety in an Industrial Society*, New York: Columbia University Press.

———. 1987. "Non-Price Competition" and "Product Differentiation," in *The New Palgrave: A Dictionary of Economics*, J. Eatwell, M. Milgate, and P. Newman (eds.), London: The Macmillan Press.

Perloff, J. M., and S. C. Salop. 1985. "Equilibrium with Product Differentiation," *Review of Economic Studies*, 52:107–20.

Schmalensee, R. 1978. "Entry Deterrence in the Ready-to-Eat Breakfast Cereal Industry," *Bell Journal of Economics*, 9:305–27.

Shaked, A., and J. Sutton. 1983. "Natural Oligopolies," *Econometrica*, 51:146–83.

Spence, A. M. 1976. "Product Selection, Fixed Costs, and Monopolistic Competition," *Review of Economic Studies*, 43:217–35.

Sweezy, P. M. 1939. "Demand Under Conditions of Oligopoly," *Review of Economic Studies*, 36:399–415.

West, D. S. 1981. "Testing for Market Preemption Using Sequential Location Data," *The Bell Journal of Economics*, 12:129–43.

PART V

Resource Markets and General Equilibrium

In Part V, we begin with input markets. In Chapter 13, we take advantage of the analytical similarities between output-market and input-market analysis to treat perfectly competitive and monopsonistic input markets in the space of a single chapter.

In Chapter 14, we introduce distribution and discover why many institutions that are intended to redistribute wealth are incompatible with economic efficiency, and in Chapter 15, we introduce the element of time into our economic analysis as we take a closer look at intertemporal resource allocation. In Chapter 16, we carefully define efficiency in a general equilibrium framework and explore the conditions under which the general competitive equilibrium is, and is not, efficient. Finally, in Chapter 17, we take up the fascinating topic of externalities and their close relatives, public goods.

CHAPTER 13

Input Markets and the Allocation of Resources

It is all too easy to lose sight of the fact that economics is essentially about the allocation of scarce resources to alternative uses. Let us glance back quickly to see in what way the analysis in the preceding four chapters was about the allocative process. In Chapter 9, we studied the concept of a scarce good by imagining an exchange economy with a limited number of rock concert tickets. Then we created a simple competitive model to analyze the allocation of tickets and money: how many tickets would be exchanged and at what price. As you discovered, the price of the tickets served as a signaling device; it guided the allocation of tickets and of money to the ten students. The competitive equilibrium price and quantity were therefore indicative of a more basic allocative process whereby certain people got scarce tickets and others got money (or command over other scarce goods).

We then extended the simple exchange model in Chapter 9 to include production. Looking back at the extended model of a perfectly competitive market in Chapter 9 and at the models of monopolistic and oligopolistic markets in Chapters 10, 11, and 12, we can see that all firms serve a similar allocative function. We can loosely regard firms as combining an assortment of scarce resources into a finished product and then offering the resulting resource "package" for sale. This vision of the role of firms allows us to see that the equilibrium price and quantity in *any* market for goods are indicative of a more fundamental allocative process in which scarce resources (packaged as finished goods) are traded by firms for consumers' dollars. For example, labor and iron ore, among other resources, are packaged as automobiles, toasters, and filing cabinets. These "processed resources" then end up in the garages, kitchens, and offices of the nation. In this sense, the price system serves to allocate resources to competing ends.

13.1

The Role of Input Markets

input markets

What we have so far ignored in our analysis is the allocative role played by resource or **input markets**. The time has come to bring input markets to center stage. For example, how does the input price of steel affect the amount of steel bought, processed, and sold by automobile, small-appliance, and office-equipment manufacturers? How do input prices of sugar and vanilla flavoring affect the amount of these inputs bought, processed, and sold by bakers and Popsicle makers? How does the input price of farm labor affect the amount of labor services bought by orange growers and lettuce producers in the Salinas Valley?

Notice, however, that in analyzing input markets, output markets cannot completely disappear from view, since an input's value to any firm depends on the price that the firm can charge for its output. For example, demand for the epoxy resins and the assembly-line labor used to make cars depends on the output prices of goods in the automobile industry. Like the output prices in goods markets, the input prices for raw and processed resources and for various kinds of labor signal where more resources are needed in input markets and from where they are to be drawn.

Input markets, like the output markets of Chapters 9–12, range all the way from *perfectly competitive markets* characterized by many insignificant buyers to what are called *monopsonistic markets* characterized by a single buyer. We will begin the analysis of input markets by developing a model of equilibrium price and quantity in a perfectly competitive input market. As we analyze the resulting allocation, we will deepen our understanding that competitive markets — unlike monopolistic or oligopolistic markets — are efficient. That is, in competitive markets, resources are successfully allocated to their most valuable uses. Next, we will develop a model of equilibrium in a monopsony. We will discover that monopsony, where there is just one firm buying an input (like monopoly, where there is just one firm selling a good), is not consistent with efficiency. Then, we will take up price discrimination in input markets and see how monopsonists (like monopolists) are able to use clever pricing strategies to exploit their market power.

13.2

Perfectly Competitive Input Markets

perfectly
competitive
input market

Let us begin with a model of equilibrium price and quantity in a **perfectly competitive input market**. A perfectly competitive input market is characterized by firms that are *price takers*, in the sense that they fail to exercise any appreciable control over the price they pay for the input. For instance, if the input market for unskilled labor in the Albuquerque area is perfectly competitive, none of the many firms hiring unskilled labor can significantly affect the wage rate.

Notice that this definition says nothing about the position of firms in their output markets, where they may be either perfectly competitive or monopolistic. For example, a lettuce grower is a perfect competitor in both the input and output markets. Lettuce growers have no real control over the prices they pay for inputs like water, seed, fertilizers, or labor, nor do they have control over the price they are paid for their lettuce. On the other hand, a local telephone company is competitive in many of its input markets but monopolistic in its output market. It may have no real control over the price it pays for inputs like secretarial services but, as the only firm selling local telephone service, it can exercise significant control over the price it charges for its service. We will include both types of firms in our analysis.

primary input
markets

intermediate
input markets

Now let us begin the analysis of supply and demand in input markets. There are two types of input markets: primary and intermediate input markets. Inputs in **primary markets**, which include resources such as land, oil, and labor, have not been processed by other firms. For convenience, we will assume that all suppliers in primary input markets are individuals. Inputs in **intermediate input markets**, which include inputs such as iron ingots, flour, hog bellies, or cold rolled steel, are the processed output of other firms. Again for convenience, we will assume that all suppliers in intermediate input markets are firms. Then the supply functions in primary input markets (the market for unskilled labor, for example) will reflect the utility-maximizing decisions of individuals. By contrast, the supply function in intermediate input markets (the iron ingot market, for instance), will reflect the profit-maximizing decisions of firms. We will also assume that the demanders in all input markets are firms, and the input demand functions will therefore reflect the profit-maximizing decisions of firms.

Our primary objective in this chapter is to derive these input supply and demand functions. Before launching into this task, however, we need to look quickly at the key assumptions about competitive input markets. Not surprisingly, they closely parallel earlier assumptions about competitive output markets. In particular, the first two assumptions are familiar and important. The first is the assumption of large numbers, which guarantees that all demanders and all suppliers are price takers in the input market:

ASSUMPTION: LARGE NUMBERS

The number of input demanders (suppliers) is large enough and each demander (supplier) is small enough so that no individual buys (sells) a significant portion of the total quantity traded.

The second is the assumption of perfect information, which guarantees that all demanders and all suppliers are perfectly informed. In other words, the demanders (firms, in this case) know the prices of all inputs and outputs as well as the relevant production functions. The suppliers (individuals in primary input markets and firms in intermediate input markets) know the prices of all goods and, in particular, the prices of all relevant inputs.

ASSUMPTION: PERFECT INFORMATION

All demanders and suppliers have perfect knowledge of the relevant prices, and all firms have perfect knowledge of the relevant production functions.

The third assumption is that inputs are homogeneous, or identical. This assumption rules out the case of differentiated inputs. For example, this means that one barrel of bunker-C oil can be substituted for any other barrel and that the labor of one systems analyst in the Atlanta labor market is indistinguishable from that of any other systems analyst.

ASSUMPTION: INPUT HOMOGENEITY

In any input market, all units of the input are identical.

The last assumption is that inputs are perfectly mobile. This implies that all units of the same input will command the same price in competitive equilibrium. However, as you will discover in Section 13.9 often this assumption is not satisfied. For example, intermediate goods like cement may not be easy to transport, and individual workers may not want to relocate. When resources are imperfectly mobile, the firms demanding these "immobile" inputs can exercise some control over input prices. The result, known as monopsony, is something very much like monopoly in output markets. For example, a fish-processing plant located in an isolated coastal community will exercise some significant control over the wages it pays its workers.

ASSUMPTION: PERFECT MOBILITY OF RESOURCES

All inputs are perfectly mobile.

If all four assumptions are satisfied, the perfectly competitive model can be applied without hesitation. But if one (or more) of the assumptions is not fulfilled, the model may or may not apply. The question in this case is whether the model continues to yield accurate predictions or not. An answer necessarily comes from empirical and experimental testing.

The Supply of Non-Labor Inputs

We can think of inputs as falling into two categories: labor and non-labor inputs. First, let us look at non-labor inputs like land, steel, cement, or chemicals. As we said, we will think of firms as the suppliers in intermediate input markets and individuals as the suppliers in primary input markets. If the supplier is a firm selling an intermediate input — say, a manufacturer of cold rolled steel — then the analysis of supply decisions is a simple matter. In this case, we can think of these firms as producing and supplying — not a consumption good — but an intermediate input, and then apply the analysis in Chapter 9 directly to input markets. It is as easy as that.

If the supplier is an individual selling a primary input that is a renewable resource such as land — a resource that can be used over and over again — we will make the simplifying assumption that the supply is perfectly inelastic with respect to input price: landowners, for example, simply offer their land at the going price in the marketplace. In making this assumption, however, we are ignoring some important questions concerning the improvement of a resource to make it fit for a specific use. If a marshland needs to be drained before it can be used for farming, for example, the supply will not be perfectly price inelastic because the price must be high enough to justify the expense of drainage.

If a supplier is an individual selling a primary input that is a nonrenewable resource like oil or iron ore — a resource that, once it is used, is gone — we will again make the simplifying assumption that the supply is perfectly price inelastic. In doing so, however, we are ignoring the question of the time period in which the resource will be supplied. In other words, when we assume that supply is perfectly price inelastic, we are analyzing the equilibrium within a single period. However, an important question in the allocation of nonrenewable resources is how much to allocate to production today and how much to keep available for allocation in some future time period. In the following chapter, we will combine the results from this one-period analysis with an analysis of multi-period, or intertemporal supply to determine the intertemporal equilibrium in a nonrenewable resource market.

The Supply of Labor

Now let us turn to the supply of labor. Analyzing labor supply is necessarily different from the supply of non-labor inputs. Labor supply depends on the decisions that individuals make about how much of their time to apportion to work rather than to other, leisure-time activities. To develop a deeper understanding of labor supply, let us return to the leisure-income model from Section 4.5. We will suppose that people divide their time between work (uses of time that generate income) and leisure (all other uses of time). We will also suppose that their preferences can be reduced to preferences over consumption bundles composed of two goods — leisure, x_1, and income, x_2. Notice that both goods are composite commodities. Leisure is a composite of time spent in activities like sleeping, eating, watching TV, exercising, reading, and so on. Income is a composite of money spent on items like food, clothing, transportation, housing, entertainment, and so on.

In this model, an individual faces two constraints. The time constraint dictates that total time devoted to work and to leisure must be equal to total time available. Letting T denote total time available in the period and h denote hours of work, the time constraint is

$$h + x_1 = T$$

Hours spent at work h plus hours spent at leisure x_1 add up to total hours available T.

The income constraint says that the individual's income is the sum of income earned from work and non-work income. Let w denote the individual's wage rate and A denote his or her non-work income from sources like savings accounts, rental income, stocks and bonds, and so on. The income constraint is

$$x_2 = wh + A$$

Income x_2 is equal to income from work wh plus non-work income A.

From the time constraint, we see that $h = T - x_1$. Using this result to eliminate h from the income constraint, we get what we will call the leisure-income budget constraint:

$$wx_1 + x_2 = A + wT$$

price of leisure

full income

As we emphasized in Section 4.5, two important insights follow from this budget constraint. First, the wage rate w can be interpreted as the **price of leisure**, since \$$w$ of income must be given up to get an additional hour of leisure. Second, $A + wT$ can be interpreted as **full income**, since it is the amount that could be earned by devoting all T hours to work.

We can then think of an individual as choosing a bundle of leisure and income so as to maximize utility, subject to the constraint that the value of leisure (wx_1) plus income (x_2) be equal to full income ($A + wT$). The solution to this problem is shown in Figure 13.1. The budget constraint has slope equal to $-w$ since the price of leisure is w. When T hours are spent working (or, when no time is apportioned to leisure), income is $A + wt$. When T hours are devoted to leisure (or, when no time is spent working) income is just A. The utility-maximizing bundle is at point E, where the indifference

---

FIGURE 13.1 **The demand for leisure and the supply of labor**

The utility-maximizing bundle of leisure and income is (x_1^*, x_2^*), which implies that the individual supplies h^* hours of labor.

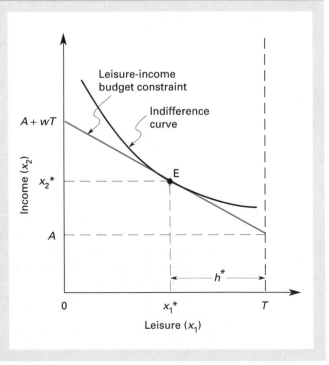

curve is tangent to the leisure-income budget constraint: this person chooses to devote x_1^* hours to leisure and to supply h^* hours of work.

In solving this problem, we have determined both this person's demand for leisure (x_1^*) and his or her supply of labor (h^*) since $h^* = T - x_1^*$. This suggests two comparative statics questions. First, how does an individual's supply of labor supply h^* and demand for leisure x_1^* respond to changes in non-work income A? Second, how do they respond to changes in the wage rate w? Notice that because hours of leisure and hours of work use up the total time available, the labor supply response and demand for leisure response will have opposite signs. For example, if labor supply increases, then the demand for leisure must decrease.

Responses to Changes in Non-Work Income

Our theory provides no definitive prediction about the first comparative statics question: What are the supply and demand responses to changes in non-work income A? However, it does yield a useful taxonomy. Leisure is a **normal good** if the response to an increase in non-work income A is an increase in hours of leisure, and therefore a decrease in hours of work. This case is shown in Figure 13.2. Non-work income is initially $500 per week, and in the initial equilibrium, this person chooses to devote 120 of the 168 hours in the week to leisure and the remaining 48 hours to work. Non-work income subsequently rises to $800 per week, and in the subsequent equilibrium, this person chooses to devote 138 hours to leisure and the remaining 30 hours to work. We see, then, that in response to a $300 increase in non-work income, this person's demand for leisure rises by 18 hours and his or her supply of labor drops by 18 hours.

In contrast, leisure is an **inferior good** if the response to an increase in non-work income A is a decrease in hours of leisure and, therefore, an increase in hours of work.

normal good

inferior good

FIGURE 13.2 **Leisure as a normal good**

In the initial equilibrium, this person demands 120 hours of leisure per week. When non-work income increases from $500 per week to $800 per week, this person's demand for leisure increases to 138 hours per week. Therefore, for this person, leisure is a normal good.

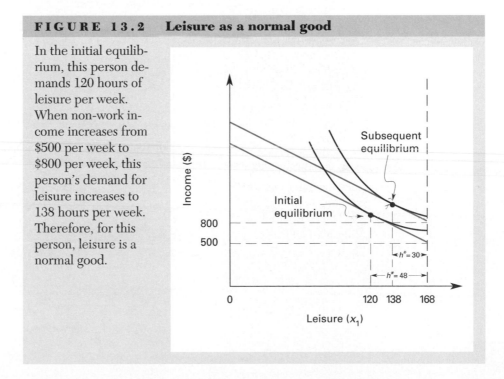

PROBLEM 13.1

Construct a diagram similar to Figure 13.2 to illustrate the case in which leisure is an inferior good.

Responses to a Change in the Wage Rate

For most people, non-work income is a relatively small proportion of income. In economies like the United States and Canada, about 80% of all income is work-generated for the economy as a whole. For average individuals, the proportion of work-generated income is even higher. Because work-generated income plays such an important role, economists have paid more attention to the second comparative statics question: How does the supply of labor — and therefore the demand for leisure — change in response to a change in the wage rate? Or, to put it another way: Does the individual's supply of labor increase or decrease as the wage rate increases? As you might have already guessed, either response is consistent with our theory.

Consider the case in Figure 13.3, where this individual has no non-work income and the wage rate is initially $10 per hour. This person selects utility-maximizing bundle A, choosing 126 hours of leisure and 42 hours of work per week and earning an income of $420 per week. What happens if the wage rate increases to $20 per hour? Given the higher wage rate, this person now selects bundle B, choosing 140 hours of leisure and 28 hours of work per week and earning an income of $560 per week. We see that in response to the $10 per hour wage increase, this person's demand for leisure increases — and supply of labor decreases — by 14 hours per week.

FIGURE 13.3 Income and substitution effects for a wage change

In response to an increase in the wage rate from $10 per hour to $20 per hour, the demand for leisure increases by 14 hours per week — from 126 hours to 140 hours. This change can be decomposed into a positive income effect of 27 hours $(140 - 113)$ and a negative substitution effect of -13 hours $(113 - 126)$.

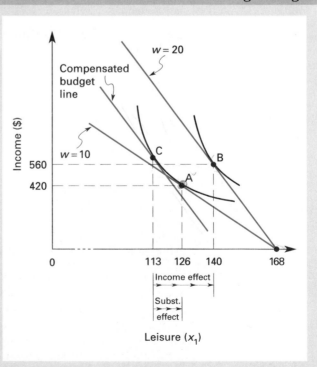

For a better understanding of these results, let us decompose the response in Figure 13.3 into income and substitution effects. Beginning at point B, imagine reducing the individual's non-work income by just enough so that he or she could attain the initial (lower) indifference curve in Figure 13.3, given the $20 per hour wage rate. The result is the compensated budget line in the figure. This person would choose point C on the compensated budget line. We see that the income effect for this wage increase is to increase hours of leisure (and therefore to decrease hours of work) by 27 hours per week. In contrast, the substitution effect for this increase in the wage rate (or price of leisure) is to reduce hours of leisure (and therefore increase hours of work) by 13 hours per week. Because the income effect is larger than the substitution effect, the net effect is an increase in hours of leisure (and a decrease in hours of work) by 14 hours per week.

In Figure 13.3, leisure is clearly a normal good. When leisure is a normal good, the income effect of a wage increase invariably leads to an increase in hours of leisure and a decrease in hours of work. But the substitution effect works in just the opposite direction: a wage increase leads to a decrease in hours of leisure and an increase in hours of work:

When leisure is a normal good, the income and substitution effects are at cross purposes, and the results are ambiguous. Whether hours of work increase or decrease in response to an increase in the wage rate depends on whether the income effect is smaller or larger than the substitution effect.

When leisure is an inferior good, however, the income and substitution effects are complementary, and the results are unambiguous:

When leisure is an inferior good, an increase in the wage rate invariably leads to a decrease in hours of leisure and an increase in hours of work.

To check your understanding of the leisure-income model, give the following problem careful attention.

PROBLEM 13.2

Indicate whether the following statements are true or false, and carefully explain your answer.
1. If in response to an increase in the wage rate, hours of work increase, then leisure is necessarily an inferior good.
2. If in response to an increase in the wage rate, hours of work decrease, then leisure is necessarily a normal good.

Labor Supply Curves

By considering a number of different wage rates, we can easily derive an individual's labor supply curve. In Figure 13.4a, we have solved an individual's utility-maximizing problem for six wage rates. The point labeled E on each of the budget lines indicates the chosen bundle of leisure and income. (For simplicity, we have suppressed the indifference curves. You will have to imagine the points of tangency between these budget lines and the suppressed indifference curves.)

The information from Figure 13.4a has been used to derive this individual's labor supply curve in Figure 13.4b. For example, we see from Figure 13.4a that when the wage rate is $25 per hour, this person demands 138 hours of leisure per week and therefore supplies (168-138) or 30 hours of labor per week. In the case shown in Figure 13.4,

FIGURE 13.4   The demand for leisure and the supply of labor

The curve EE in (a) passes through the utility-maximizing bundles that are generated as the wage rate increases from $5 to $30 in $5 increments. The information from (a) has been used to construct the labor supply curve in (b).

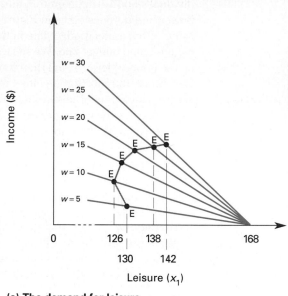

(a) The demand for leisure

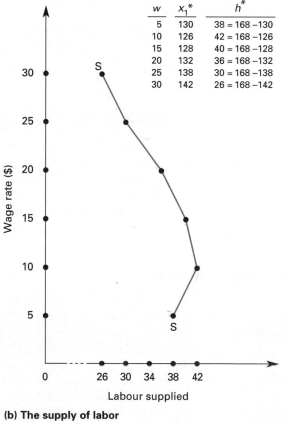

w	x_1^*	h^*
5	130	$38 = 168 - 130$
10	126	$42 = 168 - 126$
15	128	$40 = 168 - 128$
20	132	$36 = 168 - 132$
25	138	$30 = 168 - 138$
30	142	$26 = 168 - 142$

(b) The supply of labor

when the wage rate is low (less than $10 per hour), this person's labor supply increases as the wage rate increases. However, when the wage is higher (more than $10 per hour), this person's labor supply decreases as the wage rate increases. Of course, there is nothing in our theory to suggest that *all* labor supply curves look like the supply curve in Figure 13.4b. This is just one possible labor supply curve.

13.5

The Firm's Demand for One Variable Input

short-run input demand function

Now let us turn from the supply of inputs to the demand for inputs. We will begin with what we will call the **short-run input demand function** where only one input is variable. Specifically, let us imagine a firm — The Fish Company — that hires people to catch fish from a company-owned lake. To keep the analysis simple, we will initially suppose that there is just one good in the economy, namely fish. In this case, The Fish Company's profit will be measured in fish and the workers will be paid "in kind" — that is, in fish instead of dollars. The hourly wage rate, denoted by w, is the number of fish a worker is paid for an hour of fishing. After we find the firm's demand for labor in this case, we can easily generalize results to the more realistic case in which workers are paid in dollars.[1]

Input Demand in a One-Good Economy

The Fish Company's marginal product function $MP(z)$ and its average product function $AP(z)$, where z is hours of labor, are shown in Figure 13.5. Because the unit of measure on the vertical axis is numbers of fish, we can represent the wage rate w on this axis. We will find The Fish Company's demand curve by answering the following question: Given any wage rate (in fish), how many hours of labor will The Fish Company buy to maximize its profit?

Marginal product is the number of fish attributable to an additional hour of labor, and the wage rate is the number of fish that The Fish Company must pay to hire an additional hour of labor. Therefore, when marginal product exceeds the wage rate, The Fish Company's profit increases as it hires more labor. When marginal product is less than the wage rate, its profit decreases as it hires more labor. It would seem that to maximize its profit, The Fish Company should hire labor up to the point at which marginal product is equal to the wage rate. In other words, the marginal product function appears to be the firm's demand curve.

With two qualifications, the marginal product function is the demand curve. To see why we need the first qualification, suppose that the wage rate is 7 fish in Figure 13.5 — a wage rate less than the maximum value of average product, which is 9 fish. Although marginal product equals 7 fish at both 20 hours of labor and 150 hours of labor, the point of maximum profit is — as you will discover in the following problem — at 150 hours of labor on the downward-sloping portion of the marginal product function.

---

1 For a historical perspective on the material covered in the next few sections, see the entry in *The New Palgrave* by Robert Dorfman on "marginal productivity theory."

FIGURE 13.5   Input demand in a one-good economy

When the wage rate w exceeds 9, The Fish Company demands no labor because AP is less than the wage for all values of z. When the wage rate is less than 9, The Fish Company's demand function is MP. For example, if $w = 7$, The Fish Company hires 150 hours of labor.

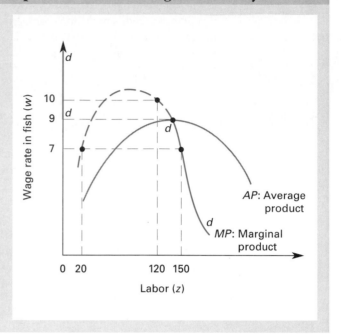

PROBLEM 13.3

Assuming that the wage rate is 7 fish, show that profit is maximal at 150 hours of labor. To do so, imagine that the firm is currently hiring 150 hours of labor, and then show that profit falls both as the firm hires more labor, and as it hires less labor. Now show that profit is minimal at 20 hours of labor.

The result from Problem 13.3 can be generalized:

For any wage less than the maximum value of average product, the firm's demand function is the downward-sloping portion of its marginal product function.

This segment of the marginal product function is labeled dd in Figure 13.5.

To see why we need a second qualification, suppose the wage rate is 10 fish in Figure 13.5. As you will discover in the following problem, since 10 exceeds the maximum value of average product, which is 9, The Fish Company maximizes its profit by deciding not to hire any workers.

PROBLEM 13.4

Given that the wage rate is 10 fish in Figure 13.5, if the company actually were to hire labor, it would hire 120 hours. On the other hand, if it hired no labor, its profit would be zero, since no fish would be caught and no wages paid. Show that the company's profit is larger if it hires no labor than if it hires 120 hours — or equivalently, that its profit is negative if it hires 120 hours of labor. Hint: The company's profit is just average product minus the wage rate multiplied by the number of hours.

The result from Problem 13.4 can also be generalized:

For any wage rate greater than the maximum value of average product, the firm maximizes profit by hiring no labor.

Thus, for wage rates greater than 9 fish in Figure 13.5, the company's demand function is the vertical axis, also labeled dd. At any of these wage rates, the firm will shut down. The Fish Company's demand for labor in this one-good economy is thus composed of the two segments labeled dd in Figure 13.5.

Now let us generalize these results. Instead of focusing on The Fish Company's demand for labor, we will think more generally about a firm's demand for a variable input. We will also move into the more realistic framework in which inputs are paid and profit is measured in money. The generalization is surprisingly simple. We need to introduce a money price for the variable input, denoted by w. And we need to transform the two measures of physical productivity, marginal and average product, into monetary units.

First let us transform marginal product MP into what is called marginal revenue product MRP. If a firm buys an additional unit of the variable input, its output will increase by approximately $MP(z)$. When the additional output is sold, the change in the firm's revenue is the additional output $MP(z)$ multiplied by marginal revenue in the firm's output market $MR(y)$. The product of marginal revenue and marginal product is called **marginal revenue product**, or $MRP(z)$:

marginal revenue product

$$MRP(z) = MR(y)MP(z)$$

If $MP(z)$ is 5 and $MR(y)$ is \$5, for example, then $MRP(z)$ is equal to \$25. $MRP(z)$ is the rate at which the firm's revenue changes as the quantity of input, z, increases. Therefore, $MRP(z)$ tells us the monetary value to the firm of an additional unit of the variable input. (Even though y and z both appear on the right side of the equality sign, marginal revenue product is written as a function of z alone because the quantity of output, y, is itself determined by the quantity of input, z.)

average revenue product

Now let us transform average product AP into what is called **average revenue product** ARP. Average revenue product is the price of the firm's output, p, multiplied by the average product of the variable input, $AP(z)$.

$$ARP(z) = pAP(z)$$

In the following problem, you can derive $MRP(z)$ and $ARP(z)$ from $MP(z)$ and $AP(z)$ for a firm that is a perfect competitor in both its input and output markets.

> **PROBLEM 13.5**
>
> First draw the standard stylizations of $MP(z)$ and $AP(z)$ from in Figure 13.5. The units on the vertical axis are measures of output. (If the output is fish, the unit might be tons of fish.) Now change the label on the vertical axis from units of output to units of money, or dollars. Suppose initially that p is \$1, and construct $MRP(z)$ and $ARP(z)$. Recall that for a perfect competitor in the output market, marginal revenue is equal to price. Next, suppose that p is \$2, and again construct $MRP(z)$ and $ARP(z)$.

The standard stylizations of $MRP(z)$ and $ARP(z)$ are illustrated in Figure 13.6. Generalizing what we learned from the encounter with The Fish Company, we see

FIGURE 13.6   The firm's demand for one variable input

If input price w exceeds 10, the firm demands nothing because the input price exceeds ARP for all z. If w is less than 10, the demand for z is MRP. For example, if $w = 6$, then the firm demands 50 units of the variable input.

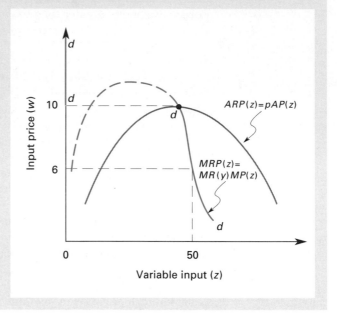

that the firm's demand function for z is composed of the two segments labeled dd.

We will look at each of the two segments of the input demand function in turn. First:

For input prices less than the maximum value of ARP, the firm's demand function is the downward-sloping portion of MRP.

If the input price, w, is $6, for example, the firm will demand 50 units of the variable input. Why? If the firm were to buy more than 50 units, its profit would fall because, when z exceeds 50 units, the rate at which its revenue increases as z increases $MRP(z)$ — is less than the rate at which its cost increases as z increases — w. And if the firm were to buy less than 50 units, its profit would fall, because when z is less than 50 units, the rate at which its revenue decreases as z decreases — $MRP(z)$ — is greater than the rate at which its cost decreases as z decreases — w. Since profit falls as the firm buys both more and less of the variable input, profit is a maximum when the firm buys 50 units.[2] Second:

---

2 When there is just one variable input, the firm's profit function is $yD(y) - wz - FC$, where FC is the firm's fixed cost and $D(\cdot)$ is the firm's price as a function of quantity produced. Of course, $y = TP(z)$. Using this fact, we can write the firm's profit as a function of z:

$$\neq(z) = TP(z)D[TP(z)] - wz - FC$$

If z^*, the profit-maximizing value of z, is positive, then $\neq'(z^*) = 0$, or

$$MP(z^*)\{D[TP(z^*)] + TP(z^*)D'[TP(z^*)]\} = w$$

since $MP(z) = TP'(z)$. The expression in braces is marginal revenue at the profit-maximizing level of output, since

$$p + yD'(y) = D[TP(z)] + TP(z)D'[TP(z)]$$

But $MP(z)MR(y)$ is just $MRP(z)$, and we see that $\neq'(z^*) = 0$ implies that

$$MRP(z^*) = w$$

For input prices greater than the maximum value of *ARP*, the firm will demand none of the variable input.

Why not? The firm's revenue is equal to $zARP(z)$ and its short-run cost is wz. Its variable profit — its revenue minus its variable cost — is therefore just

$$z[ARP(z) - w]$$

At input prices higher than $10, w exceeds $ARP(z)$ for all values of z. This means that if the firm were to buy a positive amount of the variable input, its variable profit would be negative. By contrast, if it buys none of the variable input, its revenue, its variable cost, and its variable profit will all be zero. Therefore, when the wage rate exceeds $10, it will buy none of the variable input — that is, it will shut down. The firm's demand curve is then composed of the two segments labeled *dd* in Figure 13.6.

It is useful to highlight one qualitative property of the firm's input demand function:

In response to an increase in the price of an input, a firm will not demand an increased quantity of the input. If the firm originally demanded a positive quantity of the input, the quantity demanded will decrease.

In short, we know that the firm's short-run demand function is downward sloping when only one input is variable: the lower the input price, the higher the quantity demanded of the input.

We have now looked at the firm's short-run profit-maximizing decision in two ways. In Chapters 9 and 10, we concentrated on the firm's choice in the output market. Here, we have fixed our attention on the firm's choice in the input market. In the following two problems, you can show that the two short-run profit-maximizing rules are equivalent.

PROBLEM 13.6

In Section 9.4, you saw that if the firm produces a positive output, then $SMC = MR$. You just learned that if the firm buys a positive amount of the variable input, then $w = MRP$. From Section 7.4 you know that $SMC = w/MP$. Using this relationship, show that the two profit-maximizing rules are equivalent.

PROBLEM 13.7

You know from Section 9.4 that a perfectly competitive firm will produce no output if the output price p is less than the minimum value of *AVC*. You have just learned that if the input price w exceeds the maximum value of *ARP*, the same is true. Can you show that these statements are equivalent?

Value of the Marginal Product

Now let us turn to the question of efficiency in input markets. In thinking about how efficiently inputs are allocated in input markets, we will ask: What is the value to consumers of an additional unit of an input used by a firm? For example, what is the value to consumers who buy Roquefort cheese of an additional gallon of sheep's milk used by some Roquefort cheese maker? Knowing that these consumers value the cheese, not sheep's milk, we can break this question into two parts: How much additional cheese can be made from 1 more gallon of milk? How much do the consumers value that

value of the marginal product

additional amount of cheese? The answer to the first question is, of course, $MP(z)$. If p is the price of Roquefort, the answer to the second question is just p times $MP(z)$. More generally, the **value of the marginal product** of the variable input $VMP(z)$ is output price multiplied by marginal product:

$$VMP(z) = pMP(z)$$

In the following problem you are asked to establish some important results, so give this problem special attention.

> **PROBLEM 13.8**
>
> First, show that if the firm is a perfect competitor in its output market, then $VMP = MRP$. Next, show that if the firm is a monopolist in its output market, then $VMP > MRP$. Hint: if a firm is a perfect competitor in its output market, then p is equal to MR, while if it is a monopolist MR is less than p.

VMP can be interpreted as the value to consumers of an additional unit of the variable input in a given production process. MRP is, of course, the value to a firm of an additional unit of the variable input. From Problem 13.6, you know that if a firm is a perfect competitor in its output market, its valuation of an additional unit of the variable input is identical to consumers' valuation — that is, for such a firm, $VMP = MRP$. If the firm is a monopolist in its output market, however, its valuation of an additional unit is less than consumers' valuation. That is, for such a firm, $MRP < VMP$. As we will see in Section 13.7, these observations are the keys to understanding why monopoly in the output market is inefficient whereas perfect competition is efficient.

Input Demand with Many Variable Inputs

In the preceding section, we derived the firm's input demand function when only one input was variable. What will a firm's input demand function look like when more than one input is variable — say, when two inputs are variable? We will denote quantity of input 1 by z_1 and quantity of input 2 by z_2 and their respective input prices by w_1 and w_2. We can interpret the results as either a short run in which only two of any number of inputs are variable or as a long run in which there are only two inputs. For convenience, here we will call it the long-run case.

We learned earlier that the short-run input demand function is downward sloping: the lower the input price, the higher the quantity demanded. In this section, we will argue that the long-run demand function is also downward sloping, and we will compare these two input demand functions. Our treatment will be intuitive rather than rigorous.

Downward-Sloping Long-Run Input Demand Curve

substitution effect

output effect

Firms have more flexibility in responding to an input-price change in the long run than in the short run. The added flexibility is reflected in two kinds of decisions the firm makes in response to an input-price change: it can change its mix of inputs by substituting towards the relatively cheaper input, and it can alter its total output. Thus, we will decompose the firm's response to an input-price change into a **substitution effect** and an **output effect**. Then we will argue that *both* effects tend to produce a downward-sloping, long-run input demand curve.

First, let us fix the price of both inputs at, say, $w_1 = \$15$ and $w_2 = \$12$ and then identify the initial long-run equilibrium. When a firm is in long-run equilibrium, its output — say, $y = 100$ units — is, by definition, produced at minimum cost. This means that the point of long-run equilibrium in Figure 13.7 is at E, where the steeper isocost line is tangent to the 100-unit isoquant. At input prices $w_1 = \$15$ and $w_2 = \$12$, then, this firm demands 15 units of input 1 and 30 units of input 2. Now, how will its demand for input 1 change if its price drops from $w_1 = \$15$ to $w_2 = \$10$?

Let us begin with the substitution effect. If we imagine that the firm continues to produce 100 units of output after the price change, it would substitute towards the now-cheaper input 1, moving from point E to point E' on the 100-unit isoquant in Figure 13.7. The quantity demanded of input 1 would therefore rise from 15 units to 22 units. In this case, the substitution effect produces an *inverse relationship* between the quantity demanded of an input and its price. As we saw in Section 8.6, this inverse relationship is generally true. The substitution effect therefore tends to produce a downward-sloping demand function. The cheaper input 1 becomes, the more of it the firm buys.

Now let us turn to the output effect. When the input price changes, the firm alters its level of output because its total cost function is now different. We can easily see how the firm's cost function shifts. At the original input prices, the minimum cost of producing 100 units was $\$585$ — ($\$15 \times 15$) + ($\$12 \times 30$). At the new input prices, it is only $\$472$ — ($\$10 \times 22$) + ($\$12 \times 21$). The minimum cost of producing 100 units is less after the price decrease. By extension, the cost of producing any level of output has decreased and the firm's cost function has therefore shifted downward. The output effect associated

FIGURE 13.7 **The substitution effect of an input price change**

At input prices $w_1 = \$15$ and $w_2 = \$12$, the cost-minimizing input bundle for 100 units of output is 15 units of input 1 and 30 units of input 2. Now suppose that w_1 drops from $\$15$ to $\$10$. To identify the substitution effect, hold output constant at $y = 100$, and find the cost-minimizing bundle for input prices $w_1 = \$10$ and $w_2 = \$12$. It is 22 units of input 1 and 21 units of input 2. We see that the substitution effect works

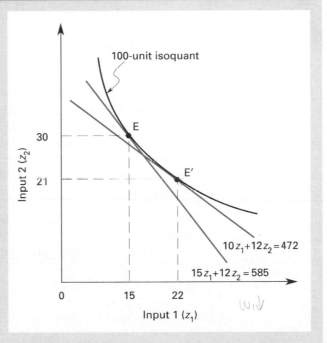

to produce a downward-sloping input demand function — as the price of an input decreases, the firm demands more of it.

with the input price change is this: because the firm's total cost function has shifted downward, its choice of output — and its demand for input 1 — will also change.[3]

Just how is the shift in the firm's cost function reflected in its choice of output? If input 1 is a normal rather than an inferior input, the input-price reduction means that not only the firm's total cost function but also its marginal cost function shift downward. (Do notice that we are only asserting this result, not proving it.) As a result, the firm will produce more output. Because input 1 is a normal input, the firm will demand even more of input 1 as it produces more output. Therefore, the output effect reinforces the substitution effect in generating a downward-sloping demand function when input 1 is a normal input.

If input 1 is instead an inferior input, will the two effects still tend to produce a downward-sloping demand curve? The direction of the substitution effect is unchanged: the firm will substitute input 1 for input 2 as w_1 drops. Surprisingly, the direction of the output effect is also unchanged. A reduction in the price of an inferior input causes the marginal cost function to shift upward. (This result, which is not particularly intuitive, is asserted rather than proved.) As a result, the firm will produce less output and, because input 1 is an inferior input, it will demand more of that inferior input as its output decreases. Again, substitution and output effects complement each other in producing a downward-sloping demand function in the long run.

To summarize:

Regardless of whether the input is normal or inferior, the substitution and output effects are complementary. Both work to produce a long-run input demand function that is donward sloping.

A Comparison of Long-Run and Short-Run Input Demand

If we compare the steepness of the long-run and the short-run demand functions, we discover that the long-run function is flatter than its short-run counterparts. In other words, the quantity response to an input-price decrease (or increase) is larger in the long run than in the short run.

The long-run input demand function in Figure 13.8 is labeled *DD*; the representative short-run function is labeled *MRP*. (We can identify any number of possible short-run demand functions, depending on the quantity of the fixed input 2.) The long-run input demand function and any short-run demand function will have one point in common because a firm in long-run equilibrium is also in a particular short-run equilibrium. Accordingly, *DD* and *MRP* intersect at point E in Figure 13.8. However, *DD* is flatter than *MRP*, indicating that the response to an input-price change is greater in the long run:

The response to an input price change in both the short and the long run is to demand more (less) of the input as its price falls (rises), and the response to any such price change is greater in the long run than in the short run.

---

3 In Chapter 8, we analyzed the firm's conditional input demand function, which gives the quantity of the input in the cost-minimizing input bundle when output y is held constant. Since output is held constant, the conditional input demand function captures only the substitution effect. The long-run input demand function that we are now considering captures the output effect as well as the substitution effect.

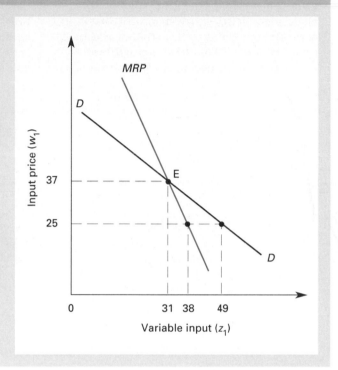

FIGURE 13.8 Comparing long-run and short-run input demand functions

DD is the long-run demand function for input 1, and MRP is a short-run input demand function. The two demand functions have one point in common, and MRP is steeper than DD.

13.7
Competitive Equilibrium in an Input Market

A long-run competitive equilibrium in an input market is presented in Figure 13.9. The market demand and market supply functions, AID and SS, are shown in Figure 13.9c. To get AID we have horizontally summed the demand functions all firms that demand the input, and to get SS we have horizontally summed the supply functions of all suppliers. Recall that we used the same aggregation procedure — horizontal summation — to get the market supply and demand functions in Chapter 9. The **competitive equilibrium** is identified in the familiar way: at the equilibrium price w^e, quantity supplied equals quantity demanded.

competitive
equilibrium

The position of a firm that is a perfect competitor in both its output market and the input market is shown in Figure 13.9b. The position of a firm that is a monopolist in its output market and a perfect competitor in the input market is shown in Figure 13.9a. Recall that we can interpret MRP as the value of one more unit of the input to the firm itself. In contrast, VMP is the value of one more unit of input to consumers of the firm's product. We can use these interpretations in conjunction with Figure 13.9 to deepen our understanding of the inefficiency of monopoly and the efficiency of perfect competition.

Let us begin with the firm shown in Figure 13.9b. In long-run equilibrium, the firm is on both its long-run demand function D_2 and its short-run demand function MRP. Since the firm is a perfect competitor in its output market, MRP is coincident with VMP. Thus, beginning at the equilibrium position of the firm, we know that if the firm

FIGURE 13.9 Equilibrium in a competitive input market

From (c), we see that w^e is the equilibrium input price. In (b), we see that a firm that is perfectly competitive in its output market buys z_2^* of the input, where VMP and MRP are

equal to the input price w^e. In (a), we see that a firm that is a monopolist in its output market buys z_1^* of the input, where MRP is equal to w^e and where VMP exceeds w^e.

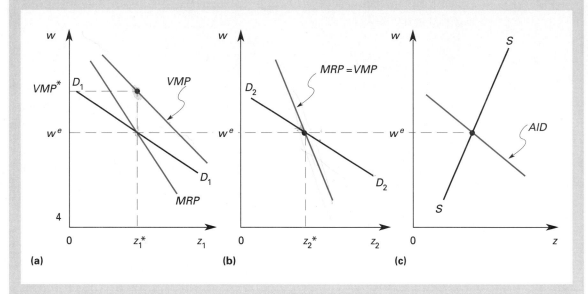

were to use one more unit of the input, the increase in its cost of production w^e would exceed the value its consumers place on the added output VMP. In other words, if these consumers were allowed to make the firm's production decisions, they would decide against buying more than z_2^* units of the input since the additional output that an additional unit of the input would produce is not worth w^e to these consumers. This property reflects the efficiency of perfect competition.

Now consider the firm shown in Figure 13.9a. In equilibrium, the monopolist, like the competitive firm, is on both its long-run demand function D_1 and its short-run demand function MRP. But, because this firm is a monopolist in its output market, MRP is less than VMP. Therefore, VMP exceeds w^e at the monopolist's point of equilibrium. If this firm's customers were put in charge, they would opt for buying more of the input because at z_1^* their valuation of the output produced by an additional unit of the input, VMP^* in Figure 13.9a, exceeds the price of the additional unit of the input w^e.

Let us summarize these important results:

In long-run equilibrium, a firm that is a perfect competitor in both its output and its input markets will choose an input bundle such that, for each input,

$$w^e = MRP(z) = pMP(z) = VMP(z)$$

In long-run equilibrium, a firm that is a perfect competitor in its input markets, but a monopolist in its output market, will choose an input bundle such that, for each input,

$$w^e = MRP(z) = MR(y)MP(z) < pMP(z) = VMP(z)$$

13.8

Monopsony in Input Markets

monopsony

Let us now begin to explore **monopsony** in an input market; that is, a market in which a monopsonist — like its logical cousin, the monopolist — is a price setter. That is, a monopsonist has significant control over the price it pays for an input. For example, the Harlem Globetrotters basketball team is a monopsonist in the market for show-biz basketball players. As far as basketball clubs that hire entertainers rather than competitors are concerned, it is metaphorically the only game in town. Any company owning a "company town" is likewise a monopsonist in the local labor market because it, too, is the only game in town. A sugar refinery in an isolated, relatively small agricultural region is a monopsonist in the local sugar beet market for precisely the same reason.

Let us look at two closely related questions. How will such a monopsonist choose input price and quantity? And what are the sources of a monopsonist's input market power? To determine how a monopsonist will set price and quantity in an input (or "factor") market, we need three new concepts: the firm's total factor cost TFC, its marginal factor cost MFC, and its average factor cost AFC.

The Monopsonist's Factor Cost Functions

market supply
function

For a monopsonist, the relationship between input price w and quantity of the input z is determined by the **market supply function** for the input:

$$w = S(z)$$

If the monopsonist wants to buy z units of the input, the price w it must pay is determined by the supply function $S(z)$. It is natural to suppose that the supply function is upward sloping. In other words, we are assuming that the more the monopsonist wants to buy, the higher the price it must pay.

average factor
cost

Keep in mind that the monopsonist buys all units at the same price. Price can then be interpreted as **average factor cost** AFC. Since all units are bought at the same price, the average amount any unit contributes to the firm's cost is the price at which it is bought. Then, for any quantity of the input z, the supply function $S(z)$ determines both price w and average factor cost AFC.

total factor cost

Total factor cost TFC is then just quantity z multiplied by average factor cost, or price $S(z)$.

$$TFC(z) = zS(z)$$

marginal factor
cost

Of course, **marginal factor cost** MFC is the rate at which total factor cost TFC changes as quantity of the input z changes. What is the relationship between input price w and marginal factor cost MFC for a monopsonist?

When the monopsonist buys a positive quantity of the input, marginal factor cost MFC exceeds price w or average factor cost AFC.

To understand this important result, recall that the monopsonist buys all units at the same price and faces an upward-sloping supply curve. Because the supply curve is upward sloping, to buy an additional unit the monopsonist must raise the price it pays for the input. Therefore MFC is greater than the price at which the additional unit is bought by an amount equal to the quantity originally bought multiplied by the price increase. Suppose, for example, that the monopsonist in Figure 13.10 is initially at point

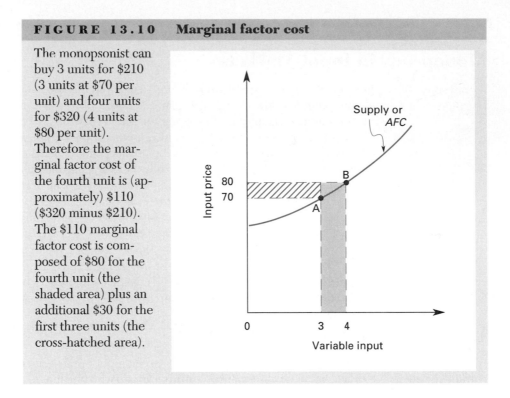

FIGURE 13.10   Marginal factor cost

The monopsonist can buy 3 units for $210 (3 units at $70 per unit) and four units for $320 (4 units at $80 per unit). Therefore the marginal factor cost of the fourth unit is (approximately) $110 ($320 minus $210). The $110 marginal factor cost is composed of $80 for the fourth unit (the shaded area) plus an additional $30 for the first three units (the cross-hatched area).

A, where it is buying 3 units of an input at a price of $70. To buy one additional unit — or 4 units of input in total — it must increase the price it pays per unit by $10 from $70 to $80. The resulting change in total factor cost, which is approximately equal to marginal factor cost, is $110 — $(4 \times \$80) - (3 \times \$70)$. This change is $30 more than the $80 price at which the fourth unit is bought. The $30 difference between the $80 price at which the fourth unit is bought and marginal factor cost *MFC* is equal to the original 3 units sold times the $10 price increase. In Figure 13.10, the shaded area represents the cost of buying the fourth unit at price $80, and the cross-hatched area represents the added cost of buying the original three units at $80 instead of $70 per unit.

For a more precise understanding of the relationship between marginal factor cost and input price or average factor cost, we will look at a more general experiment. Suppose initially that the monopsonist is on its supply curve, where it is buying z units at price w and generating total revenue equal to wz. Now suppose that it increases the input price by amount Δw and that the quantity supplied increases by amount Δz. Total factor cost is then $(w + \Delta w)(z + \Delta z)$, and the resulting change in total factor cost is

$$w\Delta z + z\Delta w + \Delta w\Delta z = (w + \Delta w)(z + \Delta z) - wz$$

Now, we divide this expression by Δz to get the rate of change of total factor cost with respect to z:

$$w + z[\Delta w/\Delta z] + \Delta w$$

The term in brackets is approximately the slope of the demand curve at the initial point. As the price change Δw gets smaller and smaller, the approximation gets better and better. As $\varnothing w$ approaches zero, the approximation is perfect, and we then have the following result

$$MFC(z) = w + z[\text{slope of the supply curve}]$$

In other words, marginal factor cost MFC is equal to input price w plus quantity z multiplied by the slope of the supply curve.[4]

In this expression, w captures the rate at which revenue increases as an infinitesimal additional amount of the input is bought at price w. This term is analogous to the added cost in Figure 13.10 when a fourth unit is bought at a price of $80. The rate at which input price must be increased in order to buy an infinitesimal additional amount is given by the slope of the supply curve. Of course, this slope is positive because the supply curve is upward sloping. Therefore, the second term — z(slope of the supply curve)— captures the rate at which the cost of the original z units rises as price is increased to buy an infinitesimal additional amount. This second term is analogous to the increase in the cost of the original three units in Figure 13.10 when price is raised from $70 to $80 to buy a fourth unit.

This result is analogous to our discovery in Section 10.2 that a monopolist's marginal revenue function lies below its demand function. As we will see, the resulting efficiency implications are also analogous.

PROBLEM 13.9

Suppose that the supply function is

$$w = 1 + z$$

Show that

$$MFC(z) = 1 + 2z$$

Hint: What is the slope of supply function?

We can generalize what you learned in Problem 13.9. If the supply function is linear,

$$w = a + bz \qquad \text{where } a > 0 \text{ and } b > 0$$

then MFC is

$$MFC(z) = a + 2bz$$

Notice, the linear supply function and its MFC intersect the input price axis at the same point, and MFC is twice as steep as the supply function.

---

4 Total factor cost is

$$TFC(z) = zS(z)$$

Marginal factor cost is the derivative of $TFC(z)$. Hence,

$$MFC(z) = S(z) + zS'(z)$$

which can be written as

$$MFC(z) = w + zS'(z)$$

because $w = S(z)$. Since $S'(z) > 0$ for a monopsonist, it is clear that when $z > 0$, $MFC(z) > w$. In contrast, $MFC(z) = w$ for a competitor, since the supply curve for a perfect competitor is horizontal.

The Short-Run Monopsony Equilibrium

We can learn the essential features of monopsony equilibrium by concentrating on the monopsonist's short-run decisions. Figure 13.11 presents a monopsonist's supply function for an input, the associated MFC, and the firm's MRP. On the one hand, MRP is the value to the firm of buying an additional unit of the input because it is the rate at which the firm's revenue increases as z increases. On the other hand, MFC is the cost to the firm of each additional unit of the input because it is the rate at which its total factor cost TFC increases as z increases.

To maximize profit the firm in Figure 13.11 will buy z^* units of the input. Why? As it moves to the right of z^*, buying more of the input, it profit decreases because MFC exceeds MRP. And as it moves to the left of z^*, buying less of the input, profit once again decreases because the rate of decrease of its costs MFC is less than the rate of decrease of its revenues MRP:

> The monopsonist maximizes profit by choosing the quantity of an input where marginal factor cost is equal to marginal revenue product: $MFC(z^*) = MRP(z^*)$.

It is useful to describe mechanically the monopsonist's profit-maximizing rule: to find the profit-maximizing level of the input z^*, first identify the intersection of MFC and MRP — point E in Figure 13.11. Then move vertically down to the z axis to find the profit-maximizing quantity of the input — z^* in Figure 13.11. To find the associated equilibrium input price w^*, move vertically up from z^* to AFC, and then horizontally over to the vertical axis.

The following problems will help you check your understanding of monopsony.

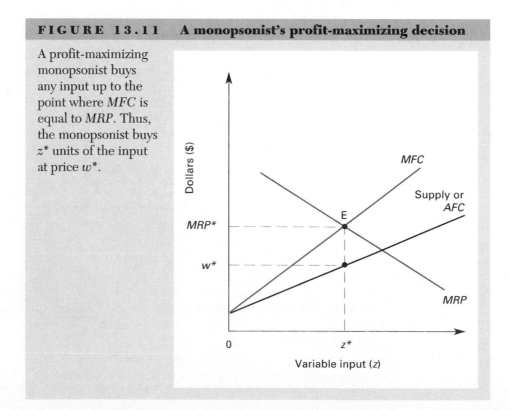

FIGURE 13.11   A monopsonist's profit-maximizing decision

A profit-maximizing monopsonist buys any input up to the point where MFC is equal to MRP. Thus, the monopsonist buys z^* units of the input at price w^*.

PROBLEM 13.10

Suppose that

$$MRP(z) = 10 - z$$

and that the supply function is

$$w = 1 + z$$

Show that $z^* = 3$ and $w^* = 4$. Carefully construct a diagram illustrating this solution.

PROBLEM 13.11

Ten suppliers of coal are spread out along a railroad line at 50, 150, 250, ... , 950 miles from the origin in Figure 13.12. The lone demander is located at the origin. Each supplier will supply 1 ton if the price offered by the demander minus the transport costs incurred by the supplier is greater than or equal to $100. It costs $0.10 to transport 1 ton of coal 1 mile. Derive the supply function faced by the demander. If the demander's MRP is $200 per ton, show that it will buy 5 tons at $145 per ton.

As we saw in Section 13.5, a firm that is competitive in its input markets buys an input up to the point where the input price is equal to MRP. Of course, for such a competitive firm, the exogenous input price is its marginal factor cost because it can buy all the labor it wants at the competitive wage rate. From this we get:

The general profit-maximizing rule in an input market is to buy an input up to the point where marginal factor cost is equal to marginal revenue product. For a perfect competitor in the input market,

$$MRP(z^*) = MFC(z^*) = w$$

For a monopsonist,

$$MRP(z^*) = MFC(z^*) > w$$

FIGURE 13.12   Monopsony in a spatial resource market

A railroad line runs from 0 to 1,000. A coal demander is located at 0, and suppliers are located at the points 50, 150, ... , 950, denoted by Xs. As long as it is costly to transport coal, the demander has monopsony power. That is, it must offer a higher price to get more coal.

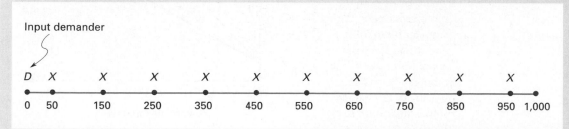

The Inefficiency of Monopsony

Now let us see why monopsony is inefficient. We can eliminate any market failure arising from the monopsonist's output market by assuming that the firm is a perfect competitor in its output market. In this case, $VMP(z)$, is equal to $MRP(z)$, and the value to consumers of the monopsonist's use of an additional unit of the input is identical to the monopsonist's value.

Suppose that the monopsonist in Figure 13.13 follows its maximizing rule by buying z^* at price w^* in a certain period. Now imagine that it "reopens" the market, as it considers buying more units of the input without increasing the price paid for the original z^* units. Can the monopsonist improve its position by buying more of the input? (Notice that this hypothetical experiment corresponds to the exercise used to demonstrate monopoly inefficiency in Section 10.4.) The answer is yes. If the firm buys one more unit at any price less than w'', its profit will increase. Furthermore, the supplier of the additional unit of labor will happily provide it at any price greater than w'. Because at any price less than w'' and greater than w' both the monopsonist and the input supplier are better off, and because no one else is worse off, the original equilibrium clearly was not Pareto-optimal, or efficient. Furthermore, we can see from this exercise that in the original equilibrium, the monopsonist fails to extract the maximum possible profit.

The monopsonistic equilibrium identified by picking the point at which MFC intersects MRP is "uninventive" in very much the same way that the monopolistic equilibrium identified by picking the point at which $MR = MC$ is unimaginative. The inventive monopsonist, like the imaginative monopolist who resorts to price discrimination to reap more of its potential harvest of profit, will therefore search for some sort of discriminatory solution. You can discover the theory of the perfectly discriminating

FIGURE 13.13   The inefficiency of monopsony

To maximize profit, the monopsonist buys z^* units at price w^*. The supplier of unit $z^* + 1$ would happily sell it at any price larger than w', and the firm would happily buy it at any price less than w''. Because any price greater than w' and less than w'' would make both the monopsonist and the supplier better off, and would leave the suppliers of the original z^* units no worse off, the monopsony equilibrium is inefficient.

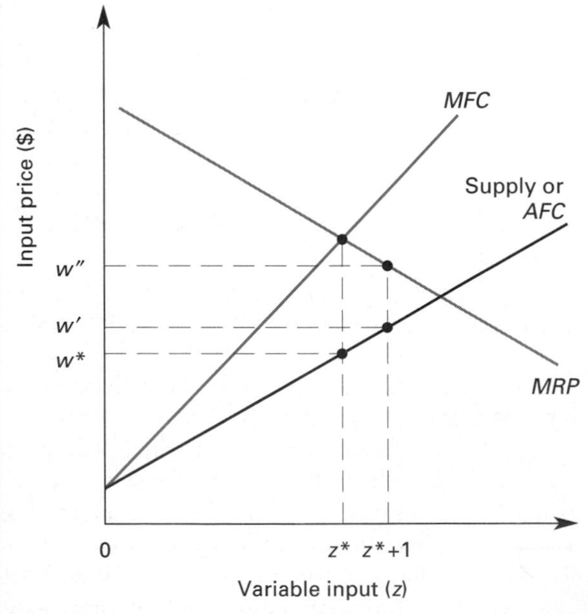

monopsonist in the following problem. We will consider monopsonistic discrimination more carefully in Section 13.10.

PROBLEM 13.12

Suppose that the setup is exactly as it was in the previous problem: a demander of coal is at one end of a railroad line, and the suppliers are spread out along the line, as shown in Figure 13.12. In contrast to that problem, however, suppose that the demander buys the coal from each supplier at the mine head and bears the transport cost itself. How much will it buy and how much will it pay for each ton? Hint: Think back to the perfectly discriminating book vendor in Problem 10.5.

13.9
Sources of Monopsony Power

monopsony power

The telltale sign of **monopsony power** is an upward-sloping supply function to the individual firm. The extent of monopsony power is determined by the responsiveness of quantity supplied to changes in input price. Let us see what we can discover about one important source of monopsony power by considering the labor supply response to a salary reduction. Imagine that Bloomingdale's department store in New York cuts its security officers' salaries and that Bell Laboratories in New Jersey cuts its computer scientists' salaries. How might the supply responses in these two cases differ?

Let us skip over each employee's labor/leisure choice by supposing that the job entails a fixed work week. The supply behavior of every employee can then be described by his or her reservation salary, the lowest possible dollar figure at which the employee will continue to work for the firm. Of course, these reservation salaries will vary from employee to employee, because each places different valuations on such factors as personal relationships on the job, the company's location, and working hours. We can array these different reservation prices from lowest to highest and then use familiar techniques to construct the supply function of current employees shown in Figure 13.14. If Bloomingdale's (or Bell Labs) is now paying its seven employees a salary of w'', we know that salary must be higher than the highest reservation salary of its current employees.

What happens if Bloomingdale's (or Bell Labs) decides to cut its security officers' (computer scientists') salary to, say, w' in Figure 13.14? Every employee whose reservation salary is above the new salary — three employees in this example — will then quit.

What determines exactly how high (or low) any individual's reservation salary will actually be? Perhaps the most important factor is the availability and the salaries of alternative jobs. Because security officers at Bloomingdale's are likely to find comparable jobs in the immediate area without too much trouble, we can reasonably expect that most of their reservation salaries will be close to the initial salary w''. If Bloomingdale's cuts their salaries by very much, the security officers will go elsewhere. In this case, the supply response to a relatively small salary reduction will presumably be large, and we might think of Bloomingdale's as a near perfect competitor in the market for security officers.

By contrast, the computer-science researchers at Bell Labs are much less likely to find similar research jobs within easy commuting distance. For Bell researchers, a job change will probably entail moving and all the consequent social and economic dis-

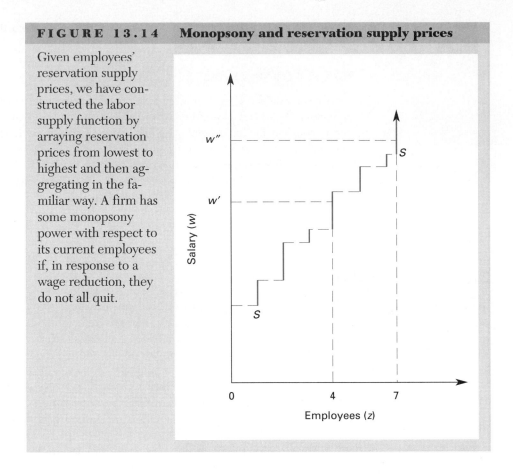

FIGURE 13.14 **Monopsony and reservation supply prices**

Given employees' reservation supply prices, we have constructed the labor supply function by arraying reservation prices from lowest to highest and then aggregating in the familiar way. A firm has some monopsony power with respect to its current employees if, in response to a wage reduction, they do not all quit.

ruption that moving implies. Even if these researchers are willing to look for nonresearch jobs in the immediate area, a career change is likely to bring a significant salary cut. Because major relocation costs or salary reductions are distinct possibilities, the supply response to a significant cut in Bell researchers' salaries will presumably be relatively small. In other words, Bell Labs differs from Bloomingdale's in having some significant *monopsony power* with respect to its employees.

Immobility

immobility of inputs

The general lesson that emerges from this labor-supply discussion and from the earlier coal-supply problems is that **immobility of inputs** can be an important source of monopsony power. The difficulty for Bell Labs' computer scientists is that they are not perfectly mobile: changing jobs is likely to be costly, and the more costly it is, the less mobile a Bell employee is. Therefore, Bell Labs' monopsony power arises from its employees' immobility. The difficulty for the coal suppliers is that coal is not perfectly mobile: transporting coal from the mine to the place where it is needed is expensive. The farther it must be shipped and the higher are the per mile costs of transporting coal, the more expensive it will be. Therefore coal demanders' monopsony power springs from the immobility of coal.

In both cases, the resource immobility is primarily due to locational considerations familiar from the address models of Chapter 12. If all the economic activity in the world were concentrated at a single point — which we might call the economist's black hole — this type of monopsony power could not arise. Because economic activity does not take place at a single point, however, monopsony power is an important feature of the input market landscape. Locational issues are therefore at least as important in input markets as in output markets.

Monopoly and Specialized Inputs

For more than 40 years, the Harlem Globetrotters have provided a unique brand of entertainment for children of all ages. As we saw in Section 13.8, the Globetrotters illustrate another (but less central) source of monopsony power: the demand by a monopolist for a specialized input. This organization — a virtual monopolist in show-business basketball — demands a specialized input: the "showboat" basketball player. Organizations like the National Basketball Association (NBA) clubs also demand the services of skilled basketball players, but they look for quite different skills. Because only the Globetrotters' organization wants players who specialize in entertainment, the club is a monopsonist in the market for show-business players.

So, too, Dow Chemical is a virtual monopolist in primary magnesium production in the United States. It demands the specialized input magnesium chloride — a salt with no other important chemical use. Because Dow is the only significant demander, it is also a virtual monopsonist in the magnesium chloride input market.

13.10

Monopsonistic Price Discrimination

Let us turn to price discrimination in a monopsonistic market.[5] Knowing how to solve the book vendor's dilemma in Problem 10.5 was the key to solving the coal buyer's dilemma in Problem 13.12 because perfect price discrimination is so similar in monopoly and monopsony. In this section, we will again exploit the similarity between monopolistic and monopsonistic price discrimination as we do a quick treatment of

ordinary monopsonistic price discrimination

ordinary monopsonistic price discrimination.

Suppose that a monopsonist can buy an input from two identifiable groups of suppliers — say, labor from women and men, or from whites and nonwhites. Suppose, too, that the supply functions of these groups are different. How will a profit-maximizing monopsonist exploit this chance to price discriminate? Let us defer the firm's profit-maximizing problem until we have answered a simpler question: What combination of labor from the first group, z_1, and the second group, z_2, will minimize the cost of hiring a fixed amount of labor, say z'?

Recall that we used a similar strategy to solve the monopolist's price-discrimination problem in Section 10.7. The monopsonist in Figure 13.15 will choose z_1 and z_2 so that $MFC(z_1)$ and $MFC(z_2)$ are equal and so that the sum of z_1 and z_2 is z'. At the solution presented in Figure 13.15, the monopsonist buys z_1^* from the first group at the price w_1^*, and z_2^* from the second group at the price w_2^*. We can see why this is the cost-minimizing solution by considering a departure from it. If the monopsonist were to buy 1 unit less from the first group and 1 unit more from the second, for example, its cost would increase because MFC at $z_1^* - 1$ units in the first market (equal to AB in Figure 13.15a) is less than MFC at $z_2^* + 1$ units in the second market (equal to A′B′ in Figure 13.15b).

Again exploiting the obvious correspondence with the discriminating monopolist's profit-maximizing rule, we have solved the discriminating monopsonist's profit-maximizing problem in Figure 13.16. The two marginal factor cost functions in Figures 13.16a and

---

5 For an introduction to the extensive economic literature on discrimination see the entry in *The New Palgrave* by Peter Mueser on "discrimination."

FIGURE 13.15   Discriminatory hiring to minimize costs

To minimize the cost of buying a fixed quantity of the input from two market segments, the firm chooses the two quantities so that MFC is identical in the two market segments. It buys z_1^* at price w_1^* in the first market segment and z_2^* at price w_2^* in the second.

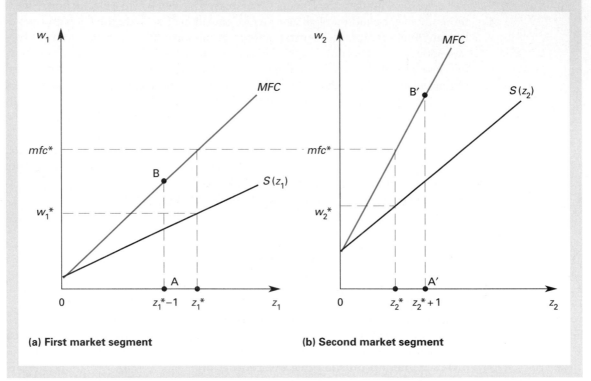

(a) First market segment

(b) Second market segment

13.16b have been horizontally summed to obtain the function labeled ΣMFC in Figure 13.16c, which gives the marginal cost of the input when the monopsonist follows its cost-minimizing rule. To maximize its profit, the monopsonist will buy the input up to the point where ΣMFC intersects MRP at z^* units in Figure 13.16c. We can identify the corresponding prices and quantities in the component submarkets simply by projecting mfc^* from Figure 13.16c into Figures 13.16a and 13.16b. To summarize:

> A profit-maximizing monopsonist will choose aggregate quantity of the input so that aggregate marginal factor cost is equal to marginal revenue product, and it will allocate purchases so that marginal factor cost is identical in all input markets.

In discussing monopoly price discrimination in goods markets, we discovered that the possibility of arbitrage significantly limited the monopolist's ability to price discriminate. For example, if the price of a new car in Vancouver exceeds the price of the same model in Seattle by more than the combined costs of transportation and import duty (soon to be eliminated), arbitragers will begin buying cars in Seattle and selling them in Vancouver. Yet we also found that when the goods are personal services, arbitrage is not possible: parents cannot have their kids buy haircuts for them at the children's price, for example. So, too, when the inputs in resource markets are labor services, arbitrage is once again impossible because employment contracts involve the employer and specific employees: women cannot have men obtain employment for

FIGURE 13.16   **Discriminatory hiring to maximize profit**

To find the profit-maximizing solution, horizontally aggregate MFC_1 and MFC_2 to obtain ΣMFC in (c). The profit-maximizing quantity z^* is the quantity such that ΣMFC is equal to

MRP. Allocate the z^* units to the two market segments so as to equalize MFC in the two segments. That is, buy z_1^* in the first market segment and z_2^* in the second.

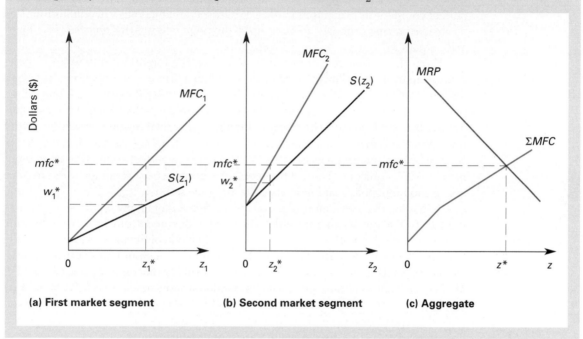

(a) First market segment   **(b) Second market segment**   **(c) Aggregate**

them at the male worker's wage rate. Because arbitrage is difficult in labor markets, we might expect to see significant monopsonistic discrimination.

    Certain conditions must prevail, however, before monopsonistic discrimination in labor markets can occur. First, the market must be characterized by monopsony power. Second, the degree of monopsony power must be different for identifiable groups of workers within that market. Although we will not examine this sort of discrimination in any detail, we can outline the important questions to be asked. First, is the labor market characterized by significant job immobility? For example, are accountants or hair stylists fairly immobile? Second, is one segment of the labor force significantly less mobile than another? For example, are female accountants or hair stylists less mobile than their male counterparts? If the answer to both questions is affirmative and if the less mobile group is paid less, we can tentatively ascribe that differential in wage rates to ordinary monopsonistic discrimination.

    The whole question of discrimination is a hotly debated issue as well as a complex economic problem. Comparable pay for comparable work and affirmative action programs for identifiable minorities are just two of the many policy issues related to labor market discrimination that regularly appear in the headlines. Many theoretical approaches have been proposed to explain this important and difficult problem. For example, Gary Becker (1958) has presented an interesting theory of discrimination that is based not on profit maximization, but on employers' utility maximization. If you are intrigued by other ways to model labor market discrimination, Kenneth Arrow (1972) provides an accessible and stimulating discussion of a number of theoretical approaches.

SUMMARY

This chapter has focused on one of the fundamental problems in economics: the allocation of resources. The results from the first nine sections are summarized in Figure 13.17, where four types of firms are characterized according to their status as either monopolists or perfect competitors in their output markets, and as either monopsonists or perfect competitors in an input market. We learned that in long-run equilibrium, any profit-maximizing firm uses an input up to the point where MRP equals MFC. Thus, MRP equals MFC in each cell of Figure 13.17.

From the perspective of resource allocation, the important differences among firms stem from the following relationships. When a firm is a monopolist in its output market, VMP (value of the marginal product) exceeds MRP because a monopolist's price is greater than its marginal revenue. When a firm is a perfect competitor in its output market, VMP equals MRP because the firm's marginal revenue equals its output price. When a firm is a monopsonist in an input market, MFC (marginal factor cost) exceeds w^e (the equilibrium wage rate). When a firm is a perfect competitor in an input market, MFC equals w^e. These differences arise because perfect competitors are price takers and monopolists and monopsonists are price setters.

The value that consumers place on an additional unit of any input used by a firm is VMP. To find out whether too little of an input is allocated to any firm in equilibrium, we can simply ask if VMP exceeds w^e. If so, then too little of the input is allocated to the firm. In Figure 13.17, VMP does exceed w^e in three of the four types of firms: II, III, and IV. In cell II, $w^e < MFC$ because this type of firm has monopsony power; in cell III, $MRP < VMP$ because this type of firm has monopoly power; and in cell IV, $w^e < MFC$ and $MRP < VMP$ because this type of firm has both monopoly and monopsony power. Only the type of firm in cell I — where $w^e = VMP$, the case of the perfect competitor in both markets — is consistent with Pareto optimality.

FIGURE 13.17　**Resource allocation summarized**

In all four cases, $MFC = MRP$, reflecting profit-maximization. In cell I, $w^e = VMP$, which reflects the efficiency of competitive markets. In cell II, $w^e < VMP$ because the input market is monopsonistic. In cell III, $w^e < VMP$ because the output market is monopolistic. Finally, in cell IV, $w^e < VMP$ because neither the input nor the output market is competitive.

	INPUT MARKET	
	Competitive	Monopsonistic
OUTPUT MARKET — Competitive	$w^e = MFC = MRP = VMP$ I Efficient allocation	$w^e < MFC = MRP = VMP$ II Inefficient allocation
OUTPUT MARKET — Monopolistic	$w^e = MFC = MRP < VMP$ III Inefficient allocation	$w^e < MFC = MRP < VMP$ IV Inefficient allocation

EXERCISES

1. If all input and output markets are competitive, then all inputs are allocated to their most productive uses in competitive equilibrium. Explain. If some input and/or output market is imperfectly competitive, however, then inputs are not allocated to their most valuable uses. Explain.

2. The City Council of Podunk has given Walley the exclusive right to sell Coke at local baseball games. The operation is very simple. Walley buys Coke from the local Coke distributor (who lives next door to Walley) for $0.40 per can and takes his supply of Coke to the ballpark in his picnic cooler. Anyone wanting to buy a Coke walks down to Walley's seat behind home plate and buys it. Since Walley would go to the ballgames even if he did not have the Coke franchise, his only cost in the short run is the $0.40 per can that he pays to buy the Coke. The demand for Coke at a typical ballgame is

$$p = 1.60 - .01y$$

For example, he could sell 100 cans for $0.60 per can, or 150 cans for $0.10 per can.

   a. First, let us focus on the output market. What is Walley's marginal revenue function and what is his marginal cost? What is his profit-maximizing level of output? How much profit does he earn? Construct a graph to illustrate Walley's position in the output market.

   b. Now let us focus on the input market. What is the single costly input? What is the marginal revenue product function? What is the input demand function? How much of the input does Walley buy? If the distributor charged $0.60 per can, how much would he buy? Construct a graph to illustrate Walley's position in the input market.

3. Suppose that a firm that is a perfect competitor in its output market can vary only input Z in the short run and that

$$AP(z) = 100 - z$$

   and

$$MP(z) = 100 - 2z$$

   a. Suppose that the price of the firm's product is $10. What are the firm's marginal and average revenue product functions? What is the firm's short-run demand function for input Z? How much input Z will the firm use when its price is $40? When its price is $60?

   b. Show that the results in a are consistent with the profit-maximizing rule in the firm's output market: produce the level of output where *SMC* is equal to output price.

   c. What is the firm's short-run demand function for input Z when the price of the firm's product is $25? How much input Z will the firm now use when the input price is $40? When the input price is $60?

4. Many countries, states, and provinces have passed "equal pay for equal work" legislation, which is intended to discourage discrimination by forcing firms to pay the same wage to all employees who do the same job. Some jurisdictions have gone even further by passing "equal pay for work of equal value" legislation, which is intended to force firms to pay the same wage to all employees whose work is of equal value, regardless of the job.

   a. Using the model of monopsony discrimination developed in this chapter, discuss the implications of equal pay for equal work.

   b. Using the productivity concepts developed in this chapter, discuss the difficulties involved in implementing "equal pay for work of equal value."

   c. Would either kind of legislation serve a useful economic purpose if all labor markets were competitive?

5. Consider a firm in which each unit of labor produces 1 unit of output that can be sold for $100. The firm faces two different supply functions from groups 1 and 2. The supply functions for the two groups are

$$w_1 = 10 + z_1$$

$$w_2 = z_2$$

   where w_1 and w_2 are wage rates and z_1 and z_2 are quantities of labor supplied.

   a. Assuming that the firm can discriminate, find the firm's profit-maximizing solution and calculate its profit. What wage is paid in each market, and how much labor is hired in each market?

b. Assuming that the firm cannot discriminate, first find its aggregate supply function, and then find the firm's profit-maximizing solution and calculate its profit.

c. Compare your results from a and b. In particular, determine who is better off in a and who is better off in b.

6. Consider a world with only two types of workers, A and B. For example, type A might be blacks (or men) and type B whites (or women). Assume that types A and B both prefer to work with others of their own type. Show that this sort of bigotry is likely to produce firms in which all workers are of the same type. Will it produce wage differentials?

7. Suppose that the demand function for some nonrenewable resource is

$$w_1 = 200 - 2z_1$$

in period 1 and

$$w_2 = 200 - 2z_2$$

in period 2. There are 100 units of the resource to be allocated for use in the two periods, and the interest rate is 50%. Find the competitive equilibrium prices in periods 1 and 2 and the competitive equilibrium allocation to the two periods.

*8. In this chapter, we ignored the possibility of *oligopsony*: the case in which more than one firm has some monopsony power in the same input market. We can alter Problem 13.11 to construct a very simple model of oligopsony to convey the flavor of such problems. Suppose that there are two demanders on the railroad — one at mile 0 and the other at mile 975 — and that the demanders bear the costs of transport. For each demander, marginal revenue product is $200 per ton of coal; otherwise, the setup is as specified in Problem 13.11.

a. Construct a table in which you identify the maximum price that each of the demanders would pay to each of the suppliers for the supplier's ton of coal. For each supplier, note which demander is willing to pay the higher price.

b. Now consider the "game" between the two demanders as they vie to buy the coal offered

by the supplier at mile 550. Suppose that prices must be announced in dollars and cents — $130.75 is a permissible price, but $130.753 is not. Show that the Nash equilibrium price offers are $155.00 for the firm located at mile 0 and $155.01 for the firm located at mile 975. Of course, the supplier sells the ton of coal to the buyer offering the higher price. (You may want to review Bertrand's oligopoly model, discussed in Section 11.16.)

c. Now find the Nash equilibrium prices offered to the nine other suppliers, and compute each demander's profit.

d. Finally, compare the prices that the suppliers receive in this oligopsony with the prices they received in Problem 13.11.

*9. In this exercise, you can explore what is called a *bilateral monopoly*. Firm A is the only demander of input Z, and its marginal revenue product function is

$$MRP(z) = 200 - 2z$$

Firm B is the only supplier of input Z, and its reservation price for each unit of input Z, $R(z)$, is

$$R(z) = z$$

You can think of $R(z)$ as firm B's marginal cost of producing input Z.

a. Suppose first that firm A can choose a price w and that firm B then decides how much input Z to sell to A at A's chosen price. What price maximizes A's profit, and what quantity will B sell to A?

b. Now reverse the exercise. Suppose that B can choose a price and that A then decides how much to sell at B's chosen price. What price maximizes B's profit, and what quantity will A buy at this price?

c. Finally, suppose that firm C were to buy both firms A and B. How much input Z would firm C produce?

*10. The Fraser River Valley is the "breadbasket" of British Columbia. The agriculture in the valley uses relatively little labor, except at harvest time. Much of the harvest labor is supplied by recent immigrants to Canada who live about 40 miles away in Vancouver, who have little or no facility in English, and who do not own cars. The market in harvest labor is mediated by labor brokers.

A labor broker typically owns a truck for transporting laborers and speaks both English and the laborers' language. The broker buys labor at one price w_1 and sells it to farmers at a higher price w_2. Assume that the demand for farm labor from a particular broker is linear and downward sloping, that the supply of labor is linear and upward sloping, and that all of the broker's costs are fixed, or independent of the quantity of labor bought and sold. Find the values of w_1 and w_2 and the quantity of labor bought and sold that maximize the labor broker's profit.

REFERENCES

Arrow, K. 1972. "Models of Job Discrimination," in *Racial Discrimination in Economic Life,* A. H. Pascal (ed.), Lexington, Mass.: D. C. Heath.

Becker, G. 1957. *The Economics of Discrimination*, Chicago: University of Chicago Press.

Dorfman, R. 1987. "Marginal Productivity Theory," in *The New Palgrave: A Dictionary of Economics*, J. Eatwell, M. Milgate, and P. Newman (eds.), London: The Macmillan Press.

Mueser, P. 1987. "Discrimination," in *The New Palgrave: A Dictionary of Economics*, J. Eatwell, M. Milgate, and P. Newman (eds.), London: The Macmillan Press.

The Distribution of Income

Chapter 13 explored how well markets performed their allocational function of directing resources to competing uses. In this chapter, we will consider how well they perform another, equally important function: the distribution of a society's product among its members. By distribution we mean, very loosely, just what share of the national product each person receives. As we turn now to the distributional function of markets, we will be focusing our attention on input markets in a partial equilibrium setting because, in a very real sense, input markets determine the size of everyone's slice of the economic pie.

We all have certain salable input endowments — certain human (labor) resources and nonhuman (property) resources. The input endowments we possess and the prices paid for those inputs in the marketplace, including the prevailing wage rates, are crucial in determining the size of our personal rewards in a market economy. For example, relative shares of the economic pie in a dental office will vary, depending on the going wage rates for different kinds of training and talents: a dentist might be earning $80 per hour, a dental technician $18 per hour, and a dental receptionist $12 per hour. Even for people who are selling resources other than labor, income still depends on the prevailing input prices. For example, one person we know inherited his grandparents' farm in what is now downtown Houston; he enjoys a relatively large claim to society's product because his land is now prime real estate. Another acquaintance inherited his grandparents' once elegant estate in the decaying core of Chicago; he has a comparably smaller claim because his property is worth less in the real estate market.

One unmistakable feature of the price system is that some people get more of the economic pie and others considerably less. In almost any large, cosmopolitan city around the globe, you can encounter people who are super-rich or desperately poor. We can trace these sometimes striking inequalities in personal claims to the national product directly to differences in input prices and input endowments. But are these inequalities in the distribution of wealth and income "right," or just? Let us look more closely at the question of distributive justice.

14.1
Distributive Justice

Economist Kenneth Arrow (1976) has commented that what Aristotle called "distributive justice" was not seen as an issue in earlier, more static societies. These societies, Arrow claims, tended to view the prevailing distribution of material goods as right, either because they reflected the long-familiar status quo or because earthly rewards were viewed as the workings of divine justice. As members of a changing society, however, we cannot simply say that "What is, is just." We recognize that the distribution of wealth and income in modern economies is, in large part, the handiwork of human beings. The social and economic institutions we create significantly affect who is rich and who is poor. Just a few of the many institutions affecting distribution in any modern economy are income taxes, inheritance taxes, gift taxes, welfare, social security, collective bargaining, public housing, zoning, public education, minimum wages, rent controls, and agricultural price supports.

Unfortunately, we have no yardstick like the economic concept of Pareto optimality that lets us judge how well the market system (or any other set of institutions) performs this distributional function. That is, we have no way to assess whether the distribution of wealth and income resulting from market forces is in some sense right or just. Indeed, determining what "justice" means is a *philosophical* rather than an economic issue — and even among philosophers, there is no consensus. Broadly speaking, two opposing approaches to this ethical issue have emerged: the *productivity principle* and the *redistributionist principle*.

The Productivity Principle

productivity
principle

In a nutshell, the **productivity principle** asserts that each of us ought to receive the monetary equivalent of what we have individually produced from our human resources (or labor) and our nonhuman resources (or property). If we ignore property and look only at labor, the appeal of the productivity principle is clear: it implies that you should reap what you have sown. In other words, the harder you work, the more you will produce — and the larger your market reward ought to be.

product-
exhaustion
criterion

Although, as economists, we cannot agree or disagree with this view, we can clarify the core concept of the productivity principle: the meaning of productivity itself. If it is to serve as a distributional principle, any definition of productivity must fulfill the **product-exhaustion criterion**. If the owners of all resources receive what their resources produce, then the individual shares of the total product pie must add up to 1. If the sum were less than 1, there would be leftover product that no one had produced; if the sum were greater than 1, there would be too little product to go around.

Surprisingly, a meaning that satisfies the product-exhaustion criterion in any general set of circumstances is not easy to find. However, we can find one set of circumstances (the case in which all production functions exhibit constant returns to scale) and one definition of productivity (the value of the marginal product) that satisfy the criterion. In other words, if all production functions exhibit constant returns to scale, then paying the owners of each input the value of the input's marginal product will exhaust (exactly use up) what we will call the value of the total product: the sum of all (output) prices multiplied by the quantities produced.

Furthermore, there is a set of institutions (the institutions of perfect competition) that guarantees that the owners of each input do, in fact, receive the value of the input's marginal product in these circumstances. Why? Recall that in Section 13.7, we discovered that when every input and output market in an economy is perfectly competitive, the owners of each input are paid the value of the input's marginal product.

Product Exhaustion

Let us see why this pattern of input payments just equals (exhausts) the value of the total product. We will look at a firm in long-run competitive equilibrium that uses just two inputs and is producing, say, y^* units of output. If the firm's input bundle is (z_1^*, z_2^*) and if p and (w_1, w_2) are the competitive equilibrium output and input prices, respectively, we want to show that

$$py^* = w_1 z_1^* + w_2 z_2^*$$

The left side is the value of the firm's output, and the right is the sum of the firm's input payments. If, at the level of the firm, the product is just used up, the two sides must be identical. We can rewrite the product-exhaustion requirement as

$$p = (w_1 z_1{}^* + w_2 z_2{}^*)/y^* = LAC(y^*)$$

The second equality follows from the definition of long-run average cost as total cost divided by output. We know from Section 9.7 that price is equal to minimum long-run average cost for any firm in long-run competitive equilibrium. The product-exhaustion criterion is therefore satisfied in a competitive equilibrium.

But just where did the condition of constant returns to scale enter this argument? In long-run competitive equilibrium, each firm is at the bottom of its U-shaped long-run average cost function, operating at the efficient scale of production. As we discovered in Section 8.3, at this level of output the firm experiences constant returns to scale. Therefore, constant returns to scale entered the picture when we observed that p is equal to $LAC(y^*)$ for a firm in long-run competitive equilibrium.

Let us view this result from a slightly different perspective. We have found a definition of productivity that can serve as a principle of distribution because this definition satisfies the product-exhaustion criterion. This definition then raises an important normative question: Is payment in accordance with the value of the marginal product an ethically appealing principle of distributive justice? As economists, we cannot answer this question, but we will suggest two thought experiments that are useful in trying to answer it. In both experiments, we will suppose that the economy produces just one good **endowment** and then examine how output of that good responds to a change in the **endowment** of an input — that is, in the total amount of an input available in an economy.

Thought Experiments for the Productivity Principle

Imagine an economy in a competitive equilibrium and consider what happens to the total output of the economy if some person — let us call her Rose — simply disappears, taking her resource endowment — including her labor and any other resources she owns — out of the economy. Total output will decrease (approximately) by the amount of Rose's income, since she must have been receiving as income the marginal contribution to the total product of her labor and her other resources. This result follows from the fact that each unit of each input is paid its marginal product in competitive equilibrium. Notice that this exercise, in which there is a *marginal change* in the economy's input endowment, seems to be consistent with the spirit of the productivity principle: Rose seems to have received just what she produced.

Now let us try a second experiment in which there is a *nonmarginal change* in the economy's input endowment. For simplicity, we will assume that the economy has only two resources (or inputs) and produces only one product. We will also assume that the specific production function below describes the entire economy's technology:

$$y = 240(z_1 z_2)^{1/2}$$

(Note, however, that the general nature of the results does not depend on any particular production function.)

The marginal product functions associated with this production function are[1]

---

1 We can use calculus to find these marginal product functions. To get MP_1, partially differentiate $240(z_1 z_2)^{1/2}$ with respect to z_1. To get MP_2, partially differentiate with respect to z_2.

$$MP_1 = 120(z_2/z_1)^{1/2}$$

$$MP_2 = 120(z_1/z_2)^{1/2}$$

Suppose that initially this economy's resource endowment consists of 64 units of input 1 and 36 units of input 2. Using this production function, we can calculate that the economy's total output is 11,520 units, and the competitive equilibrium input prices are $w_1 = 90$ and $w_2 = 160$. (Since this economy produces only one product, the unit for input prices is the unit in which output is measured.) Now suppose that the quantity of input 2 increases from 36 to 100, while the quantity of input 1 remains at 64. The total output then rises from 11,520 to 19,200, for an increase of 7,680 units. Notice, too, what happens to input prices: w_1 increases from 90 to 150, and w_2 falls from 160 to 96.

What accounts for (or produces) the 7,680-unit increase in output? Because only the quantity of input 2 changed, it seems sensible to attribute the increased output to the 74 additional units of input 2. Notice, however, that these 74 units are paid only 7,104 (74×96) units — not the 7,680 units they apparently have produced. Thus, in this thought experiment, where the change in an economy's resource endowment is a nonmarginal change, marginal product does not seem to be a reasonable measure of productivity, because when the added inputs are paid their marginal product, they do not capture all of the added output.

Notice, too, that once the endowment of input 2 increases, the change in input prices is dramatic. The price paid per unit of input 2 drops sharply, while the price paid per unit of input 1 soars. If we want to argue that marginal productivity actually captures the spirit of the productivity principle — that one should reap what one has sown — we must be prepared to accept that the productivity of each of the original 36 units of input 2 decreased from 160 to 96 and that the productivity of each of the original 64 units of input 1 increased from 90 to 150, solely as a result of the increase in the endowment of input 2.

Input Prices and Scarcity

The changes in input prices in the second thought experiment reflect a fundamental reality of the market system: *markets reward scarcity*. As input 1 became scarcer relative to input 2, the price paid per unit went up. This reward to scarcity serves an allocational function by directing resources to the uses in which their marginal productivities are greatest. Think of tennis great Steffi Graf. At least two of her personal characteristics are noteworthy: 1. she is abundantly endowed with athletic talent, and 2. she is a very wealthy person. Most economists would consider her wealth to be a reward for having a scarce natural talent. They are not implying that Graf is rewarded without having worked hard on her game. Rather, they are suggesting that no matter how hard the vast majority of us worked at tennis, we could not put together a game comparable to hers.

The size of any individual's claim on the national product therefore depends on how scarce his or her salable talents and resources are relative to the whole society's endowment of resources. If all of us were as talented at tennis as Graf, none of us — including Steffi Graf — would receive a large market reward for it. This insight parallels our earlier lesson from the ticket model in Chapter 9: the initial distribution of resources is crucial in determining the size of personal rewards in a market economy. The bigger our initial share of scarce personal or property endowments, the bigger will be our slice of the economic pie.

The Redistributionist Principle

redistributionist
principle

The **redistributionist principle** is at odds with the productivity principle. Redistributionists find significant economic inequalities ethically unacceptable and argue that a more nearly equitable distribution ought to be a social objective. Simply put, they say that wealth and income in the real world should be redistributed from the rich to the poor. The most extreme version of this position is philosopher John Rawls's **difference principle**. Taking equality as a point of reference, Rawls (1971) argues that the only acceptable inequality is one that improves the lot of the worst-off member of society. If we compare all possible distributions of wealth and pinpoint the worst-off member of a society in each distribution, the difference principle asserts that the preferred distribution is the one in which the wealth of the poorest member is largest.

difference principle

But how do redistributionists conclude that distributive justice demands less inequality? They begin by observing the difficulties in thinking objectively about distribution. For example, they note that taking from the rich and giving to the poor is not nearly as popular among wealthy people as it is among the impoverished. In an attempt to achieve an ethical standard free of personal bias, redistributionists posit a hypothetical circumstance called the **original position**. Arrow, a contemporary proponent of the redistributionist view, has summarized the philosophical arguments for reducing inequality:

original position

> The basic presupposition is that any moral judgment must be impersonal. The individual making the judgment cannot take his own situation into account. To the extent that he does, the judgment is one of his own interests and cannot be accounted a moral judgment. A principle of justice or morality is, by its nature, universalizable: an individual cannot defend an allocation of goods to himself unless others benefit similarly from this policy.
>
> The argument has been given modern form in the notion of the "original position" as developed by the economists William Vickery and John Harsanyi and the philosopher John Rawls. To make concrete the concept of an impersonal judgment, they introduce the fiction of an "original position," in which each individual knows all the possible conditions he or she can be in the society but does not know which particular condition he himself will have. The term "condition" refers to both inherent personal endowment, the individual's capacities and values, and to the social rewards to be received. In the original position, we may imagine the members of the society considering alternative social arrangements for resource allocation. Because of the symmetry of their positions, all would agree in their preferences; hence, they would arrive at a mutually beneficial contract.
>
> The contract would be in effect an arrangement for mutual insurance and have the same advantages. If a group of individuals have the same uncertain prospects, they will each prefer a situation in which beforehand they agree to share their fortunes; those who gain relatively will give up some of their winnings to those who lose relatively. This argument, to be sure, presupposes that individuals may be presumed averse to the bearing of risks; but this is surely a safe assumption.
>
> Thus, the "original position" argument shows that the impersonality which characterizes moral judgment implies that the content of that judgment will favor an equalization of outcomes. There is considerable room for differences in the precise interpretation of equality... But I would judge that the similarities are much more important than the differences; all tend to lead to the moral obligation to redistribute income and other goods more equally. (1976, 14–5)

The main tenet of the redistributionist principle, then, is that the "insurance contract" resulting from the original-position experiment leads to a more equal distribution of income as a moral principle. Try the following problem to check your understanding of this approach to distributive justice.

PROBLEM 14.1

Put yourself into the following original position. Suppose that tomorrow you will be one of two people, A or B, in a very simple two-person economy that has a fixed endowment of one good, manna. You must choose today how the manna is to be apportioned out between A and B tomorrow, but all you know is this: it is equally probable that you will be A or B. A number R greater than 0 but less than 1 is A's share of manna, and $1 - R$ is B's share. What value of R would you choose?

If you have read the material on expected utility in Chapter 5, try the following problem, designed to aid your understanding of Arrow's remarks about risk, insurance, and distribution.

PROBLEM 14.2

Show that a risk-averse person in the original position described in the previous problem, believing that he or she will be either A or B with equal probability, will choose R equal to 1/2. Notice that if both A and B are risk-averse, they will both choose R equal to 1/2. In the original position, then, this society of two would unanimously agree on a 50/50 split.

We should underline the fact that this sort of mental experiment does not inevitably lead to the conclusion that equality is necessary for distributive justice. To see why not, let us consider another two-person economy. In the first period, A is alive; in the second period, B is alive. In each period, the endowment of manna is 2 units. In period 1, A can either eat both units of manna or eat one and plant the other. If A eats both, B will have just 2 units of manna in period 2. If A eats just 1 unit, however, the planted manna will triple, so that B will have a total of 5 units in period 2. If you do not know whether you will be A or B, which scheme would you choose in the original position: A gets 1 unit and B gets 5, or A gets 2 units and B gets 2? If you are not too risk-averse, you will choose the first; if you are very risk-averse, you will choose the second. From this, we see that Rawls's difference principle can be justified on the assumption that people are completely risk-averse.

As we have said, economists have no special expertise on the ethics of distribution and cannot comment on the validity of the redistributionist stance. Nevertheless, if the redistributionist position is accepted as a normative objective, economists can say a great deal about the implication of particular schemes for achieving redistribution.

Just looking at the range and variety of institutions aimed at redistribution in modern economies, it seems fair to say that most people do not believe that the distribution resulting from pure market institutions is perfectly just. Instead, most societies devise means for redistributing wealth and income from the wealthier to the poorer members of society. In the following sections, we will analyze a range of possible redistributive institutions. As you will see, many of these schemes inevitably result in a conflict between the demands of redistribution (or equity) and of efficiency. The challenge, therefore, is to design economic institutions that achieve the desired redistribution while minimizing the adverse consequences in terms of efficiency.

14.2

Minimum-Wage Legislation

minimum-wage
legislation

One of the ever-present features of Western economies is **minimum-wage legislation** designed to provide a "living wage" to workers whose wage rate would otherwise be below a legally designated minimum. In the United States, for instance, the *Fair Labor Standards Act* of 1938 imposed a minimum wage of $0.25 per hour in specified industries. Periodic updates of the act since 1938 have increased the minimum wage and expanded the number of industries it governs. The objective of the U.S. law — and of similar schemes elsewhere — clearly is to redistribute income to less well-paid members of society.

Yet a *Time* magazine article entitled "The Incredible Shrinking Paycheck" posed the key question: "Would raising the minimum wage help or hurt the working poor?" (August 1, 1988, 36). In other words, is the objective of redistribution — helping the working poor — invariably realized under minimum-wage schemes? Are workers in the designated industries actually better off once a minimum wage is put in effect? And whose income falls to make up for the rise in minimum-wage earners' incomes? Is inefficiency invariably an unfortunate side effect of minimum-wage laws?

As you will see, the answers depend on whether labor markets are perfectly competitive or monopsonistic. In a perfectly competitive labor market, an effective minimum wage creates unemployment or underemployment; redistributes income to workers from the buyers of the goods produced in minimum-wage-designated industries; and invariably creates inefficiency. By contrast, in monopsonistic labor markets, a minimum wage is likely to increase employment, redistribute money from monopsonistic firms to their employees, and offset some of the inefficiency associated with monopsony.

To analyze the implications of a minimum wage in these two market settings — perfectly competitive and monopsonistic — we will think of the labor-supply function as an aggregation of the various reservation wages of workers from lowest to highest. We can then interpret each worker's reservation wage as the value of his or her labor in the best alternative use: work in some other market, work at home, or leisure. For convenience, we will assume that the first of these alternatives — work in some other market — is the best. Although this supply function is actually a series of vertical segments ascending from left to right, we will approximate it by a smooth curve, such as the supply function in Figure 14.1. We will also assume that all other labor markets and all output markets are perfectly competitive. Given this assumption, for any labor market in equilibrium, the wage rate will be equal to the value of the marginal product.

Competitive Labor Markets

Figure 14.1 presents the basic implications of minimum-wage legislation in a competitive labor market. Let us look at what happens before and after a minimum-wage law is introduced. Before the minimum-wage legislation is introduced, the competitive equilibrium in this market is at point E in Figure 14.1, where 270 workers are employed at a wage rate of $5 per hour. Bringing in a minimum-wage law will change the pre-legislation equilibrium at point E *only* if it is higher than the competitive equilibrium wage of $5 per hour. If the minimum wage is higher than the competitive equilibrium wage, then the post-legislation equilibrium will shift. If the minimum wage is $6 per hour, for example, the post-legislation equilibrium shifts to point E′, where just 130 workers are employed.

We can see from Figure 14.1 that one result of the legislation is inefficiency. Why? At the minimum-wage equilibrium at point E′, the value of the marginal product of an

FIGURE 14.1 Minimum-wage legislation in a competitive labor market

The competitive equilibrium is at point E. Given the minimum wage rate of $6, the equilibrium shifts to E'. The wage rate rises from $5 to $6, employment falls from 270 to 130, and labor is in excess supply because 370 people want to work at the $6 wage rate but only 130 jobs are available.

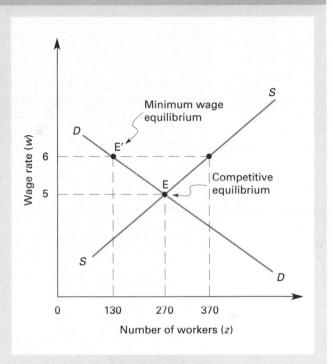

additional employee — equal to the minimum wage — is higher than the reservation wage at 130 workers on the supply function. In other words, some labor that could have been put to its most productive use in this industry will not be hired.

We can also see that labor is in excess supply at the minimum wage equilibrium at point E' because 370 workers would like to be employed at this wage rate, but only 130 will be hired. It is tempting to interpret this excess supply as unemployment. However, the unemployment created by the minimum wage will almost certainly be less than (370 − 130) or 240 workers. We can decompose the excess supply as follows:

$$370 - 130 = (370 - 270) + (270 - 130)$$

The first term in the decomposition — (370 − 270) or 100 — is the added supply of labor (over and above 270) that would be forthcoming at a wage of $6 if employment were freely available at this wage. Yet it is unlikely that this component of excess supply will actually materialize as unemployment. We know that the 100 workers in this group prefer their best alternative option to employment in this market at the $5 competitive equilibrium wage rate since their reservation wages exceed $5 per hour. Because job openings are few and far between, these workers are not likely to give up their alternative options to look for jobs in this market once the $6 minimum wage is introduced. In all likelihood, they will stay put rather than risk unemployment.

The second term in the decomposition — (270 − 130) or 140 — is the number of workers initially employed at the competitive equilibrium who are laid off once the minimum-wage law is introduced. Even these workers may or may not show up among the unemployed. If they have no other options, they may continue to look for jobs at the

under-
employment

higher, minimum wage rate of $6. In this case, they will be unemployed. On the other hand, they may look for less attractive employment in some other industry. In this case, they will instead experience **underemployment**, in the sense that they accept jobs in which the value of their marginal product is less than the competitive equilibrium wage of $5 per hour. This is just another indication that the minimum-wage equilibrium is inefficient: labor services are not allocated to their most productive uses.

In a competitive market, inefficiency is a necessary by-product of an effective minimum-wage law. As labor services are no longer put to their most productive uses, either unemployment or underemployment will signal that inefficiency.

From the perspective of efficiency, then, minimum-wage legislation in competitive markets is unsatisfactory. Nor is the legislation entirely satisfactory from a redistributional perspective. Even though the workers who manage to keep their jobs are better off, laid-off workers are clearly worse off. Moreover, the goods produced by firms employing minimum-wage labor will cost more. In effect, this means that income is redistributed from the buyers of those goods to the minimum-wage workers. Are these buyers the ones who ought to bear the burden of redistribution? Without more information, we cannot answer the question.

> ### PROBLEM 14.3
>
> Some people argue that minimum-wage legislation encourages discrimination in hiring. Can you make a supporting argument? Hint: Contrast the employer's costs of discriminating when minimum-wage legislation is and is not in effect.

Monopsonistic Labor Markets

The implications of minimum-wage legislation are very different in monopsonistic markets. Why? Notice that once a minimum wage law is brought in, the monopsonist's marginal factor cost function changes. Let w' denote the minimum wage rate and z denote the number of workers employed in this market. The monopsonist's prelegislation marginal factor cost function is the line DBC in Figure 14.2. Once the minimum wage is introduced, however, its marginal factor cost function changes: it is now composed of the two line segments w'A and BC. If this monopsonist hires an amount of labor less than or equal to z', its marginal factor cost is the minimum wage w'. If it hires beyond that point, its marginal factor cost is segment BC of its original marginal factor cost function because it can hire additional workers only at a wage higher than w'. In Problem 14.4, you can discover the most intriguing implications of a minimum-wage scheme in a monopsonistic labor market.

> ### PROBLEM 14.4
>
> Figure 14.3 illustrates the standard monopsony solution: the monopsonist employs z^* units of labor at a wage rate of w^*. First, show that if the minimum wage is higher than w^* but less than w''' in Figure 14.3, the monopsonist will increase employment. In other words, show that a minimum wage can actually reduce the inefficiency associated with monopsony by inducing the monopsonist to hire more labor. Second, identify the minimum-wage rate in Figure 14.3 that completely eliminates monopsonistic inefficiency. Finally, show that any minimum wage higher than w'''

FIGURE 14.2 Minimum wage and a monopsonist's marginal factor cost

DAS is the supply function and DBC is the ordinary marginal factor cost function. Given the minimum wage w', the monopsonist's marginal factor cost function is composed of the two green segments w'A and BC.

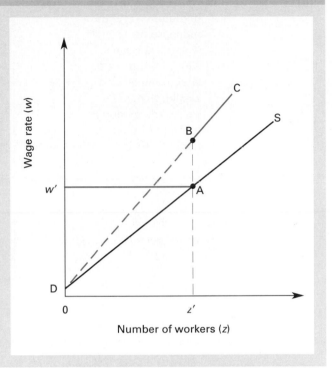

prompts the monopsonist to employ fewer than z^* units of labor. In other words, if the minimum wage is too high, it can increase inefficiency, an increase signaled by reduced employment in the industry.

As you discovered in Problem 14.4, minimum-wage legislation can promote both redistribution and efficiency in a monopsonistic labor market. In fact, if the minimum wage is cleverly chosen, monopsonistic inefficiency can be totally eliminated.

Let us look more closely at the redistributional aspects of the problem in a monopsonistic labor market. Does a minimum wage actually increase workers' incomes? The answer is a carefully qualified yes. As long as the minimum wage is not higher than w''' in Figure 14.3, some workers in the industry will be better off and none worse off. Why? At any minimum wage at or below w^*, the status quo prevails — and legislation is an empty gesture. At any minimum wage rate above w^* but below w''', workers hired before the introduction of the minimum wage will be paid more, and new workers will be hired at the new (minimum) wage rate. If the rate is w''', no new workers will be hired, but existing workers will be paid more. In any of these cases, the workers' increase in income is accomplished largely at the expense of the monopsonist. Is the monopsonist the one who ought to bear the burden of this redistribution? Again, the answer is not obvious.

The attractiveness of minimum-wage legislation thus depends on whether labor markets are competitive or monopsonistic. Empirical evidence suggests that labor markets covered by minimum-wage legislation are essentially competitive. This suggests that such legislation is problematical. Workers who remain employed are better off. It

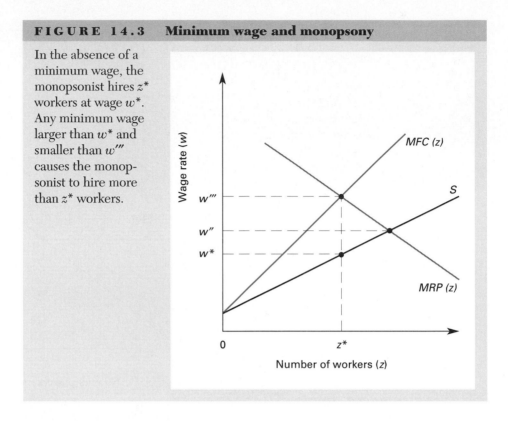

FIGURE 14.3   Minimum wage and monopsony

In the absence of a minimum wage, the monopsonist hires z^* workers at wage w^*. Any minimum wage larger than w^* and smaller than w''' causes the monopsonist to hire more than z^* workers.

is not clear at whose expense this gain is made, however, because we do not know who is footing the bill. Furthermore, by creating unemployment or underemployment, the legislation will hurt some of the people it was intended to help.

Union Wage Rates: Some Analogous Issues

Many people hold strong opinions about unions: they either hate them or love them. Although analyzing the economic consequences of unionization objectively is not easy, we can make a move in that direction by adapting our minimum-wage analysis to apply to union wage rates. In Problem 14.5, you need only reinterpret the minimum wage rate as a union wage rate, because — like a minimum wage — a union wage rate is just
wage floor   another **wage floor**. It sets the minimum wage paid in the unionized industry.

> ### PROBLEM 14.5
>
> What are the redistributional and efficiency implications of a labor union with the power to negotiate a wage rate in a competitive labor market? In a monopsonistic labor market?

> ### PROBLEM 14.6
>
> A *hiring hall* is common in unionized construction trades and elsewhere. Traditionally, the union member who has been unemployed the longest

gets the first available job. The hiring hall thus serves to distribute employment (and unemployment) among union members. If such a union has a fixed membership and (for convenience) a completely wage-inelastic, or vertical, supply function, what is the wage rate that the union would prefer? Hint: Consider the elasticity of demand and also consider the probability of being unemployed.

PROBLEM 14.7

Under a *seniority rule*, if a unionized job is eliminated, the union member most recently hired is laid off. Will a union with a seniority rule demand a higher wage than one without it? Assume that in the absence of a seniority rule, each member has the same probability of being laid off if the union-negotiated wage dictates a drop in employment. Hint: How does the private interest of a member change as his or her seniority changes?

14.3
Wage Floors in a Two-Sector Model

We can explore more fully the implications of a wage floor, such as a union wage or a minimum wage, by concentrating on a labor market divided into two sectors — say, a union (or minimum-wage-regulated) sector and a nonunion (or non-minimum-wage-regulated) sector. The market might be the construction industry, for instance, in which some workers are unionized and others are not. To keep this model simple, we will assume that a total of 100 workers are looking for jobs in these two sectors and that, in the absence of a wage floor, workers are perfectly mobile between the two sectors.

First, we will identify the competitive equilibrium wage and the allocation of the fixed supply of labor to the two sectors as a point of reference. All four quadrants in Figure 14.4 share an origin at the center of the figure. The arrows at the ends of the axes indicate the direction in which any variable is increasing. The labor demand functions for sectors 1 and 2 are shown in quadrants I and II. (Notice that in quadrant II, z_2 increases from right to left along the z_2 axis.) The line in quadrant III labeled $100 = z_1 + z_2$ tells us all the possible allocations of the 100 workers to the two sectors. For example, at point A on this line, 35 workers are allocated to sector 1 and 65 workers to sector 2. The line $z_1 = z_1$ in quadrant IV allows us to project values of z_1 from quadrant III into quadrant I, and vice versa.

The competitive equilibrium is the allocation where the wage rates are identical in both sectors. Why? If the wage rates in the two sectors were different, all workers would look for work in the sector with the higher wage rate. The allocation that does the trick is at point A in quadrant III where the wage rate in both sectors is $9 per hour and where 35 workers are employed in sector 1 and 65 workers in sector 2. (You should check to see that all the allocations to the right (left) of A imply that the wage in sector 1 will be less than (greater than) the wage in sector 2.)

The Underemployment Equilibrium

Now suppose that a wage floor — say, a union wage of $12 per hour — is imposed in sector 1. If we set aside the possibility of unemployment for the moment and concentrate on underemployment, we can easily identify the resulting wage floor equilibrium. At the $12 wage rate, only 20 workers will find jobs in sector 1. Projecting this value into quadrant III to point B, we discover that 80 workers will be hired in sector 2 and that the wage rate in sector 2 will fall from $9 to $6 per hour. In this two-sector model, then, imposing a wage floor means that some workers are reallocated from sector 1 to sector 2 and that, as a result, the wage rate in sector 2 will fall. Because $6 per hour is less than the competitive equilibrium wage of $9 per hour, we know that workers are not allocated to their most productive jobs: the wage floor results in an equilibrium with underemployment.

The Unemployment Equilibrium

Now let us reintroduce the possibility of unemployment by slightly modifying the wage-floor model in Figure 14.4. The crucial factor in determining the effect of wage floors on unemployment is what kind of institution governs the allocation of employment in the high-wage sector. The following model can be applied to any wage floor, including minimum wages. However, we will talk here in terms of a labor market characterized by unionized and nonunionized sectors, and we will assume that the governing

FIGURE 14.4 A wage floor in the two-sector model of the labor market

Any point on the line $100 = z_1 + z_2$ in quadrant III is an allocation of the 100 workers seeking jobs in sectors 1 and 2. In competitive equilibrium, the wage rate in the two sectors will be identical. The competitive equilibrium allocation at point A in quadrant III produces a $9 wage rate in both sectors. Imposing a wage floor of $12 in sector 1 forces 15 sector-1 workers into sector 2, depressing the wage rate in sector 2 to $6.

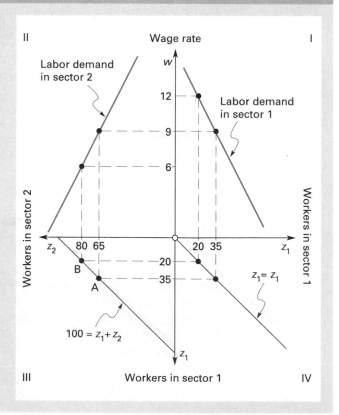

institution is what East Coast dock workers used to call the *shape-up*. In the shape-up, the union members all turned up at a certain time each day, and a union official picked the members who were to work that day from the group.

Let us assume that dock workers were free to seek work in either of two sectors. In other words, they could join the dock workers' union and take part in the union shape-up in sector 1, or they could look for work in the nonunionized sector 2. We will denote the number of dock workers looking for jobs in the union shape-up in sector 1 by z_1 and the number looking for jobs in the nonunionized sector 2 by z_2. The institution of the shape-up (like the hiring hall in Problem 14.6) means that the available employment in sector 1 — or 20 jobs at the union wage of $12 per hour in Figure 14.5 — is shared out among all the union members. If we assume that the work is shared equally, then the proportion of time that any union member will be employed is just the number of jobs divided by the number of union members, $20/z_1$. The expected wage is therefore just the union wage of $12 per hour multiplied by $20/z_1$, or $240/z_1$.

Notice that Figure 14.5 is identical to Figure 14.4 in all but one respect. In quadrant I, we have plotted — not the demand for labor in sector 1 — but the expected wage rate in sector 1, $240/z_1$. Notice, too, that the expected wage relationship passes through point G in quadrant I because when 20 union workers are looking for jobs in the shape-up, each worker is employed full-time at the union wage of $12 per hour.

Now let us identify the equilibrium in Figure 14.5. (For purposes of comparison we have included the underemployment equilibrium from Figure 14.4 at point B in quadrant

FIGURE 14.5 Wage floors and search unemployment in a two-sector model

When a $12 wage floor is imposed in sector 1, 20 workers are hired. The expected wage of a job searcher in this sector is plotted in quadrant I. In equilibrium, the expected wage is identical in the two sectors. The equilibrium allocation at point C in quandrant III produces an $8 wage rate in sector 2 and an $8 expected wage rate in sector 1. With 30 searchers in sector 1 and only 20 jobs, the $12 wage floor creates search unemployment u equal to 10 workers.

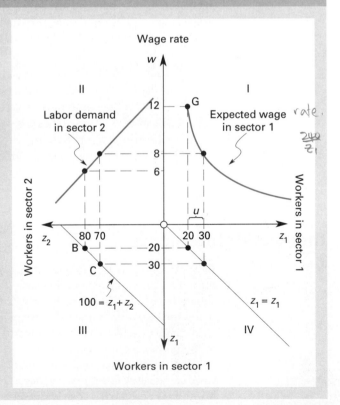

III.) To find the equilibrium allocation, let us suppose that dock workers continue to join the union until the expected wage in unionized sector 1 is equal to the wage in nonunionized sector 2. As you can see by trying out alternative allocations, the equilibrium allocation is at point C in quadrant III, where the expected wage in both sectors is $8 per hour.

In the equilibrium at point C, 30 unionized workers in sector 1 are chasing 20 union jobs paying $12 an hour. As we said, because these unionized workers split the available work equally, the expected wage in sector 1 is 240/30 or $8 an hour. As you can see from Figure 14.5, there is unemployment in sector 1 equal to the distance marked *u* in quadrant I — the equivalent of 10 full-time workers. And again in the equilibrium at point C, 70 nonunion workers in sector 2 are employed full-time at $8 an hour. By comparison, in the equilibrium in the underemployment model of Figure 14.4 (reproduced at point B in Figure 14.5), 80 nonunion workers in sector 2 are employed at $6 an hour. It is necessarily the case that the equilibrium wage rate in sector 2 of the preceding underemployment model is lower that the equilibrium wage rate in sector 2 of this unemployment model. Why? Because in this unemployment model some nonunionized workers will leave sector 2 to chase union jobs in the sector-1 shape-up, and, as a result, the smaller number of nonunionized workers remaining in sector 2 will earn a higher wage.

Notice that the equilibrium wage of $8 in this unemployment model happens to be less than the competitive equilibrium wage rate of $9 at point A in Figure 14.4. However, this is not always the case. As you may want to show, under different market conditions the equilibrium wage rate in this unemployment model may be either lower or higher than the competitive equilibrium wage rate. If it is higher, all workers are better off with the union wage floor; if it is lower, all workers are worse off with the union wage floor.

Two sources of inefficiency arise in this unemployment equilibrium. First, there is unemployment equal to the distance *u* in quadrant I of Figure 14.5. Second, the allocation of workers who are employed is inefficient because the union wage floor exceeds the equilibrium wage rate. In other words, the equilibrium in the unemployment model is characterized by both unemployment and underemployment.

> **PROBLEM 14.8**
>
> Michael Todaro (1969) used a two-sector model very much like this one to explain the shantytowns that lie around the perimeters of most large African cities. These cities are peopled by migrants from the agricultural sector who hope to find high-wage employment in the urban economy. Reinterpret our two-sector model to discover Todaro's explanation.

Income Maintenance

Despite serious disagreement among people living in economically developed societies about how income and wealth should be distributed, most agree that no one should have to live in abject poverty. Given that providing some minimum standard of living for everyone is a widely accepted social objective, what institutional arrangement can best achieve it? In other words, what institution is best for transferring income to the poorer members of society?

In the last section, we saw that there were difficulties associated with using a minimum wage law as a way to ensure everyone a "living wage." In this section, we will explore three institutions designed to transfer income directly to the poor. The first of these transfer

efficient transfer
mechanism

topping-up
mechanism

negative income
tax

mechanisms is an ideal (but impracticable) income-maintenance institution that is compatible with both redistributional and efficiency objectives. We will call it the **efficient transfer mechanism**. It serves as a benchmark against which to assess the following two more practical but problematical transfer mechanisms. The first of these is a stylized version of the standard welfare system in developed countries that we will call the **topping-up mechanism**. As you will discover, this transfer mechanism is seriously incompatible with efficiency. The second is a combination of the efficient transfer mechanism and the topping-up mechanism, sometimes called a **negative income tax**. As you will see, it at least moderates the gross inefficiency associated with the standard welfare system.

The Efficient Transfer Mechanism

utility-
maintenance
mechanism

To an economist, the words "minimum standard of living" can be directly translated into economic terms as "minimum level of utility." The first transfer mechanism we will explore is concerned, then, not with an income-maintenance program but with a **utility-maintenance mechanism**. This transfer of income allows someone who is below a socially designated minimum level of utility to attain that target indifference curve. Consider the target indifference curve in Figure 14.6, where x_1 is hours of leisure and x_2 is income (a composite commodity). Suppose, too, that the person who is a potential recipient of the income transfer has no access to income other than the opportunity to work at wage rate w. So that we can interpret w as the value of the recipient's marginal product, we will assume that the economy is perfectly competitive.

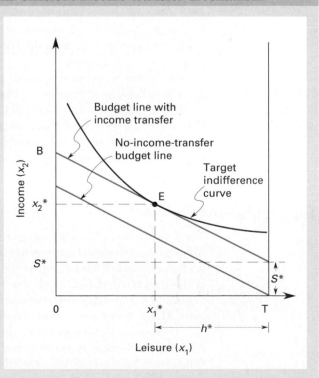

FIGURE 14.6   An efficient income-transfer mechanism

In the absence of any income transfer, this person's budget line does not permit him or her to reach the target indifference curve. The unconditional income transfer S^* both allows this person to attain the target indifference curve and is efficient because *MRS* in the equilibrium at point E is equal to the wage rate.

When there is no income transfer, the potential recipient's opportunities are determined by the budget line $x_2 + wx_1 = wT$, where T is the total time available. Notice that here we can interpret w as the price of leisure, just as we did in Section 4.5. Because this budget line lies below the target indifference curve in Figure 14.6, some social action is needed to boost this person onto the target indifference curve.

Let us look at a scheme that is ideal, in the sense that it both achieves the necessary redistribution and is consistent with efficiency. The single point on the target indifference curve consistent with efficiency is at point E in Figure 14.6, where MRS is equal to w. If this person is given an unconditional transfer of income (a no-strings-attached gift) just large enough to attain the target indifference curve, then he or she will choose the Pareto-optimal combination of income and leisure. Point E will then be the recipient's utility-maximizing combination. Given the appropriate transfer — equal to S^* in Figure 14.6 — the recipient will work h^* hours, enjoy x_1^* hours of leisure, and have income x_2^*. An unconditional lump-sum transfer of income therefore both accomplishes the mandated redistribution and is efficient.

The lump-sum transfer mechanism is ideal in yet another sense. As you will see in Problem 14.9, the transfer S^* is the smallest possible transfer that will allow this person to achieve the target indifference curve.

PROBLEM 14.9

To show that S^* is the minimum transfer, first reproduce Figure 14.6 on the top half of a sheet of paper. Next, construct a diagram on the bottom half in which you calculate for every value of x_1 the amount of income needed in addition to earned income to attain the target indifference curve.

Unfortunately, even though the lump-sum mechanism is efficient, it is not practical. First, we have no systematic way of choosing a target indifference curve for each person. Second, even if we had a way to do it, we would still face the overwhelming task of identifying everyone's individual preferences and everyone's budget line in order to pinpoint subsidy recipients.

income-
maintenance
program

As a result, maintenance policies are usually formulated in terms of target levels of income rather than utility: they are **income-maintenance programs**. The object of an income-maintenance scheme is to raise the income of anyone below a targeted level up to that level. In all practical income-maintenance schemes, the amount of the income transfer is conditional upon the amount of the recipient's earned income. As you will see, the conditional nature of these transfers creates a conflict between efficiency and distribution (or equity).

Topping Up and Welfare

The most pervasive conditional transfer mechanism is the familiar welfare system. Although real-world welfare systems are many and diverse, an essential feature of many is a *topping-up mechanism*, where the subsidy is just large enough to put the recipient at the mandated income level. The result is that potential recipients can affect the amount of income transferred to them by choosing how much (or how little) income they earn. In fact, they cannot avoid making such a choice. And that is the problem.

To see why, let us suppose that the target level of income is S' and that the potential recipient can work at wage rate w and has no wealth. Let S denote the size of the subsidy actually paid out. If the potential recipient earns as much as or more than the target level of income, S', then he or she will not be given any subsidy:

$$\text{If } wh > S' \text{ then } S = 0$$

If his or her earned income is below S', however, the amount of the subsidy will be just large enough that the earned income and the subsidy together equal the targeted income level:

$$\text{If } wh < S' \text{ then } S = S' - wh$$

We can translate this topping-up mechanism into the kinked budget line BGDE in Figure 14.7. Segment BG corresponds to the case in which earned income exceeds S' and no subsidy is paid. Segment GDE corresponds to the case in which this person earns an income that is less than S' and receives a subsidy just large enough to top his or her income up to S'.

Given this topping-up scheme, two solutions to the potential recipient's utility-maximization problem are possible. In one solution, which is not shown in Figure 14.7, this person picks some point on segment BG of the kinked budget line BGDE where earned income exceeds S'. In this case, he or she gets no income subsidy. In the other solution, this person picks point E in Figure 14.7. In this case, the recipient does not work, and all of his or her income S' comes instead from the public purse.

What the topping-up mechanism actually does, then, is to encourage potential recipients to give up all income from work (or to conceal any income actually earned). As long as earned income is less than S', the implicit marginal tax rate on that income is

FIGURE 14.7   An inefficient income-transfer mechanism

Line BGCT is the no-income-transfer budget line. The inefficient transfer mechanism simply tops up the recipient's income to a specified level S'. For example, if the recipient works h' hours, earning income NC, then the income transfer received is CD because NC + CD = S'. This mechanism produces the kinked budget line BGDE, and the recipient chooses point E. It is inefficient because the recipient's *MRS* at E is less than the wage rate w. The

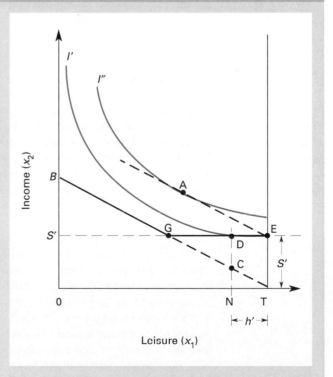

fact that segment GDE of the budget line is horizontal reflects an implicit 100% tax rate on earned income.

100% because all work-generated income is immediately deducted from the subsidy. If the potential recipient in Figure 14.7 considered working h' hours instead of zero hours, for instance, his or her earned income would rise from zero to distance NC. But the income transfer would fall by precisely the same amount, from S' to the distance CD, reflecting an implicit tax on earned income at a rate of 100%. The welfare scheme is thus associated with perverse incentives: it fails to provide recipients with any incentive to work. The topping-up mechanism is clearly inconsistent with Pareto optimality as well because at point E, MRS is less than w. We know that the potential recipient could attain point A in Figure 14.7 by receiving the transfer S' and working at the same time. Because he or she would be better off than at point E and because no one else would be worse off, we know that the equilibrium at point E is not efficient. Considerations like these have led to proposals for an alternative to the welfare system known as the negative income tax.

The Negative Income Tax

We will consider a scheme equivalent to one version of the *negative income tax* (NIT). It combines elements of the efficient lump-sum transfer mechanism and the topping-up mechanism. Though not problem-free, this combined scheme both alleviates the gross inefficiency and the perverse lack of work incentives associated with the welfare system and it redistributes income to poorer members of society.

This version of the NIT is based on a combination of an unconditional income transfer for everyone, equal to, say, S'', and a proportional (but moderate) income tax t on earned income (in the range of a 10% to 25% tax rate rather than the welfare scheme's implicit tax rate of 100%). Under this combined scheme, everyone receives the subsidy S'', pays twh in taxes, keeps $(1 - t)wh$ from his or her earned income, and therefore receives a net income of

$$x_2 = S'' + (1 - t)wh$$

We can translate this combined scheme into the budget line HES$''$ in Figure 14.8.

To compare this NIT mechanism with the welfare topping-up mechanism, we have chosen S'' and t so that this person reaches indifference curve I' under either transfer scheme. The budget line HES$''$ is therefore tangent to the indifference curve at point E in Figure 14.8, and this person is indifferent between the two schemes. Nevertheless, under the combined mechanism, this person now works h^* hours and earns income equal to wh^*. (This person's disposable income, including the income subsidy and subtracting taxes payable on earned income, is the larger sum x_2^* in Figure 14.8.) You can see that point E is not an efficient equilibrium because MRS is less than w. Nevertheless, the NIT mechanism offsets at least some of the inefficiency associated with the topping-up mechanism.

Furthermore, the NIT mechanism makes a smaller demand on the public purse. Once the taxes paid on earned income are deducted from the unconditional subsidy, the net subsidy is just the distance DE in Figure 14.8. This amount is much smaller than S', the transfer under the topping-up welfare mechanism.

This combined scheme differs from the proposed NIT only in the actual mechanics of the income transfer. Here we imagined that the government paid out the unconditional subsidy S'' and then collected the tax on earned income. Under the proposed NIT, the government would subtract the income tax due on earned income from S'' and pay only the net subsidy, distance DE in Figure 14.8.

In the case shown in Figure 14.8, a negative income tax is preferable to the welfare topping-up scheme. It avoids the totally perverse labor-supply incentives of the topping-up

FIGURE 14.8 A negative income tax

Think of the NIT as offering an unconditional subsidy S'' combined with a proportional tax on earned income, producing the budget line HES''. This individual chooses point E, working h^* hours and receiving the net subsidy DE. The negative income tax avoids the extreme work disincentive inherent in the topping-up mechanism.

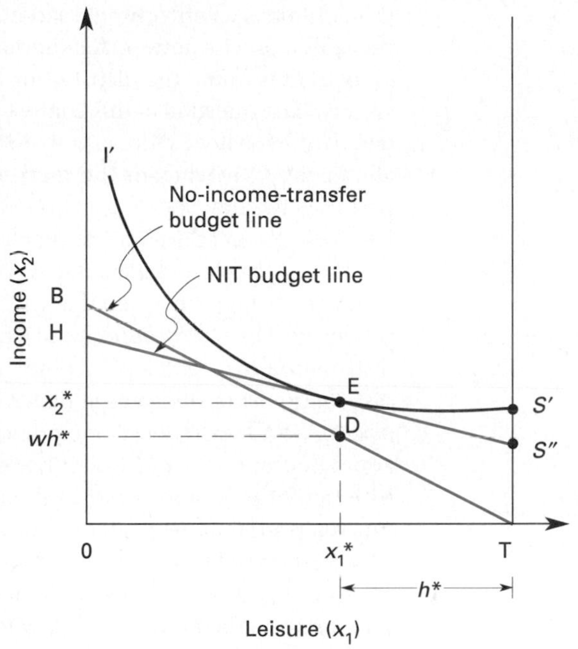

mechanism, and it requires a smaller government subsidy. As you will discover in Problem 14.10, however, these results are not the invariable outcome of a negative income tax.

PROBLEM 14.10

On a single diagram, draw the budget lines associated with the topping-up and NIT schemes. Let the target income under the topping-up mechanism, S', be greater than the unconditional transfer under the NIT, S''. Show that a person who will not receive a subsidy under the topping-up scheme might decide to work less and to receive a subsidy under NIT.

As this problem illustrates, once we leave behind the ideal world of the efficient transfer mechanism, there are no easy answers about how best to redistribute income to poorer members of society. In reality, any income-transfer mechanism that has desirable personal and social effects when applied to one person may have just the opposite effects when applied to someone else. Furthermore, conflicts between efficiency and redistributional objectives are unavoidable.

These difficulties just mean that theory can carry us only so far, not that we should throw up our hands in despair. To design a real income-transfer mechanism that successfully minimizes the tension between efficiency and redistribution, good hard evidence is required, and such evidence is being provided. (See, for example, Cogan, 1983; Hall, 1975; and Keely, 1977.) Theory identifies the potential problems that accompany any income-transfer mechanism; empirical evidence tells us how serious these potential problems are in reality.

SUMMARY

One major task of markets is to allocate resources to competing ends. The question in this context is whether input markets are or are not efficient, and the Pareto criterion provides a precise answer. Another task of markets — and particularly of input markets — is to determine the distribution of wealth and income among the members of a society. The question in this context is whether the resulting distribution is the "right" one. Unfortunately, there is no twin to the economic concept of Pareto optimality that allows us to say whether the market system, or indeed any other set of institutions, performs the function of distribution well. Determining the *just distribution of income* is essentially an ethical rather than an economic question.

Two opposing philosophical principles have been proposed. The *productivity principle* is the proposition that each of us ought to receive what we have individually produced. The *redistributionist principle* is the proposition that a more nearly equitable distribution of wealth and income ought to be a social objective. Advocates of the redistributionist position argue that ethical judgments must be impersonal: the *original position* is a hypothetical situation designed to ensure such impersonality. They also argue that in this original position, each of us would choose a more or less equal distribution of economic rewards. Finally, they assert that what we would choose in this original position is equivalent to what is just in the world we actually inhabit.

We have labeled this the redistributionist principle because it leads to the ethical position that income and wealth ought to be redistributed from the rich to the poor. Judging from the array of *redistributional institutions* we see in modern economies, it is fair to say that most of us would not regard the distribution arising from pure market institutions as perfectly just. To one degree or another, most of us are redistributionists.

Distribution and efficiency, however, are separate problems. As we saw in considering a range of *income-maintenance mechanisms*, the institutions that solve one problem regrettably do not solve the other. This presents us with a fundamental social quandary. Once we realize that the efficient income-transfer institutions are not practicable, we must conclude that any institution or set of institutions that effectively redistributes income or wealth will be inconsistent with economic efficiency, at least to some degree. Thus, a conflict between *efficiency* and *distribution* is inevitable.

The problem for economists is to design redistributionary institutions that minimize the conflict between equity and efficiency. Yet economic theory alone cannot solve this problem. It can only highlight the problems that we expect to arise in any particular institutional context. To take any further step requires empirical work to determine how serious the potential problems identified by economic theory are in reality.

EXERCISES

1. Suppose that in an economy composed of three people we can measure each person's utility cardinally. Suppose, too, that we can use three possible institutions — A, B, and C — to organize economic activity in this economy. The problem is to choose one of the three institutions. The utility of each person under each institution is given below.

Institution	Utility of 1	Utility of 2	Utility of 3
A	45	45	45
B	75	60	30
C	78	63	21

   a. According to Rawls's difference principle, which institution is preferred?

b. Suppose that none of these three people knows which person he or she will be in this economy. What institution would you choose? If each person maximizes expected utility and if each attaches probability 1/3 to being any one person, which is the preferred institution?

c. Now suppose that each of the three does know which person he or she will be. If the institution is chosen by majority rule, which one will be chosen by self-interested individuals?

2. Hilary hires labor to make fancy fishing lures in a small village. She is a profit maximizer. Her marginal revenue product function is

$$MRP(z) = 130 - z$$

and the supply of labor to her firm is

$$w = 10 + z/2$$

where z is the number of workers she hires and w is the daily wage rate.

a. What wage rate does she pay and how much labor does she hire?

b. Her workers are forming a union and need advice on what wage rate they should seek. Their advisor has told them that they should ask for a wage no lower than $50. Explain why this is good advice.

c. The workers have said that they want to ensure that employment does not fall. Given this objective, what is the maximum wage they should bargain for?

3. This problem provides an illustration of the two-sector model developed in Section 14.3. Labor demand functions in the two sectors are $w_1 = 149 - z_1/2$ and $w_2 = 100 - z_2/2$. There are 200 workers to be allocated to the two sectors.

a. Find the competitive equilibrium allocation and wage rate. Hint: Set z_2 equal to $200 - z_1$ in the second demand function. Then set the right-hand sides equal to each other and solve for z_1, the competitive allocation to sector 1.

b. Now suppose that a union wage equal to $100 is established in sector 1 and that available jobs are allocated permanently to a lucky group of 98 workers. Find the underemployment equilibrium.

c. Finally, suppose once again that a union wage equal to $100 is established in sector 1 but that jobs in this sector are now allocated by the shape-up described in Section 14.3. Find the unemployment equilibrium. What is the level of unemployment? What is the wage in sector 2? What is the expected wage of a worker looking for work in sector 1?

d. Illustrate all three equilibria on one carefully constructed graph.

4. Explain (i) why lump-sum, or unconditional, income transfers and taxes are consistent with Pareto optimality; (ii) why they are impractical as a means of achieving significant redistribution; and (iii) why income transfers and taxes that are conditional on earned income are not consistent with Pareto optimality.

5. Professional associations, such as the California Bar Association, have considerable leeway in determining both the standards that new entrants must meet and the prices of professional services.

a. First, suppose that the professional association can set prices but cannot control entry standards. What are the implications of a price increase when the demand for professional services is price inelastic? In particular, what will happen to the earnings and hours worked of an individual professional in the short run and the long run? What are the implications when demand is price elastic?

b. Second, suppose that the association can control entry standards but not prices. What are the implications of increasing the entry standard — say, by requiring entrants to spend an additional term in a training program? In particular, do the established practitioners have private incentives to increase the entry standard?

REFERENCES

Arrow, K. 1976. "The Viability and Equity of Capitalism," E. S. Woodward Lectures in Economics. Department of Economics, University of British Columbia.

Cogan, J. F. 1983. "Labor Supply and Negative Income Taxation: New Evidence from the New Jersey–Pennsylvania Experiment," *Economic Inquiry,* 21:465–83.

Cowell, F. A. 1987. "Redistribution of Income and Wealth," in *The New Palgrave: A Dictionary of Economics,* J. Eatwell, M. Milgate, and P. Newman (eds.). London: The Macmillan Press.

Hall, R. 1975. "Effects of the Experimental Negative Income Tax on Labor Supply," in *Work Incentives and Income Guarantees*, J. Peckman and P. M. Timpane (eds.), Brookings Institute.

Keely, M., et al. 1977. "The Labor Supply Effects and Costs of Alternative Negative Income Tax Programs: Evidence from the Seattle and Denver Income Maintenance Experiments," Stanford Research Institute.

Parsons, D. O. 1987. "Minimum Wages," in *The New Palgrave: A Dictionary of Economics*, J. Eatwell, M. Milgate, and P. Newman (eds.), London: The Macmillan Press.

Rawls, J. 1971. *A Theory of Justice*, Boston: Belknap Press of Harvard University.

Todaro, M. 1969. "A Model for Labor Migration and Urban Unemployment in Less Developed Countries," *American Economic Review*, 59:138–48.

Watts, H. 1987. "Negative Income Tax," in *The New Palgrave: A Dictionary of Economics*, J. Eatwell, M. Milgate, and P. Newman (eds.). London: The Macmillan Press.

Intertemporal Resource Allocation

intertemporal
resource
allocation

In exploring issues of efficiency and equity in the allocation of resources in last two chapters, we used a static model in which time played no role. Yet many interesting and important allocation problems are inherently problems about **intertemporal resource allocation** — about the allocation of resources to present and future uses. Your decisions with respect to education and occupational choice are unavoidably intertemporal. When you decide to spend money today instead of saving it for a future use, you are making an intertemporal decision. An oil company's decision to pump and sell oil today, or wait for tomorrow, is an intertemporal decision. All investment decisions are intertemporal.

Inevitably, intertemporal choices involve comparisons of sums of money at different points in time. Think, for example, about the intertemporal resource problem that arises in choosing between becoming a medical doctor or a carpenter. Medicine involves a long period of training during which the medical student earns very little income, but it promises a very high annual income once training is completed. In contrast, carpentry involves a much shorter training period, but the annual income of a journeyman carpenter is small relative to that of a practicing doctor. A person who faces the choice between these occupations needs to compare the two income streams. But how does an eighteen-year-old student trying to choose an occupation go about comparing the stream of earnings for a doctor with its high annual income but a very long training period to the stream of earnings for a carpenter with its shorter training period but smaller annual income?

interest rate

The key to making such comparisons is the ability to borrow and lend money, and the price that drives these comparisons is the **interest rate** at which borrowing and lending take place. This one very important price — the interest rate — is the price that governs all intertemporal decisions and therefore determines the intertemporal allocation of resources.

In the first part of the chapter, we see how the interest rate affects a number of important intertemporal decisions, including the major economic decisions that individuals must make over their life cycle. In the last part of chapter, we analyze how the interest rate is determined.[1]

---

1 The theory of intertemporal choice in the absence of uncertainty was developed by Irving Fisher (1907) in his great work, *The Theory of Interest*. Hirshleifer (1970) provides an excellent modern treatment. See also J. Hirshleifer's entry "investment decision criteria," in *The New Palgrave*.

15.1

Intertemporal Value Comparisons

market for
loanable funds

The fact that people can borrow and lend money in what is called the **market for loanable funds** allows them to compare different sums of money at different points in time. Your local banker, from whom you can borrow money and to whom you can lend money, works in the market for loanable funds. We will call the rate of interest at which you can borrow money from your local bank the **borrowing rate**, denoted by i_b. We usually do not think about lending money to the bank, but when you deposit money in a savings account, for example, you are in fact lending money to the bank. We will call the rate of interest you earn on money deposited in the bank the **deposit rate**, denoted by i_d.

borrowing rate

deposit rate

Typically, i_b exceeds i_d: that is, the borrowing rate of interest exceeds the deposit rate of interest. Why? Fundamentally, a bank is a business which borrows money from some people — at the deposit rate of interest i_d — and lends to other people — at the borrowing rate of interest i_b. Then, the deposit rate of interest i_d can be interpreted as either the rate of interest at which people lend money to their bank, or as the rate of interest the bank pays to borrow money from its customers. Similarly, the borrowing rate i_b can be interpreted as either the rate of interest at which people borrow money from the bank, or as the rate of interest at which the bank lends money to its customers. If the bank is to cover it transactions costs and perhaps make a profit, then i_b must exceed i_d.

Now let us see how to compare $1,000 payable today with $1,100 payable one year from today. Imagine that you have been given the choice between two windfall gains: $1,000 payable today or $1,100 payable one year from today. Which should you choose? Since the two windfall gains are separated by exactly one year, we can think of the interest rates i_b and i_d as annual rates.

future value

Suppose your preferences are such that you want to save this windfall gain for some future purpose — a trip to Argentina after you graduate, for example. The sensible way to make the comparison is to compute a **future value** FV for the $1,000 payable today, and then compare this future value with the $1,100 payable one year in the future. If you deposited $1,000 in your bank today at interest rate i_d, one year from today you would have $FV = \$1,000(1 + i_d)$, the original $1,000 plus interest equal to $1,000 times i_d. In other words, $\$1,000(1 + i_d)$ is the *future value* (one period in the future) of $1,000 payable today. Notice that FV is greater than or less than $1,100 as i_d is greater than or less than 10%. In comparing future values, then, we can use the following rule to make the choice:

Future Value Choice Rule: (i) choose $1,000 payable today if i_d exceeds 10%; (ii) choose $1100 payable in one year if i_d is less than 10%; (iii) choose either if i_d is equal to 10%.

---

present value

Now suppose your preferences are such that you want to spend this windfall gain today for a new mountain bike, for example. In this case the sensible thing to do is to compute a **present value** PV for the $1,100 payable in one year, and then compare this present value with the $1,000 payable today. The present value of $1,100 payable one year from today is the amount you could borrow from your banker in exchange for a payment of $1,100 in one year. Since for each dollar you borrow today at interest rate i_b you must pay back $1 + i_b$ dollars one year from today, we see that $PV(1 + i_b) = \$1,100$, or that $PV = \$1,100/(1 + i_b)$. In other words, $\$1,100/(1 + i_b)$ is the *present value* of $1,100 payable one year from today. Notice that PV is greater than or less than $1,000 as i_b is less than or greater than 10%. In comparing present values, then, you can use the following rule to make your choice:

Present Value Choice Rule: (i) choose $1000 payable today if i_b exceeds 10%; (ii) choose $1100 payable in one year if i_b is less than 10%; (iii) choose either if i_b is equal to 10%.

These choice rules are almost identical. The only difference is that i_d — the interest rate you earn on money deposited in the bank — is the relevant rate for the future value choice rule, while i_b — the interest rate at which you can borrow money from your bank — is the relevant rate for the present value choice rule. Remarkably, if both rates exceed 10%, or if both are less than 10%, we know what you should do: choose $1000 payable today if both rates exceed 10%, and choose $1100 payable in a year if both rates are less than 10%.

If i_b is greater than 10% and i_d is less than 10%, however, the two rules lead us to different choices and it is not clear what you should do. In fact, to determine your choice, we need to know when you intend to spent the money; that is, we need to know something about your preferences. If you want to spend this windfall gain on a new bicycle today, then the present value rule should guide your choice, since by following the present value rule you maximize the amount of money available today. In contrast, if you want to save the windfall gain for future consumption, the future value rule is the relevant rule. If you want to spend some of it today and some of it in the future, however, we need to know more about your preferences to determine which windfall gain to choose.

A Perfect Market for Loanable Funds

In certain circumstances, your choice of which windfall to pick can be separated from the way in which you intend to spend the money — that is, from your preferences. Importantly, if the two rates of interest are identical, we can *always* achieve this separation. For this reason, we will assume throughout the chapter that the borrowing and lending rates are identical, and we will denote that single interest rate by i. When this assumption is satisfied, the market for loanable funds is said to be *perfect*.

Empirically, the market for loanable funds is almost never perfect, but this assumption greatly simplifies, and more importantly, it significantly clarifies the principles of choice in situations where time matters.

The Separation Theorem

Let us generalize what we learned about the separation of your decision with respect to which windfall gain to choose from the decision about how and when you actually spend the windfall. The general lesson is this: Given a perfect market for loanable funds, we can separate the choice of income streams over time from the choice of consumption expenditures over time. The ability to neatly separate decisions in this way is called the **separation theorem**:

separation
theorem

---

1. Individuals will choose among different income streams by choosing the income stream with the largest present value.
2. They will choose consumption expenditures over time to maximize utility, given the constraint that the present value of income not exceed the present value of consumption expenditures.

Notice that the criterion for choosing among different income streams is couched in terms of present value. However, given a perfect market for loanable funds, an equivalent criterion is to choose the income stream with the largest future value (at some future point in time). For example, in choosing between the two windfall gains, we saw that when the two rates of interest are identical, the windfall gain with the larger present value is also the one with the larger future value. Though the two criteria are equivalent, it is conventional to use the present-value criterion.

Present Value

Now let us see how to calculate the *present value* of the following income stream: (I_0, I_1, I_2, …, I_T). Income I_0 is received today, income I_1 is received one period in the future, and so on. First let us calculate the present value of I_t — income that is received t periods in the future. The key to this calculation is the following definition: the present value of I_t is a sum of money PV such that, if we were to invest it today at interest rate i, it would be worth I_t in t periods.

Suppose, for example, that you deposit $1 in your savings account at interest rate i. At the end of one period, your balance will be the original dollar plus interest i on that dollar, or $(1 + i)$. At the end of two periods, your balance will be

$$\$(1 + i)^2 = \$(1 + i) + \$i(1 + i)$$

The first expression on the right, $(1 + i)$, is the balance at the end of the first period, and the second expression on the right, $i(1 + i)$, is the interest earned in the second period. As you can easily verify, at the end of t periods, the balance will be $(1 + i)^t$. Therefore, $1 invested today at interest rate i will be worth $(1 + i)^t$ in t periods.

Now we can use this result to find the present value of I_t. If you deposit PV in your savings account, at the end of t periods you will have $PV(1 + i)^t$. But this sum must be equal to I_t, since PV is the present value of I_t. By solving the following equation for PV, we have the present value of I_t.

$$\$PV(1 + i)^t = \$I_t$$

Solving for PV we have,

$$\$PV = \$I_t/(1 + i)^t$$

As you know, if today you invested PV at interest rate i, you would have I_t in t periods. Alternatively, the maximum sum your banker would lend you today in exchange for a payment of I_t in t periods is PV. In these *two* senses, then, PV today is equivalent to I_t in period t.

With the help of this formula, we can calculate the present value of income stream (I_0, I_1, I_2, …, I_T).[2]

$$\$PV = \$I_0 + \$I_1/(1 + i) + \$I_2/(1 + i)^2 + \ldots + \$I_T/(1 + i)^T$$

---

2 Interest rates often change from period to period. Letting i_t denote the interest rate in period t, the present value of income stream (I_0, I_1, I_2, …, I_T) is

$$\$PV = \$I_0 + \$I_1/(1 + i_1) + \$I_2/(1 + i_2)^2 + \ldots + \$I_T/(1 + i_T)^T$$

> **PROBLEM 15.1**
>
> The first income stream consists of $0 today, $5,000 one year from today, and $12,100 two years from today. The second income stream consists of $10,000 today, $5000 one year from today, and $0 two years from today. Which income stream has the larger present value when the annual rate of interest is 0%? When it is 5%? When it is 10%? When it is 15%? When it is 20%? There is a pattern in these results. What is it? Can you explain it?

In the next two sections, we use the separation theorem to look at two different aspects of the life cycle of individuals. First, we take income over the life cycle as given, and look at the principles that guide a person's decisions about consumption expenditure over the life cycle. Then, we look at the way in which income over the life cycle is determined by a person's decisions about education, or human capital acquisition.

15.2
The Life-Cycle Model

life cycle

A freshly minted college graduate is likely to have a substantial student loan to repay in the first few years out of college — it is not unusual for students to borrow $30,000 or more to finance their education. A married couple who are thirtysomething and "own" their own home, typically will have a sizeable mortgage debt — $200,000 or more in many cases. In contrast, a married couple who are sixtysomething typically will have substantial savings — perhaps as much as $1,000,000. These stylized facts are indicative of a **life cycle** in which individuals incur debt when they are young so that they can spend more than they earn, repay that debt and accumulate savings when they are middle aged, and consume their accumulated savings when they are old. In this section, we focus on the allocative role of the interest rate as we develop a two-period version of the life-cycle model to explore these intertemporal consumption and saving decisions.[3]

We begin our analysis of the consumption possibilities open to ordinary people by exploring the highly simplified choices available to an imaginary person named Harold. Imagine that Harold is alive for just two periods and that he has income I_0 in the initial period and income I_1 in the next period. We can think of the two periods as the two halves of Harold's life. We will call the first half of Harold's life period zero and the second half period one. Since each period is half a lifetime, the incomes I_0 and I_1 will be a great deal larger than a typical annual income. Harold's income per period will be on the order of $1,000,000. Similarly, the interest rate i will be a great deal higher than the usual annual rates of interest. These interest rates will be in the range of 100% to 400% per period.

The Budget Line

The amounts Harold spends on consumption in period zero and in period one are denoted by C_0 and C_1 respectively. What combinations of C_0 and C_1 can Harold achieve, given that his income is I_0 in period zero and I_1 in period one, and given interest rate i? In other words, what is Harold's budget line?

---

3 In its modern form, the life cycle hypothesis is due to Modigliani and Brumberg (1954) and Friedman (1957). M. R. Fisher's entry "life cycle hypothesis" in *The New Palgrave* is a useful survey of work in this area.

If Harold spends less than his full income in period zero — that is, if C_0 is less than I_0 — he will earn interest at rate i on his savings, equal to $(I_0 - C_0)$. The amount saved plus interest — equal to $(1 + i)(I_0 - C_0)$ — will then be available for consumption in period one. The total amount available for consumption in period one is then $I_1 + (1 + i)(I_0 - C_0)$. That is,

$$C_1 = I_1 + (1 + i)(I_0 - C_0)$$

That is, period one consumption C_1 is equal to period one income I_1 plus the future value of period zero savings $(1 + i)(I_0 - C_0)$. Rearranging this expression, we get

$$C_0(1 + i) + C_1 = I_0(1 + i) + I_1$$

This is Harold's budget line.

The expression on the right side of the inequality is the *future value* of the income stream I_0 in period zero and I_1 in period one. It is, in other words, the future value of Harold's lifetime income. Analogously, the expression on the left is the *future value* of the consumption bundle (C_0, C_1). The budget line tells us that the future value of Harold's consumption bundle is equal to the future value of his lifetime income.

The slope of this budget line, shown in Figure 15.1, is $-(1 + i)$, a reflection of the fact that the opportunity cost of a dollar consumed in period zero is $(1 + i)$ dollars of consumption in period one. Put another way, the *opportunity cost* of a dollar spent in period zero is the future value of a dollar in period one.

If we divide both sides of the budget line equation by $(1 + i)$, we get a second version of Harold's budget line:

$$C_0 + C_1/(1 + i) = I_0 + I_1/(1 + i)$$

Now the expression on the right is the *present value* of Harold's lifetime income, and the expression on the left is the *present value* of the consumption bundle (C_0, C_1). This version of the budget line tells us that the present value of Harold's consumption bundle is equal to the present value of his lifetime income. Of course, the two versions of Harold's budget line are equivalent.

> ### PROBLEM 15.2
>
> In deriving this budget line, we assumed that Harold consumed less than his full income in period zero and more than his full income in period one. Let us make the opposite assumption and see if we get the same budget line. If C_1 is less than I_1, then, in period zero, Harold can borrow the present value of savings in period 1 for consumption in period zero. Therefore, in period zero, he can consume the present value of $I_1 - C_1$ plus period zero income I_0. That is,
>
> $$C_0 = I_0 + \text{present value of } (I_1 - C_1)$$
>
> What is the present value of $(I_1 - C_1)$? Use this present value to rewrite the above equation, and then show that it is equivalent to the budget line above.

Three points on Harold's budget line deserve special attention. Notice first that C_0 equal to I_0 and C_1 equal to I_1 corresponds to point A on the budget line — that is, Harold can always spend what he earns in each period. Notice, too, that if he spends nothing in period

FIGURE 15.1   An intertemporal budget line

Harold's income in period zero is I_0 and income in period one is I_1. A consumption bundle (C_0, C_1) is the amount Harold spends on consumption in periods zero and one. Harold's intertemporal budget line gives us the consumption bundles that exhaust his income, given that he can borrow and lend at interest rate i. The budget line passes through point A since Harold can spend I_0 on consumption in period zero and I_1 on consumption in period one. The slope of the budget line is $-(1+i)$ since the

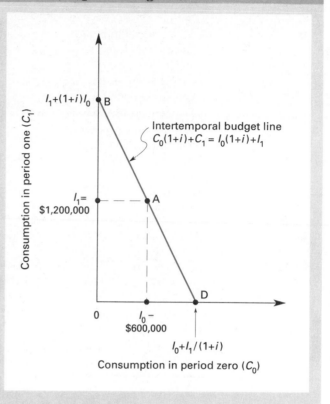

opportunity cost of a dollar spent on consumption in period zero is $(1+i)$ dollars not spent on consumption in period one.

zero, he can achieve point B in Figure 15.1 where C_1 is equal to period one income plus the future value of period zero income or $I_1 + (1+i)I_0$. Finally, notice that if he consumes nothing in period one, Harold can achieve point D in Figure 15.1 where C_0 is equal to period zero income plus the present value of period one income or $I_0 + I_1/(1+i)$.

PROBLEM 15.3

Suppose the interest rate is 300% per period and that $I_0 = \$600,000$ and $I_1 = \$1,200,000$. Construct Harold's budget line. What is the maximum amount he could consume in period one? In period zero? What is the opportunity cost of a dollar of consumption in period zero? What is the opportunity cost of a dollar of consumption in period one? What is the slope of his budget line?

In Figure 15.2 we have shown how Harold's budget line shifts as the interest rate i increases. Since the opportunity cost of a dollar consumed in period zero is $1 + i$ dollars of consumption in period one, when i increases the budget line gets steeper. And since Harold can always spend I_0 on consumption in period zero and I_1 in period one, the budget line always passes thorough point A in Figure 15.2. We see then that when the interest rate i increases, the budget line pivots clockwise around point A.

FIGURE 15.2 **The rate of interest and the intertemporal budget line**

As the rate of interest i increases, Harold's budget line pivots in the clockwise direction around point A. This reflects the fact that as i increases, the opportunity cost of consumption in period zero — equal to $(1 + i)$ — increases.

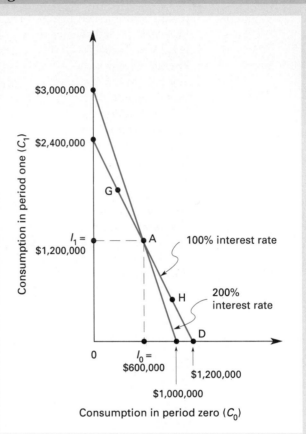

PROBLEM 15.4

In what circumstances is Harold made better off, and in what circumstances is he made worse off, by an increase in the interest rate? Hint: Suppose that prior to the increase in i, Harold's preferred bundle is at a point like G in Figure 15.2 where C_0 is less than I_0; now ask, given the increase in i, can he still achieve the consumption bundle he preferred prior to that increase? Now suppose that prior to the increase in i, his preferred bundle is at a point like H where C_0 exceeds I_0, and ask the same question.

The Intertemporal Allocation of Lifetime Income

To complete the picture of Harold's life-cycle consumption decision, we can use the composite commodity theorem to represent Harold's preferences in terms of the amount spent on consumption in the two periods; that is, in terms of C_0 and C_1. We will assume that Harold's indifference curves are smooth and convex, and, naturally, that preferred indifference curves are farther from the origin.

To maximize utility, Harold will choose a bundle (C_0^*, C_1^*) in Figure 15.3 where an indifference curve is tangent to his budget line, or where the marginal rate of substitution of consumption in period one for consumption in period zero is equal to $(1+i)$. In the current context, the marginal rate of substitution is called the **marginal rate of time preference** since it is the rate at which Harold is willing to substitute consumption in period one for consumption in period zero. In equilibrium, the marginal rate of time preference is equal to $(1+i)$.

marginal rate of
time preference

In Figure 15.3, Harold's income is $600,000 in period zero and $1,200,000 in period one, and the interest rate is 100% per half a lifetime. In equilibrium, Harold spends $800,000 in each period. In the equilibrium shown in Figure 15.3, Harold therefore borrows against period one income in order to consume more than his income in period zero. Because the interest rate is 100%, the opportunity cost of an added dollar of consumption in period zero is two dollars of consumption in period one. Accordingly, starting at the income endowment point A, as he increases period-zero consumption from $600,000 to $800,000, Harold is forced to reduce period-one consumption from $1,200,000 to $800,000. We see that Harold borrows $200,000 in period zero and pays back $400,000 in period one — the $200,000 borrowed in period one plus $200,000 in interest.

In the case shown in Figure 15.3, Harold consumes more than his income in period zero and less than his income in period one. Clearly, this is just one of three possibilities. If Harold's income endowment had been at point A′ instead of at point A,

FIGURE 15.3   **Choosing an intertemporal consumption bundle**

To maximize utility Harold chooses the consumption bundle on his intertemporal budget line where *MRS* is equal to $(1+i)$, or where the *marginal rate of time preference* is equal to $(1+i)$.

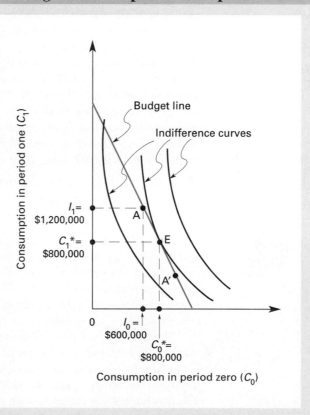

for example, he would have consumed less than his income in period zero and more than his income in period one. And if his income endowment had been at point E, his consumption would have been equal to his income in both periods.

PROBLEM 15.5

impatient

patient

It is usually assumed that people are "impatient." A person is **impatient** if, when C_0 is equal to C_1, his or her marginal rate of time preference is greater than one. And a person is **patient** if, when C_0 is equal to C_1, his or her marginal rate of time preference is less than one. From Figure 15.3, is Harold patient or impatient? Show that an impatient person will always spend more on consumption in the first period than in the second period if the interest rate is zero.

Comparative Statics

The *exogenous variables* in the life-cycle model are income and the interest rate in each of the two periods, and the *endogenous variables* are consumption in the two periods. We can develop a deeper understanding of the model by conducting a series of comparative statics exercises in which we change an exogenous variable and then analyze how the change in the exogenous variable affects the endogenous variables.

We will begin by looking at the effects of an increase in I_0 or I_1. As income in either period increases, the budget line shifts up and to the right, but its slope, equal to $-(1 + i)$, does not change. In Figure 15.4, for example, the initial income endowment is at point A on the initial budget line. By holding I_1 fixed, and increasing income in period zero by $\varnothing I_0$ we get the new income endowment at point A′ on the subsequent budget line, which is parallel to the initial budget line. Notice that we get the same subsequent budget line by holding I_0 constant and increasing I_1 by $\varnothing I_1$. Notice, too, that $\varnothing I_1$ is equal to the future value of $\varnothing I_0$.

In the case shown in Figure 15.4, the initial equilibrium is at point E and the subsequent equilibrium is at point E′. Notice that in moving from E to E′ consumption in both periods increases. In this case, consumption in period and consumption in period one are therefore both *normal* goods. Although it is possible that consumption in one period or the other is an inferior good, this seems to be an unlikely case. We will therefore adopt the following assumption:

ASSUMPTION
Both C_0 and C_1 are normal goods.

Now let us turn to the more interesting effects associated with a *change* in the interest rate. We will begin with an equilibrium based on a relatively low rate of interest, and then increase the interest rate, and we will ask: What happens to consumption in each period? As you saw from Problem 15.4, an increase in i makes someone who saves in period zero better off, and it makes someone who borrows in period zero worse off. In assessing the impact of an increase in i on consumption in the two periods, we will have to consider these two cases separately.

The case of someone who saves in period zero is shown in Figure 15.5. Given the relatively low interest rate, the initial equilibrium is at point E where this person saves in period zero — that is, consumes less than his or her income I_0. When the interest rate increases, the budget line pivots clockwise around the income endowment at point A. The new budget line is steeper than the original budget line, reflecting the fact that the opportunity cost of consumption in period zero increases when the interest rate rises.

FIGURE 15.4   Comparative statics of a change in income

As income in either period increases the budget line shifts up and to the right, but its slope does not change. Because, in this case, consumption in both periods increases as income increases, both C_0 and C_1 are normal goods.

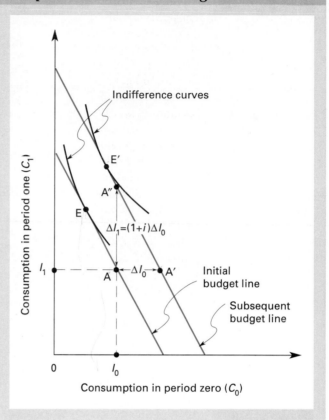

Given the higher interest rate, the subsequent equilibrium is at point E′ in Figure 15.5. Notice that in this case, consumption in both periods increases.

By looking at income and substitution effects for both goods, we will show that consumption in period one must increase when the interest rate increases, and that consumption in period zero may either increase or decrease. Notice that in identifying income and substitution effects for *both goods* we are doing something new here. And keep in mind the assumption that both C_0 and C_1 are normal goods.

To identify the income effects, we have constructed the compensated budget line, parallel to the subsequent budget line and tangent to the lower indifference curve. Since the increase in i makes the saver in Figure 15.5 better off, the compensated budget line lies below the subsequent budget line. And since both goods are normal, in the move from the equilibrium point at D on the compensated budget line to the equilibrium point at E′ on the subsequent budget line, both C_0 and C_1 necessarily increase.

> For a person who saves the initial equilibrium, the income effects associated with an increase in i lead to an increase in consumption in both periods.

To isolate the substitution effects, notice what happens in moving from point E to point D. Since indifference curves are smooth and convex, consumption in period one necessarily increases while consumption in period zero necessarily decreases. Thus, the substitution effect of an increase in the interest rate leads to a decrease in consumption in period zero and an increase in consumption in period one.

FIGURE 15.5 Comparative statics of an increase in *i* — part 1

The initial equilibrium is at point E. As *i* increases, the budget line pivots clockwise around point A and the subsequent equilibrium is at E′. As a result, consumption in both periods increases. For consumption in period one, the income and substitution effects are complementary — both lead to an increase in C_1 in response to an increase in *i*. For consumption in period zero the income and substitution effects are opposed — the income effect leads to an increase in C_0 while the substitution effect leads to a decrease.

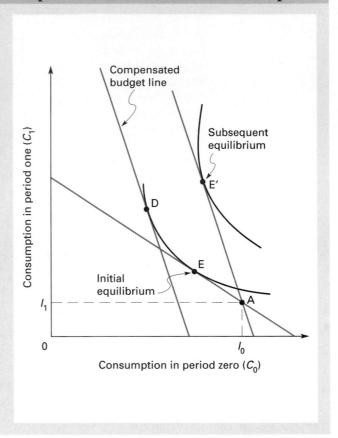

Notice that the income and substitution effects are complementary for consumption in period one — both lead to an increase in consumption:

For someone who saves in the initial equilibrium, consumption in period one necessarily increases when the interest rate increases.

In contrast, the income and substitution effects are opposed for consumption in period zero — the income effect leads to an increase in period zero consumption while the substitution effect leads to a decrease:

For someone who saves in the initial equilibrium, consumption in period zero may either increase or decrease when the interest rate increases.

In the case shown in Figure 15.5, the positive income effect dominates the negative substitution effect. Therefore, the net effect of the increase in the interest rate in this particular case is an increase in consumption in period zero. It is entirely possible, however, for the substitution effect to dominate the income effect.

The case of someone who borrows against future income in period zero is shown in Figure 15.6. Given the relatively low interest rate, the initial equilibrium is at point E, where period zero consumption exceeds period zero income I_0. When the interest rate increases, the budget line pivots clockwise around the income endowment point

A. Given the higher interest rate, the subsequent equilibrium is at E′ in Figure 15.6. Notice that in moving from point E to point E′ consumption in period zero decreases and consumption in period one increases. We will show that consumption in period zero must decrease when the interest rate increases, and that consumption in period one may either increase or decrease.

To identify the income effects, we have constructed the compensated budget line, which is parallel to the subsequent budget line and tangent to the higher indifference curve in Figure 15.6. Since an increase in i makes the borrower in Figure 15.5 worse off, the compensated budget line lies above the subsequent budget line. And since both goods are normal, in the move from the equilibrium at point D on the compensated budget line to the equilibrium at point E′ on the subsequent budget line, both C_0 and C_1 necessarily decrease:

> For someone who borrows in the initial equilibrium, the income effects associated with an increase in i lead to a decrease in consumption in both periods.

To isolate the substitution effects we observe what happens in the move from point E to point D. Since indifference curves are smooth and convex, consumption in period one necessarily increases while consumption in period zero necessarily decreases. Thus, the substitution effect of an increase in the interest rate leads to a decrease in consumption in period zero and an increase in consumption in period one.

FIGURE 15.6 **Comparative statics of an increase in i — part 2**

The initial equilibrium is at point E. As i increases the budget line pivots clockwise around point A and the subsequent equilibrium is at E′. As a result, C_0 decreases and C_1 increases. For consumption in period zero, the income and substitution effects are complementary — both lead to a decrease in C_0 in response to an increase in i. For consumption in period one, the income and substitution effects are opposed — the income effect leads to a decrease in C_1 while the substitution effect leads to an increase.

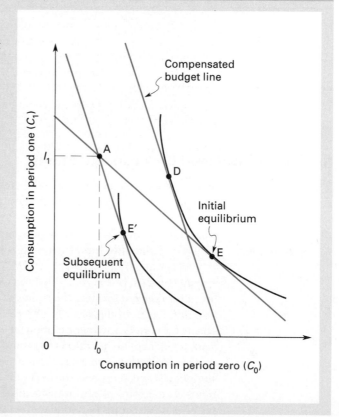

Notice that the income and substitution effects are complementary for consumption in period zero — both lead to a decrease in period zero consumption:

For someone who borrows in the initial equilibrium, consumption in period zero necessarily decreases when the interest rate increases.

In contrast, the income and substitution effects are opposed for consumption in period one — the income effect leads to a decrease in period one consumption while the substitution effect leads to an increase:

For someone who borrows in the initial equilibrium, consumption in period one may either increase or decrease when the interest rate increases.

In the case shown in Figure 15.6, the net effect is an increase in consumption in period one because the positive substitution effect dominates the negative income effect.

To check your understanding of the life-cycle model, try the following problem.

PROBLEM 15.6

1. Given the current interest rate, it is known that Rachelle would consume less than her income in period zero. Indicate whether the following statements are true, false, or uncertain.
   a. Given an increase in the interest rate, Rachelle would consume less than her income in period zero.
   b. Given a decrease in the interest rate, Rachelle would consume less than her income in period zero.
2. Given the current interest rate, it is known that Ralph would consume more than his income in period zero. Indicate whether the following statements are true, false, or uncertain.
   a. Given an increase in the interest rate, Ralph would consume more than his income in period zero.
   b. Given a decrease in the interest rate, Ralph would consume more than his income in period zero.

Supply and Demand for Loanable Funds

loanable funds

So far, we have focused on the link between the interest rate and the allocation of lifetime income to consumption in periods zero and one. It is useful to consider this exercise from a different perspective. Someone like the person in Figure 15.5 — who consumes less than his or her income in period zero — generates a supply of savings, or a *supply* of **loanable funds** in period zero. And someone like the person in Figure 15.6 — who consumes more than his or her income in period zero — generates a *demand* for loanable funds in period zero. What can we say about the way in which an individual's supply of (or demand for) loanable funds responds to a change in the rate of interest?

In the case of the saver in Figure 15.5, we saw that the income and substitution effects for period-zero consumption are opposed. The income effect for an increase in i leads to an increase in period-zero consumption, while the substitution effect leads to a decrease in period-zero consumption. Since savings is just equal to income minus consumption, we can express these results in terms of an individual's supply of loanable funds. The income effect for an increase in i leads to a decrease in the individual's supply of loanable funds in period zero while the substitution effect leads to an increase. The net effect of an increase in the interest rate on the supply of loanable funds is therefore ambiguous. If the substitution effect dominates the income effect, an increase in i will lead to an increase in the supply of loanable funds. Conversely, if the income effect dominates the substitution effect, an increase in i will lead to a decrease in the supply of loanable funds.

In the case of the borrower in Figure 15.6, we saw that the income and substitution effects for period-zero consumption are complementary. For an increase in the interest rate, both the income and substitution effects lead to a decrease in period zero consumption. In terms of an individual's demand for loanable funds, this means that for an increase in i both the income and substitution effects work to reduce an individual's demand for loanable funds. Accordingly, a borrower's demand for loanable funds is inversely related to the rate of interest.

15.3

Human Capital

In analyzing Harold's intertemporal consumption decisions we took his life-cycle income stream as given. With income in both periods fixed, Harold's only decision was how to allocate his fixed lifetime income to consumption in the two periods. Notice, however, that our decisions with respect to schooling and other forms of training allow us to exercise considerable control over our personal life-cycle income stream. When a student chooses to get a bachelor's degree in electrical engineering, for example, the student is simultaneously giving up the *current income* that could be earned by working instead of going to school and enhancing *future income*. Our analysis of the individual's life cycle to this point is seriously incomplete because it ignores the training choices that determine the individual's life-cycle income stream.[4]

In this section, we will use the separation theorem to analyze the training decision of an imaginary person named Harriet, and then we will combine the results of this analysis with results from the life-cycle model for a more complete picture of an individual's economic life cycle.

human capital

Economists call Harriet's investment in training **human capital**, and they measure her investment in human capital by adding up her direct expenditures on training and the income that she gives up by spending time in training as opposed to working, called **foregone income**. Direct expenditures include amounts spent on tuition, books, and lab fees, for example. In most training programs, however, foregone income is the most important component of investment in human capital. Adding the direct costs and the foregone income of training gives us a measure of Harriet's human capital. We will denote this investment, or Harriet's quantity of human capital, by H.

foregone
income

Harriet's return on human capital is, of course, additional income that she will earn in the future. We will denote this additional income, or return to human capital, by R. We will think of Harriet's human capital decision in the context of our two-period life-cycle model — she will make the investment H in period zero, and she will get the return R in period one. Naturally, we will assume that R increases as H increases. The larger is Harriet's investment H in period zero, the larger is the return R she enjoys in period one.

We will represent the relationship between R and H by the function $F(H)$. That is,

$$R = F(H)$$

---

4 There has been a great deal of work on human capital in the last 30 years, inspired by the pioneering work of Becker (1964), Mincer (1958), and Schultz (1961). For an overview of this vast body of work, see S. Rosen's entry "human capital" in *The New Palgrave*.

human capital
production
function

marginal
product of
human capital

$F(H)$ is called the **human capital production function**. We will assume that Harriet's production function has diminishing returns: successive equal increments in human capital, II, add less and less to her return, R. This production function is shown in Figure 15.7. The slope of the production function at any point is, of course, the **marginal product of human capital** MP. At point D in Figure 15.7, MP is the slope of the tangent line TT. MP tells us the rate at which Harriet's income in period one increases as she invests more in human capital in period zero.

We can use the separation theorem to solve Harriet's investment problem. The separation theorem tells us that Harriet will choose quantity of human capital to maximize the present value of income available for consumption, or what we will call her net income. To begin, suppose that Harriet has invested 400,000 dollars in human capital — $H = \$400,000$ — and then ask: What happens to the present value of Harriet's net income when she invests one additional dollar in human capital? Her net income for period zero decreases by \$1 because the additional dollar she invests in human capital is no longer available for consumption. And her net income for period one increases by (approximately) $\$MP(H = 400,000)$ — equal to the slope of tangent line TT in Figure 15.7. But the present value of this increase is just $\$MP(H = 400,000)/(1 + i)$, because she does not get the added income until next period. So, the change in the present value of Harriet's net income stream is

$$\$MP(H = 400,000)/(1 + i) - \$1$$

FIGURE 15.7 Investing in human capital

The human capital production function $F(H)$ gives Harriet's dollar return R in period one for every level of investment in human capital H in period zero. The separation theorem dictates that Harriet should invest in human capital up to the point where the marginal product of human capital is equal to $(1 + i)$. The optimal investment is H^*, which generates return R^*.

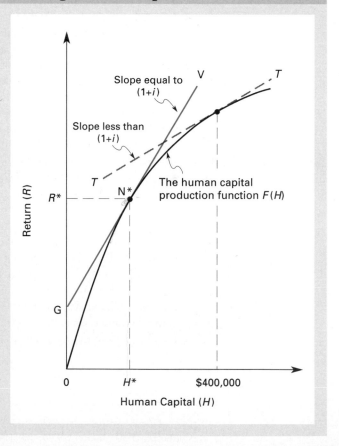

The present value of Harriet's net income increases as she invests one more dollar if this expression is positive, or if

$$MP(H = 400{,}000) > (1 + i)$$

From Figure 15.7 we see that this inequality is not satisfied when $H = \$400{,}000$ since the slope of tangent line TT is less than $(1 + i)$, so Harriet definitely should not invest another dollar in human capital.

More generally, we see that Harriet should invest an additional dollar in human capital if MP exceeds $(1 + i)$ and that she should invest one less dollar in human capital if MP is less than $(1 + i)$. That is:[5]

To maximize the present value of net income invest in human capital up to the point where MP is equal to $(1 + i)$.

In Figure 15.7, the optimal investment is H^*, since the line GN^*V, whose slope is $(1 + i)$, is tangent to the human capital production function at point N^*. At point N^* Harriet gives up H^* in income in period zero in return for an increase in income in period one equal to R^*. For any point to the left of N^* on the human capital production function, the present value of Harriet's net income increases as she invests more in human capital because MP exceeds $(1 + i)$ to the left of N^*. Conversely, for any point to the right of N^* on the production function, the present value of Harriet's net income decreases as she invests more in human capital because MP is less than $(1 + i)$.

Now let us integrate our understanding of the choice human capital into the life-cycle model. Point $0'$ in Figure 15.8 represents the income stream Harriet would enjoy if she invested nothing in human capital. Associated with this income stream is the budget line of slope $-(1 + i)$ that passes through $0'$. This budget line gives us the consumption bundles (C_0, C_1) that Harriet could buy if she invested nothing in human capital. Using point $0'$ as an origin, we have plotted Harriet's human capital production function, the line $0'SN^*G$. Notice that H increases as we leftward from $0'$. The line $0'SN^*G$ traces out the net income streams available to Harriet. We use the adjective *net* because points on $0'SN^*G$ give us Harriet's income stream minus, or net of, her investment in human capital. It is her net income stream that matters here because it is only net income that she can devote to consumption. If Harriet invests $0'H'$ in human capital, for example, her net income in period zero decreases by $0'H'$ and her income in period one increases by $H'S$. Given this investment in human capital, Harriet attains the net income stream S in

---

5 We can derive this result using calculus. The present value of income associated with the investment in human capital, or what we have called net income, is

$$\text{net income} = F(H)/(1 + i) - H$$

$F(H)$ is the return on human capital. Since it is received in period one, however, its present value is $F(H)/(1 + i)$. H is the investment in human capital, and it must be subtracted to get net income. The problem is then to maximize net income by choice of H. This requires that the derivative of net income with respect to H be equal to zero, which gives us the following first-order condition.

$$F'(H^*)/(1 + i) - 1 = 0.$$

This can be rewritten as

$$F'(H^*) = (1 + i)$$

$F'(H)$ is, of course, the marginal product of human capital. To maximize net income, the rule is to invest in human capital up to the point where the marginal product of human capital is equal to $(1 + i)$.

FIGURE 15.8 — Another perspective on the human capital investment

The human capital production function in this figure specifies the income bundles that Harriet can achieve, and the separation theorem dictates that Harriet choose the income bundle that generates the budget line farthest from the origin. The optimal income bundle is N*, where the human capital production function is tangent to the budget line for N*. At N* the marginal product of human capital is equal to $(1 + i)$ — the absolute value of the slope of the budget line.

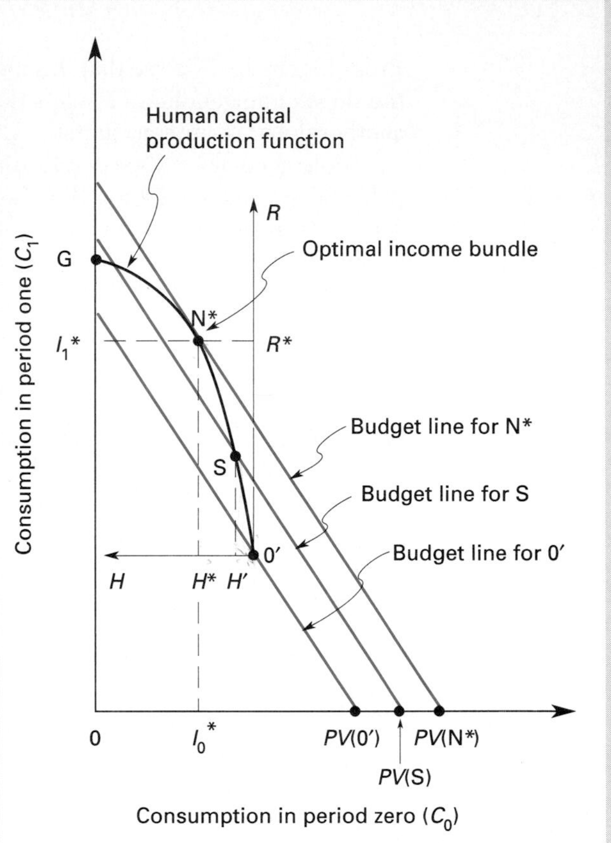

Figure 15.8. The budget line associated with the net income stream S is the line of slope $-(1 + i)$ through point S. This budget line gives us the consumption bundles (C_0, C_1) Harriet could buy if she invested $0'H'$ in human capital. Harriet is clearly better off with this investment than she is when she invests nothing in human capital. However, she can do better still by investing even more in human capital.

Her optimal investment in human capital is $0'H^*$, which gives her return H^*N^*, and the net income stream N*. This result is consistent with the result from Figure 15.7. Notice that at N* in Figure 15.8, Harriet's human capital production function is tangent to the budget line for N*. Even though, relative to the origin at 0, the slope of the budget line is $-(1 + i)$, relative to the origin at 0', the slope is $(1 + i)$, and Figures 15.7 and 15.8 give us the same result.

The advantage of Figure 15.8 is that it gives us a more direct perspective on why Harriet should choose to invest in human capital up to the point where *MP* is equal to $(1 + i)$. Notice that the budget line associated with any other investment in human capital lies closer to the origin than the budget line for N*. Therefore, by choosing point N* on her human capital production function, Harriet gets a budget line that is preferred to any other available budget line.

As we saw in the preceding section, we can find the present value of a net income stream by identifying the point where the budget line for the income stream intersects the horizontal axis. Looking at the present values on the horizontal axis in Figure 15.8, we see that by investing $0'H^*$ in human capital, Harriet maximizes the present value of income available for consumption. Of course, this result is dictated by the separation theorem.

Now we can complete this simplified presentation of an economic life cycle by introducing Harriet's consumption decision. In Figure 15.9 we have combined the analysis of Harriet's human capital decision with the analysis of her intertemporal consumption decision. The optimal point on her human capital production function is N^*, which generates net income stream N^*, composed of net income I_0^* in period zero and income I_1^* in period one. Given the budget line associated with this income stream, she chooses consumption bundle E^*, composed of consumption C_0^* in period zero and consumption C_1^* in period one.

Figure 15.9 has some interesting features that are true of the life cycle — not just of Harriet but of most people. In period zero, Harriet invests in human capital to maximize the present value of her net income over her life cycle. Consequently, the net income she actually earns in period zero is small relative to both the net income she would earn in period zero if she invested nothing in human capital and the income she earns in period one. But her preferences lead her to want a life-cycle consumption

FIGURE 15.9 **The life-cycle choice**

This figure draws together the elements of the life-cycle model. Harriet chooses to invest in human capital up to the point where the marginal product of human capital is equal to $(1 + i)$, which generates the income bundle N^*. She then uses the budget line for income bundle N^* in conjunction with her preferences to choose consumption bundle E^*, where her marginal rate of time preference is equal to $(1 + i)$.

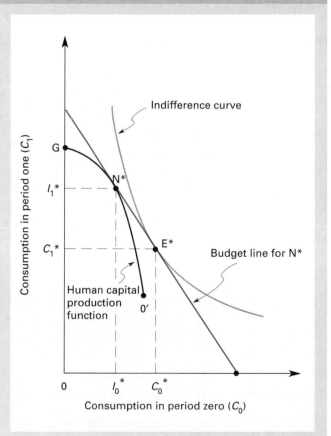

bundle that is more *balanced* than her life-cycle net income stream. As a result, in period zero Harriet borrows against future earnings to indulge in present consumption. To get a firm grasp of this life-cycle model, try the following problems.

PROBLEM 15.7

Suppose that E* is to the right of N* as in Figure 15.9, and consider a drop in the interest rate. Indicate whether the following statements are true, false, or uncertain.
a. Harriet invests more in human capital.
b. The present value of Harriet's optimal net income stream increases.
c. The future value of Harriet's optimal net income stream increases.
d. Harriet is better off.
e. Harriet consumes more in period zero.
f. Harriet consumes more in period one.

PROBLEM 15.8

If Harriet has no access to a market for loanable funds — no bank where she can borrow and/or deposit money — then her consumption in each period is equal to her net income in that period. Is she worse off when she has no access to a market for loanable funds than she is when she does have access to such a market? Construct a diagram to support your answer.

In our discussion of human capital, we have assumed that people like Harriet face a perfect market for loanable funds. In particular, we have assumed that, while they are investing in human capital, they can borrow against future income for current consumption. This is the pattern we show in Figure 15.9. In fact, the ability of young people to engage in this sort of borrowing is quite limited. Commercial institutions like banks, trust companies, and credit unions will lend large sums of money only if the loan is secured by a legally enforceable, *conditional claim* against some asset that permits the lender to seize the asset if the borrower defaults on his or her repayment obligations. If you own a home, for example, you can use it as security for a loan from a bank or credit union. The instrument that gives the lender the legally enforceable, conditional claim against the home is, of course, a **mortgage**.

mortgage

Most young people do not own their own homes or any other assets that can be used to secure large loans. Their most valuable asset is their human capital — their future earning potential — and this asset cannot be used as security for a loan. Laws against slavery and other forms of involuntary servitude mean that you cannot "mortgage" your human capital. There is, then, an important imperfection in the market for loanable funds arising from the fact that human capital cannot be used as security. In response to this imperfection, many governments have devised student loan programs. These programs can be seen as attempts to allow young people to borrow against their human capital.

15.4
Intertemporal Allocation of Nonrenewable Resources

The old aphorism, "Oil in the ground is like money in the bank," brings up an important intertemporal question: When will oil in the ground be pumped, sold, and turned into money in the bank? This kind of supply decision clearly depends on the prices that suppliers anticipate today, tomorrow, and the day after, and on the interest rate i.

To discover the basic principles that guide the intertemporal allocation of nonrenewable resources, we will develop a two-period model for a nonrenewable natural resource that is in fixed supply — oil, for example. We will start by analyzing the supply behavior of individual owners of oil and then combine these results with the tools developed in Chapter 13 to determine the intertemporal equilibrium: the price and the allocation of oil to each of the two periods.

Individual Supply Behavior

Let us begin with the supply decision of an imaginary person named Bagwell, who owns 10,000 barrels of crude oil. For simplicity, we will assume that Bagwell incurs no cost in pumping and selling his oil, and that there are only two periods in this economy — period zero and period one. We will also assume that Bagwell owns only a tiny portion of the total supply of oil and that he is therefore a price taker in the market for oil. Therefore, Bagwell's only decisions are how much of his 10,000 barrels of oil to pump and sell (or supply) in period zero, z_0, and how much in period one, z_1.

Suppose that the market for loanable funds is perfect. From the separation theorem we know that Bagwell will then choose z_0 and z_1 to maximize the present value of his oil income. If we let w_0 and w_1 denote the prices of oil in periods zero and one respectively, the present value of his oil income is

$$PV = w_0 z_0 + w_1 z_1/(1 + i)$$

Of course, since Bagwell has just 10,000 barrels of oil,

$$z_1 = 10{,}000 - z_0$$

If we then substitute this expression for z_1 in the expression for the present value of Bagwell's oil income and rearrange it, we get

$$PV = 10{,}000 w_1/(1 + i) + z_0[w_0 - w_1/(1 + i)]$$

The first term is Bagwell's wealth if he sells all of his oil in period one. The second term is the crucial one: notice that in the second term $(w_0 - w_1/(1 + i))$ is the rate of change of Bagwell's wealth as he sells one more unit of oil in period zero and therefore one less unit in period one. If this term is positive — that is, if w_0 exceeds $w_1/(1 + i)$ — then his wealth increases as z_0 increases (and z_1 correspondingly decreases). Therefore, Bagwell will sell all 10,000 barrels of his oil in period 0 and none of it in period 1 if w_0 exceeds $w_1/(1 + i)$.

To understand this result, suppose that Bagwell initially sells, say, 9,000 barrels in period zero. Now suppose that he considers selling one more unit in period zero, and therefore one less unit in period one. The increase in the present value of Bagwell's oil income from selling one more unit of oil in period zero is w_0, and the decrease in the present value of his income from selling one less unit in period one is $w_1/(1 + i)$. If w_0 exceeds $w_1/(1 + i)$, the net change in the present value of his income, $w_0 - w_1/(1 + i)$, is positive, and Bagwell therefore will sell his whole supply of oil in period zero.

This sort of reasoning also reveals that if w_0 is less than $w_1/(1 + i)$, he will sell all his oil in period one. Finally, if w_0 is equal to $w_1/(1 + i)$, the present value of Bagwell's income is independent of how much oil he sells in each period. Obviously, the rules we have just derived for Bagwell describe the supply behavior of any owner of oil:

If $w_0 > w_1/(1 + i)$, all oil is sold in period 0.

If $w_0 < w_1/(1 + i)$, all oil is sold in period 1.

If $w_0 = w_1/(1 + i)$, some oil may be sold in each period.

Hotelling's Law

Now that we know the supply response of any individual to any pair of prices for oil in the two periods, we can combine this knowledge with the tools developed earlier in Chapter 13 to determine the competitive equilibrium allocation of a fixed supply of oil and the equilibrium prices in the two periods. We will assume that each of a great many people owns a small portion of a fixed total supply of oil. We will denote the fixed total supply by z', and the quantities allocated to the two periods by z_0 and z_1. Clearly,

$$z_0 + z_1 = z'$$

We will look at the normal case in which some portion of the oil is allocated to each of the two periods — that is, the case in which the equivalent values of both z_0 and z_1 are positive. From what we just learned about the supply behavior of individuals like Bagwell, when z_0 and z_1 are both positive, the following relationship between w_0 and w_1 must hold:

$$w_0 = w_1/(1 + i)$$

If w_0 were less than $w_1/(1 + i)$, then no one would supply any oil in period zero, and if w_0 were larger than $w_1/(1 + i)$, then no one would supply any oil in period 1. Let us rewrite this equation as

$$w_1 = w_0(1 + i)$$

Hotelling's law   We can express this result, known as **Hotelling's law**, in words:[6]

The price of oil rises from one period to the next at the rate of interest.

Determining the Competitive Equilibrium

We can now use Figure 15.10 to find equilibrium prices and the equilibrium allocation of oil to the two periods. Notice that all four quadrants in Figure 15.10 share a common origin at the center of the figure and that the arrows at the ends of the axes indicate the direction in which the given price or quantity is increasing.

Hotelling's law tells us that the pair of equilibrium prices in periods 0 and 1, (w_0^e, w_1^e), will lie on the line $w_1 = (1 + i)w_0$ in quadrant I. But which point on the line represents the equilibrium-price pair, and what is the corresponding allocation of oil to the two periods? We can find out by using the ordinary tools of input supply and demand to derive a locus of market-clearing prices, labeled B'E'G'A' in quadrant 1. The equilibrium prices are then determined by the intersection of this locus with the line $w_1 = (1 + i)w_0$ that captures Hotelling's law.

6 Hotelling's law was developed in Hotelling (1931).

FIGURE 15.10   Intertemporal allocation of a nonrenewable natural resource

Since the line 0E' in quadrant I captures Hotelling's law, the equilibrium prices for oil in the two periods will lie on 0E'. The demand functions for periods 0 and 1 are constructed in quadrants IV and II, and the line AGEB in quadrant III represents all possible allocations of the fixed supply of oil to the two periods. Using these relationships, we have derived the locus of market-clearing prices in quadrant I — the curve B'E'G'A'. The equilibrium prices for oil will also lie on the

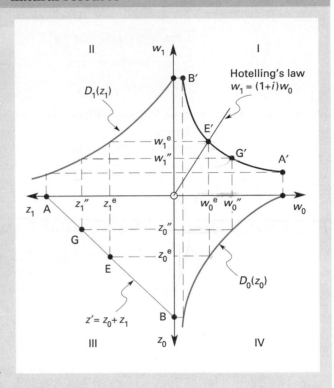

locus of market clearing prices. Hence, the equilibrium prices (w_0^e, w_1^e) are at the intersection of the line 0E' and the curve B'E'G'A'.

Any point on the line $z' = z_0 + z_1$ in quadrant III is a possible allocation of the fixed supply of oil to the two periods. By choosing any one of those allocations — say, (z_0'', z_1'') at point G in quadrant III — we can identify the corresponding pair of market-clearing prices by referring to the input demand functions in quadrants II and IV. The allocation at G gives rise to point G' on the locus of market-clearing prices in quadrant I — the competitive equilibrium price in period 0 is w_0'' when z_0'' units are supplied, and the competitive equilibrium price in period 1 is w_1'' when z_1'' units are supplied. The entire locus of market-clearing prices — the line B'E'G'A' in quadrant I — has been derived with this technique. (On this locus, the price pairs at points B', E', and A' correspond, respectively, to the allocations labeled B, E, and A in quadrant III.)

The equilibrium-price pair (w_0^e, w_1^e) is determined by the intersection of the line $w_1 = (1 + i)w_0$, which captures Hotelling's Law, and the locus of market-clearing prices at point E' in quadrant I. The corresponding equilibrium allocation (z_0^e, z_1^e) is at point E in quadrant III. Because (w_0^e, w_1^e) is on the locus of market-clearing prices, quantity demanded is equal to z_0^e in period zero and z_1^e in period one. Because the price combination (w_0^e, w_1^e) is on the line $w_1 = (1 + i)w_0$, the allocation (z_0^e, z_1^e) is consistent with the supply behavior of individual owners of oil.

Let us see why other price combinations cannot be equilibrium prices. At the prices (w_0'', w_1'') at point G', for instance, all the suppliers will want to sell all their oil in period zero because w_0 exceeds $w_1(1 + i)$. Therefore, the corresponding allocation $(z_0{''}, z_1{''})$ at point G in quadrant III, in which $z_1{''}$ is positive, will not be forthcoming. To check your understanding of this model, try the comparative statics exercise in the following problem.

PROBLEM 15.9

Suppose that the interest rate increases. Show that z_0^e increases; z_1^e decreases; w_0^e decreases; and w_1^e increases.

From Problem 15.9 you have learned that, given a fixed supply of a nonrenewable resource, the price that governs the intertemporal allocation of the fixed supply to different time periods is the rate of interest i. Thus, a drop in the interest rate serves to reallocate resource use from the present to the future.

15.5

The Firm's Demand for Capital Inputs

In our discussion of a firm's demand for inputs in Chapter 13, we focused on inputs that were rented or hired on a period by period basis. Clearly, firms not only rent and hire inputs, but they also buy inputs that provide productive services over many periods. A railroad, for example, *buys* a variety of different goods that serve as inputs over many periods — locomotives, flat cars, tanker cars, box cars, signaling equipment, rails, and real estate, to name just a few such goods — and it *hires* other inputs — principally labor. Goods that serve as inputs over many periods are called **capital inputs**. In this section, we extend the analysis of input demand to include the demand for capital inputs.

capital inputs

In Chapter 13, we discovered that the firm's input demand function for a hired input was, with some qualifications, its marginal revenue product *MRP* function. As you know, *MRP* measures the contribution of an additional unit of the input to the firm's revenue, and input price w measures the contribution of an additional unit of the input to the firm's cost. Accordingly, hiring one more unit of the input results in an increase in the firm's profit when *MRP* exceeds w, and a decrease in the firm's profit when w exceeds *MRP*. Therefore, to maximize profit the firm hires an input up to the point where *MRP* is equal to w. In this section we want to find the firm's demand function for capital inputs.

Given a particular capital input, say a truck of some description, the question we want to answer is this: How many trucks will the firm want to have? To answer this question, we need to know what the firm's objective is. In previous chapters, where the firm made decisions for just one period, we took the firm's objective to be profit maximization. We arrived at profit maximization as the firm's objective by arguing that the firm's owners would unanimously agree on the goal of profit maximization because the firm's profit is, in effect, purchasing power for the owners of the firm: by maximizing profit, the firm maximizes the purchasing power of its owners.

What is the firm's objective when there are many periods? When the market for loanable funds is perfect, we can use the separation theorem to argue that the firm's owners will unanimously agree that the firm should maximize the *present value* of the firm's profit: by maximizing the present value of its profit, the firm maximizes the purchasing power of its owners.

We will begin the analysis with a very simple, imaginary capital input, which we call a gadget. Imagine that the purchase price of a gadget is P dollars, the gadget lasts for exactly D years, it has no scrap value, and it requires no maintenance. Having mastered this simple case, we can easily generalize it to apply it to more complex capital inputs.

Since it lasts for D periods, a gadget that is bought in the current period — period zero — will contribute to the firm's revenue for exactly D periods — period zero, period one, ..., and period $D - 1$. Its contribution to the firm's revenue in period zero will be MRP_0 — the marginal revenue product of an additional gadget in period zero. Similarly, its contribution to the firm's revenue in period t will be MRP_t, where t is in the range 0 to $D - 1$. If we compute the present value of each of these MRPs and sum them, we have the present value of the gadget's contribution to the firm's revenue. This sum of present values of marginal revenue products is denoted by ΣMRP.

$$\Sigma MRP = MRP_0 + [MRP_1/(1+i)] + \ldots + [MRP_{D-1}/(1+i)^{D-1}]$$

The contribution of an additional gadget to the present value of the firm's costs is, of course, just the purchase price of the gadget, P.

Notice that if ΣMRP exceeds P, an additional gadget results in an increase in the present value of the firm's profit. On the other hand, if ΣMRP is less than P, an additional gadget results in a decrease in the present value of the firm's profit. To maximize the present value of its profit, the firm should therefore have enough gadgets so that ΣMRP is equal to P. We see, then, that ΣMRP is the firm's *demand function* for gadgets.

In Figure 15.11a, we have drawn the firm's demand function for gadgets for three different rates of interest — 5%, 10%, and 15%. In constructing Figure 15.11 we have assumed a diminishing marginal product for gadgets in all periods and the three ΣMRP functions therefore are everywhere downward sloping.

Our primary interest is the relationship between the demand for capital inputs and the rate of interest. Notice that the demand function in Figure 15.11a shifts downward as the interest rate increases. Why? Because, for every period except period zero, the present value of MRP decreases as the interest rate increases. In other words, as the interest rate increases, the contribution of an additional gadget to the present value of the firm's revenue decreases, and the demand function therefore shifts downward. Holding the price of a gadget fixed at $1,000, we see from Figure 15.11 that the firm demands 98 gadgets when the interest rate is 5%, 71 gadgets when the interest rate is 10%, and only 50 gadgets when the interest rate is 15%.

In other words, there is an inverse relation between the interest rate and the firm's demand for gadgets. The higher the interest rate, the fewer gadgets the firm will buy. We have used the information from Figure 15.11a to construct this inverse relation between quantity of gadgets demanded and the interest rate in Figure 15.11b.

PROBLEM 15.10

Consider a slightly more complex capital input, a widgit. The purchase price of a widgit is P, a widgit lasts for D periods, it has no scrap value, and it requires expenditure on maintenance equal to M at the beginning of each period, excluding period zero. Show that, to maximize its profit, the firm will buy widgits up to the point where

$$\Sigma \text{MRP} = P + [M/(1+i)] + [M/(1+i)^2] + \ldots + [M/(1+i)^{D-1}]$$

Let us generalize what you learned in this problem:

The optimal quantity of a capital input is the quantity such that the present value of all marginal revenue products over the life of the capital input is equal to the present value of all costs associated with the capital input.

FIGURE 15.11   The demand for a capital input

To maximize profit, the firm buys gadgets up to the point where ΣMRP is equal to the price of the input. As the interest rate i increases, ΣMRP shifts to the left as shown in (a), reducing the firm's demand for gadgets. In (b), we have held the price of gadgets constant at $1,000 and constructed the firm's demand for gadgets as a function of the rate of interest i. Observe that the demand for gadgets is inversely related to the rate of interest.

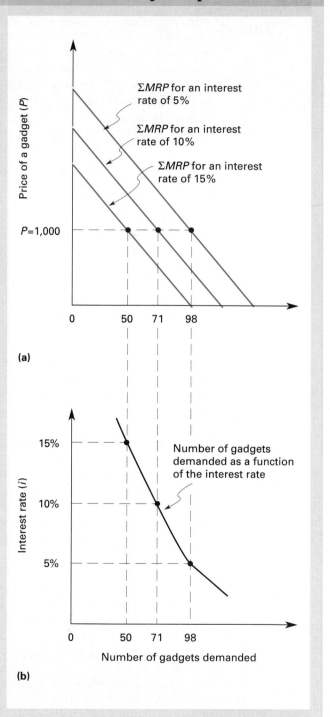

15.6

The Market for Loanable Funds

As we have seen throughout this chapter, the interest rate is the crucial price that determines the intertemporal allocation of resources. Now let us see how that very important price is set. Clearly the interest rate is determined by the forces of demand and supply in the market for loanable funds.[7] The primary actors in the market for loanable funds are individuals, firms, and governments. However, for simplicity, we will restrict our attention to individuals and firms as the actors determining the interest rate.

To further simplify the analysis, we will assume that firms remit all their profit in each period to their owners. This means that, in any given period, all the economy's income is initially in the hands of individuals. Of course, in reality, firms do retain some of their profit to finance their purchases of capital goods. Given our assumption of a perfect market for loanable funds, however, firms can never increase the present value of their profit by retaining profit for buying capital goods. In this setting, then, the assumption that firms retain no profit does not affect the analysis.

As we saw in Section 15.2, individuals create a *demand* for loanable funds when they borrow against future income to support current consumption, and they create a *supply* of loanable funds when they save current income for purposes of future consumption. Supposing that consumption in each period is a normal good, we saw that an individual borrower's demand for loanable funds is inversely related to the interest rate — the income and substitution effects both lead to decreased borrowing as the interest rate increases. In contrast, we saw that an individual saver's supply of loanable funds could be either directly or inversely related to the interest rate — the substitution effect for an increase in the interest rate leads to a larger supply of loanable funds whereas the income effect leads to a smaller supply. We will suppose, however, that the substitution effect dominates the income effect and that the saver's supply of loanable funds therefore is directly related to the interest rate.

In Section 15.5 we found the firm's demand function for a generic capital input that we called a gadget. How does the demand for capital inputs manifest itself as a demand for loanable funds? Recall that we are supposing that all the firm's profit is paid out to the owners of the firm. This means that if the firm wants to buy additional capital goods, it will have to borrow money in the market for loanable funds to finance the purchase.

Of course, if the firm had no gadgets on hand, it would buy them up to the point where ΣMRP equals the purchase price of a gadget. If the firm already owns a number of gadgets, however, the number of gadgets it actually buys will be correspondingly reduced. We will call the number of gadgets the firm buys in any period its **investment demand** for gadgets. The firm's investment demand for gadgets is just its demand for a stock of gadgets minus the quantity of gadgets that the firm already owns. (If this number is negative, then the firm's investment demand is zero.) If the firm requires a stock of 25 gadgets to maximize the present value of its profit and if it currently has 17 gadgets, its investment demand will be 8 gadgets.

It is a firm's investment demand that generates a demand for loanable funds. If a firm wants to buy 8 additional gadgets and if the price of a gadget is $1,000, it will demand $8,000 in the market for loanable funds. We saw that the firm's demand for a stock of

investment demand

---

7 See the entry by S. C. Tsiang "loanable funds" in *The New Palgrave*.

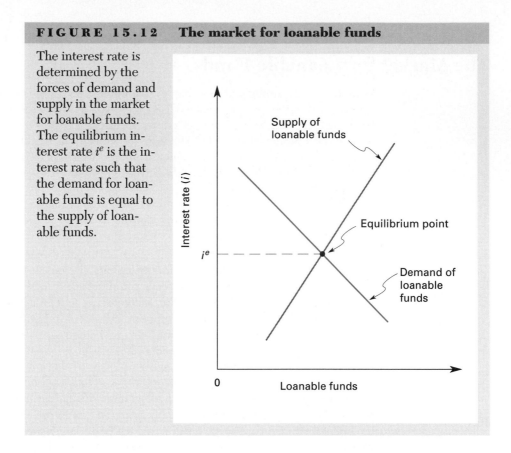

FIGURE 15.12   The market for loanable funds

The interest rate is determined by the forces of demand and supply in the market for loanable funds. The equilibrium interest rate i^e is the interest rate such that the demand for loanable funds is equal to the supply of loanable funds.

capital goods is inversely related to the rate of interest. It follows directly from this result that the firm's demand for loanable funds is likewise inversely related to the rate of interest.

By horizontally aggregating the supply of loanable funds over all individual savers, we get a positively sloped supply curve. Similarly, by horizontally aggregating the demand for loanable funds over all borrowers — individuals and firms — we get a negatively sloped demand curve. The interest rate is then determined at the intersection of the demand and supply curves as shown in Figure 15.12.

Notice that the market for loanable funds involves virtually all the actors in the economy — all individuals and all firms. Even the wealthiest person and the largest firm in the economy are insignificant relative to the market as a whole. In other words, if there is any market in the economy that is competitive, it is the market for loanable funds — and we do not need to consider the possibility of monopsony or monopoly in this market.

SUMMARY

We began this chapter with a very simple choice problem: given a choice between two windfall gains — $1,000 today or $1,100 one year from today — which should you choose? We saw that when the borrowing and deposit rates of interest are identical, there is an unambiguous best choice. You should always choose the windfall gain with the larger present value.

This is one application of what is known as the *separation theorem*. The theorem says that in an intertemporal context, an individual's utility maximization problem can be separated into two parts: the choice of an income stream and the choice of a consumption bundle. We saw that (i) given a number of possible income streams, the individual will choose the income stream with the largest present value of income, and that (ii) the individual will choose a consumption bundle to maximize utility, subject to the constraint that the present value of expenditures on consumption is equal to the present value of the individual's income. This separation is achievable only when the borrowing and lending rates of interest are identical, or when the market for loanable funds is perfect. Virtually all of the analysis in the chapter is built on the foundation of the separation theorem.

We saw how an individual allocates income to consumption over his or her economic life cycle, and we used this analysis to generate the demand and supply for loanable funds from individuals. Then, we used the separation theorem to analyze an individual's choice of human capital. We discovered that to maximize the present value of his or her lifetime income, an individual invests in human capital up to the point where the marginal product of human capital is equal to $(1 + i)$.

We then combined these two pieces of analysis to develop a larger understanding of the typical person's economic life cycle. A typical individual invests heavily in human capital in the early part of the life cycle and therefore earns an income considerably smaller than the income that could be earned in the absence of this investment in human capital. Faced with the resulting — and decidedly unbalanced — lifetime income stream, the typical individual borrows in the early part of the life cycle against his or her future income to finance consumption that exceeds income.

We then used the separation theorem in conjunction with tools developed earlier to analyze the intertemporal allocation of a nonrenewable resource like oil. We saw that the price of the nonrenewable resource will rise from one period to the next at the rate of interest — *Hotelling's law*.

In the next section, we turned to the firm's demand for *capital inputs*. Here, too, we used the separation theorem — this time to argue that the firm's objective in an intertemporal setting is to maximize the present value of its profit. We then found that the firm's demand function for a capital input was the sum of the present values of the marginal revenue products of the capital input over the good's lifetime — ΣMRP. Of course, this result is a generalization of what we learned about the demand for hired inputs in Chapter 13. We found that the firm's demand for a capital input is inversely related, not only to the purchase price of the capital input, but also to the rate of interest. The higher the interest rate, the fewer units of the capital input the firm will use.

Finally, in the last section, we turned to the *determination of the interest rate* in the market for loanable funds. We saw how to translate a firm's demand for a stock of capital goods into an investment demand for loanable funds, and we showed that this investment demand is inversely related to the rate interest. And we aggregated the elements of the demand for and supply of loanable funds to get aggregate demand and supply curves. The equilibrium interest rate is, of course, the rate of interest such that demand for loanable funds is equal to supply of loanable funds.

EXERCISES

1. Howard can borrow against future income at a 10% rate of interest, and he can earn 10% on his savings. His rich uncle has given him the choice between $50,000 now or $72,000 in four years. If he put it all in his savings account, how much would the original $50,000 be worth in four years? What is the present value of the $70,000? Which option should Howard choose?

2. Sarah has been given the following choice of inheritance packages by her parents: Package A is composed of $100,000 today and $200,000 one year from today. Package B is composed of $200,000 today and $85,000 one year from today.

   a. Assuming that the borrowing and deposit rates of interest are identical, identify the conditions under which Sarah should take package A, and the conditions under which she should take package B.

   b. Still assuming that the two rates of interest are identical, identify the conditions under which Sarah is better off when the interest rate changes from 10% to 12%.

   c. Assuming that the deposit rate is 0% and that the borrowing rate is 100%, construct the budget lines associated with both of these packages and show that it is impossible to say which package Sarah should choose without information regarding her preferences.

   d. Assuming that the borrowing rate exceeds the deposit rate, identify the circumstances under which Sarah should choose package A, the circumstances under which she should choose package B, and the circumstances under which you need information regarding her preferences to determine which package she should choose.

3. To borrow money from the public, firms sell bonds. A *bond* is just a piece of paper that obligates the firm to pay the holder of the piece of paper a fixed sum of money in each of a fixed number of periods.

   a. What is the maximum amount you would pay today for a bond that promised to pay you $1,000 at the end of each of the next three years, assuming that the interest rate is 5%? Assuming that the interest rate is 10%? Assuming that the interest rate is 15%?

   b. If this bond is sold at auction, and if the interest rate is 10%, what is your prediction with respect to its price? Explain. What sort of relationship would you expect to see between the price of bonds and the interest rate?

4. A bond that pays a fixed sum in every future period is called a *consol*. If D is the fixed payment, then just after an annual payment has been made, the present value of the stream of payments promised by the consol is

$$PV = \frac{D}{1+i} + \frac{D}{(1+i)^2} + \frac{D}{(1+i)^3} + \dots$$

Show that this expression for the present value of the payments of a consol can be reduced to the following simple expression:

$$PV = \frac{D}{i}$$

5. Suppose you borrow $1,000 from your bank today, and that, in return, you agree to repay a fixed amount F at the end of each of the next three years. Using the present value formula, show that F is $367.21 if the borrowing rate of interest is 5%. What is F if the borrowing rate of interest rate is 10%? If it is 30%?

6. Consider a capital input with the following characteristics. Its price is $5,000, it lasts for 5 years, it requires a $100 expenditure on maintenance at the end of 3 years, and it has a scrap value of $1,000 at the end of 5 periods. What is the rule that determines the profit-maximizing quantity of this input?

7. Fran runs a small delivery service. The borrowing and deposit rates of interest are identical for her. Her only inputs are her time, gasoline, and a very specialized delivery truck. The truck is so specialized to her needs that it has no scrap value. The price of a new truck is $25,000. As one of these trucks ages, maintenance gets more expensive. The required maintenance at the end of year one costs $2,000, and the maintenance cost increases each year by $2,000: at the end of year two it is $4,000, at the end of year three it is $6,000, and so on. She plans to stay in business for just five more years. Because her current truck is now exactly four years old, if she wants to use it for another year she must now spend $8,000 on maintenance. She is considering two options: option A, using her current truck for the next five years; and option B, buying a new truck today, and using it for the next five years.

   a. What is the present value of costs under option A? Under option B? Which is the better option?

   c. Given that she is going to stay in business for another five years, should she be considering other options?

8. Jerry has just discovered a cache of 100,000 returnable pop cans in an old barn on a property he recently bought. Currently, such cans can be returned for 10¢ per can. However, there has been

pressure on politicians to substantially increase the deposit on cans to assure that they are recycled instead of being discarded by the roadside. Consequently, Jerry (and everybody else) anticipates that he will get 20¢ per can if he holds on to his cans for a year.

a. Should Jerry sell the cans now, or should he wait a year?

b. Now take a broader perspective, and look at the decisions of all citizens. What is your prediction about the number of cans that will be returned in each of the next 13 months?

9. A certain plot of agricultural land is scheduled to be developed into a shopping mall in three years. The developer who now owns the land is not a farmer; however, she knows that if the land is farmed, it will generate $100,000 in revenue per year and that any farmer's costs are only $75,000 per year. She has therefore decided to sell the right to farm the land for the next three years.

a. If the interest rate is 10%, what price should she ask? If it is 20%, what price should she ask?

b. Suppose that the interest rate that farmers can earn on their savings (the deposit rate of interest) is less than the rate they must pay to borrow money (the borrowing rate of interest). Show that the opportunity to farm this land is more valuable to a farmer with lots of money in the bank than to one with very little money.

REFERENCES

Becker, G. 1964. *Human Capital*, New York: Columbia University Press.

Fisher, I. 1907. *The Theory of Interest*, New York: Macmillan.

Fisher, M. R. 1987. "Life Cycle Hypothesis," in *The New Palgrave: A Dictionary of Economics*, J. Eatwell, M. Milgate, and P. Newman (eds.), London: The Macmillan Press

Friedman, M. 1957. *A Theory of the Consumption Function*, Princeton, New Jersey: Princeton University Press.

Hirshleifer, J. 1970. *Investment, Interest, and Capital*, Englewood Cliffs, New Jersey: Prentice-Hall.

———. 1987. "Investment Decision Criteria," in *The New Palgrave: A Dictionary of Economics*, J. Eatwell, M. Milgate, and P. Newman (eds.), London: The Macmillan Press.

Hotelling, H. 1931. "The Economics of Exhaustible Resources," *Journal of Political Economy*, 39:137–75.

Mincer, J. 1958. "Investment in Human Capital and Personal Income Distribution," *Journal of Political Economy*, 66(August):281–302.

Modigliani, F. and R. Brumberg. 1954. "Utility Analysis and the Consumption Function: An Interpretation of Cross-Section Data," in *Post-Keynesian Economics*, K. K. Kurihara (ed.), New Brunswick, New Jersey: Rutgers University Press.

Rosen. S. 1987. "Human Capital," in *The New Palgrave: A Dictionary of Economics*, J. Eatwell, M. Milgate, and P. Newman (eds.), London: The Macmillan Press.

Schultz, T. 1961. "Investment in Human Capital," *American Economic Review*, 51(March):1–17.

Tsiang, S. C. 1987. "Loanable Funds," in *The New Palgrave: A Dictionary of Economics*, J. Eatwell, M. Milgate, and P. Newman (eds.), London: The Macmillan Press.

CHAPTER 16

Efficiency and the Allocation of Resources: A General Equilibrium Approach

Two problems are basic to all economic analysis. The first problem is allocation: How does an economic system allocate scarce resources to competing uses? More specifically, using the Pareto criterion as the evaluative yardstick, when does a market system successfully direct resources to alternative uses? The second problem is distribution: How are wealth and income (or command over goods and services) distributed among the individual members of society? Again specifically, what criterion should we use to evaluate distribution? And if we judge redistribution as socially desirable, what institutions are effective in moving an economy from one economic state to another, more "distributionally acceptable" state?

We looked at the question of distribution in Chapter 14. In this chapter, we will take up the allocation question once again as we finally fit all the analytical pieces of earlier chapters into one large picture of efficiency in an economy-wide context. We are now widening our perspective from the earlier partial equilibrium framework, characterized by a market-by-market analysis, to a **general equilibrium** framework, in which we simultaneously consider all markets in the economy. At every turn, we will be drawing on what we learned in earlier chapters. This chapter will integrate much of what we have learned so far and will review that material. If at any point you are uncertain about that earlier material, briefly review it before proceeding.

A recurring theme in economics concerns the extent to which the interactions of self-interested individuals yield results that are in some sense socially desirable. Adam Smith, the father of the doctrine of **natural identity of interests**, argued that every person, in pursuing his or her own self-interest, would be lead as by an "unseen hand" to behave in ways that ultimately contributed to the welfare of society as a whole. But, as George Stigler has observed, Smith's doctrine of the natural identity of interests is "not really a doctrine at all: it is a problem."[1] Smith's doctrine raises this question:

general
equilibrium

natural identity
of interests

---

1 See Stigler's (1957) introductory remarks. His *Selections from The Wealth of Nations* is an excellent introduction to Smith's great work. Karen Vaughn's entry on the "invisible hand" in *The New Palgrave* provides an interesting discussion of Smith's contribution to the natural identity of interests.

What kinds of social arrangements promote an identity between public and private interests? In this chapter, we will rise to the challenge posed by Smith's doctrine as we look for a set of institutions consistent with the natural identity of interests. As you will discover, when certain restrictive conditions are satisfied, the institutions of perfect competition promote Pareto optimality, or efficiency.

To an economist, the overriding purpose of the economic system is to transform the scarce resources belonging to individuals into consumption goods that benefit those same individuals. Individual people are therefore the leading actors in the economic drama. From them (and from nature) comes the wherewithal to produce goods, and goods are produced for their benefit. In this larger, general equilibrium drama, then, firms are the minor players. Their only role is to facilitate the process of transforming resources into consumption goods. Questions of efficiency are therefore concerned not with the profit of firms but exclusively with the well-being of individual people.

Using the Pareto criterion as our yardstick for measuring individual well-being, we can see that the general equilibrium of an economy is efficient if no person can be made better off without making another person worse off.

Let us begin our analysis by focusing on a simple economy in which goods are exchanged and consumed but not produced. We will discover exactly what efficiency means in this exchange economy, and then we will show that general competitive equilibrium is efficient if certain conditions are satisfied. We will then introduce production into the model and generalize the understanding developed in the simpler context of an exchange economy.[2]

16.1

Efficiency in an Exchange Economy

exchange economy

In the next two sections, we will look at an **exchange economy**, that is, an economy in which goods are traded and consumed but not produced. In this section, we discover how to determine which allocations of available goods to individual consumers are Pareto-optimal. In the next section, we create competitive markets in which goods can be traded, find the competitive equilibrium, and consider two results (or theorems) that are the cornerstones of what is called welfare economics.

The Edgeworth Box Diagram

Imagine, that two people — Marvin and Shelly — are living on some isolated island where there are 102 units of good 1 and 66 units of good 2. We can use a box diagram to describe all possible allocations of goods in this island exchange economy. The dimensions of the box diagram in Figure 16.1 reflect the available quantities of goods 1 and 2: the horizontal sides are 102 units long because there are 102 units of good 1 in this economy; the vertical sides are 66 units long because there are 66 units of good 2 in this economy. Possible consumption bundles for Shelly, or — to put it another way — possible allocations of goods to Shelly, are plotted relative to the origin 0_S at the lower left-hand corner of the box. Similarly, possible allocations of goods to Marvin are plotted relative to the origin 0_M at the upper right-hand corner of the box diagram.

---

2 Walras (1874, 1877) is the founder of general equilibrium theory. Jaffe (1954) is the English translator. Arrow and Hahn (1971) present a comprehensive treatment of general equilibrium theory and (in Chapter 1) an interesting history of it. Lionel McKenzie's entry titled "general equilibrium" in *The New Palgrave* provides a short, relatively accessible overview of the theory of general equilibrium.

FIGURE 16.1   The Edgeworth box diagram

Shelly's consumption bundles and indifference curves are plotted relative to 0_S; Marvin's, relative to 0_M. Because Shelly's and Marvin's indifference curves are tangent at allocation A, the allocation is Pareto-optimal. In contrast, because Shelly's and Marvin's indifference curves intersect at allocation D, the allocation is not Pareto-optimal: allocations in the shaded area are Pareto-preferred to allocation D.

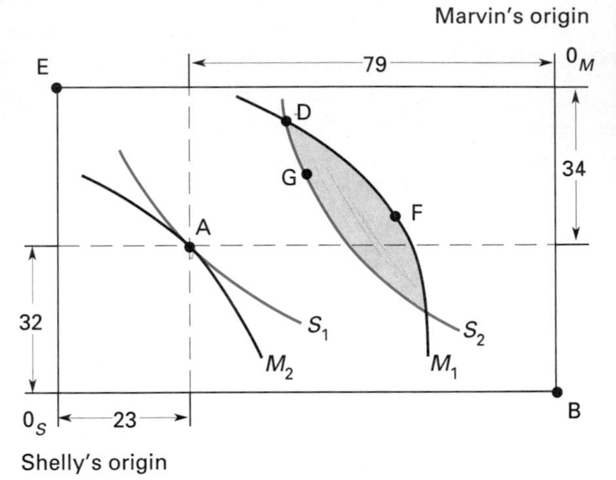

The important thing to recognize is that any point in the box is an allocation of the available quantities of the two goods to Marvin and to Shelly. Conversely, any allocation of the 102 units of good 1 and 66 units of good 2 to Marvin and Shelly is described by some point in the box.

PROBLEM 16.1

How much of each good does Marvin have, and how much does Shelly have at each of the following points in Figure 16.1? Point A; Marvin's origin 0_M; point B. Suppose that all 66 units of good 2 are allocated to Shelly and all 102 units of good 1 to Marvin. What point in Figure 16.1 describes this allocation?

Edgeworth box diagram

Notice, too, that we can plot Shelly's and Marvin's indifference curves in the box diagram. When we include indifference curves, the diagram is called an **Edgeworth box diagram**, after F. Y. Edgeworth, a late-nineteenth-century British economist who was the first to use this type of diagram. Since Shelly's indifference curves, labeled S_1 and S_2, are plotted relative to the origin 0_S, they have the familiar convex-to-the-origin shape. Marvin's indifference curves, labeled M_1 and M_2, are also standard convex-to-the-origin indifference curves, but they look odd because they are plotted relative to Marvin's origin 0_M. To see that they are convex to Marvin's origin, pick your book up and reorient it so that 0_M is at the lower left-hand corner of the box. Marvin's indifference curves will then appear in their familiar shape. To be sure that you understand the Edgeworth box diagram, try the following problem.

> **PROBLEM 16.2**
>
> What is Shelly's preference ordering of the four allocations A, D, G, and F in Figure 16.1? What is Marvin's?

Preference Assumptions

To keep our discussion as simple as possible, we will use four assumptions about preferences throughout the chapter:

1. Indifference curves are convex to the appropriate origin.
2. Indifference curves are smooth.
3. Both goods are essential for all consumers.
4. The only variables that affect an individual's economic well-being are the quantities of the two goods consumed by that person.

In Problem 16.3, you will have a chance to discover for yourself the role played by the convexity assumption. The second assumption allows us to use the marginal rate of substitution *MRS* in analyzing Pareto optimality, and the third allows us to concentrate on allocations in the interior of the Edgeworth box. (See Section 2.3 for the definition of *MRS*, and Section 3.4 for a discussion of essential and inessential goods.)

The fourth assumption rules out externalities involving consumption — in essence, it means that the only things that people care about are their own consumption bundles. In Chapter 17, which centers on externalities, you will see that consumption externalities raise some very interesting and difficult questions.

Now let us look at some specific allocations and ask if they are Pareto-optimal. Is the allocation at D in Figure 16.1, which puts Shelly on indifference curve S_2 and Marvin on indifference curve M_1, Pareto-optimal? It is, if there are no other allocations that make one of them better off while leaving the other at least as well off. Shelly prefers any allocation above and to the right of S_2 to D, and Marvin prefers any allocation below and to the left of M_1 to D. Therefore, any allocation in the shaded area above S_2 and below M_1 is preferred by both Marvin and Shelly to D; that is, any allocation in the shaded area is Pareto-preferred to D. We know, then, that the allocation at D is not Pareto-optimal.

Now let us consider the allocation at A, which puts Shelly on S_1 and Marvin on M_2. Take your pencil and first shade in the allocations above and to the right of S_1 which make Shelly better off than she is at A, and then shade in the allocations on M_2, or below and to the left of M_2, which make Marvin no worse off than he is at A. Since these two shaded areas have no points in common, it is impossible to make Shelly better off without making Marvin worse off. Similarly, given the allocation at A, it is impossible to make Marvin better off without making Shelly worse off. We know, then, that the allocation at A is Pareto-optimal.

What distinguishes allocation D from allocation A is that indifference curve M_1 intersects (or crosses) indifference curve S_2 at D, while indifference curve M_2 is tangent to indifference curve S_1 at A. As you can easily verify, any allocation in the interior of an Edgeworth box where two indifference curves intersect is not Pareto-optimal. Furthermore, the following is true:

When indifference curves are smooth and convex, if two indifference curves are tangent at a point in an Edgeworth box, then that point is a Pareto-optimal allocation.

PROBLEM 16.3

In an Edgeworth box, construct an indifference curve for Shelly that has a concave portion in the middle. Now construct an indifference curve for Marvin, convex to Marvin's origin, that is tangent to Shelly's indifference curve at one point and intersects her indifference curve at two other points. Show that the point of tangency is not a Pareto-optimal allocation, and identify the allocations that are Pareto-preferred to it.

Notice that at the Pareto-optimal allocation at A in Figure 16.1, the marginal rate of substitution *MRS* is identical for Marvin and Shelly. This follows from the definition of *MRS* as the absolute value of the slope of the indifference curve and from the fact that the indifference curves S_1 and M_2 are tangent at point A. This observation lets us restate our understanding of Pareto optimality in an exchange economy:

Given convex indifference curves, if MRS at some allocation is identical for Marvin and Shelly, then that allocation is Pareto-optimal.

Efficiency in Consumption

More generally, let us see what we can say about Pareto optimality (or efficiency) in an exchange economy composed of many people. Suppose that we have a many-person exchange economy and, for purposes of argument, that *MRS* at the current allocation is identical for everyone in that exchange economy. We could isolate any two people — with their consumption bundles in hand — to form an exchange economy very much like the one shown in Figure 16.1. In that two-person exchange economy, the initial allocation would be Pareto-optimal since *MRS* is identical for these two people. Therefore, if *MRS* is identical for every person in a many-person exchange economy, there are no bilateral (two-person) trades that are Pareto-preferred. Although we will not attempt a proof, there are also no multilateral (many-person) trades that are Pareto-preferred. Therefore, we can state the following general result:

Efficiency in Consumption: Given the assumptions we have made, an allocation of goods is Pareto-optimal in a many-person exchange economy if *MRS* is identical for all individuals.[3]

---

3 We can use the technique of constrained maximization to show this result. Pick any two consumers with utility functions $U^1(x_1^1, x_2^1)$ and $U^2(x_1^2, x_2^2)$, and any bundle of the two goods to be allocated to the two individuals— say, the bundle (x_1', x_2'). If we fix the utility level of the first individual at, say, u^1, then efficiency in consumption—Pareto optimality—clearly demands that we allocate the available bundle of goods to the two individuals so as to maximize $U^2(x_1^2, x_2^2)$, subject to the constraint that $u^1 = U^1(x_1^1, x_2^1)$. This is a standard constrained-maximization problem, and we will show that its solution implies that *MRS* is identical for the two consumers. The Lagrangian is

$$L(x_1^2, x_2^2, \lambda) = U^2(x_1^2, x_2^2) + \lambda[u^1 - U^1(x_1' - x_1^2, x_2' - x_2^2)]$$

where (x_1^2, x_2^2) is the second individual's consumption bundle and $(x_1' - x_1^2, x_2' - x_2^2)$ is the first individual's bundle. Setting the partial derivatives of $L(\cdot)$ with respect to x_1^2 and x_2^2 equal to zero, we have

$$U_1^2(x_1^2, x_2^2) - \lambda U_1^1(x_1' - x_1^2, x_2' - x_2^2) = 0$$
$$U_2^2(x_1^2, x_2^2) - \lambda U_2^1(x_1' - x_1^2, x_2' - x_2^2) = 0$$

The Contract Curve

contract curve

Given our assumptions, we know that any point in an Edgeworth box where the indifference curves of the two individuals are tangent is a Pareto-optimal allocation. By finding all the points in the Edgeworth box where the indifference curves are tangent, we can describe the entire set of Pareto-optimal allocations. This set, called the **contract curve**, is the line connecting all these points of tangency.

Line CC in Figure 16.2 is the contract curve for Marvin and Shelly. Even though we have drawn only three indifference curves for each, the box is filled with indifference curves. At any point on CC, two indifference curves, one for Marvin and one for Shelly, are tangent.

FIGURE 16.2   The contract curve

The contract curve CC passes through the points of tangency of Marvin's and Shelly's indifference curves. Allocations on the contract curve are Pareto-optimal, and allocations off it are not. For example, the shaded area represents the set of allocations that are Pareto-preferred to allocation A.

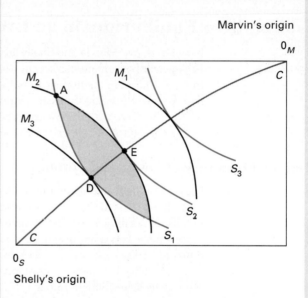

Manipulating these two expressions, we have

$$\lambda = \frac{U_1^2(x_1^2, x_2^2)}{U_1^1(x_1' - x_1^2, x_2' - x_2^2)}$$

$$= \frac{U_2^2(x_1^2, x_2^2)}{U_2^1(x_1' - x_1^2, x_2' - x_2^2)}$$

This result implies equality of the marginal rates of substitution:

$$\frac{U_1^2(x_1^2, x_2^2)}{U_2^2(x_1^2, x_2^2)}$$

$$= \frac{U_1^1(x_1' - x_1^2, x_2' - x_2^2)}{U_2^1(x_1' - x_1^2, x_2' - x_2^2)}$$

Let us see why this set of allocations is called the contract curve. Any allocation that is not on CC — point A, for example — is not Pareto-optimal. If Marvin and Shelly are initially at A, any point in the shaded area on or above S_1 and on or below M_2 Pareto-dominates A. In other words, mutually beneficial exchanges relative to point A are available to them. Segment DE of CC represents the set of Pareto-optimal allocations that are Pareto-preferred to allocation A.[4]

Imagine that Marvin and Shelly agree to an exchange that moves them from point A to some point inside the shaded area. If that agreement, or *contract*, moves them to a point that is not on DE, then both have an incentive to recontract for another mutually beneficial exchange. Because their recontracting activity will end only when they have achieved an allocation on DE, the set of Pareto-optimal allocations is called the *contract curve*. Once on the contract curve, there is no further exchange to which both Marvin and Shelly would willingly agree.

16.2

Competitive Equilibrium in an Exchange Economy

Now let us give Marvin and Shelly an initial endowment of goods at some point in their Edgeworth box, create markets in which they can buy and sell goods 1 and 2, and give them a Walrasian auctioneer to help them find the competitive equilibrium. (Recall that we introduced a Walrasian auctioneer to coordinate trading in the ticket model in Section 9.1.) We will suppose that Shelly's initial allocation is 22 units of good 1 and 56 units of good 2 and that Marvin's allocation is 80 units of good 1 and 10 units of good 2.

Budget Lines in an Exchange Economy

The first thing to notice about an exchange economy is that the prices of goods not only determine what consumption bundles a person can buy, given his or her income, but also determine what that income is. Suppose, for example, that the auctioneer announced the following prices: $p_1 = \$2$, and $p_2 = \$1$. In effect, Shelly's income is then equal to $\$100$ — ($\$2 \times 22$) + ($\$1 \times 56$) — since she could generate that amount of income by selling her initial endowment of 22 units of good 1 and 56 units of good 2. Given these prices, her budget line is

$$2x_1{}^S + x_2{}^S = 100$$

Here $x_1{}^S$ is Shelly's consumption of good 1 and $x_2{}^S$ is her consumption of good 2. More generally, for arbitrary prices p_1 and p_2, we have

$$\text{Shelly's income} = 22p_1 + 56p_2$$

since she has 22 units of good 1 and 56 units of good 2. Shelly's budget line is then

$$p_1 x_1{}^S + p_2 x_2{}^S = 22p_1 + 56p_2$$

The second thing to notice about an exchange economy with two goods is that there is really only one price to be determined in equilibrium: the price of good 1 relative to good 2, or the relative price of good 1. Notice that Shelly's budget line always

---

4 The set of Pareto-optimal allocations that are Pareto-preferred to an allocation like A in Figure 16.2 is called the *core*. Therefore, relative to initial allocation A, segment DE of the contract curve is the core.

passes through her initial endowment; that is, the consumption bundle (22 units of good 1, 56 units of good 2) is always on Shelly's budget line. The budget line will be steeper if p_1 is large relative to p_2, and it will be flatter if p_1 is small relative to p_2, but it will always pass through her initial endowment of 22 units of good 1 and 56 units of good 2. Therefore, the price of good 1 relative to the price of good 2 — or the ratio of p_1 to p_2, or the relative price of good 1 — is what really matters to Shelly. From her point of view, ($p_1 = \$2$, $p_2 = \$1$), ($p_1 = \$4$, $p_2 = \$2$), and ($p_1 = \$6$, $p_2 = \$3$) are equivalent since all three price pairs imply a budget line through her initial endowment, with slope equal to -2, and a relative price of good 1 equal to 2. Similarly, Marvin's only concern is the price of good 1 relative to the price of good 2.

We can simplify our analysis of an exchange economy by fixing the price of good 2 at \$1. When we set $p_2 = \$1$, then p_1 becomes the relative price of good 1. With this *price normalization*, Shelly's budget line becomes [5]

$$p_1 x_1^S + x_2^S = 22p_1 + 56$$

Shelly's budget line for three different values of p_1 is shown in Figure 16.3. Notice that as p_1 changes, her budget line swivels around her initial endowment of 22 units of good 1 and 56 units of good 2. Given this price normalization, Marvin's budget line is

$$p_1 x_1^M + x_2^M = 80p_1 + 10$$

since he has 80 units of good 1 and 10 units of good 2.

FIGURE 16.3   Budget lines in an exchange economy

As relative price p_1 changes, Shelley's budget line swivels around her initial endowment of 22 units of good 1 and 56 units of good 2. This reflects the fact that she can always afford her initial endowment. Given p_1 equal to 1/2, Shelly's utility-maximizing consumption bundle is at point E.

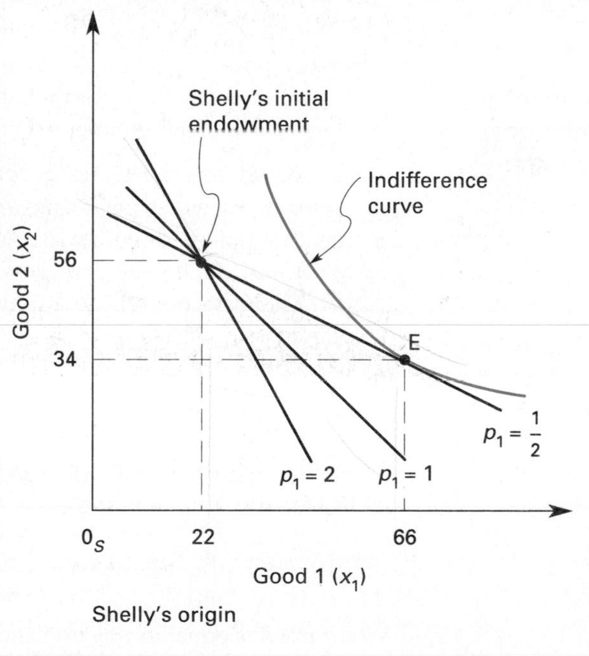

5 We are free to choose any price normalization. Another commonly used normalization is $p_2 = 1 - p_1$.

Finding the Competitive Equilibrium

net demand

net supply

gross supply

gross demand

To find the competitive equilibrium, we will use the Walrasian auctioneer, who begins the bidding process by announcing a relative price p_1. Marvin and Shelly could respond to the auctioneer by announcing a **net demand**, or supply, for each good. For example, if the auctioneer announced $p_1 = 1/2$, we see from Figure 16.3 that Shelly could respond with a *net demand* for good 1 equal to 44 units — since she wants to consume 66 units of good 1 and has 22 units — and a **net supply** of good 2 equal to 22 units — since she has 56 units of good 2 but wants to consume only 34 units.

Alternatively, Marvin and Shelly could respond to the auctioneer by reporting their **gross supply** of each good and their **gross demand** for each good. In the preceding example, if the auctioneer announced $p_1 = 1/2$, Shelly would respond by offering to supply 22 units of good 1 and 56 units of good 2 — her entire endowment of each good — and to demand 66 units of good 1 and 34 units of good 2.

In either case, at the utility-maximizing bundle, Shelly's *MRS* will be equal to the announced price p_1, since p_1 is the relative price of good 1. Similarly, at his utility-maximizing bundle, Marvin's *MRS* will be equal to the announced price p_1.

For clarity, we will suppose that Marvin and Shelly respond by reporting their gross supply of each good and their gross demand for each good. To find the competitive equilibrium, the auctioneer begins by announcing a price p_1. Given that price, Marvin and Shelly then report to the auctioneer the gross *quantity supplied* of each good and the gross *quantity demanded* of each good. The auctioneer first adds their responses to get **aggregate supply** and **aggregate demand**, and then compares aggregate supply and aggregate demand for each good.

aggregate supply

aggregate demand

1. If aggregate demand is not equal to aggregate supply for both goods, no trading takes place. Instead, the auctioneer announces another price, and the process is repeated.

2. If, for both goods, aggregate demand is equal to aggregate supply, the announced relative price is a competitive equilibrium price, goods are traded, and the auction stops. In the resulting **competitive equilibrium allocation**, both individuals get the gross demands announced to the auctioneer.

competitive equilibrium allocation

As we will see, the auctioneer can focus on just one market because when aggregate demand is equal to aggregate supply in one market, aggregate demand is equal to aggregate supply in the other as well. To see why, suppose the auctioneer has found some price p_1^e such that aggregate demand for good 1 is equal to aggregate supply of good 1. Then, since aggregate supply of good 1 is 102 units, Shelly's demand for good 1, x_1^S, plus Marvin's demand for good 1, x_1^M, must satisfy

$$x_1^S + x_1^M = 102$$

To see that aggregate demand for good 2 is also equal to its aggregate supply (66 units), let us first add Marvin's and Shelly's budget lines to get the following equation:

$$p_1(x_1^S + x_1^M) + (x_2^S + x_2^M) = 102p_1 + 66$$

When price is equal to p_1^e, demand is equal to supply of good 1, or $x_1^S + x_1^M = 102$; therefore, the first terms on the left and right cancel, and this combined budget constraint reduces to

$$x_2^S + x_2^M = 66$$

FIGURE 16.4 **Competitive equilibrium in an exchange economy**

The initial allocation is at point A. Given the announced (relative) price, the line AE* can be seen as both Shelly's budget line and as Marvin's budget line. Since both Shelly and Marvin choose the allocation at E*, the announced relative price is a competitive equilibrium price, and E* is the competitive equilibrium allocation. Since E* is on the contract curve CC, the competitive equilibrium is Pareto-optimal.

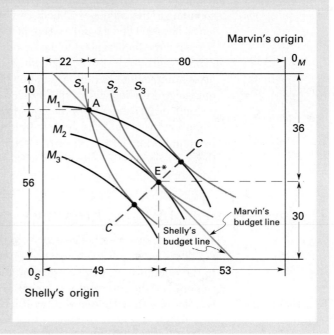

Walras' law

Recalling that the aggregate supply of good 2 is 66 units, we see that the demand for good 2 is equal to its supply. This result is known as **Walras' law:**[6]

> If at price p_1^e demand is equal to supply in one market, then demand is equal to supply in the other market as well, and p_1^e is therefore a competitive equilibrium price.

We can use the Edgeworth box diagram to illustrate the competitive equilibrium in this two-person exchange economy. In Figure 16.4, the initial endowment is at point A, point E* is the competitive equilibrium allocation, and the gray line is a common budget line whose slope reflects the competitive equilibrium price. Relative to Shelly's origin 0_S, the gray line can be seen as Shelly's budget line, and relative to Marvin's origin 0_M, it can be seen as Marvin's budget line. The utility-maximizing bundles are both at point E*, which is the competitive equilibrium allocation in this exchange economy.

PROBLEM 16.4

In this competitive equilibrium, Shelly is a net demander of one good and Marvin a net supplier of that good. Which is the good, and what is her net demand and his net supply? Similarly, Marvin is a net demander of one good and Shelly a net supplier of that good. Which is the good, and what is his net demand and her net supply? What trade will implement the competitive equilibrium allocation?

---

6 More generally, when there are n markets in a general equilibrium model, Walras' law says that if demand is equal to supply in $n - 1$ markets, then demand is equal to supply in the nth as well.

Notice that the competitive equilibrium allocation is on the contract curve in the diagram. This is a general and important result, so let us take time to examine it. In responding to the auctioneer, Shelly and Marvin solve a standard utility-maximizing problem. They each find a bundle where MRS is equal to the announced relative price p_1. That is, every time they respond to the auctioneer, they each plan to consume a bundle where MRS is equal to the price p_1 announced by the auctioneer. They cannot, and therefore do not, implement these consumption plans until their plans are mutually consistent, or until aggregate demand is equal to aggregate supply in both markets — that is, until the auctioneer has announced the equilibrium price. At the equilibrium price, their consumption plans are consistent; therefore, trades are made to implement the competitive equilibrium allocation where MRS is equal to the equilibrium price p_1^e for each of them. Shelly's MRS is therefore identical to Marvin's. Of course, this means that the equilibrium allocation is on the contract curve, or is Pareto-optimal.

The First Theorem of Welfare Economics

In a many-person exchange economy, there is an analogous result. In the competitive equilibrium of such an economy, each person consumes a bundle where MRS is equal to the equilibrium relative price for good 1. Therefore, MRS is identical for all consumers, and the competitive equilibrium allocation is Pareto-optimal. We then have what

first theorem of welfare economics

is called the **first theorem of welfare economics**:

Given the assumptions we have made, the competitive equilibrium allocation of a many-person exchange economy is Pareto-optimal.

This theorem says, in effect, that all gains from trade are realized in competitive equilibrium.[7]

The Second Theorem of Welfare Economics

Of course, any allocation on the contract curve is Pareto-optimal. The second theorem of welfare economics concerns a means of attaining any of these Pareto-optimal allocations. Suppose that we have identified some Pareto-optimal allocation that we would like to implement. The second theorem tells us first to redistribute the initial endowment and then to rely on competitive markets to achieve Pareto optimality.

To see how this works, let us reinterpret Figure 16.4 by supposing that the initial endowment is at 0_M, where Shelly owns everything. Suppose, too, that we have somehow identified point E* as the Pareto-optimal allocation that we would like to implement. How can we achieve it? We do so by first redistributing the initial endowment to attain an endowment anywhere on the budget line in Figure 16.4, and then using a competitive market to attain the desired Pareto-optimal allocation at E*. For example, we could transfer 80 units of good 1 and 10 units of good 2 from Shelly to Marvin to attain the endowment at point A, confident in the knowledge that this endowment will produce the desired Pareto-optimal allocation at E*. (After all, we initially found the equilibrium

---

7 Given the assumptions we have made, it is entirely possible that there are many competitive equilibria. If there are many equilibria, the first theorem says that they are all Pareto-optimal. You can easily construct an Edgeworth box with two competitive equilibria. Begin by drawing two budget lines through the same initial endowment, and then construct indifference curves so that there is a competitive equilibrium on both budget lines.

second theorem of welfare economics

at E* by supposing that the allocation was at A.) A little thought should convince you that any allocation on the budget line, including E* itself, will produce E* as the competitive equilibrium allocation. Thus, we have the **second theorem of welfare economics**:

If preferences satisfy the assumptions we have made, given any Pareto-optimal allocation POA, there is an initial allocation IA such that, given the initial allocation IA, the competitive equilibrium allocation is POA.

16.3
Efficiency in General Equilibrium with Production

Now it is time to introduce production into our model and to see how these two theorems of welfare economics can be extended once production is included in the model. After we have concluded this extension, we will try to put the results into perspective. Let us suppose that the number of firms producing good 1 and good 2 is fixed. Therefore, firms do not enter or exit in this general equilibrium model; they simply choose how much of the good to produce. Suppose, too, that the number of people in the economy is fixed and that their preferences satisfy the assumptions laid out in the previous section.

We will also assume that all firms producing the same good have the same constant-returns-to-scale production function. To produce their goods, firms use two primary inputs, input 1 and input 2. And we will assume that there is a fixed supply of each input. Therefore, the quantity supplied is not responsive to input price.

Production Assumptions

To keep our discussion as simple as possible, we will use five assumptions about production (or technology) throughout the chapter.

1. Isoquants are convex.
2. Isoquants are smooth.
3. Both inputs are essential in the production of both goods.
4. Production functions exhibit constant returns to scale.
5. Production involves no externalities.

The first assumption is standard. The second assumption implies that the marginal rate of technical substitution *MRTS* is well defined, and the third that all firms will use a positive quantity of both inputs. We will explain the role of the fourth assumption when we define the marginal rate of transformation. In Chapter 17, we will see how production externalities like air and water pollution, which are ruled out here by our fifth assumption, fit into the analysis.

Before plunging into the analysis, let us quickly preview this approach to efficiency in this general equilibrium model. Given the assumptions we have made, three conditions are *necessary* and *sufficient* to achieve efficiency in this model. One familiar condition concerns efficiency in consumption; a second, similar condition concerns efficiency in production; and the third condition concerns efficiency of product mix. When we say that these three conditions are *necessary* for efficiency in general equilibrium, we mean that if any of them is *not* satisfied, then the allocation of resources is not Pareto-optimal. When we say that these three conditions are *sufficient* for efficiency in general equilibrium, we mean that if *all* three conditions are satisfied, then the allocation of resources is Pareto-optimal. In discussing these conditions, we will focus almost exclusively on showing that they are necessary conditions. As a result, the discussion will be somewhat incomplete.

Efficiency in Consumption

efficiency in consumption

Efficiency in consumption means that the allocation to individual consumers of the goods actually produced in the economy must be Pareto-optimal. Therefore, the condition for efficiency in consumption for an exchange economy is directly applicable to an economy with production.

Efficiency in Consumption Condition: Efficiency in consumption requires that MRS is identical for all individuals.

Production Possibilities Set

production possibilities set

production possibilities frontier

The shaded area in Figure 16.5 represents the economy's **production possibilities set** — all the combinations of goods 1 and 2 that can be produced. The upper boundary of the production possibilties set PP is the **production possibilities frontier**. Given the economy's technology and input endowment, any combination of goods on or below PP can be produced and any combination above PP cannot be produced.

An obvious efficiency requirement is that the combination of good 1 and good 2 actually produced must be on PP rather than below it. Point B, for example, is inconsistent with efficiency. By moving upward and to the right from point B, the output of each good increases. And by giving each person some share of that increased output, everyone can be made better off. Point B is therefore inconsistent with efficiency: if the economy were at point B, Pareto-improving moves would be possible. The second efficiency condition in general equilibrium, called **efficiency in production**, is that the combination of goods actually produced must be on the production possibilities frontier.

efficiency in production

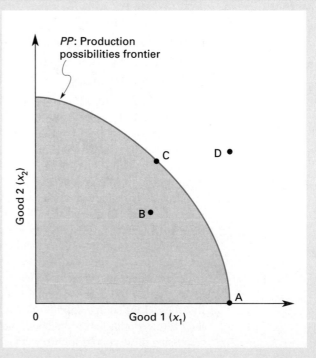

FIGURE 16.5 **The production possibilities set**

The production possibilities set, represented by the shaded area, is the set of consumption goods that this economy could produce. The bundles at points A, B, and C can be produced, whereas the bundle at D cannot be. The boundary of the production possibilities set PP is the production possibilities frontier.

PP: Production possibilities frontier

Good 2 (x_2)

Good 1 (x_1)

Efficiency in Production

An economy could become "stuck" at an inefficient point such as B in Figure 16.5 in two ways. If any inputs are unemployed, then the economy is inevitably inside *PP*. We will ignore the possibility of unemployed inputs in what follows. There is, however, a more subtle way in which the economy could end up at a point such as B. To understand this more subtle source of inefficiency, we can adapt the Edgeworth box analysis to a new purpose.

Suppose that *MRTS* is different for some pair of firms, given their current input bundles. (See Section 8.2 for the definition of *MRTS*.) Both firms might be producing the same good, or they might be producing different goods. We will show that, because *MRTS* is not identical for the two firms, the output of both firms can be increased by reallocating inputs and that the current allocation of inputs to firms is therefore not efficient.

Suppose, for example, that *MRTS* for the first firm exceeds *MRTS* for the second firm and that the first firm currently has 7 units of input 1 and 17 units of input 2, while the second firm currently has 18 units of input 1 and 3 units of input 2. Now let us put these two firms into an Edgeworth box diagram. The dimensions of the Edgeworth box in Figure 16.6 are determined by the total quantities of inputs 1 and 2 in the two input bundles — its horizontal sides are therefore 25 units long, and its vertical sides are 20 units long. The first firm's isoquants, I_1' and I_1'', are plotted relative to 0_1; the second firm's isoquants, I_2' and I_2'', relative to 0_2. The current allocation of inputs to the two firms is at point A in Figure 16.6, where *MRTS* is larger for the first firm than for the second. The first firm is currently on isoquant I'_1 and the second is on I'_2. Notice that any reallocation of inputs in the interior of the shaded area allows both firms to produce more. Therefore, the input allocation at A is not efficient.

FIGURE 16.6   An Edgeworth box for production

Here we consider the allocation of a fixed quantity of two inputs to two firms. The first firm's input bundle and isoquants are measured relative to 0_1, and the second firm's relative to 0_2. An allocation such as A, which is not on the contract curve, is inefficient. The shaded area is the set of allocations that allow both firms to produce more than they do at A. Allocations such as J and K, where *MRTS* is identical for the two firms, are on the contract curve. Efficiency in production demands that *MRTS* be identical for all firms.

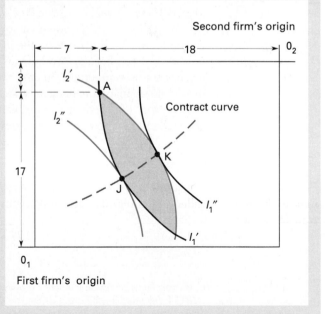

Let us see what these reallocations mean in terms of Figure 16.5. If one firm produces good 1 and the other good 2, then any reallocation from point A to the interior of the shaded area in Figure 16.6 moves the economy shown in Figure 16.5 in a northeasterly direction from a point such as B. If both firms in Figure 16.6 produce the same good — say, good 2 — then the movement in Figure 16.5 is due north. If the initial allocation had instead been on the contract curve in Figure 16.6 — that is, if $MRTS$ had been identical for the two firms — then increasing the output of one firm would have meant decreasing the output of the other firm. $MRTS$ therefore must be identical for all firms if the allocation of inputs is to be efficient.

Efficiency in Production Condition: Efficiency in production requires that $MRTS$ be identical for all firms.[8]

Why is this is a necessary condition for efficiency? If the condition was not satisfied, we could increase the output of one good while maintaining output of the other, which would allow us to make some consumers better off while leaving all others no worse off.

> **PROBLEM 16.5**
>
> Suppose that $MRTS$ for all producers of good 1 exceeds $MRTS$ for all producers of good 2. What sort of reallocation of inputs is necessary to achieve efficiency in production? Is it possible to achieve efficiency in production while holding the output of good 1 constant?

Notice that each of these efficiency conditions concerns one side of the economy in isolation from the other. The first proposition concerns consumption and the second concerns production. The third condition for efficiency in general equilibrium concerns the interface between consumption and production. It is called **efficiency of product mix**.

efficiency of product mix

To understand the nature of the product-mix problem, suppose that good 1 is food and good 2 shelter and that 99.9% of all inputs go to the production of just one good — say, shelter. If MRS is identical for all consumers, the economy will be efficient in consumption. If all firms have the identical $MRTS$, the economy will be efficient in production. But because we humans cannot live by shelter alone, the right product mix has not been produced. In other words, there is more to Pareto optimality in an entire economy than efficiency in production and efficiency in consumption. Before we can confront the product-mix problem head on, we need to understand a little more about the production possibilities frontier.

The Marginal Rate of Transformation

marginal rate of transformation

The absolute value of the slope of the production possibilities frontier at any point is called the **marginal rate of transformation** at that point and is denoted by MRT.

$$MRT = |\text{slope of } PP|$$

---

8 The calculus argument in footnote 3 is easily adapted to show that efficiency in production requires that $MRTS$ be identical for all firms. Pick any two firms with production functions $F^1(z_1^1, z_2^1)$ and $F^2(z_1^2, z_2^2)$, and any bundle of the two inputs to be allocated to the two firms — say, the bundle (z_1', z_2'). If we fix the output of the first firm at x^1, then efficiency in production clearly demands that we allocate the available bundle of inputs to the two firms so as to maximize $F^2(z_1^2, z_2^2)$, subject to the constraint that $x^1 = F^1(z_1^1, z_2^1)$. From this point, the argument exactly parallels that in footnote 3.

MRT is the *opportunity cost* for the economy as a whole of a small increase in the amount of good 1 relative to good 2. In Figure 16.7, for example, the absolute value of the slope of the tangent line *TT* is the rate at which production of good 2 must be decreased as production of good 1 is increased when the economy is at point C.

PROBLEM 16.6

Approximately how much of good 2 must be given up to get an additional unit of good 1 if *MRT* is 2? If *MRT* is 1/5? Approximately how much of good 1 must be given up to get an additional unit of good 2 if *MRT* is 3? If *MRT* is 1/3?

We have assumed in this section that all firms experience constant returns to scale in production. This assumption guarantees that *PP* will not be convex to the origin. (We will, in fact, draw *PP* as concave to the origin, as shown in Figure 16.7.) Therefore, in moving from left to right along *PP* in Figures 16.7 and 16.8, the opportunity cost of each additional unit of good 1 in terms of foregone good 2 is progressively larger; that is, *MRT* becomes progressively larger. If there were significant increasing returns to scale in the production of good 1, however, *MRT* could decrease in moving from left to right along *PP*.

We can express *MRT* in terms of the marginal product of input 1 for a representative producer of good 1 — MP_1^1 — and the marginal product of input 1 for a representative producer of good 2 — MP_1^2. To see how this is accomplished, suppose that we wanted to produce a small additional amount of good 1 — say, Δx_1. We can do it by transferring a small additional amount of input 1 — say, Δz_1 — from the repre-

---

FIGURE 16.7   The marginal rate of transformation

The marginal rate of transformation at any point on *PP* is the absolute value of the slope of *PP* at that point. *MRT* at point C, for example, is the absolute value of the slope of *TT*. *MRT* measures the opportunity cost of a small additional quantity of good 1 in terms of the foregone quantity of good 2.

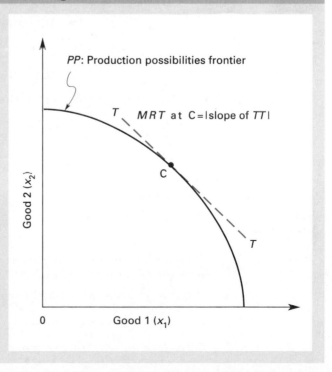

sentative producer of good 2 to the representative producer of good 1. The necessary transfer of input 1, Δz_1, (approximately) satisfies

$$\Delta x_1 = \Delta z_1 MP_1^1$$

This implies that Δx_2, the decrease in production of good 2, is (approximately)

$$\Delta x_2 = \Delta z_1 MP_1^2$$

Dividing Δx_2 by Δx_1 gives us the absolute value of the slope of PP, or MRT:

$$MRT = MP_1^2/MP_1^1$$

You may be wondering why we could not achieve this increase in the production of good 1 by transferring input 2 instead of input 1 or by transferring a small additional amount of both input 2 and input 1. The answer is that we could have done so. Suppose that we had transferred input 2 instead of input 1: by replicating the argument of the previous paragraph, we would conclude that

$$MRT = MP_2^2/MP_2^1$$

where MP_2^2 is the marginal product of input 2 for the producer of good 2 and MP_2^1 is the marginal product of input 2 for the producer of good 1.

If MRT is to be meaningful in either of these expressions, the expressions must be equivalent, and they are equivalent. Since we have efficiency in production, we know that $MRTS$ is identical for producers of good 1 and good 2:

$$MRTS_1 = MRTS_2$$

From Section 8.2, we know that any firm's $MRTS$ is equal to the ratio of the marginal product of input 1 to the marginal product of input 2 in that firm. By combining this information with the previous expression, we see that

$$MP_1^1/MP_2^1 = MP_1^2/MP_2^2$$

or that

$$MP_2^2/MP_2^1 = MP_1^2/MP_1^1$$

The two measures of MRT are therefore equivalent.[9] Thus:

The marginal rate of transformation can be expressed in terms of marginal products in two different but equivalent ways:

$$MRT = MP_1^2/MP_1^1 = MP_2^2/MP_2^1$$

These results will be quite useful in subsequent sections.

---

9 Suppose that we transfer a small amount of each input from the production of good 2 to the production of good 1. We want to show that this exercise yields an equivalent measure for MRT. To get Δx_1 additional units of good 1, we require

$$\Delta x_1 = \Delta z_1 MP_1^1 + \Delta z_2 MP_2^1$$

which means that the reduction in output of good 2 is

$$\Delta x_2 = \Delta z_1 MP_1^2 + \Delta z_2 MP_2^2$$

> **PROBLEM: 16.7**
>
> Suppose that $MRTS = 1/2$ for all firms, that $MP_1^1 = 1$, and that $MP_2^2 = 2$.
> What is MRT?

Efficiency in Product Mix

We can now return to the problem of efficiency in product mix. Imagine that we have picked an arbitrary person, Ms. C, and devised a mechanism that 1. allows her to control the allocation of resources in the whole economy by choosing a point on the production possibilities frontier, PP, and that 2. constrains her to leave everyone else in his or her initial position. Imagine, too, that the economy Ms. C is about to take charge of is initially at some point on PP — say, at point A in Figure 16.8 — where 30 units of good 1 and 34 units of good 2 are being produced. Imagine, too, that Ms. C's current consumption bundle contains 10 units of good 1 and 12 units of good 2. Taken together, the remaining individuals in this economy therefore have 20 units of good 1 $(30 - 10)$ and 22 units of good 2 $(34 - 12)$.

We will show that if this economy is efficient, then Ms. C's MRS must be equal to the economy's MRT. To do so, we will suppose that her MRS instead exceeds MRT, and then show that when she takes over, she can make herself better off without making anyone else worse off.

Now let us put Ms. C in charge of this economy and allow her to choose a point on PP that is in her own self-interest. Of course, she is constrained to keep all other consumers in their original positions. In Figure 16.8, we see how this constraint works. Point A represents the original position for the economy where there are 30 units of good 1 and 34 of good 2. If we subtract Ms. C's consumption bundle from point A, we get point B in Figure 16.8, where there are 20 units of good 1 and 22 units of good 2. This point represents the initial consumption of everyone else in the economy. Recall that Ms. C is constrained to make this combination available to them. This implies that she cannot choose any point on PP to the left of point D or to the right of point E, but she can choose any point on segment DE of PP.

Analyzing Ms. C's problem of choosing a point on segment DE is now a simple matter. We can regard point B as an origin for her private consumption bundle. Segment DE of PP, relative to the origin at B, then represents the consumption choices open to her. Now we can simply plot her indifference map relative to the origin at B in Figure 16.8. Remember that we assumed that her MRS exceeds MRT at point A. She is therefore initially on an indifference curve like I in Figure 16.8, that is steeper than PP at point A. She will obviously choose some point on PP that is to the right of A and to the left of G, a point where some indifference curve not shown in the diagram is tangent to PP.

Dividing Δx_2 by Δx_1 and rearranging, we get

$$MRT = \frac{MP_1^2(\Delta z_1 + \varnothing z_2 MP_2^2/MP_1^2)}{MP_1^1(\varnothing z_1 + \varnothing z_2 MP_2^1/MP_1^1)}$$

but, since we have efficiency in production, MP_2^2/MP_1^2 is equal to MP_2^1/MP_1^1. Hence,

$$MRT = \frac{MP_1^2}{MP_1^1}$$

FIGURE 16.8   Efficiency in product mix

Point A is the initial position in the economy, and Ms. C initially has 10 units of good 1 and 12 of good 2. Now let her choose a point on *PP*, constraining her to leave all other consumers in their original positions. To leave them in their original positions, she must make 20 units of good 1 and 22 units of good 2 available to them. Therefore, we can regard point B as Ms. C's origin and segment DE of *PP* (relative to this origin) as the

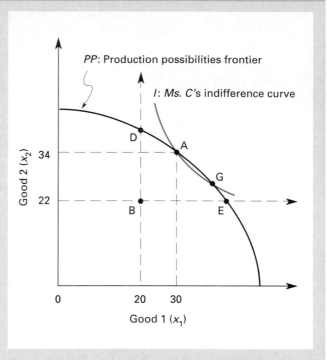

consumption choices open to her. She will choose some point other than A because her indifference curve through A intersects *PP*. The initial position is therefore not Pareto-optimal. Pareto optimality requires that her indifference curve be tangent to *PP*, or that her *MRS* be equal to the economy's *MRT*.

When she does, she is better off, and everyone else is just as well off. Therefore, we know that if her *MRS* (or any consumer's *MRS*) is not equal to *MRT*, the allocation of resources to the production of good 1 and good 2 is inefficient.

Efficiency in Product Mix Condition: Efficiency in product mix requires that each consumer's *MRS* be identical to the economy's *MRT*.

Notice how we have approached each of these efficiency conditions. We have shown that when any of these conditions is not satisfied, a Pareto-improving move is possible and the allocation is therefore inefficient. In other words, we have shown that each of these three conditions is *necessary* for an efficient allocation of resources. Although we will not show it, these three conditions are also *sufficient*: if they are satisfied, then the allocation is efficient. These three conditions thus tell us clearly what

efficiency in general equilibrium

efficiency in general equilibrium means in our general equilibrium model.

PROBLEM 16.8

Suppose that *MRT* exceeds each consumer's *MRS*. To achieve efficiency in product mix, must the economy be producing more or less of good 1?

16.4
Efficiency and General Competitive Equilibrium

What institutions and circumstances are and are not conducive to efficiency? We will begin this inquiry by recasting the first theorem of welfare economics and then showing that it is true in this general equilibrium model with production.

First Theorem of Welfare Economics: Given the assumptions we have made, the competitive equilibrium of this general equilibrium model with production is efficient.

The first theorem emphasizes the power of self-interest in directing the allocation of resources. In the perfectly competitive setting envisioned in the theorem, the pursuit of self-interest allows the collectivity of individuals to extract all the gains possible from their economic union. The theorem is, in essence, the embodiment of Smith's doctrine of the natural identity of interests, discussed at the beginning of this chapter.

We can be confident that the theorem is true if we can assure ourselves that an economy in competitive general equilibrium is efficient in production, in consumption, and in product mix. We will not consider how competitive equilibrium is attained in the model. Rather, we will suppose that we have competitive equilibrium prices for goods 1 and 2 and for inputs 1 and 2 — that is, prices such that aggregate demand is equal to aggregate supply for both goods and both inputs. Then we will use our understanding of consumer and producer behavior to show that the three conditions for efficiency are fulfilled.

Let $p_1{}^e$ and $p_2{}^e$ denote the competitive equilibrium prices for goods 1 and 2, and let $w_1{}^e$ and $w_2{}^e$ denote the competitive equilibrium prices for inputs 1 and 2. You can easily see that an economy in this competitive equilibrium is efficient in production and in consumption. From Section 8.5, we know that each firm chooses an input bundle at which its $MRTS$ is equal to $w_1{}^e/w_2{}^e$. $MRTS$ is therefore identical for all firms, and the economy is efficient in production. Similarly, from Section 3.4, we know that each consumer chooses a consumption bundle at which MRS is equal to $p_1{}^e/p_2{}^e$. MRS is therefore identical for all consumers, and the economy is efficient in consumption.[10]

Showing that an economy in competitive general equilibrium is also efficient in product mix is only slightly more complicated. To do so, we need to use what we know from Section 13.7 about a profit-maximizing firm that is a perfect competitor in its input markets and in its output market. Figure 16.9 illustrates the position of two representative producers — one of good 1 and the other of good 2 — in the market for input 1. The producer of good 1 uses 35 units of input 1 at the equilibrium price $w_1{}^e$, and the producer of good 2 uses 30 units. Both firms are in long-run equilibrium and, therefore, in short-run equilibrium as well. Accordingly,

$$w_1{}^e = p_1{}^e MP_1{}^1 = p_2{}^e MP_1{}^2$$

Rearranging, we have

$$p_1{}^e/p_2{}^e = MP_1{}^2/MP_1{}^1$$

---

10 Since there are only three independent relative prices in this model, we could eliminate one price by choosing a convenient normalization. We could, for example, set p_2 equal to 1.

FIGURE 16.9   Efficiency in product mix for general competitive equilibrium

In competitive equilibrium, we see that any producer of good 1 uses input 1 up to the point where $w_1^e = p_1^e MP_1^1$, and that any producer of good 2 uses input 1 up to the point where $w_1^e = p_2^e MP_1^2$. Therefore, $p_1^e/p_2^e = MP_1^2//MP_1^1$. But the right side of the equality is, by definition, MRT. Every consumer chooses a consumption bundle such that $MRS = p_1^e/p_2^e$. Therefore, $MRT = MRS$ for every consumer, and the economy exhibits efficiency in product mix in competitive equilibrium.

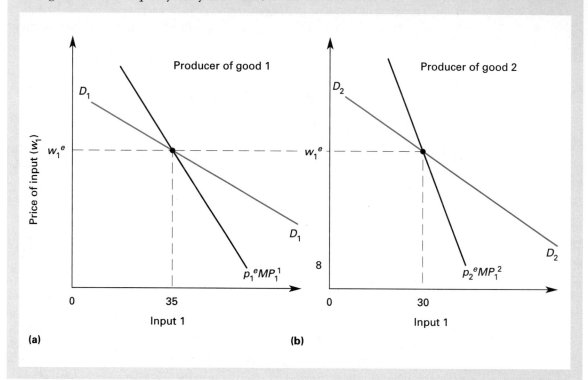

As we showed in Section 16.3, the right side of this expression is just the economy's MRT. Because every consumer chooses a bundle at which his or her MRS is equal to the left side, p_1^e/p_2^e, we see that every consumer's MRS is equal to the economy's MRT; that is, for every consumer $MRS = MRT$. Therefore, the economy produces an efficient product mix.

Although we will not consider it in great detail, the second theorem of welfare economics also holds in our model of general equilibrium with production. Recall that the second theorem concerns a two-stage procedure for attaining any Pareto-optimal allocation. In the exchange economy, the first stage of this procedure involves the redistribution of goods. In the current model with production, individuals are endowed not with goods but with inputs, which they sell in input markets to earn the incomes that they spend on goods. Therefore, in this model the second theorem relies, in effect, on the redistribution of the ownership of inputs — instead of the redistribution of goods — to redistribute purchasing power. For example, a redistribution of labor (or land), as opposed to some consumption good, might be required to achieve the given Pareto optimum as a competitive equilibrium.

Suppose, then, that we have identified an efficient allocation of goods that we would like to achieve. In the background there is, of course, a corresponding allocation of inputs to firms. But here we are interested in the allocation of goods to individuals. The second theorem is concerned with a two-stage procedure to achieve this allocation. In the first stage, the ownership of inputs is reallocated among individuals. In the second stage, the theorem tells us to rely on competitive markets to achieve efficiency.

Second Theorem of Welfare Economics: With the assumptions we have made, given any Pareto-optimal allocation of goods POA that is attainable in the model, there is a distribution of ownership of inputs DOI such that POA is the competitive equilibrium allocation associated with DOI.

The beauty of the second theorem is the neat separation of distribution and efficiency that it envisages. In effect, the second theorem tells us:

To achieve equity, redistribute the ownership of inputs; to achieve efficiency, use competitive markets.

A moment's reflection will reveal that the redistribution envisaged in the second theorem involves lump-sum taxes for some individuals and lump-sum subsidies for others. What is being redistributed in a lump-sum fashion is, of course, the ownership of inputs, not money. As we saw in a partial equilibrium context in Section 4.1, these lump-sum taxes and subsidies have some very attractive features. The second theorem reveals the source of their beauty — lump-sum taxes and subsidies do not interfere with the allocative function that competitive markets do so well, whereas other forms of tax and subsidy do. (We saw this difference clearly in our discussion of the redistribution of income in Chapter 14.)

As we also saw in Section 4.1, it is almost impossible to find a lump-sum tax or subsidy in the real world. It is clear, then, that the second theorem does not dominate the thinking of the people who design taxes. Why not? Some economists argue that such taxes and subsidies are a near impossibility. This seems to be true for the labor of individuals, which, from the point of view of generating income, is the most important input that most people have to offer. In a democratic society, it is extremely difficult to imagine significant lump-sum taxes on the labor of individuals. The real message of the second theorem, then, is that redistribution almost inevitably involves a potentially serious conflict between equity and efficiency.[11]

16.5

Sources of Inefficiency

What can go wrong? What produces an inefficient allocation of resources? Although there are many sources of inefficiency, we will look at just two of the major ones in this section: monopoly and taxation.

The Inefficiency of Monopoly

We can begin with monopoly. Suppose that there is only one producer of good 1 and that all other markets are perfectly competitive. To see why resources are inefficiently

---

11 The first essay in Koopmans' (1957) book is an excellent exposition of the relationship between efficiency and competitive equilibrium.

allocated in general equilibrium, let p_1^e, p_2^e, w_1^e, and w_2^e again represent general equilibrium prices. The equilibrium price of good 1 — p_1^e — is, of course, a monopoly price. The first two efficiency conditions still hold: because all firms face the same input prices, each chooses an input bundle at which $MRTS$ is equal to w_1^e/w_2^e. Similarly, because all consumers face the same product prices, each chooses a bundle at which MRS is equal to p_1^e/p_2^e. The economy is therefore efficient in production and in consumption in this general equilibrium.

The monopoly inefficiency arises from a distortion of product mix. This becomes apparent when considering the positions of the monopoly producer of good 1 and of any producer of good 2 in an input market. In the market for input 1, for example, both firms use the input up to the point at which marginal revenue product is equal to the price of the input:

$$w_1^e = MRP_1^1 = MRP_1^2$$

where MRP_1^1 and MRP_1^2 are the respective marginal revenue products of input 1 for the monopolist and the representative producer of good 2. But MRP_1^1 is equal to $MR_1 MP_1^1$, where MR_1 is the monopolist's marginal revenue in its output market, and MRP_1^2 is equal to $p_2^e MP_1^2$. Therefore,

$$w_1^e = MR_1 MP_1^1 = p_2^e MP_1^2$$

Furthermore, as we discovered in Section 10.2, MR_1 is less than p_1^e because a monopolist is producing good 1; that is, a profit-maximizing monopolist always produces at a point where its marginal revenue is less than its price. Combining this knowledge with knowledge from the input market, we see that

$$p_1^e/p_2^e > MP_1^2/MP_1^1$$

However, the right side of this expression is MRT, and the left side is equal to each consumer's MRS. Each consumer's MRS therefore exceeds the economy's MRT: for all consumers,

$$MRS > MRT$$

In the presence of monopoly, then, the product mix is wrong; accordingly, the allocation of resources is inefficient:

If we have only one producer of good 1 and if all other markets are perfectly competitive, resources will be inefficiently allocated in general equilibrium.

These inefficiencies arise not just in the case of a monopolist, but in any case in which there is market power — any case in which the firm's demand curve is downward sloping. In the following problem, you can see more clearly the distortions (inefficiencies) associated with market power.

PROBLEM 16.9

Taking the general equilibrium in the presence of a monopoly producer as an initial condition, construct a diagram in which you show that 1. Ms. C could make herself better off, and no one else worse off, if she could directly control the allocation of resources and that 2. the monopolist produces too little.

> ### PROBLEM 16.10
>
> Show that if the monopolist engages in ordinary price discrimination, the economy is inefficient not just in product mix, but also in consumption.

Taxation and Efficiency

Taxes not only are painful but also are a source of inefficiency in the allocation of resources. Now that you have some facility in determining whether a particular general equilibrium is efficient, you can discover in Problem 16.10 some inefficiencies associated with taxes.

> ### PROBLEM 16.11
>
> Suppose that some government authority imposes a tax equal to $\$t$ on the sale of each unit of good 2 but not on the sale of good 1. Assuming that all markets are competitive, show that competitive general equilibrium in the presence of this tax is inconsistent with efficiency. Hint: The product mix is not efficient. Is too little or too much of good 2 produced in equilibrium? Now suppose instead that a subsidy is imposed on the consumption of good 2 and repeat the exercise.

SUMMARY

In this chapter, we have drawn together in a more rigorous *general equilibrium framework* much of what we have already learned about economic efficiency and about the conditions that interfere with it or promote it. In this general equilibrium context, the allocation of resources is *efficient* when no changes of any kind will make some person better off without making someone else worse off.

This correct but imprecise definition of *economic efficiency* is equivalent to the following precise statement: given the assumptions we made in this chapter, an economy is efficient if 1. *MRTS* is identical for all producers, 2. *MRS* is identical for all consumers, and 3. the common *MRS* is equal to the economy's *MRT*. These three conditions concern *efficiency in production*, *consumption*, and *product mix*, respectively.

We showed that when certain assumptions are satisfied, an economy in general competitive equilibrium satisfies these three conditions: it is efficient. This result, the *first theorem of welfare economics*, is the modern equivalent of Adam Smith's doctrine of the natural identity of interests. Loosely speaking, the institutions that permit individuals to realize all the gains possible from their economic union are the institutions of perfect competition.

We also considered the *second theorem of welfare economics*, which outlines a two-stage procedure for attaining any Pareto-optimal allocation that is possible in the economy. In the first stage, ownership is redistributed among individuals by a set of lump-sum taxes and transfers; in the second stage, efficiency is achieved by relying on perfectly competitive markets. Unfortunately, the lump-sum taxes and transfers envisaged in the first stage are impractical in most real situations.

We found that many things could upset the efficiency applecart. Market power of any sort — monopoly, oligopoly, monopsony — creates inefficiency. As you saw in Problem 16.11, taxes and subsidies also tend to produce inefficiency. And, as we will see in Chapter 17, externalities in consumption and production also mean that competitive general equilibrium is not efficient.

From the perspective of efficiency, the economic world we inhabit is obviously imperfect. As we saw in Chapters 10 through 12, market power is unavoidable in many markets. In addition, externalities like air and water pollution (which we ignored in this chapter) are an all-too-familiar part of the economic world in which we live. Furthermore, governments are not about to eliminate their taxing and spending activities, and most of us would not want them to do so. Thus, some form of inefficiency seems to be inevitable.

This predictable inefficiency presents the economist, particularly the policy-making economist, with a real challenge. How do we measure inefficiency? How can we minimize inefficiency? One recent approach — called applied general equilibrium analysis — uses data to build general equilibrium models of the economy and extends the surplus measures familiar from earlier chapters to quantify inefficiency in a general equilibrium framework.[12] These models are one step toward meeting that challenge.

---

12 See Shoven and Whalley (1987) for a survey of work in applied general equilibrium.

EXERCISES

1. If a monopolist produces good 1 while the markets for good 2 and both inputs are perfectly competitive, then general equilibrium is inefficient because *MRS* exceeds *MRT* for all consumers. Show that a tax on the production of good 2 or a subsidy on the production of good 1 can eliminate the inefficiency of monopoly.

2. Suppose that there are immobile producers of goods 1 and 2 in each of two regions and that both inputs are completely mobile. Suppose too that input 1 is taxed in one region but not in the other. What sort of distortion (inefficiency) in the allocation of resources does this produce? Which of the efficiency conditions is violated?

3. Suppose that each firm has monopsony power with respect to input 1 and that no firm has monopoly power. What sort of distortions do these conditions produce? Which of the efficiency conditions is violated? What sort of taxes or subsidies would offset these distortions?

Appendix 16A
Efficiency

In this appendix, we will use differential calculus and the tools of constrained maximization to develop the conditions for economic efficiency for a very simple economy. We have two goods, goods 1 and 2, each produced by one firm, and two individuals, One and Two. We denote One's consumption bundle by (x_1^1, x_2^1) and Two's by (x_1^2, x_2^2). Notice that subscripts index goods and superscripts index individuals. The two utility functions are $U^1(x_1^1, x_2^1)$ and $U^2(x_1^2, x_2^2)$. We have two inputs, inputs 1 and 2, and a fixed supply of each, denoted by z_1' and z_2'. The input bundle used to produce good 1 is (z_1^1, z_2^1); the bundle used to produce good 2 is (z_1^2, z_2^2). In these input bundles, superscripts index goods; subscripts index inputs. The two production functions are $F^1(z_1^1, z_2^1)$ and $F^2(z_1^2, z_2^2)$.

First, let us simply write down the three conditions for efficiency.

1. Efficiency in consumption requires that

$$MRS^1(x_1^1, x_2^1) = MRS^2(x_1^2, x_2^2)$$

   or that

$$\frac{U_1^1(x_1^1, x_2^1)}{U_2^1(x_1^1, x_2^1)} = \frac{U_1^2(x_1^2, x_2^2)}{U_2^2(x_1^2, x_2^2)}$$

2. Efficiency in production requires that

$$MRTS^1(z_1^1, z_2^1) = MRTS^2(z_1^2, z_2^2)$$

   or that

$$\frac{F_1^1(z_1^1, z_2^1)}{F_2^1(z_1^1, z_2^1)} = \frac{F_1^2(z_1^2, z_2^2)}{F_2^2(z_1^2, z_2^2)}$$

3. Efficiency in product mix requires that

$$MRT(x_1, x_2) = MRS^1(x_1^1, x_2^1)$$
$$= MRS^2(x_1^2, x_2^2)$$

   or that

$$\frac{F_1^2(z_1^2, z_2^2)}{F_1^1(z_1^1, z_2^1)} = MRS^1(x_1^1, x_2^1)$$
$$= MRS^2(x_1^2, x_2^2)$$

Alternatively, since the economy's marginal rate of transformation can be expressed in terms of the marginal products of input 1 or of input 2, efficiency in product mix requires that

$$\frac{F_2^2(z_1^2, z_2^2)}{F_2^1(z_1^1, z_2^1)} = MRS^1(x_1^1, x_2^1)$$

$$= MRS^2(x_1^2, x_2^2)$$

Our task is to show that these three conditions are indeed implied by Pareto optimality. Let us fix the utility level of individual One at, say, u^1. Pareto optimality then demands that we allocate the fixed supplies of the two inputs to the production of the two goods and allocate the resulting quantities of the two goods to the two individuals, so that we maximize Two's utility subject to the constraint that One's utility is equal to u^1. That is, Pareto optimality, or economic efficiency, defines a somewhat complex constrained-maximization problem. We will see that the solution to this problem implies the three efficiency conditions we set down earlier.

The constrained-maximization problem is this: choose two consumption bundles — (x_1^1, x_2^1) and (x_1^2, x_2^2) — and two input bundles — (z_1^1, z_2^1) and (z_1^2, z_2^2) — to maximize $U^2(x_1^2, x_2^2)$ subject to the following constraints:

$$u^1 = U^1(x_1^1, x_2^1) \tag{1}$$

$$z_1^1 + z_1^2 = z_1' \tag{2}$$

$$z_2^1 + z_2^2 = z_2' \tag{3}$$

$$x_1^1 + x_1^2 = F^1(z_1^1, z_2^1) \tag{4}$$

$$x_2^1 + x_2^2 = F^2(z_1^2, z_2^2) \tag{5}$$

The first constraint is that the bundle allocated to One yields u^1 utility. The second and third constraints are the economy's resource constraints. The fourth and fifth constraints reflect the fact that the two individuals can consume only what the economy produces.

We can simplify the problem by combining constraints to eliminate some of the endogenous variables. First, in equation (5), use equation (2) to eliminate z_1^2 and equation (3) to eliminate z_2^2:

$$x_2^1 + x_2^2 = F^2(z_1' - z_1^1, z_2' - z_2^1) \tag{6}$$

Then write equations (4) and (6) as

$$x_1^1 = F^1(z_1^1, z_2^1) - x_1^2 \tag{7}$$

$$x_2^1 = F^2(z_1' - z_1^1, z_2' - z_2^1) - x_2^2 \tag{8}$$

Now, in equation (1), use equation (7) to eliminate x_1^1 and equation (8) to eliminate x_2^1:

$$u^1 = U^1[F^1(z_1^1, z_2^1) - x_1^2, F^2(z_1' - z_1^1, z_2' - z_2^1) - x_2^2] \tag{9}$$

We are left with just one constraint, equation (9), and only four endogenous variables: Two's consumption bundle, (x_1^2, x_2^2), and the input bundle to be devoted to good 1, (z_1^1, z_2^1).

We have reduced the original problem to this: choose (x_1^2, x_2^2) and (z_1^1, z_2^1) to maximize $U^2(x_1^2, x_2^2)$ subject to one constraint, equation (9). The Lagrangian is

$$L(x_1^2, x_2^2, z_1^1, z_2^1, \lambda) = U^2(x_1^2, x_2^2)$$
$$+ \lambda\{U^1[F^1(z_1^1, z_2^1) - x_1^2, F^2(z_1' - z_1^1, z_2' - z_2^1) - x_2^2] - u^1\}$$

Setting each of the partial derivatives of the Lagrangian equal to zero yields the following characterization of the solution, in which we have suppressed the endogenous variables.

$$U_1^2 - \lambda U_1^1 = 0 \tag{10}$$

$$U_2^2 - \lambda U_2^1 = 0 \tag{11}$$

$$\lambda(U_1^1 F_1^1 - U_2^1 F_1^2) = 0 \tag{12}$$

$$\lambda(U_1^1 F_2^1 - U_2^1 F_2^2) = 0 \tag{13}$$

$$U^1 - u^1 = 0 \tag{14}$$

Conditions (10) and (11) imply that

$$\frac{U_1^1}{U_2^1} = \frac{U_1^2}{U_2^2} \tag{15}$$

which is the condition for *efficiency in consumption*. Conditions (12) and (13) imply that

$$\frac{F_1^1}{F_2^1} = \frac{F_1^2}{F_2^2} \tag{16}$$

$$\frac{U_1^1}{U_2^1} = \frac{F_1^2}{F_1^1} \tag{17}$$

$$\frac{U_1^1}{U_2^1} = \frac{F_2^2}{F_2^1} \tag{18}$$

Condition (16) is the condition for *efficiency in production*. Condition (17) or (18), in combination with condition (15), yields the condition for *efficiency in product mix*.

REFERENCES

Arrow, K. J., and F. H. Hahn. 1971. *General Competitive Analysis*, San Francisco: Holden-Day.

Koopmans, T. C. 1957. *Three Essays on the State of Economic Science*, New York: McGraw-Hill.

McKenzie, L. W. 1987. "General Equilibrium," in *The New Palgrave: A Dictionary of Economics*, J. Eatwell, M. Milgate, and P. Newman (eds.), London: The Macmillan Press.

Shoven, J. B., and J. Whalley. 1987. *Applying General Equilibrium*, Cambridge, England: Cambridge University Press.

Stigler, G. (ed.). 1957. *Selections from The Wealth of Nations*, New York: Appleton-Century-Crofts.

Vaughn, K. I. 1987. "Invisible Hand," in *The New Palgrave: A Dictionary of Economics*, J. Eatwell, M. Milgate, and P. Newman (eds.), London: The Macmillan Press.

Walras, L. [1874, 1877] 1954. *Éléments d'économie politique pure (Elements of Pure Economics)*. Translated by W. Jaffe, London: Allen and Unwin.

CHAPTER 17

Externalities and Public Goods

externality

Every North American over the age of 40 can remember past cigarette commercial jingles: "I'd walk a mile for a Camel!"; "Call for Philip Morris!"; "Us Tareyton smokers would rather fight than switch!" A few decades ago, smoking was a pervasive, generally acceptable social activity. More recently, a new slogan has superseded those catchy old jingles: "Warning: The Surgeon General Has Determined That Cigarette Smoking Is Dangerous to Your Health." The surgeon general's 1964 report played a central role in reversing the attitude towards smoking. Today, more and more people consider cigarette smoking to be not only dangerous to smokers but also obnoxious and dangerous to nonsmokers who share the same air space. In the language of the economist, smokers' behavior imposes an **externality** on their nonsmoking neighbors because it directly affects their well-being. More generally, whenever the behavior of one economic agent affects for better or worse the well-being of another, we say that the agent is imposing an externality, either positive or negative, on the person affected.

The smoker's externality is but one example of a large class of similar problems forming the major focus of this chapter. Virtually all of the following words or phrases — none of which was in common use in 1964 — are now familiar and immediately call to mind important externality problems: acid rain, driftnets, dioxins, PCBs, greenhouse effect, nuclear winter, supertankers, clear-cutting, and ozone layer. So, too, many recent local and international news stories report on issues related to externalities. These are just a brief sample of headlines from a few of those stories: "Must spend billions to fight air pollution, report warns," "Pulp mill effluents lead to permanent ban on shellfish harvest," "Hydro demands threaten Grand Canyon," and "A nasty scrap over toxic household waste." Of course, as we noted above, not all externalities are negative. The creation of new public parks, green belts, and recreation areas, and the reclamation of marshlands for wildlife habitats are just a few examples of activities associated with positive externalities.

We will begin by using the smoker's example to show why the unrestricted, or blind, pursuit of self-interest does not produce Pareto-optimal results where externalities are concerned. Next, we will develop a taxonomy of externalities; and then examine a range of policy responses to problems created by externalities. Finally, we will investigate a set of problems that are different from, but formally similar to, externalities: the provision of public goods.[1]

---

1 Four entries in *The New Palgrave* are well worth reading in connection with this chapter: "externalities" by J. J. Laffont, "interdependent preferences" by Peter C. Fishburn, "Coase theorem" by Robert D. Cooter, and "public goods" by Agnar Sandmo.

17.1

The Smoker's Externality

In Chapter 9, we encountered the proposition that competitive markets allocate resources in a Pareto-optimal way. In this chapter, we add a very important qualification to that proposition about competitive markets. We want to show the following result:

In the presence of externalities, competitive markets ordinarily do not generate Pareto-optimal allocations.

To do so, we will consider a two-good exchange economy with a negative externality.

Let us begin by imagining an economy in competitive equilibrium that is composed of two types of consumers: smokers and nonsmokers. If there are only two goods in this economy — cigarettes, good 1, and a composite commodity, good 2 — we can represent the smokers' preferences by the standard utility function in which the quantities of cigarettes and of the composite commodity are the arguments. Let x_1' and x_2' be a representative smoker's utility-maximizing bundle, given the price of cigarettes and the smoker's income. (As usual, the price of the composite commodity is 1.)

The nonsmokers' preferences, however, are different. Because nonsmokers presumably will never buy cigarettes, their maximizing consumption bundles will contain only the composite commodity, good 2. If we let x_2^* be a representative nonsmoker's consumption of the composite commodity, x_2^* will be equal to the nonsmoker's income. If these two representative consumers regularly share the same air space, a negative externality may arise as a result of the smoker's consumption decision. It depends on whether the nonsmoker finds secondhand smoke objectionable. If so, then the smoker's decision to buy (and smoke) cigarettes is an additional argument in the nonsmoker's utility function because the smoker's decision materially affects the well-being of the nonsmoker.

Now let us take these two people from the larger social context, their maximizing consumption bundles in hand, and form a miniature exchange economy. We will assume that Shelly is the smoker and Norman is the nonsmoker. We will see that the initial endowment in this two-person exchange economy is Pareto-optimal if there is no externality but that it may not be Pareto-optimal if there is an externality.

We can use an Edgeworth box diagram, first introduced in Chapter 16, to analyze the problem. Let us begin by assuming that Norman is not bothered by secondhand smoke. The case in which no externality is at stake is shown in Figure 17.1. Shelly's origin is the northeasterly corner of the diagram, and her initial endowment of x_1' units of cigarettes and x_2' units of the composite commodity puts her at point E relative to her origin. Her indifference curve through this point is the curve labeled s_0. Norman's origin is the southwesterly corner, and his initial endowment of x_2^* of the composite commodity puts him at point E relative to his origin. Thus, E is the initial endowment point in this exchange economy.

Notice that Norman's indifference curves are horizontal lines like the two lines in Figure 17.1 labeled n_0 and n_1. Why? Norman does not want any of Shelly's cigarettes for his own use, nor does he care how many cigarettes Shelly lights up in their shared air space. In particular, he has no desire to destroy some of her cigarettes to reduce the amount of secondhand smoke in the environment. (We will assume throughout that the cigarettes can be destroyed at no cost.)

Notice, too, that if Norman's consumption of the composite commodity is fixed at x_2^* and if cigarettes are transferred from Shelly to Norman, Norman moves from left to

FIGURE 17.1 An Edgeworth box for smoking with no externality

The smoker's endowment is composed of x_1' cigarettes and x_2' units of the composite commodity, and the nonsmoker's endowment contains only x_2^* units of the composite commodity. Hence, the initial endowment is at E. The nonsmoker's indifference curves — n_0 and n_1, for example — are horizontal, reflecting the fact that he is neutral about the smoker's consumption of cigarettes. The initial endowment at E is therefore Pareto-optimal.

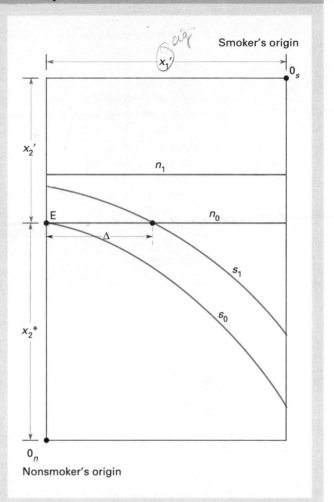

right along the horizontal indifference curve n_0 in Figure 17.1. By contrast, Shelly moves to progressively lower indifference curves. For example, if Δ cigarettes are transferred from Shelly to Norman, she moves to the less preferred indifference curve s_1. As we can see from Figure 17.1, in the absence of an externality, the allocation at point E is Pareto-optimal. No other allocation of consumption goods will leave both as well off.

PROBLEM 17.1

To convince yourself that the market-induced allocation is always Pareto-optimal in this case, identify the contract curve in Figure 17.1.

negative externality

Now let us assume that Norman does find secondhand smoke objectionable. This case, where secondhand smoke is a **negative externality**, is shown in Figure 17.2. Norman is now better off as cigarettes are transferred to him because the number of

FIGURE 17.2 An Edgeworth box for smoking with an externality

The initial endowment is at point E, as it is in Figure 17.1. In contrast to that figure, however, the nonsmoker's indifference curves — n_0 and n_1 — are negatively sloped, reflecting the fact that he finds secondhand smoke objectionable. In this case, the initial endowment is not Pareto-optimal: any allocation in the shaded area is Pareto-preferred to it.

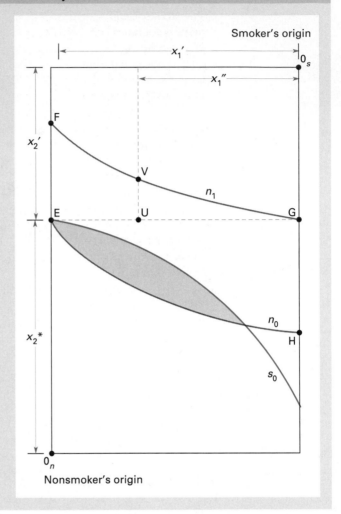

cigarettes in Shelly's hands, and therefore the amount of secondhand smoke in the air, is reduced. (Norman, of course, simply destroys any cigarettes transferred to him.) Graphically, if Norman's consumption of the composite commodity is fixed and if Shelly's consumption of cigarettes is reduced — that is, if Norman moves from left to right along any horizontal line in Figure 17.2 — he is better off.

Because Norman is now better off when Shelly smokes fewer cigarettes, his indifference curves are negatively sloped. For any small increase in the number of cigarettes allotted to Norman, there is a compensating decrease in the amount of the composite commodity he consumes that will leave him on the same indifference curve. In other words, Norman is now willing to pay to reduce Shelly's consumption of cigarettes. (For simplicity, we have drawn Norman's indifference curves in Figure 17.2, n_0 and n_1, not only as negatively sloped but also as convex to the southwesterly origin.)

Is Shelly willing to accept a bribe from Norman and to hand over some cigarettes to him? The answer is yes. The shaded area in Figure 17.2 represents all the exchanges of the composite commodity, or money, for cigarettes that both Norman and Shelly would find preferable to the initial allocation at point E. The market solution that generated the initial allocation at point E is therefore not Pareto-optimal because mutually beneficial exchanges of money for cigarettes are possible.

We can also see why the blind pursuit of self-interest is the ultimate source of that market inefficiency. If Shelly did not smoke any of her cigarettes, Norman would be at point G on indifference curve n_1 in Figure 17.2 because he could still consume x_2^* of the composite commodity. As Shelly's consumption of cigarettes increases, however, Norman falls to progressively lower and lower indifference curves until he reaches indifference curve n_0, when Shelly consumes x_1' cigarettes. Shelly's behavior clearly makes Norman less well off. We can think of Shelly as imposing an external cost on Norman.

We can measure this external cost by determining how much Norman's consumption of the composite commodity must be increased to offset the loss of utility caused by the secondary smoke from any quantity of cigarettes. For x_1' cigarettes, for example, it is the distance EF in Figure 17.2. More generally, for any given quantity of cigarettes smoked, the increase in Norman's consumption of the composite commodity required to compensate him is equal to the vertical distance from line EG to the indifference curve n_1. If Shelly smokes x_1'' cigarettes, for example, then Norman requires UV more of the composite commodity to remain as well off as he would have been in the absence of all smoking.

Although we can identify the cost of the smoker's externality to the nonsmoker, the smoker does not actually bear the costs arising from her behavior. Her failure to bear the costs means — from a social point of view — that she buys and smokes too many cigarettes. We can make the same point by considering the problem from the other side. The nonsmoker is actually willing to pay the smoker to reduce her cigarette consumption. The difficulty is that under the artificial institutional arrangements in this model, he has no way to negotiate with her. Below, we will see what happens when they can negotiate.

PROBLEM 17.2

In Figure 17.2, what is the maximum amount that Norman is willing to pay Shelly to reduce cigarette consumption from x_1' to zero?

In the following problem, you will discover that the disturbing result shown in Figure 17.2 — that in the presence of externalities, market-induced allocations are inefficient — is not an inevitable result.

PROBLEM 17.3

Construct a diagram analogous to Figure 17.2 in which a negative externality is associated with smoking and yet the market allocation is Pareto-optimal.

In summary:

Under the ordinary set of market institutions, the smoker has no incentive to take into account the cost she imposes on the nonsmoker, and the nonsmoker has no way to provide her with such an incentive. As a result, the market-induced outcome in the face of the externality may be inefficient.

As we noted earlier, externalities are not always negative. Sometimes one person's consumption of some good increases rather than detracts from the well-being of everyone materially affected by that consumption activity. For example, when one

positive externality

person with a bad cold and hacking cough buys and takes a cough suppressant, those who associate with him or her are the recipients of a **positive externality** insofar as their exposure to the cold virus (and to the noise, too) is thereby reduced.

PROBLEM 17.4

Suppose that good 1 is of no direct use to Ralph but that when Nancy buys and uses good 1, both Ralph and Nancy are better off. Show that Nancy, left to her own devices, may buy too little of good 1. Can you think of goods other than cough syrup that fit this framework? How about immunization against communicable diseases such as measles, mumps, and polio?

The smoking and cough-syrup examples are only two of a myriad of real-world externalities, both positive and negative. We can reduce all externalities to the same elements: source(s), carrier(s), and recipient(s). One or more economic agents is the source of the externality; in the smoking example, the source is the smoker. The externality is caused by a carrier; in this case, the carrier of the externality is secondary smoke. One or more economic agents is the recipient of the externality; in our example, the recipient of the external cost is the nonsmoker. The recipient fares better or worse, depending on whether the carrier creates positive or negative externalities or, more simply, external benefits or external costs. Before trying to solve (or even to ameliorate) the many real-world problems arising from externalities, we need to organize them into a few broad categories.

17.2

A Taxonomy of Externalities

We know, at least in theory, that the activity of any economic agent can indirectly affect a host of other economic agents through the operation of the price system. For example, if I decide to buy 100,000 times the number of grapefruit I usually eat, my decision will have an (admittedly small) impact on the price of grapefruit, and that impact will indirectly affect all other grapefruit buyers. Indeed, from a general equilibrium perspective, everything depends on everything else. Any choice a particular economic agent makes potentially has indirect effects on all other economic agents. By contrast, when an externality is at issue, the activity of one economic agent directly affects another economic agent (or agents). Just what do we mean by "direct" in this context?

Consumption–Consumption Externalities

consumption– consumption externality

One type of direct impact, called a **consumption–consumption externality**, occurs when consumers are both the source(s) and the recipient(s) of the externality. Massive lineups of people buying tickets on a first come, first served basis is an example of a negative consumption–consumption externality: each person in the lineup imposes a negative externality on everyone further down the line. For example, when popular musical groups come to town, their fans often pay a severe time price when they line up to buy tickets — sometimes hours or even days before the tickets go on sale. By contrast, a heavy turnout at that great American institution, the homecoming dance, is a positive consumption–consumption externality because the more people (within reason) who come to see (and to be seen), the merrier.

PROBLEM 17.5

Homecoming dances are usually organized (and often subsidized) by a student organization rather than by "leaving it to the market." Are such dances likely to be provided more efficiently through a student organization or through the market?

Production–Production Externalities

production–
production
externality

Another type of direct impact, called a **production–production externality**, arises when producers are both the source(s) and the recipient(s) of the externality. A classic case of a negative production–production externality is the pasturing of cows on the commons: any one farmer's productive activity adversely affects that of every other farmer. A major contemporary case is nickel production at INCO in Sudbury, Ontario. INCO's sulfur emissions were the largest single source of acid rain in North America — adversely affecting a host of other firms in Canada and the United States. Among the industries thought to be affected are Québec's maple sugar producers, whose trees produced less sap and died young because of acid rain fallout.

A classic case of a positive production–production externality is the shopping center. The smaller specialty stores benefit from the steady stream of potential customers attracted by the large department stores that are the cornerstones of most such developments.

Consumption–Production Externalities

consumption–
production
externality

Another type of direct impact, called a **consumption–production externality**, occurs when one or more consumers are the source(s) and one or more producers the recipient(s) of the externality. One example of a negative consumption–production externality occurred recently in Vancouver, Canada, when certain commercial blueberry producers were forced to take their blueberries off the market because the fields where their berries grew had been contaminated by lead from the emissions of cars traveling on a nearby highway. An example of a positive consumption–production externality occurs when a private flower garden provides nectar for bees from a neighboring commercial honey producer.

Production–Consumption Externalities

production–
consumption
externality

A fourth type of direct impact, called a **production–consumption externality**, arises when one or more producers are the source(s) and one or more consumers the recipient(s) of the externality. Almost inevitably in standard industrial air-pollution problems, producers are sources and consumers are recipients. The 1985 gas leak of methyl isocyanate from a Union Carbide plant in Bhopal, India, which killed more than 2,000 people in a 50-square-kilometer area, is just one tragically memorable example of a negative production–consumption externality. A positive production consumption externality arises when the bees of a commercial honey producer pollinated the fruit trees of a nearby hobby farmer.

17.3

Responses to Externalities: An Overview

So far, we have learned that externalities can arise between consumers, between firms, or between combinations of the two. When such externalities are positive, resources are *underallocated* to the source of the externality; when they are negative, resources are *overallocated* to the source. What kinds of responses to externalities can help to rectify these allocational distortions? In this section, we will briefly survey possible responses and then return to look at some of them in greater detail.

Private Negotiations

private
negotiation

So far, we have assumed that the source of the externality will turn a blind eye to the effect of its actions on the recipient, and we have seen that this blind self-interest leads directly to inefficiency. Thus, **private negotiation**, or bargaining, between the concerned parties is an obvious place to seek a remedy.

The parties concerned can actually benefit by recognizing their interdependence and negotiating an alternative, mutually beneficial solution. If the externality is positive, the recipient may be willing to pay the source to increase the amount of the carrier, and the source may be willing to accept. Apple growers in Washington State, for instance, pay an apiary fee to beekeepers for providing bees to pollinate their trees (*see* Cheung, 1973). If the externality is negative, the recipient may be willing to pay to decrease the amount of the carrier. For instance, a harassed student in the midst of final examinations might be willing to pay the music lover in the neighboring apartment $25 for 10 hours of peaceful study time. If the source and the recipient manage to negotiate a Pareto-optimal private response to the externality, then no real social problem exists.

Internalization

internalization

Another remedy is a process called **internalization**, in which a third party, who sees an opportunity to make a private gain from the presence of an externality, intervenes between the source(s) and the recipient(s) and effects an efficient private response. For example, a recent trend among hotel keepers in the United States is to offer their patrons a choice between smoking and nonsmoking rooms. In this way, they can capture the resulting benefit to nonsmokers by charging commensurately higher prices or, more realistically, by avoiding the loss of nonsmoking patrons to competing hotels that offer nonsmoking accommodation. Again, when the problem is internalized by a third party, no real social problem requiring a governmental response arises.

Governmental Responses

As we have seen, the fact that externalities are pervasive phenomena does not necessarily imply that governmental intervention must likewise be pervasive. Private parties always have the incentive (and often the means) to resolve the problems created by the blind pursuit of self-interest. Whenever such problems are not privately resolved, however, three sorts of public policy responses are possible. The first approach is to facilitate the negotiation of private solutions by assigning *property rights*. (We will soon see how property rights help the interested parties to reach a mutually acceptable resolution.) The second approach is to impose *public regulations* based on cost-benefit analysis. The third is to take *no action* at all.

Assigning Property Rights

assigning
property rights

Economists favor **assigning property rights** whenever possible because the problem is thereby resolved by the only parties having the necessary information. For example, suppose that a chemical company pours effluent into a river upstream and a household takes its drinking water out of the same river downstream. In this case, only the chemical company knows the value it places on being able to dump its wastes and only the household knows the value it places on pure drinking water. If property rights to the water are assigned to one party or the other, the two may be able to reach an efficient private solution: under a property-rights approach, each solution is tailor-made by the parties concerned.

Public Regulation

public
regulation

Because the property-rights approach is sometimes unworkable, **public regulation** based on cost-benefit analysis may be necessary. Many governmental agencies concerned with health, resource management, power, education, and recreation use cost-benefit analysis to determine a target level for the carrier of an externality and then use regulation of some sort to hit the target. Taxation is one kind of regulation. The heavy taxes imposed on cigarettes and liquor are intended, in part, to reduce consumption to more socially desirable levels. Bans on certain offensive activities are another regulatory option. For example, playing radios without earphones is now illegal in some parks in North America; smoking is typically prohibited in public buildings, hospitals, and subways; and factories emitting unacceptably high levels of pollutants are sometimes forced to shut down. Regulatory standards are yet another means of controlling externalities. Standards for lead emissions from automobiles and for sulfur emissions from industrial plants are just two of many such governmentally enforced limits.

As we will see, such regulations are necessarily crude, in the sense that a single solution is imposed on many different problems. Like an off-the-rack pair of jeans, a regulation sometimes fits, but not always. California's automobile emissions standards are applied statewide, for example, even though auto-emissions problems in such areas as Los Angeles, San Francisco, and Tahoe are quite different.

Nonintervention

nonintervention

The third possible governmental response is **nonintervention** — simply to do nothing. Because regulation itself uses up resources, including the costs of information gathering, administration, and enforcement, the best policy may be no policy. (For instance, though body odor is a negative externality, the problem in most circumstances is simply not significant enough to warrant expensive government regulation.) In the following sections, we will consider the three major types of responses in more detail and examine the conditions under which each is appropriate.

Privately Negotiated Solutions

Here we will look more carefully at the two-person smoker's externality problem, one example of the very large class of real-world externality problems well suited to negotiated solutions. Let us imagine that the two consumers are long-term roommates: Sadie is the smoker and Norma the nonsmoker. Because the problem involves only two people and because they interact over a long period of time, the resolution of the problem is best left up to Sadie and Norma themselves. In practice, they will probably negotiate some solution about when, where, and how much Sadie can smoke in their apartment. But chances are good that they will spend a great deal of time and energy arguing about their individual rights to their common air space. Sadie may insist that she has every right to smoke in her own home, and Norma may be just as vociferous in claiming her right to breathe unpolluted air.

One way to facilitate a solution to the roommates' problem, pioneered by the Nobel Prize winner Ronald Coase (1960) and subsequently applied by other economists to a wide range of externality problems, is to endow either Sadie or Norma with the exclusive right to control smoking in their shared environment. This arrangement facil-

default option

itates a solution by establishing a **default option**: the arrangement that will prevail if no settlement is reached. If Sadie has the exclusive right to the air, presumably she will smoke as much as she chooses in the apartment if the two cannot come to an agreement. Similarly, if Norma has the exclusive right, presumably she will prohibit all smoking in the apartment if they cannot agree on something else. Further, the assignment of a property right will reduce time spent bickering about who has a right to do what in the roommates' common air space.

Establishing a default option facilitates a negotiated solution in two ways. First, it narrows the range of possible solutions. Second, it establishes which of the two parties must compensate the other to move away from the default option. To explore these points let us first assign the property right to their common air to Sadie and find the set of negotiated solutions that are possible given this assignment. Then we will assign the property right to Norma and repeat the exercise. Finally, we will compare the negotiated solutions that are possible in the two cases. This comparison will reveal both how the assignment of a property right promotes a negotiated solution by narrowing the range of possibilities and how different assignments of the property right affect the welfare of Sadie and Norma.

In Figure 17.3, Sadie's position is shown on the left and Norma's on the right. Sadie's consumption of cigarettes and Norma's consumption of secondhand smoke is on the vertical axis. Sadie's consumption of her composite commodity is on the horizontal axis to the left of the origin at 0, while Norma's consumption of her composite commodity is on the horizontal axis to the right of the origin.

When the property right to the roommate's common air space is assigned to Sadie, it means that Sadie does not have to accept any solution less attractive to her than the default point at E where she simply maximizes her own utility subject to her budget constraint. In constructing Figure 17.3, we have assumed that Sadie's weekly income is $150 and that the price of a pack of cigarettes is $5. At the default point, Sadie spends $110 of her $150 weekly income on 22 packs of cigarettes, leaving her $40 to spend on her composite commodity. In this equilibrium she is on the indifference curve corresponding to 23 utils. (A util is a unit of utility. As you know from Chapter 2, since the utility function is ordinal, not cardinal, a comparison of the number of utils for two bundles reveals only which bundle is preferred.)

Under the default option, Norma finds herself at point E' where she spends all of her $180 income on the composite commodity and puts up with Sadie smoking 22 packs of cigarettes a week. At E' Norma is on her 5-util indifference curve. Keep in mind that Norma is *better off the less Sadie smokes*, so as we move down any vertical line in the right-hand portion of Figure 17.3 Norma gets progressively more utils. Notice also that as we move from left to right along one of Norma's indifference curves, the curve gets progressively flatter. This reflects the property that the more packs of cigarettes Sadie smokes, the larger is the increase in Norma's consumption of the composite commodity that is required to compensate her for the secondhand smoke from yet another pack of cigarettes.

Given the default option in which Sadie is at point E and Norma at point E', what can we say about the set of bargains that Sadie and Norma could strike which would make them both better off? Of course, these two roommates are constrained by the fact that their joint income is $330 and by the price of cigarettes, $5 per pack. To begin to answer our question, we will hold Norma on her 5-util indifference curve and then find the best consumption bundle for Sadie. In comparing points E' and A' on Norma's

FIGURE 17.3 Property rights and the smoker's externality

If Sadie has the exclusive right to their shared air space, the default option puts her at point E on her 23-util indifference curve and Norma at point E′ on her 5-util indifference curve. Since the default option is not Pareto-optimal, they can arrive at a better solution through bargaining. Holding Norma on her 5-util indifference curve, the best that Sadie can do is point F on her 27-util indifference curve, which puts Norma at point F′. Holding Sadie on her 23-util indifference curve, the best that Norma can do is point G′ on her 13-util indifference curve, which puts Sadie at point G.

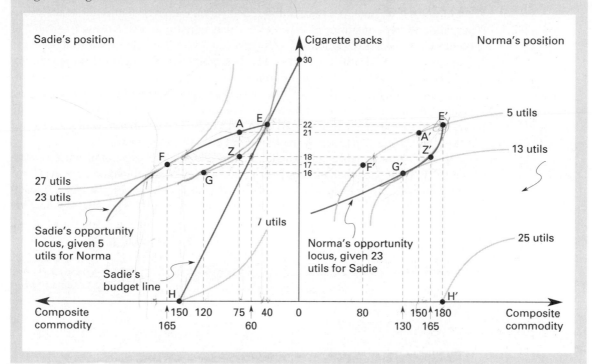

5-util indifference curve, we see that Norma would pay Sadie up to $30 to reduce cigarette consumption from 22 to 21 packs. If this bargain was struck, Sadie would have $180 (her income of $150 plus the payment of $30 from Norma); she would spend $105 of it to buy 21 packs of cigarettes, and $75 of it on her composite commodity. In other words, this bargain would allow Sadie to attain point A. Since Norma is no worse off at A′ than she is at E′, and since Sadie is better off at A than she is at E, this bargain is Pareto-preferred to their original situation.

For each point to the left of point E′ on Norma's 5-util indifference curve, we have identified the analogous bargain and the consumption bundle which that bargain allows Sadie to attain. For example, in comparing points E′ and F′ on Norma's 5-util indifference curve, we see that Norma would pay Sadie up to $100 to reduce cigarette consumption from 22 to 17 packs. If she did so, then Sadie could attain point F. The set of bundles that Sadie could attain is shown in Figure 17.3 and labeled "Sadie's opportunity locus, given 5 utils for Norma." The best point for Sadie on this opportunity locus is point F on her 27-util indifference curve, where she consumes 17 packs of cigarettes and spends $165 on the composite commodity. When Sadie is on her opportunity locus at point F, Norma is at point F′, where she puts us with the secondhand smoke from 17 packs and spends $80 on the composite commodity. We see, then, that when we hold Norma's utility at 5 utils, the best Sadie can attain for herself is 27 utils. The combination of point F for Sadie and point F' for Norma is a point of Pareto-optimality.

Now let us reverse the exercise. We will hold Sadie on her 23-util indifference curve and then find the best consumption bundle for Norma. In comparing points E and Z on Sadie's 23-util indifference curve, we see that Norma would have to pay Sadie at least $15 to reduce cigarette consumption from 22 packs to 18 packs. If this bargain was struck, Norma would have $165 to spend on her composite commodity. In other words, this bargain would allow Norma to attain point Z'. For each point to the left of point E on Sadie's 23-util indifference curve, we have identified the analogous bargain and the consumption bundle that that bargain allows Norma to attain. In Figure 17.3, the set of bundles that Norma can attain is labeled "Norma's opportunity locus, given 23 utils for Sadie." The best point for Norma on this opportunity locus is point G' on her 13-util indifference curve, where she spends $130 on her composite commodity and puts up with the secondhand smoke from 16 packs of cigarettes. When Norma is at point G', Sadie is at G. We see, then, that if we hold Sadie's utility at 23 utils, the best that Norma can attain is 13 utils. The combination of point G' for Norma and point G for Sadie is another point of Pareto-optimality.

Each Pareto-optimal combination in Figure 17.3 generates a point on what we have called the "utility possibility frontier" in Figure 17.4. The combination of point G' for Norma and point G for Sadie from Figure 17.3 generates point G in Figure 17.4. The combination of points F' for Norma and F for Sadie from Figure 17.3 generates point F on

FIGURE 17.4 The smoker's externality, property rights, and bargained solutions

If Sadie gets the property right to the shared air space, the bargained solution will be at some point like B* on segment FG of the utility possibility frontier. In contrast, if Norma gets the property right, the bargained solution will be at some point like B** on segment UV of the utility possibility frontier.

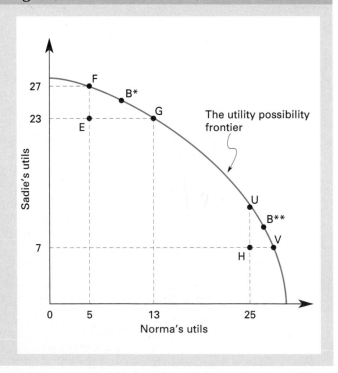

the utility possibility frontier in Figure 17.4, and so on. The default combination that is arises when we assign the property right to their common air space to Sadie — points E for Sadie and E′ for Norma — generates point E in Figure 17.4. Notice that the default combination is *below* the utility possibilities frontier because it is *not* Pareto-optimal. Notice, too, that of all the points on the utility possibilities frontier, only those on segment FG make both Sadie and Norma better off than they are at the default point E. In other words, only points on segment FG of the utility possibilities frontier are Pareto-preferred to point E. We see, then, just how the assignment of a property right narrows the range of possible solutions to the externality problem that these roommates confront. Given that the property right is assigned to Sadie, we can expect the two roommates to agree on a point like B* in which both Sadie and Norma are better off than they are at the default point E. Although we have not explicitly identified point B* in Figure 17.3, one thing is clear: Sadie will smoke fewer than 22 packs of cigarettes and Norma will have to compensate Sadie for reducing her consumption of cigarettes.

Now let us quickly consider the case in which the property right is assigned to the non-smoker, Norma. The corresponding default combination puts Norma at point H′ on her 25-util indifference curve in Figure 17.3, where she puts up with no secondhand smoke and spends her entire income on her composite commodity. The same default combination puts Sadie at point H on her 7-util indifference curve, where she consumes no cigarettes and spends her entire income on her composite commodity. In terms of Figure 17.4, when Norma gets the property right, the default option is at point H. The assignment of the property right, in this case to Norma, once again narrows the range of possible solutions to the externality problem. In this case, we expect the roommates to agree on a bargained solution at a point like B** on segment UV of the utility possibilities frontier where both roommates are better off than they are at the default point H. Any such bargain will require Sadie to compensate Norma for the privilege of smoking some cigarettes. We see, then, that if Norma gets the property right, any Pareto-optimal solution the roommates could agree to will be on segment UV of the utility possibilities frontier. On the other hand, if Sadie gets the property right, any Pareto-optimal solution they could agree to will be on segment FG.

This perspective on the problem gives rise to another important insight. The assignment of a property right is not just a solution to the roommates' externality problem. It also has important *distributional implications*. For example, Norma is clearly better off at the Pareto-inefficient point H in Figure 17.4 — the default point which arises when Norma has the property right — than she is at any of the Pareto-optimal points that could be attained when Sadie has the property right. Similarly, Sadie is better off at point E than she is at any Pareto-optimal point that could be reached when Norma has the property right.

> ## PROBLEM 17.6
>
> Find the combination in Figure 17.3 that corresponds to point V in Figure 17.4. To do so, first construct Norma's opportunity locus, given 7 utils for Sadie. Then find Norma's best point on this opportunity locus.

The parable of the two roommates illustrates three important points about externalities:

First, when the number of parties directly involved is small and when the externality itself is significant, the concerned parties have every incentive to resolve the problem themselves.

Second, from an economic perspective, these privately negotiated settlements are extremely attractive because the concerned parties are the only ones who have the information necessary to create a solution that suits them.

Third, because many externality problems arise from unspecified or incomplete property rights, one way to facilitate such privately negotiated solutions is to assign property rights, thereby defining the default option and limiting the range of possible solutions.

Is it possible to take advantage of privately negotiated arrangements when the number of sources and recipients is significantly larger? Think of the externality problem associated with residential real estate on a hill rising from the seashore, for example: everyone wants a clear view of the ocean. Owners down the hill can improve their view by building tall houses, but only at the expense of owners up the hill who lose their ocean view. The traditional regulatory solution to this problem — which is, in fact, not one problem at all but rather a whole series of discrete externality problems — is to impose a maximum height restriction on everyone. However, because one tall building creates as many different view problems as there are lots behind it and up the hill, only the owners of these building sites know in any precise sense what their particular problem may be. The umbrella, or all-encompassing, regulatory solution of a height restriction is therefore only a rough-and-ready approximation of the tailor-made solutions that individual owners might negotiate for themselves.

PROBLEM 17.7

Suppose that the municipality has imposed a maximum building height restriction of 30 feet on the seaside real estate we have described. Can you devise a better property-rights solution?

17.5

Internalizing the Externality

free rider

We now turn to problem-solving through *internalization* by a third party. Our previous example of department-store and specialized retailers in the same shopping center is an interesting case in point. If we simplify the problem by assuming that the department store is the source of the (positive) externality and the specialized retailers the recipients, then the carrier is the size of the department store. The larger it is, the more traffic it attracts, and the more benefit it confers on the smaller retailers. We can think of the specialized retailers as **free riders** on the retailing opportunities created by the department store, much as the hobos of the 1930s literally were free riders on the nation's railroad system.

Imagine a department-store firm bent on blindly pursuing its own self-interest. If it considers establishing a new branch, it will choose to build a store too small to maximize the joint profits of both that new department store and the specialized retail outlets that almost inevitably spring up to take a free ride on its traffic. Why will the store be too small? Because it cannot capture the benefits conferred on the free riders.

We can even imagine a scenario in which the joint profits from the best possible aggregation of retail activity — the best size for the department store and the best types and sizes for the specialized retailers — might be positive, whereas the profit of the department store itself might be negative. In this case, the department store would never establish its branch, even though it would see potential profits from the retail center as a whole.

How can we solve this problem of the free rider? We see the answer across the face of post-1950 North America: the shopping center. We can imagine that the shopping-center developer first calculates the profit-maximizing configuration of stores and then negotiates a series of contracts with the department store and selected specialized retailers. The contracts must guarantee only that each retailer is at least as well-off as it would be in the absence of the shopping center. By putting all the externality-producing activities under one roof, the developer can extract for itself the maximum profit from the retail agglomerate, profit that otherwise would have gone unrealized, given the blind pursuit of self-interest by the large department store. Not surprisingly, the large department stores themselves recognize that potential and often become the prime movers in shopping-center developments. So, too, Cannell Studios recognized a similar potential in the film industry. When it built its new North Shore Studios, it designed a facility in which its own studios occupied only a third of the space. All the remaining space was designated for offices to be rented to other film-related companies, including camera, lighting, and catering firms.

17.6

Regulatory Solutions

When the costs of transacting a private solution to an externality problem are prohibitively high, *public regulation* is the only effective remedy. Such high costs occur when the number of sources and recipients is relatively large or when direct contact between them is infrequent. For example, smoking in a public elevator, at a bus stop, in the corridor of a hospital, or in any other public place is an ever-changing externality problem; it changes with the number and identity of the smokers and nonsmokers present at any one time. We simply cannot expect the bus riders waiting at Fifth and Main to negotiate a solution to the smoking externality that arises if both smokers and nonsmokers are in the group: the costs of negotiation far outweigh the potential benefits. Neither can we anticipate that a third party will internalize the externality: no private person owns these public places. In this kind of circumstance, governmental regulation is apparently the only feasible option.

Many air and water pollution problems closely resemble the smoker's externality in public places. The number of individuals and firms who contribute to air pollution in Los Angeles, for instance, is as large and as continually changing as the number of individuals and firms who suffer from the resulting smog. Moreover, the air pollution problem changes as the weather changes. For example, the smog is worse when a temperature inversion occurs or when more sunshine causes chemical reactions in the atmosphere.

Because every person and every firm in Los Angeles is both a source and a recipient and because the problem itself is as changeable as the weather, the cost of privately negotiating a solution is prohibitive. And because no one owns the Los Angeles air shed, the problem cannot be internalized by a third party.

When transacting a private solution to an externality is too expensive, regulation becomes an alternative. What first strikes an economist about the regulatory approach is that policy makers need very precise information in order to identify specific regulatory targets. By contrast, the private-property approach requires only that policy makers know the gross features of the problem at hand.

Cost-Benefit Analysis

Economic cost-benefit analysis can be used to generate the information needed to stipulate regulatory targets. We can illustrate this approach by returning once more to the smoking externality. To translate that problem into the language of cost-benefit analysis, we will calculate both a representative smoker's benefits and a representative nonsmoker's costs and then subtract the costs from the benefits to determine the optimal amount of smoking in this two-person case. We will continue to call the smoker Sadie and the nonsmoker Norma.

The positions of Norma and Sadie are shown in Figure 17.5. The price of a pack of cigarettes is again $5, Sadie's weekly income is again $150, and Norma's is again $180. To compute costs and benefits of smoking, we will use the case in which no cigarettes are smoked as our point of reference. This reference point is a combination of point H for Sadie and point H′ for Norma in Figure 17.5, where Sadie is on her 7-util indifference curve and Norma is on her 25-util indifference curve.

Relative to point H, what is the benefit to Sadie — net of the cost the cigarettes — of 3 packs of cigarettes? We can put this question in a different way. Given that Sadie is currently at point H, what is the maximum amount she would pay for the right to buy 3 packs of cigarettes? From Figure 17.5 we see that the consumption bundle composed of $65 spent on her composite commodity and 3 packs of cigarettes put her on the

FIGURE 17.5   Calculating the cost and benefits of smoking

Given that Sadie is currently at point H on her 7-util indifference curve, the maximum amount she would pay for the right to smoke 3 packs of cigarettes is $70. Therefore, $70 is the benefit to Sadie of the right to smoke 3 packs of cigarettes rather than no cigarettes. Similarly, the cost to Norma of Sadie's right to smoke 3 packs of cigarettes rather than no cigarettes is $10.

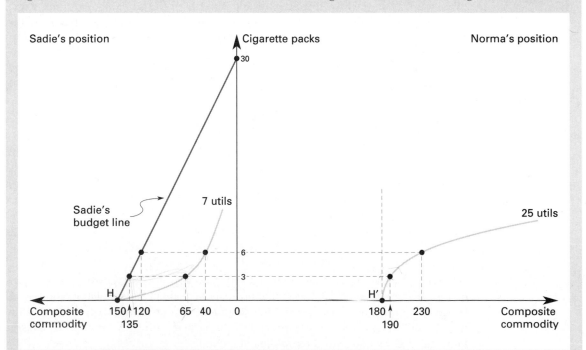

7-util indifference curve. If she paid $70 for this right and $15 for the 3 packs of cigarettes, she would have exactly $65 left to spend on her composite commodity. We therefore see that she would pay up to $70 for the right to buy 3 packs of cigarettes. Then, $70 is our measure of the benefit to Sadie of 3 packs of cigarettes. By the same logic, $80 is the benefit to Sadie of 6 packs of cigarettes. By repeatedly following this procedure, we have computed the schedule labeled "Benefit from smoking" in Figure 17.6.

Now let us turn back to Figure 17.5 to find the cost to Norma of the secondhand smoke from the cigarettes that Sadie smokes. If Sadie smoked 3 packs of cigarettes, and Norma had $190 to spend on her composite commodity, Norma would be on the 25-util indifference curve. Relative to point H′, where Sadie smokes no cigarettes and Norma spends only $180 to attain the 25-util indifference curve, we see that the cost to Norma of the secondhand smoke from 3 packs of cigarettes is $10. By the same logic, the cost to Norma of the secondhand smoke from 6 packs of cigarettes is $50. Following this procedure, we have computed the schedule labeled "Cost of smoking" in Figure 17.6.

The cost-benefit optimal quantity of cigarettes is the quantity that maximizes net social benefit — that is, benefit minus cost. Notice that the slopes of the two tangent lines in Figure 17.6 are identical. We therefore know that at 4 packs of cigarettes, the rate at which benefit increases as quantity of cigarettes increases is equal to the rate at which cost increases as quantity of cigarettes increases. In addition, as you can see from Figure 17.6, with fewer (more) than 4 packs, the rate at which benefit increases is larger (smaller) than the rate at which cost increases. We therefore know that 4 packs maximizes net social benefit. That is, relative to the reference point we used to compute costs and benefits, 4 packs of cigarettes is cost-benefit optimal. The net social benefit of 4 packs of cigarettes in this case is $63 per week (the $80 benefit minus the $17 cost associated with 4 packs). As you will see in the following problem, the choice of a reference point can have a significant impact on this analysis.

FIGURE 17.6 **Cost-benefit analysis of the smoker's externality**

Using data from Figure 17.5, we have plotted the benefits and costs of Sadie's smoking in the air space shared by Sadie and Norma. The cost-benefit optimal amount of smoking is 4 packs of cigarettes per week.

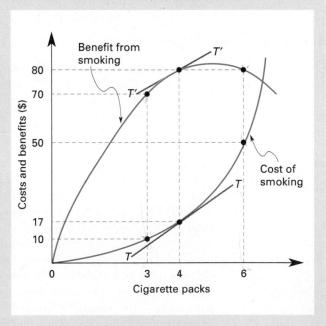

PROBLEM 17.8

Let us use a different reference point and repeat the cost-benefit calculation. In Figure 17.3 take the combination of points E for Sadie and E′ for Norma as the point of reference. Using the information in Figure 17.3, calculate the benefit to Norma and the cost to Sadie of reducing cigarette consumption from 22 packs to 21 packs; from 22 packs to 18 packs; and from 22 packs to 16 packs. Using this information, construct a diagram like Figure 17.6 and calculate the cost-benefit optimal quantity of cigarettes. (Given the limited detail in Figure 17.3, some of your calculations will be approximate.)

We can imagine extending this technique of cost-benefit analysis from our society-of-two to society at large. At least in principle, we can think either of scanning costs and benefits over a large number of individual smokers and nonsmokers, or of directly estimating the costs to nonsmokers as a group and the benefits to smokers as a group. As you will discover in Section 17.7, however, getting accurate information on personal costs and benefits can be difficult.

In principle, cost-benefit analysis allows policy makers to determine a target level for some activity that produces an externality. In practice, however, serious problems attend applications of cost-benefit analysis. As we saw in the examples concerning bus-stop smoking and Los Angeles smog, what we nominally see as "a problem" is actually a multitude of problems because the problem itself changes with each episode. The cost of gathering the information needed for this sort of cost-benefit analysis is simply prohibitive.

The best a cost-benefit analyst can do in such cases is to consider a representative problem that captures the average features of the whole gamut of real problems under study. The regulation resulting from the representative cost-benefit analysis is necessarily an umbrella solution: it covers a whole range of problems and is ideally suited to none. California's statewide auto-emissions legislation, designed to ameliorate air-pollution problems of various descriptions from the Oregon border to the Mexican border, is just one of many examples.

Hitting the Regulatory Target

regulatory
mechanisms

Suppose that policy makers, using cost-benefit analysis, have identified a *regulatory target* for some externality problem. What kind of regulation will achieve it? We can find no single answer to this question because different problems require different kinds of solutions. Yet economists do have one regulatory rule of thumb: they prefer **regulatory mechanisms** based on individual choice to mechanisms proscribing individual behavior.

Think of the emissions of sulfur from electricity-generating plants. One regulatory mechanism based on individual choice is to charge an emissions tax of t dollars per unit of sulfur. This regulation leaves the individual electricity-producing firms free to choose any level of emissions they like — as long as they are prepared to pay the price. By contrast, a proscriptive regulatory mechanism is to ban the emission of, say, more than s units of sulfur per kilowatt-hour produced. This ban means that the maximum emissions level applies across the board to every power-generating company.

Assuming that we know the values of s and t that will achieve the target level of sulfur, why is the tax preferable to the ban? If we think of the privilege of emitting sulfur into the atmosphere as an economic resource just like any other, then — in the absence of an externality — the resource is free and requires no regulatory attention. In the presence of an externality, however, only a limited amount of emission will be permitted.

The privilege of emitting sulfur is now a *scarce resource*, and the emissions tax is essentially the price per unit for that privilege. Because all firms face the same price — that is, pay the same emissions tax — the limited amount of sulfur emissions will be allocated to its most productive uses. The tax thus ensures that the limited quantity of emissions will be allocated efficiently, a result we cannot achieve with the blanket proscription.

Some government agencies are experimenting with another mechanism that invokes individual choice to allocate emission rights efficiently. Individual polluters are given marketable emission quotas, or rights. If the firm intends to emit, say, 100,000 tons of sulfur and its quota is only 70,000 tons, it must buy emission rights for 30,000 tons of sulfur from other firms. On the other hand, if the firm anticipates emitting less sulfur than allowed by its quota, it can sell its excess emission rights. For example, such "emissions trading" would let a power plant that plans to emit less than its quota of a pollutant sell the difference to another utility that plans to emit more than its quota — while the overall target for the region is still met. Like the emissions tax, this marketable emission rights solution ensures that the limited quantity of emissions will be allocated efficiently.

Using this rule of thumb, what kind of regulatory response can you devise to avert a little-publicized tragedy that now threatens much of the United States? The Ogallala Aquifer is a vast underground water reservoir lying beneath much of the Great Plains. Most of the water pumped through the impressive agricultural sprinkling systems that dot this landscape is drawn from the aquifer. As the sprinkling technology has caught on, the demands on the aquifer have grown at such an alarming rate that it may soon be sucked dry. (The aquifer is so very valuable a resource that proposals have been made to drain the Great Lakes to replenish it.)

The tragedy, of course, is the old *problem of the commons* in a new guise. Any landowner can tap into the aquifer by drilling a well. The amount of water available to any user of the aquifer next year is virtually independent of how much that person pumps this year, because any individual will use but a tiny fraction of the total. Consequently, no landowner has any incentive to conserve water for future needs. Because access is free to all, the needs of future users of this resource carry no weight in determining its present use.

A simple analogy suggests the absurdity of the problem of the Ogallala Aquifer. Imagine a thousand people on a desert island with just enough water to last them until their rescuers, known to be coming on a specified date, arrive. If each one has a straw in the common drinking supply and if no one can tell how much water anyone else is drinking, the result is almost certainly death for everyone.

> **PROBLEM 17.9**
>
> What sort of regulatory mechanism seems appropriate to control the externality problem associated with the Ogallala Aquifer?

17.7

Public Goods

public goods We now turn from externalities to **public goods** — goods characterized by a perfect positive externality to the whole community. These public goods are of a different nature from most of the goods (and services) we have considered, which have been characterized by benefits that flow to a particular consumer. When I buy and eat a

Granny Smith apple, for instance, I am the only one who gets to enjoy it. Furthermore, the apple itself is no longer available to you or to anyone else. It simply is gone. Such goods are termed **rivalrous goods**: one person's consumption of a unit of a rivalrous good precludes the possibility of anyone else enjoying it.

rivalrous goods

nonrivalrous goods

Other goods and services — those conferring positive externalities, for example — are to some extent **nonrivalrous goods**. When I enjoy my flower garden, for instance, my neighbors and occasional passers-by can also take pleasure in it without lessening my own. (Unless, of course, so many come to gawk that they interfere with my pleasure.) So, too, the presence of other sightseers does not diminish the pleasure you take in feeling the spray from the awesome force of Niagara Falls (unless the crowds are so large that they interfere with your own enjoyment). Many other goods and services are similarly nonrivalrous, differing only in degree, and a few are even purely nonrivalrous. For instance, my pleasure in the spectacle of Halley's comet zinging through the night sky is in no way diminished by the millions of other eyes turned skyward. So, too, the benefits flowing to you from a national defense program are unaffected by the benefits to me.

Nonrivalrous Goods

Many economists and others take the normative position that, for the sake of efficiency, nonrivalrous goods ought to be provided free of charge. To exclude individuals from the benefit of a *nonrivalrous good*, they argue, is inefficient, because including them makes them better off and leaves everyone else just as well off. In other words, the number of people who can enjoy the flow of benefits can be increased at virtually no cost.

Indeed, many of the services that governments commonly provide free of charge are, to some degree, nonrivalrous. National defense and navigational safety aids such as channel markers and lighthouses, for example, are, in practice, completely nonrivalrous. Roads and bridges, police and fire protection, and many public health programs — such as compulsory immunization against disease — are, to a considerable extent, nonrivalrous. The argument for publicly provided, nonrivalrous goods implies only that access should be free to all. It does not imply that taxes should not be imposed to provide the goods.

Nonexcludable Goods

nonexcludable goods

Many, but certainly not all, goods and services considered in this section are also **nonexcludable goods**, meaning that denial of access to the good or service is impossible or at least very costly. In the last century, entrepreneurs built fences along the Niagara Falls gorge and charged tourists to look at the falls through peepholes. In this case, the spectacle of Niagara Falls became an excludable good. But even P. T. Barnum, that masterly entrepreneur, could not have denied access to people refusing to pay admission to see Halley's comet. Similarly, New York State can manage to charge tolls for the use of some of its major roads, but the U.S. government would find it impossible to deny the benefits of national defense to selected residents without incurring the considerable expense of deporting them. Thus, nonrivalrous goods may or may not be excludable. By contrast, goods that are rivalrous are necessarily excludable. Once the apple is eaten, it is available to no one else.

Pure Public Goods

pure public goods

Goods that are both completely nonrivalrous and nonexcludable are called **pure public goods**. In many circumstances, if pure public goods are to be produced at all, they will be produced by some public authority rather than by profit-seeking firms because no firm can profit by providing a nonexcludable good.

One counter-example of a pure public good that is provided privately is "free" commercial TV broadcasting. At least to the viewers themselves, TV watching is both nonrivalrous and nonexcludable. No matter how many millions of people watch a TV program, the individual viewer's pleasure is unaffected, and the programming is available at no cost to anyone with a TV set. Yet, private broadcasting corporations are actually in the business of providing another, both rivalrous and excludable service: a captive audience for advertisers. The programming is merely the bait used to capture the audience. By contrast, ad-free TV programming is produced either by public corporations (such as the BBC in Britain) or by nonprofit organizations (such as PBS in the United States).

> **PROBLEM 17.10**
>
> The invention of cable TV changed forever the face of commercial broadcasting. Viewers can now be excluded from free access to programming if they refuse to pay the installation and monthly charges to private cable TV companies. Is pay TV efficient? Should it be encouraged?

Let us reconsider our short list of nonrivalrous, publicly provided goods. National defense and navigational aids are largely nonexcludable and thus qualify as pure (or nearly pure) public goods. If these are to be available, public agencies must provide them. On the other hand, roads and bridges, as well as police and fire protection, are potentially excludable and therefore are not pure public goods. These potentially excludable, nonrivalrous goods could be provided privately — and at various times and places throughout history, roads, bridges, and police and fire protection have all been financed privately for profit. Yet, the efficiency argument cited earlier suggests that such goods and services ought to be publicly funded instead.

Public Provision of Nonrivalrous Goods

Governments clearly can use some form of cost-benefit analysis to decide how much of a public good to provide. Our analytical tack in this case must be slightly different, however, because we need to imagine that the public good is actually rivalrous rather than nonrivalrous so that we can derive an ordinary demand function that answers the question: How much will an individual demand of the public good at any price p?

The ordinary demand functions for two representative citizens, A and B, are labeled AA' and BB', respectively, in Figure 17.7. If x' of the public good is supplied, the total value to citizen A is equal to the area under AA' to the left of x'; the total value to citizen B is the area under BB' to the left of x'. (To use these consumer surplus measures, we will assume that each person's demand for the public good is independent of his or her income.) More important, the marginal values of x' to citizens A and B are the distances $0H$ and $0I$, respectively. Because the good is nonrivalrous, the marginal social value is the *vertical summation* of the two individual marginal values, $0H$ and $0I$, or the distance $0J$. Notice that the vertical summation associated with public goods is different from the horizontal summation associated with rivalrous goods. Because the public good is consumed in its entirety by everyone, vertically summing marginal valuations is the appropriate aggregation procedure.

marginal social value   By vertically summing the individual marginal values for every quantity, we have derived the function labeled **marginal social value** in Figure 17.7. This function is

FIGURE 17.7 **Provision of a pure public good**

The individual demand functions for this public good are *AA'* and *BB'*. Because the good is completely nonrivalrous, to calculate the marginal social value function, we vertically add the two demand functions. For example, the marginal value of a small amount more of the public good when *x'* is already supplied is 0*H* to person A and 0*I* to person B. The marginal social value is then 0*J* = 0*H* + 0*I*. The cost-benefit criterion dictates that the public good be supplied up to the point where marginal cost *MC* is equal to marginal social value, or up to *x**.

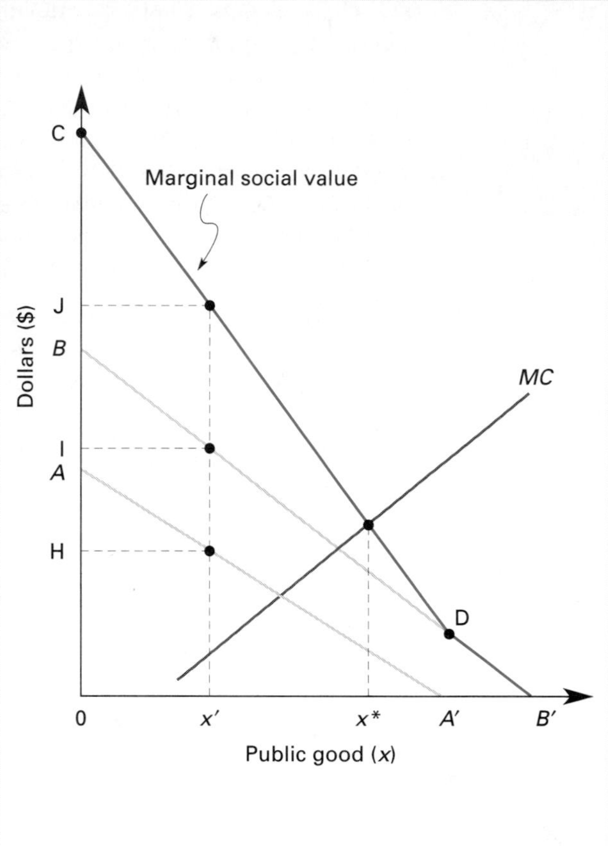

sometimes called the **demand function for public goods**, a potentially confusing label because it does not provide the ordinary information given by a demand function: the quantity demanded of a good for any given price.

From this point on, the cost-benefit analysis is completely straightforward. The optimal amount of the public good is the quantity at which the marginal social value of the good equals the marginal cost of supplying it, or *x** in Figure 17.7.

Cost-Benefit Analysis and Revealed Preference

Although applying cost-benefit analysis to public goods is theoretically straightforward, implementing it can be tricky. The problem is that individual citizens may not reveal their real demand functions for a public good. If the public good is financed by a specially earmarked tax on the citizens who benefit from it and if the more each citizen benefits, the higher his or her tax bill will be, then a self-interested citizen might think twice about reporting personal benefits accurately.

Being only one of a great many who will use the public good, the citizen might assume realistically that the amount supplied will be virtually independent of his or her reported demand function. The cagey response is to underreport the private value of the public good — or even to claim not to value it at all. In this response, we see another example of the free-rider syndrome. The self-interested citizen wants to benefit from the public good without bearing the cost of providing it. If every citizen were similarly tempted to take a free ride, they could all end up with very little of the public good, or perhaps none at all.

On the other hand, if the size of personal tax bills is independent of individually reported benefits, individuals have a clear incentive to overreport benefits. Even if they are not so devious as to distort reported benefits one way or the other, it seems clear that citizens have no particular incentive to think hard and long about the personal value of any public good and to report that valuation accurately, and this makes the whole process of social cost-benefit analysis problematical.

revealed-preference problem

Although this **revealed-preference problem** is most dramatic in the context of public goods, it also plagues the cost-benefit analysis of externalities. Suppose that a nonsmoker is told that the city council is considering a ban on smoking in public places. If asked whether he or she strongly supports the ban, moderately supports the ban, or strongly opposes the ban, the nonsmoker has no reason to weigh the personal costs and benefits thoughtfully or to report accurately. In fact, the nonsmoker may well be tempted to overestimate the value of smoke-free public places. A parallel distortion occurs if the respondent is a smoker. The resulting information from the smokers and nonsmokers whose opinions are solicited is not necessarily useful to policy makers. A hard-line economist might even argue that the only useful information this questionnaire provides is a census of smokers and nonsmokers.

SUMMARY

A major theme of economics is that the private pursuit of self-interest produces Pareto optimality, or efficiency. In Chapter 16, we identified the precise set of circumstances in which this theme is a theorem — that is, in which the pursuit of self-interest produces efficiency. We discovered that the absence of market power is essential to this result. Either monopoly or monopsony power upsets the efficiency applecart.

In Chapter 14, we saw that if society at large is not satisfied with the market determined distribution of wealth, then the institutions used to redistribute wealth inevitably create inefficiency. The general lesson is that taxes or subsidies, like market power, also tend to undermine efficiency.

In this chapter, we began by considering other situations — those involving both *positive* and *negative externalities* — in which the blind pursuit of self-interest again fails to result in efficiency. We then considered a range of possible responses to the problem posed by externalities. In many circumstances, a private resolution is feasible, either through *private negotiation* between the affected parties or through *internalization*, by putting the problem in the hands of a single decision maker. These private resolutions are appealing to economists because they rely on the only individuals who have the information needed to devise a tailor-made solution: the concerned parties themselves.

However, private solutions are not always feasible. For example, air and water pollution problems are so complicated and involve so many parties that some form of *public regulation* seems to be necessary. Given the complexity of such problems, the economist's approach to regulation, which invariably depends on some form of cost-benefit analysis, is necessarily an umbrella approach: one or perhaps a few sets of regulations that can be applied to a great many different externality problems. Although regulation is necessary in these complex cases, the economist's rule of thumb is to rely on private incentives wherever possible. For instance, taxing emissions is preferable to setting emissions standards because it serves to allocate permissible emissions to their most productive uses.

Finally, we turned to the related problem of *public goods*. A *pure public good* is both *nonrivalrous* and *nonexcludable*. In most circumstances, if such goods are to be provided, they will be publicly provided. Why? Because their nonexcludability means that no profit-seeking firm will ever produce them. Furthermore, even when a nonrivalrous good is excludable, efficiency requires that it be publicly provided at no cost.

In principle, the provision of public goods is straightforward: the rule is to provide the good up to the point where marginal social benefit is equal to marginal social cost. The problem is to estimate marginal social benefit. Here we encounter the *revealed-preference problem*, a difficulty associated not only with public goods but also with cost-benefit analysis in general. In essence, the problem is to find a mechanism that induces individuals to reveal their true preferences. In the absence of such a mechanism, we are compelled to add public goods to our list of problems that are antithetical to efficiency.

EXERCISES

1. Interpret the following laws as responses to externalities: Homeowners are required to keep their sidewalks clear of snow and ice. Drivers are required to drive on the right side of the road. Drivers are allowed to enter an intersection only if the traffic light is green. Dog owners are required to have their pets vaccinated for rabies.

2. Two types of firms emit gunk, a nasty pollutant. There are 10 firms of each type. These firms think of "gunk emissions" as a productive input much like any other input. The primary difference is that the price of gunk emissions is currently $0. Their input demand functions for gunk emissions are

$$w_1 = 100 - z_1$$

$$w_2 = 150 - z_2$$

   a. Given the current price of gunk emissions, how much does each firm emit, and what are total emissions?
   b. Suppose that we want to reduce gunk emissions to 1,000 units in total and that we must use an emission tax T per unit of gunk emitted. What value of T will induce firms to reduce emissions to the target level? Are the 1,000 units of the input gunk emissions allocated efficiently among the 20 firms?
   c. Now suppose that each of the 20 firms is given the right to emit 50 units of gunk and that firms are allowed to buy and sell these rights. What is the aggregate demand for gunk emissions? What is the aggregate supply of emissions? Think of each firm as supplying 50 units. What

is the competitive equilibrium price and allocation of gunk emissions? Are the 1,000 units allocated efficiently among the 20 firms?
   d. Finally, suppose that each of the 20 firms is given the right to emit 50 units of gunk and, in contrast to c, that the firms are forbidden to buy and sell these rights. (In other words, each firm is required to reduce its emissions to 50 units.) Are the 1,000 units allocated efficiently among the 20 firms?

3. Mosquito control at the local level is a good example of a pure public good. First, suppose that in an economy-of-two, the two people are identical and each has the following demand function for mosquito control:

$$p = 20 - y$$

   where y is quantity of mosquito control. (We are assuming for convenience that their demands for mosquito control are independent of their incomes.) The cost of mosquito control is $10 per unit.

   a. What is the socially optimal level of mosquito control? Hint: You first need to vertically sum the individual demands.
   b. Suppose that mosquito control is not publicly provided. If individual 1 provided no mosquito control, how much would individual 2 provide? If individual 1 provided 5 units of mosquito control, how much would individual 2 provide? If individual 1 provided 10 units of mosquito control, how much would individual 2 provide? Building on these results, show that in the Nash equilibrium where each

individual takes the quantity of mosquito control provided by the other as given in choosing how much mosquito control to provide — total quantity provided will be 10 units.

c. Now suppose that we have 100 people with this demand function for mosquito control. What is the socially optimal level of mosquito control? Show that in the Nash equilibrium when there are 100 people, the total quantity provided will again be 10 units.

d. In the Nash equilibria in b and c, there is a free-rider problem. Explain it in detail.

4. Imagine that a public project costs $K and provides benefits to three people: A, B, and C. Let $B_A > \$B_B > \$B_C$ be the benefits to the three individuals. Suppose that each must pay one-third of the project's cost. Show that there are circumstances in which two of the three will vote for the project, even though the total benefit from the project is less than its cost. Show that in such circumstances, C will be willing and able to bribe B to vote against the project. Suppose again that only two people will vote for the project but that the project's total benefit exceeds its cost. Is it possible in this case that C will be willing and able to bribe B to vote against the project? Would A be willing to offer B a larger bribe to vote for the project? Do these bribes serve any useful social purpose? Should such bribes be illegal?

REFERENCES

Agnello, R. J., and L. P. Donnelly. 1975. "Property Rights and Efficiency in the Oyster Industry," *Journal of Law and Economics*, 18:521–33.

Cheung, S.N.S. 1973. "The Fable of the Bees: An Economic Investigation," *Journal of Law and Economics*, 16:11–3.

Coase, R. 1960. "The Problem of Social Cost," *Journal of Law and Economics*, 3:1–44.

Cooter, R. D. 1987. "Coase Theorem," in *The New Palgrave: A Dictionary of Economics*, J. Eatwell, M. Milgate, and P. Newman (eds.), London: The Macmillan Press.

Fishburn, P. C. 1987. "Interdependent Preferences," in *The New Palgrave: A Dictionary of Economics*, J. Eatwell, M. Milgate, and P. Newman (eds.), London: The Macmillan Press.

Laffont, J. J. 1987. "Externalities," in *The New Palgrave: A Dictionary of Economics*, J. Eatwell, M. Milgate, and P. Newman (eds.), London: The Macmillan Press.

Sandmo, A. 1987. "Public Goods," in *The New Palgrave: A Dictionary of Economics*, J. Eatwell, M. Milgate, and P. Newman (eds.), London: The Macmillan Press.

ANSWERS TO PROBLEMS

PROBLEM 1.1

Just as the price of labor relative to the price of machines varies from country to country, so the price of one packaging material, say aluminum, relative to another, say steel, varies from time to time. The hypothesis that the firm chooses the technique that is least costly, applied to the choice of a packaging material, suggests the following: when aluminum is relatively cheap, it is used instead of steel and when steel is relatively cheap, it is used instead of aluminum.

PROBLEM 1.2

If there are N households drawing water from the system, and if all of them want more water than they are currently able to get in August, in August an individual householder can use only $(1/N)^{\text{th}}$ of any water conserved by that householder in July. Hence, the larger N is, the smaller the individual householder's incentive to conserve water.

PROBLEM 1.3

1. A player motivated only by private gain would reason as follows. There is nothing I can do to influence the actions of the other three players in this game, so I will concentrate on the implications of my own actions. On the one hand, if I keep the keep the $90 dollars, I am richer by $90. On the other hand, if I put the $90 in the envelope, there will be $210 additional dollars in the common pool (the $90 I put in the envelope plus the $120 the host will add to it), off which I will get only $52.50. Clearly, I am better of to keep the $90 since $90 is larger than $52.50.

2. A player motivated by self-interest will now want to know whether he or she is richer if all players keep $90 or all put $90 in their envelopes. If all four players keep the $90, each is richer by $90. In contrast, if all four players put their $90 in their envelopes, there will $840 in the common pool, and each will be richer by $210. Hence, each player will vote to require all players to put their $90 in their envelopes.

PROBLEM 1.4

Notice first that the shift in the demand curve does not affect aggregate quantity supplied — under either scheme 210 million pounds is supplied. The Agricultural Price Support Authority's costs under the buy-and-store program decrease as the demand curve gets steeper since the quantity bought by consumers at the $3.00 support price increases. Conversely, its costs under the price subsidy program increase as the demand curve gets steeper since the market clearing price for 210 million pounds decreases, necessitating an increase in the per pound subsidy.

PROBLEM 1.5

There is no right or wrong preference ordering. However, in this case, most people rank bundle d first (because it contains the most money), bundle a second, bundle c third, and bundle b fourth.

PROBLEM 1.6

This is a dual-purpose institution designed to reduce litter and encourage recycling. It works by creating a private monetary incentive to return pop bottles to the retailer or a recycling depot.

PROBLEM 1.7

Suppose that each glutton cares only about his or her own share. Beginning with any value of X, it is impossible to make one glutton better off by increasing his share of the pie without making the other worse off by reducing her share. Hence, given any X, no other attainable state is Pareto-preferred to it. Because no attainable state is Pareto-preferred to any other, every attainable state is Pareto-optimal.

PROBLEM 1.8

Using the cost-benefit criterion, we conclude that in this situation the price subsidy scheme is preferred to the buy-and-store scheme. We want to argue, however, that some people are made worse off when we move from the buy-and-store scheme to the price subsidy scheme. It is useful to focus on two types of people: a type 1 person does pay taxes but does not consume butter; a type 2 person does consume butter but does not pay taxes. There are, of course, other types of people, but we can make our point by focusing on just these two types. Clearly, individuals of type 1 prefer the buy-and-store scheme, while individuals of type 2 prefer the price support scheme. A move from the buy-and-store scheme to the price support scheme trades off losses for type 1 people against gains for type 2 people.

PROBLEM 1A.1

There are 32 customers between addresses 1/2 and 3/4, 96 between 1/4 and 1, and 16 between 0 and 1/8.

PROBLEM 1A.2

When a is 0, the point of market segmentation is 3/8, 48 customers shop at All-Valu, and All-Valu's profit is $48. When a is 1/4, the corresponding values are 1/2, 64, and $64. When a is 1/2, the corresponding values are 5/8, 80, and $80. So long as $a < b$, the number of All-Valu's customers increases as a increases.

PROBLEM 1A.3

With no loss of generality we can restrict All-Valu's location to the interval [0,1/2], since any location in the interval [1/2,1] is symmetric to a location in the interval [0,1/2]. Given a in [0,1/2], Bestway will choose to locate just to the right of a, All-Valu's market segment will extend from 0 to a, and its profit will be $(P - C)Na$. Since its profit increases as a increases, All-Valu will locate at 1/2. Bestway will then also locate at 1/2.

PROBLEM 2.1

These statements do violate the transitivity assumption. Look at the first, third, and fourth preference statements. From the first and third we infer that (11,17) is preferred to (15,8), contrary to the fourth preference statement.

PROBLEM 2.2

We will use the transitivity assumption in conjunction with the first three preference statements in the

problem to derive the fourth preference statement. First we use part 3 of the transitivity assumption in conjunction with the first two preference statements, to get a fifth preference statement — bundle 1 is preferred to bundle 3. Then, using part 1 of the transitivity assumption in conjunction with the fifth and third preference statements, we infer that bundle 1 is preferred to bundle 4. But this is the fourth preference statement, so we have accomplished our objective. The following is another of the eight statements needed to describe four-term consistency: If bundle 1 is indifferent to bundle 2, bundle 2 is indifferent to bundle 3, and bundle 3 is preferred to bundle 4, then bundle 1 is preferred to bundle 4.

PROBLEM 2.3

First observe that all bundles fit one of the following categories: A, bundles such that quantity of good 1 exceeds 2; B, bundles such that quantity of good 1 is less than 2; C, bundles such that quantity of good 1 equals 2. All bundles in A are preferred to (2,3), and (2,3) is preferred to all bundles in B. Now subdivide C as follows: C.1, bundles such that quantity of good 2 is less than 3; C.2, bundles such that quantity of good 2 is greater than 3; C.3, bundles such that quantity of good 2 equals 3. Bundle (2,3) is preferred to any bundle in C.1, and any bundle in C.2 is preferred to bundle (2,3). Hence, all bundles B that are indifferent to bundle (2,3) are in C.3. But the only bundle in category C.3 is (2, 3) itself, so we see that bundle (2,3) is a single-point indifference curve. This argument is easily adapted to show that, for Clem, each conceivable bundle is a single-point indifference curve.

PROBLEM 2.4

a. First, bundles (20,30) and (40,10); second, bundle (20,15); third, bundle (15,15); fourth, bundles (10,15) and (25,0).

b. Each of these indifference curves is a straight line with slope of −1. The indifference curves intersect the x_2 axis at the following points: (0,25), (0,50), (0,35), (0,40).

PROBLEM 2.5

The third and sixth statements violate the nonsatiation assumption.

PROBLEM 2.6

Pick an arbitrary bundle, and draw a straight line of slope −1 through the bundle. The line is one of Amy's indifference curves.

PROBLEM 2.7

1. Amy's *MRS* is 1.

2. To compensate Arno for a one pound reduction in quantity of trout (good 1), we must increase his consumption of salmon (good 2) by 1/2 a pound since he believes salmon to be twice as nutritious as trout. Hence, Arno's indifference curves are straight lines of slope −1/2. His *MRS* is therefore 1/2 (the absolute value of −1/2).

PROBLEM 2.8

Consider the indifference curve for three pairs of shoes. Clearly, it passes through the bundle with 3 right shoes and 3 left shoes, bundle (3,3), and it has a right-angled kink at this bundle. Above the kink, the indifference curve's slope is infinite, and to the right of the kink, the indifference curve's slope is zero. *MRS* is undefined at the kink, zero to the right of the kink, and infinite above the kink.

PROBLEM 2.9

The first indifference curve is a straight line of slope −1 that passes through bundles (0,2), (1,1), and (2,0); it is weakly convex. The second indifference curve is a rectangular hyperbola that passes through bundles (36,1), (18,2), (12,3), (9,4), (6,6), (4,9), (3,12), (2,18), and (1,36); it is strictly convex. The third indifference curve is a quarter circle of radius 1 centered on the origin; it is nonconvex.

PROBLEM 2.10

a. The utility numbers are 25, 50, 25, 30, 35, and 50. They reflect the preference ordering for these bundles that you found in answering Problem 2.4.

b. Notice that the utility number assigned by this function to any bundle is the number of pounds of fish in the bundle. Question 1: Since Amy is indifferent between two bundles if and only if their weight is identical, the function does assign the same utility number to bundles among which Amy is indifferent. Question 2: Since the function assigns larger numbers to heavier bundles, it does assign a larger number to the preferred bundle. Question 3: Any bundle of fish has a weight in pounds, so the function does assign a utility number to all bundles.

PROBLEM 2.11

Let us first concentrate on the function $16(x_1 + x_2)$. Since the unit of measure for both goods is the pound, and since there are 16 ounces in a pound, the utility number assigned by this function to any bundle is the number of ounces of fish in the bundle. This function assigns the same utility number to any two bundles if and only if their weight is identical, and since Amy is indifferent between two bundles if and only if their weight is identical, the function does assign the same utility number to bundles among which she is indifferent. This function assigns larger numbers to heavier bundles, so if Amy prefers one bundle to another, this function does assign a larger number to the preferred bundle. Finally, since any bundle of fish has a weight in ounces, the function does assign a utility number to all bundles. As regards the remaining three functions, the key things to notice are that each of these functions assigns the same utility number to two bundles if and only if their weight is identical, and that they assign larger utility numbers to heavier bundles.

PROBLEM 2.12

Holding x_1 (the number of $100 bills fixed), and plotting x_2 on the horizontal axis and x_3 on the vertical axis, the slope of any indifference curve is −2 since to compensate for the loss of one $20 bill, Brett must get two additional $10 bills; *MRS* of good 3 for good 2 is 2. Holding x_2 (the number of $20 bills) fixed, and plotting x_1 on the horizontal axis and x_3 on the vertical axis, the slope of any indifference curve is −10 since to compensate for the loss of one $100 bill, Brett must get ten additional $10 bills; *MRS* of good 3 for good 1 is 10. Five $20 bills will compensate for the loss of one $100 bill, so *MRS* of good 2 for good 1 is 5.

PROBLEM 3.1

The budget line is $p_1x_1 + p_2x_2 = M$. On the x_1 axis, x_2 is zero. Thus, where the budget line intersects this axis, $p_1x_1 = M$. Hence, $x_1 = M/p_1$ at the intersection. Similarly, on the x_2 axis, x_1 is zero. Hence, $x_2 = M/p_2$ at this point of intersection. The slope of the budget line is $-p_1/p_2$; hence, the individual must give up p_1/p_2 units of good 2 to get an additional unit of good 1. Conversely, he or she must give up p_2/p_1 units of good 1 to get an additional unit of good 2. As p_1 approaches zero, the budget line becomes horizontal; as p_2 approaches zero, it becomes vertical.

PROBLEM 3.2

Consider any bundle (x_1,x_2) on the budget line, and suppose that $x_1 < x_2$. The utility associated with the bundle is then $x_1 = \min(x_1,x_2)$. Then, staying on the budget line, if we increase x_1 by some very small amount, utility will increase, and we see that any bundle in which $x_1 < x_2$ cannot be the utility-maximizing bundle. Similarly, any bundle in which $x_2 < x_1$ cannot be the utility-maximizing bundle. Therefore, the quantities of good 1 and good 2 in the utility-maximizing bundle are identical; that is, $x_1{}^* = x_2{}^*$. Combining this result with the budget line, we have $p_1x_1{}^* + p_2x_1{}^* = M$. Solving for $x_1{}^*$, we have $x_1{}^* = M/(p_1 + p_2)$, which is the demand function for good 1. Finally, since $x_2{}^* = x_1{}^*$, this is also the demand function for good 2.

PROBLEM 3.3

First draw the budget line. Then draw a strictly convex indifference curve through the point where the budget line intersects the x_1 axis. At this point of intersection, the indifference curve should be *steeper* than the budget line. The result can be described as follows: If, at the point where the budget line intersects the x_1 axis, the convex indifference curve is steeper than the budget line, the consumer buys only good 1.

PROBLEM 3.4

Let us concentrate on 2. If we begin with a square of arbitrary side z, we get the following arc elasticity expression

$$E = \frac{[(z + \emptyset z)^2 - z^2]/z^2}{\emptyset z/z}$$

This can be rewritten as

$$E = \frac{z[(z + \emptyset z)^2 - z^2]}{z^2 \emptyset z}$$

which is easily reduced to

$$E = 2 + \emptyset z/z$$

Letting $\emptyset z$ approach zero, we get 2 as the marginal elasticity of the area of a square with respect to the length of side.

PROBLEM 3.5

A \$1 increase in either p_1 or p_2 causes quantity demanded of good 1 to fall from 60 units to 40 units. A \$2 increase in M causes quantity demanded of good 1 to increase from 60 to 61 units.

PROBLEM 3.6

In answering these questions, keep in mind that we are using the nonsatiation assumption, which means that the utility-maximizing consumption bundle is always on the budget line. The first statement is false, since IC is negatively sloped if either good is inferior. The second statement is true. The third statement is true — if in response to an increase in income, consumption of one good decreases, then consumption of the other necessarily increases, so both goods cannot be inferior. The fourth statement is false.

PROBLEM 3.7

This case is illustrated in Figure A3.1. For simplicity, we have set both p_1 and p_2 equal to \$1. For income greater than \$80, IC in Figure A3.1a is vertical and the Engel curve in Figure A3.1b is horizontal. Notice that for income less than \$80, the individual spends all income on good 1 and none on good 2, so when income is less than \$80, the Engel curve in Figure A3.1b has a slope of 1.

PROBLEM 3.8

At point D, expenditure on good 1 is \$66 and expenditure on good 2 is \$44; hence, the income associated with the compensated budget line is \$110. Since prices on the compensated budget line are $p_1 = \$3$ and $p_2 = \$1$, the compensated budget line is $3x_1 + x_2 = 110$. The added income necessary to attain the original indifference curve is \$50.

PROBLEM 3.9

See Figure A3.2. The substitution effect leads to an increase in consumption from 14 to 17 units, while the income effect leads to a decrease in consumption from 17 to 12 units. Since consumption decreased when income increased, good 1 is inferior.

FIGURE A3.1

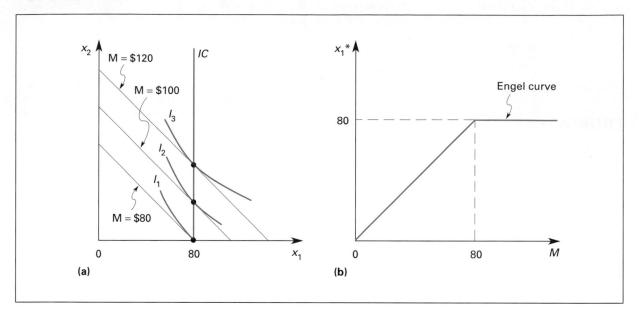

(a)

(b)

FIGURE A3.2

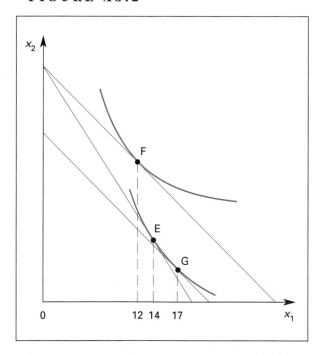

PROBLEM 3.10

In Figure A3.3, notice that the substitution effect is zero and the compensatory income $45. Since there is no substitution effect, the compensated demand curve is $x_1^{**} = 15$. Given $p_2 = \$1$ and $M = \$30$, the ordinary demand curve is $x_1^* = 30/(1 + p_1)$.

PROBLEM 3.11

For each of the proposed demand functions, we must answer the following question. Given $a > 0$, is $D_1(p_1, p_2, M)$ equal to $D_1(ap_1, ap_2, aM)$?

1. Is $M/p_1 = (aM)/(ap_1)$? Yes.
2. Is $Mp_2/p_1 = (aM)(ap_2)/(ap_1)$? No.
3. Is $M/(p_1 p_2)^{1/2} = (aM)/(ap_1 ap_2)^{1/2}$? Yes.
4. Is $1 + p_1 - 5p_2 + M/20 = 1 + ap_1 - 5ap_2 + aM/20$? No.

Thus 2 and 4 are not acceptable demand functions.

PROBLEM 3.12

System 1 is the only one of the three that satisfies Engel's aggregation law. Notice that the demand functions in system 1 are also consistent with the no money illusion property.

PROBLEM 4.1

Figure A4.1 is the graph you need. Because the indifference curve I does not intersect the budget line associated with the lump-sum tax, the consumer will choose to remain at point D when the lump-sum tax is substituted for the excise tax.

FIGURE A3.3

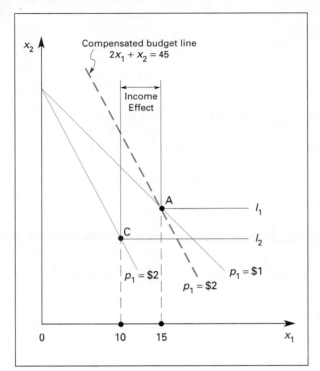

FIGURE A4.1

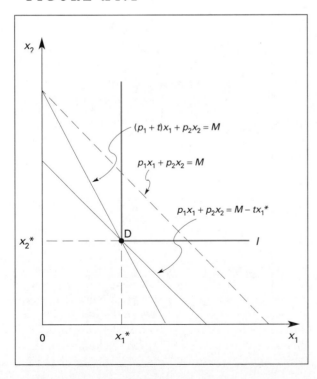

PROBLEM 4.2

Let x_2 be a composite commodity with price equal to \$1, and m the profit per meal under the first option; that is, let $m = p_1 - 50$. In Figure A4.2, m is, by construction, the profit per meal required to cover the cost per member; that is, $mx_1{}^* = 1,000$. Given this pricing scheme, the representative member chooses bundle D on indifference curve I. Notice that $DC = \$1000 = mx_1{}^*$. If the club chooses to sell meals at the \$50 per meal cost and to cover overhead costs by a membership fee equal to \$1,000, the consumer will choose some bundle on segment DE of the associated budget line. Notice, all bundles in the interior of segment DE are strictly preferred to bundle D, so the club member is better off under the second option.

FIGURE A4.2

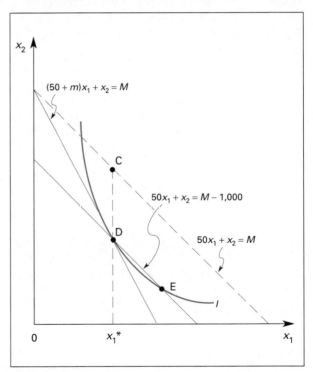

PROBLEM 4.3

First pick two prices for good 1. Then, on the same diagram, use the technique developed in Figure 4.2 to identify the CV associated with each price. You will see immediately that the CV associated with the higher price is smaller than the CV associated with the lower price. This result is consistent with common sense: it says that the dollar value of the privilege of buying good 1 at price p_1 decreases as p_1 increases.

PROBLEM 4.4

For this price decrease, the distance labeled CV in Figure 5.3 is the equivalent variation, and the distance labeled EV is the compensating variation.

PROBLEM 4.5

The benefit of a price decrease from \$60 to \$40 is \$500, and the benefit of being able to buy the good at a price of \$50, as opposed to not being able to buy it at all, is \$625.

PROBLEM 4.6

Figure A4.3 is useful here. If the price of film is equal to its \$1 cost, then the firm's profit is the area of triangle GAF less \$5, because the firm just breaks even on its film sales, the area of triangle GAF is the price of the camera, and the cost of producing the camera is \$5. At the lower price p_1', the price of the camera increases by the area of the trapezoid p_1'GFM, but the firm incurs a loss on sales of film equal to the area of the rectangle p_1'GHM. The net decrease in its profit, relative to the situation in which film is sold at cost, is the area of the triangle FHM.

PROBLEM 4.7

The relevant diagram is Figure A4.4. At wage w', the individual supplies h' hours of labor. At the higher wage w'', the individual supplies h'' hours of labor. Notice that h'' is less than h'. Leisure is a normal good in this case.

PROBLEM 4.8

Because B^1 lies above the period-0 budget line, we infer that the expenditure required to purchase B^1 at period-0 prices exceeds actual expenditure or income in period 0. This implies that L exceeds 1. Because B^0 lies above the period-1 budget line, we infer that the expenditure required to purchase B^0 at period-1 prices exceeds actual expenditure or income in period 1. This implies that P is less than 1. To see that it is impossible (without further information) to tell which is the preferred bundle, begin by drawing an indifference curve in Figure 4.14 such that the individual is indifferent between bundles B^0 and B^1.

FIGURE A4.3

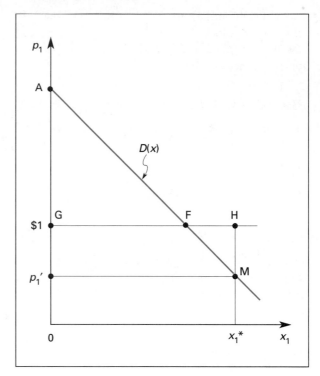

FIGURE A4.4

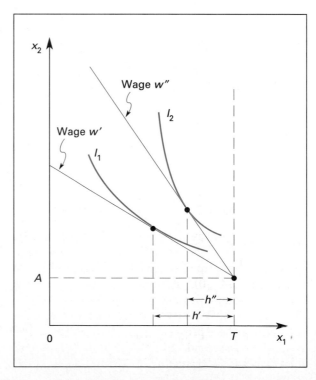

PROBLEM 4.9

The Paasche and Laspeyres quantity indexes are 120/115 and 145/120, respectively. The Paasche and Laspeyres price indexes are 120/145 and 115/120, respectively. Norm is better off in period 1.

PROBLEM 5.1

The expected monetary value of the game is $1,000,000.

PROBLEM 5.2

$950 = (2/6)$1800 + (1/6)$3000 − (3/6)$300.

PROBLEM 5.3

Chauncy's expected utility from playing Risk is 4. He is indifferent between the two options if M is equal to 50, prefers to play Risk if M is less than 50, and to take M if M exceeds 50.

PROBLEM 5.4

The first prospect pays $10,000 with probability .25, $6000 with probability .25, and $1000 with probability .5, and its expected value is $4500. The expected values of the other prospects are $5300, $7500, and $6000.

PROBLEM 5.5

For Jack, the number e^* is .75, and for Jane the number e^* is greater than .75.

PROBLEM 5.6

Jack's utility function is $U(10,000) = 1$, $U(6000) = .75$, and $U(1,000) = 0$.

PROBLEM 5.7

To find Jack's preference ordering for these prospects, we can compute their expected utilities. For the first prospect, Jack's expected utility is $(1/2 \times 1)$ plus $(1/4 \times 3/4)$ plus $(1/4 \times 0)$, or 33/48. The expected utilities for the remaining prospects are, respectively, 28/48, 36/48, 28/48, 30/48, 36/48. Hence, Jack's preference ordering for these prospects is as follows: first, $(0,1,0)$ and $(3/4,0,1/4)$; second, $(1/2,1/4,1/4)$; third, $(1/4,1/2,1/4)$; fourth, $(1/3,1/3,1/3)$ and $(7/12,0,5/12)$.

PROBLEM 5.8

For Melvin, the expected utility of the risky prospect is 2.5, and the expected utility of $25 is 5; hence, he prefers $25. For Jane, the expected utility of the risky prospect is 25, and the expected utility of $25 is also 25; hence, she is indifferent. For Baby Doe, the expected utility of the risky prospect is 2500, and the expected utility of $25 is 625; hence, she prefers the risky prospect.

PROBLEM 5.9

In Figure A5.1, EG exceeds EF, indicating that the risky prospect is preferred to the assured prospect.

FIGURE A5.1

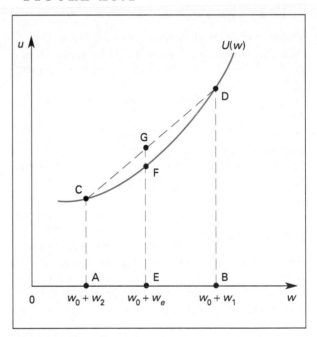

PROBLEM 5.10

The expected utility of the risk-pooling agreement is $1/100 + (18/100)(1/2)^{1/2}$, while the expected utility with no agreement is $1/10$. As you can easily verify, the risk-pooling agreement has the larger expected utility and is therefore preferred.

PROBLEM 5.11

In Figure A5.2, I_r is distance HB, whereas $pL = I_s$ is distance AB. AB exceeds HB.

FIGURE A5.2

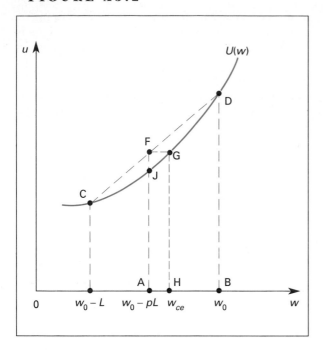

PROBLEM 5.12

Patricia will not buy this asset alone because $(100)^{1/2}$, her expected utility if she does not buy it, exceeds $(1/20)(10,000)^{1/2}$, her expected utility if she does buy it. If she joins a syndicate with 10 equal partners, her expected utility is $(1/20)(1090)^{1/2} + (19/20)(90)^{1/2}$, which exceeds $(100)^{1/2}$, so she would join the syndicate.

PROBLEM 5.13

If all three groups sold their cars, the market price would be $1920, equal to .6 multiplied by $2400 plus .4 multiplied by $1200. But this price is not large enough to induce those potential sellers of jewels whose reservations prices are $2000 to part with them. Hence, in equilibrium, all the cars will not be sold. If the last two groups sold their cars, the market price would be $1800, equal to .5 multiplied by $2400 plus .5 multiplied by $1200. Since $1800 exceeds $1600, in equilibrium, these two groups will sell their cars, but the first group will not. The market failure is that the first group of potential sellers, who would gladly sell their jewels at the $2400 value of a jewel, do not, in fact, sell them.

PROBLEM 5.14

With no signaling, the common hourly wage w is equal to $s50 + (1 - s)\$20$. If superior workers anticipate getting this hourly wage if they do not get a degree, they will acquire a degree if $10w < 500 - 200$. Substituting for w, this inequality reduces to $s < 1/3$. Hence, superior workers will acquire a degree to signal their superior productivity if s is less than 1/3.

PROBLEM 5.15

a. If the teenager could promise not to drink and drive the parents might be happy to lend the car to the teenager. But, since the action "drink and drive" is hidden from the parents, they assume the worst and refuse to lend the car.

b. The hidden action problem here is arson. Insurance companies refuse to insure a property for significantly more than its market value because this raises the possibility that the owner of the insured property might profit by intentionally burning the property. In bad economic times, the market value of some properties drops below the insured value, and some owners cannot resist the temptation to profit by burning their own property.

PROBLEM A5.1

Let us begin with prospect (1/3, 1/3, 1/3). Now let us substitute (3/4, 0, 1/4) for the $6,000 prize to produce prospect (7/12, 0, 5/12). Similarly, when we substitute (3/4, 0, 1/4) for the $6,000 prize in prospect (1/2, 1/4, 1/4), we produce prospect (11/16, 0, 5/16).

PROBLEM 6.1

The salesperson can offer to pay the customer's premium for the first year. If the customer accepts, he or she gets free insurance for 1 year and the salesperson pockets $500. If the customer then cancels the policy after the first year, the insurance company is an obvious loser. This sort of scam was recently exposed in Ontario.

PROBLEM 6.2

The CEO is (arguably) the person who makes the decisions that affect the company's profit and therefore the value of its stock. The stock option gives the CEO an incentive to make decisions that enhance the value of the company's stock. For example, if the CEO makes a decision that increases the value of the company's stock to $15, the CEO can make $50,000 by making the appropriate decision, buying 10,000 shares at $10 per share, and then selling the 10,000 shares at $15 per share. If the CEO fails to make the appropriate decision in the absence of the stock option, that option is clearly valuable to the company's stockholders — in this case, the stock option means that the value of each share will increase by $5. It is not, however, always true that a stock option is in the stockholders' interest. Consider, for example, a case in which the CEO can take an action, call it action W, that will lead to a $5 increase in the value of the stock with probability 1/2 and a $10 reduction with probability 1/2. Since the stock option offers the CEO a $50,000 gain if the price of the stock increases but does not force a loss on the CEO if the price of the stock decreases, the stock option gives the CEO an incentive to take action W, an action that is clearly not in the interest of stockholders.

PROBLEM 6.3

Regardless of the number of individuals in the partnership, the solution lies on the line $y_R = e_R$ in your diagram. Where? Suppose n is the number of individuals. The solution is at the point on this line where MRS is equal to $1/n$, because each individual gets this fraction of the total income generated by the partnership. As n increases, these solutions move toward the origin. Further, the larger n is, the smaller each individual's utility at the solution.

PROBLEM 6.4

The appropriate diagram is Figure A6.1. For larger values of B, the partnership is Pareto-preferred, and for smaller values, the one-person firm is Pareto-preferred.

PROBLEM 6.5

In Figure A6.2 the equilibrium for the owner-managed team is at D and the equilibrium for the one-person firm is at W. Clearly, the equilibrium for the owner-managed team is preferred.

PROBLEM 6.6

If in Figure 6.6 we interpret e_R as Victor's effort, Victor's income-effort relationship is composed of the two horizontal segments $0e'$ and VG. Given this income-effort relationship, Victor will supply e' units of effort. Now suppose that Victor supplies e' units of ef-

FIGURE A6.1

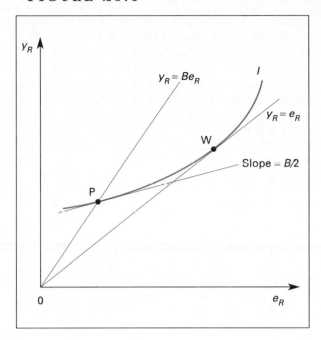

FIGURE A6.2

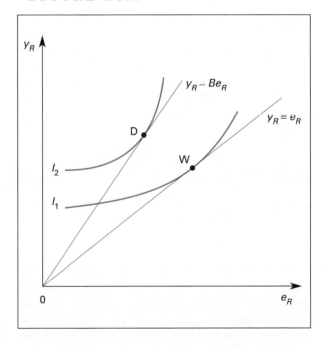

fort, and in Figure 6.6 interpret e_R as Roberta's effort. Then Roberta's income-effort relationship is the line labeled $y_R = Be_R - M/2$. Given this income-effort relationship, she too will supply e' units of effort.

PROBLEM 6.7

Figure A6.3 is the required diagram. The equilibrium for the one-person firm is at W, and the equilibrium for the owner-managed team is at V. If we increase M by a small amount, the one-person firm is Pareto-preferred. And, if we increase B by a small amount, the owner-managed firm is Pareto-preferred.

FIGURE A6.3

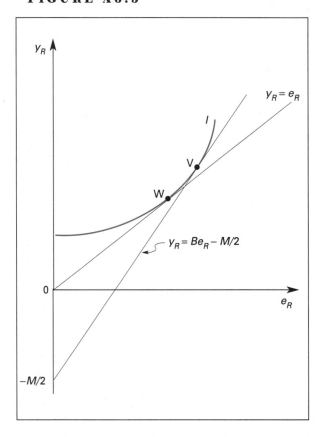

PROBLEM 6.8

If there is just one worker and if he or she has expended 180 minutes in setup time, then he or she has 300 minutes left. Dividing this time equally between the two stages, he or she can produce 15 units. If there are two workers and if one specializes in each stage, then the worker in stage 1 can process 42 units, but the worker in stage 2 can process only 36. Thus, we cannot fully utilize the effort of the stage-1 worker. To maximize productivity per worker, we want each worker to specialize so that he or she incurs only one setup cost, and we want to fully utilize the 8 hours of each worker's time. This means that the number of workers in stage 1 — let

us call this number N — multiplied by 42 must be equal to the number of workers in stage 2 — let us call this number M — multiplied by 36. That is, we want two integers — N and M — such that $42N = 36M$, or such that $N/M = 36/42 = 6/7$. Then N equal to 6 and M equal to 7 will do (as will 12 and 14, or 18 and 21, and so on). The 13 workers can produce 252 units.

PROBLEM 6.9

In many cases, it is in the property owner's self-interest. Consider, for example, an owner who is developing a property for resale. The Mechanic's Lien Act assures tradespeople that they will be paid and therefore makes it easier for the property owner to contract with tradespeople. In the absence of such an act, the tradespeople might well demand some other form of assurance that they will be paid, and the assurance is likely to be costly for the property owner.

PROBLEM 7.1

Two units of seviche use all the available red snapper, so the restaurant can make just two units of seviche. The production function is

$$y = \min(z_1/16, z_2/3, z_3, z_4/8)$$

PROBLEM 7.2

This bundle will produce at most 600 miles, and the speed required is 60 mph. If the car is driven at 40 mph, the truck can be driven only 400 miles, and if it is driven at 80 mph, it can be driven only 450 miles.

PROBLEM 7.3

The total product functions are $120(z_1)^{1/2}$ when z_2 is 12, and $180(z_1)^{1/2}$ when z_2 is 27.

PROBLEM 7.4

The associated marginal product function is

$$MP(z_1) = 1 \qquad \text{if } z_1 \leq 10$$
$$MP(z_1) = 0 \qquad \text{if } z_1 > 10$$

PROBLEM 7.5

The average product function is

$$AP(z_1) = 120/(z_1)^{1/2}$$

PROBLEM 7.6

See Figure A7.1.

FIGURE A7.1

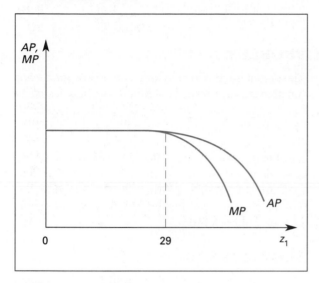

PROBLEM 7.7

From Problem 7.3, the total product function is

$$TP(z_1) = 180(z_1)^{1/2}$$

The minimum time necessary to drive y miles is then

$$z_1^* = y^2/32,400$$

and the variable cost function is

$$VC(y) = w_1 y^2/32,400$$

PROBLEM 7.8

See $AFC(y)$ in Figure 7.10b.

PROBLEM 7.9

$STC(y)$ is simply $VC(y) + FC$. Since FC does not depend on y, for any y, the slope of $STC(y)$ is equal to the slope of $VC(y)$.

PROBLEM 7.10

Since ACC_2 is always \$5 and ACC_1 is \$5 when N_1 is 3,600, if there are more than 3,600 commuters, in equilibrium, 3,600 will use Route 1 and the rest will use Route 2. If there are fewer than 3,600 commuters, all of them will use Route 1.

PROBLEM 7.11

Since MCC_2 is always \$5 and MCC_1 is \$5 when N_1 is 2,000, if there are more than 2,000 commuters, in the cost-benefit optimum, 2,000 should use Route 1 and the rest should use Route 2. If there are fewer than 2,000 commuters, all of them should use Route 1.

PROBLEM 8.1

See Figure 8.2.

PROBLEM 8.2

The $MRTS$ of wood for coal is 2.5. The $MRTS$ of coal for wood is .4.

PROBLEM 8.3

The $MRTS$ of Coke for rum is zero on the horizontal segment of the isoquant, and is infinite on the vertical segment. $MRTS$ is not defined at the kink in the isoquant, that is, at input bundle (4,12).

PROBLEM 8.4

a. Given bundle (20,8) she can produce just 4 square feet of fenced pasture since she does not have enough wire to fence a larger pasture. Given bundle (40,16) she can produce 16 square feet of pasture. Since output quadruples as the quantities of both inputs are doubled, there are increasing returns to scale.

b. Given bundle (120,48) she can produce 120 square feet of fenced pasture and she has excess barbed wire. Given bundle (240,96) she can produce 240 square feet of pasture. Since output doubles as the quantities of both inputs are doubled, there are constant returns to scale. More generally, for bundles in which there is excess land, there are increasing returns to scale, and for bundles in which there is excess barbed wire, there are constant returns to scale.

PROBLEM 8.5

Notice first that for this production function

$$F(az_1, az_2) = (a^{u+v})F(z_1, z_2)$$

Suppose $a > 1$. If $u + v > 1$, the term a^{u+v} is greater than 1, and there are increasing returns to scale. If $u + v < 1$, the term a^{u+v} is less than 1, and there are decreasing returns to scale. If $u + v = 1$, the term a^{u+v} is equal to 1, and there are constant returns to scale.

PROBLEM 8.6

If $2w_1 < 5w_2$, then $z_1{}^* = y/5$, $z_2{}^* = 0$, and $TC(w_1,w_2) = w_1 y/5$. And if $2w_1 > 5w_2$, then $z_1{}^* = 0$, $z_2{}^* = y/2$, and $TC(w_1,w_2) = w_2 y/2$. Finally, if $2w_1 = 5w_2$, any bundle on the y unit isoquant is cost-minimizing and $TC(w_1,w_2) = w_2 y/2 = w_1 y/5$.

PROBLEM 8.7

The opportunity cost of input 2 in terms of input 1 is w_2/w_1 because, to get an additional unit of input 2, one must give up w_2/w_1 units of input 1. The isocost line intersects the z_1 axis at $z_1 = c/w_1$ and the z_2 axis at $z_2 = c/w_2$. The isocost line becomes horizontal as w_1 approaches 0, and it gets vertical as w_2 approaches 0. As c gets large, the isocost line shifts out from the origin.

PROBLEM 8.8

When $w_1 = \$6$ and $w_2 = \$2$, or when $w_1 = \$12$ and $w_2 = \$4$, the conditional input demand functions are $z_1{}^* = y/60$ and $z_2{}^* = y/20$. In words, for each mile, use 1 minute of the driver's time and 1/20 of a gallon of gas. When $w_1 = \$6$ and $w_2 = \$2$, the cost function is $y/5$, and each mile costs $0.20. When we double the input prices, the cost function is $2y/5$, so each mile costs $0.40.

PROBLEM 8.9

For concreteness, suppose we want to produce 100 units of output. Initially, the cost-minimizing input bundle is the point on the 100-unit isoquant where $MRTS$ is equal to w_1/w_2. Subsequently, after the opportunity cost of input 1 increases, or after w_1/w_2 increases, the cost-minimizing bundle is the point on the 100 unit isoquant where $MRTS$ is equal to the now larger value of w_1/w_2. Since there is a diminishing $MRTS$, this cost-minimizing bundle is necessarily above and to the left of the initial cost-minimizing bundle, and therefore contains less of input 1 and more of input 2. In other words, as the opportunity cost of an input increases, the firm substitutes away from that input.

PROBLEM 8.10

Rum and coke are perfect complements in the rum-and-coke production function, so it is impossible to substitute one input for the other. As result, the cost-minimizing input bundle is unresponsive to relative input prices.

PROBLEM 8.11

The output expansion path for a homothetic production function is a ray through the origin — that is, a straight line that passes through the origin in input space. If the output expansion path is not coincident with either axis, its slope is positive, and both inputs are normal. On the other hand, if the output expansion path is coincident with one of the axes, then one input is normal and the other is neither normal nor inferior. Therefore, if the production function is homothetic, neither input is inferior.

PROBLEM 8.12

At the end of Section 8.5 we derived Tipple's long-run cost function:

$$TC(y,w_1,w_2) = y(w_1 w_2/300)^{1/2}$$

Dividing by y to get $LAC(y)$, we have

$$LAC(y) = (w_1 w_2/300)^{1/2}$$

PROBLEM 8.13

See Figure A8.1.

PROBLEM 9.1

The range of equilibrium prices is unchanged. Any price less than or equal to $60 and greater than $50 is a competitive equilibrium price. In this case, only two units are traded in the equilibrium: individuals G and J sell and C and E buy. The final allocation of tickets is the same: individuals A, B, C, D, and E end up with tickets. The individuals who are (unambiguously) better off are those who were initially given tickets this time around but not the first time around. Similarly, those who are (unambiguously) worse off are those who were not given a ticket this time but were the first time.

PROBLEM 9.2

There are two competitive equilibria. 1. Consider any price less than or equal to $10. Harry and Sarah will

FIGURE A8.1

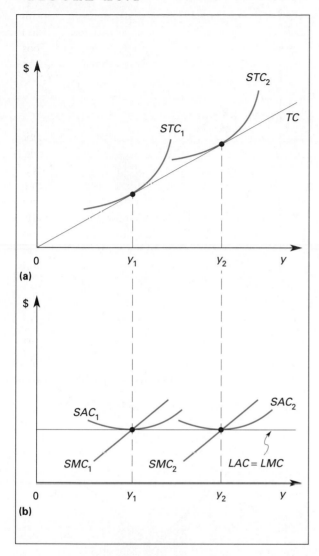

(a)

(b)

PROBLEM 9.3

In this case, any price between $45 and $50 is a market-clearing price; two units are traded; Earl and the suppliers with the three lowest reservation prices lose; the demanders with the two highest reservation prices gain.

PROBLEM 9.4

See Figure A9.1. As we have drawn the diagram, the profit-maximizing output is $y^* = 35$. Why does the firm produce anything when its profit is negative? If it produced nothing, its profit would be $-FC$, which is equal to -1 multiplied by the area of rectangle ABCD. Do you see why? By producing $y^* = 35$, the firm incurs the *smaller loss* equal to -1 multiplied by the area of rectangle GBCE. Thus, by producing 35 units, the firm incurs a smaller loss than it would if it produced nothing.

FIGURE A9.1

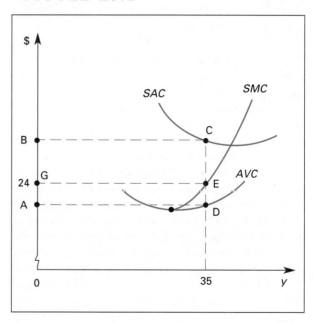

PROBLEM 9.5

It is coincident because, when price exceeds $12, one individual demands a zero quantity. Distance $0D$ is equal to 21 units.

PROBLEM 9.6

First multiply the right-hand side of the individual demand function by 1000 to get $y = 1000 - p$, and then invert this function to get $p = 1000 - y$.

buy or not sell at any such price. Similarly, Jane and Bob will sell or not buy, given that their mate does not end up with a ticket. Therefore, for any such price, we have a competitive equilibrium, with Harry and Sarah holding tickets. This equilibrium is not Pareto-optimal because Jane and Bob together would be willing to offer more than $20 to Harry and Sarah for the pair of tickets, and Harry and Sarah would be willing to accept such an offer. 2. Any price greater than $10 but less than or equal to $20 is a competitive equilibrium price, and the equilibrium allocation at this price leaves the tickets in the hands of Jane and Bob.

PROBLEM 9.7

Just multiply quantity supplied by one firm by the number of firms.

PROBLEM 9.8

The $10 excise tax shifts each firm's supply function and the industry supply function vertically upward by $10. If industry demand is perfectly inelastic, equilibrium price increases by $10 and equilibrium quantity does not change. If demand is not perfectly inelastic, equilibrium price increases by less than $10, and equilibrium quantity decreases.

PROBLEM 9.9

Equilibrium price is $500 and equilibrium quantity is 500 units. Producers' surplus and consumers' surplus are each $125,000.

PROBLEM 9.10

Figure A9.2 depicts the situation under the price subsidy program. Here, p_s is the support price, and y_s the quantity supplied at that price. The price at which y_s units can be sold is p_1. Therefore, the agency will spend $(p_s - p_1)y_s$ to achieve the support price p_s. The surplus destroyed is the shaded area in the diagram. Relative to the competitive equilibrium, it represents the excess of the cost of producing $y_s - y^e$ additional units over the consumers' willingness to pay for those units. Figure A9.3 depicts the situation under the buy-and-store program. At the support price p_s, a total of y_s units are produced: y_2 are sold in the open market and the agency buys and stores the remaining $y_s - y_2$ units. Under this scheme, the agency spends $p_s(y_s - y_2)$ plus storage costs to achieve the support price p_s. Relative to the competitive equilibrium, the surplus destroyed under this bizarre scheme is the shaded area in Figure A9.3. This is, in essence, the policy that the European Economic Community pursued for many years with respect to butter and other agricultural products.

PROBLEM 10.1

We know that $\eta(y) = p/[y(\text{slope of the demand curve})]$. In this equation, substitute $a - by$ for p, and $-b$ for "slope of the demand curve" and then rearrange to get $\eta(y) = 1 - a/(by)$. Since $y \le a/b$, price elasticity of demand is negative. Therefore, to get $|(\eta y)|$, we must

FIGURE A9.2

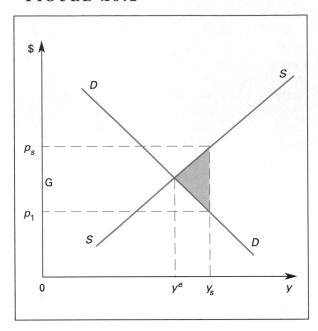

FIGURE A9.3

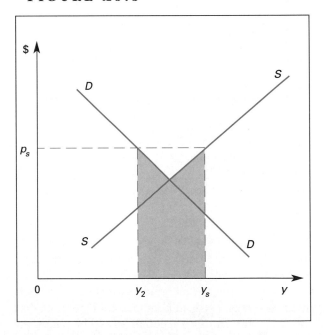

multiply by -1. We see then that $|\eta(y)| = a/(by) - 1$. To establish 1, notice that when $y < a/2b$, $MR(y) > 0$ and $|\eta(y)| > 1$. To establish 2, notice that when $y > a/2b$, $MR(y) < 0$ and $|\eta(y)| < 1$. Finally, to establish 3, notice that when $y = a/2b$, $MR(y) = 0$ and $|\eta(y)| = 1$.

PROBLEM 10.2

In Figure 10.3, MC intersects MR from above at 8 units of output. Beginning at $y = 8$ in Figure 10.3, the increase in revenue associated with an additional unit of output exceeds the increase in cost, since MR exceeds MC to the right of 8 units of output; hence, we see that profit increases as output increases. Beginning again at $y = 8$ in Figure 10.3, the decrease in revenue associated with 1 less unit of output is less than the decrease in cost, since MC exceeds MR to the left of 8 units of output, and we see that profit increases as output decreases. Thus, profit is at a minimum when output is 8 units in Figure 10.4.

PROBLEM 10.3

Let us solve the problem algebraically. The "marginal revenue equals marginal cost" condition is $100 - 2y = 40$, which yields $y^* = 30$. Price is then $p^* = 100 - 30 = 70$, and profit is $30(70 - 40)$, or 900.

PROBLEM 10.4

Beginning at the point where $MR = MC$, profit falls as the firm produces more output, and profit increases as the firm produces less output. Hence, to maximize profit, the firm produces nothing. AC must lie above AR.

PROBLEM 10.5

The answer to part 1 is to sell 5 books at a price equal to $35. Profit is $135. There are obviously unrealized gains from trade equal to $30 − $8 plus $25 − $8 plus $20 − $8 plus $15 − $8 plus $10 − $8. In part 2, the book vendor sells a book to each individual whose reservation price exceeds $8. The price charged is the individual's reservation price. The solution is efficient because the only demander who does not buy a book has a reservation price of $5, which is less than the book vendor's marginal cost. Profit is $245.

PROBLEM 10.6

In your diagram, the residual demand function should intersect the entrant's AC function at two levels of output — say y' and y'' — with $y' < y''$. Any level of output for the potential entrant larger than y' and less than y'' offers the entrant a positive profit. Therefore, this is not a case of natural monopoly.

PROBLEM 10.7

Let output y^* be the profit-maximizing output in the absence of the tax. Then we know that $\pi(y^*) > \pi(y)$ for any y not equal to y^*. Given the tax, the firm's profit is just $.9\pi(y)$. Given that $\pi(y^*) > \pi(y)$ for any y not equal to y^*, we immediately infer that $.9\pi(y^*) > .9\pi(y)$ for any y not equal to y^*. In other words, given the 10% tax on profit, y^* is still the profit-maximizing output.

PROBLEM 10.8

In each market, the monopolist will sell the quantity at which marginal revenue is zero. Hence, it will sell 24 units in the first market and 40 in the second. This result is consistent with the rule we developed.

PROBLEM 10.9

In Figure A10.1, we have drawn both demand and marginal revenue functions and the marginal cost function. The aggregated marginal revenue function is the heavy line composed of MR_1 for y less than y_1^* and $MR_2 = p_2$ for y greater than y_1^*. The profit-maximizing output is y^*, of which y_1^* is sold in the first market at price p_1^*, and $y^* - y_1^*$ is sold in the second market at price p_2.

FIGURE A10.1

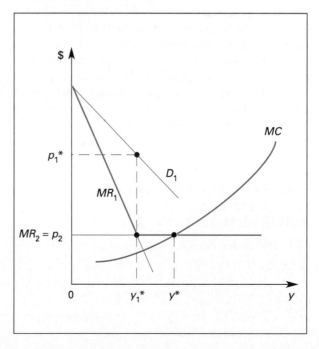

PROBLEM 10.10

First, Canadian Tire induces buyers who have ready cash to part with it rather than to use their credit cards; receiving cash is valuable to Canadian Tire because credit card companies charge the retailer for their services. Thus, there is a form of price discrimination between customers with and without ready cash. Second, among those who are entitled to receive the cash discount, some proportion do not take it because they lose the Canadian Tire money or never return to a Canadian Tire store.

PROBLEM 10.11

a. The profit-maximizing block limit is 21 units, the monopolist's profit is $366 (an increase of $42), and Sam is neither better off nor worse off.

b. The profit-maximizing block limit is 30 units, the monopolist's profit is $420, and Sam is neither better off nor worse off.

PROBLEM 11.1

The payoff matrix is presented below. Payoffs are equal to −1 multiplied by the sentence, and hence are negative. F stands for fink (provides evidence), and M stands for mum (does not provide evidence). Bonnie is the row player and Clyde is the column player. In each pair, the first element is Bonnie's payoff and the second Clyde's. Regardless of what Clyde does, fink maximizes Bonnie's payoff. Similarly, regardless of what Bonnie does, fink maximizes Clyde's payoff.

	M	**F**
M	−2/−2	−10/−1
F	−1/−10	−5/−5

PROBLEM 11.2

See Figure A11.1.

PROBLEM 11.3

The first firm's demand function is $p_1 = (100 − y_2 − y_3) − y_1$, so its marginal revenue function is $MR_1 = (100 − y_2 − y_3) − 2y_1$. Setting marginal revenue equal to marginal cost (40) and solving for y_1^*, we get the first firm's best response function:

$$y_1^* = 30 − (y_2 + y_3)/2$$

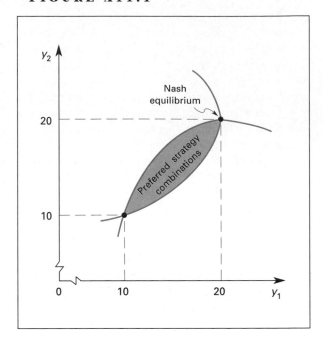

Then, using the fact that the output of all three firms will be the same in the equilibrium, we set y_1^*, y_2, and y_3 all equal to y' in this expression and solve for y', the output of each of the three firms in the Cournot equilibrium: $y' = 15$. Aggregate output is then 45 and price 55. Profit of each firm is 225.

PROBLEM 11.4

Suppose first that there are just three parties to the agreement. The cheater will produce 20 units, aggregate output will be 40 units, and price will be $60. The cheater's profit will be $400, and the inducement to cheat $100 since each firm gets $300 in the collusive agreement. If there were four parties to the agreement, the cheater would produce 18.75 units, aggregate output would be 41.25 units, and price would be $58.75. The cheater's profit would be $351.56, and the inducement to cheat $126.56, since each firm gets $225 in the collusive agreement. The inducement to cheat gets larger and larger as the number of firms in the collusive agreement increases.

PROBLEM 11.5

Suppose that a collusive solution has been in place for some time and that all sales have included the most-favored-customer clause. Then, by cheating, the firm gets the standard payoff identified above, but it incurs a loss equal to the difference between the collusive price and the discount price multiplied by the total quantity sold at the collusive price under the most-favored-customer clause. Therefore, if the most-favored-customer clause has been in effect long enough, no firm will cheat.

PROBLEM 11.6

See Figure A11.2.

FIGURE A11.2

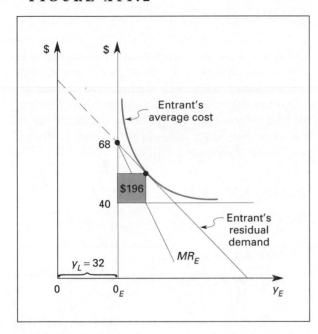

PROBLEM 11.7

In the Bertrand duopoly equilibrium, price is equal to marginal cost. An entrant would therefore anticipate price equal to marginal cost after entry. Hence the inducement to entry is $0. Therefore, if K is positive there will be no entry.

PROBLEM 11.8

Given n established firms, an entrant's profit would be $900/(n + 1) - K$. The no-entry condition is then $900/(n + 1) - K \leq 0$. Industry-wide profit, given collusive behavior and sequential entry, is $100 when K is $400 and $100 when K is $100. Using Figure 11.9, we see that industry-wide profit, given Cournot behavior and sequential entry, is $500 when K is $400 and $176 when K is $100. Given Bertrand behaviour and sequential entry, industry-wide profit is $900 − K$.

PROBLEM 12.1

Consumers 1 through 6, 19, and 20 prefer A to B and C at a common price. Customers 1, 2, and 19 switch to B, and 3, 4, and 20 switch to C as p_A rises above $p' + e$. Customers 7, 8, and 21 switch from B to A, and 13, 14, and 23 switch from C to A as p_A drops below $p' - e$. At the common price p', customers 7 through 12, 21, and 22 prefer B to A and C. As p_B drops below $p' - e$, customers 1, 2, 15, 16, 19, and 24 switch to B.

PROBLEM 12.2

In Figure A12.1, p^* is the collusive price. If one firm charges p^*, the price that maximizes the other's profit is p'.

FIGURE A12.1

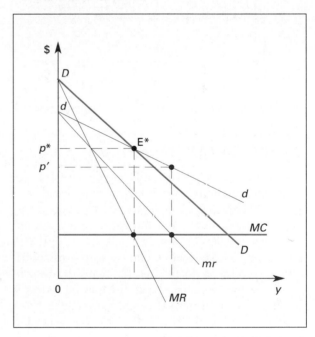

PROBLEM 12.3

The collusive solution in Figure A12.2 is for each firm to charge p^* and sell y^*. With the beliefs outlined in the problem, the demand function is the heavy line coincident with dd to the left of y^* and coincident with DD to the right of y^*. Similarly, the marginal revenue function is coincident with mr to the left of y^* and with MR to the right of y^*. Notice the discontinuity of the marginal revenue function at y^*, indicated by the heavy dashed line. With these beliefs, firms have no incentive to depart from the collusive solution.

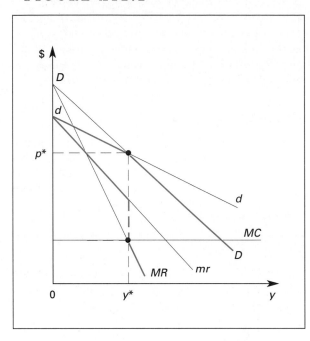

PROBLEM 12.4

Suppose that A is initially available and that B is the second product introduced. When B is introduced, consumers 1 through 6 are no better off. The amounts by which each of consumers 7 through 24 are better off, measured in units of e, are: 1, 1, 2, 3, 2, 3, 0, 0, 1, 2, 0, 1, 0, 0, 1, 2, 0, 1. The total consumers' surplus associated with the second product is thus $20e$. Similarly, the consumers' surplus associated with the fourth product is $6e$. The efficient degree of product diversity is three products because the consumers' surplus associated with the third product is $10e$, which exceeds $K = 8e$, and because the consumers' surplus associated with the fourth product is $6e$, which is less than $K = 8e$.

PROBLEM 12.5

The market boundary between the entrant and the firm to its right is $[p^e + (L/2) - p_E]/2$. Quantity demanded, y_E, is twice this amount. The entrant's demand curve is then $p_E = p^e + (L/2) - y_E$. Setting marginal revenue equal to marginal cost c, we have $y_E^* = [p^e + (L/2) - c]/2$, which is equal to $3L/4$ since $p^e = L + c$.

The other results follow from substitution of y_E^* in the entrant's demand and profit functions.

PROBLEM 12.6

An entrant between two firms L units apart would have a market equal to $L/2$, and its profit would be $(L/2) - K$. Notice that $(L/2) - K \leq 0$ implies $L \leq 2K$, the no-entry condition. An established firm's profit, given L, is $L - K$, which is equal to K when $L = 2K$.

PROBLEM 12.7

From Problem 12.6, we know that the no-entry condition is $L \leq 2K$. Because revenue is independent of the number of outlets, the profit-maximizing strategy is to establish as few (evenly spaced) outlets as possible, subject to the no-entry condition: no two outlets can be farther apart than $2K$. If C is the circumference of the circle, then the number of outlets that maximizes your profit is approximately $C/(2K)$.

PROBLEM 13.1

See Figure A13.1.

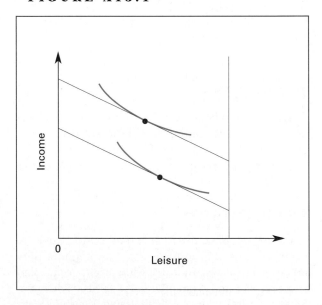

PROBLEM 13.2

1. False. Suppose leisure is a normal good and that the income effect is dominated by the substitution

effect. Then an increase in the wage rate leads to less leisure and more work.

2. True. For hours of work to fall in response to an increase in the wage rate, the income effect must dominate the substitution effect. This is possible if leisure is normal since the two effects are then opposed, but it is impossible if leisure is inferior since the two effects are then complementary.

PROBLEM 13.3

Suppose the firm is currently hiring 150 hours of labor. If it hires one more hour its costs increase by 7 fish (the wage rate) but its revenue increases by less than 7 fish since MP is less than 7 fish to the right of 150 hours of labor; consequently, profit falls as the firm hires more labor. If it hires one less hour, its costs decrease by 7 fish (the wage rate) but its revenue decreases by more than 7 fish since MP is greater than 7 fish to the left of 150 hours of labor; consequently profit falls as the firm hires less labor. Profit is therefore (locally) maximal when the firm hires 150 hours of labor.

PROBLEM 13.4

Given a wage rate of 10 fish, profit at 120 hours of labor is $120[AP(120) - 10]$ fish, which is negative since $AP(120)$ is less than 10. Hence, given a wage rate of 10 fish, the firm maximizes profit by hiring no labor and catching no fish.

PROBLEM 13.5

When $p = \$1$, simply relabel MP as MRP and AP as ARP. When $p = \$2$, shift MP and AP vertically up by a factor of 2 and attach the labels MRP and ARP.

PROBLEM 13.6

Because, by definition, $MRP(z) = MR(y)MP(z)$, we can rewrite the input market profit-maximizing rule, $w = MRP(z^*)$, as $w = MR(y^*)MP(z^*)$. Dividing both sides by $MP(z^*)$, we have $w/MP(z^*) = MR(y^*)$. But $w/MP(z^*)$ is $SMC(y^*)$. Therefore, we can again rewrite the input market rule as $SMC(y^*) = MR(y^*)$, which is the output market profit-maximizing rule.

PROBLEM 13.7

Let y^* denote the positive output at which marginal cost is equal to p. The firm will produce no output if $p < AVC(y^*)$. But from Section 7.4, we know that $AVC(y) = w/AP(z)$. Therefore, we can rewrite the shutdown condition for the output market as $p < w/AP(z^*)$ or as $pAP(z^*) < w$. But, by definition, $pAP(z) = ARP(z)$. Therefore, we can rewrite the shutdown condition as $ARP(z^*) < w$, which is the input market shutdown condition we just defined.

PROBLEM 13.8

By definition, $MRP(z) = MR(y)MP(z)$, and $VMP(z) = pMP(z)$. In a competitive output market, $MR(y^*) = p$; therefore, $VMP(z^*) = MRP(z^*)$ for a firm that is a perfect competitor in its output market. In a monopolistic output market, $MR(y^*) < p$; therefore, $VMP(z^*) > MRP(z^*)$ in this case. Be sure that you understand these simple but important relationships.

PROBLEM 13.9

The slope of the supply function is 1. Then, since $w = 1 + z$ and $MFC = w + z[$slope of the supply function$]$, $MFC = 1 + z + z = 1 + 2z$.

PROBLEM 13.10

At z^*, MRP is equal to MFC. From Problem 13.9, we know that MFC is $1 + 2z$ in this case. Hence, $10 - z^* = 1 + 2z^*$, or $z^* = 3$, and $w^* = 1 + z^* = 4$.

PROBLEM 13.11

The supply function and the marginal factor cost of each ton of coal are given below. When marginal revenue product is 200, the firm buys 5 tons.

Input Price	Tons supplied	MFC
$w < 105$	0	
$105 \leq w < 115$	1	105
$115 \leq w < 125$	2	125
$125 \leq w < 135$	3	145
$135 \leq w < 145$	4	165
$145 \leq w < 155$	5	185
$155 \leq w < 165$	6	205
$165 \leq w < 175$	7	225
$175 \leq w < 185$	8	245
$185 \leq w < 195$	9	265
$195 \leq w$	10	285

PROBLEM 13.12

The demander will obviously pay any supplier $100 per ton for any coal it buys. It will buy the coal supplied by any supplier if $100 plus the transport cost the demander must pay is less than the demander's marginal revenue product, $200. The cost of transporting a ton of coal from the most distant supplier is $95 — 950 miles multiplied by $0.10 per mile. The demander therefore will buy all 10 tons. It will pay $1000 in total to the suppliers, and $5 + $15 + $25 + … + $95 to transport the coal.

PROBLEM 14.1

This question has no "correct" answer, since each person's response depends on his or her preferences.

PROBLEM 14.2

Suppose that the fixed quantity of manna is 1. In Figure A14.1, the utility associated with $R = 1/2$ is AB, which exceeds AC, the expected utility associated with $R = 1/4$ (and $1 - R = 3/4$). It also exceeds AD, the expected utility associated with $R = 0$ (and $1 - R = 1$). As you can easily verify, the utility associated with $R = 1/2$ exceeds the expected utility associated with any other value of R, since the individual is risk-averse.

FIGURE A14.1

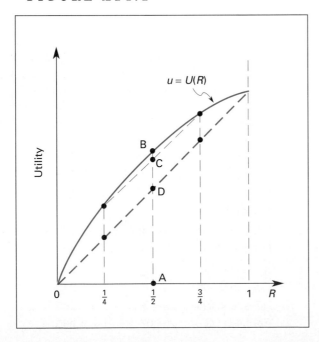

PROBLEM 14.3

An effective minimum wage implies excess supply; employers therefore can choose among applicants on the basis of sex, race, age, or any other characteristic at no cost to themselves. In the absence of a minimum wage, there is no excess supply, and if the employer does not like the applicants, it must pay a higher wage to attract more "acceptable" applicants.

PROBLEM 14.4

You can derive these results by constructing the marginal factor cost function implied by different minimum wages (as in Figure 14.2), and then finding the quantity of labor that maximizes the firm's profit.

PROBLEM 14.5

The implications of a union wage w' are identical to the implications of a minimum wage w'.

PROBLEM 14.6

Because the hiring-hall institution distributes unemployment equally and because the supply is completely inelastic, each member wants to maximize his or her earnings. The wage that such a union would seek is the wage at which the elasticity of demand for labor is 1, because the firm's total wage bill is a maximum at this point.

PROBLEM 14.7

In this case, the more junior members of the union bear all the unemployment associated with a higher wage. If the more senior members do not care about the unemployment of junior members, they will favor a much higher wage rate, knowing that they will not be unemployed as a result. The natural coalition is the coalition involving just over half of the most senior members; this coalition will seek the highest wage such that none of them is unemployed.

PROBLEM 14.8

In Figure 14.5, interpret $w = 12$ as the high urban wage and interpret "labor demand in sector 2" as the demand for labor in rural areas. Assume a casual labor market in the urban area, one with lots of job turnover, so that each urban worker gets the same share of the available urban employment. Then u is the unemployment rate among urban workers.

PROBLEM 14.9

In Figure 14.6, for any value of x_1, the subsidy required to put the individual on the target indifference curve is the vertical distance from the "No-income-transfer budget line" to the "Target indifference curve". This distance is minimized at x_1^*.

PROBLEM 14.10

In Figure A14.2, under the topping-up mechanism, the individual chooses E_1 on indifference curve I_1 and chooses not to receive the topping-up transfer S'. Given the NIT budget line, the individual chooses point E_2 on indifference curve I_2 and receives the NIT transfer S''.

FIGURE A14.2

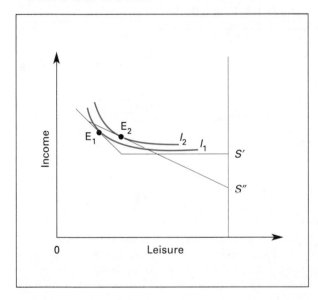

PROBLEM 15.1

The present values are identical when the interest rate is 10%. The first income stream has the larger present value for rates of interest less than 10% and the second has the larger present value for rates of interest more than 10%. Relative to each other, the first income stream is back-loaded and the second is front-loaded. The front-loaded income stream has the larger present value when the rate of interest is high, and the back-loaded income stream has the larger present value when the rate of interest is low.

PROBLEM 15.2

Note that the present value of $I_1 - C_1$ is $(I_1 - C_1)/(1 + i)$. If we substitute this expression into "$C_0 = I_0 +$ present value of $(I_1 - C_1)$" and rearrange, we get the expression we derived in the text for Harold's budget line.

PROBLEM 15.3

Harold's budget line is $C_0 + C_1/4 = 900,000$. If he consumed nothing in period one he could consume 900,000 in period zero. If he consumed nothing in period zero, he could consume $3,600,000 in period one. The opportunity cost of $1 of consumption in period zero is $4 of consumption in period one. The opportunity cost of $1 of consumption in period one is $.25 of consumption in period zero. The slope of the budget line is -4.

PROBLEM 15.4

If Harold initially chooses to borrow against future income to finance consumption in period zero, he is made worse off by an increase in the interest rate. On the other hand, if Harold initially consumes less than his income in period zero, he is made better off by an increase in the interest rate. In terms of Figure 15.2, Harold is made worse off by an increase in the interest rate if he chooses a bundle on his initial budget line that is to the right of A, and he is made better off if he chooses a bundle on his initial budget line that is to the left of A.

PROBLEM 15.5

Harold is impatient because his marginal rate of time preference is 2 at bundle E, composed of $800,000 of consumption in each period. When the interest rate is 0%, the slope of the budget line is -1 and, in addition, C_1 is equal to C_0 at the midpoint of the budget line. If the individual is impatient, the indifference curve through the midpoint of the budget line is steeper than the budget line, and the utility maximizing bundle is therefore to the right of the midpoint, where C_0 exceeds C_1.

PROBLEM 15.6

Statements 1.a and 2.b are true, and statements 1.b and 2.a are uncertain.

PROBLEM 15.7

Statements a, b, d and e are true, statement c is false, and statement f is uncertain. (Recall that we assumed that both C_0 and C_1 are normal goods. This assumption is relevant to e and f.)

PROBLEM 15.8

If Harriet has no access to a market for loanable funds, the consumption possibilities open to her are given by the human capital production function in Figure 15.8. In contrast, if she does have access, the consumption possibilities open to her are given by the line labeled "Budget line for N*" in Figure 15.8. Since this budget line has one point in common with the human capital production function (point N*) and otherwise lies above it, Harriet is clearly no worse off when she has access to a market for loanable funds. And, except in one very special case, she is definitely better off when she has access. To identify the special case, suppose she has access to a market for loanable funds. Then her budget line is the one labeled "Budget line for N*" in Figure 15.8. If, given this budget line, her utility-maximizing consumption bundle is N*, then she does not use the market for loanable funds — that is, she chooses to consume all her income in each period. In this one case, she is just as well off without access to this market as she is with access.

PROBLEM 15.9

To generate these results, simply observe that when the interest rate increases, the line in quadrant 1 of Figure 15.10 that captures Hotelling's law gets steeper, intersecting the locus of market-clearing prices at a point where w_0 is smaller and w_1 larger.

PROBLEM 15.10

The firm's objective is to maximize the present value of its profit. To do so, it should acquire widgets up to the point where the contribution of an additional widget to the present value of revenue is equal to its contribution to the present value of costs. The contribution of an additional widget to the present value of the firm's revenue is just ΣMRP, but the contribution of an additional widget to the present value of the firm's costs is no longer just P, since we must also account for the costs needed to maintain the widget in working order. The present value of these maintenance costs is $M/(1 + i) + M/(1 + i)^2 + \ldots + M/(1 + i)^{D-1}$.

PROBLEM 16.1

At point A, Shelly has 23 units of good 1 and 32 of good 2, while Marvin has 79 units of good 1 and 34 of good

2. At point 0_M, Shelly has 102 units of good 1 and 66 of good 2, while Marvin has 0 units of good 1 and 0 of good 2. At point B, Shelly has 102 units of good 1 and 0 of good 2, while Marvin has 0 units of good 1 and 66 of good 2. At point E, Shelly has 66 units of good 1 and 0 of good 2, while Marvin has 102 units of good 1 and 0 of good 2.

PROBLEM 16.2

Shelly's ordering: first, F; second, D and G; third, A. Marvin's ordering: first, A; second, G; third, D and F.

PROBLEM 16.3

All points in the shaded area in Figure A16.1 are Pareto-preferred to point T.

FIGURE A16.1

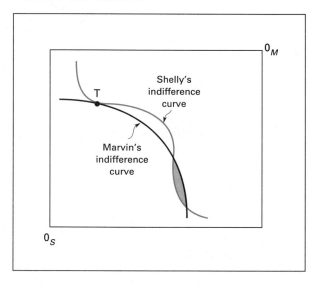

PROBLEM 16.4

Shelly's net demand for good 1 is 27 units, equal to Marvin's net supply. Marvin's net demand for good 2 is 26 units, equal to Shelly's net supply. If Marvin traded 27 units of good 1 for 26 units of good 2, and Shelly traded 26 units of good 2 for 27 units of good 1, the economy would move from the initial allocation at A to the competitive equilibrium at E.

PROBLEM 16.5

Producers of good 1 must use relatively more of input 1 and relatively less of input 2, while producers of good

2 must do the opposite. Yes, it is possible to achieve efficiency in production while maintaining a constant output of good 1.

PROBLEM 16.6

2, 1/5, 1/3, 3.

PROBLEM 16.7

MRT is 1.

PROBLEM 16.8

Less.

PROBLEM 16.9

Supposing that the monopolist produces good 1, the relevant diagram is Figure A16.2. Ms. C's origin is point B. Initially, she is at a point such as point A in the figure because, as we just discovered, her *MRS* (at the initial equilibrium) necessarily exceeds *MRT* when good 1 is produced by a monopolist. When she takes control, she will choose point Z, a point at which she consumes more good 1 and less good 2. At point Z, she is better off, and no one else, including the owner of the firm producing good 1, is worse off, because their consumption bundles have not changed. Therefore, in the general equilibrium, when good 1 is produced by a monopolist, too little of that good is produced.

PROBLEM 16.10

Assume that the price-discriminating monopolist produces good 1; let p_1' and p_1'' be the two prices it charges in the two submarkets and let p_2 be the equilibrium price of good 2. Consumers who face price p_1' will consume a bundle where *MRS* is equal to p_1'/p_2, and consumers who face price p_1'' will consume a bundle where *MRS* is equal to p_1''/p_2. The condition for efficiency in consumption — that all consumers' marginal rates of substitution be identical — is therefore violated.

PROBLEM 16.11

Let p_1, p_2, w_1, and w_2 denote equilibrium prices. Each consumer will choose a bundle where $MRS = p_1/(p_2 + t)$, and the economy is efficient in consumption. Each

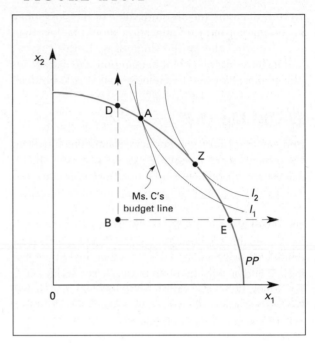

producer will use an input bundle where $MRTS = w_1/w_2$, and the economy is efficient in production. Because the prices firms receive are p_1 and p_2, $MRT = p_1/p_2$. *MRT* therefore exceeds the common value of *MRS*, and we do not have efficiency in product mix. Using a diagram like Figure 16.8, you can show that too little of good 2 is produced in general competitive equilibrium when consumption of good 2 is taxed. Similarly, if consumption of good 2 is subsidized, although we have efficiency in consumption and production, we do not have efficiency in product mix, and too much of good 2 is produced in general competitive equilibrium.

PROBLEM 17.1

The contract curve is the vertical axis through the nonsmoker's origin in Figure 17.1. Because the nonsmoker never buys cigarettes, any market-induced allocation is on the contract curve.

PROBLEM 17.2

Distance HG in Figure 17.2 is the maximum amount Norman would pay to reduce Shelly's consumption of cigarettes to 0.

PROBLEM 17.3

In your diagram, the absolute value of the slope of n_0 at the market-induced allocation should be less than the absolute value of the slope of s_0. In this case, s_0 and n_0 have just one point in common, the market-induced allocation, and that allocation is Pareto-optimal.

PROBLEM 17.4

Suppose that Nancy chooses her consumption bundle in the ordinary way, consuming, say, x_N^* of good X. Ralph values only y_R, his consumption of the composite commodity, and x_N, Nancy's consumption of X. Thus, his utility function can be written as $u = U(y_R, x_N)$. If he spends all his income, M_R, on the composite commodity, he will initially be at point E_0 in Figure A17.1. If he considers buying additional X for Nancy, his budget line is E_0A, and he will choose to buy $x_N' - x_N^*$ additional X for Nancy. Ralph is obviously better off, and so is Nancy, because she values her own consumption of X. Therefore point E_0 is not Pareto-optimal.

FIGURE A17.1

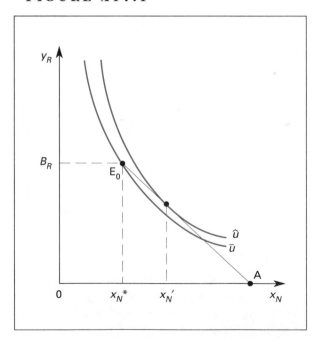

PROBLEM 17.5

The market solution is likely to be inefficient for obvious reasons, and a student organization may indeed be able to organize the dance more efficiently.

PROBLEM 17.6

The difficult part is construction of the relevant opportunity locus for Norma. Suppose Sadie smokes x packs of cigarettes, and let $\varnothing$ denote the horizontal distance from Sadie's budget line to her 7-util indifference curve. If Sadie smokes x packs of cigarettes, and if we reduce her income by $\varnothing$ she will be on her 7-util indifference curve. If we now add $\varnothing$ to Norma's \$180 income, we get one point on Norma's opportunity locus, the point $(180 + \varnothing, x)$.

PROBLEM 17.7

For simplicity, assume that when a downhill owner builds a higher house, the only view that is impaired is the view from the house immediately up the hill. A better institutional arrangement would be to let the default option be a house no higher than 30 feet and allow the neighbors the possibility of negotiating some other solution.

PROBLEM 17.8

The benefits to Norma for these three reductions are \$30, approximately \$90, and approximately \$110. The costs to Sadie of these three reductions are approximately \$5, \$15, and approximately \$50.

PROBLEM 17.9

One possible mechanism would be to establish a public property right for the whole aquifer and then to charge a fee for every gallon of water pumped from the aquifer. Some form of cost-benefit analysis would be necessary to establish the correct fee.

PROBLEM 17.10

Pay TV is clearly not efficient. It is akin to building a fence around Niagara Falls and charging tourists to look through peepholes in the fence. However, it is not obvious that it is worse than the alternatives. In the next section of the text, we will encounter the very thorny problems associated with the public provision of a service such as television. Furthermore, current pay TV channels provide many programs that ordinary commercial television stations do not offer. Both the consumers of these services and the firms that provide them are better off.

Index

Actions, 392
Address model, 412
    cost-benefit efficiency, 421–422
    equilibrium versus efficiency, 422
    product proliferation, 420
    See also Spatial competition model
Adverse selection, 161–162
Aggregate demand, 524
Akerlof, G., 161
Alchian, A., 8n, 190, 193, 198
Allen, R.D.G., 46n
Allocation of goods
    in a competitive exchange economy, 277
    in the Edgeworth box diagram, 517–522
    in general equilibrium, 528
    See also Common property problems
Allocation of output, 233
Allocation of resources
    competitive model, 275–276, 445–446,
        522–525
    in general equilibrium, 527–537
Allowed rate of return, 333
Alternatives, 14, 69–70
Appropriability problem, 349
Arbitrage, 344
Arrow, K.J., 46n, 457, 462, 466, 517n
d'Aspremont, C.J., 35n
Assigning property rights, 552–553, 558
Asymmetric information, 158
Atemporal problem, 70
Average factor cost, 447
Average fixed cost, 226
Average product
    defined, 216
    function, 217–218

Average revenue, in monopoly, 316
Average revenue product, 316
Average variable cost, 221
    deriving, 223
Average-cost-pricing policy, 331
Averch, R., 333
Axelrod, R., 379n, 392n

Bain, J.S., 380
Baltagi, B.H. 89
Barriers to entry, 380–381
Becker, G., 128, 457, 499n
Behavior of individuals, 181–182
Benefits, consumer
    compensating variation, 117, 114–116
    consumer's surplus, 118–120
    equivalent variation, 114, 117–118
Benefits, measure for new goods, 114–115
Berle, A. 179n
Bernoulli, D., 141–142
Bertrand, J., 372
Bertrand model, 372–375
    best-response function, 373
    defined, 372
Bertrand-Nash equilibrium, 372, 374–375, 377
Best response function, 360
Block pricing, 339
Boland, L., 1n
Borrowing rate, 486. *See also* Interest rate
Boulding, K., 35–36
Bounded rationality, 70n
Bradbury, H. 43
Brumberg, R., 489n
Budget constraint, 71

Budget line, 71–72
    compensated, 93
    consumer capital and, 122
    in an exchange economy, 522–523
    intertemporal, 489–492
    slope, 77
    tangent to indifference curve, 77
Burden of monopoly, 325

Capital inputs, 210
    calculating opportunity cost, 296
    defined, 508
    firm's demand for, 508–510
Certainty equivalent, 155
Chamberlin, E., 407–408
Chamberlin model
    collusive price, 405–406
    defined, 399–400
    demand functions, 401–404
    large-numbers case, 409–411
    and localized competition, 412
    Nash equilibrium, 405
    small-numbers case, 404–406
    symmetry assumption of, 400, 419
Cheung, S., 8n
Circular flow of economic activity, 23–24
Coase, R.H., 8n, 199, 554
Coate, D., 85, 91
Cogan, J.F., 481
Collinson Black, R.D., 46n
Collusive model, 375
    critique of, 396–397
    equilibrium, 376
Collusive price, 405–406
Common property problems
    first come, first served allocation, 130
    fisheries, 9
    institutional mechanisms for allocation, 131–133
    oil, 8–9
    traffic congestion problem, 230–232
    "tragedy of the commons," 129–130
    water, 3–8
    water consumption profile, 4, 15–16
Comparative statics
    analysis, 19
    for demand, 85–86
    for input prices, 254–256
    life-cycle model, 494–498
Compensated budget line, 93
Compensated demand curve, 99–100

Compensated demand function, 99n
Compensating variation (CV),
    and equivalent variation, 117
    for a new good, 114–116
    for a price change, 117
Compensation, 180
Compensatory income, 97
Competitive equilibrium, 156n, 275–277
    assumptions of, 283–284
    defined, 276
    finding intertemporal price and allocation,
      506–508
    price, 10
    price function, 278
    price-taking behavior, 281
    quantity, 10
    robustness of, 282–283
    short-run, 290–293
    See also Long-run competitive equilibrium
Competitive equilibrium allocation
    in an exchange economy, 524
    in a competitive market system, 278
Competitive labor markets, and minimum wage,
    468–470
Competitive model, 272–279
Competitive model of exchange, 272–283
    potential difficulties with, 279–283
Complements, 101
    perfect, 243
Completeness assumption, 42, 66
Composite commodity, 103–104
Conditional input demand functions, 248
Consistency assumption, 42
Constant returns to scale, 245. *See also* Returns to
    scale
Constrained maximization technique, 520n, 541–543
Constraints, 69
    budget, 71
    time, 127, 129
Consumer benefits, aggregate, 14. *See also*
    Benefits, consumer
Consumer capital, 121–124
Consumer's real income, 93
Consumer's surplus (CS), 118–120
Consumers' surplus, in competitive
    equilibrium, 295
Consumption bundles, 57–61
    attainable, 71–72
    defined, 41
    n-good case, 65
    and upward sloping indifference curves, 59–60

Consumption responses, 85
Continuity assumption, 144
Continuity of preference assumption, 45–46, 66
Contract curve, 521
Contracting costs, 193
Convexity, 52, 53
Cooter, R.D., 545n
Corner solution, 76, 78–80
Corporations, 179n
Cost-benefit analysis, 560–562
Cost-benefit criterion, 21–22, 25, 34
Cost-benefit efficient, 411
Cost functions
    average fixed cost, 226
    fixed cost, 226
    long-run average cost, 258
    long-run cost, 248–249
    long-run marginal cost, 261
    marginal cost, 225–226
    minimum average cost, 297
    monopsonist's factor, 447–449
    and product function, 224–225
    short-run average cost, 227
    short-run marginal cost, 221–222
    short-run total cost, 226
Cost minimization principle
    first, 251
    second, 251–253
Cost-minimization problem
    interior solution, 249–253
    long-run, 209, 248
    short run, 210
Costs, 3
    contracting and monitoring, 193
    time, 228
    transactions, 199–201
Cournot, A., 360
Cournot model, 375, 376, 384–385
    appeal of, 372
    central features of, 365
    defined, 365
    equilibrium strategy combination, 366–367
    finding best response function, 365–366
    generalizing results, 368
    isoprofit curves, 368–371
    key assumption of, 368
    mock dynamics of, 367–368
Cournot-Nash equilibrium. See Nash equilibrium
Cournot reversion, 395
Cross-price elasticity of demand, 102–103

Debreu, G., 46n
Decreasing returns to scale, 247
Default option, 554, 558
Delivered price schedules, 414
Demand
    aggregating, 290–291
    gross, 524
    theory of, 178
Demand curve
    compensated, 99
    inferior good, 96–97
    linear, 319–321
    market, 10, 11, 12
    normal good, 96–97
    ordinary, 91
Demand functions, 75
    finding compensated demand function, 99n
    market demand function, 273, 304
    no money illusion, 104–105
    for public goods, 566
    symmetric, 401–404
    system, 76
Demsetz, H., 8n, 190, 193, 198
Deposit rate, 486
DeVoretz, D.J. 89
Difference principle, 466
Differentiated products, 398
Diminishing marginal productivity assumption, 213
Diminishing marginal rate of substitution, assumption of, 52
Diminishing marginal rate of technical substitution, 243–244
Direct identification, in market segmentation, 344
Distributive justice, 462–463, 466–467. See also Price discrimination
Divestiture, 331
Division of labor, 197
Dixit, A., 388n, 411
Dorfman, R., 437n
Downs, A. 35n
Duopoly, 362. See also Collusive model; Cournot model; Nash equilibrium
Duopoly price equilibrium, 406

Eaton, B.C., 35n, 388n, 415n 422n
Economic activity, 14, 17
Economic models
    choice of assumptions, 28–34
    and deductive reasoning, 29

generalization, 36
and method of equilibrium, 31, 36
normative evaluation, 34–35
prediction, 19, 27, 30, 32–33, 36
robustness of, 282
and self-interest, 30, 36
Economics, 14, 36, 517
normative, 20
positive, 19–20, 25
Economies of scale, 399. *See also* Returns to scale
Economy, described, 15–17
Edgeworth box
for production, 529
diagram, 518
Edgeworth, F.Y., 518
Efficiency
address models, 421–422
Chamberlin model, 409–411
in consumption, 520, 528
criterion, 326
and general competitive equilibrium, 535–537
and Pareto optimality, 25
of product mix, 530, 533–534
in production, 528, 529–530
See also Inefficiency; Pareto optimality
Efficient scale of production, 297
Efficient transfer mechanism, 477–478
Elasticity, 81
arc, 83
cross-price elasticity of demand, 102–103, 315
income elasticity of demand, 89
marginal, 84
negative, 85
price elasticity of demand, 91–92, 319
Endogenous variables, 74–75
demand curve, 91n
Endowment, 464
Engel curve, 81–82, 87–88
Engel, E., 87
Engel's Aggregation Law, 106
Equilibrium,
concept of, 19, 24–25
finding, 30–34
method of, 19, 24, 31.
See also Competitive equilibrium; Long-run
equilibrium; Nash equilibrium
Equilibrium path, 393
Equilibrium strategy combination, 360
Equivalent variation (EV), 114
and compensating variation compared, 117–118
for a new good, 114

Essential good, 76, 79
determining factor of, 80
Excess demand, 275
Excess supply, 275
Exchange economy, 272,
competitive equilibrium in a, 522–527
defined, 517
See also Competitive model of exchange
Excise tax, 110–112
Exogenous variables, 74–75, 76
Expected monetary value hypothesis, 141
Expected-utility theorem, 171–174
Expected-utility theory, 140–146
function, 143–146
generalizations about, 146–148
hypothesis, 141–143
Externality, 545
consumption-consumption, 550
consumption-production, 551
internalization, 552
negative, 547, 551
positive, 550, 551
private negotiation, 552, 558
production-consumption, 551
production-production, 551
See also Common property problems

Factor of proportionality, 190n, 254
Factors of production, 178.
Fair Labor Standards Act, 468
Feasible input bundles, 250
Firms
collective and private objectives, 180–182
defined, 178, 205–206
demand for capital inputs, 508–510
and market structure, 265–267
theory of the firm, 178, 180, 181–183, 199–201
profit-maximizing strategy, 124–126
in pure-market economy, 23–24
structures, 179–180
See also Multiplant firms
First principle of cost minimization, 251
First theorem of welfare economics, 526, 535. *See
also* Welfare economics
Fisch, R., 301n
Fishburn, P.C., 545n
Fisher, I., 485n
Fisher, M.R., 489n
Fixed cost, 226
Fixed-proportions production function, 206–207

Forgone income, 499
Fouraker, L., 377
Franchise monopoly, 327
    responses to, 338
Free rider, 558
Free-disposal assumption, 212–213
Free-enterprise economy. *See* Pure-market economy
Friedman, J., 378, 392n
Friedman, M., 489n
Full income, 127, 432
Full information equilibrium, 160
Full price, 128
Fuss, M.A., 204n
Future value (*FV*), 486, 490

Gabsewicz, J., 35n
Game theory, 360, 364
        See also Bertrand Model; Chamberlin model;
            Cournot model; Nash equilibrium;
            Subgame perfect Nash equilibrium
General equilibrium, 516
        conditions for efficiency, 527–534
        efficiency and competitive, 535–537
        first theorem of welfare economics, 526, 535
        second theorem of welfare economics, 527,
            537
        See also Exchange economy
Good, I.J., 147n
Goods
        complementary, 121
        defined, 14
        essential, 76, 79, 80
        Giffen, 92–93, 97
        inessential, 76, 80, 81
        inferior, 86–87, 92
        luxury, 89
        necessity, 89
        nonexcludable, 564
        nonrivalrous, 564
        normal, 86–87, 96, 97
        rivalrous, 564
Goods market, 24
Government responses to externalities, 552
Government subsidies, 113–114. *See also* Price
    support programs
Griffin, J.M., 89

Hahn, F.H., 517n
Hall, R., 481

Hardin, Garrett, 129–130
Harsanyi, J., 466
Hartwick, John, 338n
Hicks, J.R., 46n, 104n, 118n, 205n
Hidden actions, 165. *See also* Assymetric information
Hidden characteristic, 158–161
Hiring hall, 472
Hirshleifer, J., 485n
Homogeneous degree of zero, 105n
Homogeneous production functions. *See* Returns
    to scale
Homogeneous products, 359
Homothetic production functions, 258
Hotelling, H., 28, 35, 35n, 506n
Hotelling model, 27–28
Hotelling's law, 506
Houthakker, H.S., 89
Human capital, 163, 499
        function, 500
Human resources endowment, 69
Hume, D., 19

Immobility of inputs, 454
Impatient person, 494
Imperfect information, 70, 142
Implicit function theorem, 51n, 244n
Incentive mechanism, 60
Income and substitution effect, for wage change,
    434–435
Income-consumption path, 86
Income effect, 93
        Giffen good, 96
        inferior good, 96, 97
        normal good, 96
        for price decrease, 95–96
        for price increase, 94
Income elasticity of demand, 89
Income maintenance program, 478
Income, real disposable, 133
Increasing returns to scale, 246
Independence assumption, 284
Index numbers, 133
Indifference curves
        continuous, 46
        and corner solutions, 79
        defined, 44
        and interior solutions, 77–78
        kinked, 52–53
        non-intersecting, 48–49
        shapes of, 53–55

and substitution effect, 96
upward sloping, 58–59
Indifference map, 47–48
Individuals, in pure-market economy, 23–24
Inducement to entry, 381–383, 385, 387
Inefficiency
of minimum wage law, 470
of monopoly, 324–326, 537–538
of monopsony, 452–453
of taxation, 539
Inefficient income-transfer mechanism, 479
Inessential good, 76, 81
determining factor of, 80
Inferior goods, 86
demand curve, 97
and income effect, 96
Informal price mechanisms, 308–309
Initial allocation, 277–278
Input bundle, defined, 206
Input demand function, short-run, 437
Input demand, in one-good economy, 437–441
Input homogeneity assumption, 430
Input market(s), 428
immediate input market, 429
long-run competitive equilibrium, 445–446
monopsony in, 447–449
perfectly competitive, 429
Input price change, demand and, 444
Input prices, cost-minimization problem, 210
Inputs, 178
capital, 210, 296, 508–510
generic, 199–200
rented, 210
Input substitution, 238
Institutional mechanisms for allocation, 131–133
Institutions
defined, 17–18
in pure-market economy, 22
Insurance, market for, 154–1577
Interest rate, 485, 511–512
and intertemporal budget line, 492
Interior solution, 76–78
Intermediate input markets, 429
Internalization, 552
Intertemporal
allocation of nonrenewable resources, 504–508
budget line, 489–492
choices, 70
consumption bundle, 493
resource allocation, 485
theory of choice, 485n

Investment demand, 511
Isocost line, 250
Isoprofit curves, 368–369
Isoquant, defined, 238

Jaffe, W., 517n
Job security, 180
Johnson, L.L., 333
Jorgenson, D.W., 205n

Kaldor, N., 420
Karni, E., 147n
Keely, M., 481
Kehoe, T., 19n
Klapholtz, K., 305n
Koopmans, T.C., 537n
Kotowitz, Y., 161n
Kreps, D., 360n

Labor supply curves, 435–437
Labor, supply of, 127–128, 431–433
Laffont, J.J., 545n
Lagrange multipliers, method of, 75n, 77n, 99n, 252n
Lancaster, K.J., 399n, 421
Large numbers assumption, 281
in Chamberlin model, 409–411
in competitive input market model, 430
in goods market model, 283
Large numbers, law of, 157
Laspeyres price index, 136
Laspeyres quantity index, 135. *See also* Quantity indexes
Legal institutions, 17
Leisure
as inferior good, 433
as normal good, 433
Leontief, W.W., 104
Lerner, A., 35n
Lewit, E.M., 85, 91
Life cycle, 489
Life-cycle model
comparative statics, 494–498
and composite commodity theorem, 492–494
consumption expenditure, 489–499
and human capital acquisition, 499–504
Limit output, 382, 383

Limit-output model, 380
 entry deterrence, 383–384
 limit price, 383
 no-entry condition, 382
 setup cost, 380
 Sylos postulate, 381, 384
Limit price, 383
Lipsey, R.G., 35n, 388n, 415n
Loanable funds, 498
Loeb, M., 335
Long-run average cost, 258
 and production choices, 296
Long-run competitive equilibrium
 individual firm in, 298
 marginal revenue, 298
 no-exit, no-entry conditions in 296–297
 price and minimum average cost, 297
Long-run cost function, 248–249. See also
 Comparative statics, for input prices
Long-run cost-minimization problem, 209, 248
Long-run costs, relationship between short-run
 costs and, 261–265
Long-run input demand function, substitution
 and output effects, 444
Long-run marginal cost, 261
Long-run reservation supply price, 309
Long-run supply function (LRS), 298
 constant-cost case, 299–300
 decreasing-cost case, 304
 increasing-cost case, 301–303
Luce, R. 143n, 364n
Lump-sum mechanism, 478
Lump-sum tax, 111–112. See also Second
 theorem of welfare economics

Machina, M.J., 143n, 146
Magat, W.A., 335
Malthus, T., 213
Malthusian hypothesis, 214
Marginal change, 51
Marginal cost,
 long-run, 261, 262
 short-run, 221, 223
Marginal elasticity, 84
Marginal factor cost, 447–449
Marginal product, 212–216
 qualitative relationships between average
 product and, 218–219
Marginal product function, 219
 and short-run marginal cost function, 225–226

Marginal product of human capital (MP), 500
Marginal rate of substitution (MRS), 50–53, 77
 defined in n-good case, 65
 and efficiency in product mix, 534
 and indifference curves, 55
 negative substitution effect, 96
Marginal rate of technical substitution (MRTS),
 240–243
 diminishing, 243–244
 and efficiency in production, 530
 and homothetic production function, 258
 as ratio of marginal products, 243
Marginal rate of time preference, 493
Marginal rate of transformation, 530–532, 534
Marginal revenue, 286
 in monopoly, 317
Marginal revenue product, 439
Marginal social value, 565
Marginal utility of wealth, 149
Market boundary, 415
Market demand function, 273, 304
 finding, 290–291
Market economy, 22–24
 and prices, 278
Market failure, 161
Market for loanable funds, 486
Market segmentation, 338, 344–345
Market structure, theory of, 265–267
Market supply functions, 274
 monopsony, 447
 long-run, in the competitive model, 298–304
 short-run, in the competitive model, 285–287
Marshall, A., 272
McKenzie, L., 517
Means, G.C., 179n
Measures of responsiveness, 81. See also Elasticity
Metered scheme, 7–8
Mincer, J., 499n
Minimum average cost, 297
Minimum differentiation, 28, 35–36
Minimum level of utility, 477
Minimum standard of living. See Minimum level
 of utility
Minimum wage, and monopsonist's marginal
 factor cost, 471
Minimum wage law, inefficiency of, 470
Minimum-wage legislation, 469
Modigliani, F., 380, 489n
Monitoring costs, 193
Monopoly
 block pricing, 339

by good management, 330, 384
defined, 315–316
equilibrium, 361–362
inefficiency of, 324–326
multipart pricing, 345–348
patent policy, 348–355
price discrimination in, 338–348
profit-maximizing problem, 321–324
revenue functions of, 316–321
sources of, 327–330
See also Regulatory responses to monopoly
Monopsonistic labor markets, and minimum wage, 470–472
Monopsony, 447
factor cost functions, 447–449
inefficiency of, 452–453
short-run equilibrium, 450–451
sources of power, 453–454
Moral hazard problems, 165. *See also* Assymetric information
Morgenstern, O., 143n 145
Mortgage, 509
Moscato, M., 43
Most-favored-customer clause, 379
Mueser, Peter, 455n
Multipart pricing, 345–348. *See also* Block pricing
Multiplant firms, 233

N-good case, 65
Nadin, M.I., 205n
Nash equilibrium, 360, 377, 378, 379, 405, 407
in duopoly, 366n, 367–370, 375
refinement of concept of, 395
Nash, J., 360
Nash price equilibrium, 405, 407
Natural identity of interests, 516
Natural monopoly, 328–329, 384
responses to, 331
Negative income tax (NIT), 480–481
Negative substitution effect, 96
Net demand, 524
Net supply, 524
New goods
consumer's surplus for, 119
measure of benefits, 114–115
No-better-than set, 65
No-entry condition
oligopoly, 382
spatial competition model, 418
No-exit, no-entry condition, 296–297

No money illusion, 104
Nonconvex indifference curve, 54–55
Nonintervention, 553
Non-labor inputs, supply of, 431
Nonmarginal rate of substitution, 51
Non-metered scheme, 4–6, 7
unbalanced profile equilibrium, 16
Nonsatiation assumption, 46–48, 56, 62
and utility-maximizing consumption bundle, 73–74, 76
Normal goods, 86
and income effect, 96
slope of demand curve, 97
No-worse-than set, 65

Oi, W., 124
Oligopoly
and collusion, 363–364, 376
theory of market structure, 385–386
theory of, 359
self-enforcing agreement, 364
static nature of oligopoly models, 377, 392
See also Bertrand model; Chamberlin model; Cournot model; Limit-output model
Oligopoly problem, 359, 363–364, 376, 407–408
One-good economy, input demand, 437–441
One-person firm, utility function of, 183–184
Opportunity cost, 72, 93, 296
and excise tax, 111
Opportunity costs, 296
Ordinal utility, 65
Ordinary monopsonistic price discrimination, 455–457. *See also* Price discrimination
Ordinary price discrimination, 338–343
Original position, 466. *See also* Price discrimination
Output effect, 442–444
Outputs, 178
Overallocation, 552
Owner-managed firm, defined, 179
monitoring costs, 194
Owner-managed team,
productivity gain, 191
symmetric equilibrium, 193–194

Paasche price index, 135
Paasche quantity index, 135
Pareto criterion, 20, 25

Pareto-optimal allocation
    in an Edgeworth box, 519
    in an exchange economy, 520, 526
    contract curve, 521
    and externalities, 546
Pareto optimality, 20, 25
    competitive equilibrium allocation, 277
    and organizational form, 189
    See also Efficiency
Pareto, V., 20
Pareto-preferred organizational forms, 191, 195–196
Partnership, defined, 179
Partnership equilibrium, 187–189, 190–191
Patent
    effects of, 352
    optimal policy, 352–355
    policy, 348–349
    protection, 350–351
Patent monopoly, 327
    responses to, 331
Patient person, 494
Payoff, 360
Perfect competition assumptions, 283–284
Perfect complements, 243
Perfect information, 70, 282
Perfect information assumption
    in competitive input market model, 430
    in goods market model, 283
Perfect market for loanable funds, 487
Perfect mobility of resources assumption
    in competitive input market model, 430
    in goods market model, 284
Perfect price discrimination, 338, 339
Perfect substitutes, 243
Perfectly competitive input market
    assumptions of, 430
    defined, 429
Perfectly competitive markets, 10
Perloff, S.C., 400
Philips, Louis, 338n
Players, 360
Plott, C.R., 377n
Positioning, 388
Postlewaite, A., 161n
Preference ordering, 15–16, 41, 43
Preference statements, 41
Preferences
    application of theory, 56–61
    assumptions of theory, 40–46
    consistency of, 41–43
    individual, 15–16, 25, 40–41

Present value (PV), 486
    calculating, 488–489
Price
    competitive equilibrium, 10, 278
    and economic decisions, 7, 11
Price ceiling, 305
Price change, measuring the cost of, 116
Price discrimination, 338, 339
    monopsonistic, 455–457
    ordinary, 338–343
    perfect, 339
Price elasticity of demand, 91–92
    for a linear demand curve, 315–321
    in monopoly, 319
Price floor, 310
Price index, 133, 135. See also Laspeyres price
    index; Laspeyres quantity index; Paasche
    quantity index
Price of leisure, 127, 432
Price manipulation, 279–281
Price mechanism, under rent control, 307–308
Price ratio, interpretations of, 72
Price reduction, consumer's surplus for, 120
Price schedule, 345
Price support programs, 11–14
Price-consumption path, 90–91
Price-taking behavior, 281
Prices, allocation function of, 278
Primary input markets, 429
Prisoners' dilemma, 364
Private incentive, 187, 188
Private negotiation, 552, 558
Producers' surplus, 295
Product
    average, 216–218, 225
    marginal, 212–216
    total, 211
Product diversity, 422
Product-exhaustion, 463–464
    criterion, 463
Production functions,
    Cobb Douglas, 209
    defined, 206
    differentiable, 258n
    finding, 208
    fixed proportions, 206–207
    homothetic, 258
    Leontief, 207
    return to scale, 247n
    variable-proportions, 207–208
Product homogeneity assumption, 283

Product proliferation, 420
Production possibilities frontier, 528
Production possibilities set, 528
Productivity gains, 189–190
Productivity principle, 463
    thought experiments, 464–465
Profit
    deriving firm's, 289
    gross, 384
    as a signal, 296
Profit function, 124–125, 285
Profit in long-run equilibrium, 418–420
Profit maximization, 209, 286
    strategy, 124–126
Profit-maximizing problem, monopolist's, 321–324
Profit rectangle
    in monopoly, 322–323
    in perfect competition, 289
Property rights, 556–558. *See also* Common
    property problems
Prospect, 143
Pseudodynamics
    constant-cost case, 300
    increasing cost case, 303
Public goods, 563
    pure, 564–565
Public regulation, 553, 559
Publicly held firm, 179
Punishment output, 393
Punishment strategies, 378–379
Pure-market economy, 22–24

Quantity demand, independent of income, 117
Quantity indexes, defined, 133

Raiffa, H., 143n, 364n
Rate-of-return regulation, 332–334, 335
Rawls, J., 466
Reacting, 388
Redistributionist principle, 465–466
Regulatory mechanisms, 562
Regulatory responses to monopoly, 330–338
    regulatory mechanisms, 334–337
Rent control model, 305–306
Rent inputs, 210
Representative consumer, 113
Reservation demand price, 155
Reservation price, 123, 272

Reservation supply price, 156
Residual
    claimancy, 188
    claimant, 179
Residual demand function, 328
Resource endowment, 15, 25
Resource market, 24
Resource-based monopoly, 327
Resources, defined, 14–15
Responses to externalities, 551–553
Returns to scale, 245–247, 259–261
    constant, 245
    decreasing, 247
    for homogeneous production functions,
        247n
    increasing, 246
    See also Market structure, theory of
Revealed-preference problem, 567
Revenue
    marginal, 286
    total, 285
Risk, 142
    attitudes towards, 148–152
    risk aversion, 149–151, 153, 157–158
    risk inclination, 149–150
    risk neutrality, 149–150
Risk pooling, 152–154
Risk spreading, 157
Roberts, K., 378n
Rosen, S., 499n
Rothschild, M.
Rule of capture, 8, 17

Saint Petersburg paradox, 141n
Salop, J.M., 400
Salvanes, K.G., 89
Samuelson, P.A., 205n
Sandmo, A., 545n
Scale of production, 245
Scarcity, 14
    and markets, 465
Schelling, T., 110
Schmalensee, R., 126n, 420n
Schultz, T., 499n
Screening, 164. *See also* Signaling
Second principle of cost minimization, 251–253
Second theorem of welfare economics, 527, 537
Self-enforcing agreement, 364
Self-interest, theory of, 16, 25, 40

Self-selection, in market segmentation, 344
Separation theorem, 487–488, 499–504, 508
Services. *See* Goods, defined.
Setup cost, 380, 387
Shape-up, 475
Sharkey, W. W., 315n
Short-run average cost, 227
Short-run competitive equilibrium, 292–294
Short-run cost-minimization problem, 210
    one variable input, 219–221
Short-run equilibrium, Chamberlin's
   large-numbers case, 409
Short-run input demand function, 437
Short-run marginal cost, 221–222
    deriving, 223
    profit maximizing rule, 286–287
Short-run marginal cost function, marginal
   product function and, 225–226
Short-run market supply function, aggregating
   short-run supply, 291–292
Short-run monopsony equilibrium, 450–451
Short-run price equilibrium, spatial competition
   model, 413–417
Short-run supply, aggregating, 291–292
Short-run supply function, 284–286
Short-run total cost, 226
Siegal, S., 377
Signaling, 162. *See also* Screening
Simon, H., 70n
Singer, H., 35n
Slutsky, E., 46
Small-numbers case, Chamberlin's, 404–405
Smith, Adam, 197, 516–517
Smith, V., 283
Smithies, A. 35n
Social benefit,
    gross, 21
    marginal, 354
    net, 21, 25
    See also Cost-benefit analysis; Cost-benefit
      criterion; Cost-benefit efficient
Social cost, 353
    aggregate, 354
    gross, 21
    marginal, 354
    social state, 18–19
    social value, 353
    aggregate, 354
Spatial competition model
    circular model, 412–413

delivered price schedules, 414
demand function in short run, 415
long-run equilibrium, 417
market boundary, 415
no-entry condition, 418
profit-maximizing output in short run, 416
profit-maximizing price in short run, 416
supranormal profits, 419
Specialization, 197
Specialized production, 198–199
Spence, A.M., 164, 384, 388, 411
Stage game, 392
State-dependent preferences, 148
Stigler, G., 379n, 392n, 516n
Stiglitz, J.E., 161n, 164, 411
Strategies, 360, 392
    dominant strategy, 363
    strategy combination, 360
    trigger, 392
Strictly convex indifference curve, 54–55
    defined mathematically, 55n
Subgame perfection, 396
Subgame perfect Nash equilibrium, 396
Subjective probabilities, 147
Subsidy scheme, 335
Substitutes, 101
    input substitute, 238
    perfect, 243
Substitution effect, 93
    and indifference curves, 95
    negative, 96
    non-zero, 112
    nonpositive, 97–99
    for price decrease, 94, 95
    for price increase, 93–94, 95
    response to input-price change, 442–444
Sunk cost, 386
Supergame, 378, 392
Supply, gross, 524
Supply, theory of, 178
Supply curve, market, 10, 11, 12
Supply function
    competitive firm's, 287–288
    long-run, 298
    short-run, 284–286
Surplus
    consumers', 295
    producers', 295
    total, 295
Sweezy, P.M., 408

Sylos postulate, 328. *See also* Limit-output model
Sylos-Labini, P., 328, 380
Symmetric equilibrium
    owner-managed team, 194
    two-person partnership, 186
Symmetric preferences, 400

Target output, 393
Tax
    excise, 110–112
    lump-sum, 111–112
Team production
    defined, 189
    and specialized production, 198
Teams, productive potential of, 190
Technically efficient technology, 206
Technological change, 17n, 304
Technological monopoly, 327–328
Technology, 15, 25
Theories of the firm, 178, 180, 181–183, 189
Thisse, J., 35n
Time price of access, 132
Todaro, M., 476
Topping-up mechanism, 477, 478–480
Total factor cost, 447
Total output, response to input-price change, 442
Total product function, 211
    stylized, 215–216
Total revenue, in monopoly, 316
Total revenue function, 285
    in monopoly, 321
Total surplus, 295. *See also* Cost-benefit analysis;
  Cost-benefit criterion; Cost-benefit efficient
Transitivity assumption, 42–43, 48–49, 66
Trigger strategy, 392
Tsang, S.C., 511n
Tucker, A.W., 364
Two-part-tariff model, 124–126. *See also* Perfect
  price discrimination
Two-person partnership
    partnership equilibrium in, 185–189
    residual claimancy, 188
Two-sector model, 473–476
    underemployment equilibrium, 474
    unemployment equilibrium, 474–476
    wage floor in, 474
Two-term consistency assumption, 42

Underallocation, 551
Underemployment equilibrium, 474
Unemployment equilibrium, 474–476
Union wage rates, 472–473
Unit-free measure of responsiveness, 82–83. *See
  also* Elasticity
Unitization, 9
Upward sloping indifference curve, 58–59
Utility function
    construction of, 61–64
    defined, 61
Utility maintenance mechanism, 477
Utility-maximizing bundle, 73–74
    corner solution, 79
    interior solution, 77–78
    of leisure and income, 432
Utility numbers, 61
    meaning of, 64

Value of the marginal product, 442
Variable cost
    average, 221
    deriving average, 223
Variable cost function, 220
    deriving, 221–222
Vaughn, Karen, 516n
Vickery, W., 466
von Neumann, J., 143n, 145
von Neumann-Morgenstern utility function, 145
von Wright, G.H. 46n

Wage floor, 472
Walras, L., 275, 517n
Walras' law, 525
Walrasian auctioneer, 275
Wasserman, J., 85, 89, 91
Weakly convex indifference curve, 54–55
Welfare. *See* Topping-up mechanism
West, D.S., 423n
West, E.G., 315n
Williamson, O., 199n
Willig, R., 120n
Wilson, C., 161n
Wooders, M.H., 422n